The Indian Act of Canada

The Indian Act of Canada

Grimes

CONTENTS

DEDICATION vii

1 The Indian Act 1

Copyright Page
© 2024 Adultbrain Publishing. All rights reserved.
Adultbrain Publishing is dedicated to breathing new life into timeless literary works by resurrecting old classics for the modern age. We meticulously curate and convert these masterpieces into high-quality digital and audio formats, making them accessible to a new generation of readers and listeners. Our commitment to preserving the essence of these works, while enhancing them with today's technology, allows us to offer immersive experiences that retain the authenticity of the original texts. Whether rediscovering a beloved classic or experiencing it for the first time, our editions invite readers to start using their Adultbrain today.
Published by Adultbrain Publishing.
ISBN: 978-1-0690495-8-2
eISBN: 978-1-0690495-9-9

Title: The Indian Act of Canada – Consolidation of Indian Legislation 1868 - 1975
Start using your Adultbrain today.
For more information, visit: www.adultbrain.ca

Adultbrain Publishing
Darren Grimes
Free Use without permission

The Indian Act

THE INDIAN ACT OF CANADA

CONSOLIDATION OF INDIAN LEGISLATION.
1868-1975

Adultbrain Publishing
Darren Grimes
Free Use without permission

INTRODUCTION

This consolidation of legislation pertaining to native peoples was prepared for the internal use of the Office of Native Claims, Department of Indian and Northern Affairs, and the legal officers. It consists of three volumes:

VOLUME I

UNITED KINGDOM AND CANADA

United Kingdom - Constitutional documents

Canada - Pre-Confederation statutes

Canada - Post-Confederation statutes

This Post-Confederation Legislation is further divided in the following order :

Administrative   Lands

Constitutional documents   Manitoba

Electoral provisions   Miscellaneous

Federal grants, assistance, etc.   Northern Canada

Federal provincial agreements   Saskatchewan and Alberta

International agreements

VOLUME II

INDIAN ACTS AND AMENDMENTS, 1868-1975

These have been set up as follows: commencing with the Revised Statute of 1886, the relevant portions of each amending statute of the revise Indian Act have been inserted directly following the provision affected. The citations to these amending acts are given in the margin. The citation to the revised statute is given at the top of each page.

VOLUME III

PROVINCIAL LEGISLATION - PRE - AND POST-CONFEDERATION

Only those provisions of the provincial legislation which specifically relate to Indians have been reproduced herein. This legislation is separated into provinces, and then further divided in the following order:

Education   Liquor provisions

Electoral   provisions Miscellaneous

Game   Provincial grants, assistance, etc.

Lands   Taxation

While attempts have been made to be exhaustive, the user is reminded that it is a consolidation for internal use of government officials.

Name of Act   Page

An Act providing for the organisation of the Department of the Secretary of State of Canada" and for the management of Indian and Ordnance Lands. S.C. 1868, c. 42. (31 Vict.)   1

An Act for the gradual enfranchisement of Indians, the better management of Indian affairs, and to extend the provisions of the Act 31st Victoria, Chapter 42. S.C. 1869, c. 6   10

An Act to provide for the establishment of "The Department of the Interior." S.C. 1873, c. 4.   15

An Act to amend certain Laws respecting Indians, and to extend certain Laws relating to matters connected with Indians to the Provinces of Manitoba and British Columbia. S.C. 1874, c. 21.   18

An Act to amend the Act providing for the organization of the Department of the Secretary of State of Canada? S.C. 18757 c- 6.   23

The Indian Act, 1876. S.C. 1876, c. 18   24

An Act to amend "The Indian Act, 1876," S.C. 1879, c. 34.   50

The Indian Act, 1880. S.C. 1880, c. 28   52

An Act to amend "The Indian Act, 1880." S.C. 1881, c. 17   78

An Act to further amend "The Indian Act. 1880." S.C. 1882, c. 30.   81

An Act to amend the Act thirty-sixth Victoria, chapter four, intituled "An Act to provide for the establishment of The Department of the Interior," and to amend "The Indian Act, 1880." S.C. 1883, c. 6   82

An Act further to amend "The Indian Act, 1880." S.C. 1884, c. 27.   83

The Indian Advancement Act, 1884. S.C. 1884, c. 28   92

Each revised Indian Act, starting with R.S.C. 1886, has the amending statutes inserted into the revised statute.

The citation to the revised statute is given at the top of the page. Citations to the amending statutes are given in the margin beside the provision which has been inserted.

The Indian Act. R.S.C. 1886, c. 43.   97

Amending Acts:

An Act to amend "The Indian Act." S.C. 1887, c. 33.

An Act further to amend "The Indian Act," Chapter forty-three of the Revised Statutes. S.C. 1888, c. 22.

An Act further to amend "The Indian Act," Chapter forty-three of the Revised Statutes. S.C. 1890, c. 29.

An Act further to amend "The Indian Act." S.C. 1891, c. 30.

An Act further to amend "The Indian Act." S.C. 1894, c. 32.

An Act further to amend the Indian Act. S.C. 1895, c. 35.

An Act further to amend the Indian Act. S.C. 1898, c. 34.

An Act to amend The Indian Act. S.C. 1906, c. 20.

    The Indian Advancement Act. R.S.C. 1886, c. 44.   157

An Act to amend "The Indian Advancement Act," chapter forty-four of the Revised Statutes'!" S.C. 1890, c. 30.   162

INDIAN ACT. R.S.C. 1906, c. 81.   164

Amending Acts:

An Act to amend the Indian Act. S.C. 1910, c. 28

An Act to amend the Indian Act. S.C. 1911, c. 14

An Act to amend the Indian Act. S.C. 1914, c. 35

An Act to amend the Indian Act. S.C. 1918, c. 26

An Act to amend the Indian Act. S.C. 1919, c. 56

An Act to amend the Indian Act. S.C. 1919-20, c. 50

An Act to amend the Indian Act. S.C. 1922, c. 26

An Act to amend the Indian Act. S.C. 1924, c. 47

An Act to amend the Indian Act. S.C. 1926-27, c. 32

INDIAN ACT. R.S.C. 1927, c. 98.   234

Amending Acts:

An Act to amend the Indian Act. S.C. 1930, c. 25.

An Act to amend the Indian Act. S.C. 1932-33, c. 42.

An Act respecting the Caughnawaga Indian Reserve and to amend the Indian Act. S.C. 1934, c. 29.

An Act to amend the Indian Act. S.C. 1936, c. 20.

An Act to amend the Indian Act. S.C. 1938, c. 31.

An Act to amend the Indian Act. S.C. 1940-41, c. 19.

The Indian Act. S.C. 1951, c. 29   300

Amending Acts:

An Act to amend The Indian Act. S.C. 1952-53, c. 41.

INDIAN ACT. R.S.C. 1952, c. 149.   340

Amending Acts:

An Act to amend the Indian Act. S.C. 1952-53, c. 41.

An Act to amend the Indian Act. S.C. 1956, c. 40.

An Act to amend the Indian Act. S.C. 1958, c. 19.

An Act to amend the Indian Act. S.C. 1960, c. 8.

An Act to amend the Indian Act. S.C. 1960-61, c. 9.
Government Organization Act. S.C. 1966-67, c. 25.
Government Organization Act. S.C. 1968-69, c. 28.
    INDIAN ACT. R.S.C. 1970, c. 1-6.   386
Amending Acts:
Federal Court Act. R.S.C. 1970 (2nd Supp.), c. 10, s. 65,
Sch. II, Item 19.
An Act to amend the Judges Act and certain other Acts for related purposes and in respect of the re-constitution of the Supreme Court of Newfoundland and Prince Edward Island. S.C. 1974-75-76, c. 48,s. 24-25

An Act providing for the organisation of the Department of the Secretary of State of Canada" and for the management of Indian and Ordnance Lands. S.C. 1868, c. 42. (31 Vict.)
    CAP. X L II.

An Act providing for the organisation of the Department
of the Secretary of State of Canada, and for the
management of Indian and Ordnance Lands.

    [Assented to 22nd May, 1868.]

HER Majesty, by and with the advice and consent of the Senate and House of ^Commons of Canada, enacts as
follows :

1. There shall be a department to be called " The Department of the Secretary of State of Canada," over which the Secretary of State of Canada for the time being, appointed by the Governor General by commission under the Great Seal, shall preside ; and the said Secretary of State shall have the management and direction of the Department, and shall hold office during pleasure.

2. The Governor General may also appoint an "Under Secretary of State," and such other officers as may be necessary for the proper conduct of the business of the said Department, all of whom shall hold office during pleasure.

3. It shall be the duty of the Secretary of State to have charge of the State correspondence, to keep all State records and papers not specially transferred to other Departments, and to perform such other duties as shall from time to time be assigned to him by the Governor General in Council.

4. The Secretary of State shall be the Registrar General of Canada, and shall as such register all Instruments of
Summons, Commissions, Letters Patent, Writs, and other Instruments and Documents issued under the Great Seal.

5. The Secretary of State shall be the Superintendent General of Indian affairs, and shall as such have the control and management of the lands and property of the Indians in Canada.

    6. All lands reserved for Indians or for any tribe, band or body of Indians, or held in trust for their benefit, shall be deemed to be reserved and held for the same purposes as before the passing of this Act, but subject to its provisions ; and no such lands shall be sold, alienated or leased until they have been released or surrendered to the Crown for the purposes of this Act

7. All moneys or securities of any kind applicable to the support or benefit of the Indians or any tribe, band or body of Indians, timber, and all moneys accrued or hereafter to accrue from the sale of any lands or of any timber on any lands reserved or held in trust as aforesaid, shall, subject to the provisions of this Act, be applicable to the same purposes, and be dealt with in the same manner as they might have been applied to or dealt with before the passing of this Act.

8. No release or surrender of lands reserved for the use of Indians or of any tribe, band or body of Indians, or of any individual Indian, shall be valid or binding, except on the following conditions:

1. Such release or surrender shall be assented to by the or if there be more than one chief, by a majority of the chiefs of the tribe, band or body of Indians, assembled at a meeting or council of the tribe, band or body summoned for that purpose according to their rules and entitled under this Act to vote thereat, and held in the presence of the Secretary of State or of an officer duly authorized to attend such council by the Governor in Council or by the Secretary of State; provided that no Chief or Indian shall be entitled to vote or be present at such council, unless he habitually resides on or near the lands in question;

2. The fact that such release or surrender has been assented to by the Chief of such tribe, or if more than one, by a majority of the chiefs entitled to vote at such council or meeting, shall be certified on oath before some Judge of a Superior, County or District Court, by the officer authorized by the Secretary of State to attend such council or meeting, and by some one of the chiefs present thereat and entitled to vote, and when so certified as aforesaid shall be transmitted to the Secretary of State by such officer, and shall be submitted to the Governor in Council for acceptance or refusal.

9. It shall not be lawful to introduce at any council or meeting of Indians held for the purpose of discussing or of assenting to a release or surrender of lands, any strong or intoxicating liquors of any kind; and any person who shall introduce at such meeting, and any agent or officer employed by the Secretary of State, or by the Governor in Council, who shall introduce, allow or countenance by his presence the use of such liquors a week before, at, or a week after, any such council or meeting, shall forfeit two hundred dollars, recoverable by action in any of the Superior Courts of Law, one half of which penalty shall go to the informer.

10. Nothing in this Act shall confirm any release or surrender would have been invalid if this Act had not been passed; and no release or surrender of any such lands to any party other than the Crown, shall be valid.

11. The Governor in Council may, subject to the provisions of this Act, direct bow, and in what manner, and by whom the moneys arising from sales of Indian Lands, and from the property held or to be held in trust for the Indians, or from any timber thereon, or from any other source for the benefit of Indians, shall be invested from time to time, and how the payments or assistance to which the Indians may be entitled shall be made or given, and may provide for the general management of such lands, moneys and property, and direct what percentage or proportion thereof shall be set apart from time to time, to cover the cost of and attendant upon such management under the provisions of this Act, and for the construction or repair of roads passing through such lands, and by way of contribution to schools frequented by such Indians.

12. No person shall sell, barter, exchange or give to any Indian man, woman or child in Canada, any kind of spirituous in any maimer or way, or cause or procure the same to be done for any pur-

pose whatsoever;—and if any person so sells, barters, exchanges or gives any such spirituous liquors to any Indian man, woman or child as aforesaid, or causes the same to be done, he shall on conviction thereof, before any Justice of the Peace upon the evidence of one credible witness, other than the informer or prosecutor, be fined not exceeding twenty dollars for each such offence, one moiety to go to the informer or prosecutor, and the other moiety to Her Majesty to form part of the fund for the benefit of that tribe, band or body of Indians with respect to one or more members of which the offence was committed; but no such penalty shall be incurred by furnishing to any Indian in case of sickness, any spirituous liquor, either by a medical man or under the direction of a medical man or clergyman.

13. No pawn taken of any Indian for any spirituous liquor, shall be retained by the person to whom such pawn is delivered, but the thing so pawned may be sued for and recovered, with costs of suit, by the Indian who has deposited the same, before any Court of competent jurisdiction.

14. No presents given to Indians nor any property purchased or acquired with or by means of any annuities granted to
Indians, or any part thereof, or otherwise howsoever, and in the possession of any Tribe, band or body of Indians or of any Indian of any such Tribe, band or body, shall be liable to be taken, seized or distrained for any debt, matter or cause whatsoever.

15. For the purpose of determining what persons are entitled to hold, use or enjoy the lands and other immoveable properly belonging to or appropriated to the use of the various tribes, bands or bodies of Indians in Canada, the following persons and classes of persons, and none other, shall be considered as
Indians belonging to the tribe, band or body of Indians interested in any such lands or immoveable property:
Firstly. All persons of Indian blood, reputed to belong to the particular tribe, band or body of Indians interested in such lands or immoveable property, and their descendants;
Secondly. All persons residing among such Indians, whose parents were or are, or either of them was or is, descended on either side from Indians or an Indian reputed to belong to the particular tribe, band or body of Indians interested in such lands or immoveable property, and the descendants of all such persons; And
Thirdly. All women lawfully married to any of the persons included in the several classes hereinbefore designated; the children issue of such marriages, and their descendants.

16. Indians and persons intermarried with Indians, residing upon any Indian Lands, and engaged in the pursuit of agriculture as their then principal means of support, shall be liable, if so directed by the Secretary of State, or any officer or person by him thereunto authorized, to perform labor on the public roads laid out or used in or through or abutting upon such Indian lands, such labor to be performed under the sole control of the said Secretary of State, officer or person, who may direct when, where and how and in what manner, the said labor shall be applied, and to what extent the same shall be imposed upon Indians or persons intermarried with Indians, who may be resident upon any of the said lands; and the said Secretary of State, officer or person shall have the like power to enforce the performance of all such labor by imprisonment or otherwise, as may be done by any power or authority under any law, rule or regulation in force in that one of the Provinces of Canada

in which such lands lie, for the non-performance of statute labor ; But the labor to be so required of any such Indian or person intermarried with an Indian, shall not exceed in amount or extent what may be required of other inhabitants of the same province, county or other local division, under the laws requiring and regulating such labor and the performance thereof.

17. No persons other than Indians and those intermarried with Indians, shall settle, reside upon or occupy any land or road, or allowance for roads running through any lands belonging to or occupied by any tribe, band or body of Indians ; and all mortgages or hypothecs given or consented to by any Indians or any persons intermarried with Indians, and all leases, contracts and agreements made or purporting to be made, by any Indians or any person intermarried with Indians, whereby persons other than Indians are permitted to reside upon such lands, shall be absolutely void.

18. If any persons other than Indians or those intermarried with Indians do, without the license of the Secretary of State, (which license, however, he may at any time revoke,) settle, Indian reside upon or occupy any such lands, roads or allowances for roads, the Secretary of State, or such officer or person as he may thereunto depute and authorize, shall, on complaint made to him, and on proof of the fact to his satisfaction, issue his warrant signed and sealed, directed to the sheriff of the proper county or district, or if the said lands be not situated within any county or district, then directed to any literate person willing to act in the premises, commanding him forthwith to remove from the said lands or roads, or allowances for roads, all such persons and their families, so settled, residing upon or occupying the same ; and such sheriff or other person shall, accordingly, remove such persons, and for that purpose shall have the same powers as in the execution of criminal process ; but the provisions in this and the four next following sections shall extend to such Indian lands only, as the Governor, from time to time, by Proclamation published in the Canada Gazette, declares and makes subject to the same, and so long only as such proclamation remains in force.

19. If any person alter having been removed as aforesaid returns to, settles upon, resides upon, or occupies, any of the said lands or roads or allowances for roads, the Secretary of State removed, if or any officer or person deputed and authorized, as aforesaid, upon view, or upon proof on oath made before him or to his satisfaction, that the said person has returned to, settled or resided upon or occupied any of the said lands or roads or allowances for roads, shall direct and send his warrant signed and sealed, to the Sheriff of the proper County or District, or to any literate person therein, and if the said lands be not situated within any County, then to any literate person, commanding him forthwith to arrest such person and commit him to the Common Gaol of the said County or District or to the Common Gaol of the nearest County or District to the said lands, if the said lands be not within any County or District, there to remain for the time ordered by such warrant, but which shall not exceed thirty days.

20. Such Sheriff or other person shall accordingly arrest the said party, and deliver him to the Gaoler or Sheriff of the proper County or District who shall receive such person, and imprison him in the said Common Gaol for the term aforesaid, there to remain without bail and without being entitled to the liberties or limits of the said Gaol. -

21. The said Secretary of Slate, or such officer or person as aforesaid, shall cause the judgment or order against the offender to be drawn up, and such judgment shall not be removed by Certiorari or otherwise, or be appealed from, but shall be final.

22. If any person without the license in writing of the Secretary of State, or of some officer or person deputed by him for that purpose, trespasses upon any of the said lands or roadster allowances for roads, by cutting, carrying away or removing therefrom, any of the trees, saplings, shrubs, underwood or timber thereon, or by removing any of the stone or soil of the said lands, roads or allowances Tor roads, the person so trespassing shall for every tree he cuts, carries away or removes, forfeit and pay the sum of twenty dollars, and for cutting, carrying or removing any of the saplings, shrubs, underwood or timber, if under the value of one dollar, the sum of four dollars, but if over the value of one dollar, then the sum of twenty dollars, and for removing any of the stone or soil aforesaid, the sum of twenty dollars, such fine to be recovered by the said Secretary of State, or any officer or person by him deputed by distress and sale of the goods and chattels of the party or parties fined, or the said Secretary of State, officer or person without proceeding by distress and sale as aforesaid, may, upon the non-payment of the said fine, order the party or parties to be imprisoned in the Common Gaol as aforesaid, for a period not exceeding thirty days, when the fine does not exceed twenty dollars, or for a period not exceeding three months, where the fine does exceed twenty dollars; and upon the return of any warrant for distress or sale, if the amount thereof has not been made, or if any part of it remains unpaid, the said Secretary of State, officer or person, may commit the party in default upon such warrant, to the Common Gaol as aforesaid, for a period not exceeding thirty days if the sum claimed by the Secretary of State, upon the said warrant, does not exceed twenty dollars, or for a time not exceeding three months if the sum claimed does exceed twenty dollars ; all such fines shall be paid to the Receiver General, to be disposed of for the use and benefit of the Tribe, band or body of Indians for whose benefit the lands are held, in such manner as the Governor may direct.

23. In all orders, writs, warrants, summonses and proceedings whatsoever made, issued or taken by the Secretary of State, or any officer or person by him deputed as aforesaid, it shall not be necessary for him or such officer or person, to insert or express the name of the person summoned, arrested, distrained upon, imprisoned or otherwise proceeded against therein, except when the name of such person is truly given to or known by the Secretary of State, officer or person, and if the name be not truly given to or known by him, he may name or describe the person by any part of the name of such person given to or known by him;
and if no part of the name be given to or known by him he may describe the person proceeded against in any manner by which he may be identified ; and all such proceedings containing or purporting to give the name or description of any such person as aforesaid shall prima facie be sufficient.

24. All Sheriffs, Gaolers or Peace Officers to whom any such process is directed by the said Secretary of State, or by any officer or person by him deputed as aforesaid, shall obey the same, and all other officers upon reasonable requisition shall assist in the execution thereof.

25. If any Railway, road or public work passes through or causes injury to any land belonging to or in possession of any tribe, band or body of Indians, compensation shall be made to them therefor, in the same manner as is provided with respect to the lands or rights of other persons ; the Secretary of State shall act for them in any matter relating to the settlement of such compensation, and the amount awarded in any case shall be paid to the Receiver General for the use of the tribe, band or body of Indians for whose benefit the lands are held.

26. The Secretary of State is hereby substituted for the Commissioner of Indian Lands for Lower Canada, under the fourteenth chapter of the Consolidated Statutes for Lower Canada, respecting Indians and Indian lands, which shall continue to apply to Indians and Indian lands, in the Province of Quebec, in so far as it is not inconsistent with this Act, and shall have all the powers and duties assigned to such. Commissioner by the said Act, except that the lands and property heretofore vested in the said Commissioner shall henceforth be vested in the Crown, and shall be under the management of the Secretary of State, who shall manage the same on behalf of the Crown, and the suits respecting them shall be brought in the name of the Crown, and the said Secretary of State shall not be bound to have any domicile in the Province of Quebec or to give security ; and so much of the said Act as is inconsistent with this Act is repealed.

27. The period limited by the sixth section of the Act last cited, as that within which informations may be brought under that Act, shall be one year instead of six months.

28. In all cases of encroachment upon any lands set apart for Indian reservations or for the use of the Indians, not herein before provided for, it shall be lawful to proceed by information in the name of Her Majesty in the Superior Courts of Law or Equity, notwithstanding the legal title may not be vested in the Crown.

29. The Governor may authorize surveys, plans and reports to be made of any lands reserved for Indians shewing and distinguishing the improved lands, the forests and lands fit for settlement, and such other information as may be required.

30. The proceeds arising from the sale or lease of any Indian lands or from the timber thereon shall be paid to the Receiver General to the credit of Indian Fund.

31. The fifty-seventh chapter of the Revised Statutes of Nova Scotia, Third Series, is hereby repealed, and the chief Commissioner and Deputy Commissioners under the said chapter, shall forthwith pay over all monies in their hands arising from the selling or leasing of Indian lands, or otherwise under the said chapter, to the Receiver General of Canada by whom they shall be credited to the Indian Fund of Nova Scotia and all such monies in the hands of the Treasurer of Nova Scotia, shall be paid over by him to the Receiver General of Canada, by whom they shall be credited to the said Indian Fund. And all Indian lands and property now vested in the said Chief Commissioner, Deputy Commissioner, or other persona whomsoever, for the use of Indians, shall henceforth be vested in the Crown and shall be under the management of the Secretary of State.

32. The eighty-fifth chapter of the Revised Statutes of New Brunswick respecting Indian Reserves is hereby repealed, and the Commissioners under the said chapter, shall forthwith pay over all monies in their hands arising from the selling or leasing of Indian Lands or otherwise under the said chapter, to the Receiver General of Canada, by whom they shall be credited to the Indians of New Brunswick, and all such monies now in the hands of the Treasurer of New Brunswick shall be paid over to the Receiver General of Canada, to be credited to the said Indians. And all Indian lands and property now vested in the said Commissioner, or other person whomsoever, for the use of Indians, shall henceforth be vested in the Crown and shall be under the management of the Secretary of State.

33. Nothing in this Act contained shall affect the provisions of the ninth chapter of the Consolidated Statutes of Canada, intituled: An Ad respecting the civilization and enfranchisement of cer-

tain Indians, in so far as respects Indians in the Provinces of Quebec and Ontario, nor of any other Act when the same is not inconsistent with this Act.

34. The Secretary of State is hereby substituted for the Commissioner of Crown Lands as regards the Ordnance and admiralty lands transferred to the late Province of Canada and lying in the Provinces of Quebec and Ontario.

35. All powers and duties vested in the Commissioner of Crown Lands with respect to the said Ordnance or Admiralty Lands, in the Provinces of Quebec and Ontario, by the Act of the Parliament of the late Province of Canada, passed in the twenty third year of Her Majesty's reign, and chaptered two, intituled : An Act respecting the sale and management of the Public Lands, or by the twenty-third chapter of the Consolidated Statutes of the said late Province, intituled : An Act respecting the sale and management of Timber on Public Lands, (both which Acts shall continue to apply to the said lands ;)—or by any other Act or law in force in any of the Provinces now composing the Dominion of Canada, at the time of the Union of the said Provinces, are hereby transferred to and vested in the said Secretary of State, and shall be exercised and performed by him ; Provided that in construing the two Acts cited in this Section, with reference to the said lands, the words " Secretary of State " shall be substituted for the words Commissioner of Crown Lands," and for the words " Registrar of the Province,"—the words " Governor General " shall be substituted for the word " Governor " and the words " Governor General in Council " for the words " Governor in Council,"—and the Governor General in Council may direct that the said two Acts or either of them, or any part or parts of either or both of them shall apply to the Indian Lands in the Provinces of Quebec and Ontario, or to any of the said lands, and may from time to time repeal any such Order in Council and make another or others instead thereof ; and provided further, that all the powers and duties by this section vested in the Secretary of State, shall be deemed to have been so vested from and after the first day of July now last past, and may be by him exercised with reference to any act or thing done or performed since that date, in connection with Ordnance or Indian Lands.

36. The Secretary of State shall also have the control and management of all Crown Lands being the property of the Dominion, that are not specially under the control of the Public Works Department.

37. The Governor in Council may, from time to time, make such Regulations as he deems expedient for the protection and management of the Indian lands in Canada or any part thereof, and of the timber thereon or cut from off the said lands, whether surrendered for sale or reserved or set apart for the Indians, and for ensuring and enforcing the collection of all moneys payable in respect of the said lands or timber, and for the direction and government of the officers and persons employed in the management thereof or otherwise with reference thereto, and generally for carrying out and giving effect to the provisions of this Act ;—and by such Regulations the Governor in Council may impose such fines not exceeding in any case two hundred dollars, as he deems necessary for ensuring the due observance of such Regulations, the payment of all such moneys as aforesaid, and the enforcing of due obedience to the provisions of this Act,—and may by such Regulations provide for the forfeiture, or the seizure and detention of any timber in respect of which the said Regulations have been infringed, or on which any sum payable in respect thereof has not been paid, and for the sale of such timber (if not forfeited,) in case the dues, damages and fine be not paid within the time

limited by such regulations, and the payment thereof out of the proceeds of the sale; and if forfeited such timber shall be dealt with as the regulation may direct :—and may appropriate any such fines in such manner he may see fit ; and the Governor in Council may by such regulations provide for the forfeiture of any lease, licence of occupation, licence to cut timber, or other licence or permission of any kind with respect to such lands, if the conditions on which such licence or permission is granted are not observed ; but no such provision imposing any penalty or forfeiture shall impair or diminish any right or remedy of the Crown to recover any money or enforce the performance of the conditions of any such sale, lease, contract, obligation, licence, or permission in the ordinary course of law.

38. All Regulations or Orders in Council made under the next preceding section shall be published in the Canada Gazette, and being so published shall have the force of law, from the date of their publication or from such later date as may be therein appointed for their coming into force ; and any such regulation maybe repealed, amended or re-enacted by any subsequent regulation, and shall be in force until so repealed or amended unless an earlier period be therein appointed for their ceasing to be in force ; and a copy of any such Regulations purporting to be printed by the Queen's Printer shall be prime facie evidence thereof.

39. The Governor may, from time to time, appoint officers and agents to carry out this Act, and any Orders in Council made under it, which officers and agents shall be paid in such manner and at such rates as the Governor in Council may direct.

46. The Governor in Council may at any time assign any the duties and powers hereby assigned to and vested in the Secretary of State, to any other member of the Queen's Privy Council for Canada, and his department, and from the period appointed for that purpose by any order in Council such duties and powers shall be transferred to, and vested in such other member of Her Majesty's Privy Council for Canada and his department.

41. The Secretary of State shall annually lay before Parliament within ten days after the meeting thereof, a report of the proceedings, transactions and affairs of the department during the year then next preceding.

42. So much of any Act or law as may be inconsistent with this Act, or as makes any provision in any matter provided for by this Act, other than such as is hereby made, is repealed, except only as to things done, obligations contracted, or penalties incurred before the coming into force of this Act.

An Act for the gradual enfranchisement of Indians, the better management of Indian affairs, and to extend the provisions of the Act 31st Victoria, Chapter 42. S.C. 1869, c. 6. (32-33 Vict.)
CAP VI.
An Act for the gradual enfranchisement of Indians, the better management of Indian affairs, and to extend the provisions of the Act 31st Victoria, Chapter 4-2.
[Assented to 22nd June, 1869.]
Her Majesty, by and with the advice and consent of the Senate and House of Commons of Canada, enacts as follows :

1. In Townships or other tracts of land set apart or reserved for Indians in Canada, and subdivided by survey into lots, no Indian or person claiming to be of Indian blood, or intermarried with an In-

dian family, shall be deemed to be lawfully in possession of any land in such Townships or tracts, unless he or she has been - or shall be located for the same by the order of the Superintendent General of Indian affairs ; and any such person or persons, assuming possession of any lands of that description, shall be dealt with as illegally in possession, and be liable to be summarily ejected therefrom, unless that within six months from the passing of this Act, a location title be granted to such person or persons by the said Superintendent General of Indian affairs or such officer or person as he may thereunto depute and authorize ; but the conferring of any such location title shall not have the effect of rendering the land covered thereby transferable or subject to seizure under legal process.

2. Any person liable to be summarily ejected, under the next preceding section, may be removed from the land of which ho May have assumed possession, in the manner provided by the eighteenth section of the Act passed in the thirty-first year of Her Majesty's reign, chapter forty-two, with respect to persons other than Indians or those intermarried with Indians settling on the lands therein referred to without license of the Secretary of Shite ; and the said section and the nineteenth, twentieth and twenty-first sections of the said Act, are hereby extended to and shall apply to persons liable to be summarily ejected under this Act, as fully in all respects as to poisons liable to be removed from lands under the said Act.

3. Any person who shall sell, barter, exchange or give to any Indian man, woman, or child, any kind of spirituous or other intoxicating liquors, or cause or procure the same to be done, or open and keep or cause to be opened and kept, on any land set apart or reserved for Indians a tavern, house or building where spirituous or intoxicating liquors are sold or disposed of, shall, upon conviction in the manner provided by section twelve of the said Act thirty-first Victoria, chapter forty-two, be subject to the fine therein mentioned ; and in default of payment such fine, or of any fine imposed by the above mentioned twelfth section of the said Act, any person no offending may be committed to prison by the Justice of the Peace before whom the conviction shall take place, for a period not more than three months, or until such fine be paid; and the commander of any steamer or other vessel, or boat, from on board or on board of which, any spirituous or other intoxicating liquor shall have been, or may be sold or disposed of to any Indian man, woman, or child, shall be liable to a similar penalty.

4. In the division among the members of any tribe, bond, or body of Indians, of any annuity money, interest money or rents, no person of less than ono-fourth Indian blood, born after the passing of this Act, shall be deemed entitled to share in any annuity, interest or rents, after a certificate to that effect is given by the Chief or Chiefs of the hand or tribe in Council, and sanctioned by the Superintendent General of Indian affairs.

5. Any Indian or person of Indian blood who shall be convicted of any crime punishable by imprisonment in any Penitentiary or other place of confinement, shall, during such imprisonment, be excluded from participating in the annuities, interest money, or rents payable to the Indian tribe, band, or body, of which he or she is a member ; and whenever any Indian shall be convicted of any crime punishable by imprisonment in a Penitentiary, or other place of confinement, the legal costs incurred in procuring such conviction, and in carrying out the various sentences recorded, may be defrayed by the Superintendent General of Indian Affairs, and paid out of any annuity or interests coming to such Indian, or to the band or tribe, as the case may be.

6. The fifteenth section of the thirty-first Victoria, Chapter forty-two, is amended by adding to it the following proviso :

"Provided always that any Indian woman marrying any other than an Indian, shall cease to be an Indian within the meaning of this Act, nor shall the children issue of such marriage be considered as Indians within the meaning of this Act ; Provided also, that any Indian woman marrying an Indian of any other tribe, band or body shall cease to be a member of the tribe, band or body to which she formerly belonged, and become a member of the tribe, band or body of which her husband is a member, and the children, issue of this marriage, shall belong to their father's tribe only."

7. The Superintendent General of Indian affairs shall have power to stop the payment of the annuity and interest money of any person of Indian blood who may be proved to the satisfaction of the Superintendent General of Indian affairs to have been guilty of deserting his wife or child, and the said Superintendent may apply the same towards the support of any woman or child so deserted.

8. The Superintendent General of Indian Affairs in cases where sick or disabled, or aged and destitute persons are not provided for by the tribe, band or body of Indians of which they are members, may furnish sufficient aid from the funds of each tribe, band or body, for the relief of such sick, disabled, aged or destitute persons.

9. Upon the death of any Indian holding under location title any lot or parcel of land, the right and interest therein of such deceased Indian shall, together with his goods and chattels, devolve upon his children, on condition of their providing for the maintenance of their mother, if living ; and such children shall have a life estate only in such land which shall not be transferable or subject to seizure under legal process, but should such Indian die without issue, such lot or parcel of land and goods and chattels shall be vested in the Crown for the benefit of the tribe, band or body of Indians, after providing for the support of the widow (if any) of such deceased Indian.

10. The Governor may order that the Chiefs of any tribe, band or body of Indians shall be elected by the male members of each Indian Settlement of the full age of twenty-one years at such time and place, and in such manner, as the Superintendent General of Indian Affairs may direct, and they shall in such case be elected for a period of three years, unless deposed by the Governor for dishonesty, intemperance, or immorality, and they shall be in the proportion of one Chief and two Second Chiefs for every two to hundred people ; but any such band composed of thirty people' may have one Chief; Provided always that all life Chiefs now living shall continue as such until death or resignation, or until their removal by the Governor for dishonesty, intemperance or immorality.

11. The Chief or Chiefs of any tribe, band or body of Indians Shall be bound to cause the roads, bridges, ditches and fences within their Reserve to be put and maintained in proper order, in accordance with the instructions received from time to time from the Superintendent General of Indian Affairs ; and whenever in the opinion of the Superintendent General of "Indian Affairs the same are not so put or maintained in order, he may cause the work to be performed at the cost of the said tribe, band or body of Indians, or of the particular Indian in default, as the case may be either out of their annual allowances, or otherwise.

12. The Chief or Chiefs of any Tribe in Council may frame, subject to confirmation by the Governor in Council, rales and regulations for the following subjects, viz :

1. The care of the public health.

2. The observance of order and decorum at assemblies of the people in General Council, or on other occasions.

3. The repression of intemperance and profligacy.

4. The prevention of trespass by cattle.

5. The maintenance of roads, bridges, ditches and fences.

6. The construction of and maintaining in repair of school houses, council houses and other Indian public buildings.

7. The establishment of pounds and the appointment of pound-keepers.

13. The Governor General in Council may on the report of the Superintendent General of Indian Affairs order the issue of Letters Patent granting to any Indian who from the degree of civilization to which he has attained, and the character for integrity and sobriety which he bears, appears to be a safe and suitable person for becoming a proprietor of land, a life estate in the land which has been or may be allotted to him within the Reserve belonging to the tribe band or body of which he is a member ; and in such case such Indian shall have power to dispose of the' same by will, to any of his children, and id he dies intestate as to any such lands, the same shall descend to his children according to the laws of that portion of the Dominion of Canada in which such lands are situate, and the said children to whom such land is so devised or descends shall have the fee simple thereof.

14. If any enfranchised Indian owning land by virtue of the thirteenth and sixteenth sections of this Act, dies without loaving any children, such land shall escheat to the Crown for the benefit of the tribe, band, or body of Indians to which ho, or his father, or mother (as the ease may be) belonged ; but if ho leaves a widow, she shall, instead of Dower to which she shall not be entitled, have the said land for life or until her re-marriage, and upon her death or re-marriage it shall escheat to the Crown for the benefit of the tribe, band or body of Indians to which lie, or his father, or mother (ns the case may be) belonged.

15. The wife or unmarried daughters of any deceased Indian who may, in consequence of the operation of the thirteenth and sixteenth sections of this Act be deprived of all benefit from their husband's or father's land, shall in the periodical division of the annuity and interest money or other revenues of their husband's or father's tribe or band, and so long as she or they continue to reside upon the reserve belonging to the tribe or band, and remain in widowhood or unmarried, be entitled to and receive two shaves instead of one share of such annuity and interest money.

16. Every such Indian shall, before the issue of the letters patent mentioned in the thirteenth section of this Act, declare to the Superintendent General of Indian Affairs, the name and surname by which he wishes to be enfranchised and thereafter known, and on his receiving such letters patent, in such name and surname, ho shall be hold to be also enfranchised, and he shall thereafter be known by such name and surname, and his wife and minor unmarried children, shall be held to be enfranchised ; and from the date of such letters patent, the provisions of any Act or law making any distinction between the legal rights and liabilities of Indians and those of Her Majesty's other subjects shall cease to apply to any Indian, his wife or minor children as aforesaid, so declared to be enfranchised, who shall no longer be deemed Indians within the meaning of the laws relating to Indians, except in so far as their right to participate in the annuities and interest money and rents, of the tribe, hand, or body of Indians to which they belonged is concerned ; except that the

twelfth, thirteenth, and fourteenth sections of the Act thirty-first Victoria, chapter forty-two, and the eleventh section of this Act, shall apply, to such Indian, his wife and children.

17. In the allotting of locations, and in the issue of Letters Patent to Indians for land, the quantity of land located or to be located or passed into Patent, shall, except in special cases to be reported upon to the Governor in Council, hear (as nearly as may be) the same proportion to the total quantity of land in the Reserve, as the number of persons to whom such lands are located or patented bears to the total number of heads of families of the tribe, hand or body of Indians and male members thereof not being hoods of families, but being above the age of fourteen years, in such reserve.

18. If any Indian enfranchised under this Act dies leaving any child under the age of twenty-one years, the Superintendent of General of Indian Affairs shall appoint same person to be the tutor or guardian the case may be of such child as to property and rights until it attains the age of twenty-one years ; and the widow of such Indian, being also the mother of any such child, shall receive its share of the proceeds of the estate of such Indian during the minority of the child, and shall be entitled to reside on the land left by such Indian, so long ns in the opinion of the Superintendent General she lives respectably.

19. Any under this Act when he is not so, shall be liable, on conviction before any one Justice of the Peace, to imprisonment for any period not exceeding three months.

20. Such lands in any Indian Reserve as may be conveyed to any enfranchised Indian by Letters Patent, shall not, as long as the life estate of such Indian continues, be subject to seizure under legal process, or be mortgaged, hypothecated, sold, exchanged, transferred, leased, or otherwise disposed of

21. Indians not enfranchised shall have the right to sue for Debt duo to them, or for any wrong inflicted upon them, or to compel the performance of obligations made with them.

22. The Under Secretary of State shall be charged, under the Secretary of State of Canada, with the performance of the Departmental duties of the Secretary of State under the said Act, and with the control and management of the officers, clerics, and servants of the Department, and with such other powers and duties as may be assigned to him by the Governor in Council.

23. Chapter nine of the Consolidated Statutes of Canada is hereby repealed.

24. This Act shall be construed as one Act with the Act thirty first Victoria, chapter forty-two.

An Act to provide for the establishment of "The Department of the Interior." S.C. 1873, c. 4. (36 Vict.)

CHAP. 4.

An Act to provide for the establishment of " The Department of the Interior."

[Assented to 3rd May, 1873.]

HER Majesty, by and with the advice and consent of the Senate and House of Commons of Canada, enacts as follows:—

1. There shall be a Department of the Civil Service of Canada to be called " The Department of the Interior," over which the Minister of the Interior, for the time being, appointed by the Governor General, by Commission under the Great Seal of Canada, shall preside; and he shall hold office daring pleasure, and shall have the management of the Department of the Interior.

2. The Minister of the Interior shall have the control and management of the affairs of the North West Territories.

3. The Minister of the Interior shall be the Superintendent General of Indian affairs, and shall, as such, have the control and management of the lands and property of the Indians in Canada.

4. The Minister of the Interior shall have the control and management of all Crown Lands being the property of the Dominion, including those known as Ordnance and Admiralty Lands, and all other public lands not specially under the control of the Public Works Department, or of that of Militia and Defence, (and excepting also Maxine Hospitals and Light Houses and land connected therewith, and St. Paul's, Sable and Portage Islands,) and he is hereby substituted for the former Commissioner of Crown Lands, as regards Ordnance and Admiralty Lands, transferred to the late Province of Canada, and lying in Ontario and Quebec.

5. The Minister of the Interior is hereby substituted for the Secretary of State of Canada in all the powers, attributes, functions, restrictions, and duties laid down and prescribed in the " Dominion Lands Act, 1872 and wherever the words " Secretary of State " are used in that Act, the words " Minister of the Interior " shall be deemed to be substituted therefor; and wherever the words " Department of the Secretary of State " are used, the words " Department of the Interior " shall be deemed to be substituted therefor; and all the provisions of the said Act shall be and continue obligatory upon the Minister of the Interior ; and all the officers appointed under the said Act shall become, and continue to be officers of the Department of the Interior.

6. The Governor may appoint, and at his pleasure remove, a " Deputy of the Minister of the Interior," who shall be charged, under the Minister of the Interior, with the performance of the Departmental duties of the Minister of the Interior, and with the control and management of the Officers, Agents, Clerks and Servants of the Department, and with such other powers and duties as may be assigned to him by the Minister of the Interior ; and the fourteenth section of " The Canada Civil Service. Act. 1868," 'shall apply to the Deputy of the Minister of the Interior, as if the Department of the Interior were mentioned in Schedule A to that Act ; and the words " Deputy of the Minister of the Interior," shall be deemed to be substituted for the words " Under Secretary of State for the Provinces " in that Schedule.

7. The Governor may also appoint, subject to the " Civil Service Act, 1868," and at his pleasure remove such Departmental Officers, agents, clerks and servants as may be requisite for the proper conduct of the business of the Department at Ottawa, and also such agents, officer's, clerks and servants as may be necessary for the same purpose in the North West Territories, and amongst the Indians, and elsewhere, in the Dominion.

8. The several clauses of chapter forty-two of the Statutes passed in the thirty-first year of Her Majesty's reign, entitled "An Act providing for the organization of the Department of the Secretary of Stale of Canada, and for the management of Indian and Ordnance Lande," relating to the management of Indian affairs and lands, and of Ordnance Lands, shall govern the Minister of the Interior in the several matters to which they relate ; and wherever the words " Secretary of State " or " Department of the Secretary of State " occur in those clauses, the words " Minister of the Interior " and "Department of the Interior " shall be deemed to be substituted therefor.

9. The Governor in Council may, by proclamation, from time to time, exempt from the operation

of this Act, and of the said Act, chapter forty-two of the Statutes passed in the thirty-first year of Her Majesty's reign, or of any one or more of the clauses thereof the Indians, or any tribe of them, or the Indian Lands, or any portion of them, in the North West Territories, or in the Province of Manitoba, or in the Province of British Columbia, and may again, by like proclamation, from time to time, remove such exemption.

10. The Geological Survey of Canada as now existing shall be attached to the Department of the Interior.

11. The Minister of the Interior shall annually lay before Parliament within fifteen days after the meeting thereof, a report of the proceedings, transactions and affairs of the Department during the year then next preceding.

12. The Secretary of State of Canada shall have charge of the State Correspondence with the Governments of the several Provinces included, or which may be hereafter included within the Dominion of Canada.

13. The remaining duties hitherto discharged by the Secretary of State for the Provinces, as regards matters other than those relating to the subjects by this Act transferred to the Department of the Interior, shall devolve upon, and be discharged by the Secretary of State of Canada, to whom also is transferred the duty of supplying the stationery required by the several Departments of the Government, and the charge of that Branch of the Public Service ; and the Queen's Printer shall he held to be an officer of tins Department.

14. The Office of Secretary of State for the Provinces is and stands abolished.

15. This Act shall only come into force after the expiration of one month from the publication in the Canada Gazette of a Proclamation to that effect under an order of the Governor in Council.

16. So much of any Act or law as may be inconsistent with Act, or as makes any provision in any matter provided for by this Act, other than such as is hereby made is repealed, excepting as to things done, obligations contracted or penalties incurred before the coining into force of this Act.

An Act to amend certain Laws respecting Indians, and to extend certain Laws relating to matters connected with Indians to the Provinces of Manitoba and British Columbia. S.C. 1874, c. 21. (37 Vict.)

An Ad to amend certain Laws respecting Indians, And to extend certain Laws relating to matters connected with Indians to the Provinces of Manitoba and British Columbia.

[Absented to 26ih May, 1874.]

HER Majesty, by and with the advice and consent of the Senate and House of Commons of Canada, enacts as follows :—

1. The twelfth section of the Act thirty-first Victoria, chapter forty-two, intituled "An Act 'providing for the organization of the Department of the Secretary of State of Canada, and for the management of Indian and Ordnance Lands," and the third section of the Act thirty-second and thirty-third Victoria, chapter six, intituled "An Act for the gradual enfranchisement of Indians, the better' management of Indian affairs, and to extend the provisions of the Act thirty-first, Victoria, chapter forty-two of are hereby repealed, and the following shall he read in lieu of the last mentioned section :—

"3. 1. Whoever sells, exchanges with, barters, supplies, or gives to any Indian man, woman or child in Canada, any kind of intoxicating liquor, or causes or procures the same to be done, or connives or attempts thereat or opens or keeps, or causes to be opened or kept on any land set apart or reserved for Indians, a tavern, house, or building where intoxicating liquor is sold, bartered, exchanged, or given, or is found in possession of intoxicating liquor in the house, tent, wigwam, or place of abode of any Indian, shall, on conviction thereof before any Justice of the Peace upon the evidence of one credible witness other than the informer or prosecutor, to liable to imprisonment for a period not exceeding two years, and be fined not more than five hundred dollars, one moiety to go to the informer or prosecutor, and the other moiety to Her Majesty, to inform part of the fund for the benefit of that tribe or body of Indians with respect to one or more members of which the offence was committed ; and the commander or person in charge of any steamer or other vessel, or boat, from or on board of which any into intoxicating liquor shall have been sold, bartered, exchanged, supplied or given to Any Indian man, woman or child, shall be liable, on conviction thereof before any Justice of the Peace, upon the evidence of one credible witness other than the informer or prosecutor, to be fined not exceeding five hundred dollars for each such offence, the moieties thereof to be applicable as hereinbefore mentioned, and in default of immediate payment of such fine any person so fined may be committed to any common gaol, house of correction, lock-up, or other place of confinement by the Justice of the Peace before whom the conviction shall take place, for a period of not more than twelve months, or until such fine shall be paid ; and in all cases arising under this section, shall be competent witnesses : but no penalty shall be incurred in case of sickness where any intoxicating liquor is made use of under the sanction of any medical man or under the directions of a minister of religion."

" 2. The keg, barrel, case, box, package or receptacle whence Intoxicating liquor has been sold, exchanged, bartered, supplied or given, and as well that in which the original supply was contained as the vessel wherein any portion of such original supply was supplied as aforesaid, and the balance of the contents thereof, if such barrel, keg, ease, box, package, receptacle or vessel aforesaid respectively, can be identified, and any intoxicating liquor imported or manufactured or brought into and upon any land set apart or reserved for Indians, or into the house, tent, wigwam or place of abode of any Indian, may be seized by any constable wheresoever found on such land ; and on complaint before any Judge, Stipendiary Magistrate or Justice of the Peace, he may, on the evidence of any credible witness that this Act has been contravened in respect thereof, declare the same forfeited, and cause the same to be forthwith destroyed; and the person in whose- possession they were found may be condemned to pay a penalty not exceeding one hundred dollars, nor less than fifty dollars, and the costs of prosecution ; and one-half of such penalty shall belong to the prosecutor, the other half to Her Majesty for the purposes hereinbefore mentioned, and in default of immediate payment the offender may he committed to any common gaol, house of correction, lock-up or other place of confinement for any time not exceeding six months unless such fine and costs are sooner paid."

"3. When it shall be proved before any Judge, Stipendiary Magistrate or Justice of the Peace that any vessel, boat, canoe, or conveyance of any description upon the sea or sea-coast, Or upon any river, lake or stream in Canada, is employed in carrying in intoxicating liquor, to be supplied to any Indian or Indians, such vessel, boat, canoe, or conveyance so employed may be seized and declared forfeited as in the last sub-section mentioned, and sold, and the proceeds thereof paid to Her Majesty for the purposes hereinbefore mentioned."

"4. It shall be lawful for any constable, without process of law, to arrest any Indian whom he may find in a state of intoxication, and to convey him to any common gaol, house of correction, lock-up or other place of confinement, there to be kept until he shall have become sober ; and such Indian shall, when sober, be brought before any Judge, Stipendiary Magistrate, or Justice of the Peace, and if convicted of being so found in a state of intoxication, shall be liable to imprisonment in any common gaol, house of correction, lock-up or other place of confinement, for any period not exceeding one month. And if any Indian having been so convicted as aforesaid, shall refuse, upon examination, to state or give information of the person, place, and time from whom, where and when he procured intoxicating liquor, and if from any other Indian, then, if within his knowledge, from whom, where and when such intoxicating liquor was originally procured or received, he shall be liable to imprisonment as aforesaid for a further period not exceeding fourteen days."

" 5. The words 'intoxicating liquor ' shall mean and include all spirits, strong waters, spirituous liquors, wines, or fermented or compounded liquors or intoxicating drink of any kind whatsoever, and intoxicating liquor or fluid; as also opium and any preparation thereof, whether liquid or solid ; and any other intoxicating drug or substance, and tobacco or tea mixed or compounded or impregnated with opium or with other intoxicating drug or substance, and whether the same, or any of them, be liquid or solid."

6. No prosecution, conviction or commitment under this Act shall be invalid on account of want of form so long as the same is according to the true meaning of this Act."

2. The following shall be taken and read as part of the fourteenth section of the thirty-first Victoria, chapter forty-two, that is to say :—

"Nor shall the same be sold, bartered, exchanged or given by any tribe, band or body of Indians or any Indian of any such tribe, band or body to any person or persons other than a tribe, band or body of Indians or any Indian of any tribe ; and any such sale, barter, exchange or gift, shall be absolutely null or void, unless any such sale, barter, exchange or gift be made with the written assent of the Indian agent; and any person who may buy or otherwise acquire any presents or property purchased as aforesaid without the written consent of the Indian agent as aforesaid shall be guilty of a misdemeanor, and be punishable by fine not exceeding two hundred dollars, or by imprisonment not exceeding six months in any place of confinement other than a Penitentiary."

3. Upon any inquest, or upon any enquiry into any matter Involving a criminal charge, or upon the trial of any crime or offence whatsoever, or by whomsoever committed, it shall be lawful for any Court Judge, Stipendiary Magistrate, Coroner or Justice of the Peace to receive the evidence of any Indian or aboriginal native or native of mixed blood, who is destitute of the knowledge of God, and of any fixed and clear belief in religion or in a future state of rewards and punishments, without administering the usual form of oath to any such Indian, aboriginal native or native of mixed blood as aforesaid, upon his solemn affirmation or declaration to tell the truth, the whole truth and nothing but the truth, or in such form as may be approved by such Court, Judge, Stipendiary Magistrate, Coroner or Justice of the Peace, as most binding in his conscience.

4. Provided that in the case of any inquest, or upon any inquiry into any matter involving a criminal

charge, or upon the trial of any crime or offence whatsoever, the substance of the evidence or information of any such Indian, aboriginal native or native of mixed blood as aforesaid, shall be reduced to writing, and signed by a mark of the person giving the same, and verified by the signature or mark of the person acting as interpreter (if any), and of the judge, Stipendiary Magistrate, Coroner or Justice of the Peace or person before whom such information shall have been given.

5. The court, judge, Stipendiary Magistrate, or Justice of the Peace shall, before taking any such evidence, information or examination, caution every such Indian, aboriginal native or native of mixed blood as aforesaid, that he will be liable to incur punishment if he do not so as aforesaid tell the truth.

6. The written declaration or examination made, taken and verified in manner aforesaid, of any such Indian, aboriginal native or native of mixed blood as aforesaid, may be lawfully read and received as evidence upon the trial of any criminal suit or proceedings when, under the like circumstances, the written affidavit, examination, deposition or confession of any person, might be lawfully read and received as evidence.

7. Every solemn affirmation or declaration in whatever form Effect of made or taken by any person as aforesaid shall be of the same force and effect, as if such person had taken an oath in the usual form, and shall, in like manner, incur the penalty of perjury in of falsehood.

8. An Indian is hereby defined to be a person within the definition contained in the fifteenth section of the thirty-first Victoria, chapter forty-two, as amended by the sixth section of the thirty second and thirty-third Victoria, chapter six, and who shall participate in the annuities and interest moneys and rents of any tribe, band or body of Indians.

9. Upon, from and after the passing of this Act, the Acts and portions of Acts hereinafter mentioned of the Parliament of Canada shall be and are hereby extended to and shall be in force the Provinces of Manitoba and of British Columbia : and all enactments and laws theretofore in force in the said Provinces, inconsistent with the said Acts, or making any provision in any matter provided for by the said Acts, other than such as is made by the said Acts, shall be repealed on and after the passing of this Act.

10. The Acts and portions of Acts hereinbefore mentioned And hereby extended to and to be in force in the Provinces of Manitoba and of British Columbia, are as follows :—

1. Sections six to twenty-five both inclusive and sections twenty eight, twenty-nine, thirty, thirty-seven, thirty eight, thirty-nine and forty-two, of the Act passed in the thirty-first year of Her Majesty's reign, and intituled: "An Act providing for the organisation of the Department of the Secretary of State of Canada, and for the management of Indian and Ordnance Lands;"

2. Sections one to twenty-one, both inclusive, and section twenty-four of the Act passed in the thirty-second and thirty third years of Her Majesty's reign, intituled : " An Act for the gradual enfranchisement of Indians, the better management of Indian affairs, and to extend the provisions of the Act thirty-first Victoria, chapter forty-two;"

3. Sections one, three, six, seven, eight, nine and sixteen, of the Act passed in the thirty-sixth year of Her Majesty's reign, and intituled : " An Act to provide for the establishment of the Department of the Interior.

11. The Governor in Council may, by proclamation from time to time, exempt from the operation

of the Act passed in the thirty-first year of Her Majesty's reign, and intituled : "An Act providing for the organization of the Department of the Secretary of State of Canada, and for the. management of Indian and Ordnance Lands," or from the operation of an Act passed in the thirty-second and thirty-third years of Her Majesty's reign, intituled " An Act for the gradual enfranchisement of Indians, the better management of Indian affairs, and to extend the proto visions of the Act thirty-first Victoria, chapter forty-two? or from the operation of the Act passed in the thirty-first year of Her Majesty's reign, and intituled: "An Act to provide for the establishment of the Department of the Interior," or from the operation of this Act, or from the operation of any one or more of the clauses of any one or more of the said Acts, the Indians or any of them, or any tribe of them or the Indian lands or any portions of them in the Province of Manitoba, of in the Province of British Columbia, or in either of them, and may again, by proclamation, from time to time, remove such exemption.

12. The Governor in Council may, by proclamation from time to time, direct the application of the Act passed in the thirty-first year of Her Majesty's reign, and intituled "An Act providing for the organization of the Department of the Secretary of State of Canada, and for the management of Indian and Ordnance Lands and of an Act passed in the thirty-second and thirty third yearn of Her Majesty's reign, intituled "An Act for the. gradual enfranchisement of Indians, the better management of Indian affairs, and to extend the provisions of the Act thirty first Victoria, chapter forty-two and an Act passed in the thirty sixth year of Her Majesty's reign, and intituled "An Act to provide for the establishment of the Department of the Interior;" or of any one or more of the clauses of any one or more of the said Acts to the Indians or any of them or any tribe of them or the Indian lands or any portions of them, or that the same be in force generally in the North West Territories.

13. The second, third, and seventh sections of the Ordinance, No. 85, of the Revised Statutes of British Columbia are hereby repealed.

14. This Act shall be construed as one Act with the Acts thirty-first Victoria, chapter forty-two, and thirty-second thirty- third Victoria, chapter six.

An Act to amend the Act providing for the organization of the Department of the Secretary of State of Canada? S.C. 18757 c- 6.

CHAP. 6.

An Act to amend the Act providing for the organization of the Department of the Secretary of State of Canada.

[Assented to 8th April, 1875.]

HER Majesty, by and with the advice of the Senate and House of Commons of Canada, enacts as follows :—

1. The following words are hereby added to, and shall form part of the fourth section of the said Act, passed in the thirty-first year of Her Majesty's reign, chapter forty-two, that is to say :—

" And the Deputy Registrar-General of Canada from time " to time appointed under the second section of this Act, may " sign and certify the registration of all instruments and documents required to be registered, and all such copies of " the same, or of any records in the custody of the Registrar "General as may be required to be certified or autnenticated as being copies 01 any instruments or documents as " aforesaid."

The Indian Act, 1876. S.C. 1876, c. 18. (39 Vict.)
CHAP. 18.
An Act to amend and consolidate the laws respecting Indians.
[Assented to 12th April, 1876.]
WHEREAS it is expedient to amend and consolidate the laws respecting Indians : Therefore Her Majesty, by and with the advice and consent of the Senate and House of Commons of Canada, enacts as follows :—

1. This Act shall be known and may be cited as "The Indian Act, 1876 ; " and shall apply to all the Provinces, and to the North West Territories, including the Territory of Keewatin.

2. The Minister of the Interior shall be Superintendent General of Indian Affairs, and shall be governed in the supervision of the said affairs, and in the control and management of the reserves, lands, moneys and property of Indians in Canada by the provisions of this Act.

TERMS.

3. The following terms contained in this Act shall be held to have the meaning hereinafter assigned to them, unless such meaning be repugnant to the subject or inconsistent with the context :—

1. The term " band" means any tribe, band or body of Indians who own or are interested in a reserve or in Indian lands in common, of which the legal title is vested in the Crown, or who share alike in the distribution of any annuities or interest moneys for which the Government of Canada is responsible ; the term " the band " means the band to which the context relates ; and the term " band," when action is being taken by the band as such, means the band in council.

2. The term " irregular band" means any tribe, band or body of persons of Indian blood who own no interest in any reserve or lands of which the legal title is vested in the Crown, who possess no common fund managed by the Government of Canada, or who have not had any treaty relations with the Crown.

3, The term " Indian " means First. Any male person of Indian blood reputed to belong to a particular band ; Secondly. Any child of such person ; Thirdly. Any woman who is or was lawfully married to such person :

(a) Provided that any illegitimate child, unless having shared with the consent of the band in the distribution moneys of such baud for a period exceeding two years, may, at any time, be excluded from the membership thereof by the band, if such proceeding be sanctioned by the Superintendent-General :

(b) Provided that any Indian having for five years continuously resided in a foreign country shall with the sanction of the Superintendent-General, cease to be a member thereof and shall not be permitted to become again a member thereof, or of any other band, unless the consent of the band with the approval of the Superintendent-General or his agent, be first had and obtained ; but this provision shall not apply to any professional man, mechanic, missionary, teacher or interpreter, while discharging his or her duty as such : .

(c) Provided that any Indian woman marrying any other than an Indian or a non-treaty Indian shall cease to be an Indian in any respect within the meaning of this Act, except that she shall be entitled to share equally with the members of the band to which she formerly belonged, in the annual or semi-annual distribution of their annuities, interest moneys and rents ; but this income may be commuted to her at any time at ten years' purchase with the consent of the band :

(d) Provided that any Indian woman marrying an Indian of any other band, or a non-treaty Indian shall cease to be a member of the band to which she formerly belonged, and become a member of the band or irregular band of which her husband is a member:

(e) Provided also that no half-breed in Manitoba who see has shared in the distribution of half-breed lands shall be accounted an Indian ; and that no half-breed head of a family (except the widow of an Indian, or a half-breed who has already been admitted into a treaty), shall, unless under very special circumstances, to be determined by the Superintendent- General or his agent, be accounted au Indian, or entitled to be admitted into any Indian treaty.

4. The term " non-treaty Indian " means any person of Indian blood who is reputed to belong to an irregular band, or who follows the Indian mode of life, even though such person be only a temporary resident in Canada.

5. The term "enfranchised Indian " means any Indian, his wife or minor unmarried child, who has received letters patent granting him in fee simple any portion of the reserve which may have been allotted to him, his wife and minor children, by the band to which he belongs, or any unmarried Indian who may have received letters patent for an allotment of the reserve.

6. The term " reserve " means any tract or tracts of land set apart by treaty or otherwise for the use or benefit of or granted to a particular band of Indians, of which the legal title is in the Crown, but which is unsurrendered, and includes all the trees, wood, timber, soil, stone, minerals, metals, or other valuables thereon or therein.

7. The term " special reserve " means any tract or tracts of land and everything belonging thereto set apart for the use or benefit, of any band or irregular band of Indians, the title of which is vested in a society, corporation or community legally established, and capable of suing and being sued, or in a person or persons of European descent, but which land is held in trust for, or benevolently allowed to be used by, such band or irregular band of Indians

8. The term " Indian lands " means any reserve or portion of a reserve which has been surrendered to the Crown.

9. The term " intoxicants " means and includes all spirits, strong waters, spirituous liquors, wines, or fermented or compounded liquors or intoxicating drink of any kind whatsoever, and any intoxicating liquor or fluid, as also opium and any preparation thereof whether liquid or solid, and any other intoxicating drug or substance, and tobacco or tea mixed or compounded or impregnated with opium or with other intoxicating drugs, spirits or substances, and whether the same or any of them be liquid or solid

10. The term " Superintendent-General " means the Superintendent-General of Indian Affairs.

11. The term " agent " means a commissioner, superintendent, agent, or other officer acting under the instructions of the Superintendent-General.

12. The term " person " means an individual other than an Indian, unless the context clearly requires another construction.

RESERVES.

4. All reserves for Indians or for any band of Indians, or in trust for their benefit, shall be deemed to

be reserved and held for the same purposes as before the passing of this Act, but subject to its provisions.

5. The Superintendent-General may authorize surveys, plans and reports to be made of any reserve for Indians, shewing and distinguishing the improved lands, the forests and lands fit for settlement, and such other information as may be required; and may authorize that the whole or any portion of a reserve be subdivided into lots.

6. In a reserve, or portion of a reserve, subdivided by survey into lots, no Indian shall be deemed to be lawfully in possession of one or more of such lots, or part of a lot, unless he or she has been or shall be located for the same by the band, with the approval of the Superintendent- General :

Provided that no Indian shall be dispossessed of any lot or part of a lot, on which he or she has improvements, without receiving compensation therefor, (at a valuation to be approved by the Superintendent-General) from the Indian who obtains the lot or part of a lot, or from the funds of the band, as may be determined by the Superintendent-General.

7. On the Superintendent-General approving of any location as aforesaid, he shall issue in triplicate a ticket granting a location title to such Indian, one triplicate of which he shall retain in a book to be kept for the purpose ; the other two he shall forward to the local agent, one to be delivered to the Indian in whose favor it was issued, the other to be filed by the agent, who shall permit it to be copied into the register of the band, if such register has been established :

8. The conferring of any such location title as aforesaid shall not have the effect of rendering the land covered thereby subject to seizure under legal process, or transferable except to an Indian of the same band, and in such case, only with the consent of the council thereof and the approval of the Superintendent-General, when the transfer shall be confirmed by the issue of a ticket in the manner prescribed in the next preceding section.

9. Upon the death of any Indian holding under location or other duly recognized title any lot or parcel of land, the right and interest therein of such deceased Indian shall, together with his goods and chattels, devolve one-third upon his widow, and the remainder upon his children equally ; and such children shall have a like estate in such land as their father; but should such Indian die without issue but leaving a widow, such lot or parcel of land and his goods and chattels shall be vested in her, and if he leaves no widow, then in the Indian nearest akin to the deceased, but if he have no heir nearer than a cousin, then the same shall be vested in the Crown for the benefit of the band : But whatever may be the final disposition of the land, the claimant or claimants shall not be held to be legally in possession until they obtain a location ticket from the Superintendent- General in the manner prescribed in the case of new locations.

10. Any Indian or non-treaty Indian in the Province of British Columbia, the Province of Manitoba, in the North West Territories, or in the Territory of Keewatin, who has, or shall have, previously to the selection of a reserve, possession of and made permanent improvements on a plot of land which has been or shall be included in or surrounded by a reserve, shall have the same privileges, neither more nor less, in respect of such plot, as an Indian enjoys who holds under a location title.

PROTECTION OF RESERVES.

11. No person, or Indian other than an Indian of the band, shall settle, reside or hunt upon, occupy or use any land or marsh, or shall settle, reside upon or occupy any road., or allowance for roads run-

ning through any reserve belonging to or occupied by such band ; and all mortgages or hypothecs given or consented to by any Indian, and all leases, contracts and agreements made or 'purporting to be made by any Indian, whereby persons or Indians other than Indians of the band are permitted to reside or hunt upon such reserve, shall be absolutely void.

12. If any person or Indian other than an Indian of the without the license of the Superintendent-General (which license, however, he may at any time revoke), settles, resides or hunts upon or occupies or uses any such land or marsh ; or settles, resides upon or occupies any such roads or allowances for roads, on such reserve, or if any Indian is illegally in possession of any lot or part of a lot in a sub-divided reserve, the Superintendent-General or such officer or person as he may thereunto depute and authorize, shall, on complaint made to him, and on proof of the fact to his satisfaction, issue his warrant signed and sealed, directed to the sheriff of the proper county or district, or if the said reserve be not situated within any county or district, then directed to any literate person willing to act in the premises, commanding him forthwith to remove from the said land or marsh or roads or allowances for roads, or lots or parts of lots, every such person or Indian and his family so settled residing or hunting upon or occupying, or being illegally in possession of the same, or to notify such person or Indian to cease using as aforesaid the said lands, marshes, roads or allowances for roads ; and such sheriff or other person shall accordingly remove or notify such person or Indian, and for that purpose shall have the same powers as in the execution of criminal process ; and the expenses incurred in any such removal or notification shall be borne by the party removed or notified, and may be recovered from him as the costs in any ordinary suit :

Provided that nothing contained in this Act shall prevent an Indian or non-treaty Indian, if five years a resident in Canada, not a member of the band, with the consent of the band and the approval of the Superintendent-General, from residing upon the reserve, or receiving a location thereon.

13. If any person or Indian, after having been removed or notified as aforesaid, returns to, settles upon, resides or hunts upon or occupies, or uses as aforesaid, any of the said land, marsh or l0ts, or parts of lots ; or settles, resides upon or occupies any of the said roads, allowances for roads, or lots or parts of lots, the Superintendent-General, or any officer or person deputed and authorized as aforesaid, upon view, or upon proof on oath made before him, or to his satisfaction, that the said person or Indian has returned to, settled, resided or hunted upon or occupied or used as aforesaid any of the said lands, marshes, lots or parts of lots or has returned to, settled or resided upon or occupied any of the said roads or allowances for roads or lots or parts of lots, shall direct and send his warrant signed and sealed to the sheriff of the proper county or district, or to any literate person therein, and if the said reserve be not situated within any county or district, then to any literate person, commanding him forthwith to arrest such person or Indian, and commit him to the common gaol of the said county or district, or if these be no gaol in the said county or district, then to the gaol nearest to the said reserve in the Province or Territory there to remain for the time ordered by such warrant, but which shall not exceed thirty days.

14. Such sheriff or other person shall accordingly arrest the party, and deliver him to the gaoler or sheriff of the proper county, district, Province or Territory, who shall receive such person -or Indian and imprison him in the said gaol for the term aforesaid.

15. The Superintendent-General, or such officer or person as aforesaid, shall cause the judgment or

order against the offender to be drawn up and filed in his office, and such judgment shall not be removed by certiorari or otherwise, or be appealed from, but shall be final.

16. If any person or Indian other than an Indian of the band to which the reserve belongs, without the license in writing of the Superintendent-General or of some officer or reserves. person deputed by him for that purpose, trespasses upon any of the said land, roads or allowances for roads in the said reserve, by cutting, carrying away or removing therefrom any of the trees, saplings, shrubs, underwood, timber or hay thereon, or by removing any of the stone, soil, minerals, metals or other valuables of the said land, roads or allowances for roads, the person or Indian so trespassing shall, for every tree he cuts, carries away or removes forfeit and pay the sum of twenty dollars ; and for cutting, carrying away or removing any of the saplings, shrubs, underwood timber or hay, if under the value of one dollar, the sum of four dollars, but if over the of one dollar, then the sum of twenty dollars ; and for removing any of the stone, soil, minerals, metals or other valuables aforesaid, the sum of twenty dollars, such fine to be recovered by the Superintendent-General, or any officer or person by him deputed, by distress and sale of the goods and chattels of the party or parties fined : or the Superintendent General, or such officer or person, without proceeding by distress and sale as aforesaid, may, upon the non-payment of the said fine, order the party or parties to be imprisoned in the common gaol as aforesaid, for a period not exceeding thirty flays, when the fine does not exceed twenty dollars, or for a period not exceeding three months when the fine does exceed twenty dollars : and upon the return of any warrant for distress or sale, if the amount thereof has not been made, or if any part of it remains unpaid, the said Superintendent- General, officer or person, may commit the party in default upon such warrant, to the common gaol as aforesaid for a period not exceeding thirty days if the sum claimed by the Superintendent-General, upon the said warrant does not exceed twenty dollars, or for a time not exceeding three months if the sum claimed does exceed twenty dollars : all such fines shall be paid to the Receiver-General, to be disposed of for the use and benefit of the band of Indians for whose benefit the reserve is held, in such manner as the Governor in Council may direct.

17. If any Indian, without the license in writing of the Superintendent-General, or of some officer or person deputed by him for that purpose, trespasses upon the land of an Indian who holds a location title, or who is otherwise recognized by the department as the occupant of such land, by cutting, carrying away, or removing therefrom, any of the trees, saplings, shrubs, underwood, timber or hay thereon, or by removing any of the stone, soil, minerals, metals or other valuables off the said land ; or if any Indian, without license as aforesaid, cuts, carries away or removes from any portion of the reserve of his band for sale (and not for the immediate use of himself and his family) any trees, timber or hay thereon, or removes any of the stone, soil, minerals, metals, or other valuables therefrom for sale as aforesaid, he shall be liable to all the fines and penalties provided in the next preceding section in respect to Indians of other hands and other persons.

18. In all orders, writs, warrants, summonses and proceeding whatsoever made, issued or taken by the Superintendent-General, or any officer or person by him deputed as aforesaid, it shall not be necessary for him or such officer or person to insert or express the name of the person or Indian summoned, arrested, distrained upon, imprisoned, or otherwise proceeded against therein, except when the name of such person or Indian is truly given to or known by the Superintendent-General,

or such officer or person, and if the name be not truly given to or known by him. he may name or describe the person or Indian by any part of the name of such person or Indian given to or known by him ; and if no part of the name be given to or known by him he may describe the person or Indian proceeded against in any manner by which he may be identified ; and all such proceedings containing or purporting to give the name or description of any such person or Indian as aforesaid shall prima facie be sufficient.

19. All sheriffs, gaolers or peace officers to whom any such process is directed by the Superintendent-General, or by any officer or person by him deputed as aforesaid, shall obey the same, and all other officers upon reasonable requisition shall assist in the execution thereof.

20. If any railway, road, or public work passes through or causes injury to any reserve belonging to or in possession of any band of Indians, or it any act occasioning damage t0 any reserve be done under the authority of any Act of Parliament, or of the legislature of any province, compensation shall be made to them therefor in the same manner as is provided with respect to the lands or rights of other persons ; the Superintendent-General shall in any case in which an arbitration may be had, name the arbitrator on behalf of the Indians, and shall act for them in any matter relating to the settlement of such compensation; and the amount awarded in any case shall be paid to the Receiver General for the use of the band of Indians for whose benefit; the reserve is held, and for the benefit of any Indian having improvements thereon..

SPECIAL RESERVES.

21. In all cases of encroachment upon, or of violation of trust respecting any special reserve, it shall be lawful to proceed by information in the name of Her Majesty, in the superior courts of law or equity, notwithstanding the legal title may not be vested in the Crown.

22. if by the violation of the conditions of any such trust as aforesaid, or by the breaking up of any society, corporation, or community, or if by the death of any person or persons without a legal succession of trusteeship, in whom the title to a special reserve is held in trust, the said title lapses or becomes void in law, then the legal title shall become vested in the Crown in trust, and the property shall be managed for the band or irregular band previously interested therein, as an ordinary reserve.

REPAIR OF ROADS.

28. Indians residing upon any reserve, and engaged in the pursuit of agriculture as their then principal means of support, shall be liable, if so directed by the Superintendent- General, or any officer or person by him thereunto authorized, to perform labor on the public roads laid out or used in or through, or abutting upon such reserve, such labor to be performed under the sole control of the said Superintendent- General, officer or person, who may direct when, where and how and in what manner the said labor shall be applied, and to what extent the same shall be imposed upon Indians who may be resident upon any of the said lands ; and the said Superintendent-General, officer or person shall have the like power to enforce the performance of all such labor by imprisonment or otherwise, as may be done by any power or authority under any law, rule or regulation in force in the province or territory in which such reserve lies, for the non-performance of statute labor ; but the labor to be so required of any such Indian shall not exceed in amount or extent what may be required of other inhabitants of the same province, territory, county, or other local division, under

the laws requiring and regulating such labor and the performance thereof.

24. Every band of Indians shall be bound to cause the roads, bridges, ditches and fences within their reserve to be put and maintained in proper order, in accordance with the instructions received from time to time from the Superintendent- General, or from the agent of the Superintendent- General ; and whenever in the opinion of the Superintendent-General the same are not so put or maintained in order he may cause the work to be performed at the cost of such band, or of the particular Indian in default, as the case may be, either out of their or his annual allowances, or otherwise.

SURRENDERS.

25. No reserve or portion of a reserve shall be sold, alienated or leased until it has been released or surrendered to the Crown for the purposes of this Act.

26. No release or surrender of a reserve, or portion of a reserve, held for the use of the Indians of any band or of any individual Indian, shall be valid or binding, except on the following conditions

1. The release or surrender shall be assented to by a majority of the male members of the band of the full age of twenty-one years, at a meeting or council thereof summoned for that purpose according to their rules, and held in the presence of the Superintendent-General, or of an officer duly authorized to attend such council by the Governor in Council or by the Superintendent-General ; Provided, that no Indian shall be entitled to vote or be present at such council, unless he habitually resides on or near and is interested in the reserve in question ;

2. The fact that such release or surrender has been assented to by the band at such council or meeting, shall be certified on oath before some judge of a superior, county, or district court, or stipendiary magistrate, by the Superintendent- General or by the officer authorized by him to attend such council or meeting, and by some one of the chiefs or principal men present thereat and entitled to vote, and when so certified as aforesaid shall be submitted to the Governor in Council for acceptance or refusal ;

3. But nothing herein contained shall be construed to prevent the Superintendent-General from issuing a license to any person or Indian to cut and remove trees, wood, timber and hay, or to quarry and remove stone, and gravel on and from the reserve ; Provided he, or his agent acting by his instructions, first obtain the consent of the band thereto in the ordinary manner as hereinafter provided.

27. It shall not be lawful to introduce at any council or meeting of Indians held for the purpose of discussing or of assenting to a release or surrender of a reserve or portion thereof, or of assenting to the issuing of a timber or other license, any intoxicant ; and any person introducing at such meeting, and any agent or officer employed by the Superintendent- General, or by the Governor in Council, introducing, allowing or countenancing by his presence the use of such intoxicant among such Indians a week before, at, or a week after, any such council or meeting, shall forfeit two hundred dollars, recoverable by action in any of the superior courts of law, one half of which penalty shall go to the informer.

28. Nothing in this Act shall confirm any release or surrender which would have been invalid if this Act had not been passed ; and no release or surrender of any reserve to any party other than the Crown, shall be valid.

MANAGEMENT AND SALE OF INDIAN LANDS.

29. All Indian lands, being reserves or portions of reserves surrendered or to be surrendered to the Crown, shall be deemed to be held for the same purposes as before the passing of this Act ; and shall be managed, leased and sold as the Governor in Council may direct, subject to the conditions of surrender, and to the provisions of this Act.

30. No agent for the sale of Indian lands shall, within his division, directly or indirectly, unless under an order the Governor in Council, purchase any land which he is appointed to sell, or become proprietor of or interested in any such land, during the time of his agency ; and any such purchase or interest shall be void ; and if any such agent offends in the premises, he shall forfeit his office and the sum of four hundred dollars for every such offence, which may be recovered in action of debt by any person who may sue for the same.

31. Every certificate of sale or receipt for money received the sale of Indian lands, heretofore granted or made or to be granted or made by the Superintendent-General or any or agent of his, so long as the sale to which such receipt or certificate relates is in force and not rescinded, shall entitle the party to whom the same was or shall be made or granted, or his assignee, by instrument registered under this or any former Act providing for registration in such cases, to take possession of and occupy the land therein comprised, subject to the conditions of such sale, and thereunder, unless the same shall have been revoked or cancelled, to maintain suits in law or equity against any wrongdoer or trespasser, as effectually as he could do under a patent from the Crown ;—and such receipt or certificate shall be prima facie evidence for the purpose of possession by such person, or the assignee under an instrument registered as aforesaid, in any such suit ; but the same shall have no force against a license to cut timber existing at the time of the making or granting thereof.

32. The Superintendent-General shall keep a book for registering (at the option of the parties interested) the particulars of any assignment made, as well by the original purchaser or lessee of Indian lands or his heir or legal representative, as by any subsequent assignee of any such lands, or the heir or legal representative of such assignee;— and upon any such assignment being produced to the Super- intendent-General, and, except in cases where such assignment is made under a corporate seal, with an affidavit of due execution thereof, and of the time and place of such execution, and the names, residences and occupations of the witnesses, or, as regards lands in the province of Quebec, upon the production of such assignment executed in notarial form, or of a notarial copy thereof, the Superintendent- General shall cause the material parts of every such assignment to be registered in such book of registry, and shall cause to be endorsed on every such assignment a certificate of such registration, to be signed by himself or his deputy, or any other officer of the department by him authorized to sign such certificates ;—And every such assignment so registered shall be valid against any one previously executed, but subsequently registered, or unregistered ; but all the conditions of the sale, grant or location must have been complied with, or dispensed with by the Superintendent-General, before such registration is made.

33. If any subscribing witness to any such assignment is deceased, or has left the province, the Superintendent- General may register such assignment upon the production of an affidavit proving the death or absence of such witness and his handwriting, or the handwriting of the party making such

assignment.

34. On any application for a patent by the heir, assignee or devisee of the original purchaser from the Crown, the Superintendent-General may receive proof in such manner as he may direct and require in support of any claim for a patent when the original purchaser is dead, and upon being satisfied that the claim has been equitably and justly established, may allow the same, and cause a patent to issue accordingly ; but nothing in this section shall limit the right of a party claiming a patent to land in the province of Ontario to make application at any time to the commissioner, under the " Act respecting claims to lands in Upper Canada for which no " patents have issued."''

35. If the Superintendent-General is satisfied that any purchaser or lessee of any Indian lands, or any assignee claiming under or through him, has been guilty of any fraud or imposition, or has violated any of the conditions of sale or lease, or if any such sale or lease has been or is made or issued in error or mistake, he may cancel such sale or lease, and resume the land therein mentioned, or dispose of it as if no sale or lease thereof had ever been made ; and all such cancellations heretofore made by the Governor in Council or the Superintendent-General shall continue valid until altered.

36. When any purchaser, lessee or other person refuses or neglects to deliver up possession of any laud after revocation or cancellation of the sale or lease as aforesaid, or when any person is wrongfully in possession of any Indian lands and refuses to vacate or abandon possession of the same, the Superintendent-General may apply to the county judge of the county, or to a judge of the superior court in the circuit, in which the land lies in Ontario or Quebec, or to any judge of a superior court of law or any county judge of the -county in which the land lies in any other province, or to any stipendiary magistrate in any territory in which the land lies, for an order in the nature of a writ of habere facias possessionem, or writ of possession, and the said - judge or magistrate, upon proof to his satisfaction that the Tight or title of the party to hold such land has been revoked or cancelled as aforesaid, or that such person is wrongfully in possession of Indian lands, shall grant an order upon the purchaser, lessee or person in possession, to deliver up the same to the Superintendent- General, or person by him authorized to receive the same ; and such order shall have the same force as a writ of habere facias possessionem, or writ of possession ; and the sheriff, or any bailiff or person to whom it may have been trusted for execution by the Superintendent-General, shall execute the same in like manner as he would execute such writ in an action of ejectment or possessory action.

37. Whenever any rent payable to the Crown on any lease , -of Indian lands is in arrear, the Superintendent-General, or any agent or officer appointed under this Act and authorized by the Superintendent-General to act in such cases, may issue a warrant, directed to any person or persons by him named therein, in the shape of a distress warrant as in ordinary cases of landlord and tenant, or as in the case of distress and warrant of a justice of the peace for non-payment of a pecuniary penalty; and the same proceedings may be had thereon for the collection of such arrears as in either of the said last mentioned cases ; or an action of debt as in ordinary cases of rent in arrear may be brought therefor in the name of the Superintendent-General ; but demand of rent shall not be necessary in any case.

38. When by law or by any deed, lease or agreement relation to any of the lands herein referred to, any notice is required to be given, or any act to be done, by or on behalf of the Crown, such notice may be given and act done by or by the authority of the Superintendent-General.

39. Whenever letters patent have been issued to or in the name of the wrong party, through mistake, or contain any clerical error or misnomer, or wrong description of any material fact therein, or of the land thereby intended to be granted, the Superintendent-General (there being no adverse -claim,) may direct the defective letters patent to be cancelled and a minute of such cancellation to be entered in the margin of the registry of the original letters patent, and correct letters patent to be issued in their stead, which corrected letters patent shall relate back to the date of those so cancelled, and have the same effect as if issued at the date of such cancelled letters patent.

40. In all cases ill which grants or letters patent have issued for the same land inconsistent with each other through error, and in all cases of sales or appropriations of the same land inconsistent with each other, the Superintendent- General may, in cases of sale, cause a repayment of the purchase money, with interest, or when the land has passed from the original purchaser or has been improved before a discovery of the error, he may in substitution assign land or grant a certificate entitling the party to purchase Indian lands, of such value and to such extent as to him, the Superintendent General, may seem just and equitable under the circumstances ; but no such claim shall be entertained unless it be preferred within five years from the discovery of the error.

41. "Whenever by reason of false survey or error in the books or plans in the Indian Branch of the Department of the Interior, any grant, sale or appropriation of land is found to be deficient, or any parcel of land contains less than the quantity of land mentioned in the patent therefor, the Superintendent- General may order the purchase money of so much land as is deficient, with the interest thereon from the time of the application therefor, or, if the land has passed from the original purchaser, then the purchase money which the claimant (provided he was ignorant of a deficiency at the time of his purchase) has paid for so much of the land as is deficient, with interest thereon from the time of the application therefor, to be paid to him in land or in money, as he, the Superintendent-General, may direct ;—But no such claim shall be entertained unless application has been made within five years from the date of the patent, nor unless the deficiency is equal to one-tenth of the whole quantity described as being contained in the particular let or parcel of land granted.

42. In all cases wherein patents for Indian lands have issued through fraud or in error or improvidence, the Exchequer Court of Canada, or a superior court of law or equity in any province may, upon action, bill or plaint, respecting such lands situate within their jurisdiction, and upon hearing of the parties interested, or upon default of the said parties after such notice of proceeding as the said courts shall respectively order, decree such patents to be void ; and upon a registry of such decree in the office of the Registrar General of Canada, such patents shall be void to all intents. The practice in court, in such cases, shall be regulated by orders to be from time to time made by the said courts respectively ; and any action or proceeding commenced under any former - Act may be continued under this section, which, for the purpose of any such action or proceeding shall be construed as merely continuing the provisions of such former Act.

43. If any agent appointed or continued in office under this Act knowingly and falsely informs, or causes to be informed, any person applying to him to purchase any land within his division and agency, that the same has already been purchased, or refuses to permit the person so applying to purchase the same according to existing regulations, such agent shall be liable therefor to the person so applying in the sum of five dollars for each acre of land which the person so applying offered

to purchase, to be recovered by action of debt in any court, having jurisdiction in civil cases to the amount.

44. If any person, before or at the time of the public sale of any Indian lands, by intimidation, combination, or unfair management, hinders or prevents, or attempts to hinder or prevent, any person from bidding upon or purchasing any lands so offered for sale, every such offender, his, her, or their aiders and abettors, shall, for every such offence, be guilty of a misdemeanor, and on conviction thereof shall be liable to a fine not exceeding four hundred dollars, or imprisonment for a term not exceeding two years, or both, in the discretion of the court.

MANAGEMENT AND SALE OF TIMBER.

45. The Superintendent-General, or any officer or agent authorized by him to that effect, may grant licenses to cut timber on reserves and ungranted Indian lands at such rates, and subject to such conditions, regulations and restrictions, as may from time to time be established by the Governor in Council, such conditions, regulations and restrictions to be adapted to the locality in which such reserves or lands are situated.

46. No license shall be so granted for a longer period than twelve months from the date thereof ; and if in consequence of any incorrectness of survey or other error, or cause what- soever, a license is found to comprise land included in a license or a prior date, or land not being reserves or ungranted Indian lands, the license granted shall be void in so far as it comprises such land, and the holder or proprietor of the license so rendered void shall have no claim upon the Government for indemnity or compensation by reason of such avoidance.

47. Every license shall describe the lands upon which the timber may be cut, and shall confer for the time being on the nominee, the right to take and keep exclusive possession of the land so described, subject to such regulations and restrictions as may be established ;— And every license shall vest in the holder thereof all rights of property whatsoever in all trees, timber and lumber cut within the limits of the license during the term thereof, whether such trees, timber and lumber are cut by authority of the holder of such license or by any other person, with or without his consent ;— And every license shall entitle the holder thereof to seize in revendication or otherwise, such trees, timber or lumber where the same are found in the possession of any unauthorized person, and also to institute any action or suit at law or in equity against any wrongful possessor or trespasser, and to prosecute all trespassers and other offenders to punishment, and to recover damages, if any :— And all proceedings pending at the expiration of any license may be continued to final termination as if the license had not expired.

48. Every person obtaining a license shall, at the expiration thereof make to the officer or agent granting the same, or to the Superintendent-General a return of the number and kinds of trees cut and of the quantity and description of sawlogs, or of the number and description of sticks of square timber, manufactured and carried away under such license ; and such statement shall be sworn to by the holder of the license, or his agent, or by his foreman ; And any person refusing or neglecting to furnish such statement, or evading or attempting to evade any regulation made by Order in Council, shall be held to have cut without authority, and the timber made shall be dealt with accordingly.

49. All timber cut under license shall be liable for the payment of the dues thereon, so long as and

wheresoever the said timber or any part of it may be found, whether in the original logs or manufactured into deals, boards or other stuff,—and all officers or agents entrusted with the collection of such dues may follow' all such timber and seize and detain the same wherever it is found, until the dues are paid or secured.

50. Bonds or promissory notes taken for the dues, either before or after the cutting of the timber, as collateral security or to facilitate collection, shall not in any way affect the lien of the Crown on the timber, but the lien shall subsist until the said dues are actually discharged.

51. If any timber so seized and detained for non-payment of dues remains more than twelve months in the custody of the agent or person appointed to guard the same, without the dues and expenses being paid,—then the Superintendent- General, with the previous sanction of the Gover-- nor in Council, may order a sale of the said timber to be made after sufficient notice,—and the balance of the proceed of such sale, after retaining the amount of dues and costs incurred, shall be handed over to the owner or claimant of such timber.

52. If any person without authority cuts or employs or induces any other person to cut, or assists in cutting any timber of any kind on Indian lands, or removes or carries or employs or induces or assists any other person to remove or carry away any merchantable timber of any kind so cut from Indian lands aforesaid, he shall not acquire any right to the timber so cut, or any claim to any remuneration for cutting, preparing the same for market, or conveying the same to or towards market,—and when the timber or saw-logs made, has or have been removed out of the reach of the officers of the Indian Branch of the Department of the Interior, or it is otherwise found impossible to seize the same, he shall in addition to the loss of his labour and disbursements, forfeit a sum of three dollars for each tree (rafting stuff excepted), which he is proved to have cut or caused to be cut or carried away,—and such sum shall be recoverable with costs, at the suit and in the name of the Superintendent-General or resident agent, in any court having jurisdiction in civil matters to the amount of the penalty ;—And in all such cases it shall be incumbent on the party charged to prove his authority to cut ; and the averment of the party seizing or prosecuting, that he is duly employed under the authority of this Act, shall be sufficient proof thereof, unless the defendant proves the contrary.

53. Whenever satisfactory information, supported by affidavit made before a justice of the peace or before any other competent authority, is received by the Superintendent- General, or any other officer or agent acting under him that any timber or quantity of timber has been cut without authority on Indian lands, and describing where the said timber can be found, the said Superintendent-General, officer, or agent, or any one of them, may seize or cause to be seized, in Her Majesty's name, the timber so reported to have been cut without authority, wherever it is found, and place the same under proper custody, until a decision can be had in the matter from competent authority ;

2. And where the timber so reported to have been cut without authority on Indian lands, has been made with other timber into a crib, dram or raft, or in any other manner has been so mixed up at the mills or else- as to render it impossible or very difficult to distinguish the timber so cut on reserves or Indian lands without license, from other timber with which it is mixed up the whole of the timber so mixed shall be held to have been out without authority on Indian lands, and shall be liable to seizure and forfeiture accordingly, until satisfactorily separated by the holder.

54. Any officer or person seizing timber, in the discharge of his duty under this Act, may in the name

of the Crown call in any assistance necessary for securing and protecting the timber so seized ; and whosoever under any pretence, either by assault, force or violence, or by threat of such assault, force or violence, in any way resists or obstructs any officer or person acting in his aid, in the discharge of his duty under this Act, is guilty of felony, and liable to punishment accordingly.

55. Whosoever, whether pretending to be the owner or not either secretly or openly, and whether with or without force or violence, takes or carries away, or causes to be taken or carried away, without permission of the officer or person who seized the same, or of some competent authority, any timber seized and detained as subject to forfeiture under this Act, before the same has been declared by competent authority to have been seized without due cause, shall be deemed to have stolen such timber being the property of the Crown, and guilty of felony, and is liable to punishment accordingly ;

2. And whenever any timber is seized for non-payment of Crown dues or for any other cause of forfeiture, or any prosecution is brought for any penalty or forfeiture under this Act, and any question arises whether the said dues have been paid on such timber, or whether the said timber was ' cut on other than any of the lauds aforesaid, the burden of proving payment, or on what land the said timber was cut, shall lie on the owner or claimant of such timber, and not on the officer who seizes the same, or the party bringing such prosecution.

56. All timber seized tinder this Act shall be deemed to be condemned, unless the person from whom it was seized, or the owner thereof within one month from the day of the seizure, gives notice to the seizing officer, or nearest officer or agent of the Superintendent-General, that he claims or intends to claim the same ; failing such notice, the officer or agent seizing shall report the circumstances to the Superintendent- General, who may order the sale of the said timber by the said officer or agent, after a notice on the spot, of at least thirty days:

2. And any Judge having competent jurisdiction, may, whenever he deems it proper, try and determine such seizures, and may order the delivery of the timber to the alleged owner, on receiving security by bond with two good and sufficient sureties to be first approved by the said agent, to pay double the value in case of condemnation,—and such bond shall be taken in the name of the Superintendent- General, to Her Majesty's use, and shall be delivered up to and kept by the Superintendent-General,—and if such seized timber is condemned, the value thereof shall be paid forthwith to the Superintendent-General, or agent, and the bond cancelled, otherwise the penalty of such bond shall be enforced and recovered.

57. Every person availing himself of any false statement or oath to evade the payment of dues under this Act, shall forfeit the timber on which dues are attempted to be evaded.

MONEYS.

58. All moneys or securities of any kind applicable to the support or benefit of Indians, or any band of Indians, and all moneys accrued or hereafter to accrue from the sale of any Indian lands or of any timber on any reserves or Indian lands shall, subject to the provisions of this Act, be applicable to the same purposes, and be dealt with in the same manner as they might have been applied to or dealt with before the passing of this Act.

59. The Governor in Council may, subject to the pro- visions of this Act, direct how, and in what manner, and by whom the moneys arising from sales of Indian lands, and from the property held or to be held in trust for the Indians, or from any timber on Indian lands or reserves, or from any other

source for the benefit of Indians (with the exception of any small sum not exceeding ten per cent, of the proceeds of any lands, timber or property, which may be agreed at the time of the surrender to be paid to the members of the band interested therein), shall be invested from time to time, and how the payments or assistance to which the Indians may be entitled shall be made or given, and may for the general management of such moneys, and direct what percentage or proportion thereof shall be set apart from time to time, to cover the cost of and attendant upon the management of reserves, lands, property and moneys under the provisions of this Act. and for the construction or repair of roads passing through such reserves or lands, and by way of contribution to schools frequented by such Indians.

60. The proceeds arising from the sale or lease of any Indian lands, or from the timber, hay, stone, minerals or other valuables thereon, or on a reserve, shall be paid to the Receiver General to the credit of Ihe Indian fund.

COUNCILS AND CHIEFS.

61. At the election of a chief or chiefs, or the «ranting of any ordinary consent required of a band of Indians under this Act. those entitled to vote at the council or meeting thereof shall be the male members of the band of the full age of twenty-one years; and the vote of a majority of such members at a council or meeting of the band summoned according to their rules, and held in the presence of the Superintendent-General, or an agent acting under his instructions, shall be sufficient to determine such election, or grant such consent ;

Provided that in the case of any band having a council of chiefs or councillors, any ordinary consent required of the band may be granted by a vote of a majority of such chiefs or councillors at a council summoned according to their rules, and held in the presence of the Superintendent- General or his agent.

62. The Governor in Council may order that the chiefs of any band of Indians shall be elected, as hereinbefore provided, at such time and place, as the Superintendent- General may direct, and they shall in such case be elected for a period of three years, unless deposed by the Governor for dishonesty, intemperance, immorality, or incompetency ; and they may be in the proportion of one head chief and two second chiefs or councillors for every two hundred Indians ; but any such band composed of thirty Indians may have one chief : Provided always, that all life chiefs now living shall continue as such until death or resignation, or until their removal by the Governor for dishonesty, intemperance, immorality, or incompetency.

63. The chief or chiefs of any band in council may frame, subject to confirmation by the Governor in Council, rules and regulations for the following subjects, viz. :

1. The care of the public health ;
2. The observance of order and decorum at assemblies of the Indians in general council, or on other occasions ;
3. The repression of intemperance and profligacy ;
4. The prevention of trespass by cattle ;
5. The maintenance of roads, bridges, ditches and fences ;
6. The construction and repair of school houses, council houses and other Indian public buildings ;

7. The establishment of pounds and the appointment of pound-keepers;
8. The locating of the land in their reserves, and the establishment of a register of such locations.

PRIVILEGES OF INDIANS.

64. No Indian or non-treaty Indian shall be liable to taxed for any real or personal property, unless he holds real estate under lease or in fee simple, or personal property, outside of the reserve or special reserve, in which case he shall be liable to be taxed for such real or personal property at the same rate as other persons in the locality in which it is situate.

65. All land vested in the Crown, or in any person or body corporate, in trust for or for the use of any Indian or non-treaty Indian, or any band or irregular band of Indians or non-treaty Indians shall be exempt from taxation.

66. No person shall take any security or otherwise obtain any lien or charge, whether by mortgage, judgment or otherwise, upon real or personal property of any Indian or non-treaty Indian within Canada, except on real or personal property subject to taxation under section sixty-four of this Act: Provided always, that any person selling any article to an Indian or non-treaty Indian may, notwithstanding this section, take security on such article for any part of the price thereof which may be unpaid.

67. Indians and non-treaty Indians shall have the right to sue for debts due to them or in respect of any tort or wrong inflicted upon them, or to compel the performance of obligations contracted with them.

68. No pawn taken of any Indian or non-treaty Indian for any intoxicant shall be retained by the person to whom such pawn is delivered, but the thing so pawned may be sued for and recovered, with costs of suit, by the Indian or non-treaty Indian who has deposited the same, before any court of competent jurisdiction.

69. No presents given to Indians or non-treaty Indians, nor any property purchased, or acquired with or by means of any annuities granted to Indians or any part thereof or otherwise howsoever, and in the possession of any band of such Indians or of any Indian of any band or irregular band, shall be liable to be taken, seized or distrained for any debt, matter or cause whatsoever. Nor in the province of British Columbia, the province of Manitoba, the North-West Territories or in the territory of Keewatin, shall the same be sold, bartered, exchanged or given by any band or irregular band of Indians or any Indian of any such band to any person or Indian other than an Indian of such band; and any such sale, barter, exchange or gift shall be absolutely null and void, unless such sale, barter, exchange or gift be made with the written assent of the Superintendent-General or his agent; and whosoever buys or otherwise acquires any presents or property purchased as aforesaid, without the written consent of the Superintendent- General, or his agent as aforesaid, is guilty of a misdemeanor, and is punishable by fine not exceeding two hundred dollars, or by imprisonment not exceeding six months, in any place of confinement other than a penitentiary.

DISABILITIES AND PENALTIES.

70. No Indian or non-treaty Indian, resident in the province of Manitoba, the North-West Territories or the territory of Keewatin, shall be held capable of having' acquired or acquiring a homestead or pre-emption right to a quarter section, or any portion of laud in any surveyed or unsurveyed lands in the said province of Manitoba, the North-West Territories or the territory of Keewatin, or the

right to share in the distribution of any lands allotted to half breeds, subject to the following exceptions :

(a) He shall not be disturbed in the occupation of any plot on which he has or may have permanent improvements prior to his becoming a party to any treaty with the Crown :

(b) Nothing in this section shall prevent the Government of Canada, if found desirable, from compensating any Indian for his improvements on such a plot of land without obtaining a formal surrender therefor from the band :

(c) Nothing in this section shall apply to any person who withdrew from any Indian treaty prior to the first day of October, in the year one thousand eight hundred and seventy four.

71. Any Indian convicted of any crime punishable by imprisonment in any penitentiary or other place of confinement, shall, during such imprisonment, be excluded from participating in the annuities, interest money, or rents payable to the band of which he or she is a member ; and whenever any Indian shall be convicted of any crime punishable by imprisonment in a penitentiary or other place of confinement, the legal costs incurred in procuring such conviction, and in carrying out the various sentences recorded, may be defrayed by the Superintendent-General, and paid out of any annuity or interest coming to such Indian, or to the band, as the case may be.

72. The Superintendent-General shall have power to stop the payment of the annuity and interest money of any Indian who may be proved, to the satisfaction of the Superintendent General to have been guilty of deserting his or her family, and the said Superintendent-General may apply the same towards the support of any family, woman or child so deserted ; also to stop the payment of the annuity and interest money of any woman having no children, who deserts her husband and lives immorally with another man.

73. The Superintendent-General in cases where sick, or disabled, or aged and destitute persons are not provided for by the band of Indians of which they are members, may furnish sufficient aid from the funds of the band for the relief of such sick, disabled, aged or destitute persons.

EVIDENCE OF NON-CHRISTIAN INDIANS.

74. Upon any inquest, or upon any enquiry into any matter involving a criminal charge, or upon the trial of any crime or offence whatsoever or by whomsoever committed, it shall be lawful for any court, judge, stipendiary magistrate, coroner or justice of the peace to receive the evidence of any Indian or non-treaty Indian, who is destitute of the knowledge of God and of any fixed and clear belief in religion or in a future state of rewards and punishments, without administering the usual form of oath to any such Indian, or non-treaty Indian, as aforesaid, upon his solemn affirmation or declaration to tell the truth, the whole truth and nothing but the truth, or in such form as may be approved by such court, judge, stipendiary magistrate, coroner or justice of the peace as most binding on the conscience of such Indian or non-treaty Indian

75. Provided that in the case of any inquest, or upon any inquiry into any matter involving a criminal charge, or upon the trial of any crime or offence whatsoever, the substance of the evidence or information of any such Indian, or nontreaty Indian, as aforesaid, shall be reduced to writing, and signed by the person (by mark if necessary) giving the same, and verified by the signature or mark of the person acting as interpreter (if any) and by the signature of the judge, stipendiary magistrate or coro-

ner, or justice of the peace or person before whom such evidence or information has been given.

76. The court, judge, stipendiary magistrate, or justice of the peace shall, before taking any such evidence, information or examination, caution every such Indian, or nontreaty Indian, as aforesaid, that lie will be liable to incur punishment if he do not so as aforesaid toil the truth.

77. The written declaration or examination, made taken and verified in manner aforesaid, of any such Indian or non-treaty Indian as aforesaid, may be lawfully read and received as evidence upon the trial of any criminal suit or proceedings, when under file like _____ the written affidavit, examination, deposition or confession of any other person, might be lawfully read and received as evidence.

75. Every solemn affirmation or declaration in whatever Form taken by any Indian or non-treaty Indian as aforesaid shall be of the same force and effect as if such Indian or non-treaty Indian had taken an oath in the usual form, and he or she shall in like manner incur the penalty of perjury in case of falsehood.

INTOXICANTS.

79. Whoever sells, exchanges with, barters, supplies or gives to any Indian, or non-treaty Indian in Canada, any kind of intoxicant, or causes or procures the same to be done, or connives or attempts thereat, or opens or keeps, or causes to be opened or kept, on any reserve or special reserve, a tavern, house or building where any intoxicant is sold, bartered, exchanged or given, or is found in possession of any intoxicant in the house, tent, wigwam or place of abode of any Indian or non-treaty Indian, shall, on conviction thereof before any judge, stipendiary magistrate or two justices of the peace, upon the evidence of one credible witness other than the informer or prosecutor, be liable to imprisonment for a period not less than one month nor exceeding six months, with or without hard labor, and be fined not less than fifty nor more than three hundred dollars, with costs of prosecution,—one moiety of the fine to go to the informer or prosecutor, and the other moiety to Her Majesty, to form part of the fund for the benefit of that body of Indians or non-treaty Indians, with respect to one or more members of which the offence was committed : and the commander or person in charge of any steamer or other vessel, or boat, from or on board of which any intoxicant has been sold, bartered, exchanged, supplied or given to any Indian or non-treaty Indian, shall be liable, on conviction thereof before any judge, stipendiary magistrate or two justices of the peace, upon the evidence of one credible witness other than the informer or prosecutor, to be fined not less than fifty nor exceeding three hundred dollars for each such offence, with costs of prosecution,— the moieties of the fine to be applicable as hereinbefore mentioned ; and in default of immediate payment of such fine and costs any person so fined shall be committed to any common gaol, house of correction, lock-up, or other place of confinement by the judge, stipendiary magistrate or two justices of the peace before whom the conviction has taken place, for a period of not less than one nor more than six months, with or without hard labor, or until such line and costs are paid : and any Indian or non-treaty Indian who makes or manufactures any intoxicant, or who has in his possession, or concealed, or who sells, exchanges with, barters, supplies or gives to any other Indian or non-treaty Indian in Canada any kind of intoxicant shall, on conviction thereof, before any judge, stipendiary magistrate or two justices of the peace, upon the evidence of one credible witness other than the in-

former or prosecutor, be liable to imprisonment for a period of not less than one month nor more than six months, with or without hard labor; and in all cases arising under this section, Indians or non-treaty Indians, shall be competent witnesses : but no penalty shall be incurred in case of sickness where the intoxicant is made use of under the sanction of a medical man or under the directions of a minister of religion.

80. The keg, barrel, case, box, package or receptacle whence any intoxicant has been sold, exchanged, bartered. supplied or given, and as well that in winch the original supply was contained as the vessel wherein any portion of such original supply was supplied as aforesaid, and the remainder of the contents thereof, if such barrel, keg, case, box, package, receptacle or vessel aforesaid respectively, can be identified, and any intoxicant imported or manufactured or brought into and upon any reserve or special reserve, or into the house, tent, wigwam or place of abode of any Indian or non-treaty Indian, may be seized by any constable whosesoever found on such land or in such place ; and on complaint before any judge, stipendiary magistrate or justice of the peace, he may, on the evidence of any credible witness that this Act has been contravened in respect thereof, declare the same forfeited, and cause the same to be forthwith destroyed ; and may condemn, the Indian or other person m whose Person in possession they were found to pay a penalty not exceeding one hundred dollars nor less than fifty dollars, and the costs of prosecution ; and one-half of such penalty shall belong to the prosecutor and the other half to Her Majesty for the purposes hereinbefore mentioned ; and in default of immediate payment, the offender may be committed to any common goal, house of correction, lock-up or other place of confinement with or without hard labor, for any time not exceeding six nor less than two months unless such fine and costs are sooner paid.

81. When it is proved before any judge, stipendiary magistrate or two justices of the peace that any vessel, boat, canoe or conveyance of any description upon the sea or sea coast, or upon any river, lake or stream in Canada, is employed in carrying any intoxicant, to be supplied to Indians or non-treaty Indians, such vessel, boat, canoe or conveyance so employed may be seized and declared Forfeited, as in the next preceding section, and sold, and the proceeds thereof paid to Her Majesty for the purposes hereinbefore mentioned.

82. Every article, chattel, commodity or thing in the purchase, acquisition, exchange, trade or barter of which in contravention of this Act the consideration, either wholly be any intoxicant, shall be forfeited to Her Majesty and shall be seized as in the eightieth section in respect to any-receptacle of any intoxicant, and may be sold and the proceeds thereof paid to Her Majesty for the purposes herein before mentioned.

83. It shall be lawful for any constable, without process of law, to arrest any Indian or non-treaty Indian whom he may find in a state of intoxication, and to convey him to any common gaol, house of correction, lock-up or other place of confinement, there to be kept until he shall have become sober ; and such Indian or non-treaty Indian shall, when sober, be brought before any judge, stipendiary magistrate, or justice of the peace, and if convicted of being so found in a state of intoxication shall be liable to imprisonment in any common gaol, house of correction, lock-up or other place of confinement, for any period not exceeding one month. And if any Indian or non-treaty Indian, having

been so convicted as aforesaid, refuses upon examination to state or give information of the person, place and time from whom, where and when, he procured such intoxicant, and if from any other Indian or non-treaty Indian, then, if within his knowledge, from whom, where and when such intoxicant was originally procured or received, he shall be liable to imprisonment as aforesaid for a further period not exceeding fourteen days.

84. No appeal shall lie from any conviction under the five year preceding sections of this Act, except to a Judge of any superior court of law, county, or circuit, or district the Chairman or Judge of the Court of the Sessions of the Peace, having jurisdiction where the conviction was had, and such appeal shall be heard, tried, and adjudicated upon by such judge without the intervention of a jury ; and no such appeal shall be brought after the expiration of thirty days from the conviction.

83. No prosecution, conviction or commitment under this Act shall be invalid on account of want of form, so long; as the same is according to the true meaning of this Act.

ENFRANCHISEMENT

80. Whenever any Indian man, or unmarried woman, of the full age of twenty-one years, obtains the consent of the band of which he or she is a member to become enfranchised and whenever such Indian has been assigned by the band a suitable allotment of land for that purpose, the local agent shall report such action of the band, and the name of the applicant to the Superintendent-General ; whereupon the said Superintendent-General, if satisfied that the proposed allotment of land is equitable, shall authorize some competent person to report whether the applicant is an Indian who, from the degree of civilization to which he or she has attained, and the character for integrity, morality and sobriety which he or she bears, appears to be qualified to become a proprietor of land in fee simple ; and upon the favorable report of such person, the Superintendent-General may grant such Indian a location ticket as a probationary Indian, for the land allotted to him or her by the band.

(1.) Any Indian who may be admitted to the degree of Doctor of Medicine, or to any other degree by any University of Learning, or who may be admitted in any Province of the Dominion to practice law either as an Advocate or as a Barrister or Counsellor or Solicitor or Attorney or to be a Notary Public, or who may enter Holy Orders or who may be licensed by any denomination of Christians as a Minister of the Gospel, shall ipso facto become and be enfranchised under this Act.

87. After the expiration of three years (or such longer period as the Superintendent-General may deem necessary in the event of such Indian's conduct not being satisfactory), the Governor may, on the report of the Superintendent- General, order the issue of letters patent, granting to such Indian in fee simple the land which had, with this object in view, been allotted to him or her by location ticket.

88. Every such Indian shall, before the issue of the letters patent mentioned in the next preceding section, declare to the Superintendent-General the name and surname by which he or she wishes to be enfranchised and thereafter known, and on his or her receiving such letters patent, in such name and surname, he or she shall be held to be also enfranchised, and he or she shall thereafter be known by such name or surname, and if such Indian be a married man his wife and minor unmarried children also shall be held to be enfranchised ; and from the date of such letters patent the provisions of this Act and of any Act or law making any distinction between the legal rights, privileges, dis-

abilities and liabilities of Indians and those of Her Majesty's other subjects shall cease to apply to any Indian, or to the wife or minor unmarried children of any Indian as aforesaid, so declared to be enfranchised, who shall no longer be deemed Indians within the meaning of the laws relating to Indians, except in so far as their right to participate in the annuities end interest moneys. and rents and councils of the band of Indians to which they belonged is concerned: Provided always. that any children of a probationary Indian, who being minors and unmarried when the probationary ticket probation granted to such Indian, arrive at the full age of twenty one years before the letters patent are issued to such Indian, may, at the discretion of the Governor in Council, receive letters patent in their own names for their respective shares of the land allotted under the said ticket, at the same time that letters patent are granted to their parent : and provided, that if any Indian child having arrived at the full age of twenty one years, during his or her parents' probationary period,, be unqualified for enfranchisement, or if any child of such parent, having been a minor at the commencement of such, period, be married during such period, then a quantity of land equal to the share of such child shall be deducted in such manner as may be directed by the Superintendent- General, from the allotment made- to such Indian parent on receiving his probationary ticket.

89. If any probationary Indian should fail in qualifying, to become enfranchised, or should die before the expiration of the required probation, his or her claim, or the claim his or her heirs to the land, for which a probationary ticket was granted, or the claim of any unqualified Indian, or of any Indian who may marry during his or her parents' probationary period, to the land deducted under the operation of the next preceding section from his or her parents' probationary allotment, shall in all respects be the same as that conferred by an ordinary location ticket, as provided in the sixth, seventh, eighth and ninth sections of this Act.

90. The children of any widow who becomes either a probationary or enfranchised Indian shall be entitled to the same privileges as those of a male head of a family in like circumstances.

91. In allotting land to probationary Indians, the quantity to be located to the head of a family shall be in proportion to the number of. such family compared with the total quantity of land in the reserve, and the whole number of the band, but any band may determine what quantity shall be allotted to each member for enfranchisement purposes, provided each female of any age, and each male member under fourteen years of age receive not less than one-half the quantity allotted to each male member of fourteen years of age and over.

92. Any Indian, not a member of the band, or any non-treaty Indian, who, with the consent of the band and the approval of the Superintendent-General, has been permitted to reside upon the reserve, or obtain a location thereon, may, on being assigned a suitable allotment of land by the band for enfranchisement, become enfranchised on the same terms and conditions as a member of the band ; and such enfranchisement shall confer upon such Indian the same legal rights and privileges, and make such Indian subject to such disabilities and liabilities as affect Her Majesty's other subjects ; but such enfranchisement shall not confer upon such Indian any right to participate in the annuities, interest moneys, rents and councils of the band.

93. "Whenever any band of Indians, at a council summoned for the purpose according- to their rules, and held in the presence of the Superintendent-General or of an agent duly authorized by him to attend such council, decides to allow every member of the band who chooses, and who may be

found qualified, to become enfranchised, and to receive his or her share of the principal moneys of the band, and sets apart for such member a suitable allotment of land for the purpose, any applicant of such band after such a decision may be dealt with as provided in the seven next preceding sections until his or her enfranchisement is attained ; and whenever any member of the band, who for the three years immediately succeeding the date on which he or she was granted letters patent, or for any longer period that the Superintendent-General may deem necessary, by his or her exemplary good conduct and management of property, proves that he or she is qualified to receive his or her share of such moneys, the Governor may, on the report of the Superintendent-General to that effect, order that the said Indian be paid his or her share of the capital funds at the credit of the band, or his or her share of the principal of the annuities of the band, estimated as yielding five per cent, out of such moneys as may be provided for the purpose by Parliament ; and if such Indian be a married man then he shall also be paid his wife and minor unmarried children's share of such funds and other principal moneys, and if such Indian be a widow, she shall also lie paid her minor unmarried children's share : and the unmarried children of such married Indians, who become of age during either the probationary period for enfranchisement or for payment of such moneys, if qualified by the character for integrity, morality and sobriety which they bear, shall receive their own share of such moneys when their parents are paid, and if not so qualified, before they can become enfranchised or receive payment of such moneys they must themselves pass through the probationary periods ; and all such Indians and their unmarried minor children who are paid their share of the principal moneys of their band as aforesaid, shall thenceforward cease in every respect to be Indians of any class within the meaning of this Act, or Indians within the meaning of any other Act or law.

94. Sections eighty six to ninety three, both inclusive of this Act, shall not apply to any band of Indians in the Province of British Columbia, the Province of Manitoba, the North-Most Territories, or the Territory of Keewatin, save in so far as the said sections may, by proclamation of the Governor-General, be from time to time extended, as they may be, to any band of Indians in any of the said provinces or territories.

MISCELLANEOUS PROVISIONS.

95. All affidavits required under this Act, or intended to be reference to any claim, business or transaction in this the Indian Branch of the Department of the Interior, may be taken before the judge or clerk of any county or circuit court, or any justice of the peace, or any commissioner for taking affidavits in any of the courts, or the Superintendent- General, or any Indian agent, or any surveyor duly licensed and sworn, appointed by the Superintendent-General to enquire into or take evidence or report in any matter submitted or pending before such Superintendent General, or if made out of Canada, before the mayor or chief magistrate of, or the British consul in, any city, town or other municipality ; and any wilful false swearing in any such affidavit shall be perjury.

96. Copies of any records, documents, books or papers belonging to or deposited in the Department of the Interior, to attested under the signature of the Superintendent-General or of his deputy shall be competent evidence in all cases in which the original records, documents, books or papers, could be evidence.

97. The Governor in Council may, by proclamation from time to time, exempt from the operation

of this Act, or from the operation of any one or more of the sections of this Act, Indians or non-treaty Indians, or any of them, or any band or irregular band of them, or the reserves or special reserves, or Indian lands or any portions of them, in any province, in the North-West Territories, or in the territory of Keewatin, or in either of them, and may again, by proclamation from time to time, remove such exemption.

98. The Governor may, from time to time, appoint officers and agents to carry out this Act, and any Orders in. Council made under it, which officers and agents shall be paid in such manner and at such rates as the Governor in Council , may direct out of any fund that may be appropriated by law for that purpose.

99. Section fitty-six of chapter sixty-one and section fifty chapter sixty-eight of the Consolidated Statutes of Canada, section twenty-nine of chapter forty-nine of the Consolidated Statutes for Upper Canada, and so much of chapter eighty one of the said Consolidated Statutes for Upper Canada as relates to Indians or Indian lands, sections five to thirty- three, inclusive, and sections thirty-seven and thirty-eight of the Act passed in the session held in the thirty-first year of Her Majesty's reign, chaptered forty-two, and the Act passed in the session held in the thirty-second and thirty-third years of Her Majesty's reign, chaptered six, and the Act passed in the thirty-seventh year of Her Majesty's reign, chaptered twenty-one, are hereby repealed, with so much of any Act or law as may be inconsistent with this Act, or as makes any provision in any matter provided for by this Act, except only as to things done, Tights acquired, obligations contracted, or penalties incurred before the coming into force of this Act ; and this Act shall be construed not as a new law but as a consolidation of those hereby repealed in so far as they make the same provision that is made by this Act in any matter hereby provided for.

100. No Act or enactment repealed by any Act hereby repealed shall revive by reason of such repeal.

An Act to amend "The Indian Act, 1876," S.C. 1879, c. 34. (42 Vict.)
    CHAP. 34.
An Act to amend "The Indian Act, 1876."
[Assented to 15th May, 1879.]
HER Majesty, by and with the advice and consent of the XI Senate and House of Commons of Canada, enacts as follows :—

1. Paragraph (e) of sub-section three, of section three of The Indian Ac 1876," is hereby amended by adding at the end thereof the words " And any half-breed who may have been admitted into a treaty shall be allowed to withdraw therefrom on refunding all annuity money received by him or her under the said treaty, or suffering a corresponding reduction in the quantity of any land, or scrip, which such half-breed as such may be entitled to receive from the Government."

2. Section sixteen of the '.Act aforesaid is hereby repealed. repealed, and the following section substituted in lieu thereof :—

" 16. If any person or Indian, other than an Indian of the band to which the reserve belongs, without the license in writing of the Superintendent-General, or of some officer or person deputed by him for that purpose, trespasses upon any of the said land, roads or allowances for roads in the said reserve, by cutting, carrying away, or removing therefrom any of the trees, saplings, shrubs, underwood, timber or hay thereon, or by removing any of the stone, soil, minerals, metals or other valuables, off the sand land, roads or allowances for roads, the person or Indian so trespassing shall, on conviction thereof before any Stipendiary Magistrate, Police Magistrate or Justice of the Peace, for every tree he cuts, carries away or removes, forfeit and pay the sum of twenty dollars ; and for cutting, carrying away, or removing any of the saplings, shrubs, underwood, timber or hay, if under the value of one dollar, the sum of four dollars ; but if over the value of one dollar, then the sum of twenty dollars ; and for removing any of the stone, soil, minerals, metals or other valuables aforesaid, the sum of twenty dollars, with costs of prosecution in all cases ; and in default of immediate payment of the said penalties and costs, the Superintendent-General, or such other person as he may have authorized in that behalf, may issue a warrant, directed to any person or persons by him named therein, to levy the amount of the said penalties and costs by distress and sale of the goods and chattels of the person liable to pay the same ; and similar proceedings may be had upon such warrant as if it had been issued by the magistrate or Justice of the Peace before whom the person was convicted ; or the Superintendent-General, or such other person as aforesaid, without proceeding by distress or sale, may, upon non-payment of the said penalties and costs, order the person liable therefor to be imprisoned in the common gaol of the county or district in which the said reserve or any part thereof lies, for, a period not exceeding thirty days when the penalty does not exceed twenty dollars, or 'for a period not exceeding three months when the penalty does exceed twenty dollars; and upon the return of any warrant for distress or sale, if the amount thereof has not been made, or if any part of it remains unpaid, the said Superintendent General, or such other person as aforesaid, may commit the person in default to the common gaol, as aforesaid, for a period not exceeding thirty days, if the sum claimed upon the said warrant does not exceed twenty dollars, or for a time not exceeding three months if the sum does exceed twenty dollars : all such penalties shall be paid to the Receiver-General to be disposed of for the use and benefit of the band of Indians for whose benefit the reserve is held, in such manner as the Governor in Council may direct."

3. Section seventeen of the said Act is hereby amended by adding thereto the words "and similar proceedings maybe had for the recovery thereof as are provided for in the next preceding section."

4. Section sixty-three of the said Act is hereby amended by adding to the fourth subsection thereof the words " also or the protection of sheep

And by substituting for the words "maintenance of" in the fifth subsection thereof, the words "construction and maintenance of water courses

And by adding to the said section the two following subsections:—

" 9. The repression of noxious weeds ;

" 10. The imposition of punishment, by fine or penalty, or by imprisonment, or both, for infraction of any of such rules or regulations,—the fine or penalty in no case to exceed thirty dollars, and the imprisonment in no case to exceed thirty days."

5. Section sixty-nine of the said Act is hereby amended by striking out the words " or otherwise, howsoever." in the fourth line thereof and by adding at the end of the said section the words " If any presents given to Indians or non-treaty Indians, or any property purchased or acquired with or by to Indians means of any annuities granted to Indians be unlawfully in the possession of any person, within the true intent and meaning of this section, any person acting under the authority (either

general or special) of the Superintendent- General, may, with such assistance in that behalf as he may think necessary, seize and take possession of the same, and he shall deal therewith as the Superintendent-General may direct."

6. Section eighty-seven is hereby amended by adding thereto the words " and in such cases compliance with the provisions of sections twenty-five and twenty-six and the sub-sections thereof shall not be necessary."

7. If any person, being the keeper of any house, allows or suffers any Indian woman to be or remain in such house, knowing, or having probable cause for believing, that such Indian woman is in or remains in such house with the intention of prostituting herself therein, such person shall be deemed guilty of an offence against this Act, and shall, on conviction thereof, in a summary way, before any Stipendiary Magistrate, Police Magistrate or Justice of the Peace, be liable to a fine of not less than ten dollars, or more than one hundred dollars, or to imprisonment in any gaol or place of confinement other than a penitentiary, for a term not exceeding six months.

8. Any person who appears, acts or behaves as master or mnsteVor1 mistress, or as the person having the care, government or management of any house in which any Indian woman is, the purpose of prostituting herself therein, shall be deemed and taken to be the keeper thereof, notwithstanding he or she may not in fact be the real keeper thereof.

The Indian Act, 1880. S.C. 1880, c. 28. (43 Vict.)

CHAP. 28

An Act to amend and consolidate the laws respecting Indians.

[Assented to 7th May, 1880.]

WHEREAS it is expedient to amend and consolidate the laws respecting Indians : Therefore Her Majesty, by and with the advice and consent of the Senate and House of Commons of Canada, enacts as follows :—

1- This Act shall be known and may be cited as " The Indian Act, 1880;" and shall, subject to the exceptions herein contained, apply to all the Provinces, and to the North-West Territories, including the District of Keewatin.

2 The following terms contained in this Act shall be held to have the meaning hereinafter assigned to them, unless such meaning be repugnant to the subject or inconsistent with the context :—

1. The term "band" means any tribe, hand or body of Indians who own or are interested in a reserve or in Indian lands in common, of which the legal title is vested in the Crown, or who share alike in the distribution of any annuities or interest moneys for which the Government of Canada is responsible ; the term " the band " means the band to which the context relates; and the term "band," when action is being taken by the hand as such, means the band in council.

2. The term " irregular band " means any tribe, band or body of persons of Indian blood who own no interest in any reserve or lands of which the legal title is vested in the Crown, who possess no common fund managed by the Government of Canada, or who have not had any treaty relations with the Crown.

3. The term " Indian " means— First. Any male person of Indian blood reputed to belong to a particular band ; Secondly. Any child of such person ; Thirdly. Any woman who is or was lawfully married to such person.

4. The term "non-treaty Indian" means any person of Indian blood who is reputed to belong to an irregular band, or who follows the Indian mode of life, even though such person be only a temporary resident in Canada.

5. The term "enfranchised Indian" means any Indian, his wife or minor unmarried child, who has received letters patent granting him in fee simple any portion of the reserve which may have been allotted to him, his wife and minor children, by the band to which he belongs, or any unmarried Indian who may have received letters patent for an allotment of the reserve.

6. The terra " reserve " means any tract or tracts of land set apart by treaty or otherwise for the use or benefit of or granted to a particular band of Indians, of which the legal title is in the Crown, but which is unsurrendered, and includes all the trees, wood, timber, soil, stone, minerals, metals and other valuables thereon or therein.

7. The terra " special reserve " means any tract or tracts of land and everything belonging thereto set apart for the use or benefit of any band or irregular band of Indians, the title of which is vested in a society, corporation or community legally established, and capable of suing and being sued, or in a person or persons of European descent, but which land is held in trust for such band or irregular band of Indians.

8. The term " Indian lands " means any reserve or portion of a reserve which has been surrendered to the Crown.

9. The term " intoxicants " means and includes all spirits, strong waters, spirituous liquors, wines, or fermented or compounded liquors or intoxicating drink of any kind whatsoever, and any intoxicating liquor or fluid, as also opium and any preparation thereof, whether liquid or solid, and any other intoxicating drug or substance, and tobacco or tea mixed or compounded or impregnated with opium or with other intoxicating drugs, spirits or substances, and whether the same or any of them be liquid or solid.

10. The term " Superintendent-General " means the Superintendent General of Indian Affairs.

11. The term "agent" includes a commissioner, superintendent, agent, or other officer acting under the instructions of the Superintendent-General.

12. The term " person " means an individual other than an Indian, unless the context clearly construction.

3. The Minister of the Interior shall be the Superintendent- General of Indian Affairs.

4. There shall be a Department of the Civil Service of Canada to be called the Department of Indian Affairs, over which the Superintendent-General of Indian Affairs shall preside.

5. The Governor General in Council may, by commission under the Great Seal, appoint a Deputy of the Superintendent- General of Indian Affairs, who shall be charged under the Superintendent-General with the performance of his Departmental duties, and with the control and management of the officers, clerks and servants of the Department, and with such other powers and duties as may be assigned to him by the Governor in Council.

6. Schedule A of the " Canada Civil Service Act, 1868," is hereby amended by adding thereto the words "Deputy of the Superintendent-General of Indian Affairs."

7. Upon the passing of this Act, so much of the business of the Department of the Interior as relates to Indian Affairs, and which has hitherto been conducted in what is usually known as the " Indian

Branch" of that Department, shall fall under the management, charge and direction of the Department of Indian Affairs ; and the Governor in Council may from time to time assign to the Department of Indian Affairs any of the present officers and employees of the Department of the Interior, or may direct any one or more of the officers and employees of the last-named Department to act as an officer of both Departments.

8. The Governor in Council may also appoint, subject to " The Canada Civil Service Act, 1868," such officers, clerks and servants as may be requisite for the proper conduct of the business of the Department of Indian Affairs.

9. The Governor in Council may appoint an Indian Commissioner for Manitoba. Keewatin and the North-West Territories, or an Indian Commissioner for Manitoba and Keewatin and as Indian Commissioner for the North-West Territories, with such powers and duties as may be provided by Order in Council. The Governor in Council may also appoint an Indian Superintendent for the Province of British Columbia, with such powers and duties as may be provided by Order in Council.

10. Any illegitimate child, unless having shared with the consent of the band whereof the father or mother of such child is a member in the distribution moneys of such bands, band for a period exceeding two years, may, at any time, be excluded from the membership thereof by the Superintendent- General.

11. Any Indian having for five years continuously resided in a foreign country without the consent in writing of the Superintendent-General or his agent, shall cease to be a member of the band of which he or she was formerly member, nor shall he or she become again a member of that band, or become a member of any other band, unless the consent of the band with the approval of the Superintendent General or his agent, be first had and obtained.

12. Any Indian woman marrying any other than an Indian or a non-treaty Indian shall cease to be an Indian in any respect within the meaning of this Act, except that she shall be entitled to share equally with the members of the band to which she formerly belonged, in the annual or semi-annual distribution of their annuities, interest moneys and rents ; but this income may be commuted to her at any time at ten years' purchase with the consent of the band.

13. Any Indian woman marrying an Indian of any other band, or a non-treaty Indian, shall cease to be a member of the band to which she formerly belonged, and become a member of the band or irregular band of which her husband is a member ; but should she marry a non-treaty Indian, while becoming a member of the irregular band of which her husband is a member, she shall be entitled to share equally with the members of the band of which she was formerly a member in the distribution of their moneys ; but this income may be commuted to her at any time at ten years' purchase with the consent of the band.

14. No half-breed in Manitoba who has shared in the distribution of half-breed lands shall be accounted an Indian; and no half-breed head of a family (except the widow of an Indian or a half-breed who has already been admitted into a treaty) shall, unless under very special circumstances, to be determined by the Superintendent- General or his agent, be accounted an Indian, or entitled to be admitted into any Indian treaty ; and any half-breed who may have been admitted into a treaty shall be allowed to withdraw therefrom on refunding all annuity money Withdrawal received by him or

her under the said treaty, or suffering a corresponding reduction in the quantity of any land, or scrip, which such half-breed, as such, may be entitled to receive from the Government.

2. The Half-breeds who are by the father's side either wholly or partly of Indian blood now settled in the Seigniory of Caughnawaga, and who have inhabited the said Seigniory for the last twenty years, are hereby confirmed in their possession and right of. residence and property, but not beyond the tribal rights and usages which others of the band enjoy.

15. All reserves for Indians or for any band of Indians, or held in trust for their benefit, shall be deemed to be reserved and held for the same purposes as before the passing of this Act, but subject to its provisions.

16. The Superintendent-General may authorize surveys, plans and reports to be made of any reserve for Indians, shewing and distinguishing the improved lands, the forests and lands fit for settlement, and such other information as may be required ; and may authorize that the whole or any portion of a reserve be subdivided into lots.

17. No Indian shall be deemed to be lawfully in possession of any land in a reserve, unless he or she has been or shall be located for the same by the band or council of the band, with the approval of the Superintendent-General : Provided that no Indian shall be dispossessed of any land on which he or she has improvements, without receiving compensation therefor (at a valuation to be approved by the Superintendent-General) from the Indian who obtains the land, or from the funds of the band, as may be determined by the Superintendent-General.

18. On the Superintendent-General approving of any location as aforesaid, he shall issue in triplicate a ticket granting a location title to such Indian, one triplicate of which he shall retain in a book to be kept for the purpose ; the other two he shall forward to the local agent,—one to be delivered to the Indian in whose favor it was issued, the other to be filed by the agent, who shall also cause the same to be copied into a register of the band to be provided for the purpose.

19. The conferring of any such location title as aforesaid shall not have the effect of rendering the land covered thereby subject to seizure under legal process, and such title shall be transferable only to an Indian of the same band, and then only with the consent and approval of the Superintendent-General, whose consent and approval shall be given only by the issue of a ticket in the manner proscribed in the next preceding section.

20. Upon the death of any Indian holding under location or other duly recognized title any parcel of land, the right and interest therein of such deceased Indian shall, together with his goods and chattels, devolve one-third upon his widow (if any), and the remainder upon his children in equal shares ; and such children shall have a like estate in such land as their father had. During the minority of such children the administration and charge of such land and goods and chattels as they may be entitled to under this clause, shall devolve upon the widow (if any) of such deceased Indian. As each male child attains the age of twenty-one, and as each female child attains that age, or marries before that age with the consent of the said widow, his or her share is to be handed to him or her : Provided always, that the Superintendent general may, at any time, remove the widow from such administration and charge, and confer the same upon Some other person, and in like manner remove such other person and appoint another, and so on as occasion may require. Should such Indian die without issue but leaving a widow, such lot or parcel of land and his goods and chattels shall be vested

in her, and if he leaves no widow, then in the Indian nearest akin to the deceased ; but if ho have no heir nearer than a cousin, then the same shall be vested in the Crown for the benefit of the band ; but whatever may be the final disposition of the land, the claimant or claimants shall not be held to be legally in possession until he, she or they obtains or obtain a location ticket from the Superintendent- General in the manner prescribed in the case of new locations : Provided always, that the Superintendent General may, whenever there are minor children, appoint a fit and proper person to take charge of such children and their property, and remove such person and appoint another, and so on as occasion may require ; Provided also, that the Superintendent-General shall have power to decide all questions which may arise respecting the distribution, among those entitled, of the land and goods and chattels of a deceased Indian ; also to do whatever he may, under the circumstances, think will best give to each claimant his or her share, according to the true meaning and spirit of this Act, whether such share be a part of the lands or goods and chattels themselves, or be part of the proceeds thereof, in case it be thought best to dispose thereof,—regard always being had m any such disposition to the restrictions upon the disposition of property in a reserve.

21. Any Indian or non-treaty Indian in the Province of British Columbia, in the Province of Manitoba, in the North West Territories, or in the District of Keewatin, who has or shall have, previously to the selection of a reserve, possession include session of and made permanent improvements on a plot of land which has been or shall be included in or surrounded provinces, by a reserve, shall have the same privileges, neither more nor less, in respect of such plot, as an Indian enjoys who holds under a location title.

22. No person, or Indian other than an Indian of the band, shall settle, reside or hunt upon, occupy or use any land or marsh, or shall settle, reside upon or occupy any road, or allowance for roads running through any reserve belonging to or occupied by such band ; and all mortgages or hypothecs given or consented to by any Indian, and all leases, contracts and agreements made or purporting to be made by any Indian, whereby persons or Indians other than Indians of the band are permitted to reside or hunt upon such reserve, shall be absolutely void.

23. If any person or Indian other than an Indian of the band, without the license of the Superintendent-General (which license, however, he may at any time revoke), settles, ' resides or hunts upon or occupies or uses any such land or marsh ; or settles, resides upon or occupies any such roads or allowances, for roads, on such reserve, or if any Indian is illegally in possession of any land in a reserve, the Superintendent-General, or such officer or person as he may thereunto depute and authorize, shall, on complaint made to him, and on proof of the fact to his satiation, issue his warrant signed and sealed, directed to the sheriff of the proper county or district, or if the said reserve be not situated within any county or district, then directed to any literate person willing to act in the premises, commanding him forthwith to remove from the said land or marsh, or roads or allowances for roads, or land, every such person or Indian and his family, so settled, residing or hunting upon or occupying, or being illegally in possession of the same, or to notify such person or Indian to cease using as aforesaid the said lands, marshes, roads or allowances for roads ; and such sheriff or other person shall accordingly remove or notify such person or Indian, and for that purpose shall have the same powers as in the execution of criminal process ; and the expenses incurred in any such removal or notification shall be borne by the party removed or notified, and may be recovered from him as the

costs in any ordinary suit :

Provided that nothing contained in this Act shall prevent an Indian or non-treaty Indian, if five years a resident in Canada, not a member of the band, with' the consent of the band and the approval of the Superintendent-General from residing on the reserve or receiving a location thereon.

24. If any parson or Indian, after having been removed or notified as aforesaid, returns to, settles, resides or hunts upon or occupies, or uses as aforesaid, any of the said land, marsh or lots or parts of lots ; or Betties or resides upon or occupies any of the said roads, allowances for roads, or lots or parts of lots, the Superintendent-General, or any officer or person deputed and authorized as aforesaid, upon view, or upon proof on oath made before him, or to his satisfaction, that the said person or Indian has returned to, settled, resided or hunted upon or occupied or used as aforesaid any of the said lands, marshes, lots or parts of lots, or has returned to, settled or resided upon or occupied any of the said roads or allowances for roads, or lots or parts of lots, shall direct and send his warrant signed and sealed to the sheriff of the proper county or district, or to any literate person therein and if the said reserve be not situated within any county or district, then to any literate person, commanding him forth- with to arrest such person or Indian, and bring him before any Stipendiary Magistrate, Police Magistrate or Justice of the Peace, who may, on conviction, commit him to the common gaol of the said county or district, or if there be no gaol in the said county or district, then to the gaol nearest . to the said reserve in the Province or Territory, there to remain for the time ordered by such warrant, but which shall not exceed thirty days for the first offence, and thirty additional for each subsequent offence.

25. Such sheriff or other person shall accordingly arrest the said party, and deliver him to the gaoler or sheriff of the proper county, district, Province or Territory, who shall receive such person or Indian and imprison him in the said gaol for the term aforesaid.

26. The Superintendent-General, or such officer or person aforesaid, shall cause the judgment or order against the P. offender to be drawn up and filed in his office; and such to be final judgment shall not he removed by certiorari or otherwise, or be appealed from, hut shall be final.

27. If any person or Indian, other than an Indian of the band to which the reserve belongs, without the license in writing of the Superintendent-General, or of some officer or person deputed by him for that purpose, trespasses upon any of the said land, roads, or allowances for roads in the said reserve, by cutting, carrying away, or removing therefrom any of the trees, saplings, shrubs, underwood, timber, or hay thereon, or by removing any of the stone, soil, for minerals, metals, or other valuables, oil the sand land, roads, or allowances for roads, the person or Indian so trespassing shall, on conviction thereof before any Stipendiary Magistrate, Police Magistrate or Justice of the Peace, for every tree he cuts, carries away, or removes, forfeit and pay the sum of twenty dollars ; and for cutting, carrying away, or removing any of the saplings, shrubs, underwood, timber or have, if under the value of one dollar, the sum of four dollars ; but if over the value of one dollar, then the sum of twenty dollars ; and for removing any of the stone, soil, minerals, metals, or other value aforesaid, the sum of twenty dollars, with costs of prosecution in all cases. And in default of immediate payment of the said penalties and Forth with Si the Superintendent-General, or such other person as paid. he may have authorized in that behalf, may issue a warrant, directed to any person or persons by him

named therein, to levy the amount of the said penalties and costs by distress and sale of the goods and chattels of the person liable to pay the same ; and similar proceedings may be had upon such warrant as if it had been issued by the Magistrate or Justice of the Peace before whom the person was convicted ; or the Superintendent-General, or such other person as aforesaid, without proceeding by distress or sale, may, upon non-payment of the said penalties and costs, order the person, liable therefor to be imprisoned in the common gaol of the county or district in which the said reserve or any part thereof lies, for a period not exceeding thirty days when the penalty does not exceed twenty dollars, or for a period not exceeding three months when the penalty does exceed twenty dollars; and upon the return of any warrant for the amount thereof has not been made, or if any part of it remains unpaid, the said Superintendent General, or such other person as aforesaid, may commit the person in default to the common gaol, as aforesaid, for a period not exceeding thirty days, if the sum claimed upon the said warrant does not exceed twenty dollars, or for a time not exceeding three months if the sum does exceed twenty dollars. All such -penalties shall be paid to the Receiver-General to be disposed of for the use and benefit of Indians fop whose benefit the reserve is held, in such manner as the Governor in Council may direct.

2. But nothing herein contained shall be construed to the Superintendent-General from issuing a license to any person or Indian to cut and remove trees, wood, timber and hay, or to quarry and remove stone and gravel on and from the reserve. Provided he, or his agent acting by his instructions, first obtain the consent of the band thereto in the ordinary manner as hereinafter provided.

28. If any Indian, without the license in writing of the Superintendent-General, or of some officer or person deputed by him for that purpose, trespasses upon the land of an Indian who holds a location title, or who is otherwise recognized by the Department as the occupant of such land, by cutting, carrying away, or removing therefrom, any of the trees, saplings, shrubs, underwood, timber or hay thereon, or by removing any of the stone, soil, minerals, metals or other valuables off the said land : or if any Indian, without license as aforesaid, cuts, carries away or removes from any portion of the reserve of his band, for sale (and not for the immediate use of himself and his family), any trees, timber or hay thereon, or removes any of the stone, soil, minerals, metals, or other valuables therefrom for sale as aforesaid, he shall be liable to all the fines and penalties provided in the next preceding section in respect to Indians of other bands and other persons, and similar proceedings may be had for the recovery thereof as are provided for in the next preceding section.

29. In all orders, writs, warrants, summonses and proceeding whatsoever made, issued or taken by the Superintend General, or any officer or person by him deputed as aforesaid, it shall not be. necessary for him or such officer or person to insert or express the name of the person or Indian summoned, arrested, distrained upon, imprisoned, or otherwise proceeded against therein, except when the name of such person or Indian is truly given to or known by the Superintendent-General, or such officer or person ; and if the name be not truly given to or known by hint, he may name or describe the person or Indian by any part of the name of such person or Indian given to or known by him ; and if no part of the name be given to or known by him he may describe the person or Indian proceeded against in any manner by which he may be identified ; and all such proceedings containing or purporting to give the name or description of any such person or Indian as aforesaid shall prima facie be sufficient.

30. All sheriffs, gaolers or peace officers to whom any such process is directed by the Superintendent-General, or by any officer or person by him deputed as aforesaid, shall obey the same; and all other officers upon reasonable requisition shall assist in the execution thereof.

31. If any railway, road or public work passes through causes injury to any reserve belonging to or in possession to of any band of Indians, or if any act occasioning damage any reserve be done under the authority of any Act of Parliament, or of the Legislature of any Province, compensation shall be made to them therefor in the same manner as is provided with respect to the lands or rights of other persons; the Superintendent-General shall, in any case in which an arbitration may be had, name the arbitrator on behalf of the Indians, and shall act for them on any matter relating to the settlement of such compensation; and the amount awarded in any case shall be paid to the Receiver-General for the use of the band of Indians for whose benefit the reserve is held, and for the benefit of any Indian having Improvement thereon.

32. In all cases of encroachment upon, or of violation of trust respecting any special reserve, it shall he lawful to proceed by information in the name of Her Majesty, in the superior courts of law or equity, notwithstanding the legal title may not be vested m the Crown.

33. If by the violation of the conditions of any such trust as aforesaid, or by the breaking up of any society, corporation, or community, or if by the death of any person or persons without a legal succession of trusteeship, in whom the title to a special reserve is held in trust, the said title lapses or becomes void in law, then the legal title shall become vested in the Crown in trust, and the property shall be managed for the band or irregular baud previously interested therein, as an ordinary reserve. The trustees of any special reserve may at any time surrender the same to Her Majesty in trust, whereupon the property shall be managed for the band or irregular band previously interested therein as an ordinary reserve.

34. Indians residing upon any reserve, and engaged in pursuit of agriculture as their then principal means of support, shall De liable, if so directed by the General, or any officer or person by him thereunto authorized, to perform labour on the public roads laid out or used in or through, or abutting upon such reserve,—such labour to be performed under the sole control of the said Superintendent- General, officer or person, who may direct when, where and how and in what manner the said labour shall be applied, and to what extent the same shall be imposed upon Indians who may be resident upon any of the said lands; and the said Superintendent-General, officer or person have the like power to enforce the performance of all such labour by imprisonment or otherwise, as may be done by any power or authority under any law, rule or regulation in force in the Province or territory in which such reserve lies, for the non-performance of statute labour; but the labour to be so required of any such Indian shall not exceed extent what may be required of other inhabitants of the same Province, territory, county, or other local division, under the laws requiring and regulating such labour and the performance thereof.

35. Every band of Indians shall be bound to cause the roads, bridges, ditches and fences within their reserve to be put and maintained in proper order, in accordance with the instructions received from time to time from the Superintendent- General, or from the agent of the Superintendent- General; and whenever in the opinion of the Superintendent-General the same are not so put or maintained in order, he may cause the work to be performed at the cost of such band, or of the particular Indian

in default, as the case may be, either out of their or his annual allowances, or otherwise.

36. No reserve or portion of a reserve shall be sold alienated or leased until it has been released or surrendered to the Crown for the purpose of this Act, excepting that in cases of aged, sick and infirm Indians and widows or children left without a guardian, the Superintendent-General ' shall have the power to lease the lands to which they may be entitled for their support or benefit.

37. No release or surrender of a reserve, or portion of a reserve, held for the use of the Indians of any band or of any individual Indian, shall be valid or binding, except on the following conditions :—

1. The release or surrender shall be assented to by majority of the male members of the band of the full age of twenty-one years, at a meeting or council thereof summoned for that purpose according to their rules, and held in the presence of the Superintendent-General, or of an officer duly authorized to attend such council by the Governor in Council or by the Superintendent-General : Provided, that no Indian shall be entitled to vote or be present at such council, unless he habitually resides on or near, and is interested in the reserve in question :

2. The fact that such release or surrender has been Proof of a8- assented to by the band at such council or meeting, shall be certified on oath before some judge of a superior, county or district court, or Stipendiary Magistrate, by the Superintendent- General, or by the officer authorized by him to attend such council or meeting, and by some one of the chiefs or principal men present thereat and entitled to vote, and when so certified as aforesaid shall be submitted to the Governor in Council for acceptance or refusal.

38. It shall not be lawful to introduce, at any council or meeting of Indians held for the purpose of discussing or of assenting to a release or surrender of a reserve or portion council or 3 thereof, or of assenting to the issuing of a timber or other license, any intoxicant ; and any person introducing at such under the meeting, and any agent or officer employed by the Superintendent-General, or by the Governor in Council, introducing, or countenancing by his presence the use of such intoxicant among such Indians a week before, at, or a week after, any such council or meeting, shall forfeit two hundred dollars, recoverable by action in any of the superior courts of law, one-half of which penalty shall go to the informer.

39. Nothing in this Act shall confirm any release or Act not to surrender which would have been invalid if this Act had not been passed ; and no release or surrender of any reserve or portion of a reserve to any party other than the Crown, be valid.

40. All Indian lands, being reserves or portions of reserves surrendered or to be surrendered to the Crown, shall be deemed to be held for the same purposes as before the passing of this Act ; and shall be managed, leased and sold as the Governor in Council may direct, subject to the conditions of surrender and the provisions of this Act.

41. No agent for the sale of Indian lands shall, within his division, directly or indirectly, unless under an order of the Governor in Council, purchase any land which he is appointed to sell, or become proprietor of or interested in any such land, during the time of his agency; and any such purchase or interest shall be void ; and if any such agent offends in the premises, he shall forfeit his office and the sum of four hundred dollars for every such offence, which may be recovered in action of debt by any person who may sue for the same.

42. Every certificate of sale or receipt for money received on the sale of Indian lands, heretofore

granted or made or to be granted or made by the Superintendent-General or any agent of his, so long as the sale to which such receipt or certificate relates is in force and not rescinded, shall entitle the party to whom the same was or shall be made or granted, or his assignee, by instrument registered under this or any former Act providing for registration in such cases, to take possession of and occupy the land therein comprised, subject to the conditions of such sale, and thereunder, unless the same shall have been revoked or cancelled, to maintain suits in law or equity against any wrongdoer or trespasser, as effectually as he could do under a patent from the Crown ;— and such receipt or certificate shall be prima facie evidence for the purpose of possession by such person, or the assignee under an instrument registered as aforesaid, in any such suit ; but the same shall have no force against a license to cut timber existing at the time of the making or granting thereof.

43. The Superintendent-General shall keep a book for registering (at the option of the parties interested) the particulars of any assignment made, as well by the original purchaser or lessee of Indian lands or his heir or legal representative, as by any subsequent assignee of any such lands, or the heir or legal representative of such assignee ;—and upon any such assignment being produced to the Superintendent- General, and, (except in cases where such assignment is made under a corporate seal), with an affidavit of due execution thereof, and of the time and place of such execution, and the names, residences and occupations of the witnesses, or, as regards lands in the Province of Quebec, upon the production of such assignment executed in notarial form, or of a notarial copy thereof, the Superintendent General shall cause the material parts of every such assignment to be registered in such book of registry, and shall cause to be endorsed on every such assignment a certificate of such registration, to be signed by himself or his deputy, or any other officer of the department by him authorized to sign such certificates : And every such assignment Their effect, so registered shall be valid against any one previously executed, but subsequently registered, or unregistered ; but all the conditions of the sale, grant or location must have been complied with, or dispensed with by the Superintendent- General, before such registration is made. But any assignment to be registered as aforesaid must be unconditional in its terms.

44. If any subscribing witness to any such assignment is deceased, or has left the province, the Superintendent- General may register such assignment upon the production of an affidavit proving the death or absence of such witness and his handwriting, or the handwriting of the party making such assignment.

45. On any application for a patent by the heir, assignee devisee of the original purchaser from the Crown, the Superintendent-General may receive proof in such manner as he may direct" and require in support of any claim for a patent when the original purchaser is dead, and upon being satisfied that the claim has been equitably and justly established, may allow the same, and cause a patent to issue accordingly ; but nothing in this section shall limit the right of a party claiming a patent to land in the Province of Ontario to make application at any time to the Commissioner, under the "'Act respecting the Heir, Devisee and Assignee Commission being chapter twenty-five of the Revised Statutes of Ontario.

46. If the Superintendent-General is satisfied that any purchaser or lessee of any Indian lands, or any assignee claiming under or through him, has been guilty of any fraud in cases of or imposition, or has violated any of the conditions of sale or lease, or if any such sale or lease has been or is made or

issued in error or mistake, he may cancel such sale or lease, and resume the land therein mentioned, or dispose of it as if no sale or lease thereof had ever been made ; and all such cancellations heretofore made by the Governor in Council or the Superintendent-General shall continue valid until altered.

47. When any purchaser, lessee or other person refuses or neglects to deliver up possession of any land after revocation or cancellation of the sale or lease as aforesaid, or when any person is wrongfully in possession of any Indian lands and refuses to vacate or abandon possession of the same, the Superintendent-General may apply to the county judge of the county, or to a judge of the Superior Court in the circuit, in which the land lie in Ontario or Quebec, or to any judge of a superior court of law or any county judge of the county in which the land lies in any other province or to any Stipendiary Magistrate in any territory in which the land lies, for an order in the nature of a writ of habere facias possessionem or writ of possession, and the said judge or magistrate, upon proof to his satisfaction that the right or title of the party to hold such land has been revoked or cancelled as aforesaid, or that such person is wrongfully in possession of Indian lands, shall grant an order upon the purchaser, lessee or person in possession, to deliver up the same to the Superintendent-General, or person by him authorized to receive the same ; and such order shall have the same force as a writ of habere facias possessionem, or writ of possession ; and the sheriff, or any bailiff or person to whom it may have been trusted for execution by the Superintendent- General, shall execute the same in like manner as he would execute such writ in an action of ejectment or possessory action.

48. "Whenever any rent payable to the Crown on any lease of Indian lands is in arrear, the Superintendent-General, or any agent or officer appointed under this Act and authorized by the Superintendent-General to act in such cases, may issue a warrant, directed to any person or persons by him named therein, in the shape of a distress warrant as in ordinary cases of landlord and tenant, or as in the case of distress and warrant of a justice of the peace for non-payment of a pecuniary penalty ; and the same proceedings may be had thereon for the collection of such arrears as in either of the said last-mentioned cases ; or an action of debt as in ordinary cases of rent in arrear may be brought therefor in the name of the Superintendent-General ; but demand of rent shall not be necessary in any case.

49. When by law OT by any deed, lease or agreement relating to any of the lands herein referred to, any notice is required to be given, or any act to be done, by or oil behalf of the Crown, such notice may be given and act done by or by the authority of the Superintendent-General.

50. Whenever letters patent have been issued to or in the name of the wrong party, through mistake, or contain any clerical error or misnomer, or wrong description of any material fact therein, or of the land thereby intended to be granted, the Superintendent-General (there being no adverse claim) may direct the defective letters patent to be cancelled and a minute of such cancellation to be entered in the margin of the registry of the original letters patent, and correct letters patent to be issued in their stead,—which corrected letters patent shall relate ha k to the date of those so cancelled, and have the same effect as if issued at the date of such cancelled letters patent.

51. In all cases in which grants or letters patent have for the same land inconsistent with each other through error, and in all cases of sales or appropriations of the same land inconsistent with each other, the Superintendent- General may, in cases of sale, cause a repayment of the purchase money, with interest, or when the land has passed from the original purchaser or has been improved before

a discovery of the error, he may in substitution assign land or grant a certificate entitling the party to purchase Indian lands, of such value and to such extent as to him, the Superintendent- General, may seem just and equitable under the circumstances ; but no such claim shall be entertained unless it be preferred within five years from the discovery of the error.

52. Whenever by reason of false survey or error in the books or plans in the Department of Indian Affairs, in the late Indian Branch of the Department of the Interior, any grant, sale or appropriation of land is found to be deficient, or any parcel of land contains less than the quantity of land mentioned in the patent therefor, the Superintendent- General may order the purchase money of so much land as is deficient, with the interest thereon from the time of the application therefor, or. if the land has passed from the original purchaser, then the purchase money which the claimant (provided he was ignorant of a deficiency at the time of his purchase) has paid for so much of the land as is deficient, with interest thereon from the time of the application therefor, to be paid to him in land or in money, as he, the Superintendent-General, may direct ;—But no such claim shall be entertained unless application has been made within five years from the date of the patent, nor unless the deficiency is equal to one-tenth of the whole quantity described as being contained in the particular lot or parcel of land granted.

53. In all cases patents for Indian lands have issued through fraud superior or improvidence, the Exchequer Court of Canada, superior court of law or equity in issued any Province may, bill or plaint, respecting such lands situate within their jurisdiction, and upon hearing of the parties interested, or upon default of the said parties after such notice of proceeding as the said courts shall respectively order, decree such patents to be void; and upon a registry of such decree in the office of the Registrar-General of Canada, such patents shall be void to all intents. The practice in court, in such cases, shall be regulated by orders Practice in to be, from time to time, made by the said courts respectively ; and any action or proceeding commenced under any former Act may be continued under this section,—which, for the purpose of any such action or proceeding shall be construed as merely continuing the provisions of such former Act.

54. If any agent appointed or continued in office under this Act knowingly and falsely informs, or causes to be informed, any person applying to him to purchase any land within his division and agency, that the same has already been purchased, or refuses to permit the person so applying to purchase the same according to existing regulations, such agent shall be liable therefor to the person so applying- in the sum of lire dollars for each acre of land which the person so applying offered to purchase, to be recovered by action of debt in any court having jurisdiction in civil cases to the amount.

55. If any person, before or at the time of the public sale Of any Indian lands, by intimidation, combination or unfair management, hinders or prevents, or attempts to hinder or prevent any person from bidding upon or purchasing any lands so offered for sale, every such offender, his, her or Misdemeanor, their aiders and abettors, shall, for every such offence, be misdemeanor, and on conviction thereof shall be liable to a fine not exceeding four hundred dollars, or imprisonment for a term not exceeding two years, or both, in the discretion of the court.

56. The Superintendent-General, or any officer or agent authorized by him to that effect, may grant licenses to cut trees on reserves and ungranted Indian lands at such rates, subject to such conditions, regulations and restrictions, as may, from time to time, be established by the Governor in Coun-

cil,—such conditions, regulations and restrictions to be adapted to the locality in which such reserves or lands are situated.

57. No license shall be so granted for a longer period than twelve months from the date thereof: and if, in consequence of any incorrectness of survey or other error, or cause whatsoever, a license is found to comprise land included in a license of a prior date, or land not being reserve's or ungranted Indian lands, the license granted shall be void in so far as it comprises such land, and the holder or proprietor of the license so rendered void shall have no claim upon the Government for indemnity or compensation by reason of such avoidance.

58. Every license shall describe the lands upon which the trees may be cut and the kind of trees to be cut, and shall confer for the time being on the nominee, the right to take and keep exclusive possession of the land so described, subject to such regulations and restrictions as may be established ; and every license shall vest in the holder thereof all rights of property whatsoever in all trees of the kind specified cut within the limits of the license during the term thereof, whether such trees are cut by authority of the holder of such license or by any other person, with or without his consent ; and every license shall entitle the holder thereof to seize in revendication or otherwise, such trees -and the logs, timber or other product thereof where the same are found in the possession of any unauthorized person, and also to institute any action or suit at law or in equity Against any wrongful possessor or trespasser, and to prosecute all trespassers and other offenders to punishment, and to recover damages, if any ; and all proceedings pending at the expiration of any license may be continued to final termination as if the license had not expired.

59. Every person obtaining a license shall, at the expiration thereof, make to the officer or agent granting the same, or to the Superintendent-General, a return of the number and kinds of trees cut, and of the quantity and description of saw-logs, or of the number and description of sticks of square or other timber, manufactured and carried away under such license ; and such statement shall be sworn to by the holder of the license, or his agent, or by his foreman : and any person refusing or neglecting to furnish such statement, or evading or attempting to evade any regulation made by Order in Council, shall be held to have cut without authority, and the timber or other product made shall be dealt with accordingly.

60. All trees cut, and the logs, timber or other products thereof, shall be liable for the payment of the dues thereon so long as and wheresoever the same or any part thereof for the may be found, whether in the original logs or manufactured into deals, boards or other stuff ; and all officers or agents e ' entrusted with the collection of such dues may follow and seize and detain the same wherever it is found, until the dues are paid or secured.

61. Any instrument or security taken for the dues, either before or after the cutting of the trees, as collateral security or to facilitate collection, shall not in any way affect the lien, but the lien shall subsist until the said dues are actually discharged.

62. If any timber so seized and detained for non-payment of dues remains more than twelve months in the custody of the agent or person appointed to guard the same, without the dues and expenses being paid,—then the Superintendent- General, may order a sale of the said timber to be made after sufficient notice ; and the balance of the proceeds of such sale, after retaining the amount of dues and cost» incurred, shall be handed over to the owner or claimant of such timber, upon his apply-

ing therefor and proving his right thereto

63. If any person without authority cuts, or employs or induces any other person to cut, or assists in cutting any trees of any kind on Indian lands, or removes or carries away, or employs or induces or assists any other person to remove or carry away, any trees of any kind so cut from Indian lands aforesaid, he shall not acquire any right to the trees so cut, or any claim to any remuneration for cutting, preparing the same for market, or conveying the same to or towards market,—and when the trees or logs OT timber, or other products thereof, have been removed, so that the same cannot, in the opinion of the Superintendent-General, conveniently be seized, he shall in addition to the loss of his labour and disbursements, forfeit a sum of three dollars for each tree (rafting stuff excepted), which he is proved to have cut or caused to be cut or carried away ; and such sum shall be recoverable with costs, at the suit and in the name of the Superintendent-General or resident agent, in any court having jurisdiction in civil matters to the amount of the penalty : and in all such cases it shall be incumbent on the party charged to prove his authority to cut ; and the averment of the party seizing or prosecuting, that he is duly employed under the authority of this Act, shall be sufficient proof thereof, unless the defendant proves the contrary.

64. Whenever satisfactory information, supported by affidavit made before a Justice of the Peace or before any other competent authority, is received by the Superintendent- General, or any other officer or agent acting under him, that any trees have been cut without authority on Indian lands, and describing where the same or the logs, timber or other products thereof can be found, the said Superintendent- General, officer or agent, or any one of them, may seize or cause to be seized the same in Her Majesty's name, wherever found, and place the same under proper custody, until a decision can be had in the matter from competent authority :

2. And where the wood, timber, logs or other products thereof so reported to have been cut without authority on Indian lands, have been made up or intermingled with other timber, logs or other products thereof into a crib, dram or raft, or in any other manner, so that it is difficult to distinguish the timber cut on reserves or Indian land without license, from the other timber with which.it is made up or intermingled, the whole of the timber so made up or intermingled shall be held to have been cut without authority on Indian lands, and shall be seized and forfeited and sold by the Superintendent-General, or any other officer or agent acting under him, unless evidence satisfactory to him is adduced shewing the probable quantity not cut on Indian lands.

65. Any officer or person seizing trees, logs, timber or Seizing other products thereof, in the discharge of his duty under this Act, may, in the name of the Crown, call in any assistance necessary for securing and protecting the same ; and whosoever under any pretence, either by assault, force or violence, or by threat of such assault, force or violence, in any way resists or obstructs any officer or person acting in his aid, in the discharge of his duty under this Act, shall, on conviction thereof in a summary manner before a Justice of Punishment the Peace or other proper functionary, be liable to a fine not resisting exceeding one hundred dollars, or to imprisonment not exceeding twelve months, or to both, in the discretion of the convicting justice or other functionary.

66. Whosoever, whether pretending to be the owner or not, either secretly or openly, and whether with or without force or violence, takes or carries away, or causes to be taken or carried away, without permission of the officer or person who seized the same, or of some competent authority, any trees,

logs, timber or other product thereof, seized and detained as subject to forfeiture under this Act, before the same, has been declared by competent authority to have been seized without due cause, shall be deemed to have stolen the same, as being the property of the Crown, and guilty of felony, and is liable to punishment accordingly :

2. And whenever any trees, logs, timber or other products thereof are seized for non-payment of Crown dues or for any other cause of forfeiture, or any prosecution is brought for any penalty or forfeiture under this Act, and any question arises whether the said dues have been paid or whether the same were cut on other than any of the lands aforesaid, the burden of proving payment, or on what land the same were cut, shall lie on the owner or claimant and not on the officer who seizes the same, or the party bringing such prosecution.

67. All trees, logs, timber or other products thereof seized under this Act shall be deemed to be condemned, unless the person from whom the same are seized, or the owner thereof, within one month from the day of the seizure, gives notice to the seizing officer, or nearest officer or agent of the Superintendent-General, that he claims or intends to claim the same ; failing such notice, the officer or agent seizing shall report the circumstances to the Superintendent-General, who may order the sale of the same by the said officer or agent :

2. And any judge of a superior, county or district court, or any Stipendiary Magistrate, may, in a summary way, and following the procedure on summary trials before Justices of the Peace out of sessions, try and determine such seizures, and may, pending the trial,-Order the delivery of the trees, logs, timber or other products thereof to the alleged owner, on receiving security by bond with two good and sufficient sureties, to be first approved by the said agent, to pay double the value in case of condemnation,—and such bond shall be taken in the name of the Superintendent- General, to Her Majesty's use, and shall be delivered up to and kept by the Superintendent-General ; and if such seized trees, logs, timber or other products thereof are condemned, the value thereof shall be paid forthwith to the Superintendent- General, or agent, and the bond cancelled, otherwise the penalty of such bond shall be enforced and recovered.

68. Every person availing himself of any false statement or oath to evade the payment of dues under this Act, shall forfeit the timber on which dues are attempted to be evaded.

69. All moneys or securities of any kind applicable to the support or benefit of Indians, or any band of Indians, and all moneys accrued or hereafter to accrue from the sale of any Indian lands or of any timber on any reserves or Indian lands, shall, subject to the provisions of this Act, be applicable to the same purposes, and be dealt with in the same manner as they might have been applied to or-dealt with before the passing of this Act.

70. The Governor in Council may, subject to the provisions of this Act, direct how, and in what manner, and by whom the moneys arising from sales of Indian lands, and from the property held or to be held, in trust for the Indians, or from any timber on Indian lands or reserves, or from any other source for the benefit of Indians (with the exception of any small sum not exceeding ten per cent, of the proceeds of any lands, timber or property, which may be agreed at the time of the surrender to be paid to the members of the band interested therein), shall be invested from time to time, and how the payments or assistance to which the Indians may be entitled shall be made or given, and may provide for the general management of such moneys, and direct what percentage or proportion

thereof shall be set apart from time to time, to cover the cost of and attendant upon the management of reserves, lands, property and moneys under the provisions of this Act, and for the construction or repair of roads passing through such reserves or lands, and by way of contribution to schools frequented by such Indians.

71. The proceeds arising from the sale or lease of any Indian lands, or from the timber, hay, stone, minerals or other valuables thereon, or on a reserve, shall be paid to the Receiver-General to the credit of the Indian fund.

72. Whenever the Governor in council deems it advice able for the good government of a band to introduce the election system of chiefs, he may by Order in Council pro-election vide that the chiefs of any band of Indians shall be elected, as hereinafter provided, at such time and place as the Superintendent-General may direct ; and they shall, in such case, be elected for a period of three years, unless deposed by the Governor for dishonesty, intemperance, immorality or incompetency ; and they may be in the proportion of one head chief and two second chiefs or councillors for every two hundred Indians : Provided, that no band shall have more than six head chiefs and twelve second chiefs, but any band composed of thirty Indians may have one chief : Provided always, that all life chiefs now living shall continue to hold the rank of chief until death or resignation, or until their moval by the Governor for dishonesty, intemperance, immorality or incompetency: Provided also, that in the event of His Excellency ordering that the chiefs of a band shall be elected, then and in such case the life chiefs shall them. not exercise the powers of chiefs unless elected under such order to the exercise of such powers.

73. At the election of a clerk or chief or the granting of any ordinary consent required of a band of Indians under this Act, those entitled to vote at the council or meeting thereof shall be the male members of the band of the full age of twenty-one years ; and the vote of a majority of such members at a council or meeting of the band summoned according to their rules, and held in the presence of the Superintendent-General, or an agent acting under his instructions, shall be sufficient to determine such election, or grant such consent

Provided that in the case of any band having a council of chiefs or councillors, any ordinary consent required of the band may be granted by a vote of a majority of such chiefs or councillors at a council summoned according to their rules, and held in the presence of the Superintendent- General or his agent.

74. The subject to confirmation by the Governor in Council, rules and regulations for the following subjects, viz. :—

1. As to what religious denomination the teacher of the school established on the reserve shall belong to ; provided always, that he shall be of the same denomination as the majority of the band; and provided that the Catholic or Protestant minority may likewise have a separate school with the approval of and under regulations to be made by the Governor in Council ;

2. The care of the public health ;

3. The observance of order and decorum at assemblies of the Indians in general council, or on other occasions;

4. The repression of intemperance and profligacy ;

5. The prevention of trespass by cattle,—also for the protection of sheep, horses, mules and cattle;

6. The construction and maintenance of water-courses, roads, bridges, ditches and fences ;
7. The construction and repair of school houses, council houses and other Indian public buildings;
8. The establishment of pounds and the appointment of pound-keepers ;
9. The locating of the land in their reserves, and the establishment of a register of such locations;
10. The repression of noxious weeds ;
11. The imposition of punishment, by fine or penalty, or by imprisonment, or both, for infraction of any of such rules or regulations ; the fine or penalty in no case to exceed thirty dollars, and the imprisonment in no case to exceed thirty days ; the proceedings for the imposition of such punishment to be taken in the usual summary way before a Justice of the Peace, following the procedure on summary trials before a justice out of sessions.
75. No Indian or non-treaty Indian shall be liable to be taxed for any real or personal property, unless he holds in his individual right real estate under a lease or in fee simple, or personal property, outside of the reserve or special reserve,—in which ease he shall be liable to be taxed for such real or personal property at the same rate as other persons in the locality in which it is situate.
76. All land vested in the Crown, or in any person or body corporate, in trust for or for the use of any Indian or non-treaty Indian, or any band or irregular baud of Indians or non-treaty Indians, shall be exempt from taxation.
77. No person shall take any security or otherwise obtain any lien or charge, whether by mortgage, judgment or otherwise, upon real or personal property of any Indian non-treaty Indian within Canada, except on real or personal property subject to taxation under section seventy-five of this Act: Provided always, that any person selling any article to an Indian or non-treaty Indian may, not withstanding this section, take security on such article for any part of the price thereof which may be unpaid.
78. Indians and non-treaty Indians shall have the right to sue for debts due to them or in respect of any tort or wrong inflicted upon them, or to compel the performance of obligations contracted with them.
79. No pawn taken of any Indian or non-treat Indian for any intoxicant shall be retained by the person to for whom such pawn is delivered, but the thing so pawned may be sued for and recovered, with costs of suit, by the Indian or non-treaty Indian who has deposited the same, before any court of competent jurisdiction.
80. No presents given to Indian or no-treaty Indians, nor any property purchased or acquired with or by means Indiana of any annuities granted to Indians or any part thereof, and in the possession of any band of such Indians or of any Indian of any band or irregular band, shall be liable to be taken, seized or distrained for any debt, matter or cause whatsoever. Nor in the Province of British Columbia, the Province of Manitoba, the North-West Territories, or in the District of Keewatin, shall the same be sold, bartered, exchanged or given by any band or irregular band of Indians, or any Indian of any such band, to any person or Indian other than an Indian of such band ; and any such barter, exchange or gift shall be absolutely null and void, unless such sale, barter, exchange or gift be made with the written assent of the Superintendent-General or his agent ; and whosoever buys or otherwise acquires any presents or property purchased as aforesaid, without the written mention consent of the Superintendent-General, or his agent, as aforesaid, is guilty of a misdemeanor, and is punish-

able by fine not exceeding two hundred dollars, or by imprisonment not exceeding six months, in any place of confinement other than a penitentiary. If any presents given to Indians or Present, non-treaty Indians, or any property purchased or acquired with or by means of any annuities granted to Indians, be possession of unlawfully in the possession of any person, within the true intent and meaning of this section, any person acting under the authority (either general or special) of the Superintendent- General, may, with such assistance in that behalf as he may think necessary, seize and take possession of the same, and he shall deal therewith as the Superintendent-General may direct.

DISABILITIES AND PENALTIES.

81. No Indian or non-treaty Indian, resident in the province of Manitoba, the North-West Territories or the District home the of Keewatin, shall be held capable of having acquired or acquiring a homestead or pre-emption right to a quarter section, or any portion of land in any surveyed or unsurveyed lands in the said Province of Manitoba, the North-west Territories or the District of Keewatin, or the right to share in the distribution of any lands allotted to half-breeds, subject to the following exceptions

(a) He shall not be disturbed in the occupation of any plot on which he has or may have permanent improvements prior to his becoming a party to any treaty with the Crown ;

(b) Nothing in this section shall prevent the- Government of Canada, if found desirable, from compensating any Indian for his improvements on such a plot of land without obtaining a formal surrender therefor from the band ;

(c) Nothing in this section shall apply to any person who withdrew' from any Indian treaty prior to the first day of October, in the year one thousand eight hundred and seventy four.

82. Any Indian convicted of any crime punishable by imprisonment in any penitentiary or other place of confinement, shall, during such imprisonment, be excluded from participating in the annuities, interest money, or rents able to the band of which he or she is a member ; and Indian shall be convicted of any crime punishable by imprisonment in a penitentiary or other place of confinement, the legal costs incurred in procuring such conviction, and in carrying out the various sentences recorded, may be defrayed by the Superintendent-General, and paid out of any annuity or interest coming to such Indian, or to the band, as the case may be.

83. The Superintendent-General shall have power to stop the payment of the annuity and interest money of any Indian who may be proved, to the satisfaction of the Superintendent general to have been guilty of deserting his or her family and the said superintendent general may apply the same towards the support of any family, women or child so deserted of any woman having no children. Who desert her husband and lives immorally with another man.

84. 'The Superintendent-General, in cases where sick or disabled, or aged and destitute persons are not provided for by the band of Indians of which they are members, may furnish sufficient aid from the funds of the band for the relief of such sick, disabled, aged or destitute persons.

85. Upon any inquest, or upon any enquiry into any matter involving a criminal charge, or upon the trial of any crime or offence whatsoever or by whomsoever committed, it shall be lawful for any court, judge, Stipendiary Magistrate, coroner or justice of the peace to receive the evidence of any Indian or non-treaty Indian, who is destitute of the knowledge of God and of any fixed and clear belief in religion or in a future state of rewards and punishments without administering the usual

form of oath to any such Indian, or non-treaty Indian, as aforesaid, upon his solemn affirmation or declaration to tell the truth, the whole truth and nothing but the truth, or in such form as may be approved by such court, judge, Stipendiary Magistrate, coroner or justice of the peace as most binding on the conscience of such Indian or non-treaty Indian.

88. Provided that in the case of any inquest, or upon any enquiry into any matter involving a criminal charge, or upon the trial of any crime or offence whatsoever, the substance of the evidence or information of any such Indian, or non- treaty Indian, as aforesaid, shall be reduced to writing and signed by the person (by mark if necessary) giving the same, and verified by the signature or mark of the person acting as interpreter (if any) and by the signature of the judge, Stipendiary Magistrate or coroner, or justice of the peace or person before whom such evidence or information has been given.

87. The court, judge, Stipendiary Magistrate or justice of the peace shall, before taking any such evidence, information or examination, caution every such Indian, or non-treaty Indian, as aforesaid, that he will be liable to incur punishment if he do not so as aforesaid tell the truth.

88. The written declaration or examination, made, taken and verified in manner aforesaid, of any such Indian or non- declarations, treaty Indian as aforesaid, may be lawfully read and received as evidence upon the trial of any criminal suit or proceedings. when under the like circumstances the written affidavit, examination, deposition or confession of any other person, might be lawfully read and received as evidence.

89. Every solemn affirmation or declaration in whatever Effect of form made or taken by any Indian or non-treaty Indian as aforesaid shall be of the same force and effect as if such Indian or non-treaty Indian had taken an oath in the usual form, and he or she shall, in like manner, incur the penalty of perjury in case of falsehood.

90. Whoever sells, exchanges with, barters, supplies or gives to any Indian or non-treaty Indian in Canada, any for furnishing kind of intoxicant, or causes or procures the same to be done, or connives or attempts thereat, or opens or keeps, or causes to be opened or kept on any reserve or special reserve, a tavern, house or building where any intoxicant is sold, bartered, exchanged or given, or is found in possession of any intoxicant in the house, tent, wigwam or place of abode of any Indian or non-treaty Indian, shall, on conviction thereof before any judge, Stipendiary Magistrate or two justices of the peace, upon the evidence of one credible witness other than the informer or prosecutor, or in the Province of Manitoba, in the District of Keewatin, in the north-West Territories or in the Province of British Columbia, upon the evidence of the informer alone if he be a credible person, be liable to imprisonment for a period not less than one month nor exceeding six months, with or without hard labour, or be fined not less than fifty nor more than three hundred dollars, with costs of prosecution,- one moiety of the fine to go to the informer or prosecutor, and the other moiety to Her Majesty, to form part of the fund for the benefit of that body of Indians or non treaty Indians, with respect to one or more members of which the offence was committed, or he shall be liable to both fine and imprisonment in the discretion of the convicting judge, Stipendiary Magistrate or justices of the peace ; and the commander or person in charge of any steamer or other vessel, or boat, from or on board of which any intoxicant has been sold, bartered, exchanged, supplied or given to any Indian or non treaty Indian, shall be liable, on conviction thereof before any judge,

Stipendiary Magistrate or two justices of the peace, upon the evidence of one credible witness other than the informer or prosecutor, or in the Province of Manitoba, in the District of Keewatin, in the North-West Territories or in the Province of British Columbia, upon the evidence of the informer alone if he be a credible person, to be fined not less than fifty nor exceeding three hundred dollars for each such offence, with costs of prosecution, the moieties of the fine to be applicable as hereinbefore mentioned ; and in default of immediate payment of such fine and costs any person so fined shall be committed to any common gaol, house of correction, lock-up or other place of confinement by the judge, Stipendiary Magistrate or two justices of the peace before whom the conviction has taken place, for a period of not less than one nor more than six months, with or without hard labour, or until such fine and costs are paid ; and any Indian or non-treaty Indian who makes or manufactures any intoxicant, or who has in his possession, or concealed, or who sells, exchanges with, barters, supplies or gives to any other Indian or non-treaty Indian in any kind of intoxicant, shall, on conviction to other thereof, before any judge, Stipendiary Magistrate or two justices of the peace, upon the evidence of one credible witness other than the informer or prosecutor, or in the Province of Manitoba, in the District of Keewatin, in the North-West Territories or in the Province of British Columbia, upon the evidence of the informer alone if h» be a credible person be liable to imprisonment for a period of not less than one month nor more than six months, with or without hard labour, or a fine of not less than twenty-five or more than one hundred dollars, or to both fine and imprisonment in the discretion of the convicting judge, Stipendiary Magistrate or justices of the peace ; and in all cases arising under this of section, Indians or non-treaty Indians shall be competent witnesses : but no penalty shall be incurred in case of sickness where the intoxicant is made use of under the sanction of & medical man or under the directions of a minister of religion.

91. The keg, barrel, case, box, package or receptacle whence any intoxicant has been sold, exchanged, bartered, supplied or given, and as well that in which the original curried to supply was contained as the vessel wherein any portion of forfeited, such original supply was supplied as aforesaid, and the remainder of the contents thereof, if such barrel, keg, case, box, package, receptacle or vessel aforesaid respectively, can be identified,—and any intoxicant imported or manufactured Intoxicants or brought into and upon any reserve or special reserve, or containing8 into the house, tent, wigwam or place of abode, or on the them may be person of any Indian or non-treaty Indian be searched for, and if found seized by any Indian superintendent, agent or bailiff, or other officer connected with the Indian Department, or by any constable wheresoever found on such land or in such place or on the person of such Indian or non-treaty Indian: and on complaint before any judge. Stipendiary Magistrate or justice of the peace, he may, on the evidence of any credible witness that this Act has been contravened in respect thereof, declare the same forfeited, and cause the same to be forthwith destroyed ; and may condemn the Persons in Indian or other person in whose possession they were found are to pay a penalty not exceeding one hundred dollars nor less than fifty dollars, and the costs of prosecution ; and one-half of such penalty shall belong to the prosecutor and the other half to Her Majesty, for the purposes hereinbefore mentioned ; and in default of immediate payment, the offender may be Imprisonment committed to any common gaol, house of correction, lock-up or other place of confinement, with or without hard labour, for any time not exceeding six nor less than two months, unless such fine and costs are sooner paid.

92. When it is proved before any judge, Stipendiary Magistrate or two justices of the peace that any vessel, boat canoe or conveyance of any description upon the sea or sea coast, or upon any river, lake or stream in Canada, is employed in carrying any intoxicant, to be supplied to Indians or non-treaty Indians, such vessel, boat, canoe or conveyance so employed may be seized and declared forfeited, as in the next preceding section, and sold, and the proceeds thereof paid to Her Majesty for the purpose hereinbefore mentioned.

93. Every article, chattel, commodity or thing in the purchase, acquisition, exchange, trade or barter of which, in contravention of this Act, the consideration, either wholly or in part, maybe any intoxicant, shall be forfeited to Her Majesty and shall be seized as in the ninety-first section in respect to any receptacle of any intoxicant, and may be sold, and the proceeds thereof paid to Her Majesty for the purposes hereinbefore mentioned.

94. it shall be lawful for any constable, without process of law, to arrest any Indian or non-treaty Indian whom he may find in a state of intoxication, and to convey him to any common gaol, house of correction, lock-up or other place of confinement, there to be kept until he shall have become sober; and such Indian or non-treaty Indian shall, when sober, be brought before any judge, Stipendiary Magistrate or justice of the peace, and if convicted of being so found in a state of intoxication shall be liable to imprisonment in any common gaol, house of correction, lock-up or other place of confinement, for any period not exceeding one month ; and if any Indian or non-treaty Indian, having been so convicted as aforesaid, refuses upon examination to state or give information of the person, place and time from whom, where and when, he procured such intoxicant, and if from any other Indian or non-treaty Indian, then, if within his knowledge, from whom, where and when such intoxicant was originally procured or received, he shall be liable to imprisonment as aforesaid for a further period not exceeding fourteen days.

95. If any person, being the keeper of any house, allows or suffers any Indian woman to be or remain in such house, knowing, or having probable cause for believing, that such Indian woman is in or remains in such house with the intention of prostituting herself therein, such person shall be deemed guilty of an offence against this Act, and shall, on conviction thereof, in a summary way, before any Stipendiary Magistrate, police magistrate or justice of the peace, be liable to a fine of not less than ten dollars, or more than one hundred dollars, or to imprisonment in any gaol or place of confinement other than a penitentiary", for a term not exceeding six months.

96. Any person who appears, acts or behaves as master or mistress, or as the person having the care, government or management of any house in which any Indian woman is, or remains for the purpose of prostituting herself therein, shall be deemed and taken to be the keeper thereof, notwithstanding he or she may not in fact be the real keeper thereof.

97. No appeal shall lie from any conviction under the seven next preceding sections of this Act, except to a judge of any superior court of law, county", or circuit, or district court or to the chairman or judge of the court of the sessions of the peace, having jurisdiction where the conviction was had ; and such appeal shall be heard, tried, and adjudicated upon by 6uch judge without the intervention of a jury ; and no such appeal shall- be brought after the expiration of thirty days from the conviction.

98. No prosecution, conviction or commitment under Want of form this Act shall be invalid on ac-

count of want of form, so long , as the same is according to the true meaning of this Act.
ENFRANCHISEMENT.
99. Whenever any Indian man, or unmarried woman, of the full are of twenty-one years, obtains the consent of the band of which he or she is a member to become enfranchised, and whenever such Indian has been assigned by the band a suitable allotment of land for that purpose, the local agent shall report such action of the band, and the name of the applicant to the Superintendent-General ; whereupon the Superintendent-General, if satisfied that the proposed allotment of land is equitable, shall authorize some competent person to report whether the applicant is an Indian who, from the degree of civilization to which he or she has attained, and the character for integrity, morality and sobriety which he or she bears, appears to be qualified to become a proprietor of land in fee simple ; and upon the favorable Location report of such person, the Superintendent-General may grant such Indian a location ticket as a probationary Indian, for the land allotted to him or her by the band.
(1.) Any Indian who may be admitted to the degree of Indians Doctor of Medicine, or to any other decree by any University of Learning, or who may be admitted in any Province of the Dominion to practice law either as an Advocate or as a Barrister or Counsellor, or Solicitor or Attorney or to be a Notary Public, or who may enter Holy Orders, or who may be allotment licensed by any denomination of Christians as a Minister of the Gospel, may, upon petition to the Superintendent General, ipso facto become and be enfranchised under this Act, and he shall then be entitled to all the rights and privileges to which any other member of the band to which he belongs would be entitled were he enfranchised under the provisions of this Act; and the Superintendent-General may give him a suitable allotment of laud from the lands belonging to the band of which he is a member.
100. After the expiration of three years (or such longer period as the Superintendent-General may deem necessary in the event of such Indian's conduct not being satisfactory), the Governor on the report of the Superintendent- General, order the issue of letters patent, granting to such Indian in fee simple the land which had, with this object in view, been allotted to him or her by location ticket. And : as in such cases compliance with the provisions of sections thirty-six and thirty-seven and the sub-sections thereof shall not be necessary.
101. Every such Indian shall, before the issue of the letters patent mentioned in the next preceding section, and declare to the Superintendent-General the name and surname which he or she wishes to be enfranchised and thereafter known, and on his or her receiving such letters patent, in such name and surname, he or she shall be held to be also enfranchised, and he or she shall thereafter be known by such name or surname, and if such Indian be a married man his wife and minor unmarried children also shall be held to he enfranchised, enfranchised ; and from the date of such letters patent the pro- visions of this Act and of any Act or law making any distinction between the legal rights,. privileges, disabilities and liabilities of Indians and those of Her Majesty's other subjects shall cease to apply to such Indian, or to the wife or minor unmarried children of such Indian as aforesaid, so declared to be enfranchised, who shall no longer be deemed Indians within the meaning of the laws relating to Indians, except in so far as their right to participate in the annuities and interest moneys, and rents and councils of the band of Indians to which they belonged, is concerned : Provided always, that any children of a probationary Indian, who being minors and unmarried when the probationary ticket was granted to such Indian, arrive at the full age of twenty one years before

the letters patent are issued to such Indian, may, at the discretion of the Governor in Council, receive letters patent in their own names for their respective shares of the land allotted under the said ticket, at the same time that letters patent are granted to their parent ; and provided, that if any Indian child having arrived at the full age of twenty one years, during his or her parents' probationary period, be unqualified for enfranchisement, or if any child of such parent, having been a minor at the commencement of such period, be married during such period, then a quantity of land equal to the share of such child shall be deducted in such manner as may he directed by the Superintendent-General, from the allotment made to such Indian parent on receiving his probationary ticket.

102. If any probationary Indian should fail in qualifying to become enfranchised, or should die before the expiration of the required probation, his or her claim, or the claim of his or her heirs, to the land for which a probationary ticket was granted, or the claim of any unqualified. Indian, or of any Indian who may marry during his or her parents' probationary period, to the land deducted under the operation of the next preceding section from his or her parents' probationary allotment, shall in all respects he the same as that conferred by an ordinary location ticket, as provided in the seventeenth, eighteenth, nineteenth and twentieth sections of this Act.

103. The children of any widow who becomes either a probationary or enfranchised Indian shall be entitled to the same privileges as those of a male head of a family in like circumstances.

104. In allotting land to probationary Indians, the quantity, to be located to the head of a family shall be in portion to the number of such family, compared with the total quantity of land in the reserve, and the whole number the band ; but any band may determine what quantity shall be allotted to each member for enfranchisement purposes, provided each female of any age, and each male member under fourteen years of age, receive not less than one-half the quantity allotted to each male member of fourteen years of age and over.

105. Any Indian, not a member of the band, or any non- treaty Indian, who, with the consent of the band and the approval of the Superintendent-General, has been permitted to reside upon the reserve, or obtain a location thereon, may, on being assigned a suitable allotment of land by the band for enfranchisement, become enfranchised on the same terms and conditions as a member of the band ; and such enfranchisement. shall confer upon such Indian the same legal rights and privileges, and make such Indian subject to such disabilities and liabilities as affect Her Majesty's other subjects ; but such enfranchisement shall not confer upon such Proviso. Indian any right to participate in the annuities, interest moneys, rents or councils of the band.

106. Whenever any band of Indians, at a council summoned for the purpose according to their rules, and held in the presence of the Superintendent General, or an agent duly authorized by him to attend such council, decides to allow every member of the band who chooses, and who may be fond qualified, to become enfranchised, and to receive his or her share of the principal moneys of the band, and sets apart for such member a suitable allotment of land for the purpose, any applicant of such band, after such a decision, may be dealt with as provided in the seven next preceding sections until his or her enfranchisement is attained ; and whenever any member of the band, who for the three years immediately succeeding the date on which he or she was granted letters patent, (or for any longer period that the Superintendent-General may deem necessary,) by his or her exemplary good conduct and management of property, proves that he or she is qualified to receive his or her

share of such moneys, the Governor may, on the report of the Superintendent- General to that effect, order that the said Indian be paid or her share of the capital funds at the credit of the band, or his or her share of the principal of the annuities of the band, estimated as yielding five per cent., out of such moneys as may' be provided for the purpose by Parliament ; and if such Indian be a married man then he shall also be paid his wife's and minor unmarried children's share of such funds and other principal moneys, and if such Indian be a widow, she shall also be paid her minor unmarried children's share ; and the unmarried children of such married Indians, who become of age during the probationary period either for enfranchisement or for payment of such moneys, qualified by the character for integrity, morality and. sobriety which they bear, shall receive their own share of such moneys when their parents are paid ; and if not so qualified before they can become enfranchised or receive payment of such moneys they must themselves pass through the probationary periods ; and all such Indians and their unmarried minor children who are paid their share of the principal moneys of their band as aforesaid, shall thenceforward cease in every respect to be Indians of any class within the meaning of this Act, or Indians within the meaning of any other Act or law.

107. Sections ninety-nine to one hundred and six, both inclusive Act, shall not apply to any band of Indians in the Province of British Columbia, the Province of Manitoba, Territories North-West Territories, or the District of Keewatin, save or so far as the said sections may, by proclamation of the Governor- General, be from time to time extended, as they may be, to any band of Indians in any of the said provinces or territories.

MISCELLANEOUS PROVISIONS.

108. All affidavits required under this Act, or intended to Be used in reference to any claim, business or transaction in connection with Indian Affairs, may be taken before the Judge or Clerk of any County or Circuit Court, or any Justice of the Peace, or any Commissioner for taking affidavits in any of the Courts, or the Superintendent-General, or his Deputy, or any Inspector of Indian Agencies, or any Indian Agent, or any Surveyor duly licensed and sworn, appointed by the Superintendent-General to enquire into or take evidence or report in any matter submitted or pending before such Superintendent-General, or if made out of Canada, before the Mayor or Chief Magistrate of, or the British Consul in, any city, town or municipality, or before any Notary Public; and any wilfully false swearing in any such affidavit shall be perjury.

109. Copies of any records, documents, books or papers belonging to or deposited in the Department of Indian Affairs attested under the signature of the Superintendent-General to be or of his Deputy shall be competent evidence in all cases in which the original records, documents, books or papers, could be evidence.

110. The Governor in Council may, by proclamation from time to time, exempt from the operation of this Act, or from the operation of any one or more of the sections of this Act, Indians or non-treaty Indians, or any of them, or any band or irregular band of them, or the reserves or special reserves, or Indian lands or any portions of them, in any Province, in the North-West Territories, or in the District of Keewatin, or in either of them, and may again, by proclamation from time to time, remove such exemption.

111. The Governor may, from time to time, appoint Governor to officers and agents to carry out this Act, and any Orders in Council made under it,—which officers and agents shall be paid in such

manner and at such rates as the Governor in Council may direct out of any fund that may be appropriated by law for that purpose.

112. The Act passed in the thirty-ninth year of Her Majesty's reign and chaptered eighteen, and the Act passed in the forty-second year of Her Majesty's reign and chaptered thirty-four, are hereby repealed, with so much of any other Act or law as may be inconsistent with this Act, or as makes any provision in any matter provided for by this Act, except only as to things done, rights acquired, obligations contracted, or penalties incurred before the coming into force of this Act ; and this Act shall be construed not as a new law but as a consolidation of those hereby repealed in so far as they make the same provision that is made by this Act in any matter hereby provided for.

113. No Act or enactment repealed by any Act hereby repealed shall revive by reason of such repeal.

An Act to amend "The Indian Act, 1880." S.C. 1881, c. 17. (44 Vict.)
CHAP. 17.
An Act to amend " The Indian Act, 1880."
[Assented to 21st March, 1881.]
Her Majesty, by and with the advice and consent of the Senate and House of Commons of Canada, enacts as follows :—

1. The Governor in Council may make such provisions and regulations as may, from time to time, seem advisable for prohibiting or regulating the sale, barter, exchange or gift, by any band or irregular band of Indians, or by any Indian prohibiting of any band or irregular band, in the North-West Territories, the Province of Manitoba, or the District of Keewatin of any grain or root crops, or other produce grown upon any Indian Reserve in the North-West Territories, the Province of Manitoba, or the District of Keewatin ; and may further provide that such sale, barter, exchange or gift shall be absolutely null and void unless the same be made in accordance with the provisions and regulations made in that behalf. All provisions and regulations made under this Act shall be published in the Canada Gazette.

2. Any person who buys or otherwise acquires from any such Indian, or band, or irregular band of Indians, contrary to any provisions or regulations made by the Governor in Council under this Act, is guilty of an offence, and is punishable upon summary conviction, by fine, not exceeding one hundred dollars, or by imprisonment for a period not exceeding three months, in any place of confinement other than a penitentiary, or by both fine and imprisonment.

3. If any such grain or root crops or other produce aforesaid, be unlawfully in the possession of any person within the intent and meaning of this Act, and of any provisions or regulations made by the Governor in Council, under this Act, any person acting under the authority, either general or special, of the Superintendent General may, with such assistance in that behalf as he may think necessary, seize and take possession of the same, and he shall deal therewith as the Superintendent General or any officer or person thereunto by him authorized, may direct.

4. The Governor in Council may make such provisions and regulations as may, from time to time, seem advisable,- for prohibiting the cutting, carrying away or removing from any reserve or special reserve, of any hard or sugar-maple tree or sapling.

5. Any person who outs, carries away or removes from any reserve or special reserve any hard or

sugar-maple tree or sapling, or buys or otherwise acquires from any Indian or non-treaty Indian or other person, any hard or sugar maple tree or sapling so cut, carried away or removed from any reserve or special reserve, contrary to any provisions or regulations made by the Governor in Council under this Act, is guilty of an offence, and is punishable upon summary conviction by fine not exceeding one hundred dollars, or by imprisonment for a period not exceeding three months, or by both fine and imprisonment.

6. Any one Judge, Judge of Sessions of the Peace, Recorder, Police Magistrate, District Magistrate or Stipendiary Magistrate, sitting at a police court or other place appointed in that behalf, for the exercise of the duties of his office, shall have full power to do alone whatever is authorized by " The Indian Art, 1880," to be done by a Justice of the Peace or by two Justices of the Peace.

7. Any Recorder, Police Magistrate or Stipendiary Magistrate, appointed for or having jurisdiction to act in any city or town shall, with respect to offences and matters under The Indian Act, 1880," have and exercise jurisdiction over the whole county or union of counties or judicial district in which the city or town for which he has been appointed or in which he has jurisdiction, is situate.

8. Section twenty-three of " The Indian Act, 1880," is hereby repealed, and the following substituted therefor:—

" 23. If any person or Indian other than an Indian of the band, without the license of the Superintendent General (which license, however, he may at any time revoke) settles, resides, or hunts upon, or occupies, or uses, any such land or marsh ; or settles, resides upon, or occupies any such roads or allowances for roads, on such reserve ; or if any Indian is illegally in possession of any land in a reserve,—the Superintendent General, or such officer or person as he may thereunto depute and authorize, shall, on complaint made to him, and on proof of the fact to his satisfaction, issue his warrant, signed and sealed, directed to any literate person willing to act in the premises, commanding' him forthwith to remove from the said land, or marsh, or roads or allowances for roads or land, every such person or Indian and his family, so settled, residing, or hunting upon, or occupying, or being illegally in possession of the same, or to notify such person or Indian to cease using as aforesaid the said lands, marshes, roads or allowances for roads ; and such person shall accordingly remove or notify every such person or Indian, and for that purpose shall have the same powers as in the execution of criminal process ; and the expenses incurred in any such removal or notification shall be borne by the party removed or notified, and may be recovered from him as the costs in any ordinary suit"

9. Section thirty of " The Indian Act, 1880," is hereby repealed, and the following substituted therefor:—

" 30. All sheriffs, gaolers or peace officers, to whom any such process is directed by the Superintendent General, or by any officer or person by him Reputed as aforesaid, and all other persons to whom such process is directed with their consent, shall obey the same ; and all other officers shall, upon reasonable requisition, assist in the execution thereof."

10. Section ninety of the said Act is hereby amended by adding after the words, "or non-treaty Indian," in the ninth line thereof, the words, " or of any person, or upon any other part of the reserve or special reserve, or sells, exchanges with, barters, supplies or gives to any person on any reserve or special reserve, any kind of intoxicant—.

11. Section ninety-one of " The Indian Act, 1880," is hereby amended by striking out of the

eleventh line thereof the word "may," and inserting in lieu thereof the words, "or suspected to be upon any reserve or special reserve, may, upon a search warrant in that behalf being granted by any Judge, Stipendiary Magistrate or Justice of the Peace—."

12. Every Indian Commissioner, Assistant Indian Commissioner, Indian Superintendent, Indian Inspector or Indian Agent shall be ex officio a Justice of the Peace for the purposes of this Act.

13. In all cases in " The Indian Act, 1830," where it is provided that the conviction must take place on the evidence of one credible witness other than the informer or prosecutor, the informer or prosecutor shall nevertheless be allowed to give evidence.

14. The Governor in Council may appoint an Assistant Indian Commissioner for Manitoba, Keewatin and the North- West Territories or an Assistant Indian Commissioner for Manitoba and Keewatin, and an Assistant Indian Commissioner for the North-West Territories, with such of the powers and duties of the Commissioner, and such other powers and duties as may be provided by Order in Council.

An Act to further amend "The Indian Act. 1880." S.C. 1882, c. 30. (45 Vict.)
CHAP. 30
An Act to further amend " The Indian Act, 1880."
[Assented to 17th May, 1882.]
Her Majesty, by and with the advice and consent of the Senate and House of Commons of Canada, enacts as follows :—

1. The sixth sub-section of the second section of " The Indian Act, 1880" is hereby amended by striking out of the fourth line thereof the words "but which is unsurrendered," and inserting in lieu thereof the words " and which remains a portion of the said Reserve. "

2. The twenty-seventh section of " The Indian Act, 1880 " is hereby amended by striking out of the twelfth line there of the word "Justice" and inserting in lieu thereof the words " any two Justices," and by striking out of the twenty-ninth line thereof the word "Justice " and inserting in lieu thereof the word "Justices."

3. "Wherever, in "the Indian act 1880" or in the act passed in the forty-fourth year of Her Majesty's reign, chaptered seventeen, amending the said Act,—or in this Act, power powers of is given to any Stipendiary Magistrate or Police Magistrate to dispose of cases of infraction of the provisions of the said Acts brought before him, any Indian Agent shall have the same power as a Stipendiary Magistrate or a Police Magistrate has in respect to such cases.

4. The seventy-eighth section of " The Indian Act, 1880 " is hereby amended by adding thereto the following words : amended. " But in any suit between Indians no appeal shall lie from an order made by any District Magistrate, Police Magistrate, Stipendiary Magistrate or two Justices of the Peace, when the sum adjudged does not exceed ten dollars."

5. The ninety-fourth section of " The Indian Act, 1880 " is hereby amended by adding after the word " month " in the eleventh line thereof the words : " or to a fine of not less than five nor more than thirty dollars, or to both fine and imprisonment in the discretion of the convicting Judge, Stipendiary Magistrate or Justice of the Peace," and by adding after the word " days " in the nineteenth line the following words : "or to an additional fine of not less than three nor more than fif-

teen dollars, or to both fine and imprisonment at the discretion of the convicting Judge, Stipendiary Magistrate or Justice of the Peace."

6. The second section of the Act passed in the forty-fourth year of Her Majesty's reign, chaptered seventeen, intituled " An Act to amend the Indian Act, 1880" is hereby amended by adding after the word " conviction " in the fifth line thereof, the words : " before a Stipendiary Magistrate, Police Magistrate, or two Justices of the Peace."

An Act to amend the Act thirty-sixth Victoria, chapter four, intituled "An Act to provide for the establishment of The Department of the Interior," and to amend "The Indian Act, 1880." S.C. 1883, c. 6 (46 Vict.)

CHAP. 6.

An Act to amend the Act thirty sixth Victoria, chapter four, intituled
"An Act to provide for the establishment of The Department of the Interior,"
and to amend "The Indian Act, 1880"

[Assented to 25th May, 1883.]

HER Majesty, by and with the advice and consent of the A-L Senate and House of Commons of Canada, enacts as follows:—

1. The third section of the Act passed in the thirty-sixth year of Her Majesty's reign, chapter four, intituled "An Act to provide for the establishment of " The Department of the Interior " and the third section of " The Indian Art, 1880," are hereby repealed and the following section is substituted for each such section respectively :—

3. The Minister of the Interior or the Head of any other Department appointed for that purpose by order of the Governor in Council shall be the Superintendent General of Indian Affairs and shall, as such, have the control and management of the lands and property of the Indians in Canada.

2. So much of any Act or law as may be inconsistent with this Act, or make any provision in the matter provided for by this Act contrary hereto, is hereby repealed.

An Act further to amend "The Indian Act, 1880." S.C. 1884, c. 27. (47 Vict.)

CHAP. 27.

An Act further to amend " The Indian Act, 1880."

[Assented to 19th April, 1884.]

In further amendment of " The Indian Act, 1880," Her Majesty, by and with the advice and consent of the Senate and House of Commons of Canada, enacts as follows : —

1. "Whoever induces, incites or stirs up any three or more Indians, non-treaty Indians, or half-breeds apparently acting in concert,—

(a.) To make any request or demand of any agent or servant of the Government in a riotous, routous, disorderly or threatening manner, or in a manner calculated to-cause a breach of the peace ; or—

(b.) To do an act calculated to cause a breach of the peace,—

Is guilty of a misdemeanor, and shall be liable to be imprisoned for any term not exceeding two years, with or without hard labor.

2. The Superintendent General may, when he considers it the public interest to do so, prohibit, by public notice to that effect, the sale, gift or other disposal, to any Indian in the Province of Manitoba or in any part thereof, or in the North West Territories or in any part thereof, of any fixed ammunition or ball cartridge ; and every person who, after such notice, without the permission in writing of the Superintendent General, sells or gives or, in any other manner, the conveys to any Indian in the section of country thus prohibited any fixed ammunition or ball cartridge, shall incur a penalty of not more than two hundred dollars, or shall be liable to imprisonment for a term of not more than six months, or to both fine and imprisonment within the limits aforesaid, at the discretion of the court before which the conviction is had ; and every offender against the provisions of this section may be tried in a summary manner by two Justices of the Peace or by any stipendiary or other magistrate having the power of two Justices of the Peace.

3. Every Indian or other person who engages in or assists celebrating the Indian festival known as the "Potlach or in the Indian dance known as the " Tamanawas " is guilty Of a misdemeanor, and shall be liable to imprisonment" for a term of not more than six nor less than two months in any Gaol or other place of confinement ; and any Indian or other person who encourages, either directly or indirectly, an Indian or Indians to get up such a festival or dance, or to celebrate the same, or who shall assist in the celebration of the same is guilty of a like offence, and shall be liable to the same punishment.

4. Sub-section one of the fourteenth section of the said Act is hereby amended by striking out all the words after the word " on," in the tenth line thereof, and substituting therefor the words : " signifying in writing his or her desire so to do,—which signification in writing shall be signed by him or her in the presence of two witnesses, who shall certify the same on oath before some person authorized by law to administer the same."

5. The twentieth section of the said Act is hereby repealed and the following is substituted therefor:—

" 20. Any Indian who holds, under location ticket or other duly recognized title, any parcel or parcels of land upon the reserve of his band, or upon a reserve of any other band, upon which he or he and his family or any of them resided at the date of his death, may devise the same by will, as well as his personal effects or other property of which he is the recognized owner, to such member or members of his family or relative or relatives, as to him seems proper, provided the said will, after his death, is consented to by the band owning the said reserve, and approved of by the Superintendent, General of Indian Affairs, and provided that he does not devise the same or any part thereof to any relative not entitled to reside upon the reserve of the band on which the property devised is situated, or to any relative farther removed than a second cousin ; and the devise may be made subject to such trust or trusts as to the devisor seems proper, provided the are within the provisions of this or any other Act in force or that may hereafter be enacted respecting Indian Affairs : in case such will is not assented to or approved of as aforesaid the Indian shall be held to have died intestate :

" 2. Upon the death of any Indian holding, under location ticket or other duly recognized title, any parcel of land, if such Indian has died intestate, the right and interest therein of such deceased Indian shall, together with his goods and chattels, devolve one-third upon his widow (if any) provided she be a woman of good moral character and that she was living with her husband at the date of his death, and the remainder upon his children (provided that they are Indians within the meaning of " The Indian Act, 1880,") in equal shares ; and such children shall have a like estate in such land as their father had : Provided, that the Superintendent General may, in his discretion, direct that the widow, if of the character above described, shall have the right to occupy such parcel of land and to have the use of such goods and chattels during the term of her widowhood :

" 3. During the minority of such children the administration and charge of such land and goods and chattels as they may be entitled to under this section, shall devolve upon the widow (if any) of such deceased Indian, provided she be a woman of good moral character and that she was living with her husband at the date of his death ; as each male child attains the age of twenty-one, and as each female child attains that age, or marries before that age with the consent of the said widow, his or her share shall be handed to him or her : Provided always, that the Superintendent General may, at any time, remove the widow from such administration and charge, and confer the same upon some person, and in like manner remove such other person and appoint another, and so on as occasion requires :

" 4. If any such Indian dies without issue but leaving a widow of the character above described, such lot or parcel of land and his goods and chattels shall be vested in her, issue, and if he leaves no widow, then in the Indian nearest akin to the deceased ; but if he have no heir nearer than a cousin, then the same shall be vested in the Crown for the benefit of the band :

" 5. Whatever may be the final disposition of the land the claimant or claimants shall not be held to be legally m possession until he, she or they obtains or obtain a location ticket from the Superintendent General in the manner prescribed in the case of new locations :

"6. The Superintendent General may, whenever there are minor children, appoint a fit and proper person to take charge of such children and their property, and remove such person and appoint another, and so on as occasion requires :

"7. The Superintendent General shall have power to decide all questions which may arise respecting the distribution, among those entitled, of the land and goods and chattels of a deceased Indian, and also to do whatever he may, under the circumstances, think will best give to each claimant his or her share, according to the true meaning and spirit of this Act, whether 6uch share be a part of the lands or goods and chattels themselves, or be part of the proceeds thereof, in case it be thought best to dispose thereof, regard always being had in any such disposition to restrictions upon the disposition of property in a reserve. "

6. The twenty-fourth section of the said Act is hereby amended by inserting after the word " aforesaid " in the second line thereof, the words " or after any cattle or other animals, owned by him, or in his charge, have been removed as aforesaid," and by inserting after the words "parts of lots " in the fourth line thereof, the words " or causes or permits any cattle or other animals owned by him, or in his charge, to return to any of the said land, marsh or lots or parts of lots, or returns to any marsh, river, stream or creek, on or running through a reserve, for the purpose of fishing therein and also by inserting after the words " parts of in the thirteenth line thereof the words " or has caused or permitted any cattle or other animals owned by him, or in his charge, to return to any of the said land, marsh or lots or parts of lots, or has returned to any marsh, river, stream or creek, on or running through a reserve, for the purpose of fishing therein."

7. Sub-section one of the twenty-seventh section of the said Act is hereby repealed, and the following is substituted therefor :-

" 27. If any person or Indian, other than an Indian of the Band to which the reserve belongs, without the license in writing of the Superintendent General, or of some officer or person deputed by him for that purpose, trespasses upon any of the said land, roads or allowances for roads in the said reserve, by cutting, carrying away or removing there- from any of the trees, saplings, shrubs, underwood, timber or hay thereon, or by removing any of the stone, soil, minerals, metals or other valuables off the said land, roads or allowances for roads, the person or Indian so trespassing shall, on conviction thereof before any Stipendiary Magistrate, Police Magistrate or any two Justices of the Peace, for every tree he cuts, carries away or removes, forfeit and pay the sum of twenty dollars,-and for cutting, carrying away or removing any of the saplings, shrubs, underwood, timber or hay, if under the value of one dollar, the sum of four dollars, but if over the value of one dollar, then the sum of twenty dollars,-and for removing any of the stone, soil, minerals, metals or other valuables aforesaid, the sum of twenty dollars,-with costs of prosecution in all cases. And in default of immediate payment of the said penalties and costs, such magistrate, or Justices of the Peace, or the Superintendent General, or such other person as he has authorized in that behalf, may issue a warrant, directed to any person or persons by him or them named therein, to levy the amount of the said penalties and costs by distress and sale of the goods and chattels of the person liable to pay the same; and similar proceedings may be had upon such warrant issued by the Superintendent General, or such other person as aforesaid, as if it had been issued by the magistrate or Justices of the Peace before whom the person was convicted; or such magistrate or Justices of the Peace, or the Superintendent General, or such other person as aforesaid, without proceeding by distress and sale, may, upon non-payment of the said penalties and costs, order the person liable therefore to be imprisoned in the common goal of the county or district in which the said reserve or any part thereof lies, for a term not exceeding thirty days when the penalty does not exceed twenty dollars, or for a term not exceeding three months when the penalty exceeds twenty dollars; and upon the return of any warrant for distress and sale, if the amount thereof has not been made, or if any part of it remains unpaid, such magistrate or Justices of the Peace, or the said Superintendent General, or such other person as aforesaid, may commit the person in default to the common gaol, as aforesaid, for a term not exceeding thirty days, if the sum claimed upon the said warrant does not exceed twenty dollars, or for a term not exceeding three months if the sum exceeds twenty dollars. All such penalties shall be paid to the Minister of Finance and Receiver General to be disposed of for the use and benefit of the band of Indians for whose benefit the reserve is held, in such manner as the Governor in Council directs."

8. The thirty-sixth section of the said Act is hereby amended by inserting after the word "guardian" in the fifth line thereof) the following words : " or in the cases of Indians engaged in the practice of any one of the learned professions, or in teaching schools, or in pursuing a trade which interferes with their cultivating land on the reserve."

9. The seventy-second section of the said Act is hereby amended by adding thereto the following sub-section :-

" 2. An election may be set aside by the Governor in Council, on the report of the Superintendent General, should it be proved by two witnesses before the Indian Agent for the locality or such other person as may be deputed by the Superintendent General to take evidence in the matter, that fraud or gross irregularity as practiced at the said election ; and any Indian proved to have been guilty of such fraud or irregularity or connivance thereat may be declared ineligible for re-election for six years, if so directed by the Governor in Council, on the report of the Superintendent General. "

10. Sub-section seven of the seventy-fourth section of the said Act is hereby amended by adding thereto the words " And the attendance at school of children between the ages of six and fifteen years. "

11. The seventy fifth section of the said Act is hereby amended by adding the following words thereto : "And no taxes shall be levied on the real property of any Indian, acquired under the enfranchisement clauses of this Act, until the same has been declared liable to taxation by proclamation of the Governor General, published in the Canada Gazette."

12. The eighty-second section of the said Act is hereby amended by striking out all the words preceding the word " whenever " in the fifth and sixth lines thereof.

13. The ninetieth section of the said Act is hereby amended by adding thereto the words " Any person giving or supplying an intoxicant to an Indian or non-treaty Indian on an order, verbal or -written, shall be liable to all the penalties to which he would have been liable if he had sold the same without such order ; and any person found drunk in the house, tent, wigwam or other domicile of an Indian, or gambling therein, and any person found within an Indian village, settlement or reserve after sunset, and who refuses to leave, after having been requested to do so by an Indian agent or chief, shall be liable to all the fines and penalties to which he would have been liable had he supplied intoxicants to Indians, and under similar process."

14. The ninety-fifth section of the said Act is hereby amended by inserting in the first, third and fourth lines, after the word " house, " the words " tent or wigwam," and by adding thereto after the word " months," in the twelfth line, the words " and any Indian man or woman who keeps, frequents or is found in a disorderly house, tent or wigwam used for such a purpose, shall be liable to the same penalty on similar process."

15. The ninety-seventh section of the said Act is hereby amended by adding the following thereto, as sub-section two:-

"2. No such conviction shall be quashed for want of form, Or be removed by certiorari into any of Her Majesty's certiorari. superior courts of record ; and no warrant of commitment shall be held void by reason of any defect therein, provided it is therein alleged that the person has been convicted, and there is a good and valid conviction to sustain the same."

16. The ninety-ninth section of the said Act is hereby repealed and the following substituted therefor :-

" 99. Whenever any male Indian or unmarried Indian woman, of the full age of twenty-one years, makes application to the Superintendent General to be enfranchised, the Superintendent General shall instruct the agent of the band, of which the applicant is a member, to call upon the latter to furnish a certificate, to be made under oath before a judge of any court of justice by the priest, clergyman or minister of the religious denomination to which the applicant belongs or by two Justices of the Peace, to the effect that, to the best of the knowledge and belief of the deponent or deponents, the applicant for enfranchisement is and had been for at least five years previous, a person of good moral character, temperate in his or her habits, and of sufficient intelligence to be qualified to hold land in fee simple and otherwise to exercise all the rights and privileges of an enfranchised person :

"2. Upon receipt of such a certificate the agent shall, with the least possible delay, submit the same to a council of the band of which the applicant is a member, and he shall then inform the Indians assembled at such council, that thirty days will be given within which affidavits will be received, to be made before a judge or a Stipendiary Magistrate, containing reasons, if any there be, of a personal character affecting the applicant, why such enfranchisement should not be granted to the applicant :

" 3. At the expiration of thirty days aforesaid, the agent shall forward to the Superintendent General all affidavits received by him in the case, if any have been filed with him, as well as one made by himself, also before a judge or a Stipendiary Magistrate, containing his reasons for or against the enfranchisement of the applicant ; and if the Superintendent General, after examining the evidence decides in favor of the applicant, he may grant him or her a location ticket as a probationary Indian, for the land occupied by him or her or for such proportion thereof as appears to the Superintendent General fair and proper :

"4. Every Indian who is admitted to the degree of doctor of medicine, or to any other degree by any university of learning, or who is admitted in any Province of Canada to practice law either as an advocate, or as a barrister or counselor or solicitor or attorney or a notary public, or who enters holy orders, or who is licensed by any denomination of Christians as a minister of the gospel, may, upon petition to the Superintendent General, ipso facto become and be enfranchised under this Act, and he shall then be entitled to all the rights and privileges to which any other member of the band to which he belongs would be entitled if he was enfranchised under the provisions of this Act ; and the Superintendent General may give him a suitable allotment of land from the lends belonging to the band of which he is a member : Provided, that if he is not the recognized holder of a location on the reserve by ticket or otherwise, he shall first obtain the consent of the band and the approval of the Superintendent General of Indian Affairs to such allotment."

17. The one hundredth section of the said Act is hereby repealed, and the following substituted therefor:-

" 100. After the expiration of three years (or such longer period as the Superintendent General deems necessary in the event of such Indian's conduct not being satisfactory), the Governor may', on the report of the Superintendent General, order the issue of letters patent, granting to such Indian the land in fee simple, which had, with this object in view, been allotted to him or her by location ticket, but without power to sell, lease or otherwise alienate the land, unless with the sanction of the Governor in Council ; and provisos to such effect shall be inserted in the letters patent conveying the land to the said Indian : and in such cases compliance with the provisions of sections thirty-six and thirty-seven of this Act shall not be necessary."

18. The one hundred and first section of the said Act is hereby amended by adding thereto, after the word "names," in the twenty-sixth line thereof the words " subject to the same restrictions and reservations as are contained in the letters patent issued to their parent."
19. The one hundred and fourth section of the said Act is hereby amended by striking out the words "any band," in the fifth line thereof, and substituting therefor the words "the Superintendent General."
20. The one hundred and fifth section of the said Act is hereby amended by striking out the word " band " in the fifth line thereof, and substituting therefor the words " Superintendent General."

21. The eighth section of the Act forty-fourth Victoria, chapter seventeen, is hereby repealed, and the following is hereby substituted for section twenty-three of " The Indian Act, 1880 "
" 23. If any person or Indian, other than an Indian of the band, without the license of the Superintendent General (which license, however, he may at any time revoke), settles, resides, or hunts upon, or occupies, or uses, or causes or permits any cattle or other animals, owned by him or in his charge, to trespass on any such land or marsh, or fishes in any marsh, river, stream or creek on or running through a reserve ; or settles, resides upon, or occupies any such roads or allowances for roads, on such reserve ; or if any Indian is illegally in possession of any land in a reserve,-the Superintendent General, or such officer or person as he thereunto deputes and authorizes, shall, on complaint made to him, and on proof of the fact to his satisfaction, issue his warrant, signed and sealed, directed to any literate person willing to act in the premises, commanding him forthwith to remove from the said land or marsh, or roads or allowances for roads, every such person or Indian and his family, so settled, residing or hunting upon or occupying or being illegally in possession of the same,-or to remove such cattle or other animals from such land or marsh,-or to cause such person or Indian to cease fishing in any marsh, river, stream or creek, as aforesaid,-or to notify such person or Indian to cease using as aforesaid the said lands, river, streams, creeks or marshes, roads or allowances for roads ; and such person shall accordingly remove or notify every such person or Indian, or remove such cattle or other animals, or cause such person or Indian to cease fishing as aforesaid, and for that purpose shall have the same powers as in the execution of criminal process ; and the expenses incurred in any such removal or notification shall be borne by the person removed or notified, or owning the cattle or other animals removed, or having them in charge, and may be recovered from him as the costs in any ordinary suit,-or if the trespasser is an Indian, such expenses may be deducted from his or her share or shares of annuity and interest money, if any such be due to him or her."
22. The twelfth section of the Act forty-fourth Victoria, chapter seventeen, is hereby amended by adding at the end thereof the words, " with jurisdiction where so ever any contravention of the provisions of * The Indian Act, 1880,' occurs, or wheresoever it is considered by him most conducive to the ends of justice that any contravention aforesaid shall be tried."
23. The third section of the Act forty-fifth Victoria, chapter thirty, is hereby amended by adding at the end thereof the words "or in any other matter affecting Indians, with jurisdiction wheresoever any contravention of the provisions of the said Acts occurs, or wheresoever it is considered by him most conducive to the ends of justice that the trial be held And such officer shall have the same powers in respect to infractions of this Act.

24. The fourth section of the Act forty-fifth Victoria, chapter thirty, is hereby mended by striking out all the words after "following words" in the second line of the said section and by inserting the following in lieu thereof:-
" But in any suit between Indians or in a case of assault in which the offender was an Indian or the offenders were Indians, no appeal shall lie from an order made by any District Magistrate, Police Magistrate, Stipendiary Magistrate or two Justices of the peace, when the sum adjudged, or the fine inflicted, does not exceed ten dollars."
25. This Act shall not come into force until the first day of January, in the year of Our Lord one thousand eight hundred and eighty-five.

The Indian Advancement Act, 1884. S.C. 1884, c. 28. (47 Vict.)
CHAP. 28.
An Act for conferring certain privileges on the more advanced Bands of the Indians of Canada, with the view of training them for the exercise of municipal powers.
[Assented to 19th April, 1884.]
Whereas it is expedient to provide means by which Indians on reserves in divers parts of the Dominion, may be trained for the future exercise of municipal privileges and powers : Therefore Her Majesty, by and with the advice and consent of the Senate and House of Commons of Canada, enacts as follows :-
1. This Act shall be known and may be cited as " The Indian Advancement Act, 1884," and may be made applicable as hereinafter provided, to any band or bands of Indians in any of the Provinces or the North-West Territories, including the District of Keewatin, except in so far only as it is herein otherwise provided.
2. The terms used in this Act shall have the same meaning respectively as the like terms have in "The Indian Act, 1880", but the term reserve" include two or more reserve the term " band " includes two or more bands, united for the purposes of this Act by the Order in Council applying it.
3. Whenever any band or bands of Indians shall be declared by Order of the Governor in Council to be considered fit to have this Act applied to them, it shall so apply from the time to be appointed in such Order, which shall not be earlier than the first of January, one thousand eight hundred and eighty five.
4. Any reserve to which this Act is to apply shall, by the order applying it, be divided into sections,- the number of which shall be not less than two nor more than six, having in each a number of male Indians of full age, equal as nearly as may be found convenient to such proportion of the male Indians of full age resident on the reserve, as one section of the reserve will bear to all the sections ; each section shall be distinguished by a number from one upwards ; the reserve shall be designated in the Order as " The Indian Reserve," inserting such name as may be thought proper, and the sections by the numbers assigned to them respectively.

5. On a day and at a place and between Hours to be designated in such Order, the male Indians of the full age of twenty-one years, resident on the reserve (hereinafter termed electors) shall meet for

the purpose of electing the members of the council of the reserve ; one or more members (as may be provided in such Order in Council) to represent each section thereof shall be elected by the electors resident in such section; and the Indian or Indians (as the case may be) having the votes of the greatest number of electors for each section shall be the councillor or councillors (as the case may be) therefor, provided he or they be possessed of, and living in, a house in the reserve, and subject to the provision hereinafter made in case of ties by an equal number of votes for two or more. The agent of the Superintendent General for the reserve shall preside at the election (or in his absence some person appointed by him as his deputy, with the consent of the Superintendent General or his deputy, or some person appointed by the Superintendent General or his deputy may preside at the said election) and shall take and record the votes of the electors, and shall have full power, subject to appeal to the Superintendent General by or on behalf of any Indian or Indians deeming himself or themselves to be aggrieved by the action of such agent or deputy or of such agent or person appointed as aforesaid, to admit or reject the claim of any Indian to be an elector, and to determine who are the councillors for the several sections, and shall report the same to the Superintendent General.

6. On a day, and at a place, and between hours to be designated by the Superintendent General or his deputy, (provided the day fixed for the same be within eight days from the date at which the councillors were elected), the said councillors shall meet and elect one of their number to act as chief councillor ; and the councillor so elected shall be the chief councillor.

7. The councillors shall remain in office until others are elected in their stead ; and an election for that purpose shall be held in like manner at the same place and between the like hours on the like day in each succeeding year if it be not a Sunday or holiday,-in which case it shall be held on the next day after which shall not be a holiday. In case of the failure of any election on the day appointed for it, the Superintendent General or his deputy shall appoint another day on which it shall be held.

8. In the case of vacancy in the Council by death or inability to act of any councillor, more than three months before the time for the next election, an election shall be held by the agent or his deputy, after such notice to the electors concerned as the Superintendent General or his deputy may direct, to fill such vacancy, and at which only the elector-; of the section represented by the councillor to be replaced shall vote,-and to such election the provisions respecting other elections shall apply, so far as they are applicable ; but if the councillor to be replaced is the chief, then an election of a chief councillor shall be held in the manner already provided, but the day fixed for such election shall be at least one week from the date when the new councillor is elected : Provided always, that during such vacancy the remaining councillors shall constitute the council and may in case of vacancy of the office appoint a chief from among themselves pro tempore.

9. The council shall meet for the despatch of business, at such place on the reserve, and at such times as the agent for the reserve shall appoint, not being less than four nor more than twelve times in the year for which it is elected, and due notice of the time and place of each meeting shall be given to each councillor by the agent; at such meeting the agent for the reserve or his deputy, to be appointed for the purpose with the consent of the Superintendent General or his deputy, shall preside and record the proceedings, and shall have full power to control and regulate all matters of procedure and form, and to adjourn the meeting to a time named or sine die, and to report and certify

all by-laws and other acts and proceedings of the council to the Superintendent General ; and full faith and credence shall be given to his certificate thereof in all courts and places whatsoever: he shall address the council and explain and advise them upon their powers and duties, and any matter requiring their consideration, but shall have no vote on any question to be decided by the council ; but each councillor present shall have a vote thereon, and it shall be decided by the majority of votes,-the chief voting as a councillor and having also a casting vote in case the votes would otherwise be equal ; four councillors shall be a quorum for the despatch of any business.

10.The council shall have power to make by-laws, rules and regulations, which, if approved and confirmed by the Superintendent General, shall have force as law within and with respect to the reserve, and the Indians residing thereon, upon all or any of the following subjects, that is to say :-

1. The religious denomination to which the teacher or teachers of the school or schools established on the reserve shall belong, as being that of the majority of the Indians resident on the reserve; provided that the Roman Catholic or Protestant minority on the reserve may also have a separate school or schools with the approval of and under regulations to be made by the Governor in Council ;

2. The care of the public health ;

3. The observance of order and decorum at elections of councillors, meetings of the council, and assemblies of Indians on other occasions or generally on the reserve, by appointing constables and erecting lock-ups or by the adoption of other legitimate means ;

4. The repression of intemperance and profligacy ;

5. The sub-division of the land in the reserve, and the Sub-division distribution of the same among the members of the band; also the setting apart for common use, wood land and land for other purposes ;

6. The protection of and the prevention of trespass by cattle, sheep, horses, mules and other domesticated animals ; and the establishment of pounds, the appointment of pound-keepers, and the regulation of their duties, fees and charges ;

7. The construction and repair of school houses, council houses, and other buildings for the use of the Indians on the reserve ;

8. The construction, maintenance and improvement of roads and bridges, and the contributions in money or labor and other duties of residents on the reserve in respect thereof ; and the appointment of road masters and fence viewers, and their powers and duties ;

9. The construction and maintenance of water courses, ditches and fences, and the obligations of vicinage, and the destruction and repression of noxious weeds ; the preservation of the wood on the various holdings or elsewhere in the reserve ;

10. The removal and punishment of persons trespassing upon the reserve, or frequenting it for improper purposes ;

11. The raising of money for any or all of the purposes for which the council is empowered to make by-laws as aforesaid, by assessment and taxation on the lands of Indians enfranchised, or in possession of lands by location ticket in the reserve,-the valuation for assessment being made yearly in such manner and at such times as shall be appointed by the by-law in that behalf, and being subject to revision and correction by the agent, for the reserve, of the Superintendent General, and in force

only after it has been submitted to him and corrected if and as he may think justice requires, and approved by him,-the tax to be imposed for the year in which the by-law is made, and not to exceed one-half of one percent, on the assessed value of the land on which it is to be paid : and if such tax be not paid at the time prescribed by the by-law, the amount thereof with the addition of one-half of one percent, thereon, may be paid by the Superintendent General to the treasurer out of the share of the Indian in default in any moneys of the band; or if such share be insufficient to pay the same, the defaulter shall be subject to a fine equal to the deficiency for infraction of the by-law imposing the tax, by such default : Provided always, that any Indian deeming himself aggrieved by the decision of the agent, made as hereinbefore provided, may appeal to the Superintendent General, whose decision in the case shall be final ;

12. The appropriation and payment to the local Agent as Treasurer by the Superintendent General of so much of the moneys of the band as may be required for defraying expenses necessary for carrying out the by-laws made by the council, including those incurred for assistance absolutely necessary for enabling the council or the agent to perform the duties assigned to them by this Act ;

13. The imposition of punishment by fine or penalty or by imprisonment or both, for any infraction of or disobedience to any by-law, rule or regulation made under this Act committed by any Indian of the reserve ; the fine or penalty in no case (except only for non-payment of taxes) to exceed thirty dollars, and the imprisonment in no case to exceed thirty days,-the proceedings for the imposition of such punishment to be taken in the usual summary way before a Justice of the Peace, following the procedure under the " Act respecting the duties of Justices of the Peace, out of Sessions, in relation to summary convictions and orders " ; and the amount of any such fine shall be paid over to the treasurer of the band to which the Indian incurring it belongs, for the use of such band ;

14. The amendment, repeal or re-enactment of any such by-laws. by-law, by a subsequent by-law made and approved as hereinbefore provided.

11. Any member of a council elected under the provisions of this Act who shall be proved to be a habitual Drunkard or to be living in immorality, or to have accepted a bribe, or to have been guilty of dishonesty or of malfeasance of office of any kind,-shall, on proof of the fact to the satisfaction of the Superintendent General, be disqualified from acting as a member of the council, and shall, on being notified, cease forthwith so to act ; and the vacancy occasioned thereby shall be filled in the manner provided by the eighth section of this Act.

12. A copy of any by-law, rule or regulation under this Act approved by the Superintendent General or his deputy, and purporting to be certified by his agent for the band to which it relates, to be a true copy thereof, shall be evidence of such by-law, rule or regulation, and of such approval, without proof of the signature of such agent, unless such signature be formally disputed ; and no such by-law, rule or regulation shall be invalidated by any defect of form, provided it be substantially consistent with the provisions and spirit of this Act.

13. The provisions of "The Indian Act, 1880," and of any Act amending it, shall continue to apply to any band to which this Act has been declared to apply, in so far, but in so far only, as they are not inconsistent with this Act : Provided always, that if it shall thereafter appear to the Governor in Council that this Act cannot be worked satisfactorily by any band to which it has been declared to

apply, he may be Order in Council, declare that, after a day named therein, it shall no longer apply to such band, and such band shall thereafter be subject to the provisions of the said " Indian Act, 1880," as amended by any subsequent Act, except that by-laws, rules and regulations theretofore made under this Act and not inconsistent with the seventy-fourth section of the said Indian Act, shall continue in force under that Act, unless and until they are repealed by Order of the Governor in Council.

The Indian Act. R.S.C. 1886, c. 43.
CHAPTER 43.
An Act respecting Indians.
Her Majesty, by and -with the advice and consent of the Senate and House of Commons of Canada, enacts as follows :-
SHORT TITLE.
1. This Act may be cited as " The Indian Act." 43 V., c. 28, s. 1.
INTERPRETATION.
2. In this Act, unless the context otherwise requires,- (a.) The expression " Superintendent General " means the Superintendent General of Indian Affairs, and the expression " Deputy Superintendent General" means the Deputy Superintendent General of Indian Affairs;
(b.) The expression "Agent," or "Indian Agent," means and includes a commissioner, assistant commissioner, superintendent, agent or other officer acting under the instructions of the Superintendent General;
(c.) The expression "person" means any individual other than an Indian ;
(d.) The expression " band " means any tribe, band or body of Indians who own or are interested in a reserve or in Indian lands in common, of which the legal title is vested in the Crown, or who share alike in the distribution of any annuities or interest moneys for which the Government of Canada is responsible;
(e.) The expression "the band" means the band to which the context relates ;
(f) The expression "band," when action is being taken by the band as such, means the band in council,
(g.) The expression "irregular band" means any tribe, band or body of persons of Indian blood who own no interest in any reserve or lands of which the legal title is vested in the Crown, who possess no common fund managed by the Government of Canada, and who have not had any treaty relations with the Crown ;
(h) The expression " Indian " means-
First. Any male person of Indian blood reputed to belong to a particular band ;
Secondly. Any child of such person ;

Thirdly. Any woman who is or was lawfully married t such person ;
(i} The expression " non-treaty Indian " means any person of Indian blood who is reputed to belong to an irregular band, or who follows the Indian mode of life, even if such person is only a temporary resident in Canada;

(j) The expression "enfranchised Indian" means any Indian, his wife or minor unmarried child, who has received letters patent granting to him in fee simple any portion of the reserve which has been allotted to him or to his wife and minor children, by the band to which he belongs, or any unmarried Indian who has received letters patent for an allotment of the reserve;

(k.) The expression "reserve" means any tract or tracts of land set apart by treaty or otherwise for the use or benefit of or granted to a particular band of Indians, of which the legal title is in the Crown, and which remains a portion of the said reserve, and includes all the trees, wood, timber, soil, stone, minerals, metals and other valuables thereon or therein :

(l) The expression "special reserve" means any tract or tracts of land, and everything belonging thereto, set apart for the use or benefit of any band or irregular band of Indians, the title of which is vested in a society, corporation or community legally established, and capable of suing and being sued, or in a person or persons of European descent, -but which land is held in trust for such band or irregular band of Indians ;

(m) The expression "Indian lands " means any reserve or portion of a reserve which has been surrendered to the Crown;

(n) The expression "intoxicants" means and includes all spirits, strong waters, spirituous liquors, wines, or fermented or compounded liquors or intoxicating drink of any kind whatsoever, and any intoxicating liquor or fluid, and opium and any preparation thereof, whether liquid or solid, and any other intoxicating drug or substance, and tobacco or tea mixed or compounded or impregnated with opium or with other intoxicating drugs, spirits or substances, and whether the same or any of them are liquid or solid. 43 V. c. 28, s. 2 ;- 45 V., c. 30, s. 1.

APPLICATION OF ACT

3. The Governor in Council may, by proclamation, from time to time, exempt from the operation of this Act, or from the operation of any one or more of the sections of this Act,. Indians or non-treaty Indians, or any of them, or any band or irregular band of them, or the reserves or special reserves, or Indian lands, or any portions of them, in any Province, or in the North-West Territories, or in the District of Keewatin, or in any of them ; and may again, by proclamation, from time to time, remove such exemption. 43 V., c. 28, s. 110.

DEPARTMENT OF INDIAN AFFAIRS.

4. The Minister of the Interior, or the head of any other department appointed for that purpose' by the Governor in Council, shall be the Superintendent General of Indian Affairs, and shall, as such, have the control and management of the lands and property of the Indians in Canada. 46 V., c. 6, s. 1.

5. There shall be a department of the Civil Service of Canada which shall be called the Department of Indian Affairs, over which the Superintendent General shall preside. 43 Y., c. 28, s. 4.

6. The Department of Indian Affairs shall have the management, charge and direction of Indian Affairs. 43 V., c. 28, s. 7, part.

7. The Governor in Council may appoint an officer who Deputy shall be called the Deputy of the Superintendent General of Indian Affairs, and may also appoint such other officers, clerks and servants as are requisite for the proper conduct of the business of the department. 43 V., c. 28, ss. 5 and

8. parts.

8. The Governor in Council may appoint an Indian Commissioner for Manitoba, Keewatin and the North-West Territories, or an Indian Commissioner for Manitoba and Keewatin, and an Indian Commissioner for the North-West Territories, and may also appoint an Indian Superintendent for British Columbia, who shall have, respectively, such powers and duties as are assigned to them, respectively, by the Governor in Council :

2. The Governor in Council may also appoint an Assistant Indian Commissioner for Manitoba, Keewatin and the North-West Territories, or an Assistant Indian Commissioner for Manitoba and Keewatin, and an Assistant Indian Commissioner for the North-West Territories, "who shall have such of the powers and duties of the Commissioner, and such other powers and duties as are assigned to him by the Governor in Council :

3. The Governor in Council may, also, from time to time, appoint officers and agents to carry out this Act, and Orders in Council made under it-which officers and agents shall be paid in such manner and at such rates as the Governor in Council directs, out of any fund that is appropriated by law for that purpose :

4. The Governor General may appoint a Deputy Governor, who shall have the power, in the absence of or under instructions of the Governor General, to sign letters patent for Indian lands ; and the signature of such Deputy Governor to such patents shall have the same force and virtue as if such patents were signed by the Governor General. 43 V., c. 28, ss. 9 and 111;-44 V., c. 17, s.14; 49 V.. c 7, s. 1.

MEMBERSHIP OF BAND

9. Any illegitimate child may,-unless he has, with the Consent of the band whereof the father or mother of such Child is a member, shared in the distribution moneys of such band for a period exceeding two years,-be, at any time, excluded from the membership thereof by the Superintendent General. 43 V., c. 28, s. 10.

10. Any Indian who has for five years continuously resided in a foreign country without the consent, in writing, of the Superintendent General or his agent, shall cease to be a member of the band of which he or she was formerly a member ; and he shall not again become a member of that band, or of any other band, unless the consent of such band, with the approval of the Superintendent General or his agent, is first obtained. 43 V., c. 28, s. 11.

11. Any Indian woman who marries any person other than Indian, or a non-treaty Indian, shall cease to be an Indian in every respect within the meaning of this Act, except that she shall be entitled to share equally with the members of the band to which she formerly belonged, in the annual or semi-annual distribution of their annuities, interest moneys and rents ; but such income may be commuted to her at any time at ten years' purchase, with the consent of the band. 43 V., c. 28, s. 12.

1. Section eleven of "The Indian Act," is hereby amended by adding the following sub-section thereto :-

"2. Where a band has become enfranchised, or has otherwise ceased to exist, such commutation may take place upon the approval of the Superintendent General."

12. Any Indian woman who marries an Indian of any other band, or a non-treaty Indian, shall cease

to be a member of the band to which she formerly belonged, and shall become a member of the band or irregular band of which her husband is a member; but if she marries a non-treaty Indian, while becoming a member of the irregular band of which her husband is a member, she shall be entitled to share equally with the members of the band of which she was formerly a member, in the distribution of their moneys ; but such income may be commuted to her at any time at ten years' purchase, with the consent of the band. 43 V. c. 28, s. 13.

13. No half-breed in Manitoba who has shared in the distribution of half-breed lands shall be accounted an Indian ; and no half-breed head of a family, except, the widow of an Indian, or a half-breed who "has already been admitted into a treaty, shall, unless under very special circumstances, which shall be determined by "the Superintendent General or his agent, be accounted an Indian, or entitled to be admitted into any Indian treaty; and any half-breed who has been admitted into a treaty shall be allowed to withdraw therefrom on signifying in writing his desire so to do,-which signification in writing shall be signed by him in the presence of two witnesses, who shall certify the same on oath before some person authorized by law to administer the same :

1. Sub-section one of section thirteen of "The Indian Act " is hereby repealed and the following substituted therefor:

"13. No half-breed in Manitoba who has shared in the distribution of half-breed lands shall be accounted an Indian ; and no half-breed head of a family, except the widow of an Indian or a half-breed who has already been admitted into a treaty, shall, unless under very special circumstances, which shall be determined by the Superintendent General or his agent, be accounted an Indian or entitled to be admitted into any Indian treaty ; and any half-breed who has been admitted into a treaty shall, on obtaining the consent in writing of the Indian Commissioner or in his absence the Assistant Indian Commissioner, be allowed to withdraw therefrom on signifying in writing his desire so to do,-which signification in writing shall be signed by him in the presence of two witnesses, who shall certify the same on oath before some person authorized by law to administer the same ; and such withdrawal shall include the minor unmarried children of such half-breed."

2. The half-breeds who are by the father's side either Wholly or partly of Indian blood' now settled in the seigniory of Caughnawaga. and who have inhabited the said seigniory for the last twenty years, are hereby confirmed their possession and right of residence and property, but not beyond the tribal rights and usages which others of the band enjoy. 43 V., c. 28, s. 14 ;-47 V., c. 27, s. 4.

RESERVES.

14. All reserves for Indians, or for any band of Indians, or held in trust for their benefit, shall be deemed to be reserved and held for the same purposes as they were held before the passing of this Act, but shall be subject to the provisions of this Act. 43 V.. c. 28, s. 15.

15. The Superintendent General may authorize surveys, plans and reports to be made of any reserve for Indians, showing and distinguishing the improved lands, the forests and lands fit for settlement, and such other information as is required ; and may authorize the whole or any portion of a reserve to be sub-divided into lots. 43 V., c. 28, s. 16.

16. No Indians shall be deemed to be lawfully in possession of any land in a reserve, unless he has been or is located for the same by the band, or council of the band, with the approval of the Super-

intendent General: but no Indian shall be dispossessed of any land on which he has improvements, without, receiving compensation therefor, at a valuation approved by the Superintendent General, from the Indian who obtains the land, or from the funds of the band as is determined by the Superintendent General 43 V., c.28.s17

2. Section sixteen of the said Act is hereby amended, by adding the following words at the end thereof : "Provided always, that prior to the location of an Indian under this section, the Indian Commissioner for Manitoba, Keewatin and The Western Territories may issue a certificate of occupancy to any Indian belonging to a band residing upon a reserve in the aforesaid Province, District or Territories, of so much land, (in no case however to exceed one hundred and sixty acres,) as the Indian, with the approval of the Commissioner, selects ; and such certificate may be cancelled at any time by the Indian Commissioner, but shall, while it remains in force, vest in the holder thereof, as against all others, lawful possession of the lands described therein.

17. When the Superintendent General approves of any location as aforesaid, he shall issue, in triplicate, a ticket granting a location title to such Indian, one triplicate of which he shall retain in a book to be kept for the purpose; and the other two of which he shall forward to the local agent-one' to be delivered to the Indian in whose favor it was issued, and the other to be filed by the agent, who shall also cause the same to be copied into a register of the band, provided for the purpose. 43 V., e. 28, s. 18.

18. The conferring of any such location title shall not have the effect of rendering the land covered thereby subject to seizure under legal process, and such title shall be transferable only to an Indian of the same band, and then only with the consent and approval of the Superintendent General, whose consent and approval shall be given only by the issue of a ticket, in the manner prescribed in the next preceding section. 43 V., c. 28, s. 19.

19. Every Indian and every non-treaty Indian, in the Province of British Columbia, in the Province of Manitoba, in the North-West Territories or in the District of Keewatin, who has previously to the selection of a reserve, possession of and who has made permanent improvements on a plot of land which is or shall he included in, or surrounded by, a reserve, shall have the same privileges, in respect of such plot, as an Indian enjoys who holds under a location title. 43 V., c. 28, s. 21.

DESCENT OF PROPERTY.

20. Any Indian who holds, under location ticket or other Duly recognized title, any parcel of land upon the reserve of his band, or upon a reserve of any other band, upon which he, or he and his family, or any of them, resided at the date of his death, may devise the same by will, as well as his personal effects or other property of which he is the recognized owner, to such member or members of his family, or relative or relatives, as to him seems proper ; provided the said will after his death, is consented to by the band owning the said reserve, and approved of by the Superintendent General, and that such devise is not to any relative who is not entitled to reside upon the reserve of the band on which the property devised is situated, or to any relative farther removed than a second cousin :

2. The devise may be made subject to such trusts as to the devisor seems proper, if the same are within the provisions of this Act, or any other Act respecting Indian affairs :

3. If such will is not assented to or approved of, as aforesaid, the Indian shall be deemed to have died intestate:

4. Upon the death of any Indian who holds, under location Ticket or other duly recognized title, any parcel of land, and Who had died intestate, the right and interest therein of such deceased Indian shall, together with his goods and chattels, devolve one-third upon his widow, if any, if she is a woman of good moral character and was living with her husband at the time of his death, and the remainder upon his children, in equal shares, if they are Indians within the meaning of this Act, and such children shall have a like estate in such land as their father had ; but the Superintendent General may, in his discretion, direct that the widow, if she is of good moral character, shall have the right to occupy such parcel of land, and have the use of such goods and chattels during the term of her widowhood:

5. During the minority of such children, the administration And charge of such land and goods and chattels as they minora. are entitled to, as aforesaid, shall devolve upon the widow, if any, of such deceased Indian, if she is a woman of good moral character and was living with her husband at the time of his death ; and as each male child attains the age of twenty-one years, and each female child attains that age or marries before that age. with the consent of the said widow the share of such male or female child shall be conveyed or delivered, as the case may be, to him or her; but the Superintendent General may, at any time, remove the, widow from such administration and charge, and confer the same upon some other person, and, in like manner, may remove such other person and appoint another, and so, from time to time, as occasion requires:

6; If any such Indian dies without issue, leaving a widow of good moral character, such lot or parcel of land, and his goods and chattels, shall be vested in her, and if he leaves issue no widow, then they shall be vested in the Indian nearest of kin to the deceased ; but if he has no heir nearer than a cousin, the same shall be vested in Her Majesty for the benefit of the band :

7. Whatever is the final disposition of the land, the claim- ant shall not be held to be lawfully in possession until he obtains a location ticket from the Superintendent General, in the manner prescribed in regard to new locations:

8. The Superintendent General may, whenever there are minor children, appoint a fit and proper person to take charge of such children and their property, and may remove such person and appoint another, and so, from time to time, as occasion requires:

9. The Superintendent General may decide all questions which arise respecting the distribution, among those entitled, of the lands and goods and chattels of a deceased. Indian, and may also do whatsoever he, under the circumstances, thinks will best give to each claimant his share, according to the true, intent and meaning of this Act, whether such share is part of the lauds or goods and chattels themselves, or is part of the proceeds thereof, if it is thought best to dispose thereof- regard always being had in any such disposition to restrictions upon the disposition of property in a reserve. 47 V., c. 27, s. 5.

1. Section twenty of The Indian Act, chapter forty-three, of the Revised Statutes, is hereby repealed and the following substituted therefor :-

" 20. Indians may devise or bequeath property of any kind in the same manner as other persons :

Provided that no devise or bequest of land in a reserve or of any interest therein shall be made to any one not entitled to reside on such reserve, except when the devise or bequest of land is made to the daughter, sister or grand-children of the testator, and that no will purporting to dispose of land in a reserve or any interest therein shall ,be of any force or effect unless or until the will has been approved by the superintendent general, and that if a will be disapproved by the superintendent general the Indian making the will shall be deemed to have died intestate; and provided further that the superintendent general may approve of a will generally and disallow any disposition thereby made of land in a reserve or of any interest in such land, in which case the will so approved shall have force and effect except so far as such disposition is concerned and the Indian making the will shall be deemed to have died intestate as to the land or interest as to which such disallowance takes place.

" 2. Upon the death of an Indian intestate his property of all kinds, real and personal, movable and immovable, including any interest he may have in land in a reserve, shall de- volve one-third upon his widow, if any, if she is a woman of good moral character, as to which fact the superintendent general shall be the sole and final judge, and the remainder (or the whole if there is no widow or if the widow is not of good moral character) upon the children in equal shares if they are Indians Within the meaning of this Act : provided that if one or more of the children of such intestate Indian are living and one or more are dead the inheritance shall devolve upon the children who are living and the descendants of such children as have died, so that each child who is living shall receive such share as would have descended to him if all the children of the intestate who have died leaving issue had been living, and so that the descendants of each child who is dead shall inherit in equal shares the share which their parent would have received if living, and the rule of descent thus prescribed shall apply in every case where the descendants of the intestate, entitled to share in the inheritance, are of unequal degrees of consanguinity to the intestate, so that those who are in the nearest degree of consanguinity shall take the shares which would have descended to them, had all the descendants in the same degree of consanguinity who have died leaving issue, been living, and so that the issue of the descendants, who have died, shall respectively take the shares which their parents, if living, would have received: provided that the superintendent general may in his discretion direct that the widow, if she is of good moral character, shall have the right during her widowhood to occupy any land in the reserve of the band to which the deceased belonged of which he was the recognized owner and to have the use of any property of the deceased for which under section seventy-seven of this Act he was not liable to taxation.

"3. During the minority of the children of an Indian who dies intestate the administration and charge of the property to which they are entitled as aforesaid shall devolve upon the widow, it any, of the intestate, if she is of good moral character, and in such case, as each male child attains the age of twenty-one years, and as each female child attains that age or with the consent of the widow marries before that age, the share of such child, shall, subject to the approval of the superintendent general, be conveyed or delivered to him or her ; but the superintendent general may at any time remove the widow from such administration and charge and confer the same upon some other person and in like manner may remove such other person and appoint another and so from time to time as occasion requires.

" 4. In case any Indian dies intestate without issue, leaving a widow of good moral character, all his property of whatever kind shall devolve upon her, and if he leaves no widow the same shall devolve upon the Indian nearest of kin to the deceased ; any interest which he may have had in land in a reserve shall be vested in Her Majesty for the benefit of the band owning such reserve if his nearest of kin is more remote than a brother or sister.

" 5. The property of a married Indian woman who dies intestate shall descend in the same manner and be distributed in the same proportions as that of a male Indian under the like circumstances, her widower, if any, taking the share which the widow of such male Indian would take ; and the other provisions of this section shall in like manner apply to the case of an intestate married woman, the word " widower " being substituted for the word " widow " in each case. The property of an unmarried Indian woman who dies intestate shall descend in the same manner as if she had been a male.

" 6. A claimant of land in a reserve or of any interest therein as devisee or legatee or heir of a deceased Indian shall not be held to be lawfully in possession thereof or to be the recognized owner thereof until he shall have obtained a location ticket therefor from the superintendent general.

" 7. The superintendent general may, whenever there are minor children, appoint a fit and proper person to take charge of such children and their property and may remove such person and appoint another and so from time to time as occasion requires.

"8. The superintendent general may decide all questions which arise under this Act, respecting the distribution among entitled thereto of the property of a deceased Indian, and he shall be the sole and final judge as to who the' persons so entitled are. The superintendent general may do whatsoever in his judgment will best give to each claimant his share according to the true intent and meaning of this Act, and to that end if he thinks fit may direct the sale, lease or other disposition of such property or any part thereof and the distribution or application of the proceeds or income thereof, regard being always had in any such disposition to the restrictions upon the disposition of property in a reserve.

" 9. Notwithstanding anything in this Act it shall be lawful for the courts having jurisdiction in that regard in the case of persons other than Indians, with but not without the consent of the superintendent general, to grant probate of the wills of Indians and letters of administration of the estate and effects of intestate Indians, in which case such courts and the executors and administrators obtaining such probate or thereby appointed shall have the like jurisdiction and powers as in other cases, except that no disposition shall, without the consent of the superintendent general, be made of or dealing had with regard to any right or interest in land in a reserve or any property for which, under section seventy-seven of this Act, an Indian is not liable to taxation."

TRESPASSING ON RESERVES.

21. No person, or Indian other than an Indian of the band, shall settler, reside or hunt upon, occupy or use any land or marsh, or shall settle, reside upon or occupy any road, or allowance for road, running through any reserve belonging to or occupied by such band ; and all mortgages given or consented to by any Indian, and all leases, contracts and agreements made or purporting to be made by any Indian, whereby persons or Indians other than Indians of the band are permitted to reside or hunt upon such reserve, shall be void. 43 V., c. 28, s. 22.

2. Section twenty-one of The Indian Act is hereby repealed and the following substituted therefor :-
"21. Every person, or Indian other than an Indian of the band, who, without the authority of the superintendent general, resides or bunts upon, occupies or uses any land or marsh, or who resides upon or occupies any road, or allowance for road, running through any reserve belonging to or occupied by such band, shall be liable, upon summary conviction, to imprisonment for a term not exceeding one month or to a penalty not exceeding ten dollars and not less than five dollars, with costs of prosecution, half of which penalty shall belong to the informer ; and all deeds, leases, contracts, agreements or instruments of whatsoever kind made, entered into, or consented to by any Indian, purporting to permit persons or Indians other than Indians of the band to reside or hunt upon such reserve, or to occupy or use any portion thereof, shall be void."
22. If any person, or Indian other than an Indian of the band., without the license of the Superintendent General (which license he may at any time revoke', settles, resides or hunts upon, occupies, uses, or causes or permits any cattle or other animals owned by him, or in his charge, to trespass on any such land or marsh, or fishes in any marsh, river, stream or creek on or running through a reserve, or settles, resides upon or occupies any such road, or allowance for road, on such reserve,-or it any Indian is illegally in possession of any land in a reserve-the Superintendent General, or such officer or person as he thereunto deputes and authorizes, shall, on complaint made to him, and on proof of the fact to his satisfaction, issue his warrant, signed and sealed, directed to any literate person willing to act in the premises, commanding him forthwith-

(a.) To remove from the said land, marsh or road, or allowance for road, every such person or Indian and his family, so settled, or who is residing or hunting upon, or occupying, or is illegally in possession of the same ; or-
(b.) To remove such cattle or other animals from such land or marsh ; or-
(c.) To cause such person or Indian to cease fishing in any marsh, river, stream or creek, as aforesaid ; or-
(d) To notify such person or Indian to cease using, as aforesaid, the said lands, river, streams, creeks or marshes, roads or allowance for roads ;
And such person shall accordingly remove or notify every such person or Indian, or remove such cattle or other animals, or cause such person or Indian to cease fishing, as aforesaid, and for that purpose shall have. the same powers as in the execution of criminal process ; and the expenses incurred in any such removal or notification shall be borne by the person removed or notified, or who owns the cattle or other animals removed, or who has them in charge, and may be recovered from him as the costs in any ordinary action or suit, or if the trespasser is an Indian, such expenses may be deducted from his share of annuity and interest money, if any such are due to him. 47 V., c. 27, s. 21.
1. Section twenty-two of " The Indian Act," chapter forty- three of the Revised Statutes, is hereby amended by adding the following sub-section thereto :-
2. Or any such person or Indian other than an Indian of the band may be required orally or in writing by an Indian agent, a chief of the band occupying the reserve, or a constable-
"(a) To remove (with his family, if any) from the land, marsh or road, or allowances or road upon which he is or has so settled, or is residing or hunting, or which he so occupies ; or-

" (b.) To remove his cattle from such land or marsh ; or-
" (c.) To cease fishing' in any such marsh, river, stream or creek as aforesaid ; or-
" (d) To cease using as aforesaid any such land, river, stream, creek, marsh, road or allowance for road :

"And any such person or Indian who fails to comply with such requirement, shall, upon summary conviction, be liable to a penalty of not less than five and not more than ten dollars for every day during which such failure continues, and in default of payment to be imprisoned for a term not exceeding three months."

23. If any person or Indian, after he has been removed Or notified as aforesaid, or after any cattle or other animals owned by him or in his charge have been removed, as aforesaid returns to, settles, resides or hunts upon, or occupies or uses, as aforesaid, any of the said land, marsh or lots, or parts of lots, or causes or permits any cattle or other animals owned by him or in his charge, to return to any of the said land, marsh, or lots or parts of lots, or returns to any marsh, river, stream or creek on or running through a reserve, for the purpose of fishing therein, or settles or resides upon or occupies any of the said roads, allowances for roads, or lots or parts of lots, the Superintendent General, or any officer or person deputed and authorized, as aforesaid, upon view, or upon proof on oath made before him, or to his satisfaction, that the said person or Indian has returned to, settled, resided or hunted upon, or occupied or used, as aforesaid, any of the said lands, marshes, lots or parts of lots, or has returned to settled or resided upon or occupied any of the said roads, or allowances for roads, or lots or parts of lots, or has caused or permitted any cattle or other animals owned by him, or in his charge, to return to any of the said land, marsh or lots or parts of lots, or has returned to any marsh, river, stream or creek, on or running through a reserve,' for the purpose of fishing therein, shall direct and send his warrant, signed and sealed, to the sheriff of the proper county or district, or to any literate person therein ; and if the said reserve is not situated within any county or district, then to any literate person, commanding him forthwith to arrest such person or Indian, and bring him before any stipendiary magistrate, police magistrate, justice of the peace, or Indian agent, who may, on conviction, commit him to the common goal of the said county or district ; or if there is no goal in the said county or district, then to the goal nearest to the said reserve in the Province or Territory, there to remain for the time ordered in such warrant, but which shall not exceed thirty days for the first offence, and thirty days additional for each subsequent offence. 43 Y., c. 28, s. 24 ;-45 V., c. 30, s. 3 ;-47 V., c. 27, s. 6.

24. Such sheriff or other person shall accordingly arrest the said person or Indian, and deliver him to the gaoler or sheriff of the proper county, district, Province or Territory, who shall receive such person or Indian, and imprison him in the said goal for the term aforesaid. 43 Y., c. 28. s. 25.

25. The Superintendent General, or such officer or person aforesaid, shall cause the judgment or order against the offender to be drawn np and filed in his office ; and such judgment shall not be appealed from, or removed by certiorari or otherwise, but shall be final. 43 V., c. 28, s. 26.

26. Every person, or Indian other than an Indian of the band to which the reserve belongs, who, without the license in writing of the Superintendent General, or of some officer or person deputed

by him for that purpose, cuts, carries away, or removes from any of the said land, roads or allowances for roads, in the said reserve, any of the trees, saplings, shrubs, underwood, timber or hay thereon, or removes any of the stone, soil, minerals, metals or other valuables from the said land, mads or allowances for roads, shall, on conviction thereof before any stipendiary magistrate, police, magistrate, or any two justices of the. peace or Indian agent, incur-

(a.) For every tree he cuts, carries away or removes, a penalty of twenty dollars ;

(b.) For cutting, carrying away or removing any of the saplings, shrubs, underwood, timber or hay. if under the value of one dollar, a penalty of four dollars ; but if over the value of one dollar, a penalty of twenty dollars ;

(c.) For removing any of the stone, soil, minerals, metals or other valuables aforesaid, a penalty of twenty dollars, - and the costs of prosecution in each case :

3. Sub-section one of section twenty-six of the said Act is hereby repealed, and the following substituted therefor :-

"26. Every person, or Indian, other than an Indian of the band to which the reserve belongs, who, without the license in writing of the Superintendent General, or of some officer or person deputed by him for that purpose, cuts, carries away or removes from any of the said land, roads or allowances for roads, in the said reserve, any of the trees, saplings, shrubs, underwood. timber, cordwood or part of a tree, or hay thereon, or remove any of the stone, soil, minerals, metals or other valuables from the said land, roads or allowances for roads, shall, on conviction thereof before any stipendiary magistrate, police magistrate or any two justices of the peace or Indian agent, incur-

"(a) For every tree he cuts, carries away or removes, a penalty of twenty dollars ;

"(b) For cutting, carrying away or removing any of the saplings, shrubs, underwood, timber, cordwood or part of a tree or hay, if under the value of one dollar, a penalty of four dollars ; but, if over the value of one dollar, a penalty of twenty dollars ;

"(c) For removing any of the stone, soil, minerals, metals, or other valuables aforesaid, a penalty of twenty dollars :- " And the costs of prosecution in each case : "

2. In default of immediate payment of the said penalties and costs, such magistrate, justices of the peace, or Indian agent, or the Superintendent General, or such other officer or person as he has authorized in that behalf, may issue a warrant, directed to any person or persons by him or them named therein, to levy the amount of the said penalties and costs by distress and sale of the goods and chattels of the person or Indian liable to pay the same; and similar proceedings may be had upon such warrant issued by the Superintendent General, or such other officer or person as aforesaid, as if it had been issued by the magistrate, justices of the peace or Indian agent, before whom the person was convicted ; or such magistrate, or justices of the peace, or Indian agent, or the Superintendent General, or such other officer or person as aforesaid, without proceeding by distress and sale, may, upon non-payment of the said penalties and costs, order the person or Indian liable therefor to be imprisoned in the common goal of the county or district in which the said reserve or any part thereof lies, for a term not exceeding thirty days, if the penalty does not exceed twenty dollar's, or for a term not exceeding three months if the penalty exceeds twenty dollars :

3. If upon the return of any warrant for distress and sale, the amount thereof has not been made,

or if any part of it remains unpaid, such magistrate, or justices of the peace, or Indian agent, or the Superintendent General, or such other officer or person as aforesaid, may commit the person in default to the common gaol, as aforesaid, for a term not exceeding thirty days, if the sum claimed upon the said warrant does not exceed twenty dollars, or for a term not exceeding three months if the sum exceeds twenty dollars:

4. All such penalties shall be paid to the Minister of Finance and Receiver General, and shall be disposed of for the use and benefit of the band of Indians for whose benefit the reserve is held, in such manner as the Governor in Council directs :

5. Nothing herein contained shall be construed to prevent the Superintendent General from issuing a license to any person or Indian to cut and remove trees, wood, timber and hay, or to quarry and remove stone and gravel on and from the reserve, if he, or his agent, acting by his instructions. first obtains the consent of the band thereto in the. Ordinary manner, as hereinafter provided. 4o V., e. 28, s. 27. part ;-45 V., c. 30, s. 3 ;-47 V., c. 27, s. 7.

3. Sub-section five of section twenty-six of the said Act Is hereby repealed.

27. Every Indian who. without the license in writing of the Superintendent General, or of some officer or person deputed by him for that purpose, cuts, carries away or removes from the land of an Indian who holds a location-title, or who is otherwise recognized by the department as the occupant of such land, any of the trees, saplings. shrubs, underwood, timber or hay thereon, or removes any of the stone, soil, minerals, metals or other valuables off the said land ; and every Indian who, without license as aforesaid, cuts, carries away or removes from any portion of the reserve of his band, for sale and not for the immediate use of himself and his family, any trees, timber or hay thereon, or removes any of the stone, soil, minerals, metals or other valuables therefrom, for sale, as aforesaid, shall incur the penalties provided in the next preceding section in respect to Indians of other bands and other persons, and similar proceedings may be had for the recovery thereof as are provided for in the said section. 43V., c. 28, s. 28.

"4. The twenty-seventh section of the said Act is hereby repealed and the following section, substituted therefor :-

"27. Every Indian who, without the license in writing Of the Superintendent General, or of some officer or person deputed by him for that purpose, cuts, carries away or removes from the land of an Indian who holds a location title, or who is otherwise recognized by the department as the occupant of such land, any of the trees, saplings, shrubs, underwood, timber or hay thereon, or removes any of the stone, soil, minerals, metals or other valuables off the said land; and every Indian who, without license as aforesaid, cuts, carries away or removes from any portion of the reserve of his band, for sale and not for the immediate use of himself and his family, any trees, timber or hay thereon, or removes any of the stone, soil, minerals, metals or other valuables therefrom, for sale, as aforesaid, or who cuts or uses any pine or large timber for any other purpose than for budding on his own location or farm, unless with the consent the band and the approval of the Superintendent General, shall incur the penalties provided in the next preceding section in respect to Indians of other bands and other persons, and the, same proceedings may be had for the recovery thereof as are provided for in the said section."

28. In all orders, writs, warrants, summonses and proceedings whatsoever made, issued or taken by the Superintendent General, or any officer or person by him deputed as aforesaid, or by any stipendiary magistrate, police magistrate, justice of the peace or Indian agent, it shall not be necessary to insert or express the name of the person or Indian summoned, arrested, distrained upon, imprisoned or otherwise proceeded against therein, except when the name of such person or Indian is truly given to or known by the Superintendent General, or such officer or person, or such stipendiary magistrate, police magistrate, justice of the peace or Indian agent; and if the name is not truly given to or known by him, he may name or describe the person or Indian by any part of the name of such person or Indian given to or known by him : and if no part of the name is given to or known by him, he may describe the person or Indian proceeded against in any manner by which he may be identified ; and all such proceedings, containing or purporting to give the name or description of any such person or Indian, as aforesaid, shall prima facie be sufficient. 43 V., c. 28, s. 29.

29. All sheriffs, gaolers or peace officers, to whom any such process is directed by the Superintendent General, or by any officer or person by him deputed as aforesaid, or by any stipendiary magistrate, police magistrate, justice of the peace or Indian agent, and all other persons to whom such process is directed with their consent, shall obey the same; and all other officers shall, upon reasonable requisition so to do, assist in the execution thereof. 44 V., c. 17, s. 9.

SALE OR BARTER OF PRODUCE AND MAPLE TREES GROWN ON RESERVES.

30. The Governor in Council may make such regulations As from time to time, seem advisable for prohibiting or regulating the sale, barter, exchange or gift, by any baud or irregular band of Indians, or by any Indian of any band or irregular band, in the Province of Manitoba, the North-West Territories or district of Keewatin, of any grain or root crops or other produce Grown upon any Indian reserves in the Province of Manitoba, the North-West Territories or the District of Keewatin; and may further provide that such sale, barter, exchange or gift shall be null and void, unless the same are made in accordance with regulations made in that behalf:

 2. Every person who buys or otherwise acquires from such Indians or band, or irregular band of Indians, any such grain, root crops or other produce, contrary to any such regulations, shall, on summary conviction before a stipendiary magistrate, police magistrate, or two justices of the peace or an Indian agent, be liable to a penalty not exceeding one hundred dollars, or to imprisonment for a term not exceeding three months, or to both. 44 V., c. 17, s. 1, part, and s. 2 ;-45 V., o. 30, ss. 3 and 6.

31. If any such grain or root crops, or other produce as aforesaid, are unlawfully in the possession of any person, within the intent and meaning of this Act, and of any regulations made by the Governor in Council under this Act, any person acting under the authority, either general or special, of the Superintendent General, may, with such assistance in that behalf as he thinks necessary, seize and take possession of the same ; and he shall deal therewith as the Superintendent General, or any officer or person thereunto by him authorized, directs. 44 V., c. 17, s. 3.

32. The Governor in Council may, from time to time, make regulations for prohibiting the cutting, carrying away or removing from any reserve or special reserve, of any hard or sugar-maple tree or

sapling; and every person who cuts, carries away or removes from any reserve or special reserve, any hard or sugar-maple tree or sapling, or buys or otherwise acquires from any Indian or non-treaty Indian, or other person, any hard or sugar-maple tree or sapling so cut, carried away or removed from any reserve or special reserve, contrary to any such regulation, shall, on summary conviction before a stipendiary magistrate, police magistrate, or two justices of the peace or an Indian agent, be liable to a penalty not exceeding one hundred dollars, or to imprisonment for a term not exceeding three months, or to both. 44 V., c. 17, ss. 4 and 5 ;-45 V., o. 30, s. 3.

ROADS AND BRIDGES.

33. Indians residing upon any reserve, and engaged in the pursuit of agriculture as their then principal means of support; shall be liable, if so directed by the Superintendent General, or any officer or person by him thereunto authorized, to perform labor on the public roads laid out or used in or through, or abutting upon such reserve,-which labor shall be performed under the sole control of the Superintendent General, or officer or person aforesaid, who may direct when, where and how and in what manner such labor shall be applied, and to what extent the same shall be imposed upon Indians who are resident upon any of the said lands ; and the Superintendent General, or officer or person aforesaid, shall have the like power to enforce the performance of such labor by imprisonment or otherwise, as may be done by any power or authority under any law, rule or regulation in force in the Province or Territory in which such reserve is situate, for the non-performance of statute labor ; but the labor to be so required of any such Indian shall not exceed in amount or extent what may be required of other inhabitants of the same Province, Territory, county or other local division, under the laws requiring and regulating such labor and the performance thereof. 43 V., c. 28, s. 34.

1. Section 33 of The Indian Act, chapter 48 of the Revised Statutes, is hereby repealed and the following is substituted therefor :-

"38. Indians residing upon any reserve shall be liable, if so directed by the Superintendent General, or any officer or person by him thereunto authorized, to perform labour upon the public roads laid out or used in or through, or abutting upon such reserve, which labour shall be performed under the sole control of the Superintendent General, or officer or person aforesaid, who may direct when, where and how and in what manner such labour shall be applied, and to what extent the same shall be imposed upon Indians who are resident upon any of the said

lands ; and the Superintendent General, or officer or person aforesaid, shall have the like power to enforce the performance of such labour by imprisonment or otherwise, as may be done by

any power or authority under any law, rule or regulation in force in the province or territory in which such reserve is situate, for the non-performance of statute labour ; but the labour to be

so required of any such Indian shall not exceed in amount or extent what may be required or of other local inhabitants division, under the laws requiring and regulating such labour and the performance thereof!

84. Every band of Indians shall cause the roads, bridges, ditches and fences within its reserve to be put and maintained in proper order, in accordance with the instructions received, from time to time, from the Superintendent General, or from the agent of the Superintendent General; and Power of the whenever, in the opinion of the Superintendent General, the same are not so put or maintained

in order, he may cause the work to be performed at the cost of such band, or of the particular Indian in default, as the case may be. either out of its or his annual allowances, or otherwise. '43 V., c. 28, s. 85.

COMPENSATION FOR PORTION OF RESERVE USED FOR ANY PURPOSE OR TRESPASSED UPON.

35. If any railway, road or public work passes through or causes injury to any reserve belonging to or in possession any band of Indians, or if any act occasioning damage to any reserve is done under the authority of an Act of Parliament, or of the Legislature of any Province, compensation shall be made to them therefor in the same manner as is provided with respect to the lands or rights of other persons ; and the Superintendent General shall, in any case in which an arbitration is had, name the arbitrator on behalf of the Indians, and shall act for them in any matter relating to the settlement of such compensation ; and the amount awarded in any case shall be paid to the Minister of Finance and Receiver General for the use of the band of Indians for whose benefit the reserve is held, and for the benefit of any Indian who has improvements thereon. 42 V., c. 9, a. 9, sub-s. 37 ;-43 V., c. 28, s. 31.

5. The thirty-fifth section of the said Act is hereby amended by striking out the words " If any " in the first line thereof and by substituting therefor the words following, that is to say :-" No portion of any reserve shall be taken for the purposes of any railway, road or public work without the consent of the Governor in Council, and if any."

36. In all cases of encroachment upon, or of violation of trust respecting any special reserve, proceedings may be taken in the name of Her Majesty, in any superior court, notwithstanding the legal title is not vested in Her Majesty. 43 Y, c. 28, s. 32.

SURRENDER AND FORFEITURE OF LANDS IN RESERVE.

37. If, by the violation of the conditions of any such as aforesaid, or by the breaking up of any society, corporation or community, or if by the death of any person or persons without a legal succession of trusteeship, in whom the title to a special reserve is held in trust, the said title lapses or becomes void in law, the legal title shall become vested in Her Majesty in trust, and the property shall be managed for the band or irregular band previously interested therein as an ordinary reserve :

2. The trustees of any special reserve may, at any time, surrender the same to Her Majesty in trust, whereupon the property shall be managed for the band or irregular band previously interested therein as an ordinary reserve. 43 V., c. 28, s. 33.

38. No reserve or portion of a reserve shall be sold, alienated or leased until it has been released or surrendered to the Crown for the purposes of this Act. excepting that in cases of aged, sick and infirm Indians and widows or children left without a guardian, or in the cases of Indians engaged in the practice of any one of the learned professions, or in teaching schools, or in pursuing a trade which interferes with their cultivating land on the reserve, the Superintendent General shall have the power to lease, for their support or benefit, the lands to which they are entitled. 43 V., c. 28, s. 36 47 V., c. 27, s 8.

3. Section thirty-eight of The Indian Act is hereby repealed and the following substituted therefor :-

"38. No reserve or portion of a reserve shall be sold, alienated or leased until the same has been released or surrendered to the Crown for the purposes of this Act ; but the superintendent general may lease, for the benefit of Indians engaged in occupations which interfere with their cultivating land on the reserve, and of sick, infirm or aged Indians, and of widows and orphans or neglected children, lands to which they are entitled without the same being released or surrendered."

1. The section substituted for section thirty-eight of The Indian Act, chapter forty-three of the Revised Statutes, by section three of chapter thirty-two of the Statutes of 1894 hereby repealed and the following substituted therefor :-
" 38. No reserve or portion of a reserve shall be sold, alienated or leased until the same has been released or surrendered to the Crown for the purposes of this Act ; provided that the superintendent general may lease, for the benefit of any Indian, upon his application for that purpose, the land to which he is entitled without the same being released or surrendered."
2. The section substituted for section 38 of the said Act by section 1 of chapter 35 of the statutes of 1895, is hereby repealed and the following is substituted therefor :-
"38. No reserve or portion of a reserve shall be sold, alienated or leased until it has been released or surrendered the Crown for the purposes of this Act : provided that the Superintendent General may lease, for the benefit of any Indian, upon his application for that purpose, the land to which he is entitled without such land being released or surrendered, and may, without surrender, dispose to the best advantage; in the interests of the Indians, of wild grass and dead or fallen timber."
39. No release or surrender of a reserve, or portion of a render of a reserve, held for the use of the Indians of any band, or of any individual Indian, shall be valid or binding, except on the following conditions :-
(a.) The release or surrender shall be assented to by a majority of the male members of the band, of the full age of twenty-one years, at a meeting or council thereof summoned for that purpose, according to the rules of the band, and held in the presence of the Superintendent General, or of an officer duly authorized to attend such council, by the Governor in Council or by the Superintendent General ; but no Indian shall be entitled to vote or be present at such council unless he habitually resides on or near and is interested in the reserve in question ;
(b.) The fact that such release or surrender ha6 been assented to by the band at such council or meeting, shall be certified on oath before some judge of a superior, county or district court, or stipendiary magistrate, by the Superintendent General, or by the officer authorized by him to attend such council or meeting, and by some one of the chiefs or principal men present thereat and entitled to vote ; and when such assent has been so certified, as aforesaid, such release or surrender shall be submitted to the Governor in Council for acceptance or refusal. 43 V., c. 28, s. 37.
2. Section thirty-nine of the said Act is hereby amended by inserting in the eighteenth line thereof, after the word "magistrate," the words " or, in the case of reserves in Manitoba or the North-West Territories, before the Indian Commissioner for Manitoba and the North-West Territories, and in the case of reserves in British Columbia, before the Visiting Indian Superintendent for British Columbia, or, in either case, before some other person or officer specially thereunto authorized by the Governor in Council."

3. Subsection (b) of section 39 of the said Act, as amended by section 2 of chapter 30 of the statutes of 1891, is hereby repealed and the following is substituted therefor :- "

(b.) The fact that such release or surrender has been assented to by the land at such council or meeting shall be certified on oath by the Superintendent General, or by the officer authorized by him to attend such council or meeting, and by some one of the chiefs or principal men present thereat and entitled to vote, before some judge of a superior, county or district court, stipendiary magistrate or justice of the peace, or, in the case of reserves in Manitoba or the North-west Territories, before the Indian Commissioner for Manitoba and the North-west Territories, and in the case of reserves in British Columbia, before the visiting Indian Superintendent for British Columbia, or, in either case, before some other person or officer specially thereunto authorized by the Governor in Council ; and when such assent has been so certified, as aforesaid, such release or surrender shall be submitted to the Governor in Council for acceptance or refusal."

40. Nothing in this Act shall confirm any release or surrender which , but for this Act, would have been invalid and no release or surrender of any reserve, or portion of a reserve, to any person other than Her Majesty, shall be valid. 43 V., c. 28, s. 39.

41. All Indian lands, which are reserves, or portions of reserves, surrendered or to be surrendered to Her Majesty, shall be deemed to be held for the same purposes as before the passing of this Act ; and shall be managed, leased and sold as the Governor in Council directs, subject to the conditions of surrender and the provisions of this Act. 43 V., c. 28, s. 40.

SALE AND TRANSFER OF LANDS IN RESERVES.

42. Every certificate of sale or receipt for money received on the sale of Indian lands granted or made by the Superintendent General or any agent of his, so long as the sale to which such receipt or certificate relates is in force and not rescinded, shall entitle the person to whom the same is granted/or his assignee, by instrument registered under this or any former Act providing for registration in such cases, to take possession of and occupy the land therein comprised, subject to the conditions of such sale, and thereunder, unless the same has been revoked or cancelled, to maintain actions and suits against any wrongdoer or trespasser, as effectually as he could do under a patent from the Crown ; and such receipt or certificate shall be prima facie evidence for the purpose of possession by such person, or assignee, under an instrument registered as aforesaid, in any such action or suit ; but the same shall have no force against a license to cut timber existing at the time of the making or granting thereof. 43 V., c. 28, s. 42.

48. The Superintendent General shall keep a book for registering, at the option of the persons interested, the particulars of any assignment made, as well by the original ° p purchaser or lessee of Indian lands, or his heirs or legal representatives, as by any subsequent assignee of any such lands, or the heirs or legal representatives of such assignee,:

2. Upon any such assignment being produced to the Superintendent General, and, except in cases where such assignment is made under a corporate seal, with an affidavit of due execution thereof, and of the time and place of such execution, and the names, residences and occupations of the witnesses; or, as regards lands in the Province of Quebec, upon the production of such assignment,

executed in notarial form, or of a notarial copy thereof, the Superintendent General shall cause the material parts of every such assignment to be registered in such book of registry, and shall cause to be indorsed on every such assignment a certificate of such registration, signed by himself, or by the Deputy Superintendent General or any other officer of the department by him authorized to sign such certificates :

4. Sub-section two of section forty-three of the said Act is hereby repealed, and the following substituted therefor :-

" 2. Upon any such assignment being produced to the Superintendent General, and, except in cases where such assignment is made under a corporate seal, with an affidavit of due execution thereof, and of the place of such execution, and the names, residences and occupations of the witnesses,- or, as regards lands in the Province of Quebec, upon the production of such assignment, executed in notarial form, or of a notarial copy thereof,-the Superintendent General shall cause the material parts of every such assignment to be registered in such book of registry, and shall cause to be indorsed on every such assignment a certificate of such registration, signed by himself, or by the Deputy Superintendent General, or any other officer of the department by him authorized to sign such certificates :

3. Every such assignment so registered shall be valid against any assignment previously executed, which is subsequently registered or is unregistered ; and no such registration shall be made until all the conditions of the sale, grant or location are complied with or dispensed with by the Superintendent General, and every assignment registered, as aforesaid, shall be unconditional in its terms. 43 V., c. 28, s. 43.

2. Section forty-three of the said Act is hereby amended by adding the following sub-sections thereto :-

" 4. Whenever the proper municipal officer having, by the law of the Province in which the land affected is situate, authority to make or execute deeds or conveyances of lands sold for taxes, makes or executes any deed or conveyance purporting to convey any land, or portion of land, the fee of which is vested in the Crown or any person in trust for or for the use of any Indian or non-treaty Indian or band or irregular baud of Indians or non-treaty Indians, but which has been surrendered under the provisions of this Act, or purporting to grant or convey the interest of any locatee or purchaser from the Crown, and such deed or conveyance recites or purports to be based upon a sale of such laud or such interest for taxes, the Superintendent General may act upon and treat such deed or conveyance as a valid transfer of all the right and interest of the original locatee or purchaser from the Crown, and of every person claiming under him, in or to such land to the grantee named in such deed or conveyance :

"5. So soon as the Superintendent General has signified his approval of such deed or conveyance by endorsement thereon, the grantee shall be substituted in all respects, in relation to the land so conveyed, for the original locatee or purchaser from the Crown, but no such deed or conveyance shall be deemed to confer upon the grantee any greater right or interest in the land than that possessed by the original loeatee or purchaser from the Crown :

" 6. The Superintendent General may cause a patent to be issued to the grantee named in such deed or conveyance on, the completion of the original conditions of the location or sale, unless such deed or conveyance is declared invalid by a court of competent jurisdiction in a suit or action instituted by some person interested in such land within two years of the date of such sale for taxes, and unless within such delay notice of such contestation has been given to the Superintendent General :

" 7. Every such deed or conveyance shall be registered in the office of the Superintendent General within two years from the date of the sale for taxes ; and unless the same is so registered, it shall not be deemed to have preserved its priority, as against a purchaser in good faith from the original locatee or purchaser from the Crown, in virtue of au assignment registered in like manner previously to the date of the registration of the deed or conveyance based upon a sale for taxes as aforesaid."

44. If any subscribing witness to any such assignment is dead, or is absent from Canada, the Superintendent General may register such assignment upon the production of an affidavit proving the death or absence of such witness, and his handwriting, or the handwriting of the person making such assignment. 43 Y., c. 28, s. 44.

45. Every patent for Indian lands shall be prepared in the Department of Indian Affairs, and shall be signed by the Superintendent General of Indian Affairs or his deputy, or ' by some other person thereunto specially authorized by order of the Governor General in Council, and when so signed, shall be registered by an officer specially appointed for that purpose by the Registrar General, and then transmitted to the Secretary of State of Canada, by whom", or by the Under Secretary of State, the same shall be counter- . signed, and the Great Seal of Canada thereto caused to be affixed : Provided, that every such patent for land shall be signed by the Governor or by the Deputy Governor; appointed under this Act for that purpose :

2. On any application for a patent by the heir, assignee or devisee of the original purchaser from the Crown, the Superintendent General may receive proof, in such manner ' as he directs and requires, in support of any claim for a patent, when the original purchaser is dead ; and upon being satisfied that the claim has been equitably and justly established, may allow the same, and cause a patent to issue accordingly: but nothing in this section shall limit the right of a person claiming a patent to land in the Province of Ontario to make application at any time to the Commissioner, under the " Act respecting the Heir, Devisee and Assignee Commission," being chapter twenty-five of the revised Statutes of Ontario (1877) or the corresponding provision in any subsequent revision of the said Statutes. 43 V.. c. 28, s. 45 49 V., c. 7, s. 2.

46. If the Superintendent General is satisfied that any purchaser or lessee of any Indian lands, or any assignee claiming under or through him has been guilty of any fraud or imposition, or has violated any of the conditions of sale or lease, or if any such sale or lease has been made or issued in error or mistake, he may cancel such sale or lease, and resume the land therein mentioned, or dispose of it as if no sale or lease thereof had ever been made; and all such cancellations heretofore made by the Governor in Council, or by the Superintendent General, shall continue valid until altered. 43 V., c. 28, s. 40.

47. Whenever any purchaser, lessee or other person refuses or neglects to deliver up possession of any land after revocation or cancellation of the sale or lease, as aforesaid, or when ever any person is wrongfully in possession of any Indian lands and refuses to vacate or abandon possession of the same, the Superintendent General may apply to the judge of the county court of the county, or to a judge of the superior court in the district in which the land lies, in Ontario or Quebec respectively,

or to any judge of a superior court, or to any judge of a county court of the county in which the land lies, in any other Province, or to a judge of the Supreme Court of the North-West Territories in the said Territories, or to any stipendiary magistrate in any other Territory or district in which the land lies, for an order in the nature of a writ of habere facias possessionem or writ of possession ; and the said judge or magistrate, upon proof to his satisfaction that the right or title of the person to hold such land has been revoked or cancelled, as aforesaid, or that such person is wrongfully in possession of Indian lands, shall grant an order upon the purchaser, lessee or person in possession, to deliver up the same to the Superintendent General, or person by him authorized to receive the same ; and such order shall have the same force as a writ of habere facias possessionem. or writ of possession : and the sheriff, or any bailiff or person to whom it has been intrusted for execution by the Superintendent General, shall execute the same in like manner-as he would execute such writ in an action of ejectment or a possessory action. 43 V.. c. 28, s. 47 ;-49 V., c. 25. s. 30.

3. Section forty-seven of the said Act is hereby amended by adding the following sub-section thereto :

" 2. The costs of an incident to any proceedings under this section or any part thereof shall be paid by any party to such proceedings or by the Superintendent General, as the judge or magistrate orders."

48. Whenever any rent payable to the Crown on any lease of Indian lands is in arrear, the Superintendent General, or any agent or officer appointed under this Act and authorized by the Superintendent General to act in such cases, may issue a warrant, directed to any person or persons by him named therein, in the form of a distress warrant, as in ordinary cases of landlord and tenant, or as in the case of distress and warrant of a justice of the peace for non-payment of a pecuniary penalty ; and the same proceedings may be had thereon, for the collection of such arrears, as in either of the said last-mentioned cases : or an action of debt, as in ordinary cases of rent in arrear, may be brought therefor in the name of the Superintendent General ; but demand of rent shall not be necessary in any case. 43 V., c. 28, s. 48.

49. When by law or by any deed, lease or agreement relating to any of the lands herein referred to, any notice is required to be given, or any act to be done, by or on behalf of the Crown, such notice may be given and act done by or by the authority of the Superintendent General. 43 V., c. 28, s. 49.

50. Whenever letters patent have been issued to or in the name of the wrong person, through mistake, or contain any clerical error or misnomer, or wrong description of any material fact therein, or of the land thereby intended to be granted, the Superintendent General, if there is no adverse claim, may direct the defective letters patent to be cancelled and a minute of such cancellation to be entered in the margin of the registry of the original letters patent, and correct letters patent to be issued in their stead,-which corrected letters patent shall relate back to the date of those so cancelled, and have the same effect as if issued at the date of such cancelled letters patent. 43 V., c. 28, s.50.

51. In all cases in which grants or letters patent have issued for the same land, inconsistent with each other, through error, and in all cases of sates or appropriations of the same land, inconsistent with each other, the Superintendent General may, in cases of sale, cause a repayment of the purchase money, with interest ; or when the land has passed from the original purchaser or has been improved

before a discovery of the error, he may, in substitution, assign land or grant a certificate entitling the person to purchase Indian lands, of such value and to such extent as the Superintendent General deems just and equitable under the circumstances ; but no such claim shall be entertained unless it is preferred within five years from the discovery of the error. 43 V., c. 28, s. 51.

52. Whenever, by reason of false survey or error in the Books or plans in the department, or in the late Indian branch of the Department of the Interior, any grant, sale or appropriation of land is found deficient, or any parcel of land contains less than the quantity of land mentioned in the patent therefor, the Superintendent General may order the purchase money of so much land as is deficient, with the interest thereon from the time of the application therefor, -or, if the land has passed from the original purchaser, the purchase money which the claimant, if he was ignorant of a deficiency at the time of his purchase, has paid for so much of the land as is deficient, with interest thereon from the time of the application therefor,-to be paid to him in land or money, as the Superintendent General directs ; but no such claim shall be entertained unless application is made within five years from the date of the patent, and unless the deficiency is equal to one-tenth of the whole quantity described. as contained in the particular lot or parcel of land granted. 43 V., c. 28, s. 52.

53. Whenever patents for Indian lauds have issued through fraud or in error or improvidence, the Exchequer Court of Canada, or a superior court in any Province may, upon action, bill or plaint, respecting such lands situate within its jurisdiction, and upon hearing the parties interested, or upon default of the said parties after such notice of proceeding as the said courts shall respectively order, decree such patents to be void; and upon a registry of such decree in the office of the Registrar General of Canada, such patents shall be void to all intents ;

5. Sub-section one of section fifty three of the said act is hereby amended by substituting for the words "office of the Registrar General of Canada," in the ninth line thereof, the

words " Department of Indian Affairs."

2. The practice in court, in such cases, shall be regulated by orders, from time to time, made by the said courts respectively. 43 V., c. 28, s. 53.

TIMBER LANDS.

54. The Superintendent General, or any officer or agent authorized by him to that effect, may grant licenses to cut trees on reserves and ungranted Indian lands, at such rates, and subject to such conditions, regulations and restrictions, as are, from time to time, established by the Governor in Council, and such conditions, regulations and restrictions shall be adapted to the locality in which such reserves or lands are situated. 43 V., c. 28, s. 56.

55. No license shall be so granted for a longer period than twelve months from the date thereof: and if. in consequence of any incorrectness of survey or other error, or cause what- soever, a license is found to comprise land included in a license of a prior date, or land not being reserve, or ungranted Indian lands, the license granted shall be void in so far as it comprises such laud, and the holder or proprietor of the license so rendered void shall have no claim upon the Crown for indemnity or compensation by reason of such avoidance. 43 V., c. 28, s. 57.

56. Every license shall describe the lands upon which the trees may be cut, and the kind of tree which

may be cut and shall confer, for the time being, on the licensee the right to take and keep exclusive possession of the land so described, subject to such regulations as are made; and every license shall vest in the holder thereof all rights of property whatsoever in. all trees of the kind specified, curt within the limits of the license, during the term thereof, whether such trees are cut by the authority of the holder of such license or by any other person, with or without his consent ; and every license shall entitle the holder thereof to seize, in revendication or otherwise, such trees and the logs, timber or other product thereof, if the same are found in the possession of any unauthorized person, and also to institute any action or suit against any wrongful possessor or trespasser, and to prosecute all trespassers and other offenders to punishment, and to recover damages, if any ; and all proceedings pending at expiration of any license may be continued to final termination, as if the license had not expired. 43 V., c. 28, s. 58.

4. Section 56 of the said Act, is hereby repealed and the following is substituted therefor :-

"56. Every license shall describe the lands upon which the trees may be cut, and the kind of trees which may be cut, and shall confer, for the time being, on the licensee the right to take and keep possession of the land so described, subject to such regulations as are made ; and every license shall vest in the holder thereof all rights of property in all trees of the kind specified, cut within the limits of the license during the term thereof, whether such trees are cut by the authority of the holder of such license or by any other person, with or without his consent; and every license shall entitle the holder thereof to seize, in revendication or otherwise, such trees and the logs, timber or other product thereof, if found in the possession of any unauthorized person, and also to institute any action or suit against any wrongful possessor or trespasser, and to prosecute all trespassers and other offenders to punishment, and to recover damages, if any ; and all proceedings pending at the expiration of any license may be continued to final termination, as if the license had not expired."

57. Every person who obtains a license shall, at the expiration thereof, make to the officer or agent granting the same, or to the Superintendent General, a return of the number and kinds of trees cut, and of the quantity and description of saw-logs, or of the number and description of sticks of square or other timber, manufactured and earned away under such license ; and such statement shall be sworn to by the holder of the license, or his agent, or by his foreman ; and every person who refuses or neglects to furnish such statement, or who evades or attempts to evade any regulation made by the Governor in Council, shall be held to have cut without authority, and the timber or other product made shall be dealt with accordingly. 43 V., c. 28, s. 59.

58. All trees cut, and the logs, timber or other product shall be liable for the payment of the dues thereon, so long as and wheresoever the same, or any part thereof, are ' found whether in the original logs or manufactured into deals, boards or other stuff ; and all officers or agents in trusted with the collection of such dues, may follow and seize and detain the same wherever they are found, until the dues are paid or secured. 43 Y., c. 28, s. 60.

59. No instrument or security taken for the dues, either before or after the cutting of the trees, as collateral security, or to facilitate collection, shall in any way affect the lien for such dues, but the lien shall subsist until the said dues are actually discharged. 43 V., c. 28, s. 61.

60. If any timber so seized and detained for non-payment of dues remains more than twelve months

in the custody of the agent or person appointed to guard the same, without the dues and expenses being paid, the Superintendent General may order a sale of the said timber to be made after sufficient notice ; and the balance of the proceeds of such sale, after retaining the amount of dues and costs incurred, shall be handed over to the owner or claimant of such timber, upon his applying therefor and proving his right thereto. 43 V., c. 28, s. 62.

61. If any person, without authority, cuts, or employs induces any other person to cut, or assists in cutting any trees of any kind on Indian lands, or removes or carries away, or employs, or induces or assists any other person to remove or carry away, any trees of any kind so cut from Indian lands, he shall not acquire any right to the trees so cut, or any claim to any remuneration for cutting or preparing the same for market, or conveying the same to or towards market ; and when the trees, or logs or timber, or other product thereof, have been removed, so that the same cannot, in the opinion of the Superintendent General, conveniently be seized, he shall, in addition to the loss of his labor and disbursements, incur a penalty of three dollars for each tree, rafting stuff excepted, which he is proved to have cut or caused to be cut or carried away ; and such penalty shall be recoverable with costs, at the suit and in the name of the Superintendent General or resident agent, in any court having jurisdiction in civil matters to the amount of the penalty ; and in all such cases it shall be incumbent on the person charged to prove his authority to cut ; and the averment of the person seizing or prosecuting, that he is duly employed under the authority of this Act, shall be sufficient proof thereof, unless the defendant proves the contrary. 43 Y., c. 28, s. 63.

62. When the Superintendent General, or any officer or agent acting under him, receives satisfactory information, supported by affidavit made before a justice of the peace or before any other competent authority, that any trees have been cut without authority on Indian lands, describing where the trees, logs, timber or other product thereof are to be found, the Superintendent General, officer or agent, may seize, or cause to be seized, the same in Her Majesty's name, whosesoever found, and place the same under proper custody, until the matter is decided by competent authority. 43 V., c. 28. s. 64, part.

6. The sixty-second section of the said Act is hereby repealed and the following section substituted therefor :-

"62. Any officer or agent acting under the Superintendent General may seize or cause to be seized in Her Majesty's name any logs, timber, wood or other products of trees or any trees themselves, cut without authority on Indian lands or on an Indian reserve, wherever they are found, and place the same under proper custody until a decision can be had in the matter from competent authority."

63. When the tress, timber, logs or other product thereof so reported to have been cut without authority, on Indian on Indian lands, have been made up or intermingled with other trees timber, logs or other product thereof, into a crib, dram or raft or in any other manner, so that it is difficult to distinguish the trees, timber, logs or other product thereof, cut on reserves on reserves or Indian land, without license, from that with which it is made up or intermingled, the whole of the trees, timber, logs or other product thereof, so made up or inter- mingled, shall be held to have been cut without authority on Indian lands, and shall be seized, and forfeited, and sold, by the Superintendent General, or any other officer or agent acting under him, unless evidence satisfactory to him is adduced,

showing the probable quantity not cut on Indian lands. 43 Y., c. 28, s. 64, part.

7. The sixty-third section of the 6aid Act is hereby repealed, and the following section substituted therefor :-

"63. When the logs, timber, wood or other products of trees cut without authority, or the trees themselves so cut without authority on Indian lands or on an Indian reserve, have been made up or intermingled with other trees, wood, timber, logs or other products thereof, into a crib, dram or raft, or in any other manner, so that it is difficult to distinguish the timber cut on a reserve or on Indian lands without license from the other timber with which it is made up or intermingled, the whole of the timber so made up or intermingled shall be held to have been cut without authority on a reserve or on Indian lands, and shall be seized and forfeited and sold by the Superintendent General or any officer or agent acting under him, unless evidence satisfactory to him is adduced showing the probable quantity not cut on a reserve or on Indian lands."

64. Every officer or person seizing trees, logs, or other product thereof, in the discharge of his duty under this Act, may, in the name of the Crown, call in any assistance necessary for securing and protecting the same. 43 V., c. 28, s. 65, part.

65. Whenever any tree, logs, timber or other product thereof are seized for non-payment of Crown dues, or for any other cause of forfeiture, or whenever any prosecution is brought in respect of any penalty or forfeiture under this Act. and any question arises whether the said dues have been paid or whether the trees, logs, timber or other product were cut on lands other than any of the lands aforesaid, the burden of proving payment, or on what land the same were cut, as the case may be, shall lie on the owner or claimant and not on the officer who seizes the same, or the person who brings such prosecution. 43 V., c. 28, s. 66, part.

66. All trees, logs, timber or other product thereof seized This act, shall be deemed to be condemned, unless the person from whom the same are seized, or the owner thereof, within one month from the day of the seizure, gives notice to the seizing officer or nearest officer or agent of the Superintendent General, that he claims or intends to claim the same; and in default of such notice, the officer or agent seizing shall report the circumstances to the Superintendent General, who may order the sale of the same by the said officer or agent. 43 V., c. 28, s. 67, part.

5. Section 66 of the said Act is hereby repealed and the following is substituted therefor:-

66. All trees, logs, timber or other product thereof seized Under this Act, shall be deemed to be condemned, unless the person from whom they are seized, or the owner thereof, within one month from the day of the seizure, gives notice to the seizing officer, or nearest officer or agent of the Superintendent General, that he claims, or intends to claim them, and unless within one month from the day of giving such notice he initiates, in some court of competent jurisdiction, proceedings for the purpose of establishing his claim ; and in default of such notice and initiation of proceedings, the officer or agent seizing shall report the circumstances to the Superintendent General, who may order the sale, by the said officer or agent, of such trees, logs, timber or other product thereof."

67. Any judge of any superior, county or district court, or any stipendiary magistrate, police magistrate or Indian agent, may, in a summary way, under the " Act respecting summary proceedings before Justices of the Peace," try and determine such seizures,-and may, pending the trial, order the

delivery of the trees, logs, timber or other product thereof to the alleged owner, on receiving security by bond, with two good and sufficient sureties, first approved by the said agent, to pay double the value of such trees, logs, timber or other product, in case of their condemnation ; and such bond shall be taken in the name of the Superintendent General, for Her Majesty, and shall be delivered up to and kept by the Superintendent General ; and if such seized trees, logs, timber or other product-thereof are condemned, the value thereof shall be paid forthwith to the Superintendent General or agent. and the bond cancelled, otherwise the penalty of such bond shall be enforced and recovered. 43 V., c. 28, s. 67, part 45 V., c. 30, s. 3.

68. Everyone who avails himself of any false statement or false oath to evade the payment of dues under this Act, shall forfeit the. timber in respect of which the dues are attempted to be evaded. 43 V., c. 28, s. 68.

MANAGEMENT OF INDIAN MONEYS.

60. All moneys or securities of any kind applicable to the support or benefit of Indians, or any band of Indians, and all moneys accrued or hereafter to accrue from the sale of any Indian lands or of any timber on any reserves or Indian lands, shall, subject to the provisions of this Act. be applicable to the same purposes and be dealt with in the same manner as they might have been applied to or dealt with but for the passing of this Act. 43 V., c. 28, s. 69.

70. The Governor in Council may, subject to the provisions of this Act, direct how, and in what manner, and by whom, the moneys arising from sales of Indian lands, and from the property held or to be held in trust for the Indians, or from any timber on Indian lands or reserves, or from any other source, for the benefit of Indians, (with the exception of any sum not exceeding ten per cent, of the proceeds of any lands, timber or property, which is agreed at the time of the surrender to be paid to the members of the band interested therein,) shall be invested, from time to time, and how the payments or assistance to which the Indians are entitled shall be made or given,-and may provide for the general -management of such moneys, and direct what percentage or proportion thereof shall be set apart, from time to time, to cover the cost of and incidental to the management of reserves, lands, property and moneys under the provisions of this Act, and for the construction or repair of roads passing through such reserves or lands, and by way of contribution to schools attended by such Indians. 43 V., c. 28. s. 70.

2. Section seventy of The Indian Act is hereby repealed and the following substituted therefor:-

70. The Governor in Council may, subject to the provisions of this Act, direct how, and in what manner, and by whom, the moneys arising from the disposal of Indian lands, or of property held or to be held in trust for Indians, or timber on Indian lands or reserves, or from any other source for the benefit of Indians, (with the exception of such sum not exceeding ten percent of the proceeds of any lands, timber or property, from, as is agreed at the time of the surrender to be paid to the members of the band interested therein,) shall be invested, from time to time, and how the payments or assistance to which the Indians are entitled shall be made or given ; and may provide for the general management of such moneys, and direct what percentage or proportion thereof shall be set apart, from time to time, to cover the cost of and incidental to the management of reserves, lands, property and moneys under the provisions of this Act, and may authorize and direct the expenditure of such

moneys for the construction or repair of roads, bridges, ditches and watercourses on such reserves or lands, for the construction of school buildings, and by way of contribution to schools attended by such Indians."

6. The section substituted for section 70 of the said Act by section 2 of chapter 35 of the statutes of 1895, is hereby repealed and the following is substituted therefor :-

"70. The Governor in Council may, subject to the provisions of this Act, direct how, and in what manner and by whom, the moneys arising from the disposal of Indian lands, or of property held or to be held in trust for Indians, or timber on Indian lands or reserves, or from any other source for the benefit of Indians (with the exception of such sum, not exceeding ten per cent of the proceeds of any lands, timber, or property, as is agreed at the time of the surrender to be paid to the members of the band interested therein), shall be invested from time to time, and how the payments or assistance to which the Indians are entitled shall be made or given ; and he may provide for the general management of such moneys, and direct what percentage or proportion thereof shall be set apart, from time to time, to cover the cost of and incidental to the management of reserves, lands, property and moneys under the provisions of this Act, and may authorize and direct the expenditure of such moneys for surveys, for compensation to Indians for improvements or any interest they have in lands taken from them, for the construction or repair of roads, bridges, ditches and watercourses on such reserves or lands, for the construction of school buildings, and by way of contribution to schools attended by such Indians."

1. Section 6 of chapter 34 of the statutes of 1898 is repealed and the following is enacted as section 70 of The Indian Act, chapter 43 of the Revised Statutes:-

"70. The Governor in Council may, subject to the provisions of this Act, direct how, and in what manner, and by whom, the moneys arising from the disposal of Indian lands, or of property held or to be held in trust for Indians, or timber on Indian lands or reserves, or from any other source for the benefit of Indians (with the exception of such sum, not exceeding fifty percent of the proceeds of any lands, and not exceeding ten percent of the proceeds of any timber or other property, as is agreed at the time of the surrender to be paid to the members of the band interested therein), shall be invested from time to time, and how the payments or assistance to which the Indians are entitled shall be made or given; and he may provide for the general management of such moneys, and direct what percentage or proportion thereof shall be set apart, from time to time, to cover the cost of and incidental to the management of reserves, lands, property and moneys under the provisions of this Act, and may authorize and direct the expenditure of such moneys for surveys, for compensation to Indians for improvements or any interest they have in lands taken from them, for the construction or repairs of roads, bridges, ditches and watercourses on such reserves or lands, for the construction and repair of school buildings and charitable institutions, and by way of contribution to schools attended by such Indians."

71. The proceeds arising from the sale or lease of any Indian lands, or from the timber, hay, stone, minerals or other valuables thereon. or on a reserve, shall be paid to the Minister of Finance and Receiver General to the credit of Indian fund. - 43 V., c. 28, s. 71.

72. The Superintendent General may stop the payment of the annuity and interest money of any Indian who is proved to the satisfaction of the Superintendent General, guilty of deserting his family and the Superintendent General may apply the same towards the support of any family, woman or child, so deserted. 43 V., c. 28, s. 83, part.

8. The seventy-second section of the said Act is hereby repealed and the following section substituted therefor :---

72. The Superintendent General may stop the payment of the annuity and interest money of, as well as deprive . any participation in the real property of the band, an Indian who is proved, to the satisfaction of the Superintendent General, guilty of deserting his family ; and the Superintendent General may apply the same towards the support of any family, woman or child, so deserted."

4. The section substituted for section seventy-two of The Indian Act by section eight of chapter thirty-three of the Statutes of 1887 Is hereby repealed and the following substituted therefor:-

72. The superintendent general may stop the payment of the annuity and interest money of, as well as deprive of any participation in the real property of the band, any Indian who is proved, to the satisfaction of the superintendent general, guilty of deserting his family, or of conduct justifying his wife or family in separating from him, or is separated from his family by imprisonment ; and the superintendent general may apply the same towards the support of the wife or family of such Indian."

7. Section 72 of the said Act, as enacted by section 4 of chapter 32 of the statutes of 1894, is hereby repealed and the following is substituted therefor :-

"72. The Superintendent General may stop the payment of the annuity and interest money of, as well as deprive of any participation in the real property of the band, any Indian who is proved, to the satisfaction of the Superintendent General, guilty of deserting his family, or of conduct justifying his wife or family in separating from him, or who is separated from his family by imprisonment; and the Superintendent General may apply the same towards the support of the wife or family of such Indian. The Superintendent General may also stop the payment of the annuity and interest money of any Indian parent of an illegitimate child, and apply the same to the support of the child."

73. The Superintendent General may also stop the payment of the annuity and interest money of any woman who has no children, and who deserts her husband and lives immorally with another man. 43 V., c. 28, s. 83, part .

9. The seventy-third section of the said Act is hereby repealed and the following section substituted therefor:-

" 73. The Superintendent General may also stop the payment of the annuity and interest money of, as well as deprive of any participation in the real property of the band any woman who has no children, and who deserts her husband and lives immorally -with another man."

8. The section substituted for section 73 of the said Act by section 9 of chapter 33 of the statutes of 1887, is hereby repealed and the following is substituted therefor :-

"73. The Superintendent General may also stop the payment of the annuity and interest money of, as well as deprive of any participation in the real property of the band, any woman who deserts her husband or family and lives immorally with another man, and the Superintendent General may apply the same to the support of the family so deserted."

74. The Superintendent General may, whenever sick or disabled, or aged or destitute Indians are not provided for by the band of which they are members, furnish sufficient aid from the funds of the band for the relief of such sick, disabled, aged or destitute Indians. 43 V., c. 28, s. 84.

ELECTION OF CHIEFS.

75. Whenever the Governor in Council deems it advisable, for the good government of a band, to introduce the system election of election of chiefs, he may provide that the chiefs of any band of Indians shall be elected, as hereinafter provided, at such time and place as the Superintendent General directs; and they shall, in such case, he elected for a term of three years, but may be deposed by the Governor in Council for dishonesty, intemperance, immorality or incompetency; and they may be in the proportion of one head chief and two second chiefs or councilors for even- two hundred Indians :

5. Subsection one of section seventy-five of The Indian Amended hereby amended by inserting after the word "deposed " in the seventh line thereof the following words "and declared ineligible for re-election for three years."

2. No band shall have more than six head chiefs and twelve second chiefs, but any baud, composed of thirty Indians, may have one chief:

3. Provided that life chiefs, now living, shall continue to hold the rank of chief until death or resignation, or until their removal, by the Governor in Council, for dishonesty, intemperance, immorality or incompetency ; but in the event of the Governor in Council providing that the chiefs of a band shall be elected, the life chiefs shall not exercise the powers of chiefs, unless elected, under the provision aforesaid, to the exercise of such powers :

4. An election may be set aside by the Governor in Council on the report of the Superintendent General, if it is proved by two witnesses before the Indian agent for the locality or such other person as is deputed by the Superintendent General to take evidence in the matter, that fraud or gross irregularity was practiced at the said election ; and every Indian who is proved guilty of such fraud or irregularity, or connivance thereat, may be declared ineligible for re-election for six years, if the Governor in Council, on the report of the Superintendent General, so directs. 43 Y., c. 28, s. 72;-47 V., c. 27, s. 9.

3. Section seventy-five of The Indian Act is hereby repealed and the following substituted therefor :-

" 75. Whenever the Governor in Council deems it advisable, for the good government of a band, to introduce the system of election of chiefs or headmen, he may provide that the chiefs or headmen of any band of Indians shall be elected, as hereinafter provided, at such time and place as the superintendent general directs ; and they shall, in such case, be elected for a term of three years :

2. Bands containing thirty or more Indians shall be entitled to elect chiefs or headmen in the proportion of one for each thirty members ; but no band shall have more than fifteen chiefs or headmen : Provided that life chiefs, now living, shall continue to hold the rank of chief until death or resignation, or until their removal, by the Governor in Council, for dishonesty, intemperance, immorality or incompetency ; but in the event of the Governor in Council providing that the chiefs or headmen of a band shall be elected, the life chiefs or headmen shall not exercise the powers of chiefs or

headmen, unless elected, under the provision aforesaid, to the exercise of such powers :

" 3. An election may be set aside by the Governor in Council on the report of the superintendent general, if it is proved by two witnesses before the Indian agent for the locality or such other person as is deputed by the superintendent general to take evidence in the matter, that fraud or gross irregularity was practiced at the said election ; and every Indian who is proved-guilty of such fraud or irregularity, or connivance thereat, may be declared ineligible for re-election for six years, if the Governor in Council, on the report of the superintendent general, so directs :

"4. Any elected or life chief or headman, or any chief or headman chosen according to the custom of any band, may, on the ground of dishonesty, intemperance, immorality or incompetency, be deposed by the Governor in Council and declared ineligible to hold the office of chief or headman for three years."

9. The section substituted for section 75 of the said Act by section 8 of chapter 35 of the statutes of 1895, is hereby repealed and the following is substituted therefor :-

"75. Whenever the Governor in Council deems it advisable, for the good government of a band, to introduce the elective system of chiefs and councillors or headmen, he may provide that the chief and councillors or headmen of any band shall he elected, as hereinafter provided, at such time and place as the Superintendent General directs ; and they shall in such ease be elected for a term of three years. The councillors or headmen may he in the proportion of two for every two hundred Indians ; but no hand shall have more than one chief and fifteen councillors or headmen : provided, however, that any band composed of at least thirty members may have a chief.

"2. Life chiefs and councillors or headmen now living may continue to hold rank until death or resignation, or until their removal by the Governor in Council for dishonesty, intemperance, immorality or incompetency ; but in the event of the Governor in Council providing that the chief and councillors or headmen of a band shall be elected, the life chiefs and councillors or headmen shall not exercise powers as such unless elected under the provision aforesaid.

"3. An election may be set aside by the Governor in Council, on a report of the Superintendent General, if it is proved by two witnesses before the Indian agent for the locality, or such other person as is deputed by the Superintendent General to take evidence in the matter, that fraud or gross irregularity was practiced at the said election ; and every Indian who is proved guilty of such fraud or irregularity, or connivance thereat, may be declared ineligible for re-election for a period not exceeding six years, if the Governor in Council, on the report of the Superintendent General, so directs.

"4. Any elected or life chief and any councillor or headman, or any chief or councillor or headman chosen according to the custom of any band, may, on the ground of dishonesty, intemperance, immorality or incompetency, be deposed by the Governor in Council and declared ineligible to hold the office of chief or councillor or headman for a period not exceeding three years."

REGULATIONS TO BE MADE BY CHIEFS.

76. The chief or chiefs of any band in council may frame, subject to confirmation by the Governor in Council, rules and regulations in respect of the subjects following, that is to say :-

(a.) As to what religious denomination the teacher of the school established on the reserve shall belong to : Provided always, that he shall he of the same denomination as the majority of the band ; and that the Protestant or Catholic minority may likewise hare a separate school, with the approval of and under regulations made by the Governor in Council ;

(b.) The care of the public health;

(c.) The observance of order and decorum at assemblies of Order, the Indians in general council, or on other occasions ;

(d.) The repression of intemperance and profligacy ;

(e.) The prevention of trespass by cattle, and the protection of sheep, horses, mules and cattle;

(f.) The construction and maintenance of water-courses, roads, bridges, ditches and fences ;

(g.) The construction and repair of school houses, council houses and other Indian public buildings, and the attendance at school of children between the ages of six and fifteen years ;

(h.) The establishment of pounds and the appointment of pound-keepers ;

(i) The locating of the land in their reserves, and the establishment of a register of such locations ;

(j.) The repression of noxious weeds ;

(k) The imposition of punishment, by fine, penalty or punishment imprisonment, or both, for violation of any of such rules or regulations ; but the fine or penalty shall in no case exceed thirty dollars, and the imprisonment shall in no case exceed thirty days ; and the proceedings for the imposition of such punishment shall be taken under the " Act respecting' summary proceedings before Justices of the Peace." 43 V ., c. 28, s. 74 47 V., c. 27, s. 10.

EXEMPTION FROM TAXATION.

77. No Indian or non-treaty Indian shall be liable to be taxed for any real or personal property, unless he holds, in his individual right, real estate under a lease or in fee simple, or personal property outside of the reserve or special reserve- in which case he shall be liable to be taxed for such real or personal property at the same rate as other persons in the locality in which it is situate:

2. No taxes shall be levied on the real property of any Indian, acquired under the enfranchisement clauses of this Act, until the same has been declared liable to taxation by proclamation of the Governor in Council, published in the Canada Gazette :

3. All land vested in the Crown or in any person, in trust for or for the use of any Indian or non-treaty Indian, or any from taxation, band or irregular band of Indians or non-treaty Indians, shall be exempt from taxation. 43 V., c. 28, ss. 75 and 76;- 47 V., c. 27, s. 11.

3. Sub-section three of section seventy-seven is hereby repealed and the following substituted therefor :-

" 3. All land vested in the Crown or in any person, in for or for the use of any Indian or non-treaty Indian, or any band or irregular band of Indians or non-treaty Indians, shall be exempt from taxation, except those lands which, having been surrendered by the bands owning them, though unpatented, have been located by or sold or agreed to be sold to any person ; and, except as against the Crown and any Indian located on the land, the same shall be liable to taxation in like manner as other lands in the same locality ; but nothing herein contained shall interfere with the right of the Superintendent General to cancel the original sale or location of any land, or shall render such land liable to taxation until it is again sold or located."

LEGAL, RIGHTS OF INDIAN'S.

78. No person shall take any security or otherwise obtain Any lien or charge, whether by mortgage,

judgment or otherwise, upon real or personal property of any Indian or Indian non-treaty Indian, except on real or personal property subject to taxation under the next preceding section ; but any person selling any article to an Indian or non-treaty Indian may take security on such article for any part of the price thereof which is unpaid. 43 V., c. 28, s. 77.

79. Indians and non-treaty Indians shall have the right To sue for debts due to them, or in respect of any tort or wrong inflicted upon them, or to compel the performance of obligations contracted with them ; but in any suit or action between Indians, or in any case of assault in which the offender is an Indian, no appeal shall lie from any judgment, order or conviction by any police magistrate, stipendiary magistrate, or two justices of the peace or an Indian agent, when the sum adjudged or the penalty imposed does not exceed ten dollars. 43 V., c. 28, s. 78 ;-45 V., c. 30, s. 3 ;- 47 V., c. 27, s. 24.

80. No pawn taken from any Indian or non-treaty Indian for any intoxicant, shall be retained by the person to whom such pawn is delivered ; but the thing so pawned may be sued for and shall be recoverable, with costs of suit, in any court of competent jurisdiction by the Indian or non-treaty Indian who pawned the same. 43 V., c. 28, s. 79.

81. No presents given to Indians or non-treaty Indians, And no property purchased or acquired with or by means of any annuities granted to Indians, or any part thereof, and in the possession of any band of such Indians, or of any Indian of any band or irregular band, shall be liable to be taken, seized or distrained for any debt, matter or cause whatsoever :

2. No such presents or property shall, in the Province of British Columbia, the Province of Manitoba, the North- West Territories or in the District of Keewatin, be sold, bartered, exchanged or given by any band or irregular band of Indians, or any Indian of any such band, to any person or Indian other than an Indian of such band :

3. Every such sale, barter, exchange or gift shall be null And void, unless such sale, barter, exchange or gift is made with the written assent of the Superintendent General or his agent ; and everyone who buys or otherwise acquires any presents or property purchased as aforesaid, without the written consent of the Superintendent General or his agent, as aforesaid, is guilty of a misdemeanor, and liable to a fine not exceeding two hundred dollars, or to imprisonment for a term not exceeding six months :

6. Sub-section three of section eighty-one of the said Act is hereby amended by adding the following words at the end thereof : " and the burden of proof, concerning such written consent of the Superintendent General or his agent, shall lie on the accused."

4. If any presents given to Indians or non-treaty Indians, or any property purchased or acquired with or by means of any annuities granted to Indians, are or is unlawfully in the possession of any person, within the true intent and meaning of this section, any person acting under the authority of the Superintendent General may, with such assistance in that behalf as he thinks necessary, seize and take possession of the same, and he shall deal therewith as the Superintendent General directs. 43 V., c. 28, s. 80.

7. The said section eighty-one is hereby further amended by adding the following sub-section thereto :-

" 5. Animals given to Indians under treaty stipulations, and the progeny thereof, and farming implements, tools and any other articles given to Indians under treaty stipulations, shall be held to be presents within the meaning of this section."

ENFRANCHISEMENT.

82. The eleven sections next following, shall not apply to any band of Indians in the Province of British Columbia, the Province of Manitoba, the North-West Territories or the District of Keewatin, except in so far as the said sections are, by proclamation of the Governor in Council, from time to time, extended to any band of Indians in any of the said Provinces, Territories or District. 48 V., c. 28, s. 107.

88. Whenever any male Indian or unmarried Indian woman,-of the full age of twenty-one years, makes application to the Superintendent General to be enfranchised, the Superintendent General shall instruct the agent of the band of which the applicant is a member, to call upon the latter to furnish a certificate, under oath, before a judge of any court of justice, by the priest, clergyman or minister of the religious denomination to which the applicant belongs, or by a stipendiary magistrate or two justices of the peace, to the effect that to the best of the knowledge and belief of the deponent or deponents, the applicant for enfranchisement is, and has been for at least five years previously, a person of good moral character, temperate in his or her habits, and of sufficient intelligence to be qualified to hold land in fee simple, and otherwise to exercise all the rights and privileges of an enfranchised person. 47 V., c. 27, s. 16, part.

84. Upon receipt of such a certificate, the agent shall, with the least possible delay, submit the same to a council of the band of which the applicant is a member ; and he shall then inform the Indians assembled at such council, that thirty days will be given within which affidavits made before a judge or a stipendiary magistrate will be received, containing reasons, if any there are, of a personal character affecting the applicant, why such enfranchisement should not be granted to the applicant. 47 V., c. 27, s. 16, part.

85. At the expiration of the thirty days aforesaid, the agent shall forward to the Superintendent General all affidavits which have been filed with him in the case, as well as one made by himself before a judge or a stipendiary magistrate, containing his reasons for or against the enfranchisement of the applicant; and if the Superintendent General, after examining the evidence, decides in favor of the applicant, he may grant him or her a location ticket as a probationary Indian for the land occupied by him or her or for such proportion thereof as appears Superintendent General fair and proper. 47 V., c. 27, s. 16, part.

86. Every Indian who is admitted to the degree of doctor of medicine, or to any other degree, by any University of learning, or who is admitted, in any Province of Canada, to practice law, either as an advocate, a barrister, solicitor or attorney, or a notary public, or who enters holy orders, or who is licensed by any denomination of Christians as a minister of the gospel, may, upon petition to the Superintendent General, ipso facto become and be enfranchised under this Act, and he shall then be entitled to all the rights and privileges to which any other member of the band to which he belongs would be entitled if he was enfranchised under the provisions of this Act ; and the Superintendent General may give him a suitable allotment of land from the lands belonging to the band of which

he is a member ; but if he is not the recognized holder of a location on the reserve, by ticket or otherwise, he shall first obtain the consent of the band and the approval of the Superintendent General to such allotment. 47 V., c. 27, s. 16, part.

87. After the expiration of three years, or such longer period as the Superintendent General deems necessary in the event of the conduct of such Indian not being- satisfactory, the Governor in Council may, on the report of the Superintendent General, order the issue of letters patent, granting to such Indian the land in fee simple, which has, with this object in view, been allotted to him by location ticket, but without power to sell, lease or otherwise alienate the land, except with the sanction of the Governor in Council ; and provisos to such effect shall be inserted in the letters patent conveying the land to the said Indian, and in such cases compliance with the provisions of sections thirty-eight and thirty-nine of this Act shall not be necessary. 47 V., c. 27, s. 17.

88. Every such Indian shall, before the issue of such letters patent, declare to the Superintendent General the name and surname by which he wishes to be enfranchised and thereafter known, and on his receiving such letters patent, in such name and surname, he shall be held to be also enfranchised, and he shall thereafter be known by such name or surname; and if such Indian is a married man, his wife and minor unmarried children shall also be held to be enfranchised; and from the date of such letters patent the provisions of this Act and of any Act or law making any distinction between the legal rights, privileges, disabilities and liabilities of Indians and those of Her Majesty's other subjects, shall cease to apply to such Indian, or to the wife or minor unmarried children of such Indian as aforesaid, so declared to be enfranchised, who shall no longer be deemed Indians within the meaning of the laws relating to Indians, except in so far as regards their right to participate in the annuities and interest moneys, and rents and councils of the band to which they belonged :

2. Any children of a probationary Indian, who, being minors and unmarried when the probationary ticket was granted to such Indian, arrive at the full age of twenty one years before the letters patent are issued to such Indian, may, at the discretion of the Governor in Council, receive letters patent in their own names, subject to the same restrictions and reservations as are contained in the letters patent issued to their parent, for their respective shares of the land allotted under the said ticket, at the same time that letters patent are granted to their parent :

3. If any Indian child who arrives at the full age of twenty-one years, during his or her parent's probationary period, is not qualified for enfranchisement, or if any child of such parent, who was a minor at the commencement of such period, is married during such period, a quantity of land equal to the share of such child shall be deducted, in such manner as the Superintendent General directs, from the allotment made to such Indian parent on receiving his probationary ticket. 43 V., c. 28, s. 101 ;-47 V., c. 27, s. 18.

4. The Indian Act is hereby amended by adding the following section thereto, immediately after section eighty-eight :-

88A. Whenever any member of a band, for three years Indian's of immediately succeeding the date on which he was granted letters patent, or for any longer period that the superintendent general deems necessary, by his exemplary good conduct and management of property proves that he is qualified to receive his share of the moneys of such band, the Governor in Council may, on the report of the superintendent general to that effect, order that the said Indian be paid his share of the capital funds at the credit of the band, or his share of the principal of the annuities of the band, estimated as yielding five per cent, out of such moneys as are provided for the purpose by Parliament :

" 2. If such Indian is a married man he shall also be paid his wife's and minor unmarried children's shares of such funds and principal moneys, and if such Indian is a widow, she shall also be paid her minor unmarried children's shares :

"8. The unmarried children of such married Indians who become of age during the probationary period, for payment of such moneys, if qualified by the character for integrity, morality and sobriety which they bear, shall receive their own share of such moneys, when their parents are paid ; and if not so qualified, before they receive payment of such moneys they must themselves pass through the probationary period :

" 4. All such Indians, and their unmarried minor children, who are paid their shares of the principal moneys of their band, as aforesaid, shall thenceforward cease, in every respect, to be Indians of any class within the meaning of this Act, or Indians within the meaning of any other Act or law."

89. If any probationary Indian fails in qualifying to become enfranchised, or dies before the expiration of the required probation, his claim, or the claim of his heirs, to the laud for which a probationary ticket was granted, or the claim of any unqualified Indian, or of any Indian who marries during his or her parent's probationary period, to the land deducted, under the operation of the next preceding section, from his or her parent's probationary allotment, shall, in all respects, be the same as that conferred by an ordinary location ticket under this Act. 43 Y.. c. 28, s. 102.

90. The children of any widow who becomes either a probationary or enfranchised Indian shall be entitled to the same privileges as those of a male head of a family in like circumstances. 43 V., c. 28, s. 103.

91. In allotting land to probationary Indians, the quantity to be allotted to the head of a family shall be in proportion. to the number of such family, compared with the total quantity of land in the reserve, and the whole number of the band : but the Superintendent General may determine what quantity shall be allotted to each member for enfranchisement purposes, provided that each -female of any age, and each male under fourteen years of age, shall receive at one-half the quantity allotted to each male of fourteen years of age and over. 43 V., c. 28,s 194; - 47 V., c. 27, s19.

92. Every Indian who is not a member of the band, and every non-treaty Indian, who, with the consent of the band but and the approval of the Superintendent General, has been permitted to reside upon the reserve, or to obtain a location thereon, may, on being assigned a suitable allotment of land by the Superintendent General for enfranchisement, become enfranchised on the same terms and conditions as a member of the band ; and such enfranchisement shall confer upon such Indian the same legal rights and privileges, and make such Indian subject to such disabilities and liabilities as after her Majesty's other subjects; but such enfranchisement shall not confer upon such Indian any right to participate in the annuities, interest moneys, rents or councils of the band. 43 V., c. 28, s. 105 47 V., c. 27, s. 20.

93. If any band, at a council summoned for the purpose according to their rules, and held in the

presence of the Superintendent General, or an agent duly authorized by him to attend such council, decides to allow every member of the band who chooses, and who is found qualified, to become enfranchised, and to receive his or her share of the principal moneys of the band, and sets apart for such member a suitable allotment of land for the purpose, any applicant belonging to such band, after such a decision, may be dealt with as provided in the foregoing provisions respecting enfranchisement, until his or her enfranchisement is attained ; and whenever any member of the band, who, for the three years immediately succeeding the date on which he was granted letters patent, or for any longer period that the Superintendent General deems necessary, by his exemplary good conduct and management of property proves that he is qualified to receive his share of such moneys, the Governor in Council may, on the report of the Superintendent General to that effect, order that the said Indian be paid his share of the capital funds at the credit of the band, or his share of the principal of the annuities of the band, estimated as yielding five per cent., out of such moneys as are provided for the purpose by Parliament :

2. If such Indian is a married man he shall also be paid his wife's and minor unmarried children's share of such funds and other principal moneys, and if such Indian is a widow, she shall also be paid her minor unmarried children's share : -

3. The unmarried children of such married Indians, who become of age during the probationary period, either for enfranchisement or for payment of such moneys, if qualified by the character for integrity, morality and sobriety which they bear, shall receive their own share of such moneys, when their parents are paid ; and if not so qualified, before they can become enfranchised or receive payment of such moneys they must themselves pass through the probationary periods :

4. All such Indians, and their unmarried minor children who are paid their share of the principal moneys of their band, as aforesaid, shall thenceforward cease, in every respect, to be Indians of any class within the meaning of this Act, or Indians within the meaning of any other Act or law. 48 V., c.28, e. 106.

3. Section ninety-three of The Indian Act is hereby repealed and the following substituted therefor :-

" 93. If any band, at a council summoned for the purpose Provision according to their rules, and held in the presence of the superintendent general, or an agent duly authorized by him to attend such council, decides to allow every member of the band who chooses, and who is found qualified, to become enfranchised, and to receive his or her share of the principal moneys of the band, and sets apart for such member a suitable allotment of land for the purpose, any applicant belonging to such band, or the wife and children of any such applicant, may, after such decision, be dealt with as provided in the foregoing provisions respecting enfranchisement and the payment to enfranchised Indians of their shares of the capital funds at the credit of the hand or of the estimated principal of the annuities of the band to which they are entitled."

OFFENCES AND PENALTIES.

94. Everyone who sells, exchanges with, barters, supplies Or gives to any Indian or non-treaty Indian, any intoxicant, or causes or procures me same to be done, or attempts the same or connives thereat, or opens or keeps, or causes to be opened or kept, on any reserve or special reserve, a tavern, house or

building in which any intoxicant is sold, bartered,-exchanged or given, or who is found in possession of any intoxicant in the house, tent, wigwam or place of abode of any Indian or non-treaty Indian, or of any person, or upon any other part of the reserve or special reserve, or who sells, exchanges with, barters, supplies or gives to any person, on any reserve or special reserve, any intoxicant, shall, on summary conviction before any judge, police magistrate, stipendiary magistrate or two justices of the peace, or Indian agent, upon the evidence of one credible witness, other than the informer or prosecutor,-or in the Province of Manitoba, the Province of British Columbia, the North-West Territories or the District of Keewatin, upon the evidence of the informer alone, if he is a credible person,-be liable to imprisonment for a term not exceeding six months and not less than one month, with or without hard labor, or to a penalty not exceeding three hundred dollars and not less than fifty dollars, with costs of prosecution, a moiety of which penalty shall belong to the informer or prosecutor, and the other moiety whereof shall belong to Her Majesty, to form part of the fund for the benefit of that body of Indians or non-treaty Indians, with respect to one or more members of which the' offence was committed, or he shall liable to both penalty and imprisonment in the discretion of the convicting judge, magistrate, or justices of the peace or Indian agent. 43 V., c. 28. s. 90, part ;-44 V., c.17, s. 10 ;-45 V., c. 30. s. 3.

4. Section ninety-four of the said Act is hereby repealed and the following substituted therefor:-
"94. Everyone, who by himself, his clerk, servant or agent, and every one who in the employment or on the premises of another directly or indirectly on any pretence or by any device sells barters, supplies or gives to any Indian or nontreaty Indian any intoxicant, or causes procures the same to be done or attempts the same or connives thereat, or opens or keeps, or causes to be opened or kept on any reserve or special reserve, a tavern, house or building in which any intoxicant is sold, bartered, supplied or given, or who is found in possession of any intoxicant in the house, tent, wigwam or place of abode of any Indian or non-treaty Indian or of any person, or upon any other part of the reserve or special reserve, or who sells, barters, supplies or gives to any person on any reserve or special reserve any intoxicant, shall, on summary conviction before any judge, police magistrate, stipendiary magistrate or two justices of the peace or Indian agent, upon the evidence of one credible witness other than the informer or prosecutor -or in the Province of Manitoba, the Province of British Columbia, the North-West Territories or the District of Keewatin, upon the evidence of the informer alone if he is a credible person-be liable to imprisonment for a term not exceeding six months and not less than one month, with or without hard labor, or to a penalty not exceeding three hundred dollars and not less than fifty dollars with costs of prosecution, or he shall be liable to both penalty and imprisonment in the discretion of the convicting judge, magistrate, stipendiary magistrate, justices of the peace or Indian agent ; and a moiety of every such penalty shall belong to the informer or prosecutor, and the other moiety thereof shall belong to Her Majesty to form part of the fund for the benefit of that body of Indians or non-treaty Indians with respect to one or more members of which the offence was committed."
6. The section substituted for section ninety-four of The Indian Act by section four of chapter twenty-two of the Statutes of 1888, is hereby amended by adding thereto the following subsection :-

" 2. In this section the expression 'Indian,' in addition to its ordinary signification as defined in section two of this Act, shall extend to and include any person, male or female, who is reputed to belong to a particular band, or who follows the Indian mode of life, or any child of such person."

95. The commander or person in charge of any steamer or other vessel, or boat, from or on board of which any intoxicant has been sold, bartered, exchanged, supplied or given to any Indian or non-treaty Indian, shall, on summary conviction before any judge, police magistrate, stipendiary magistrate or justice of the peace, or Indian agent, upon the evidence of one credible witness, other than the informer or prosecutor.-or in the Province of Manitoba, the Province of British Columbia, the North-West Territories or the District of Keewatin. Upon the evidence of the informer alone, if he is a credible person,-be liable to a penalty not exceeding three hundred dollars and not less than fifty dollars for each offence, with costs of prosecution,-which penalty shall be applied as provided in the next preceding section ; and in default of immediate payment of such penalty and costs, any person so convicted shall be committed to any common gaol, house of correction, lock-up or other place of confinement by the judge, magistrate or two justices of the peace, or Indian agent, before whom the conviction has taken place, for a term not exceeding six months and not less than one month, with or without hard labor, or until such penalty and costs are paid. 43 V., c. 28, s. 90, part.

96. Every Indian or non-treaty Indian who makes or manufactures any intoxicant, or who has in his possession, or concealed, or who sells, exchanges with, barters, supplies or gives to any other Indian or non-treaty Indian, any intoxicant, shall, on summary conviction before any judge, police magistrate, stipendiary magistrate or two justices of the peace, or Indian agent, upon the evidence of one credible witness, other than the informer or prosecutor.-or in the Province of Manitoba, the Province of British Columbia, the North-West Territories or the District of Keewatin, upon the evidence of the informer alone, if he is a credible person,-be liable to imprisonment for a term not exceeding six months and not less than one month, with or without hard labor, or to a penalty not exceeding one hundred dollars and not less than twenty-five dollars, or to both penalty and imprisonment, in the discretion of the convicting judge, magistrate, or justices of the peace or Indian agent. 43 V., c. 28, s. 90, part.

97. In all cases arising under the three sections next preceding, Indians or non-treaty Indians shall be competent witnesses. 43 Y.. c. 28, s. 90, part.

98. No penalty shall be incurred when the intoxicant is Made use of in case of sickness under the sanction of a medical man or under the directions of a minister of religion 43 V., c. 28, s. 90, part.

8. Section ninety-eight of the said Act is hereby amended by adding the following words at the end thereof : " And the burden of proof that the intoxicant has been so made use of shall be on the accused."

99. Everyone who gives or supplies an intoxicant to an Indian or non-treaty Indian on an order, verbal or written. shall he liable to all the penalties to which he would have been liable if he had sold the same without sue order ; and every person found drunk in the bouse, tent, wigwam or other domicile of an Indian, or gambling therein, and every person found within an Indian village, settlement or reserve after sunset, and who refuses to leave after having been requested so to do by an Indian

agent or chief, shall be liable to all the fines and penalties to which he would have been liable if he had supplied intoxicants to Indians, and under similar process. 47 V., c. 27, 6.13.

7. Section ninety-nine of The Indian Act is hereby repealed and the following substituted therefor :-

" 99. Any constable or peace officer may arrest without warrant any person or Indian found gambling, or drunk, or with intoxicants in his possession, on any part of a reserve, and may detain him until he can be brought before a justice of the peace, and such person or Indian shall be liable upon summary conviction to imprisonment for a term not exceeding three months or to a penalty not exceeding fifty dollars ana not less than ten dollars, with costs of prosecution, half of which penalty shall belong to the informer."

100. The keg, barrel, case, box, package or receptacle from Keg any intoxicant has been sold, exchanged, bartered, supplied or given, as well that in which the original supply was contained as the vessel wherein any portion of such original supply was supplied as aforesaid, and the remainder of the contents thereof, if such barrel, keg, case, box, package, receptacle or vessel aforesaid, respectively, can be identified, -and any intoxicant imported, manufactured or brought into and upon any reserve or special reserve, or into the house, tent, wigwam or place of abode, or on the person of any Indian or non-treaty Indian, or suspected to be upon any reserve or special reserve, may, upon a search warrant in that behalf being granted by any judge, police magistrate, stipendiary magistrate or justice of the peace be searched, and if found, seized by any Indian superintendent, agent or bailiff, or other officer connected with the Indian Department, or by any constable, wheresoever found on such land or in such place or on the person of such Indian or nontreaty Indian; and on complaint before any judge, police magistrate, stipendiary magistrate, justice of the peace or Indian agent, he may, on the evidence of any credible witness that, this Act has been violated in respect thereof declare the same forfeited, and cause the same to be forthwith destroyed; and may condemn the Indian or person in whose possession the same is found to pay a penalty not exceeding one hundred dollars and not less than fifty dollars, and the costs of prosecution :

2. A moiety of such penalty shall belong to the prosecutor and the other moiety to Her Majesty, for the purposes hereinbefore mentioned ; and in default of immediate payment, the offender may be committed to any common gaol. House of correction, lock-up or other place of confinement, with or without hard labor, for any term not exceeding six months, and not less than two months, unless such penalty and costs are sooner paid. 43 V., c. 28, s. 01 ;-44 V.. c. 17. s. 11 :-45 V. c. 00, s. 3.

101. If it is proved before any judge, police magistrate. stipendiary magistrate or two justices of the peace, or Indian agent, that any vessel, boat, canoe or conveyance of any description, upon the sea or sea coast, or upon any river, lake or stream, is employed in carrying any intoxicant, to be supplied to Indians or non-treaty Indians, such vessel, boat, canoe or conveyance so employed may he seized and declared forfeited, as in the next, preceding section mentioned, and sold, and the proceeds thereof paid to Her Majesty for the purposes hereinbefore mentioned. 43 V., c. 28, s. 92;- 4-5 V., c. 30, s. 3.

102. Every article, chattel, commodity' or thing in the purchase, acquisition, exchange, trade or barter of which, in violation of this Act, the consideration, either wholly or in part, is an intoxicant, is forfeited to Her Majesty and may be seized, as is hereinbefore provided in respect to any receptacle

of any intoxicant, and may be sold, and the proceeds thereof paid to Her Majesty, for the purposes hereinbefore mentioned 4-3 V., c. 28, s. 93.

103. No one shall introduce any intoxicant at any council or meeting of Indians held for the purpose of discussing or of assenting to a release or surrender of a reserve or portion thereof, or for the purpose of assenting to the issuing of a timber or other license ; and every person who introduces, at such meeting, and every agent or officer employed by the Superintendent General, or by the Governor in Council, who introduces, allows or countenances by his presence, the use of such intoxicant among such Indians, a week before, or at, or a week after, any such council or meeting, shall incur a penalty of two hundred dollars, recoverable by action in any court of competent jurisdiction,-a moiety' of which penalty shall belong to the informer. 43 V., c. 28, s. 38.

104. Any' constable may', without process of law, arrest any Indian or non-treaty Indian whom he finds in a state of intoxication, and convey him to any common gaol, house of correction, lock-up or other place of confinement, there to be kept until he is sober; and such Indian or non-treaty Indian shall, when sober, be brought before any judge, police magistrate, stipendiary magistrate, or justice of the peace or Indian agent, and if convicted of being so found in a state of intoxication, shall be liable to imprisonment in any' common gaol, house of correction, lock-up or other place of confinement, for a term not exceeding one month, or to a penalty not exceeding thirty dollars and not less than five dollars, or to both penalty and imprisonment, in the discretion of the convicting judge, magistrate, justice of the peace or Indian agent. 43 V., c. 28, s. 94, part ;-45 V., c. 30, ss. 3 and 5, part.

10. The one hundred and fourth section of the said Act is hereby repealed and the following section substituted therefor :-

" 104. Every Indian who is found in a state of intoxication shall be liable on summary conviction thereof to imprisonment for any term not exceeding one month or to a penalty not exceeding thirty dollars and not less than five dollars, or to both penalty and imprisonment, in the discretion of the convicting judge, magistrate, justice of the peace or Indian agent."

" 2 Any constable or other peace officer may, without warrant, arrest any Indian or non-treaty Indian found in a state of intoxication, and convey him to any common gaol house of correction, lockup or other place of confinement, there to be kept until he is sober ; and such Indian or nontreaty Indian shall, when sober, be brought for trial before any judge, police magistrate, stipendiary magistrate, or justice of the peace or Indian agent.

105. If any Indian or non-treaty Indian who has been So convicted, refuses, upon examination, to state or give information of the person, place and time from whom, where and when he procured such intoxicant, and if from any other Indian or non-treaty Indian, then, if within his knowledge, from whom, where and when such intoxicant was originally procured or received, he shall be liable to imprisonment. as aforesaid for a further period not exceeding fourteen days, or to an additional penalty not exceeding fifteen dollars and not less than three dollars, or to both penalty and imprisonment, in the discretion of the convicting judge, magistrate, justice of the peace or Indian agent. 43 V., e. 28, s. 94, part 45 V., c. 30, ss. 3 and 5, part.

106. Every person who, being the keeper of any house, tent or wigwam, allows or suffers any Indian woman to be or remain in such house, tent or wigwam, knowing, or having probable cause for be-

lieving, that such Indian woman is in or remains in such house, tent or wigwam, with the intention of prostituting herself therein, is guilty of an offence against this Act, and shall, on summary conviction before any stipendiary' magistrate, police magistrate, justice of the peace or Indian agent, be liable to a penalty not exceeding one hundred dollars and not less than ten dollars, or to imprisonment in any gaol or place of confinement for a term not exceeding six months :

2. Every Indian who keeps, frequents, or is found in a disorderly house, tent or wigwam used for such a purpose as aforesaid, shall be liable to the same penalty and on similar process. 43 V., c. 28, s. 95 ;-45 V., c. 30. s. 3 ;-47 Y., e. 27, s. 14.

11.Sub-section one of the one hundred and sixth section of the said Act is hereby repealed and the following sub-section substituted therefor :-

106. Every person and Indian who, being the keeper of any house, tent or wigwam, allows or suffers any Indian woman to be or remain in such house, tent or wigwam, knowing, or having probable cause for believing, that such Indian woman is in or remains in such house, tent or wigwam, with the intention of prostituting herself therein, or who, being an Indian woman, prostitutes herself therein, is guilty of an offence against this Act, and shall, on summary conviction before any stipendiary magistrate, police magistrate, justice of the peace or Indian agent, be liable to a penalty not exceeding one hundred dollars and not less than ten dollars, or to imprisonment in any gaol or place of confinement for a term not exceeding six months. "

107. Every person who appears, acts or behaves as master or mistress, or as the person who has the care or management of any house, tent or wigwam, in which any Indian woman is, or remains, for the purpose of prostituting herself therein, shall be deemed and taken to be the keeper thereof, notwithstanding he or she is not in fact the real keeper thereof. 43 V., c. 28, s. 96.

108. No appeal shall lie from any conviction under the fourteen sections next preceding, except to a judge of a superior court, county, circuit or district court, or to the chairman or judge of the court of the sessions of the peace, preceding having jurisdiction where the conviction was had ; and such appeal shall be heard, tried and adjudicated upon by such .judge or chairman without the intervention of a jury : and no such appeal shall be brought after the expiration of thirty days from the conviction:

2. No such conviction shall be quashed for want of form or be removed by certiorari into any superior court ; and no warrant of commitment shall be held void by reason of any defect therein, if it is therein alleged that the person has been convicted, and if there is a good and valid conviction to sustain the same. 43 V.. e. 28, s. 97 ;-47 V.. e. 27, s. 15.

109. Every agent who knowingly and falsely informs, or causes to be informed, any person applying to him to purchase any land within his division and agency, that the same has already been purchased, or who refuses to permit the person so applying to purchase the same according to existing regulations, shall be liable therefor to the person so applying, in the sum of five dollars for each acre of land which the person so applying offered to purchase, recoverable by action of debt in any court of competent jurisdiction. 43 Y., c. 28, s. 54.

110. No agent for the sale of Indian lands shall, within his division, directly or indirectly, except under an order of the Governor in Council, purchase any land which he is appointed to sell, or become

proprietor of or interested in any such land, during the time of his agency ; and every such purchase or interest shall be void :

2. Every such agent who so offends shall forfeit his office and incur a penalty of four hundred dollars for every such offence, recoverable in an action of debt by any person who sues for the same. 43 V., c. 28, s. 41.

111. Everyone who induces, incites or stirs up any three or more Indians, non-treaty Indians, or half-breeds apparently acting in concert-

(a) To make any request or demand of any agent or servant of the Government in a riotous, riotous, disorderly or threatening manner, or in a manner calculated to cause a breach of the peace ; or-

(b) To do any act calculated to cause a breach of the peace, -is guilty of a misdemeanor, and liable to imprisonment for a term not exceeding two years. 47 V., c. 27, s. 1.

112. Everyone who incites any Indian to commit any indictable offence is guilty of felony and liable to imprisonment for any term not exceeding five years. C. S. U. C., c. 128, s. 104.

113. The Superintendent General may, when he considers it in the public interest so to do, prohibit, by public notice to that effect, the sale, gift, or other disposal, to any Indian in the Province of Manitoba or in any' part thereof, or in the North-West Territories or in any part thereof, of any fixed ammunition or ball cartridge ; and every person who, after such notice, without the permission in writing of the Superintendent General, sells or gives, or in any other manner conveys to any Indian, in the section of country thus prohibited, any fixed ammunition or ball cartridge, shall incur a penalty not exceeding two hundred dollars, or shall be liable to imprisonment for a term not exceeding six months, or to both penalty and imprisonment within the limits aforesaid, at the discretion of the court before which the conviction is had :

2. Every offender against the provisions of this section may be tried in a summary manner by any stipendiary or police magistrate or by any two justices of the peace, or by an Indian agent. 45 V., e. 30, s. 3 ;-47 V., c. 27, s. 2.

114. Every Indian or person who engages in or assists in celebrating the Indian festival known as the "Potlach " or the Indian dance known as the "Tamauawas," is guilty of a misdemeanor, and liable to imprisonment for a term not exceeding six months and not less than two months:

2. Every Indian or person who encourages either directly or indirectly, an Indian to get up such a festival or dance, or to celebrate the same, or who assists in the celebration of the same, is guilty of a like offence, and shall he liable to the same punishment. 47 V., c. 27, s. 3.

6. Section one hundred and fourteen of The Indian Act is hereby repealed and the following substituted therefor:---

"114. Every Indian or other person who engages in, or assists in celebrating or encourages either directly or indirectly another to celebrate, any Indian festival, dance or other ceremony of which the giving away or paying or giving back of money, goods or articles of any sort forms a part, or is a feature, whether such gift of money, goods or articles takes place before, at, or after the celebration of the same, and every Indian or other person who engages or assists in any celebration or dance of which the wounding or mutilation of the dead or living body of any human being or animal forms a part or is a feature, is guilty of an indictable offence and is liable to imprisonment for a term not exceeding six months and not less than two months ; but nothing in this section shall be construed to prevent the holding of any agricultural show or exhibition or the giving of prizes for exhibits thereat."

115. Any judge of a court, judge of sessions of the peace, recorder, police magistrate or stipendiary magistrate, shall have full power to do alone whatever is authorized by this Act to be done by a justice of the peace or by two justices of the peace. 44 V., c. 17. s. 6.

116. Any recorder, police magistrate or stipendiary magistrate, appointed for or having jurisdiction to act in any city or town shall, with respect to offences and matters under this Act, have and exercise jurisdiction over the whole country or union of counties or judicial district in which the city or town for which he' has been appointed or in which he has jurisdiction is situate. 44 V., c. 17. s. 7.

117. Every Indian agent shall be ex officio a justice of the peace for the purposes of this Act, and shall have the power and authority of two justices of the peace, with jurisdiction wheresoever any violation of the provisions of this Act occurs,- or wheresoever it is considered by him most conducive to the ends of justice that any violation aforesaid shall be tried. 44 Y., c. 17, s. 12;-4-5 Y., c. 30, s. 3 ;- 47 V., c. 27, ss. 22 and 23.

9. Section one hundred and seventeen of the said Act is hereby repealed, and the following substituted therefor:--

"117. Every Indian agent shall be ex officio a justice of the peace for the purposes of this Act and shall have the power and authority of two justices of the peace, with jurisdiction wheresoever any violation of the provisions of this Act occurs, and in all cases of infraction, by Indians, of any of the provisions of chapter one hundred and fifty-seven of the Revised Statutes, intituled "An Act respecting Offences against Public Morals and Public Convenience," or wheresoever it is considered by him most conducive to the ends of justice that any violation aforesaid shall be tried."

8. The section substituted for section one hundred and seventeen of The Indian Act by section nine of chapter twenty-nine of the Statutes of 1890, is hereby repealed and the following substituted therefor :-

" 117. Every Indian agent shall, for all the purposes of this Act, or of any other Act respecting Indians, and with respect to any offence against the provisions thereof or against the provisions of section ninety-eight or section one hundred and ninety of The Criminal Code, 1892, and with respect to any offence by an Indian against any of the provisions of part XIII. Of the said Code, be ex officio a justice of the peace, and have the power and authority of two justices of the peace, anywhere within the territorial limits of his jurisdiction as a justice, as defined in his appointment or otherwise defined by the Governor in Council, whether the Indian or Indians charged with or in any way concerned in or affected by the offence, matter or thing to be tried, investigated or dealt with, are or are not within his ordinary jurisdiction, charge or supervision as an Indian agent.

" 2. In the North-west Territories and the provinces of Manitoba and British Columbia every Indian agent shall for all such purposes and with respect to any such offence be ex officio a justice of the peace and have the power and authority of two justices of the peace anywhere in the said Territories or provinces within which his agency is situated, whether or not the territorial limits of his jurisdiction as a justice, as defined in his appointment or otherwise defined as aforesaid, extend to the place where he may have occasion to act as such justice or to exercise such power or authority, and whether the Indians charged with or in any way concerned in or affected by the offence, matter or thing to be tried, investigated or otherwise dealt with, are or are not within his ordinary jurisdiction, charge or supervision as Indian agent."

7. Section one hundred and seventeen of The Indian Act as enacted by section eight of chapter thirty-two of the Statutes of 1894, is hereby repealed, and in lieu thereof it is hereby enacted that every Indian' agent shall, for all the purposes of The Indian Act or of any other Act respecting Indians, and with respect to any offence against the provisions thereof or against the provisions of section ninety-eight or section one hundred and ninety of The Criminal Code, 1892, and with respect to any offence by an Indian or non-treaty Indian against any of the provisions of parts XIII. and XV. of the said Code, be ex officio a justice of the peace, and have the power and authority of two justices of the peace, anywhere within the territorial limits of his jurisdiction as a justice, as defined in his appointment or otherwise defined by the Governor in Council, whether the Indian or non-treaty Indian charged with or in any way concerned in or affected by the offence, matter or thing to be tried, investigated or dealt with, is or is not within his ordinary jurisdiction, charge or supervision as an Indian agent.

"2. In the North-west Territories and the provinces of Manitoba and British Columbia every Indian agent shall for all such purposes and with respect to any such offence be ex officio a justice of the peace and have the power and authority British Co- 0f two justices of the peace anywhere in the said territories or provinces, whether or not the territorial limits of his jurisdiction as a justice, as defined in his appointment or otherwise defined as aforesaid, extend to the place where he may have occasion to act as such justice or to exercise such power or authority, and whether the Indians charged with or in any way concerned in or affected by the offence, matter or thing to be tried, investigated or otherwise dealt with, are or are not within his ordinary jurisdiction, charge or supervision as Indian agent."

118. If any Indian is convicted of any crime punishable by imprisonment in a penitentiary or other place of confinement, the costs incurred m procuring such conviction, and in carrying out the various sentences recorded, may be defrayed by the Superintendent General, and paid out of any annuity or interest coming to such Indian, or to the band. As the case may be. 48 V.. c. 28, s. 82 ;-47 V., c. 27. s. 12.

119. Whenever in this Act in which it is provided that the conviction shall take place, on the evidence of one credible witness other than the informer or prosecutor, the informer or prosecutor shall, nevertheless, be allowed to give evidence. 44 Y., c. 17, s. 13.

120. Upon any inquest, or upon any inquiry into any Matter involving a criminal charge, or upon the trial of any crime or offence whatsoever or by whomsoever committed, any court, judge, police or stipendiary magistrate, recorder, coroner, justice of the peace or Indian agent, may receive the evidence of any Indian or non-treaty Indian, who is destitute of the knowledge of God or of any fixed and clear belief in religion, or in a future slate of rewards and punishments, without administering the usual form of oath to any such Indian or non-treaty Indian, as aforesaid, upon his solemn affir-

mation or declaration to tell the truth, the whole truth and nothing hut the truth, or in such form as is approved by such court, judge, magistrate, recorder, coroner, justice of the peace or Indian agent, as most binding on the conscience of such Indian or non-treaty Indian. 43 V., c. 28, s. 8-5 ;-45 V., c. 30, s. 3, part.

121. In the case of any inquest, or upon any inquiry into any matter involving a criminal charge, or upon the trial of any crime or offence whatsoever, the substance of the evidence or information of any such Indian or nontreaty Indian, as aforesaid, shall be reduced to writing and signed by the Indian (by mark if necessary), giving the same, and verified by the signature or mark of the person acting as interpreter, if any, and by the signature of the judge, magistrate, recorder, coroner, justice of the peace, Indian agent or person before whom such evidence or information is given. 43 V., c. 28, s. 86 ;-45 V., c. 30, s. 3.

122. The court, judge, magistrate, recorder, coroner, justice of the peace or Indian agent shall, before taking any such evidence, information or examination, caution every such Indian or non-treaty Indian, as aforesaid, that he will be liable to incur punishment if he does not tell the truth, the whole truth and nothing but the truth. 43 V., c. 28, s. 87 ;-4-5 V., c. 30, s. 3.

123. The written declaration or examination so made, taken and verified of any such Indian or non-treaty Indian, as aforesaid, may be lawfully read and received as evidence upon the trial of any criminal proceeding, when under the like circumstances the written affidavit, examination, deposition or confession of any person might be lawfully read and received as evidence. 43 V., c. 28, s. 88.

124. Every solemn affirmation or declaration, in whatsoever form made or taken, by any Indian or non-treaty Indian, Indian as aforesaid, shall be of the same force and effect as if such Indian or non-treaty Indian had taken an oath in the usual form. 43 V., c. 28, s. 89, part.

125. No prosecution, conviction or commitment under this Act shall be invalid for want of form, so long as the same is according to the true meaning of this Act. 43 V., c. 28, s. 98.

GENERAL PROVISIONS.

126. No Indian or non-treaty Indian, resident in the Province of Manitoba, the North-West Territories or the District of Keewatin, shall be held capable of having acquired or of acquiring a homestead or pre-emption right to a quarter section, or any portion of land in any surveyed or unsurvey lands in the Province of Manitoba, the North-West Territories or in the District of Keewatin, or the right to share in the distribution of any lands allotted to half-breeds, subject to the following exceptions :-

(a.) He shall not be disturbed in the occupation of any plot on which he has permanent improvements prior to his becoming a party to any treaty with the Crown ;

(b.) Nothing in this section shall prevent the Superintendent General, if found desirable, from compensating any Indian for his improvements on such a plot of land, without obtaining a formal surrender thereof from the band ;

(c.) Nothing in this section shall apply to any person who withdrew from any Indian treaty prior to the first day of October, in the year one thousand eight hundred and seventy four. 43 V., c. 28, s. 81.

127. At the election of a chief or chiefs, or at the granting of any ordinary consent required of a band under this Act. those entitled to vote at the council or meeting thereof shall be the male members

of the baud, of the full age of twenty-one years ; and the vote of a majority of such members, at a council or meeting of the band summoned according to its rules, and held in the presence of the Superintendent General, or of an agent acting under his instructions, shall be sufficient to determine such election or gran: such consent 43 V., c. 28, s. 73, part.

128. If any band has a council of chiefs or councillors any ordinary consent required of the band may be granted by a vote of a majority of such chiefs or councillors, at a council summoned according to its rules, and held in the presence of the Superintendent General or his agent. 43 V. c. 28, s. 73, part.

129. All affidavits required under this Act or intended to be used m reference to any claim, business or transaction in connection with Indian affairs, may be taken before the judge or clerk of any county or circuit court, or any justice of the peace, or any commissioner for taking affidavits in any court, or the Superintendent General, or the deputy of the Superintendent General, or any inspector of Indian agencies, or any Indian agent, or any surveyor duly licensed and sworn, appointed by the Superintendent General to inquire into, or to take evidence, or report in any matter submitted to or pending before the Superintendent General, or if made out of Canada, before the mayor or chief magistrate of, or the British consul in, any city, town or municipality, or before any notary public. 43 V., c. 28, s. 108, part.

130. Copies of any records, documents, books or papers belonging to or deposited in the department, attested under the signature of the Superintendent General, or of the deputy of the Superintendent General, shall be evidence in all cases in which the original records, documents, hooks or papers would be evidence. 43 V., e. 28, s. 109.

131. All regulations made under this Act shall be published in the Canada Gazette. 44 V., c. 17, s. 1, part.

5. The said Act is hereby amended by adding the following section thereto :-

"132. Notwithstanding anything contained in this Act The governor in Council may, from time to time direct that any fine penalty or forfeiture or any portion thereof which would otherwise belong to the Crown for the public uses of Canada, or be paid to the Minister of Finance and Receiver General for the use of any band of Indians or which would belong to Her Majesty to form part of the fund for anybody of Indians or non-treaty Indians, or which is ordered to be disposed of in any particular manner, be paid to any Provincial, municipal or local authority."

9. Section one hundred and thirty-two, as added to Indian Act by section five of chapter twenty-two of the Statutes of 1888, is hereby repealed and the following substituted therefor:-

"132. Every fine, penalty or forfeiture under this Act, except so much thereof as is payable to an informer or person suing therefore, shall belong to Her Majesty for the benefit of the band of Indians with respect to which or to one or more members of which the offence was committed, or to which the offender if an Indian belongs; but the Governor General in Council may from time to time direct that the same be paid to any provisional, municipal or local authority which wholly in part bears the expense of administering the law under which such fine, penalty or forfeiture is imposed, or that the same be applied in any other manner deemed best adapted to attain the objects of such law or to secure its due administration ; and may in case of doubt decide what band is entitled to the benefit of any such fine, penalty or forfeiture."

10. The said Act is hereby amended by adding the following sections thereto :-

" 133. The Superintendent General may, from time to time, by public notice, declare that, on and after a day therein named, the laws respecting game in force in the Province of Manitoba, or the Western Territories, or respecting such game as is specified in such notice, shall apply to Indians within the said Province or Territories, as the case may be, or to Indians in such parts thereof as to him seems expedient."

" 134. No official or employee connected with the inside or outside service of the Department of Indian Affairs, and no missionary in the employ of any religious denomination, or otherwise employed in mission work among Indians, and no school teacher on an Indian reserve, shall trade with any Indian, or sell to him, directly or indirectly, any goods or supplies, cattle or other animals :

" 2. In Manitoba and the North-West- Territories no person or persons shall be allowed, on an Indian reserve, to barter, directly or indirectly, with any Indian, or sell to him any goods or supplies, cattle or other animals, without the special license in writing of the Superintendent General,-which license he may at any time revoke :

" 3. Every offender against the provisions of this section shall be liable to a fine equal in amount to double the sum received for the goods, supplies, cattle or other animals sold, and in addition to the costs of prosecution before a police magistrate, a stipendiary magistrate, a justice of the peace or the Indian agent for the locality where the offence occurs ; and the evidence of the Indian to whom the sale was made, and the production to, or view by, the magistrate or Indian agent of the article or animal sold, shall be sufficient evidence on which to convict."

10. Subsection one of section one hundred and thirty-four added to The Indian Act by section ten of chapter twenty- nine of the Statutes of 1890, is hereby amended by inserting after the word "shall," in the fifth line thereof, the following words: "without the special license, in writing, of the Superintendent General of Indian Affairs, which license he may at any time revoke."

133. Any offender sentenced by a magistrate or Indian agent, under any provision of this Act or of any amendment thereof, to the payment of a penalty or of costs, or of both, shall, in default of payment, be liable to imprisonment, notwithstanding that such provision does not expressly authorize such imprisonment to be imposed in the event of non-payment of the penalty ; but the term of such imprisonment shall not exceed that to which the offender may be sentenced for the offence."

4. The said Act is hereby further amended by adding the following section thereto :-

" 136. Where shooting privileges over a reserve or part of a reserve, or fishing privileges in any marsh, pond, river, stream or creek, upon or running through a reserve, have, with the consent of the Indians of the band, been leased or granted to any person, it shall not be lawful for any person not under such lease or grant entitled so to do, or for any Indian other than an Indian of the band, to hunt, shoot, kill or destroy any game animals or birds, or to fish for, take, catch or kill any fish to which such exclusive privilege extends, upon the reserve or part of a reserve, or in any marsh, pond, river, stream or creek covered by such lease or grant ; and any person or Indian acting in contravention of this section shall, in addition to any other penalty or liability thereby incurred, be liable, on summary conviction, for every such offence to a penalty not exceeding ten dollars and not less than five dollars, and, in default of payment, to imprisonment for any term not exceeding one month."

11. The Indian Act is hereby amended by adding the following sections thereto :-

"137. The Governor in Council may make regulations, either general or affecting the Indiana of any province or of any named band, to secure the compulsory attendance of children at school.

" 2. Such regulations, in addition to any other provisions deemed expedient, may provide for the arrest and conveyance to school, and detention there, of truant children and of children who are prevented by their parents or guardians from attending: and such regulations may provide for the punishment, upon summary conviction, by fine or imprisonment, or both, of parents and guardians, or persons having the charge of children, who fail, refuse or neglect to cause such children to attend school."

" 138. The Governor in Council may establish an industrial school or a boarding school for Indians, or may declare any existing Indian school to be such industrial school or boarding school for the purposes of this section.

" 2. The Governor in Council may make regulations, which shall have the force of law, for the committal by justices or Indian agents of children of Indian blood under the age of sixteen years, to such industrial school or boarding school, there to be kept, cared for and educated for a period not extending beyond the time at which such children shall reach the age of eighteen years.

"3. Such regulations may provide, in such manner as to the Governor in Council seems best, for the application of the annuities and interest moneys of children committed to such industrial school or boarding school, to the maintenance of such schools respectively, or to the maintenance of the chil-

"139. The Governor in Council may, with the consent of a band, authorize and direct the expenditure of any capital moneys standing at the credit of such band, in the purchase of land as a reserve for the band or as an addition to its reserve, or in the purchase of cattle for the band, or in the construction of permanent improvements upon the reserve of the band, or such works thereon or in connection therewith as, in his opinion, will be of permanent value to the band, or will, when ; completed, properly represent capital."

8. The Indian Act is hereby amended by adding the following sections thereto :-

" 140. "When by a majority vote of a band, or the council of a band, an Indian of one band is admitted into membership in another band, and his admission thereinto is assented to by the superintendent general, such Indian shall cease to have any interest in the lands or moneys of the band of which he was formerly a member, and shall be entitled to share in the lands and moneys of the band to which he is so admitted ; but the superintendent general may cause to be deducted from the capital of the band of which such Indian was formerly a member his per capita share of such capital and place the same to the credit of the capital of the band into membership in which he had been admitted in the manner aforesaid.

" 141. The Governor in Council may reduce the purchase money due or to become due on sales of Indian lands, or reduce or remit the interest on such purchase money, or reduce the rent at which Indian lands have been leased, when he considers the same to be excessive ; and all such reductions heretofore made are hereby confirmed.

" 2. A return setting forth all the reductions and remissions made under this section during the preceding fiscal year shall be submitted to both Houses of Parliament on or before the twentieth day of July in each year, if Parliament be then sitting, and otherwise within twenty days after the opening of the then ensuing session of Parliament.".

CHAP. 33.
An Act to amend " The Indian Act."
     [Assented to 23rd June, 1887.]
WHEREAS it is expedient to amend the Revised Statutes 0f Canada, chapter forty-three intituled "An Act respecting Indians : " Therefore Her Majesty, by and with the advice and consent of the Senate and House of Commons of Canada, enacts as follows :-

1.Superintendent General, may, from time to time, upon the report of an officer, or other person specially appointed by him to make an inquiry, determine who is or who is not a member of any band of Indians entitled to share in the property and annuities of the band ; and the decision of the Superintendent General in any such matter shall be final and conclusive, subject to an appeal to the Governor in Council.

2. The Superintendent General, his deputy, or other person specially authorized by the Governor in Council, shall have power, by subpoena issued by him, to summon any person before him and to examine such person under oath in respect to any matter affecting Indians, and to compel the production of papers and writings before him relating to such matters ; and if any person duly summoned neglects or refuses to appear at the time and place specified in the subpoena upon such person duly served, or refuses to give evidence or to produce the papers or writings demanded of him, may, by warrant under his hand and seal, cause such person, so refusing or neglecting, to be taken into custody and to be imprisoned in the nearest common gaol, as for contempt of court, for a period not exceeding fourteen days.

12- All regulations made by the Governor in Council under this Act shall be published in the Canada Gazette, and shall be laid before both Houses of Parliament within the first fifteen days of the session next after the date thereof.

The Indian Advancement Act. R.S.C. 1886, c. 44. (49 Vict.)
CHAPTER 44.
The Indian Advancement Act.
HER Majesty, by and with the advice and consent of the Senate and House of Commons of Canada, enacts as follows :-
INTERPRETATION.
1- In this Act, unless the context otherwise requires, the expressions used in this Act shall have the same meaning as the same expressions have in " The Indian Act," but the expression "reserve" in this Act, includes two or more reserves, and the expression " band " includes two or more bands united for the purposes of this Act by the Order in Council applying it. 47 Y., c. 28, s. 2.
APPLICATION OF ACT.
"2. This Act may be made applicable, as hereinafter provided, to any band of Indians in any of the

Provinces, or in the North-West Territories of Canada, or in the District of Keewatin, except in so far as it is herein otherwise provided

2. The. provisions of " The Indian Art " shall continue to apply to every band to which this Act is, from time to time, declared to apply, in so far only as they are not inconsistent with this Act : Provided always, that if it thereafter appears to the Governor in Council that this Act cannot be worked satisfactorily by any band to which it has been declared to apply, the Governor in Council may declare that after a day named in the Order in Council, this Act shall no longer apply to such band, and such band shall thereafter be subject only to " The Indian Act," except that by-laws, rules and regulations theretofore made under this Act. and not inconsistent with the seventy-sixth section of " The Indian Act," shall continue in force until they are repealed by the Governor in Council. 47 V., c. 28, ss. 1 and 13.

GENERAL PROVISIONS.

3. Whenever any band of Indians is declared by the Governor in Council to be considered fit to have this Act applied to them, this Act shall so apply, from the- time appointed in such Order in Council. 47 V., c. 2S, s. 3.

4. Every reserve to which this Act is to apply shall, by the Order in Council applying it, be divided into sections, the number of which shall not exceed six or be less than two, and each section shall have therein a number of male Indians of full age, equal, as nearly as is found convenient, to such proportion of the male Indians of full age resident on the reserve, as one section of the reserve bears to all the sections :

2. The sections shall be distinguished by numbers from one upwards, and the reserve shall be designated in the Order in Council as "The Indian Reserve," inserting such name as is thought proper, and the sections shall be designated by the numbers assigned to them respectively. 47 V., c. 28, s 4.

3. On a day and at a place, and between the hours prescribed in the Order in Council, the male Indians of the full age of twenty-one years, resident on the reserve, hereinafter termed electors, shall meet for the purpose of electing the members of the council of the reserve :

2. One or more members, as provided in such Order in Council to represent each section thereof, shall be elected by the electors resident in such section, and the Indian or Indians, as the case may be, having the votes of the greatest number of electors for each section, shall be the councillor or councillors, as the case may be, therefor, provided he or they are respectively possessed of, and living in, a house in the reserve :

3. The agent for the reserve shall preside at the election, or in his absence some person appointed by him as his deputy, with the consent of the Superintendent General, or some person appointed by the Superintendent General may preside at the said election, and shall take and record the votes of the electors, and may,-subject to appeal to the Superintendent General by or on behalf of any Indian or Indians who deems himself or themselves aggrieved by the action of such agent or deputy, or of such agent or person appointed as aforesaid,-admit or reject the claim of any Indian to be an elector, and may determine who are the councillors for the several sections, and shall report the same to the Superintendent General. 47 V., c. 28, s. 5.

4. In any case of an equality of votes at any such election the agent or person presiding thereat shall

have the casting vote.

6. On a day and at a place, and between the hours prescribed by the Superintendent General, if the day fixed for the same is within eight days from the date at which the councillors were elected, the said councillors shall meet and elect one of their number to act as chief councillor, and the councillor so elected shall be the chief councillor. 47 V., c. 28, s. 6.

7. The councillors shall remain in office until others are elected in their stead, and an election for that purpose shall be held in like manner, at the same place and between the like hours on the like day, in each succeeding year, if it is not a Sunday or holiday, in which case it shall be held on the next day thereafter which is not a Sunday or a holiday

2. If there is a failure to elect on the day appointed for the election, the Superintendent General shall appoint another day on which it shall be held. 47 V., c. 28, s. 7.

8. In the event of a vacancy in the council, by the death or inability to act of any councillor, more than three months before the time for the next election, an election to fill such vacancy shall be held by the agent or his deputy, after such notice to the electors concerned as the Superintendent General directs, at which only the electors of the section represented by the councillor to be replaced shall vote, and to such election the provisions respecting other elections shall apply, so far as they are applicable :

2. If the councillor to be replaced is the chief councillor, then an election of a chief councillor shall be held in the manner already provided, but the day fixed for such election shall be at least one week after the date when the new councillor is elected :

3. Daring the time of any vacancy the remaining councillors shall constitute the council, and they may, in the event of a vacancy in the office, appoint a chief from among them- selves for the time being. 47 V., c. 28, s. 8.

9. The council shall meet for the dispatch of business, at such place on the reserve and at such times as the agent for the reserve appoints, but which shall not exceed twelve times or be less than four times in the year for which it is elected, and due notice of the time and place of each meeting shall be given to each councillor by the agent :

2. At -such meeting the agent for the reserve, or his deputy appointed for the purpose, with the consent of the Superintendent General, shall preside and record the proceedings, and may control and regulate all matters of procedure and form, adjourn the meeting to a time named, or sine die, and report and certify all by-laws and other acts and proceedings of the council to the Superintendent General, to which certificate full faith and credence shall be given in all courts and places whatsoever :

3. He shall address the council and explain and advise them upon their powers and duties, and any matter requiring their consideration, but he shall have no vote question to be decided by the council:

4. Each councillor present shall have a vote on every question to be decided by the council, and such question shall be decided by the majority of votes, the chief councillor voting as a councillor and having also a casting- vote, in case the votes would otherwise be equal:

5. Four councillors shall be a quorum for the dispatch of any business. 47 V., c. 28. s. 9.

10. The council may make by-laws, rules and regulations winch, if approved and confirmed by the Superintendent General, shall have force as law within and with respect to the reserve, and the Indians residing thereon, upon all or any of the following subjects, that is to say :-

(a.) The religious denomination to which the teacher or teachers of the school or schools established on the reserve shall belong, as being that of the majority of the Indians resident on the reserve ; but the Protestant or Roman Catholic minority on the reserve may also have a separate school or schools, with the approval of and under regulations made by the Governor in Council ;
(b.) The care of the public health;
(c.) The observance of order and decorum at elections of councillors, meetings of the council, and assemblies of Indians on other occasions, or generally, on the reserve, by the appointment of constables and erection of lock-up houses, or by the adoption of other legitimate means ;
(d.) The repression of intemperance and profligacy;
(e.) The sub-division of the laud in the reserve, and the distribution of the same amongst the members of the band : also, the setting apart, for common use, of woodland and land for other purposes ;
(f.) The protection of and the prevention of trespass by cattle, sheep, horses, mules and other domesticated animals : and the establishment of pounds, the appointment of pound keepers and the regulation of their duties, fees and charges ;
(g.) The construction and repair of school houses, council houses and other buildings for the use of the Indians on the reserve, and the attendance at school of children between the ages of sis and fifteen years ;
(h.) The construction, maintenance and improvement of roads and bridges, and the contributions, in money or labor, and other duties of residents on the reserve, in respect thereof; and the appointment of road masters and fence viewers, and their powers and duties ;
(i.) The construction and maintenance of water courses. ditches and fences, and the obligations of vicinage, the destruction and repression of noxious weeds and the preservation of the wood on the various holdings, or elsewhere, in the reserve ;
(j.) The removal and punishment of persons trespassing Upon the reserve, or frequenting it for improper purposes :
(k.) The raising of money for any or all of the purposes for which the council may make by-laws, as aforesaid, by assessment and taxation on the lauds of Indians enfranchised, or in possession of lands by location ticket in the reserve, the valuation for assessment being made yearly, in such manner and at such times as are appointed by the by-law in that behalf, and being subject to revision and correction by the agent for the reserve, and in force only after it has been submitted to him and corrected, if, and as he thinks justice requires, and approved by him,-the tax to be imposed for the year in which the by-law is made, and mot to exceed one-half of one per cent, on the assessed value of the land on which it is to be paid ; and if such tax is not paid at the time prescribed by the by-law, the amount thereof, with the addition of one-half of one per cent, thereon, may be paid by the Superintendent General to the treasurer out of the share of the Indian in default in any moneys of the band ; or if such share is insufficient to pay the same, the defaulter shall, for violation of the by-law imposing the

tax, be liable to a penalty equal to the deficiency caused by such default : Provided always, that any Indian deeming himself aggrieved by the decision of the agent, made as hereinbefore provided, may appeal to the Superintendent General, whose decision in the matter shall be final ;

(l.) The appropriation and payment to the local agent, as treasurer, by the Superintendent General, of so much of the moneys of the band as are required for defraying expenses necessary for carrying out the by-laws made by the council, including those incurred for assistance absolutely necessary for enabling the council or the agent to perform the duties assigned to them ;

(m.) The imposition of punishment by penalty or by imprisonment, or by both, for any -violation of or disobedience to any by-law, rule or regulation made under this Act, committed by any Indian of the reserve; but such penalty shall, in no case, except for non-payment of taxes, exceed thirty dollars, nor the imprisonment thirty days ; the proceedings for the imposition of such punishment may be taken before one justice of the peace, under the "Act respecting 'summary proceedings before Justices of the Peace ; " and the amount of any such penalty shall be paid over to the treasurer of the band to which the Indian incurring it belongs, for the use of such band ;

(n.) The amendment, repeal or re-enactment of any such by-law, by a subsequent by-law, made and approved as hereinbefore provided. 47 V., c. 28, s. 10.

11. Every member of a council elected under the provisions of this Act, who is proved to be a habitual drunkard or to be living in immorality, or io have accepted a bribe, or to have been guilty of dishonesty or of malfeasance of office of any kind, shall, on proof of the fact to the satisfaction of the Superintendent General, be disqualified from acting as a member of the council, and shall, on being notified, cease forthwith so to act ; and the vacancy occasioned thereby shall be filled in the manner hereinbefore provided. 47 V., c. 28, s. 11.

12. A copy of any by-law, rule or regulation under this Act, approved by the Superintendent General, and purporting to be certified by the agent for the band to which it relates to be a true copy thereof, shall be evidence of such by-law, rule or regulation, and of such approval, -without proof of the signature of such agent ; and no such by-law, rule or regulation shall be invalidated by any defect of form, if it is substantially consistent with the intent and meaning of this Act. 47 V., c. 28, s. 12.

An Act to amend "The Indian Advancement Act," chapter forty-four of the Revised Statutes'!"
S.C. 1890, c. 30. (53 Vict.)
CHAP. 30
An Act to amend "The Indian Advancement Act," chapter forty-four of the Revised Statutes.
[Assented to 16th May, 1890.]
HER Majesty, by and with the advice and consent of the Senate and House of Commons of Canada, enacts as follows :-

1. Sub-section one of section four of " The Indian Advancement Act," is hereby repealed and the following substituted therefor :-

" 4- Every reserve to which this Act is to apply may, by the Order in Council applying it, be divided into sections, the number of which shall not exceed six or be less than two, and each section shall have therein a number of male Indians of full age, equal, as nearly as is found convenient, to such proportion of the male Indians of full age resident on the reserve, as one section of the reserve bears to all the sections ; or, should the majority of the Indians of the reserve so desire, the whole reserve may form one section,-the wishes of the Indians in respect thereto being first ascertained, in the manner prescribed in " The Indian Act," in like matters, and certified to the Superintendent General by the Indian agent.

2. Paragraph (h) of section ten of the said Act, is hereby repealed, and the following substituted therefor :-

"(h.) The construction, maintenance and improvement of roads and bridges, and the contributions, in money or labor and other duties of residents on the reserve, in respect thereof the size and kind of sleighs to be used on the roads in the winter season, and the manner in which the horse or horses or other beasts of burden shall be harnessed to such sleighs; and the appointment of road masters and fence viewers, and their powers and duties;"

3. The said Act is hereby amended by adding the following section thereto :-

"13- On a day, being one week previous to the day on which the election of the councillors is to be held on any reserve under section five of this Act, and at a place to be appointed by the Indian agent, and between the hours of ten in the forenoon and twelve at noon, a meeting of the electors,- of which meeting due notice shall be given in the manner customary in the band for calling meetings for public purposes-shall be held for the purpose of nominating candidates for election as councillors as aforesaid :

" 2. The Indian agent, or in his absence such person as is appointed by the Superintendent General, or failing such appointment, a chairman to be chosen by the meeting, shall preside over such meeting and shall take and keep the minutes thereof :

" 3. Only Indians nominated at such meeting shall be recognized as, or permitted to become, candidates for election as aforesaid ; and each nomination to be valid must be made on the motion of an elector of the section of the reserve for the representation whereof the nominee is proposed as a candidate, and the motion must be seconded by another elector of that section :

" 4. The nominations of the candidates shall, so far as practicable, be made consecutively and previously to any speeches being made by the movers and seconders or by any other persons, but nominations may be made up to the hour of twelve o'clock noon :

" 5. If only one candidate for any councillorship is proposed, the Indian agent or chairman shall, at twelve o'clock noon, declare such candidate duly elected ; and if two or more candidates are proposed for any councillorship, an election shall be held under the provisions of section five of this Act."

INDIAN ACT. R.S.C. 1906, c. 81.
CHAPTER 81.
An Act respecting Indians.
SHORT TITLE.
1, This Act may be cited as the Indian Act. R.S., c. 43,
INTERPRETATION.
2. In this Act, unless the context otherwise requires,-

(a) 'Superintendent General' means the Superintendent General of Indian Affairs, and 'Deputy Superintendent General' means the Deputy Superintendent General of Indian Affairs;
(b) 'agent' or 'Indian agent' means and includes a com-. missioner, assistant commissioner, superintendent, agent or other officer acting under the instructions of the Superintendent General;
(c) 'person' means an individual other than an Indian;
(d) 'band ' means any tribe, band or body of Indians who own or are interested in a reserve or in Indian lands in common, of which the legal title is vested in the Crown, or who share alike in the distribution of any annuities or interest moneys for which the Government of Canada is responsible; and, when action is being taken by the band as such, means the band in council ;
(e) ' irregular band ' means any tribe, band or body of persons of Indian blood who own no interest in any reserve or lands of which the legal title is vested in the Crown, who possess no common fund managed by the Government of Canada, and who have not had any treaty relations with the Crown ;
(f) ' Indian ' means
(i) any male person of Indian blood reputed to belong to a particular band,
(ii) any child of such person,
(iii) any woman who is or was lawfully married to such person ;
(g) 'non-treaty Indian' means any person of Indian blood who is reputed to belong to an irregular band, or who follows the Indian mode of life, even if such person is only a temporary resident in Canada;

(h) ' enfranchised Indian ' means any Indian, his wife or minor unmarried child, who has received letters patent granting to him .in fee simple any portion of the reserve which has, upon his application for enfranchisement, been allotted to him, or to his wife and minor children, or any unmarried Indian who has received letters patent for an allotment of the reserve;
(i) ' reserve ' means any tract or tracts of land set apart by treaty or otherwise for the use or benefit of or granted to a particular band of Indians, of which the legal title is in the Crown, and which remains so set apart and has not been surrendered to the Crown, and includes all the trees, wood, timber, soil, stone, minerals, metals and other valuables thereon or therein ;
(j) ' special reserve 'means any tract or tracts of land, and everything belonging thereto, set apart for the use or benefit of and held in trust for any band or irregular band of Indians, the title of which is vested in a society, corporation or community legally established, and capable of suing and being sued, or in a person or persons of European descent;
(k) ' Indian lands ' means any reserve or portion of a reserve which has been surrendered to the Crown;
(l) ' intoxicants ' means and includes all spirits, strong waters, spirituous liquors, wines, or fermented or compounded liquors, or intoxicating drink of any kind whatsoever, and any intoxicating liquor or fluid, and opium, and any preparation thereof, whether liquid or solid, and any other intoxicating drug or substance, and tobacco or tea mixed or compounded or impregnated with opium or with other intoxicating drugs, spirits or substances, and whether the same or any of them are liquid or solid;

(m) 'Territories' means the Northwest Territories and the Yukon Territory. R.S., c. 43, s. 2.

PART I.

INDIANS.

Application.

3. The Governor in Council may, by proclamation, from time to time, exempt from the operation of this Part, or from the operation of any one or more of the sections of this Part, Indians or non-treaty Indians, or any of them, or any band or irregular band of them, or the reserves or special reserves, or Indian lands, or any portions of them, in any province or in the Territories, or in any of them ; and may again, by proclamation, from time to time, remove such exemption. R.S., c. 43, s. 3.

Department of Indian Affairs.

4. The Minister of the Interior, or the head of any other department appointed for that purpose by the Governor in Council, shall be the Superintendent General of Indian Affairs, and shall, as such, have the control and management of the lands and property of the Indians in Canada. R.S., c. 43, s. 4.

1. Section four of the Indian Ad, chapter eighty-one of the Revised Statutes of Canada, 1906, is amended by adding thereto the following subsection:-

" (2) The Superintendent General of Indian Affairs shall have charge of Eskimo affairs."

5. There shall be a department of the Civil Service of Canada which shall be called the Department of Indian Affairs, over which the Superintendent General shall preside. R.S., c. 43, s. 5.

6. The Department of Indian Affairs shall have the management, charge and direction of Indian affairs. R.S., c. 43. s. 6.

7. The Governor in Council may appoint,-

(a) an officer who shall be called the Deputy of the Superintendent General of Indian Affairs, and such other officers, clerks and servants as are requisite for the proper conduct of the business of the Department ;

(b) an Indian commissioner and an assistant Indian commissioner for the provinces of Manitoba, Saskatchewan and Alberta, and the Territories, or an Indian commissioner and an assistant Indian commissioner for Manitoba and that portion of Canada formerly known as the district of Keewatin, and an Indian commissioner and an assistant Indian commissioner for the provinces of Saskatchewan and Alberta and the Territories, except that portion formerly known as the district of Keewatin. and for the Yukon Territory;

(c) an Indian superintendent for British Columbia ;

(d) a deputy governor. R.S., c. 43, ss. 7 and 8.

8. The Deputy Governor shall have the power, in the absence of or under instructions of the Governor General, to sign letters patent for Indian lands.

2. The signature of the Deputy Governor to such patents shall have the same force and virtue as if such patents were signed by the Governor General. R.S., c. 43, s. 8.

Schools

9. The Governor in Council may make regulations, either general or affecting the Indians of any

province or of any named band, to secure the compulsory attendance of children at school.

2. Such regulations, in addition to any other provisions deemed expedient, may provide for the arrest and conveyance to school, and detention there, of truant children and of children who are prevented by their parents or guardians from attending; and such regulations may provide for the punishment, upon summary conviction, by fine or imprisonment, or both, of parents and guardians, or persons having the charge of children, who fail, refuse, or neglect to cause such children to attend school. 57-58 V., c. 32, s. 11.

10. The Governor in Council may establish an industrial school or a boarding school for Indians, or may declare any existing Indian school to be such industrial school or boarding school for the purposes of this and the next following section. 57-58 V., c. 32, s. 11.

1. Section 10 of the Indian Act, chapter 81 of the Revised Statutes of Canada, 1906, is repealed and the following is substituted therefor:-

"10. The Governor in Council may establish an industrial school or a boarding school for Indians, or may declare any school or institution where children are provided with board and lodging as well as instruction, and with the managing authorities of which the Superintendent General has made an agreement for the admission of an Indian child or children, and for the inspection of the school or institution, to be an industrial school or boarding school for the purposes of this and the next following section. "

11. The Governor in Council may make regulations, which shall have the force of law, for the committal by justices or Indian agents of children of Indian blood under the age of sixteen years, to such industrial school or boarding school, there to be kept, cared for and educated for a period not extending beyond the time at which such children shall reach the age of eighteen years.

2. Such regulations may provide, in such manner as to the Governor in Council seems best, for the application of the annuities and interest moneys of children committed to such industrial school or boarding school, to the maintenance of such schools respectively, or to the maintenance of the children themselves. 57-58 V., c. 32, s. 11.

2. The following section is inserted in the said act immediately after section 11:---

11A. The Governor in Council may take the land of an Indian held under location ticket or otherwise for school purposes upon payment to such Indian of the compensation agreed upon, or in case of disagreement such compensation as may be determined in such manner as the Superintendent General may direct."

1. Sections nine and eleven of the Indian Act, Revised , Statutes of Canada, 1906, chapter eighty-one, and section ten of the said Act as enacted by chapter thirty-five of the statutes of 1914, are repealed and the following are substituted therefor:-

"9. (1) The Governor in Council may establish,-

"(a) day schools in any Indian reserve for the children of such reserve;

"(b) industrial or boarding schools for the Indian children of any reserve or reserves or any district or territory designated by the Superintendent General.

"(2) Any school or institution the managing authorities of which have entered into a written agreement with the Superintendent General to admit Indian children and provide them with board, lodging and instruction may be declared by the Governor in Council to be an industrial school or a boarding school for the purposes of this Act.

"(3) The Superintendent General may provide for the transport of Indian children to and from the boarding or industrial schools to which they are assigned, including transportation to and from such schools for the annual vacations.

"(4) The Superintendent General shall have power to make regulations prescribing a standard for the buildings, equipment, teaching and discipline of and in all schools, and for the inspection of such schools.

"(5) The chief and council of any band that has children in a school shall have the right to inspect such school at such reasonable times as may be agreed upon by the Indian agent and the principal of the school.

"(6) The Superintendent General may apply the whole or any part of the annuities and interest moneys of Indian children attending an industrial or boarding school to the maintenance of such school or to the maintenance of the children themselves.

" 10. (1) Every Indian child between the ages of seven and fifteen years who is physically able shall attend such day, industrial or boarding school as may be designated by the Superintendent General for the full periods during which school is open each year. Provided however that such school shall be nearest school of the kind required, and that no Protestant child shall be assigned to a Roman Catholic school or a school conducted under Roman Catholic auspices, and no Roman Catholic child shall be assigned to a Protestant school or a school conducted under Protestant auspices.

" (2) The Superintendent General may appoint any officer or person to be a truant officer to enforce the attendance of Indian children at school, and for such purpose a truant officer shall be vested with the powers of a peace officer, and shall have authority to enter any place where he has reason to believe there are Indian children between the ages of seven and fifteen years, and when requested by the Indian agent, a school teacher or the chief of a band shall examine into any case of truancy, shall warn the truants, their parents or guardians or the person with whom an Indian child resides, of the consequences of truancy, and notify the parent, guardian or such person in writing to cause the child to attend school.

"(3) Any parent, guardian or person with whom an Indian child is residing who fails to cause such child, being between the ages aforesaid, to attend school as required by this section after having received three days' notice so to do by a truant officer shall, on the complaint of the truant officer, be liable on summary conviction before a justice of the peace or Indian agent to a fine of not more than two dollars and costs, or imprisonment for a period not exceeding ten days or both, and such child may be arrested without a warrant and conveyed to school by the truant officer: Provided that no parent or other person shall be liable to such penalties if such child, (a) is unable to attend school by reason of sickness or other unavoidable cause; (b) has passed the entrance examination for high schools; or, (c) has been excused in writing by the Indian agent or teacher for temporary absence to assist in husbandry or urgent and necessary household duties."

Membership of Band.

12. Any illegitimate child may, unless he has, with the consent of the band whereof the father or mother of such child is a member, shared in the distribution moneys of such band for a period ex-

ceeding two years, be, at any time, excluded from the membership thereof by the Superintendent General. R.S., c. 43, s. 9.

13. Any Indian who has for five years continuously resided in a foreign country without the consent, in writing, of the Superintendent General or his agent, shall cease to be a member of the band of which he was formerly a member; and he shall not again become a member of that band, or of any other band, unless the consent of such band, with the approval of the Superintendent General or his agent, is first obtained. R.S., c. 43, s. 10.

14. Any Indian woman who marries any person other than An Indian or a non-treaty Indian, shall cease to be an Indian in every respect within the meaning of this Act, except that she shall be entitled to share equally with the members of the band to which she formerly belonged, in the annual or semi- annual distribution of their annuities, interest moneys and rents: Provided that such income may be commuted to her at any time at ten years' purchase, with the consent of the band.

2. Where a band has become enfranchised, or has otherwise ceased to exist, such commutation may take place upon the approval of the Superintendent General. R.S., c. 43, s. 11 ; 53 V., c. 29, s. 1.

2. Section fourteen of the said Act is repealed and the following is substituted therefor:-
" 14. Any Indian woman who marries any person other than an Indian, or a non-treaty Indian, shall cease to be an Indian in every respect within the meaning of this Act, except that she shall be entitled to share equally with the members of the band to which she formerly belonged, in the annual or semi-annual distribution of their annuities, interest moneys and rents: Provided that such income may be commuted to her at any time at ten years' purchase, with the approval of the Superintendent General."

15. Any Indian woman who marries an Indian of any other band, or a non-treaty Indian, shall cease to be a member of the band to which she formerly belonged, and shall become a member of the band or irregular band of which her husband is a member.

2. If she marries a non-treaty Indian, while becoming a member of the irregular band of which her husband is a member, she shall be entitled to share equally with the members of the band of which she was formerly a member, in the distribution of their moneys; but such income may be commuted 1» her at any time at ten years' purchase, with the consent of the band. R.S., c. 43, s. 12.

18. No half-breed in Manitoba who has shared in the distribution of half-breed lands shall be accounted an Indian.

2. No half-breed head of a family, except the widow of an Indian or a half-breed who has already been admitted into a treaty, shall, unless under very special circumstances, which, shall be determined by the Superintendent General or his agent, be accounted an Indian or entitled to be admitted into any Indian treaty.

3. Any half-breed who has been admitted into a treaty shall, on obtaining the consent in writing of the Indian commissioner, or in his absence the assistant Indian commissioner, be allowed to withdraw therefrom on signifying his desire so to do in writing, signed by him in the presence of two witnesses, who shall attest his signature on oath before some person authorized by law to administer such oath.

3. Subsection 3 of section 16 of the said Act is amended by striking out the words " Indian Commis-

sioner or in his absence the Assistant Indian Commissioner " in the second and third lines thereof and substituting therefor the words " Superintendent General."

4. Such withdrawal shall include the minor unmarried children of such half-breed.

4. Subsection 4 of section 16 of the said Act is amended by inserting the words " wife and " after the word " the " in the first line thereof.

17. When, by a majority vote of a band, or the council of a band, an Indian of one band is admitted into member- ship in another band, and his admission thereinto is assented to by the Superintendent General, such Indian shall cease to have any interest in the lands or moneys of the band of which he was formerly a member, and shall be entitled to share in the lands and moneys of the band to which he is so admitted.

2. The Superintendent General may cause to be deducted from the capital of the band of which such Indian was formerly a member his per capita share of such capital and place the same to the credit of the capital of the band into membership in which he has been admitted in the manner aforesaid. 58-59 V., c. 35, s. 8.

18. The Superintendent General may, from time to time, upon the report of an officer, or other person specially appointed by him to make an inquiry, determine who is or who is not a member of any band of Indians entitled to share in the property and annuities of the band.

2. The decision of the Superintendent General in any such matter shall be final and conclusive, subject to an appeal to the Governor in Council. 50-51 V., c. 33, s. 1.

Reserves

19. All reserves for Indians, or for any band of Indians, or held in trust for their benefit, shall be deemed to be reserved and held for the same purposes as they were held heretofore, but shall be subject to the provisions of this Part. R.S., c. 43, s. 14.

20. The Superintendent General may authorize surveys, plans and reports to be made of any reserve for Indians, showing and distinguishing the unproved lands, the forests and lands fit for settlement, ana such other information as is required ; and may authorize the whole or any portion of a reserve to be subdivided into lots. R.S., c. 43, s. 15.

21. No Indian shall be deemed to be lawfully in possession of any land in a reserve, unless he has been or is located for the same by the band, or council of the band, with the approval of the Superintendent General; but no Indian shall be dispossessed of any land on which he has improvements, without receiving compensation for such improvements, at a valuation approved by the Superintendent General, from the Indian who obtains the land, or from the funds of the band, as is determined by the Superintendent General: Provided that prior to the location of an Indian under this section, in the province of Manitoba, Saskatchewan - or Alberta, or the Territories, the Indian commissioner may issue a certificate of occupancy to any Indian belonging to a band residing upon a reserve in the aforesaid provinces or territories, of so much land, not exceeding in any case one hundred and sixty acres, as the Indian, with the approval of the commissioner, selects.

2. Such certificate may be cancelled at any time by the Indian commissioner, but shall, while it remains in force, entitle the holder thereof, as against all others, to lawful possession of the lands described therein. R.S., c. 43, s. 16; 53 V., c. 29, s. 2.

22. When the Superintendent approves of any location as aforesaid, he shall issue, in triplicate, a ticket granting a location title to such Indian, one triplicate of which he shall retain in a book to be kept for the purpose ; and the other two of which he shall forward to the local agent.

2. The local agent shall deliver to the Indian in whose favour it is issued one of such duplicates so forwarded, and shall cause the other to be copied into a register of the band, provided for the purpose, and shall file the same. R.S., c. 43, s. 17.

23. The conferring of any such location title shall not have the effect of rendering the land covered thereby subject to seizure under legal process, and such title shall be transferable only to an Indian of the same band, and then only with the consent and approval of the Superintendent General, whose consent and approval shall be given only by the issue of a ticket, in the manner prescribed in the last preceding section. R.S., c. 43, s. 18.

24. Every Indian and every non-treaty Indian, in the province of Manitoba, British Columbia, Saskatchewan or Alberta, the Territories, who had, previously to the selection of a reserve, possession of and who has made permanent improvements on a plot of land which upon such selection becomes included in, or surrounded by, a reserve, shall have the same privileges, in respect of such plot, as an Indian enjoys who holds under a location title. R.S., c. 43, s. 19.

Descent of Property.

25. Indians may devise or bequeath property of any kind in the same manner as other persons: Provided that no devise or bequest of land in a reserve or of any interest therein unless to the daughter, sister or grand-children of the testator, shall be made to any one not entitled to reside on such reserve, and that no will purporting to dispose of land in a reserve or any interest therein shall be of any force or effect unless or until the will has been approved by the Superintendent General, and that if a will be disapproved by the Superintendent General the Indian making the will shall be deemed to have died intestate ; and the Superintendent General may approve of a will generally and disallow any disposition thereby made of land in a reserve or of any interest in such land, in which case the will so approved shall have force and effect except so far as such disallowed disposition is concerned, and the Indian making the will shall be deemed to have died intestate as to the land or interest the disposition of which is so disallowed. 57-58 V., e. 32, s. 1.

1. (1) Section twenty-five of the Indian Act, chapter eighty-one of the Revised Statutes of Canada, 1906, is amended by striking out the words " no devise or bequest of land in a reserve or of any interest therein unless to the daughter, sister or grandchildren of the testator, shall be made to any one not entitled to reside on such reserve, and that."

(2) Section twenty-five of the said Act is further amended by adding thereto the following subsection:-

"(2) No one who is not entitled to reside on the reserve shall by reason of any devise or bequest or by reason of any intestacy be entitled to hold land in a reserve, but any land in a reserve devised by will or devolving on an intestacy, to someone not entitled to reside on the reserve, shall be sold by the Superintendent General to some member of the band and the proceeds thereof shall be paid to such devisee or heir."

26. Upon the death of an Indian intestate his property of all kinds, real and personal, movable and immovable, including any recognized interest he may have in land in a reserve, shall descend as follows:-

(a) one-third of the inheritance shall devolve upon his widow, if she is a woman of good moral character, and the remainder upon his children, if all are living, or, if any who are dead have died without issue; or,

(b) If there is no widow, or if the widow is not of good moral character, the whole inheritance shall devolve upon his children in equal shares, if all are living, or, if any who are dead have died without issue;

(c) If one or more of the children are living, and one or more are dead, having had lawful issue, the inheritance so far as the same does not descend to the widow, shall devolve upon the children who are living, and the descendants of such children as have died, so that each child who is living shall receive such share as would have descended to him if all the children of the intestate who have died leaving issue had been living, and so that the descendants of each child who is dead shall inherit in equal shares the share which their parent would have received if living;

(d) If the descendants of the intestate entitled to share in the inheritance are of unequal degrees of consanguinity to the intestate, the inheritance shall devolve so that those who are in the nearest degree of consanguinity shall take the shares which would have descended to them, had all the descendants in the same degree of consanguinity who have died leaving issue, been living, and so that the issue of the descendants who have died shall respectively take the shares which their parents, if living, would have received: Provided that the Superintendent General may, in his discretion direct that the widow, if she is of good moral character, shall have the right, during her widowhood, to occupy any land in the reserve of the band to which the deceased belonged of which he was the recognized owner, and to have the use of any property of the deceased for which, under the provisions of this Part, he was not liable to taxation.

2. The Superintendent General shall be the sole and final judge as to the moral character of the widow of any intestate Indian. 57-58 V:, c. 32, s. 1.

27. During the minority of the children of an Indian who dies intestate, the administration and charge of the property to which they are entitled as aforesaid shall devolve upon the widow, if any, of the intestate, if she is of good moral character ; and, in such case, as each male child attains the age of twenty-one years, and as each female child attains that age, or with the consent of the widow, marries before that age, the share of such child shall, subject to the approval of the Superintendent General, be conveyed or delivered to him or her.

2. The Superintendent General may, at any time, remove the widow from such administration and charge and confer the same upon some other person, and, in like manner, may remove such other person and appoint another, and so, from time to time, as occasion requires.

3. The Superintendent General may, whenever there are minor children, appoint a fit and proper person to take charge of such children and their property, and may remove such person and appoint another, and so, from time to time, as occasion requires. 57-58 V., c. 32, s. 1.

5. The following section is inserted in the said Act " immediately after section 27 :-

" 27A. The Superintendent General may appoint a person or persons to administer the estate of any deceased Indian and may make such general regulations and such orders in particular cases as he deems necessary to secure the satisfactory administration of such estates."

2. Section twenty-seven of the said Act, as enacted by section five of chapter thirty-five of the statutes of 1914, is repealed, and the following is substituted therefor:-

"27A. The Superintendent General may appoint a person or persons to administer the estate of any deceased or insane Indian, and may make such general regulations and such orders in particular cases as he deems necessary to secure the satisfactory administration of such estates."

28. In case any Indian dies intestate without issue, leaving a widow of good moral character, all his property of whatever kind shall devolve upon her, and if he leaves no widow the widow to same shall devolve upon the Indian nearest of kin to the deceased: Provided that any interest which he may have had in land in a reserve shall be vested in His Majesty for the benefit of the band owning such reserve if his nearest of kin is more remote than a brother or sister. 57-58 V., c. 32, s. 1.

3. Section twenty-eight of the said Act is repealed, and the following is substituted therefor:-

"28. In case any Indian dies intestate without issue, leaving a widow, all his property of whatever kind shall devolve upon her, and if he leaves no widow the same shall devolve upon the nearest of kin to the deceased: Provided that any interest which he may have had in land in a reserve shall be vested in His Majesty for the benefit of the band owning such reserve if his nearest of kin is more remote than a brother or sister."

29. The property of a married Indian -woman -who dies in- testate shall descend in the same manner and be distributed in the same proportions as that of a male Indian who dies intestate, her widower, if any, taking the share which the widow of such male Indian would take.

2. The other provisions of this Part respecting the descent of property shall in like manner apply to the case of an intestate married woman, the word -widower being substituted for the word widow in each case.

3. The property of an unmarried Indian woman who dies intestate shall descend in the same manner as if she had been a male. 57-58 V., c. 32, s. 1.

30. A claimant of land in a reserve or of any interest there- in as devisee or legatee or heir of a deceased Indian shall not be held to be lawfully in possession thereof or to be the recognized owner thereof until he shall have obtained a location ticket therefor from the Superintendent General. 57-58 V., c. 32, s. 1.

31. The Superintendent General may decide all questions which arise under this Part, respecting the distribution among those entitled thereto of the property of a deceased Indian, he shall be the sole and final judge as to who the persons so entitled are.

2. The Superintendent General may do whatsoever in his judgment will best give to each claimant his share according to the true intent and meaning of this Part, and to that end, if he thinks fit, may direct the sale, lease or other disposition oi such property or any part thereof, and the distribution or application of the proceeds or income thereof, regard being always had in any such disposition to the restriction upon the disposition of property in a reserve. 57-58 V., c. 32, s. 1.

32. Notwithstanding anything in this Part it shall be lawful for the courts having jurisdiction in that regard in the case of persons other than Indians, -with but not without the consent of the Superin-

tendent General, to grant probate of the wills of Indians and letters of administration of the estate and effects of intestate Indians, in which case such courts and the executors and administrators obtaining such probate, or thereby appointed, shall have the like jurisdiction and powers as in other cases, except that no disposition shall, without the consent of the Superintendent General, be made of or dealing had with regard to any right or interest in land in a reserve or any property for which, under the provisions of this Part, an Indian is not liable to taxation. 57-58 V., c. 32, s. 1.

Trespassing, on Reserves.

33. No person, or Indian other than an Indian of the band, shall without the authority of the Superintendent General, reside or hunt upon, occupy or use any land or marsh, or reside upon or occupy any road, or allowance for road, running through any reserve belonging to or occupied by such band.

2. All deeds, leases, contracts, agreements or instruments of whatsoever kind made, entered into, or consented to by any Indian, purporting to permit persons or Indians other than Indians of the band to reside or hunt upon such reserve, or to occupy or use any portion thereof, shall be void. 57-58 V. c. 32. s. 2.

34. If any Indian is illegally in possession of any land on a reserve, or if any person, or Indian other than an Indian of the band, without the license of the Superintendent General,-

(a) settles, resides or hunts upon, occupies, uses, or causes or permits any cattle or other animals owned by him, or in his charge, to trespass on any such land or marsh; or'

(b) fishes in any marsh, river, stream or creek on or running through a reserve; or,

(c) settles, resides upon or occupies any road, or allowance for road, on such reserve ;

the Superintendent General or such other officer or person as he thereunto deputes and authorizes, shall, on complaint made to him, and on proof of the fact to his satisfaction, issue his warrant, signed and sealed, directed to any literate person willing to act in the premises, commanding him forthwith as the case may be,-

(a) to remove from the said land, marsh or road, or allowance for road, every such person or Indian and his family, so settled, or who is residing or hunting upon, or occupying, or is illegally in possession of the same; or,

(b) to remove such cattle or other animals from such land or marsh; or,

(c) to cause such person or Indian to cease fishing in any marsh, river, stream or creek, as aforesaid; or,

(d) to notify such person or Indian to cease using, as aforesaid, the said lands, river, streams, creeks or marshes, roads or allowance for roads.

2. The person to whom such warrant is directed, shall execute the same, and, for that purpose, shall have the same powers as in the execution of criminal process.

3. The expenses incurred in any such removal or notification , or causing to cease fishing, shall be borne, as the case may be, by the person removed or notified, or caused to cease fishing, or who owns the cattle or other animals removed, or who has them in charge, and may be recovered from him as the costs in any ordinary action or suit, or if the trespasser is an Indian, such expenses may be deducted from his share of annuity and interest money, if any such are due to him.

4. Any such person or Indian other than an Indian of the band may be required orally or in writing

by an Indian agent, a chief of the band occupying the reserve, or a constable, as the case may be,-

(a) to remove with his family, if any, from the land, marsh or road, or allowance for road, upon which he is or has so settled, or is residing or hunting, or which he so occupies ; or,

(b) to remove his cattle from such land or marsh ; or,

(c) to cease fishing in any such marsh, river, stream or creek as aforesaid ; or,

(d) to cease using as aforesaid any such land, river, stream, creek, marsh, road or allowance for road. R.S., c. 43, s. 22; 54-55 V., c. 30, s. 1.

35. If any person or Indian, after he has been removed or notified as aforesaid, or after any cattle or other animals owned by him or in his charge have been removed as aforesaid,-

(a) returns to, settles, resides or hunts upon or occupies or uses as aforesaid any of the said land or marsh ; or,

(b) causes or permits any cattle or other animals owned by him or in his charge to return to any of the said land or marsh; or,

(c) returns to any marsh, river, stream or creek on or running through a reserve, for the purpose of fishing therein ; or,

(d) returns to, settles or resides upon or occupies any of the said roads or allowances for roads;

the Superintendent General, or any officer or person deputed or authorized, as aforesaid, upon view, or upon proof on oath before him, to his satisfaction, that the person or Indian has,--

(a) returned to, settled, resided or hunted upon or occupied or used as aforesaid any of the said lands or marshes ; or,

(b) caused or permitted any cattle or other animals owned by him, or in his charge, to return to any of the said land or marsh ; or,

(c) returned to any marsh, river, stream or creek on or running through a reserve for the purpose of fishing therein ; or,

(d) returned to, settled or resided upon or occupied any of the said roads or allowances for roads;

shall direct and send his warrant, signed and sealed, to the sheriff of the proper county or district, or to any literate person therein, commanding him forthwith to arrest such person or Indian, and bring him before any stipendiary magistrate, police magistrate, justice of the peace or Indian agent, who may, on summary conviction, commit him to the common gaol of the said county or district, or if there is no gaol in the said county or district, or if the reserve is not situated within any county or district, then the gaol nearest to the said reserve in the province, there to remain for the time ordered in the warrant of commitment.

2. The length of imprisonment aforesaid shall not exceed thirty days for the first offence, and thirty days additional for each subsequent offence.

3. If the said reserve is not situated within any county or district, such warrant shall be directed and sent to some literate person within such reserve. R.S., c. 43, s. 23.

36. Such sheriff or other person shall accordingly arrest the said person or Indian, and deliver him to the keeper of the proper gaol, who shall receive such person or Indian, and imprison him in the said gaol for the term aforesaid. R.S., c. 43, s. 24.

37. The Superintendent General, or such officer or person aforesaid, shall cause the judgment or

order against the offender to be drawn up and filed in his office.

2. Such judgment shall not be appealed from, or removed by certiorari or otherwise, but shall be final. R.S., c. 43, s. 25.

1. The Indian Act, chapter 81 of the Revised Statutes, 1906, is amended by inserting the following heading and section immediately after section 37 thereof:-

" Recovery of Possession of Reserves.

"37A. If the possession of any lands reserved or claimed to be reserved for the Indians is withheld, or if any such lands are adversely occupied or claimed by any person, or if any trespass is committed thereon, the possession may be recovered for the Indians, or the conflicting claims may be adjudged and determined, or damages may be recovered, in an action at the suit of His Majesty on behalf of the Indians, or of the band or tribe of Indians claiming possession or entitled to the declaration, relief or damages claimed.

"2. The Exchequer Court of Canada shall have jurisdiction to hear and determine any such action.

"3. Any such action may be instituted by information of the Attorney General of Canada upon the instructions of the Superintendent General of Indian Affairs.

"4. Nothing in this section shall impair, abridge or in anywise affect any existing remedy or mode of procedure provided for cases, or any of them, to which this section applies."

4. Subsection 1 of section 37A of the said Act, as enacted by section 1 of chapter 28 of the statutes of 1910, is hereby repealed \ and the following is substituted therefor:-

"37A. If the possession of any lands reserved or claimed to be reserved for the Indians, or of any lands of which the Indians or any Indian or any band or tribe of Indians claim the possession or any right of possession, is withheld, or if any such lands are adversely occupied or claimed by any person, or if any trespass is committed thereon, the possession may be recovered for the Indians or Indian or band or tribe of Indians, or the conflicting claims may be adjudged and determined or damages may be re- covered in an action at the suit of His Majesty on behalf of the Indians or Indian or of the band or tribe of Indians entitled to or claiming the possession or right of possession or entitled to or claiming the declaration, relief or damages."

Sale or Barter.

38. The Governor in Council may make regulations for prohibiting or regulating the sale, barter, exchange or gift by any band irregular band of Indians, or by any Indian of any band or irregular band, in the province of Manitoba, Saskatchewan or Alberta, or the Territories of any given or root crops or other produce grown upon any reserve, and may further provide that such sale, barter, exchange or gift shall be null and void, unless the same are made in accordance with such regulations. R.S., c. 43, s. 30.

39. No person shall buy or otherwise acquire from any band or irregular band of Indians, or from any Indian, any grain, root crops, or other produce from upon any reserve in the province of Manitoba, Saskatchewan or Alberta, or the Territories. R.S., c. 43, 8. 30.

40. If any such grain or root crops, or other produce as aforesaid, are unlawfully in the possession of any person with in the intent and meaning of this Part, or of any regulations made by the Governor in Council under this Part, any person acting under the authority, either general or special, of the

Superintendent General, may, with such assistance in that behalf as he thinks necessary, seize and take possession of the same; and he shall deal therewith as the Superintendent General, or any officer or person thereunto by him authorized, directs. R.S., c. 43, s. 31.

41. The Governor in Council may make regulations for prohibiting the cutting, carrying away or removing from any reserve or special reserve, of any hard or sugar-maple tree or sapling. R.S., c. 43, s. 32.

42. No official or employee connected with the inside or outside service of the of the Department of Indian Affairs, and no missionary in the employ of any religious denomination, or otherwise employed in mission work among Indians, and no school teacher on an Indian reserve, shall, without the special license in writing of the Superintendent General, trade with any Indian, or sell to him directly or indirectly, any goods or supplies, cattle or other animals.

2. The Superintendent General may at any time revoke the license so given by him. 53 V., c. 29, s. 10; 57-58 V., c. 32, s. 10.

43. No person shall barter directly or indirectly with any Indian on a reserve in the province of Manitoba, Saskatchewan or Alberta, or the Territories, or sell to any such Indian any goods or supplies, cattle or other animals without the special license in writing of the Superintendent General.

2. The Superintendent General may, at any time, revoke the license by him given.

3. Upon prosecution of any offender against the provisions of this and the last preceding section, the evidence of the Indian to whom the sale was made, and the production to, or view by, the magistrate or Indian agent of the article or animal sold, shall be sufficient evidence on which to convict. 53 V., c. 29, s. 10.

Roads and Bridges.

44. Indians residing upon any reserve shall be liable, if so directed by the Superintendent General, or any officer or person by him thereunto authorized, to perform labour upon the public roads laid out or used in or through, or abutting upon such reserve, which labour shall be performed under the sole control of the Superintendent General, or officer or person aforesaid, who may direct when, where and how and in what manner such labour shall be applied, and to what extent the same shall be imposed upon any Indian who is a resident upon the reserve.

2. The Superintendent General, or person or officer aforesaid shall have the like power to enforce the performance of such labour by imprisonment or otherwise, as may be done by any power or authority under any law, rule or regulation in force in the province or territory in which such reserve is situate, for the non-performance of statute labour; but the labour to be so required of any such Indian shall not exceed in amount or extent what may be required of other inhabitants of the same province, territory, county or other local division, under the laws requiring and regulating such labour and the performance thereof. 61 V., c. 34, s. 1.

45. Every band of Indians shall cause the roads, bridges, ditches and fences within its reserve to be put and maintained in proper order, in accordance with the instructions received, from time to time, from the Superintendent General, or from the agent of the Superintendent General.

2. Whenever in the opinion of the Superintendent General, such roads, bridges, ditches and fences are not so put or maintained in order, he may cause the work to be performed at the cost of the band,

or of the particular Indian in default, as the case may be, either out of its or his annual allowances or otherwise. R.S., c. 43, s. 34.

Land taken for Public Purposes.
48. No portion of any reserve shall be taken for the purposes of any railway, road or public work without the consent of the Governor in Council, and, if any railway, road, or public work passes through or causes injury to any reserve, or, if any act occasioning damage to any reserve is done under the authority of an Act of Parliament or of the legislature of any province, compensation shall be made therefor to the Indians of the band in the same manner as is provided with respect to the lands or rights of other persons.
2. The Superintendent General shall, in any case in which an arbitration is had, name the arbitrator on behalf of the Indians, and shall act for them in any matter relating do the settlement of such compensation.
3. The amount awarded in any case shall be paid to the Minister of Finance for the use of the band of Indians for whose benefit the reserve is held, and for the benefit of any Indian who has improvements taken or injured. R.S., c. 43, s. 35 ; 50-51 V., c. 33, s. 5.
1. Subsection 1 of section 46 of The Indian Act, chapter 81 of the Revised Statutes, 1906, is repealed, and the following is substituted therefor:-
"46. No portion of any reserve shall be taken for the purpose of any railway, road, public work, or work designed for any public utility without the consent of the Governor in Council, but any company or municipal or local authority having statutory power, either Dominion or provincial, for taking or using lands or any interest in lands without the consent of the owner may, with the consent of the Governor in Council as aforesaid, and subject to the terms and conditions imposed by such consent, exercise such statutory power with respect to any reserve or portion of a reserve; and in any such case compensation shall be made therefor to the Indians of the band, and the exercise of such power, and the taking of the lands or interest therein and the determination and payment of the compensation shall, unless otherwise provided by the order in council evidencing the consent of the Governor in Council, be governed by the requirements applicable to the like proceedings by such company, municipal or local authority in ordinary cases."
Surrender and Forfeiture of Lands in Reserve.
47. If, by the violation of the conditions of any trust respecting any special reserve, or by the breaking up of any society, corporation or community, or, if by the death of any person or persons without a legal succession or trusteeship, in whom the title to a special reserve is held in trust, the said title lapses or becomes void in law, the legal title shall become vested in His Majesty in trust, and the property shall be managed for the band or irregular band previously interested therein as an ordinary reserve.
2. The trustees of any special reserve may, at any time, surrender the same to His Majesty in trust, whereupon the property shall be managed for the band or irregular band previously interested therein as an ordinary reserve. R.S., c. 43, s. 37.

48. Except as in this Part otherwise provided, no reserve or portion of a reserve shall be sold, alienated

or leased until it has been released or surrendered to the Crown for the purposes of this Part: Provided that the Superintendent General may lease, for the benefit of any Indian, upon his application for that purpose, the land to which he is entitled without such land being released or surrendered, and may, without surrender, dispose to the best advantage, in the interests of the Indians, of wild grass and dead or fallen timber. 61 V., c. 34, s. 2.

1. Section forty-eight of the Indian Act, chapter eighty-one of the Revised Statutes of Canada, 1906, is amended by adding thereto the following clause immediately after the last word thereof:-

"Provided also that the Governor in Council may make regulations enabling the Superintendent General without surrender to issue leases for surface rights on Indian reserve, upon such terms and conditions as may be considered proper in the interest of the Indians covering such area only as may be necessary for the mining of the precious metals by anyone otherwise authorized to mine such metals, said terms to include provision of compensating any occupant of land for any damage that may be caused thereon as determined by the Superintendent General."

49. Except as in this Part otherwise provided, no release or surrender of a reserve, or a portion of a reserve, held for the use of the Indians of any band, or of any individual Indian, shall be valid or binding, unless the release or surrender shall be assented to by a majority of the male members of the band of the full age of twenty-one years, at a meeting or council thereof summoned for that purpose, according to the rules of the band, and held in the presence of the Superintendent General, or of an officer duly authorized to attend such council, by the Governor in Council or by the Superintendent General.

2. No Indian shall be entitled to vote or be present at such council, unless he habitually resides on or near, and is interested in the reserve in question.

3. The fact that such release or surrender has been assented Proof to by the band at such council or meeting shall be certified on oath by the Superintendent General, or by the officer authorized by him to attend such council or meeting, and by some of the chiefs or principal men present thereat and entitled to vote, before some judge of a superior, county or district court, stipendiary magistrate or justice of the peace, or, in the case of reserves in the province of Manitoba, Saskatchewan or Alberta, or the Territories, before the Indian commissioner, and in the case of reserves in British Columbia, before the visiting Indian Superintendent for British Columbia, or, in either case, before some other person or officer specially thereunto authorized by the Governor in Council.

2. Subsection three of section forty-nine of the said Act is amended by striking out all of the subsection after the word " before " in the sixth line thereof and substituting therefor the words " any person having authority to take affidavits and having jurisdiction within the place where the oath is administered."

4. When such assent has been so certified, as aforesaid. such release or surrender shall be submitted to the Governor in Council for acceptance or refusal. R.S., c. 43, s. 39; 61 V., c. 34, s. 3.

2. The said Act is amended by inserting the following section immediately after section 49 thereof:-

"49A. In the case of an Indian reserve which adjoins or is situated wholly or partly within an incorporated town or city having a population of not less than eight thousand, and which reserve has not been released or surrendered by the Indians, the Governor in Council may, upon the recommendation of the Superintendent General, refer to the judge of the Exchequer Court of Canada for inquiry' and report the question as to whether it is expedient, having regard to the interest of the public and of the Indians of the band for whose use the reserve is held, that the Indians should be removed from the reserve or any part of it.

" 2. The order in council made in the case shall be certified by the Clerk of the Privy Council to the Registrar of the Exchequer Court of Canada, and the judge of the court shall thereupon proceed as soon as convenient to fix a time and place, of which due notice shall be given by publication in The Canada Gazette, and otherwise as may be directed by the judge, for taking the evidence and hearing and investigating the matter.

"3. The judge shall have the like powers to issue subpoenas, compel the attendance and examination of witnesses, take evidence, give directions, and generally to hear and determine the matter and regulate the procedure as in proceedings upon information by the Attorney General within the ordinary jurisdiction of the court, and shall assign counsel to represent and act for the Indians who may be opposed to the proposed removal.

"4. If the judge finds that it is expedient that the band of Indians should be removed from the reserve or any part of it, he shall proceed, before making his report, to ascertain the amounts of compensation, if any, which should be paid respectively to individual Indians of the band for the special loss or damages which they will sustain in respect of the buildings or improvements to which they are entitled upon the lands of the reserve for which they are located; and the judge shall, moreover, consider and report upon any of the other facts or circumstances of the case which he may deem proper or material to be considered by the Governor in Council.

"5. The judge shall transmit his findings, with the evidence and a report of the proceedings, to the Governor in Council, who shall lay a full report of the proceedings, the evidence and the findings before Parliament at the then current or next ensuing, session thereof, and upon such findings being approved by resolution of Parliament the Governor in Council may thereupon give effect to the said findings and cause the reserve, or any part thereof from which it is found expedient to remove the Indians, to be sold or leased by public auction after three months advertisement in the public press, upon the best terms which, in the opinion of the Governor in Council, may be obtained therefor.

"6. The proceeds of the sale or lease, after deducting the usual percentage for management fund, shall be applied in compensating individual Indians for their buildings or improvements as found by the judge, in purchasing a new reserve for the Indians removed, in transferring the said Indians with their effects thereto, in erecting buildings upon the new reserve, and in providing the Indians with such other assistance as the Superintendent General may consider advisable ; and the balance of the proceeds, if any, shall be placed to the credit of the Indians: Provided that the Government shall not cause the Indians to be removed, or disturb their possession, until a suitable reserve has been obtained and set apart for them in lieu of the reserve from which the expediency of removing the Indians is so established as aforesaid.

" 7. For the purpose of selecting, appropriating and acquiring the lands necessary to be taken, or which it may be deemed expedient to take, for any new reserve to be acquired for the Indians as authorized by the last preceding sub-section, whether they are Crown lands or not, the Superintendent General shall have all the powers conferred upon the Minister by The Expropriation Ad, and such new' reserve shall, for the purposes aforesaid, be deemed to be a public work within the definition -of that expression in The Expropriation Act; and all the provisions of The Expropriation Act, in so far as applicable and not inconsistent with this Act, shall apply in respect of the proceedings for the selection, survey, ascertainment and acquisition of the lands required and the determination and payment of the compensation therefor: Provided, however, that the Superintendent General shall not exercise the power of expropriation unless authorized by the Governor in Council."

50. Nothing in this Part shall confirm any release or surrender which, but for this Part, would have been invalid ; and no release or surrender of any reserve, or portion of a reserve, to any person other than His Majesty, shall be valid. R.S., c. 43, s. 40.

51. All Indian lands which are reserves or portions of reserves surrendered, or to be surrendered, to His Majesty, shall be deemed to be held for the same purpose as heretofore; and shall be managed leased and sold as the governor in Council directs, subject to the conditions of surrender and the provisions of this Part. R.S., c. 43, s. 41.

Sale and Transfer of Indian Lands.

52. Every certificate of sale or receipt for money received on the sale of Indian lands granted or made by die Superintendent General or any agent of his, so long as the sale to which such certificate or receipt relates is in force and not rescinded, shall entitle the person to whom the same is granted, or his assignee, by instrument registered under this or any former Act providing for registration in such cases, to take possession of and occupy the land therein comprised, subject to the conditions of such sale, and unless the same has been revoked or cancelled, to maintain thereunder actions and suits against any wrongdoer or trespasser, as effectually as he could do under a patent from the Crown ; but the same shall have no force against a license to cut timber existing at the time of the granting or making thereof.

2. Such certificate or receipt shall be prima facie evidence of possession by such person, or the assignee, under an instrument registered as aforesaid in any such action or suit. R.S., c. 43, s. 42.

53. The Superintendent General shall keep a book for registering, at the option of the persons interested, the particulars of any assignment made, as well by the original purchaser or lessee of Indian lands, or his heirs or legal representatives, as by any subsequent assignee of any such lauds, or the heirs or legal representatives of such assignee. R.S., c. 43, s. 43.

54. Upon any such assignment being produced to the Super- intendent General, and, except in cases where such assignment is made under a corporate seal, with an affidavit of due execution thereof, and of the place of such execution, and the names, residences and occupations of the witnesses, or, as to lands in the province of Quebec, upon the production of any such assignment executed in notarial form, or of a notarial copy thereof, the Superintendent General shall cause the material parts of the assignment to be registered in the said book, and shall cause to be endorsed on the assignment a certificate of such registration signed by himself or by the Deputy Superintendent General, or any other officer of the Department by him authorized to sign such certificates. 53 V., c. 20, s. 4.

55. Every such assignment so registered shall be valid against any assignment previously executed, which is subsequently registered or is unregistered.

2. No such registration shall be made until all the conditions Of the sale, grant or location are com-

plied with or dispensed with by the Superintendent General.

3. Every assignment registered as aforesaid shall be unconditional in its terms. R.S., c. 43, s. 43.

56. If any subscribing witness to any such assignment is dead, or is absent from Canada, the Superintendent General may register such assignment upon the production of an affidavit proving the death or absence of such witness, and his hand- Writing, or the handwriting of the person making such assignment R.S., c. 43, s. 44.

57. No agent for the sale of Indians lands shall within his division, directly or indirectly, except under an order of the Governor in Council, purchase any land which he is appointed to sell, or become proprietor of or interested in any such land, during the time of his agency; and every such purchase or interest shall be void. R.S., c. 43, s. 110.

Tax Sales.

58. Whenever the proper municipal officer having by the law of the province in which the land affected is situate, authority to make or execute deeds or conveyances of lands sold for taxes, makes or executes any deed or conveyance purporting to grant or convey Indian lands which have been sold or located, but not patented, or the interest therein of the locatee or purchaser from the Crown, and such deed or conveyance recites or purports to be based upon a sale of such lands or such interest for taxes, the Superintendent General may approve of deed or conveyance, and act upon and treat it as a valid transfer of all the right and interest of the original locatee or purchaser from the Crown, and of every person claiming under him in or to such land to the grantee named in such deed or conveyance.

2. When the Superintendent General has signified his approval of such deed or conveyance by endorsement thereon, the grantee shall be substituted in all respects, in relation to the land so conveyed, for the original locate or purchaser from the Crown, but no such deed or conveyance shall be deemed to confer upon the grantee any greater right or interest in the land than that possessed by the original locate or purchaser from the Crown. 51 V., c. 22, s. 2.

59. The Superintendent General may cause a patent to be issued to the grantee named in such deed or conveyance on the completion of the original conditions of the location or sale, unless such deed or conveyance is declared invalid by a court of competent jurisdiction in a suit or action instituted by some person interested in such land within two years after the date of the sale for taxes, and unless within such delay notice of such contestation has been given to the Superintendent General. 51 V., c. 22, s. 2.-,

60. Every such deed or conveyance shall be registered in the office of the Superintendent General within two years from the date of the sale for taxes; and unless the same is so registered, it shall not be deemed to have preserved its priority, as against a purchaser in good faith from the original locate or purchaser from the Crown, in virtue of an assignment registered prior to the date of the registration of the deed or conveyance based upon a sale for taxes as aforesaid. 51 V., c. 22, s.2.

Cancellation.

61. If the Superintendent General is satisfied that any purchaser or lessee of any Indian lands, or any person claiming under or through him, has been guilty of any fraud or imposition, or has violated any of the conditions of the sale or lease, or if any such sale or lease has been made or issued in error or mistake, he may cancel such sale or lease and resume the land therein mentioned, or dispose of it

as if no sale or lease thereof had ever been made. R.S., c. 43, s. 46.

4. Section sixty-one of the said Act is amended by adding thereto the following subsections:—

"(2) (a) In any case where the Superintendent or the Deputy Superintendent General gives or has given notice to a purchaser or lessee of Indian lands or to his assignee, agent, executor, administrator or representative, of his intention to cancel a sale or lease under the provisions of this section, and in pursuance of such notice enters or has entered in the records of the Department the formal cancellation of such sale or lease, such entry of cancellation shall be and be deemed to have been effective from the date thereof to cancel and annul the said sale or lease, and any payments made on account of such sale or lease shall be and be deemed to have been forfeited.

(b) In any such case as described in the preceding subsection the notice of cancellation shall be deemed to be and to have been sufficient if signed by the Superintendent General, the Deputy Superintendent General, or by any officer of the Department of Indian Affairs by the direction and with the authority of the Superintendent General or the Deputy Superintendent General; and moreover the notice shall be deemed to be and to have been duly given and served upon or delivered to the purchaser or lessee, or to his assignee, agent, executor, administrator or representative as aforesaid if posted prepaid or franked to his last known address.

(3) No action, suit or other proceeding, either at law or in equity, shall lie or be instituted, prosecuted or maintained against His Majesty or against the Superintendent General, or the Attorney General, or any officer of the Government of Canada, claiming any relief or declaration against or in respect of the cancellation or forfeiture of any such sale or lease, or payments on account thereof by means of any such notice as aforesaid, unless the same was or shall have been instituted within one year from the date of the giving of the said notice.

(4) Within the first fifteen days of each session of Parliament, the Superintendent General shall cause to be laid before both Houses of Parliament a list of all such sales or leases, cancelled during the twelve months next preceding that session, or since the date of the beginning of the then last session.

(5) This Act shall not affect any rights under any judgment rendered before the date of the passing of this Act, or under any action, suit or other proceeding instituted before the first day of May, nineteen hundred and twenty-four."

Ejectment.

62. Whenever any purchaser, lessee or other person refuses or neglects to deliver up possession of any land after revocation or cancellation of the sale or lease thereof, as aforesaid, or whenever any person is wrongfully in possession of any Indian lands and refuses to vacate or abandon possession of the same, the Superintendent General may apply to the judge of the county court of the county or district in which the land lies, or to any judge of a superior court, or in the Northwest Territories to any stipendiary magistrate, for an order in the nature of a writ of habere facias possessionem, or writ of possession.

2. The said judge or magistrate, upon proof to his satisfaction that the right or title of the person to hold such land has been revoked or cancelled, as aforesaid, or that such person is wrongfully in possession of Indian lands, shall grant an order requiring the purchaser, lessee or person in possession to deliver up the same to the Superintendent General, or person by him authorized to receive such

possession.

3. The order shall have the same force as a writ of habere facias possessionem, or writ of possession.

4. The sheriff, or any bailiff or person to whom it has been entrusted for execution by the Superintendent General, shall execute the same in like manner as he would execute such writ in an action of ejectment or a possessory action.

5. The costs of and incident to any proceedings under this section or any part thereof shall be paid by any party to such proceedings or by the Superintendent General, as the judge or magistrate orders. R.S., c. 43, s. 47 ; 54-55 V., c. 30, s. 3.

Rent.

63. Whenever any rent payable to the Crown on any lease of Indian lands is in arrear, the same may be recovered,—

(a) by warrant of distress issued by the Superintendent General or any agent or officer appointed under this Part and authorized by the Superintendent General to act in such cases, and with like proceedings thereon as in ordinary cases of landlord and tenant directed to any person or persons by him named therein ; or

(b) by warrant of distress, and with like proceedings thereon as in case of a distress warrant by a justice of the peace for non-payment of a pecuniary penalty issued by him and directed as aforesaid; or

(c) by action of debt, as in ordinary cases of rent in arrear, brought therefor in the name of the Superintendent General.

2. Demand of rent shall not be necessary in any case. R.S., c. 43, s. 48.

Powers of Superintendent General.

64. When by law or by any deed, lease or agreement relating to Indian lands, any notice is required to be given, or any act to be done by or on behalf of the Crown, such notice may be given and act done by or by the authority of the Superintendent General. R.S., c. 43, s. 49.

65. Whenever it is found that, by reason of false survey or error in the books or plans in the Department of Indian Affairs, or in the late Indian branch of the Department of the Interior, any grant, sale or appropriation of land is deficient, or whenever any parcel of land contains less than the quantity of land mentioned in the patent therefor, the Superintendent General may order the purchase money of so much land as is deficient with the interest thereon from the time of the application therefor to be paid to the original purchaser in land or money as the Superintendent General directs.

2. If the land has passed from the original purchaser, and the claimant was ignorant of a deficiency at the time of his purchase, the Superintendent General may order payment as aforesaid of the purchase money for so much of the land as is deficient which the claimant has paid.

3. No such claim shall be entertained unless application is made within five years from the date of the patent, and unless the deficiency is equal to one-tenth of the whole quantity described as contained in the particular lot or parcel of land granted. R.S., c. 43, s. 52.

66. The Superintendent General may, from time to time, by public notice, declare that, on and after a day therein named, the laws respecting game in force in the province of Manitoba, Saskatchewan or Alberta, or the Territories, or respecting such game as is specified in such notice, shall apply to Indians within the said province or Territories, as the case may be, or to Indians in such parts thereof

as to him seems expedient. 53 V., c. 29, s. 10.

67. The Superintendent General, his deputy, or other person specially authorized by the Governor in Council, shall have , power, by subpoena issued by him, to require any person to appear before him, and to bring with him any papers or writings relating to any matter affecting Indians, and to examine such person under oath in respect to any such matter.

2. If any person duly summoned by subpoena as aforesaid neglects or refuses to appear at the time and place specified in the subpoena, or refuses to give evidence or to produce the papers or writings demanded of him, the Superintendent General, his deputy or such other person may, by warrant under his hand and seal, cause such person so refusing or neglecting to be taken into custody and to be imprisoned in the nearest common goal as for contempt of court, for a period not exceeding fourteen days. 50-51 V., c. 33, s. 2.

8. (1) Section sixty-seven of the said Act is amended by inserting the words " or Indian " immediately after the word person in the third line thereof.

(2) Subsection two of section sixty-seven is amended by adding the words "or Indian" immediately after the word "person" in the first and sixth lines thereof.

Patents.

68. Every patent for Indian lands shall be prepared in the Department of Indian Affairs, and shall be signed by the Superintendent General or his deputy or by some other person thereunto specially authorized by order of the Governor in Council, and, when so signed, shall be registered by an officer specially appointed for that purpose by the Registrar General, and then transmitted to the Secretary of State of Canada, by whom, or by the Under Secretary of State, the same shall be countersigned and the Great Seal thereto caused to be affixed: Provided that every such patent for land shall be signed by the Governor or by the Deputy Governor appointed under this Part for that purpose. R.S., c. 43, s. 45.

69. On any application for a patent by the heir, assignee or devisee of the original purchaser from the Crown, the Super- intendent General may receive proof, in such manner as he directs and requires, in support of any claim for a patent, when the original purchaser is dead; and upon being satisfied that the claim has been equitably and justly established, may allow the same, and cause a patent to issue accordingly : Provided that nothing in this section shall limit the right of a person claiming a patent to land in the province of Ontario to make application at any time to the Commissioner, under the Act respecting claims to lands in Upper Canada for which no patents have been issued, being chapter eighty of the Consolidated Statutes of Upper Canada. R.S., c. 43, s. 45.

70. Whenever letters patent have been issued to or in the name of the wrong person, through mistake, or contain any clerical error or misnomer, or wrong description of any mate- rial fact therein, or of the land thereby intended to be granted, the Superintendent General, if there is no adverse claim, may direct the defective letters patent to be cancelled, and a minute of such cancellation to be entered in the margin of the registry of the original letters patent, and correct letters patent to be issued in their stead.

2. Such correct letters patent shall relate back to the date of those so cancelled, and have the same effect as if issued at the date of such cancelled letters patent. R.S., c. 43, s. 50.

71. In all cases in which grants or letters patent have issued for the same land, inconsistent with

each other, through error, and in all cases of sales or appropriations of the same land, inconsistent with each other, the Superintendent General may, in cases of sale, cause a repayment of the purchase money, with interest.

2. When the land has passed from the original purchaser, or has been improved before a discovery of the error, the Superintendent General may, in substitution, assign land or grant a certificate entitling the person to purchase Indian lands of such value, and to such extent as he deems just and equitable under the circumstances: Provided that, no such claim shall be entertained unless it is preferred within five years from the discovery of the error. R.S., c. 43, s. 51.

72. Whenever patents for Indian lands have issued through fraud or in error or improvidence, the Exchequer Court of Canada or a superior court in any province may, in respect of lands situate within its jurisdiction, upon information, action, bill or plaint, respecting such lands, and upon hearing the parties interested, or upon default of the said parties after such notice of proceeding as the said courts shall respectively order, decree such patents to be void; and, upon a registry of such decree in the Department of Indian Affairs, such patents shall be void to all intents.

2. The practice in such cases shall be regulated by orders, from time to time, made by the said courts respectively. R.S., c. 43, s. 53 ; 53 V., c. 29, s. 5.

Timber Lands.

73. The Superintendent General, or any officer or agent authorized by him to that effect, may grant licenses to cut trees on ungranted Indian lands, or on reserves at such rates and subject to such conditions, regulations and restrictions, as are, from time to time, established by the Governor in Council, and such conditions, regulations and restrictions shall be adapted to the locality in which such reserves or lands are situated. R.S., c. 43, s. 54.

74. No license shall be so granted for a longer period than twelve months from the date thereof; and if, in consequence of any incorrectness of survey or other error or cause whatsoever, a license is found to comprise land included in a license of a prior date, or land not being reserve, or ungranted Indian lands, the license granted shall be void in so far as it comprises such land, and the holder or proprietor of the license so rendered void shall have no claim upon the Crown for indemnity or compensation by reason of such avoidance. R.S., c. 43, s. 55.

75. Every license shall describe the lands upon which the trees may be cut, and the kind of trees which may be cut, and shall confer, for the time being, on the licensee the right to take and keep possession of the land so described, subject to such regulations as are made.

2. Every license shall vest in the holder thereof all rights of property in all trees of the kind specified, cut within the limits of the license during the term thereof, whether such trees are cut by the authority of the holder of such license or by any other person, with or without his consent.

3. Every license shall entitle the holder thereof to seize, in revendication or otherwise, such trees and the logs, timber or other product thereof, if found in the possession of any unauthorized person, and also to institute any action or suit against any wrongful possessor or trespasser, and to prosecute all trespassers and other offenders to punishment, and to recover damages, if any.

4. All proceedings pending at the expiration of any license may be continued to final termination, as if the license had not expired. 61 V., c. 34, s. 4.

76. Every person who obtains a license shall, at the expiration thereof, make to the officer or agent

granting the same, or to the Superintendent General, a return of the number and kinds of trees cut, and of the quantity and description of sawlogs, or of the number and description of sticks of square or other timber, manufactured and carried away under such license, which return shall be sworn to by the holder of the license or his agent, or by his foreman.

2. Every person who refuses or neglects to make such return, or who evades, or attempts to evade, any regulation made by the Governor in Council in that behalf, shall be held to have cut without authority, and the timber or other product made shall be dealt with accordingly. R.S., c. 43, s. 57.

77. All trees cut, and the logs, timber or other product thereof, shall be liable for the payment of the dues thereon, so long as and wheresoever the same, or any part thereof, are found, whether in the original logs or manufactured into deals, boards or other stuff.

2. All officers or agents entrusted with the collection of such dues may follow and seize and detain the same wherever they are found until the dues are paid or secured. R.S., c. 43 s. 58.

78. No instrument or security taken for dues, either before or after the cutting of the trees, as collateral security, or to facilitate collection, shall in any way affect the lien for such dues, but the lien shall subsist until the said dues are actually discharged. R.S., c. 43, s. 59.

79. If any timber so seized and detained for non-payment of dues remains more than twelve months in the custody of the agent or person appointed to guard the same, without the dues and expenses being paid, the Superintendent General may order a sale of the said timber to be made after sufficient notice.

2. The net proceeds of such sale, after deducting the amount of dues, expenses, and costs incurred, shall be handed over to the owner or claimant of such timber, upon his applying therefor and proving his right thereto. R.S., c. 43, s. 60.

80. Any officer or agent acting under the Superintendent General may seize or cause to be seized in His Majesty's name any logs, timber, wood or other products of trees, or any trees themselves, cut without authority on Indian lands or on a reserve, wherever they are found, and place the same under proper custody until a decision can be had in the matter from competent authority. 50-51 V., c. 33, s. 6.

81. When the logs, timber, wood, or other products of trees, or the trees themselves cut without authority on Indian lands or on a reserve, have been made up or intermingled with other trees, wood, timber, logs, or other products of trees into a crib, dram or raft, or in any other manner, so that it is difficult to distinguish the timber cut on Indian lands or on a reserve without license, from the other timber with which it is made up or intermingled, the whole of the timber so made up or intermingled shall be held to have been cut without authority on Indian lands or on a reserve, and shall be seized and forfeited and sold by the Superintendent General or any officer or agent acting under him, unless evidence satisfactory to him is adduced showing the probable quantity not cut on Indian lands Sor on a reserve. 50-51 V., c. 33, s. 7.

82. Every officer or person seizing trees, logs, timber or other products of trees in the discharge of his duty under this Part may, in the name of the Crown, call in any assistance necessary for securing and protecting the same. R.S., c. 43, s. 64.

83. Whenever any trees, logs, timber or other product of trees are seized for non-payment of Crown

dues, or for any other cause of forfeiture, or whenever any prosecution is brought in respect of any penalty or forfeiture under this Part, and any question arises whether said dues have been paid or whether the trees, logs, timber or other product were cut on lands other than any of the lands aforesaid, the burden of proving payment, or on what land the same were cut, as the case may be, shall lie on the owner or claimant and not on the officer who seizes the same, or the person who brings such presentation. R.S., c. 43, s. 65.

84. All trees, logs, timber or other product of trees seized under this Part shall be deemed to be condemned unless the person from whom they are seized, or the owner thereof within one month from the day of the seizure, gives notice to the seizing officer, or nearest officer or agent of the Superintendent General that he claims, or intends to claim them, and unless within one month from the day of giving such notice he initiates, in some court of competent jurisdiction, proceedings for the purpose of establishing his claim.

2. In default of such notice and initiation pf proceedings, the officer or agent seizing shall report the circumstances to the Superintendent General, who may order the sale by the said officer or agent of such trees, logs, timber or other products. 61 V., c. 34, s. 5.

85. Any judge of any superior, county or district court, or any stipendiary magistrate, police magistrate or Indian agent, may, in a summary way, under the provisions of Part XV. of that Criminal Code, try and determine such seizures ; and may, pending the trial, order the delivery of the trees, or the logs, timber or other product to the alleged owner, on receiving security by bond, with two good and sufficient sureties, first approved by the said agent, to pay double the value of such trees, logs, timber or other product, in case of their condemnation.

2. Such bond shall he taken in the name of the Superintend- Ent General, for His Majesty, and shall be delivered up to and kept by the Superintendent General.

3. If such seized trees, logs, timber or other product are con- demned, the value thereof shall be paid forthwith to the Super- intendent General or agent, and the bond cancelled, otherwise the penalty of such bond shall be enforced and recovered. R.S., C. 43, S. 67.

86. Everyone who avails himself of any false statement or false oath to evade the payment of dues under this Part, shall forfeit the timber in respect of which the dues are attempted to be evaded. R.S., c. 43, s. 68.

Management of Indian Moneys.

87. All moneys or securities of any kind applicable to the support or benefit of Indians, or any band of Indians, and all moneys accrued or hereafter to accrue from the sale of any Indian lands or the proceeds of any timber on any Indian lands or a reserve shall, subject to the provisions of this Part, be applicable to the same purposes, and be dealt with in the same manner as they might have been applied to or dealt with but for the passing of this Part. R.S., c. 43, s. 69.

2. Section 87 of the said Act is amended by adding thereto the following subsection:—

"2. No contract or agreement binding or purporting to bind, or in any way dealing with the moneys or securities moneys and referred to in this section, or with any moneys appropriated by Parliament for the benefit of Indians, made either by the chiefs or councilors of any band of Indians or by the members of the said band, other than and except as authorized by and for the purposes of this Part of the Act, shall be valid or of any force or effect unless and until it has been approved in writing by the Superintendent General."

88. The Governor in Council may reduce the purchase money due or to become due on sales of Indian lands, or re- duce or remit the interest on such purchase money, or reduce the rent at which Indian lands have been leased, when he con- siders the same excessive.

2. A return setting forth all the reductions and remissions made under this section during the fiscal year shall be submitted to both Houses of Parliament within twenty days after the expiration of such year, if Parliament is then sitting, and, if Parliament is not then sitting, within twenty days after the opening of the next ensuing session of Parliament. 58-59 V., c. 35, s. 8.

89. With the exception of such sum not exceeding fifty per centum of the proceeds of any land, and not exceeding ten per centum of the proceeds of any timber or other property, as is agreed at the time of the surrender to be paid to the members of the band interested therein, the Governor in Council may, subject to the provisions of this Part, direct how and in what manner, and by whom, the moneys arising from the disposal of Indian lands, or of property held or to be held in trust for Indians, or timber on Indian lands or reserves, or from any other source for the benefit of Indians, shall be invested from time to time, and how the payments or assistance to which the Indians are entitled shall be made or given.

2. Subjection one of section eighty-nine is amended by striking out the words "and not exceeding ten per centum of the proceeds of any" in the second and third lines thereof.

2. The Governor in Council may provide for the general management of such moneys, and direct what percentage or proportion thereof shall be set apart, from time to time, to cover the cost of and incidental to the management of reserves, lands, property and moneys under the provisions of this Part, and may authorize and direct the expenditure of such moneys for surveys, for compensation to Indians for improvements or any interest they had in lands taken from them, for the construction or repair of roads, bridges, ditches and watercourses on such reserves or lands, for the construction and repair of school buildings and charitable institutions, and by way of contribution to schools attended by such Indians. 6 E. VII., c. 20, s. 1.

1. Subsection two of section eighty-nine of the Indian Act, chapter eighty-one of The Revised Statutes of Canada, 1906, is amended by adding thereto the following proviso:—

"Provided, however, that where the capital standing to the credit of a band does not exceed the sum of two thousand dollars the Governor in Council may direct and authorize the expenditure of such capital for any purpose which may be deemed to be for the general welfare of the band." Power of Governor in Council as to direction of expenditure of capital of band.

90. The Governor in Council may, with the consent of a band, authorize and direct the expenditure of any capital moneys standing at the credit of such band, in the purchase of laud as a reserve for the band or as an addition to its reserve, or in the purchase of cattle for the band, or in the construction of permanent improvements upon the reserve of the band, or such works thereon or in connection therewith as, in his opinion, will be of permanent value to the band, or will, when completed, properly represent capital. 57-58 V., c. 32, s. 11.

5. Subsection one of section ninety of the said Act is repealed and the following is substituted therefor:—

"90. (1) The Governor in Council may, with the consent of a band, authorize and direct the expenditure of any capital moneys standing at the credit of such band, in the purchase of land as a reserve for the band or as an addition to its reserve, or in the purchase of cattle, implements or machinery for the band, or in the construction of permanent improvements upon the reserve of the band, or such works thereon or in connection therewith as, in his opinion, will be of permanent value to the band, or will, when completed, properly represent capital or in the making of loans to members of the band to promote progress, no such loan, however, to exceed in amount one-half of the appraised value of the interest of the borrower in the lands held by him."

4. Section ninety of the said Act is amended by adding thereto the following subsections:—

"(2) In the event of a band refusing to consent to the expenditure of such capital moneys as the Superintendent General may consider advisable for any of the purposes mentioned in subsection one of this section, and it appearing to the Superintendent General that such refusal is detrimental to the progress or welfare of the band, the Governor in Council may, without the consent of the band, authorize and direct the expenditure of such capital for such of the said purposes as may be considered reasonable and proper.

" (3) Whenever any land in a reserve whether held in common or by an individual Indian is uncultivated and the band or individual is unable or neglects to cultivate the same, the Superintendent General, notwithstanding anything in this Act to the contrary, may, without a surrender, grant a lease of such lands for agricultural or grazing purposes for the benefit of the band or individual, or may employ such persons as may be considered necessary to improve or cultivate such lands during the pleasure of the Superintendent General, and may authorize and direct the expenditure of so much of the capital funds of the band as may be considered necessary for the improvements of such land, or for the purchase of such stock, machinery, material or labour as may be considered necessary for the cultivation or grazing of the same, and in such case all the proceeds derived from such lands, except a reasonable rent to be paid for any individual holding, shall be placed to the credit of the band: Provided that in the event of improvements being made on the lands of an individual the Superintendent General may deduct the value of such improvements from the rental payable for such lands."

91. The proceeds arising from the sale or lease of any Indian lands, or from the timber, hay, stone, minerals or other valuables thereon, or on a reserve, shall be paid to the Minister of Finance to the credit of the Indian fund, R.S., c. 43, s. 71.

92. The Superintendent General may,— (a) stop the payment of the annuity and interest money of' as well as deprive of any participation in the real property of the band, any Indian who is proved, to the satisfaction of the Superintendent General, guilty of deserting his family, or of conduct justifying his wife or family in separating from him, or who is separated from his family by imprisonment, and apply the same towards the support of the wife or family of such Indian; or, (b) stop the payment of the annuity and interest money of any Indian parent of an illegitimate child, and apply the same to the support of such child; or, (c) stop the payment of the annuity and interest money of, as well as deprive of any participation in the real property of the band, any woman who deserts her husband or family and lives immorally with another man, and apply the same to the support of the family so deserted ; or,

(d) whenever sick or disabled, or aged or destitute Indians are not provided for by the band of which they are members, furnish sufficient aid from the funds of the band for the relief of such sick, disabled, aged or destitute Indians. R.S., c. 43, s. 74; 61 V., c. 34, ss. 7 and 8.

6. Section 92 of the said Act is amended by adding thereto the following: —

"(e) Make such regulations as he deems necessary for prevention or mitigation of disease; the frequent and effectual cleansing of streets, yards and premises; the removal of nuisances and unsanitary conditions; the cleansing, purifying, ventilating and disinfecting of premises by the owners and occupiers or other persons having the care or ordering thereof; the supplying of such medical aid, medicine and other articles and accommodation as the Superintendent General may deem necessary for preventing or mitigating an outbreak of any communicable disease. entering and inspecting any premises used for human habitation in any locality in which conditions exist which in the opinion of the Superintendent General are unsanitary, or such as to render the inhabitants specially liable to disease, and for directing the alteration or destruction of any such building which is, in the opinion of the Superintendent General, unfit for human habitation; preventing the overcrowding of premises used for human habitation by limiting the number of dwellers in such premises; preventing and regulating the departure of persons from, and the access of persons to, infected localities; preventing persons or conveyances from passing from one locality to another; detaining persons or conveyances who or which have been exposed to infection for inspection or disinfection until the danger of infection is past; the removal or keeping under surveillance of persons living in infected localities; and any other matter which, in the opinion of the Superintendent General, the general health of the Indians of any locality may require.

"2. In the event of any conflict between any regulation made by the Superintendent General and any rule or regulation made by any band, the regulations made by the- Superintendent General shall prevail."

5. (1) Section ninety-two of the said Act, as amended by section six of chapter thirty-five of the statutes of 1914, is amended by adding thereto the following paragraph:—

"(f) May make by-laws for the taxation, control and destruction of dogs and for the protection of sheep, and such by-laws may be applied to such reserves or parts thereof from time to time as the Superintendent General may direct."

(2) The said section is further amended by adding thereto the following subsection:—

"(3) In any regulations or by-laws made under the provisions of this section, the Superintendent General may provide for the imposition of a fine not exceeding thirty dollars or imprisonment not exceeding thirty days, for the violation of any of the provisions thereof."

2. Subsection one of section ninety-two of the said Act, as amended by section six of chapter thirty-five of the statutes of 1914, and by section five of chapter twenty-six of the statutes of 1918, is further amended by adding thereto the following paragraph:—

"(g) Make regulations governing the operation of pool rooms, dance halls and other places of amusement on Indian Reserves."

Election of Chiefs.

93. Whenever the Governor in Council deems it advisable for the good government of a band, to introduce the elective system of chiefs and councillors or headmen, he may provide that the chief

and councillors or headmen of any band shall be elected, as hereinafter provided, at such time and place as the Superintendent General directs; and they shall in such case be elected for a term of three years.

2. The councillors or headmen may be in the proportion of two for every two hundred Indians.

3. No band shall have more than one chief and fifteen councillors or headmen.

4. Any band composed of at least thirty members may have a chief. 61 V., c. 34, s. 9.

94. Life chiefs and councillors or headmen now living may continue to hold rank until death or resignation, or until their removal by the Governor in Council for dishonesty, in- temperance, immorality or incompetency.

2. In the event of the Governor in Council providing that the chief and councillors or headmen of a band shall be elected, the life chiefs and councillors or headmen shall not exercise powers as such unless elected under the provision aforesaid. 61 V., c. 34, s. 9.

95. An election may be set aside by the Governor in Council, on a report of the Superintendent General, if it is proved by two witnesses before the Indian agent for the locality, or such other person as is deputed by the Superintendent General to take evidence in the matter, that fraud or gross irregularity was practised at the said election.

2. Every Indian who is proved guilty of such fraud or irregularity, or connivance thereat, may be declared ineligible for re-election for a period not exceeding six years, if the Governor in Council, on the report of the Superintendent General, so directs. 61 V., c. 34, s. 9.

96. Any elected or life chief and any councillor or head- man, or any chief or councillor or headman chosen according to the custom of any band, may, on the ground of dishonesty, intemperance, immorality or incompetency, be deposed by the Governor in Council and declared ineligible to hold the office of chief or councillor or headman for a period not exceeding three years. 61 V., c. 31, s. 9.
Regulations to be made by Chiefs.

97. The chief or chiefs of any band in council may, subject to confirmation by the Governor in Council, make rules and regulations as to the religious denomination to which the teacher of the school established on the reserve shall belong.

2. If the majority of the band belongs to any one religious denomination, the teacher of the school established on the reserve shall belong to the same denomination.

3. The Protestant or Catholic minority of any band may, with the approval of and under regulations made by the Governor in Council, have a separate school established on the reserve. R.S., c. 43,, s. 76.

98. The chief or chiefs of any band in council may likewise and subject to such confirmation, make rules and regulations as to,—

(a) the care of the public health;

(b) the observance of order and decorum at assemblies of the Indians in general council, or on other occasions;

(c) the repression of intemperance and profligacy ;

3. Paragraph (c) of subsection one of section ninety-eight of the said Act is repealed and the following is substituted therefor:—

"(c) The prevention of disorderly conduct and nuisances."

(d) the prevention of trespass by cattle, and the protection of sheep, horses, mules and cattle;

(e) the construction and maintenance of watercourses, roads, bridges, ditches and fences;

(f) the construction and repair of school houses, council houses and other Indian public buildings, and the attendance at school of children between the ages of six and fifteen years;

(g) the establishment of pounds and the appointment of pound-keepers;

(h) the locating of the band in their reserves, and the establishment of a register of such locations;

(i) the repression of noxious weeds.

2. The Governor in Council may by the rules and regulations aforesaid provide for the imposition of punishment by fine, penalty or imprisonment, or both for violation of any of such rules or regulations.

3. The fine or penalty shall in no case exceed thirty dollars, and the imprisonment shall in no case exceed thirty days.

4. The proceedings for the imposition of such punishment shall be taken under Part XV. of the Criminal Code. R.S., c. 43, s. 76.

Taxation.

99. No Indian or non-treaty Indian shall be liable to be taxed for any real or personal property, unless he holds, in his individual right, real estate under a lease or in fee simple, or personal property outside of the reserve or special reserve, in which case he shall be liable to be taxed for such real or personal property at the same rate as other persons in the locality in which it is situate. R.S., c. 43, s. 77.

100. No taxes shall be levied on the real property of any Indian, acquired under the enfranchisement clauses of this of Part, until the same has been declared liable to taxation by pro- clamation of the Governor in Council, published in the Canada Gazette. R.S., c. 43, s. 77.

101. All land vested in the Crown or in any person in trust or for the use of any Indian or non-treaty Indian or any band or irregular band of Indians or non-treaty Indians shall be exempt from taxation, except those lands which, having been surrendered by the bands owning them, though unpatented, have been located by or sold or agreed to be sold to any person; and, except as against the Crown and any Indian located on the land, the same shall be liable to taxation in like manner as other lands in the same locality: Provided that nothing herein contained shall interfere with the right of the Superintendent General to cancel the original sale or location of any land, or shall render such land liable to taxation until it is again sold or located. 51 V., c. 22, s. 3.

Legal Rights of Indians.

102. No person shall take any security or otherwise obtain any lien or charge, whether by mortgage, judgment or otherwise, upon real or personal property of any Indian or non-treaty Indian, except on real or personal property subject to taxation under the last three preceding sections: Provided that any person selling any article to an Indian or non-treaty Indian may take security on such article for any part of the price thereof which is unpaid. R.S., c. 43, s. 78.

103. Indians and non-treaty Indians shall have the right to sue for debts due to them, or in respect of any tort or wrong inflicted upon them, or to compel the performance of obligations contracted with them: Provided that, in any suit or action between Indians, or in any case of assault in which the offender is an Indian, no appeal shall lie from any judgment, order or conviction by any police

magistrate, stipendiary magistrate, or two justices of the peace or an Indian agent, when the sum adjudged or the penalty imposed does not exceed ten dollars. R.S., c. 43, s. 79.

104. No pawn taken from any Indian or non-treaty Indian for any intoxicant shall be retained by the person to whom such pawn is delivered ; but the thing so pawned may be sued for and shall be recoverable, with costs of suit, in any court of competent jurisdiction by the Indian or non-treaty Indian who pawned the same. R.S., c. 43, s. 80.

105. No presents given to Indians or non-treaty Indians, and no property purchased or acquired with or by means of any annuities granted to Indians, or any part thereof, and in the possession of any band of such Indians, or of any Indian of any band or irregular band, shall be liable to be taken, seized or distrained for any debt, matter or cause whatsoever.

3. Subsection 1 of section 105 of the said Act is repealed and the following is substituted therefor:—

'105. No presents given to Indians or non-treaty Indians, and no annuities or interest on funds, and no moneys appropriated by Parliament, held for any band of Indians, and no property purchased or acquired with or by means of any such annuities or income or moneys, and whether in the possession of any band of such Indians or of any Indian of any band or irregular band or not, shall be liable to be taken, seized, distrained, attached or in any way made the subject of judicial process for any debt, matter or cause whatsoever."

2. No such presents or property shall, in the province of Manitoba, British Columbia, Saskatchewan or Alberta, or in the Territories be sold, bartered, exchanged, or given by any band or irregular band of Indians, or any Indian of any such band to any person or Indian other than an Indian of such band.

3. Animals given to Indians under treaty stipulations, and the progeny thereof, and farming implements, tools and any other articles given to Indians under treaty stipulations shall be held to be presents within the meaning of this section.

4. Every such sale, barter, exchange or gift shall be null and void unless such sale, barter, exchange or gift is made with the written assent of the Superintendent General or his agent. R.S., c. 43, s. 81 ; 53 V., c. 29, s. 7.

7. Section 105 of the said Act is amended by adding the following subsection thereto:—

"5. No Indian or non-treaty Indian in the provinces of Manitoba, British Columbia, Saskatchewan or Alberta, or in the Territories, shall without the written consent of the Indian Agent sell, barter, exchange or give to any person or Indian other than an Indian of such band, or kill or destroy any animal or the progeny thereof given to him or to the band under treaty stipulations, or loaned or conditionally given to him or to the band by the Government. Any Indian who violates any of the provisions of this subsection shall be liable on summary conviction to a penalty, not exceeding twenty-five dollars with costs of prosecution or to imprisonment not exceeding two months, or to both fine and imprisonment."

106. If any presents given to Indians or non-treaty Indians, or any property purchased or acquired with or by means of any annuities granted to Indians, are or is unlawfully in the possession of any person, within the true intent and meaning of the last preceding section, any person acting under the authority of the Superintendent General may, with such assistance in that behalf as he thinks

necessary, seize and take possession of the same, and shall deal therewith as the Superintendent General directs. R.S., c. 43, s. 81.

4. The said Act is amended by inserting the following section immediately after section one hundred and six thereof:—

"106A. No title to any Indian grave-house, carved grave-pole, totem-pole, carved house-post or large rock embellished with paintings or carvings on an Indian reserve, shall be acquired by any means whatsoever by any person without the written consent of the Superintendent General of Indian Affairs, and no Indian grave-house, carved grave pole, totem-pole, carved house-post or large rock embellished with paintings or carvings, on an Indian reserve shall be removed, taken away, mutilated, disfigured, defaced or destroyed without such written consent.

Any person violating any of the provisions of this section shall be liable on summary conviction to a penalty not exceeding two hundred dollars, with costs of prosecution, and in default of payment to imprisonment for a term not exceeding three months, and any article removed or taken away contrary to the provisions of this section may be seized on the instructions of the Superintendent General and dealt with as he may direct."

Enfranchisement.

107. The provisions of this Part respecting enfranchisement of Indians shall not apply to any band of Indians in the province of Manitoba, British Columbia, Saskatchewan or Alberta, or the Territories, except in so far as such provisions are, by proclamation of the Governor in Council, from time to time, extended to any band of Indians in any of the said provinces or territories. R.S., c. 43, s. 82.

3. Paragraph (h) of section two, and sections one hundred and seven to one hundred and twenty-three, both inclusive, of the said Act are repealed and the following are substituted therefor:—

"107. (1) The Superintendent General may appoint a Board to consist of two officers of the Department of Indian Affairs and a member of the Band to which the Indian or Indians under investigation belongs, to make enquiry and report as to the fitness of any Indian or Indians to be enfranchised. The Indian member of the Board shall be nominated by the council of the Band, within thirty days after the date of notice having been given to the council, and in default of such nomination, the appointment shall be made by the Superintendent General. In the course of such enquiry it shall be the duty of the Board to take into consideration and report upon the attitude of any such Indian towards his enfranchisement, which attitude shall be a factor in determining the question of fitness. Such report shall contain a description of the land occupied by each Indian, the amount thereof and the improvements thereon, the names, ages and sex of every Indian whose interests it is anticipated will be affected, and such other information as the Superintendent General may direct such Board to obtain.

1. Subsection one of section one hundred and seven of the Indian Act, Revised Statutes of Canada, 1906, chapter eighty-one, as enacted by chapter fifty of the statutes of 1920, is repealed, and the following is substituted therefor:—

"107. (1) Upon the application of an Indian of any band, or upon the application of a band on a vote of a majority of the male members of such band of the full age of twenty-one years at a meeting or council thereof summoned for that purpose, according to the rules of the band and held in the presence of the Superintendent General or of an officer duly authorized to attend such council, by the Governor in Council or by the Superintendent General, a Board may be appointed by the Superintendent General to consist of two officers of the Department of Indian Affairs and a member of the band to which the Indian or Indians under investigation belongs, to make enquiry and report as to the fitness of any Indian or Indians to be enfranchised. The Indian member of the Board shall be nominated by the council of the band, within thirty days after the date of notice having been given to the council, and in default of such nomination, the appointment shall be made by the Superintendent General. In the course of such enquiry it shall be the duty of the Board to take into consideration and report upon the attitude of any such Indian towards his enfranchisement, which attitude shall be a factor in determining the question of fitness. Such report shall contain a description of the land occupied by each Indian, the amount thereof and the improvements thereon, the names, ages and sex of every Indian whose interests it is anticipated will be affected, and such other information as the Superintendent General may direct such Board to obtain".

"(2) On the report of the Superintendent General that any Indian, male or female, over the age of twenty-one years is fit for enfranchisement, the Governor in Council may by order direct that such Indians shall be and become enfranchised at the expiration of two years from the date of such order or earlier if requested by such Indian, and from the date of such enfranchisement the provisions of the Indian Act and of any other Act or law making any distinction between the legal rights, privileges, disabilities and liabilities of Indians and those of His Majesty's other subjects, shall cease to apply to such Indian or to his or her minor unmarried children, or, in the case of a married male Indian, to the wife of such Indian, and every such Indian and child and wife shall thereafter have, possess and enjoy all the legal powers, rights and privileges of His Majesty's other subjects, and shall no longer be deemed to be Indians within the meaning of any laws relating to Indians.

6. Subsection two of section one hundred and seven of the said Act as enacted by section three of chapter fifty of the statutes of 1920 is amended by adding at the end thereof the following:—
"Provided that where a wife is living apart from her husband, the enfranchisement of the husband shall not carry with it the enfranchisement of his wife except on her own written request to be so enfranchised."

"(3) An Indian over the age of twenty-one years shall have the right to choose the christian name and surname by which he or she wishes to be enfranchised and thereafter known, and from the date of the order of enfranchisement such Indian shall thereafter be known by such names, and if no such choice is made such Indian shall be enfranchised by and bear the name or names by which he or she has been theretofore commonly known.

"(4) Upon the issue of an order of enfranchisement the Superintendent General shall, if any Indian enfranchised holds any land on a reserve, cause letters patent to be issued to such Indian for such land: Provided that such Indian shall pay to the funds of the band such amount per acre for the land he holds as the Superintendent General considers to be the value of the common interest of the band in such land, and such payment shall be a charge against the share of such Indian in the funds of the band. The Superintendent General shall also pay to each Indian upon enfranchisement his or her share of the funds to the credit of the band, including such amount as the Superintendent General determines to be his or her share of the value of the common interest of the band in the lands of the reserve or reserves, or share of the principal of the annuities of the band capitalized at five per centum, out of such moneys as are provided by Parliament for the purpose or which may be otherwise available for such purpose. The land and money of any minor, unmarried children may be held for the benefit of such minor or may be granted or paid in whole or in part to the father, or, if the father is dead, to the mother, or in either case to such person as the Superintendent General may select for such purpose for the maintenance of such minor, and the land and money of the wife shall be granted and paid to the husband, unless in any case the Superintendent General shall direct that the whole or any part thereof be granted or paid to the wife herself, in which case the same shall be granted or paid to the wife.

"(5) If such Indian holds no land in a reserve he or she shall be paid from the funds of the band such amount as the Superintendent General determines to be his or her share of the value of the common interest of the band in the lands of the reserve or reserves, and shall also be paid his or her share of the funds or annuities of the band capitalized as aforesaid.

"(6) Every Indian who is not a member of the band and every non-treaty Indian who, with the acquiescence of the band and approval of the Superintendent General, has been permitted to reside on the reserve or to obtain a holding or location thereon, may be enfranchised and given letters patent for such land as a member of the band, provided that such Indian or non-treaty Indian shall pay to the credit of the band the value of the common interest of the band in the land for which he receives a patent.

" (7) On the issue of the letters patent to any enfranchised Indian for any land he may be entitled to, or the payment from the capital funds or annuities of the band, as above provided, such Indian and his or her minor unmarried children and, in the case of a male married Indian, the wife of such Indian shall cease to have any further claims whatsoever against any common property or funds of the band.

7. Section one hundred and seven of the said Act as enacted by section three of chapter fifty of the statutes of 1920, and as amended by section one of chapter twenty-six of the statutes of 1922, is further amended by adding thereto the following subsection:—

"(8) Section one hundred and twenty-two A as enacted section six, chapter twenty-six of the statutes of 1918, was not intended to and shall be deemed not to have been repealed by section three of chapter fifty of the statutes of 1920, and any act or thing done under the provisions of said section one hundred and twenty-two A shall be and is hereby declared to be valid and effective."

108. Whenever any male Indian or unmarried Indian woman, of the full age of twenty-one years, makes application to the Superintendent General to be enfranchised, the Superintendent General shall instruct the agent of the band of which the applicant is a member, to call upon the latter to furnish a certificate, under oath, before a judge of any court of justice, by the priest, clergyman or minister of the religious denomination to which the applicant belongs, or by a stipendiary magistrate or two justices of the peace, to the effect that to the best of the knowledge and belief of the deponent or deponents, the applicant for enfranchisement is, and has been for at least five years previously, a

person of good moral character, temperate in his or her habits, and of sufficient intelligence to be qualified to hold land in fee simple, and otherwise to exercise all the rights and privileges of an enfranchised person. R.S., c. 43, s. 83.

"108. Where an Indian is undergoing a period of probation in accordance with the provisions of sections one hundred and seven to one hundred and twenty-two, inclusive, heretofore in force, such Indian may on the recommendation of the Superintendent General be enfranchised by order of the Governor in Council, and given letters patent for the lands held by such Indian under location ticket issued to him or her in respect of such enfranchisement, and paid his or her share of the capital funds at the credit of the band or share of the principal of the annuities of the band capitalized at five per centum as aforesaid, out of such moneys as are provided for the purpose by Parliament or which may be otherwise available few such purpose.

109. Upon receipt of such a certificate, the agent shall, the least possible delay, submit the same to a council of the band of which the applicant is a member; and he shall then inform the Indians assembled at such council, that thirty days will be given within which affidavits made before a judge or a stipendiary magistrate will be received, containing reasons, if any there are, of a personal character affecting the applicant, why such enfranchisement should not be granted to the applicant. R.S., c. 43, a. 84.

"109. When a majority of the members of a band is enfranchised, the common land or other public property of the band shall be equitably allotted to members of the band, and thereafter the residue, if any, of such land or public property may be sold by the Superintendent General and the proceeds of such sale placed to the credit of the funds of the band to be divided as provided in section one hundred and seven: Provided, however, that the Governor in Council may reserve and set apart from the funds of the band such sum as the Superintendent General may consider necessary for the perpetual care and protection of any Indian cemetery or burial plot belonging to such Indians, and any other common property which in the opinion of the Superintendent General should be preserved as such. And provided also that no part of such land or other property shall be sold to any person other than a member of the band except by public auction after three months' advertisement in the public press.

110. At the expiration of the thirty days aforesaid, the agent shall forward to the Superintendent General all affidavits which have been filed with him in the case, as well as one made by himself before a judge or a stipendiary magistrate, containing his reasons for or against the enfranchisement of the applicant.

2. If the Superintendent General, after examining the evidence, decides in favour of the applicant, he may grant to the applicant a location ticket for the land occupied by him or her as a probationary Indian, or for such proportion thereof as appears to the Superintendent General fair and proper. R.S., c. 43, s. 85.

"110. The Governor in Council shall have power to make regulations for the carrying out of the provisions of the three sections immediately preceding this section, and subject to the provisions of this Act for determining how the land, capital moneys and other property of a band, or any part thereof, shall be divided, granted and paid, upon the enfranchisement of any Indian or Indians belonging to such band or having any interest in any of the property of such band, and to decide any questions arising under the said sections, and the decision of the Governor in Council thereon shall be final and conclusive.

111. Every Indian who is admitted to the degree of doctor of medicine, or to any other degree, by any university of learning, or who is admitted, in any province of Canada, to practise law, either as an advocate, a barrister, solicitor or attorney, or a notary public, or who enters holy orders, or who is licensed by any denomination of Christians as a minister of the gospel, may, upon petition to the Superintendent General, ipso facto become and be enfranchised under this Part, and he shall then be entitled to all the rights and privileges to which any other member of the band to which he belongs would be entitled if he was enfranchised under the provisions of this Part.

2. The Superintendent General may give him a suitable allotment of land from the lands belonging to the band of which he is a member: Provided that, if he is not the recognized holder of a location on the reserve by ticket or otherwise, he shall first obtain the consent of the band and the approval of the Superintendent General to such allotment. R.S., c. 43. s. 86.

"111. The Minister shall, within fifteen days after the opening of each session of Parliament, submit to both Houses of Parliament a list of the Indians enfranchised under this Act during the previous fiscal year, and the amount of land and money granted and paid to each Indian so enfranchised."

112. After the expiration of three years, or, if the conduct of such Indian has not been satisfactory, after such longer period as the Superintendent General deems necessary, the Governor in Council may, on the report of the Superintendent General, order the issue of letters patent, granting to such Indian the land in fee simple, which has been allotted to him by location ticket.

2. Such letters patent shall contain a provision that such Indian shall not have power to sell, lease or otherwise alienate the land except with the sanction of the Governor in Council.

3. In such cases compliance with the provisions of this Part respecting leases or surrender of lands in a reserve shall not be necessary. R.S., c. 43, s. 87.

113. Every such Indian shall, before the issue of such letters patent, declare to the Superintendent General the name and surname by which he wishes to be enfranchised and there- after known, and, on his receiving such letters patent, in such name and surname, he shall be held to be enfranchised, and he shall thereafter be known by such name or surname; and, if such Indian is a married man, his wife and minor unmarried children shall also be held to be enfranchised.

2. From the date of such letters patent, the provisions of this Part and of any Act or law making any distinction between the legal rights, privileges, disabilities and liabilities of Indians and those of His Majesty's other subjects, shall cease to apply to such Indian, or his wife or his minor unmarried children, and he and they shall no longer be deemed Indians within the meaning of the laws relating to Indians, except in so far as regards their right to participate in the annuities and interest moneys, and rents and councils of the band to which they belonged. R.S., c. 43, s. 88.

114. Any children of a probationary Indian, who, having Been minors and unmarried when the probationary ticket was granted to such Indian, arrive at the full age of twenty-one years before the letters patent are issued to such Indian, may, at the discretion of the Governor in Council, receive

letters patent in their own names, subject to the same restrictions and reservations as are contained in the letters patent issued to their parent, for their respective shares of the land allotted under the said ticket, at the same time that letters patent are granted to their parent. R.S., c. 43, s. 88.

115. If any Indian child who arrives at the full age of twenty-one years, during his or her parent's probationary period, is not qualified for enfranchisement, or if any child of such parent, who was a minor at the commencement of such period, is married during such period, a quantity of land equal to the share of such child shall be deducted, in such manner as the Superintendent General directs, from the allotment made to such Indian parent on receiving his probationary ticket. R.S., c. 43, s. 88.

116. The children of any widow who becomes either a probationary or enfranchised Indian shall be entitled to the same privileges as those of a male head of a family in like circumstances. R.S., c. 43, s. 90.

117. Whenever any member of a band, for three years immediately succeeding the date on which he was granted letters patent upon his enfranchisement as aforesaid, or for any longer period that the Superintendent General deems necessary, by his exemplary good conduct and management of property proves that he is qualified to receive his share of the moneys of such band, the Governor in Council may, on the report of the Superintendent General to that effect, order that the said Indian be paid his share of the capital funds at the credit of the band, or his share of the principal of the annuities of the band, estimated as yielding five per centum out of such moneys as are provided for the purpose by Parliament.

2. If such Indian is a married man he shall be paid his wife's and minor unmarried children's shares of such funds and principal moneys, and if such Indian is a widow, she shall also be paid her minor unmarried children's shares. 58-59 V., c. 35, s. 4. 118. The unmarried children of such married Indians who, during the probationary period for payment of such moneys become of age, if qualified by the character for integrity, morality and sobriety which they bear, shall receive their own share of such moneys, when their parents are paid.

2. If not so qualified, before they receive payment of such moneys, they must themselves pass through the probationary period. 58-59 V., c. 35, s. 4.

119. All such Indians, and their unmarried minor children, are paid their shares of the principal moneys of their band, as aforesaid, shall thenceforward cease, in every respect, to be Indians of any class within the meaning of this Part, or Indians within the meaning of any other Act or law. 58-59 V., c. 35, s. 4.

120. If any probationary Indian fails in qualifying to become enfranchised, or dies before the expiration of the required probation, his claim, or the claim of. his heirs, to the land for which a probationary ticket was granted, or the claim of any unqualified Indian, or of any Indian who marries during his or her parent's probationary period, to the land deducted under the operation of this Part from his or her parent's probationary allotment, shall, in all respects, be the same as that conferred by an ordinary location ticket under this Part. R.S., c. 43, s. 89.

121. In allotting land to probationary Indians, the quantity to be allotted to the head of a family shall be in proportion to the number of such family, compared with the total quantity of land in

the reserve, and the whole number of the band: Pro- vided that the Superintendent General may determine what quantity shall be allotted to each member for enfranchisement purposes, and that each female of any age, and each male under fourteen years of age, shall receive at least one-half the quantity allotted to each male of fourteen years of age and over. R.S., c. 43, 8. 91.

122. Every Indian who is not a member of the band, and every non-treaty Indian, who, with the consent of the band and the approval of the Superintendent General, has been permitted to reside upon the reserve, or to obtain a location thereon, may, on being assigned a suitable allotment of land by the Superintendent General for enfranchisement, become enfranchised on the same terms and conditions as a member of the band : Pro- vided that such enfranchisement shall not confer upon such Indian any right to participate in the annuities, interest moneys, rents or councils of the band.
2. Such enfranchisement shall confer upon such Indian the same legal rights and privileges, and make such Indian subject to such disabilities and liabilities as affect His Majesty's other subjects. E.S., c. 43, s. 92.
6. The following section is inserted immediately after section one hundred and twenty-two:— "
122A. (1) If an Indian who holds no land in a reserve, does not reside on a reserve and does not follow the Indian mode of life, makes application to be enfranchised, and satisfies the Superintendent General that he is self-supporting and fit to be enfranchised, and surrenders all claims what- soever to any interest in the lands of the band to which he belongs, and accepts his share of the funds at the credit of the band including the principal of the annuities of the band, to which share he would have been entitled had he been enfranchised under the foregoing sections of the Act, in full of all claims to the property of the band, or in case the band to which he belongs has no funds or principal of annuities, surrenders all claim whatsoever to any property of the band, the Governor in Council may order that such Indian be enfranchised and paid his said share if any, and from the date of such order such Indian, together with his wife and unmarried minor children, shall be held to be enfranchised.
"(2) Any unmarried Indian woman of the age of twenty-one years, and any Indian widow and her minor unmarried children, may be enfranchised in the like manner in every respect as a male Indian and his said children.
"(3) This section shall apply to the Indians in any part of Canada."
123. If any band, at a council summoned for the purpose according to their rules, and held in the presence of the Superintendent General, or an agent duly authorized by him to attend such council, decides to allow every member of the band who chooses, and who is found qualified, to become enfranchised, and to receive his or her share of the principal moneys of the band, and sets apart for each such member a suitable allotment of land for the purpose, any applicant belonging to such band, or the wife and children of any such applicant, may, after such decision, be dealt with as provided in the foregoing provisions respecting enfranchisement and the payment to enfranchised Indians of their shares of the capital funds at the credit of the band or of the estimated principal of the annuities of the band to which they are entitled. 58-59 V., c. 35, s. 5.

Offences and Penalties.

124. Every person, or Indian other than an. Indian of the band, who, without the authority of the Superintendent General, resides or hunts upon, occupies or uses any land or marsh, or who resides upon or occupies any road, or allowance for road, running through any reserve belonging to or occupied by such band shall be liable, upon summary conviction, to imprisonment for a term not exceeding one month or to a penalty not exceeding ten dollars and not less than five dollars, with costs of prosecution, half of which penalty shall belong to the informer. 57-58 V., c. 32, s. 2.

125. Any person or Indian who, being lawfully required by an Indian agent, a chief of the band occupying a reserve, or a constable,—

(a) to remove with his family, if any, from the land, marsh, road, or allowance for road upon which he is or has settled or is residing or hunting, or which he occupies; or,

(b) to remove his cattle from such land or marsh ; or,

(c) to cease fishing in any marsh, river, stream or creek on or running through a reserve ; or,

(d) to cease using, occupying, settling or residing upon any land, river, stream, creek, marsh, road or allowance for a road in a reserve ; fails to comply with such requirement, shall, upon summary conviction, be liable to a penalty of not less than five dollars and not more than ten dollars for every day during which such failure continues, and, in default of payment, to be imprisoned for a term not exceeding three months. 54-55 V., c. 30, s. 1.

126. Every Indian, not being an Indian of the band, who, in the case where shooting privileges over a reserve or part of a reserve, or fishing privileges in any marsh, pond, river, stream or creek upon or running through a reserve, have, with the consent of the Indians of the hand, been leased or granted to any person, and, in such case, every person not, under such lease or grant, entitled so to do, who hunts, shoots, kills or destroys any game animals or birds, or who fishes for, takes, catches or kills any fish to which such exclusive privilege ex- tends, upon the reserve or part of a reserve,-or in any marsh, pond, river, stream or creek covered by such lease or grant, shall, in addition to any other penalty or liability thereby incurred, be liable, on summary conviction, for every such offence to a penalty not exceeding ten dollars and not less than five dollars, and, in default of payment, to imprisonment for any term not exceeding one month. 54-55 V., c. 30, s. 4.

127. Every person, or Indian, other than an Indian of the band to which the reserve belongs, who, without the license in writing of the Superintendent General, or of some officer or person deputed by him for that purpose, cuts, carries away or removes from any of the lands, roads or allowances for roads in a reserve, any of the trees, saplings, shrubs, underwood, timber, cordwood or part of a tree, or hay, or removes any of the stone, soil, minerals, metals or other valuables from the said lands, roads or allowances for roads, shall, on summary conviction thereof before any stipendiary magistrate, police magistrate or any two justices of the peace or an Indian agent, incur in each case the costs of prosecution and,—

(a) for every tree he cuts, carries away or removes, a penalty of twenty dollars;

(b) for cutting, carrying away or removing any of the sap- lings, shrubs, underwood, timber, cordwood or part of a tree or hay, if under the value of one dollar, a penalty of four dollars ; and, if over the value of one dollar, a penalty of twenty dollars ;

(c) for removing any of the stone, soil, minerals, metals, or other valuables aforesaid, a penalty of twenty dollars.

2. In default of immediate payment of the said penalties and costs, such magistrate, justices of the peace, or Indian agent may issue a warrant directed to any person or persons by him or them named therein, to levy the amount of the said penalties and costs by distress and sale of the goods and chattels of the person or Indian liable to pay the same, or may, without proceeding by distress and sale, upon non-payment of such penal- ties and costs, order the person or Indian liable therefor to be imprisoned in the common gaol of the county or district in which the said reserve or any part thereof lies for a term not exceeding thirty days, if the penalty does not exceed twenty dollars, or for a term not exceeding three months, if the penalty exceeds twenty dollars.

3. The Superintendent General, or such other officer or person as he shall authorize in that behalf may issue the warrant on any such conviction; or may, without proceeding by distress and sale, make such order upon such conviction as such magistrate, justices of the peace or Indian agent could make; and similar proceedings may be had upon the warrant so issued as if it had been issued by the magistrate, justices of the peace or Indian agent before whom the person was convicted.

4. If upon the return of any warrant for distress and sale, the amount thereof has not been made, or if any part of it re- mains unpaid, such magistrate, or justices of the peace, or Indian agent, or the Superintendent General, or such other officer or person as aforesaid, may commit the person in default to the common gaol, as aforesaid, for a term not exceeding thirty days, if the sum claimed upon the said warrant does not exceed twenty dollars, or for a term not exceeding three months if the sum exceeds twenty dollars.

5. All such penalties shall be paid to the Minister of Finance, and shall be disposed of for the use and benefit of the band of Indians for whose benefit the reserve is held, in such manner as the Governor in Council directs. R.S., c. 43, s. 26; 53 V., c. 29, s. 3.

128. Every Indian of the band who, without the license in writing of the Superintendent General, or of some officer or person deputed by him for that purpose,—

(a) cuts, carries away or removes from land in a reserve held by another Indian under a location title or by an Indian otherwise recognized by the Department as the occupant thereof any of the trees, cordwood, or part of a tree, sap- lings, shrubs, underwood, timber or hay thereon, or removes from such land any of the stone, soil, minerals, metals or other valuables ; or,

(b) cuts, carries away or removes from any portion of the reserve of his band, for sale and not for the immediate use of himself and his family any trees, timber, cordwood or part of a tree, saplings, shrubs, underwood or hay thereon, or removes any of the stone, soil, minerals, metals or other valuables therefrom, for sale, as aforesaid ; or,

(c) unless with the consent of the band and the approval of the Superintendent General, cuts or uses any pine or large timber for any purpose other than for building on his own location or farm; shall incur the penalties provided in the last preceding section in respect to Indians of other bands and other persons.

2. The same proceedings may be had for the recovery thereof as are provided for in the said section. 50-51 V., c. 33, s. 4.

129. Every person who buys or otherwise acquires from any Indian or band or irregular band of Indians in the province of Manitoba, Saskatchewan or Alberta, or the Territories, any grain, root crops or other produce contrary to regulations made by the Governor in Council in that behalf, shall, on

summary conviction before a stipendiary magistrate, police magistrate or two justices of the peace or an Indian agent, be liable to a penalty not exceeding one hundred dollars, or to imprisonment for a term not exceeding three months, or to both. R.S., c. 43, s. 30.

130. Every person who cuts, carries away or removes from any reserve or special reserve, any hard or sugar-maple tree or sapling, or buys or otherwise acquires from any Indian or non- treaty Indian, or other person, any hard or sugar-maple tree or sapling so cut, carried away or removed from any reserve or special reserve in the province of Manitoba, Saskatchewan or Alberta, or the Territories, contrary to regulation made in that behalf by the Governor in Council, shall, on summary conviction before a stipendiary magistrate, police magistrate, or two justices of the peace or au Indian agent, be liable to a penalty not exceeding one hundred dollars or to imprisonment for a term not exceeding three months, or to both. R.S., c. 43, s. 32.

131. Every person being,—

(a) an official or employee connected with the inside or out- side service of the Department of Indian Affairs; or,

(b) a missionary in the employ of any religious denomination or otherwise employed in mission work among Indians; or,

(c) a school teacher on an Indian reserve; and,

(d) in the province of Manitoba, Saskatchewan or Alberta, or the Territories ;

who, on a reserve, without the special license in writing of the Superintendent General, trades with any Indian or directly or indirectly sells to him any goods or supplies, cattle or other animals, shall be liable to a fine equal in amount to double the sum received for the goods, supplies, cattle or other animals sold, and, in addition, to the costs of prosecution before a police magistrate, a stipendiary magistrate, a justice of the peace or the Indian agent for the locality where the offence occurs. 53 V., c. 29, s. 10; 57-58 V., c. 32, s. 10.

132. If any person without authority, cuts or employs, or induces any other person to cut, or assists in cutting any trees of any kind on Indian lands or on any reserve, or removes or carries away, or employs, or induces or assists any other person to remove or carry away any trees of any kind so cut from any Indian lands or reserve, he shall not acquire any right to the trees so cut, or any claim to any remuneration for cutting or preparing the same for market, or conveying the same to or towards market.

2. When the trees or logs or timber or any products thereof have been removed, so that the same cannot, in the opinion of the Superintendent General, conveniently be seized, he shall, in addition to the loss of his labour and disbursements, incur a penalty of three dollars for each tree, rafting stuff excepted, which he is proved to have cut or caused to be cut or carried away.

3. Such penalty shall be recoverable with costs at the suit and in the name of the Superintendent General or resident agent in any court having jurisdiction in civil matters to the amount of the penalty.

4. In all such cases, it shall be incumbent on the person charged to prove his authority to cut.

5. The averment of the person seizing or prosecuting that he is duly employed under the authority of this Part shall be sufficient proof thereof, unless the defendant proves the contrary. R.S., c. 43, s.

61.

133. Every person or Indian other than an Indian of the band who, without the written consent of the Superintendent General or his agent, the burden of proof concerning which shall be on the accused, buys or otherwise acquires any presents given to Indians or non-treaty Indians, or any property purchased or acquired with or by means of any annuities granted to Indians or any part thereof, is guilty of an offence, and liable on summary conviction, to a fine not exceeding two hundred dollars, or to imprisonment for a term not exceeding six months. R.S., c. 43, s. 81; 53 V., c. 29, s. 6.

134. Every agent for the sale of Indian lands who, within his division, directly or indirectly, except under an order of the Governor in Council, purchases any land which he is appointed to sell, or becomes proprietor of or interested in any such land, during the time of his agency shall forfeit his office and incur a penalty of four hundred dollars for every such offence, recoverable in an action of debt by any person who sues for the same. R.S., c. 43, s. 110.

135. Every one who by himself, his clerk, servant or agent, and every one who in the employment or on the premises of another directly or indirectly on any pretense or by any device,—

(a) sells, barters, supplies or gives to any Indian or non- treaty Indian, or to any person male or female who is reputed to belong to a particular band, or who follows the Indian mode of life, or any child of such person any intoxicant, or causes or procures the same to be done or attempts the same or connives thereat; or,

(b) opens or keeps or causes to be opened or kept on any reserve or special reserve a tavern, house or building in which any intoxicant is sold, supplied or given ; or,

(c) is found in possession of any intoxicant in the house, tent, wigwam, or place of abode of any Indian or non- treaty Indian or of any person on any reserve or special reserve, or on any other part of any reserve or special reserve; or,

(d) sells, barters, supplies or gives to any person on any reserve or special reserve any intoxicant;

shall, on summary conviction before any judge, police magistrate, stipendiary magistrate, or two justices of the peace or Indian agent, be liable to imprisonment for a term not exceeding six months and not less than one month, with or without hard labour, or to a penalty not exceeding three hundred dollars and not less than fifty dollars with costs of prosecution, or to both penalty and imprisonment in the discretion of the convicting judge, magistrate, justices of the peace or Indian agent.

2. A moiety of every such penalty shall belong to the in- former or prosecutor, and the other moiety thereof to His Majesty to form part of the fund for the benefit of that body of Indians or non-treaty Indians with respect to one or more members of which the offence was committed. 51 V., c. 22, s. 4 ; 57-58 V., c. 32, s. 6. .

136. The commander or person in charge of any steamer or other vessel, or boat, from or on board of which any intoxicant has been sold, bartered, exchanged, supplied or given to any Indian or non-treaty Indian, shall, on summary conviction before any judge, police magistrate, stipendiary magistrate or two justices of the peace, or Indian agent, be liable to a penalty not exceeding three hundred dollars and not less than fifty dollars for each such offence, with costs of prosecution, and in default of immediate payment of such penalty and costs, any person so convicted shall be committed to any common gaol, house of correction, lock-up or other place of confinement by the judge, magistrate

or two justices of the peace, or Indian agent, before whom the conviction has taken place, for a term not exceeding six months and not less than one month, with or without hard labour, or until such penalty and costs are paid.

2. The penalty shall be applied as provided in the last pre- ceding section. R.S., c. 43, s. 95.

137. Every Indian or non-treaty Indian who makes or manufactures any intoxicant, or who has in his possession, or concealed, or who sells, exchanges with, barters, supplies or gives to any other Indian or non-treaty Indian, any intoxicant, shall, on summary conviction before any judge, police magistrate, stipendiary magistrate or two justices of the peace, or Indian agent, be liable to imprisonment for a term not exceeding six months and not less than one month, with or without hard labour, or to a penalty not exceeding one hundred dollars and not less than twenty-five dollars, or to both penalty and imprisonment, in the discretion of the convicting judge, magistrate, or justices of the peace or Indian agent. R.S., c. 43, s. 96.

138. No penalty shall be incurred when the intoxicant is made use of in case of sickness under the sanction of a medical man or under the directions of a minister of religion.

2. The burden of proof that the intoxicant has been so made use of shall be on the accused. R.S., c. 43, s. 98; 53 V., c. 29, s. 8.

139. Any constable or, peace officer may arrest without warrant any person or Indian found gambling, or drunk, or with intoxicants in his possession, on any part of a reserve, and may detain him until he can be brought before a justice of the peace, and such person or Indian shall be liable upon Penalty. summary conviction to imprisonment for a term not exceeding three months or to a penalty not exceeding fifty dollars and not less than ten dollars, with costs of prosecution, half of which pecuniary penalty shall belong to the informer. 57-58 V., c. 32, s. 7.

4. Section one hundred and thirty-nine of the said Act is amended by adding thereto the following subsection:—

"(2) Any person or Indian who has been gambling or has been drunk on an Indian reserve, or has-had liquor in his possession on an Indian reserve, shall be liable on summary conviction to imprisonment for any term not exceeding three months, or to a penalty not exceeding fifty dollars and not less than ten dollars, with costs of prosecution, half of which pecuniary penalty shall belong to the informer."

140. The keg, barrel, case, box, package or receptacle which any intoxicant has been sold, exchanged, bartered, sup- plied or given, as well that in which the original supply was contained as the vessel wherein any portion of such original supply was supplied as aforesaid, and the remainder of the contents thereof, if such barrel, keg, case, box, package, receptacle or vessel aforesaid, respectively, can be identified; and any intoxicant imported, manufactured or brought into and upon any reserve or special reserve, or into the house, tent, wigwam or place of abode, or on the person of any Indian or non-treaty Indian, or suspected to be upon any reserve or special reserve, may be searched for under a search warrant in that behalf granted by any judge, police magistrate, stipendiary magistrate or justice of the peace, and, if found, seized by any Indian superintendent, agent or bailiff, or other officer connected with the Department of Indian Affairs, or by any constable, wheresoever found on such land or in such place or on the person of such Indian or non-treaty Indian.

2. On complaint before any judge, police magistrate, stipendiary magistrate, justice of the peace or Indian agent, he may, on evidence that this Act has been violated in respect of any such intoxicant or of any such keg, barrel, case, box, package, receptacle or vessel, or contents thereof, declare the same forfeited, and cause the same to be forthwith destroyed.

3. Such judge, magistrate, justice of the peace or Indian agent may condemn the Indian or person in whose possession the same is found to pay a penalty not exceeding one hundred dollars and not less than fifty dollars, and the costs of prosecution ; and, in default of immediate payment, the offender may be committed to any common gaol, house of correction, lock-up or other place of confinement, with or without hard labour, for any term not exceeding six months, and not less than two months, unless such penalty and costs are sooner paid.

4. A moiety of such penalty shall belong to the prosecutor, and the other moiety to His Majesty for the purpose herein- before mentioned. R.S., c. 43, s. 100.

141. If it is proved before any judge, police magistrate. stipendiary magistrate or two justices of the peace, or Indian agent, that any vessel, boat, canoe or conveyance of any description, upon the sea or sea-coast, or upon any river, lake or stream, is employed in carrying any intoxicant, to be supplied to Indians or non-treaty Indians, such vessel, boat, canoe or conveyance so employed may be seized and declared forfeited, as in the last preceding section mentioned, and sold, and the proceeds thereof paid to His Majesty for the purpose herein- before mentioned. R.S., c. 43, s. 101.

148. Every article, chattel, commodity or thing in the purchase, acquisition, exchange, trade or barter of which, in violation of this Act, the consideration, either wholly or in part, is an intoxicant, shall be forfeited to His Majesty and may be seized, as is hereinbefore provided in respect to any receptacle of any intoxicant, and may be sold, and the proceeds thereof paid to His Majesty, for the purpose hereinbefore mentioned. R.S., c. 43, s. 102.

143. Every person who introduces any intoxicant at any council or meeting of Indians held for the purpose of dis- cussing or assenting to a release or surrender of a reserve or portion thereof or for the purpose of assenting to the issuing of a license, and every agent or officer employed by the Superintendent General, or by the Governor in Council, who introduces, allows or countenances by his presence the use of such intoxicant among such Indians during the week before or at or the week after such council or meeting, shall incur a penalty of two hundred dollars recoverable by action in any court of competent jurisdiction.

2. A moiety of such penalty shall belong to the informer. R.S., c. 43, s. 103.

144. Every Indian who is found in a state of intoxication shall be liable on summary conviction thereof to imprisonment for any term not exceeding one month, or to a penalty not exceeding thirty dollars and not less than five dollars, or to both penalty and imprisonment, in the discretion of the convicting judge, magistrate, justice of the peace or Indian agent. 50-51 V., c. 33, s. 10.

145. Any constable or other peace officer may, without warrant, arrest any Indian or non-treaty Indian found in a state of intoxication, and convey him to any common gaol, house of correction, lock-up, or other place of confinement, there to be kept until he is sober; and such Indian or non-treaty Indian shall, when sober, be brought for trial before any judge, police magistrate, stipendiary magistrate, or justice of the peace or Indian agent. 50-51 V., c. 33, s. 10.

146. If any Indian or non-treaty Indian who has been so convicted, refuses, upon examination, to state or give information of the person from whom, the place where, and the time when, he procured such intoxicant, and if from any other Indian or non-treaty Indian, then, if within his knowledge, from whom, where and when such intoxicant was originally procured or received, he shall be liable to imprisonment as aforesaid for a further period not exceeding fourteen days, or to an additional penalty not exceeding fifteen dollars and not less than three dollars, or to both penalty and imprisonment, in the discretion of the convicting judge, magistrate, justice of the peace or Indian agent R.S., c. 43, s. 105.

5. The said Act is amended by inserting the following section immediately after section one hundred and forty- six thereof:—
"146A. In any prosecution under this Act the certificate of analysis of a provincial or dominion analyst shall be accepted as prima facie evidence of the fact stated therein as to the alcoholic or narcotic content of the sample analyzed."
147. Every agent who knowingly and falsely informs, or causes to be informed, any person applying to him to purchase any land within his division and agency, that the same has already been purchased, or who refuses to permit the person so applying to purchase the same according to existing regulations, shall be liable therefor to the person so applying, in the sum of five dollars for each acre of land which the person so applying offered to purchase, recoverable by action of debt in any court of competent jurisdiction. R.S., c. 43, s. 109.
148. Every person who, after public notice by the Superintendent General prohibiting the sale, gift, or other disposal to Indians in any part of the province of Manitoba, Saskatchewan or Alberta, or the Territories, of any fixed ammunition or ball cartridge, without the permission in writing of the Superintendent General, sells or gives, or in any other manner conveys to any Indian, in the portion of the said provinces or Territories to which such notice applies, any fixed ammunition or ball cartridge, shall, on summary conviction before any stipendiary or police magistrate or by any two justices of the peace, or by an Indian agent, be liable to a penalty not exceeding two hundred dollars, or to imprisonment for a term not exceeding six months, or to both penalty and imprisonment, within the limits aforesaid, at the discretion of the court before which the conviction is had. R.S., c. 43, s. 113.
149. Every Indian or other person who engages in, or assists in celebrating or encourages either directly or indirectly another to celebrate any Indian festival, dance or other ceremony of which the giving away or paying or giving back of money, goods or articles of any sort forms a part, or is a feature, whether such gift of money, goods or articles takes place before, at, or after the celebration of the same, or who engages or assists in any celebration or dance of which the wounding or mutilation of the dead or living body of any human being or animal forms a part or is a feature, is guilty of an indictable offence and is liable to imprisonment for a term not exceeding six months and not less than two months: Provided that nothing in this section shall be construed to prevent the holding of any agricultural show or exhibition or the giving of prizes for exhibits thereat. 58-59 V., c. 35, s. 6.
7. Section one hundred and forty-nine of the said Act is amended by striking out the word " indictable " in the tenth line thereof, and by inserting after the word " liable " in the eleventh line the

words " on summary conviction."

8. Section 149 of the said Act is amended by adding the following subsection thereto :—
"2. Any Indian in the province of Manitoba, Saskatchewan, Alberta, British Columbia, or the Territories who participates in any Indian dance outside the bounds of his own reserve, or who participates in any show, exhibition, performance, stampede or pageant in aboriginal costume without the consent of the Superintendent General of Indian Affairs or his authorized Agent, and any person who induces or employs any Indian to take part in such dance, show, exhibition, performance, stampede or pageant, or in- duces any Indian to leave his reserve or employs any Indian for such a purpose, whether the dance, show, exhibition, stampede or pageant has taken place or not, shall on summary conviction be liable to a penalty not exceeding twenty-five dollars, or to imprisonment for one month, or to both penalty and imprisonment."

6. The said Act is amended by inserting the following section immediately after section one hundred and forty- nine thereof: —
"149A. Every person who, without the consent of the Superintendent General expressed in writing, receives, obtains, solicits or requests from any Indian any payment or contribution or promise of any payment or contribution for the purpose of raising a fund or providing money for the prosecution of any claim which the tribe or band of Indians to which such Indian belongs, or of which he is a member, has or is represented to have for the recovery of any claim or money for the benefit of the said tribe or band, shall be guilty of an offence and liable upon summary conviction for each such offence to a penalty not exceeding two hundred dollars and not less than fifty dollars or to imprisonment for any term not exceeding two months."

150. Every fine, penalty or forfeiture under this Act, except so much thereof as is payable to an informer or person suing therefor, shall belong to His Majesty for the benefit, of the band of Indians with respect to which or to one or more members of which the offence was committed, or to which the Governor in offender, if an Indian, belongs: Provided that the Governor in Council may from time to time direct that the same be paid to any provincial, municipal or local authority which wholly or in bears the expense of administering the law under which such fine, penalty or forfeiture is imposed, or that the same be applied in any other manner deemed best adapted to attain the objects of such law or to secure its due administration, and may in case of doubt decide what band is entitled to the benefit of any such fine, penalty or forfeiture. 57-58 V., c. 32, s. 9.

Evidence and Procedure.

151. Upon any inquest, or upon any inquiry into any matter involving a criminal charge, or upon the trial of any crime or offence whatsoever or by whomsoever committed, any court, judge, police or stipendiary magistrate, recorder, coroner, jus- tice of the peace or Indian agent, may receive the evidence of any Indian or non-treaty Indian, who is destitute of the knowledge of God or of any fixed and clear belief in religion, or in a future state of rewards and punishments, without administering the usual form of oath to any such Indian or non-treaty Indian, as aforesaid, upon his solemn affirmation or declaration to tell the truth, the whole truth and nothing but the truth, or in such form as is approved by such court, judge, magistrate, recorder, coroner, justice of the peace or Indian agent, as most binding on the conscience of such Indian or non-treaty Indian. R.S., c. 43, s. 120.

152. In the case of any inquest, or upon any inquiry into any matter involving a criminal charge, or upon the trial of any crime or offence whatsoever, the substance of the evidence or information of any such Indian or non-treaty Indian, as afore- said, shall be reduced to writing and signed by the Indian, by mark if necessary, giving the same, and verified by the signature or mark of the person acting as interpreter, if any, and by the signature of the judge, magistrate, recorder, coroner, justice of the peace, Indian agent or person before whom such evidence or information is given. R.S., c. 43, s. 121.

153. The court, judge, magistrate, recorder, coroner, justice Of the peace or Indian agent shall, before taking any such evidence, information or examination, caution every such Indian or non-treaty Indian, as aforesaid, that he will be liable to incur punishment if he does not tell the truth, the whole truth and nothing but the truth. R.S., c. 43, s. 122.

154. Every solemn affirmation or declaration, in whatsoever Form made or taken, by any Indian or non-treaty Indian, as aforesaid, shall be of the same force and effect as if such Indian or non-treaty Indian had taken an oath in the usual form. R.S., c. 43, s. 124.

155. The written declaration or examination so made, taken and verified, of any such Indian or non-treaty Indian, as aforesaid, may be lawfully read and received as evidence upon the trial of any criminal proceeding when under the like circumstances the written affidavit, examination,' deposition or confession of any person might be lawfully read and received as evidence.

2. Copies of any records, documents, books or papers belonging to or deposited in the Department, attested under the signa- of the Superintendent General or of the Deputy of the Superintendent General, shall be evidence in all cases in which the original records, documents, books or papers would be evidence. R.S., c. 43, ss. 123 and 130.

156. In any order, writ, warrant, summons and proceeding whatsoever made, issued or taken by the Superintendent General, or any officer or person by him deputed as aforesaid, or by any stipendiary magistrate, police magistrate, justice of the peace or Indian agent, it shall not be necessary to insert or express the name of the person or Indian summoned, arrested, distrained upon, imprisoned or otherwise proceeded against therein, except when the name of such person or Indian is truly given to or known by the Superintendent General, or 6uch officer or person, or such stipendiary magistrate, police magistrate, justice of the peace or Indian agent.

2. If the name is not truly given to or known by him, he name or describe the person or Indian by any part of the name of such person or Indian given to or known by him.

3. If no part of the name is given to or known by him, he may describe the person or Indian proceeded against in any manner by which he may be identified. `

4. All such proceedings containing or purporting to give the name or description of any such person or Indian, as afore- said, shall prima facie be sufficient. E.S., c. 43, s. 28.

157. All sheriffs, gaolers or peace officers, to whom any such process is directed by the Superintendent General, or by any officer or person by him deputed as aforesaid, or by any stipendiary magistrate, police magistrate, justice of the peace or Indian agent, and all other persons to whom such process is directed with their consent, shall obey the same; and all other officers shall, upon reasonable requisition so to do, assist in the execution thereof. R.S., c. 43, s. 29.

158. In all cases of encroachment upon, or of violation of respecting any special reserve, proceedings

may be taken in the name of His Majesty, in any superior court, notwithstanding the legal title is not vested in His Majesty. R.S., c. 43, a. 36.

159. Any judge of a court, judge of sessions of the peace, recorder, police magistrate or stipendiary magistrate, shall have full power to do alone whatever is authorized by this Part to be done by a justice of the peace or by two justices of the peace. R.S., c. 43, s. 115.

160. Any recorder, police magistrate or stipendiary magistrate, appointed for or having jurisdiction to act in any city or town shall, with respect to offences and matters under this Part, have and exercise jurisdiction over the whole county or union of counties or judicial district in which the city or town for which he has been appointed or in which he has jurisdiction is situate. R.S., c. 43, a. 116.

161. Every Indian agent shall for all the purposes of this Act or of any other Act respecting Indians, and with respect to, —

(a) any offence against the provisions of this Act or any other Act respecting Indians; or,

(b) any offence against the provisions of the Criminal Code respecting the inciting of Indians to commit riotous acts or,

(c) any offence by any Indian or non-treaty Indian against any of the provisions of those parts of the Criminal Code relating to vagrancy and offences against morality. be ex officio a justice of the peace and have the power and authority of two justices of the peace, anywhere within the territorial limits of his jurisdiction as a justice, as defined in his appointment or otherwise defined by the Governor in Council, whether the Indian or non-treaty Indian charged with or in any way concerned in or affected by the offence, matter or thing to be tried, investigated or dealt with, is or is not within his ordinary jurisdiction, charge or supervision as an Indian agent. 58-59 V., c. 35, s. 7.

162. In the provinces of Manitoba, British Columbia, diction. Saskatchewan and Alberta, and in the Territories, every Indian agent shall, for all such purposes and with respect to any such offence, be ex officio a justice of the peace and have the power and authority of two justices of the peace, whether or not the territorial limits of his jurisdiction as a justice, as defined in his appointment or otherwise defined as aforesaid, extend to the place where he may have occasion to act as such justice or to exercise such power or authority, and whether the Indians charged with or in any way concerned in or affected by the offence, matter or thing, to be tried, investigated or otherwise dealt with, are or are not within his ordinary jurisdiction, charge or supervision as Indian agent. 58-59 V., c. 35, s. 7.

163. If any Indian is convicted of any crime punishable imprisonment in a penitentiary or other place of confinement, the costs incurred in procuring such conviction, and in carrying out the various sentences recorded, may be defrayed the Superintendent General, and paid out of any annuity or interest coming to such Indian, or to the band, as the case may be. R.S., c. 43, s. 118.

General.

164. No Indian or non-treaty Indian resident in the pro- Vince of Manitoba, Saskatchewan or Alberta, or the Territories, shall be held capable of having acquired or of acquiring a home- stead or pre-emption right under any Act respecting Dominion lands, to a quarter-section, or any parcel of land in any surveyed or Un surveyed lands in the said provinces or territories, or the right to share in the distribution of any lands allotted to half breeds: Provided that, —

(a) he shall not be disturbed in the occupation of any plot on which he had permanent improvements prior to his becoming a party to any treaty with the Crown.

(b) nothing in this section shall prevent the Superintendent General, if found desirable, from compensating any Indian for his improvements on such a plot of land, without obtaining a formal surrender thereof from the band; and,

(c) nothing in this section shall apply to any person who withdrew from any Indian treaty prior to the first day of October, in the year one thousand eight hundred and seventy-four. R.S., c. 43, s. 126.

165. Where shooting privileges over a reserve or part of a reserve, or fishing privileges thereon have, with the consent of the Indians of the band, been leased or granted to any person, it shall not be lawful for any person, not under such lease or grant entitled so to do, or for any Indian other than an Indian of the band, to hunt, shoot, kill or destroy any game animals or birds, or to fish for, take, catch or kill any fish to which such exclusive privilege extends, upon the reserve or part of a reserve. 64-55 V., c. 30, s. 4.

166. At the election of a chief or chiefs, or at the granting of any ordinary consent required of a band under this Part, those entitled to vote at the council or meeting thereof shall be the male members of the band, of the full age of twenty-one years; and the vote of a majority of such members, at a council or meeting of the band summoned according to its rules, and held in the presence of the Superintendent General, or of an agent acting under his instructions, shall be sufficient to deter- mine such election or grant such consent. R.S., c. 43, s. 127.

167. If any band has a council of chiefs or councilors, any ordinary consent required of the band may be granted by a vote of a majority of such chiefs or councilors, at a council summoned according to its rules, and held in the presence of the Superintendent General or his agent. R.S., c. 43, s. 128.

168. No one shall introduce any intoxicant at any council or meeting of Indians held for the purpose of discussing or of assenting to a release or surrender of a reserve or portion thereof, or for the purpose of assenting to the issuing of a timber or another license. R.S., c. 43, s. 108.

169. All affidavits required under this Act or intended to be used in reference to any claim, business or transaction in connection with Indian affairs, may be taken before the judge or clerk of any county or circuit court, or any justice of the peace, or any commissioner for taking affidavits in any court, or the Superintendent General, or the deputy of the Superintendent General, or any inspector of Indian agencies, or any Indian agent, or any surveyor duly licensed and sworn, appointed by the Superintendent General to inquire into, or to take evidence, or report in any matter submitted to or pending before the Superintendent General, or if made out of Canada, before the mayor or chief magistrate of, or the British consul in, any city, town or municipality, or before any notary public. R.S., c. 43, s. 129.

170. All regulations made by the Governor in Council under this Part shall be published in the Canada Gazette, and shall be laid before both Houses of Parliament within the first fifteen days of the session next after the date thereof. R.S., c. 43, s. 131; 57-58 V., c. 32, s. 12.

171. There shall be payable, out of any unappropriated moneys forming part of the Consolidated Revenue Fund of Canada, for Indian annuities for Ontario and Quebec, twenty- Six thousand six

hundred and sixty-four dollars per annum. R.S., c. 4, a. 5.

8. Section 171 of the said Act is repealed and the following is substituted therefor: —

"171. The annuities payable to Indians in pursuance of the conditions of any treaty expressed to have been entered into on behalf of His Majesty or His predecessors, and for the payment of which the Government of Canada is responsible, shall be a charge upon the Consolidated Revenue Fund of Canada, and be pay- able out of any unappropriated moneys forming part thereof.

PART II.

INDIAN ADVANCEMENT.

Interpretation.

172. In this Part, unless the context otherwise requires, —

(a) 'reserve' includes two or more reserves, and 'band' includes two or more bands united for the purposes of this Part by the order in council applying it.

(b) 'electors' means the male Indians of the full age of twenty-one years resident on any reserve to which this Part applies. R.S., c. 44, ss. 1 and 5.

Application of this Part.

173. This Part may be made applicable, as hereinafter provided, to any band of Indians in any of the provinces, or in the Territories, except in so far as it is herein otherwise provided. R.S., c. 44, s. 2.

174. Whenever any band of Indians is declared by the Governor in Council to be considered fit to have this Part applied to it, this Part shall so apply from the time appointed in such order in council. R.S., c. 44, s. 3.

Application of Part I.

175. The provisions of Part I, of this Act shall continue to apply to every band to which this Part is, from time to time, Declared to apply, in so far only as they are not inconsistent with this Part: Provided that, if it thereafter appears too the Governor in Council that this Part cannot be worked satisfactorily by any band to which it has been declared to apply, the Governor in Council may by order in council, declare that after a day named in the order in council, this Part shall no longer apply to such band, and such band shall thereafter be subject only to Part I., except that by-law, rules and regulations theretofore made under this Part, and not ultra vires of the chiefs in council under Part I., shall continue in force until they are repealed by the Governor in Council. R.S., c. 44, s. 2.

Division of Reserves.

176. Every reserve to which this Part is to apply may, by the order in council applying it, be divided into sections, the number of which shall not exceed six, and each section shall have therein, as nearly as is found convenient, an equal number of male Indians of the full age of twenty-one years, or should the majority of the Indians of the reserve so desire, the whole reserve may form one section, the wishes of the Indians in respect thereto being first ascertained in the manner prescribed in Part I. in like matters, and certified to the Superintendent General by the Indian agent.

2. The sections shall be distinguished by numbers from one upwards, and the reserve shall lie designated in the order in council as The Indian Reserve, inserting such name as is thought proper, and the sections shall be designated by the numbers assigned to them respectively. R.S., c. 44, s. 4; 53 V., c. 30, s. 1.

THE INDIAN ACT — | 185 |

Nominations for Election of Councilors.

177. A meeting of the electors for the purpose of nominating candidates for election as councilors shall be held between the hours of ten o'clock in the forenoon and twelve o'clock at noon, at a place to be appointed by the Indian agent, on a day being one week previous to the day on which the election of councilors are to be held on any reserve as hereinafter provided.

2. Due notice of such meeting shall be given in the manner customary in the band for calling meetings for public purposes. 53 V., c. 30, s. 3.

178. The Indian agent, or in his absence such person as is appointed by the Superintendent General, or failing such appointment, a chairman to be chosen by the meeting, shall preside over such meeting and shall take and keep the minutes thereof. 53 V., c. 30, s. 3.

179. Only Indians nominated at such meeting shall be recognized as, or permitted to become candidates for election as aforesaid; and each nomination to be valid must be made on the motion of an elector of the section of the reserve for the representation whereof the nominee is proposed as a candidate, and the motion must be seconded by another elector of that section. 53 V., c. 30, s. 3.

180. The nominations of the candidates shall, so far as practicable, be made consecutively and previously to any speeches being made by the movers and seconders or by any other persons, but nominations may be made up to the hour of twelve o'clock noon. 53 V., c. 30, s. 3.

181. If only one candidate for any councillorship is pro- posed, the Indian agent or chairman shall, at twelve o'clock noon, declare such candidate duly elected; and if two or more candidates are proposed for any councillorship, an election shall be held under the provisions of this Part. 53 V., c. 30, s. 3.

Elections.

182. On a day and at a place, and between the hours pre- scribed in the order in council, the electors shall meet for the purpose of electing the members of the council of the reserve. R.S., e. 44, s. 5.

183. One or more members to represent each section of the reserve, as provided in such order in council, shall be elected by the elector's resident in each section, and the Indian or Indians, as the case may be, having the votes of the greatest number of electors for each section, shall be the councillor or councilors, as the case may be therefor, provided he or they are respectively possessed of, and living in, a house in the reserve. R.S., c. 44, s. 5.

184. The agent for the reserve shall preside at the election, or in his absence some person appointed by him as his deputy, with the consent of the Superintendent General, or some person appointed by the Superintendent General may preside at the said election, and shall take and record the votes of the electors, and may, subject to appeal to the Superintendent General by or on behalf of any Indian or Indians who deems himself or themselves aggrieved by the action of such agent or deputy, or of such agent or person appointed as aforesaid, admit or reject the claim of any Indian to be an elector, and may determine who are the councilors for the several sections, and shall report? the same to the Superintendent General.

2. In any case of an equality of votes at any such election the agent or person presiding thereat shall have the casting vote. R.S., c. 44, s. 5.

Meetings of Council.

185. On a day and at a place, and between the hours pre- scribed by the Superintendent General, if

the day fixed for the same is within eight days from the date at which the councillors were elected, the said councilors shall meet and elect one of their number to act as chief councillor, and the councillor so elected shall be the chief councillor. R.S., c. 44, s. 6.

186. The council shall meet for the dispatch of business, at such place on the reserve and at such times as the agent for the reserve appoints, but which shall not exceed twelve times or be less than four times in the year for which it is elected, and due notice of the time and place of each meeting shall be given to each councillor by the agent. R.S., c. 44, s. 9.

187. At such meeting of the council the agent for the reserve, or his deputy appointed for the purpose with the consent of the Superintendent General, shall, —

(a) preside and record the proceedings.

(b) control and regulate all matters of procedure and form and adjourn the meeting to a time named or sine die.

(c) report and certify all by-laws and other acts and proceedings of the council to the Superintendent General.

(d) address the council and explain and advise the members thereof upon their powers and duties.

2. No such agent or deputy shall vote on any question to be Not to vote, decided by the council. R.S. c. 44, s. 9.

188. Full faith and credence shall be given in all courts and places whatsoever to any certificate given by such agent or deputy under the provisions of paragraph (c) of the last preceding section. R.S., c. 44, s. 9.

189. Each councillor present shall have a vote on every question to be decided by the council, and such question shall be decided by the majority of votes, the chief councillor voting as a councillor and having also a casting vote, in case the votes would otherwise be equal. Quorum.

2. Four councilors shall be a quorum for the dispatch of any business. R.S., c. 44, s. 9.

Term of Office, Vacancies, Etc.

190. The councilors shall remain in office until others are elected, in their stead, and an election for that purpose shall be held in like manner, at the same place and between the like hours on the like day, in each succeeding year, if it is not a Sunday or holiday, in which case it shall be held on the next day thereafter which is not a Sunday or a holiday.

2. If there is a failure to elect on the day appointed for the election, the Superintendent General shall appoint another day on which it shall be held. R.S., c. 44, s. 7.

191. In the event of a vacancy in the council, by the death or inability to act of any councillor, more than three months before the time for the next election, an election to fill such vacancy shall be held by the agent or his deputy, after such notice to the electors concerned as the Superintendent General directs, at which only the electors of the section represented by the councillor to be replaced shall vote, and to such election the provisions respecting other elections shall apply, so far as they are applicable.

2. If the councillor to be replaced is the chief councillor, then an election of a chief councillor shall be held in the manner already provided, but the day fixed for such election shall be at least one week after the date when the new councillor is elected. R.S., c. 44, s. 8.

192. During the time of any vacancy in the council the remaining councilors shall constitute the

council, and they may, in the event of a vacancy in the office, appoint a chief from among themselves for the time being. R.S., c. 44, s. 8.

193. Every member of a council elected under the provi- sions of this Part, who is proved to be a habitual drunkard or to be living in immorality, or to have accepted a bribe, or to have been guilty of dishonesty or of malfeasance of office of any kind, shall, on proof of the fact to the satisfaction of the Superintendent General, be disqualified from acting as a member of the council, and shall, on being notified, cease forthwith so to act; and the vacancy occasioned thereby shall be filled in the manner hereinbefore provided. R.S., c. 44, a. 11.

Powers of Council.

194. The council may, by by-law, rule or regulation, ap- proved and confirmed by the Superintendent General, provide that the religious denomination to which the teacher or teachers of the school or schools established on the reserve shall belong, shall be that of the majority of the Indians resident on the reserve: Provided that the Protestant or Roman Catholic minority on the reserve may also have a separate school or schools,' with the approval of and under regulations made by the Governor in Council.

2. The council may also make by-laws, rules and regulations, approved and confirmed by the Superintendent General, regulating all or any of the following subjects and purposes, that is to say: —

(a) The care of the public health.

(b) The observance of order and decorum at elections of councilors, meetings of the council, and assemblies of Indians on other occasions, or generally, on the reserve, by the appointment of constables and erection of lock-up houses, or by the adoption of other legitimate means.

(c) The repression of intemperance and profligacy.

7. Paragraph (c) of subsection two of section one hundred and ninety-four of the said Act is hereby repealed and the following is substituted therefor: —

"(c) The prevention of disorderly conduct and nuisances." S.C. 1926-27, c. 32, s. 7.

(d) The subdivision of the land in the reserve, and the distribution of the same amongst the members of the band; also, the setting apart, for common use, of wood- land and land for other purposes.

(e) The protection of and the prevention of trespass by cattle, sheep, horses, mules and other domesticated animals; and the establishments of pounds, the appointment of pound keepers and the regulation of their duties, fees and charges.

(f) The construction and repairs of schoolhouses, council houses and other buildings for the use of the Indians on The reserve, and the attendance at school of children between the ages of six and fifteen years.

(g) the construction, maintenance and improvement of roads and bridges, and the contributions, in money or labor, and other duties of residents on the reserve, in respect thereof; the size and kind of sleighs to be used on the roads in the winter season, and the manner in which the horse or horses or other beasts of burden shall be harnessed to such sleighs; and the appointment of road- masters and fence-viewers, and their powers and duties.

5. Subsection two of section one hundred and ninety- four 0f the said Act is amended by inserting the following paragraph immediately after paragraph (g) thereof:

"(gg) the construction, maintenance and improvement of water, sewerage and lighting works and systems.".

(h) The construction and maintenance of watercourses, ditches and fences, and the obligations of vicinage, the destruction and repression of noxious weeds and the pre- serration of the wood on the various holdings, or else- were, in the reserve.

(i) The removal and punishment of persons trespassing upon the reserve or frequenting it for improper purposes.

(j) The raising of money for any or all of the purposes for which the council may make by-laws as aforesaid, by assessment and taxation of the lands of Indians enfranchised, or in possession of lands by location ticket in though reserve: Provided that the valuation for assessment shall be made yearly, in such manner and at such times as are appointed by the by-law in that behalf, and be subject to revision and correction by the agent for the reserve, and shall come into force only after it has been submitted to him and corrected, if and as he thinks justice requires, and approved by him, and that the tax shall be imposed for the year in which the by-law is made, and shall not exceed one-half of one per centum on the assessed value of the land on which it is to be paid; and provided also that any Indian deeming himself aggrieved by the decision of the agent, made as hereinbefore provided, may appeal to the Superintendent General, whose decision in the matter shall be final.

(k) The appropriation and payment to the local agent, as treasurer, by the Superintendent General, of so much of the moneys of the band as are required for defraying ex- pensées necessary for carrying out the by-laws made by the council, including those incurred for assistance absolutely necessary for enabling the council or the agent to perform the duties assigned to them.

(l) The imposition of punishment by penalty or by imprisonment, or by both, for any violation of or disobedience to any law, rule or regulation made under this Part, committed by any Indian of the reserve; but such penalty shall, in no case, except for non-payment of taxes, exceed thirty dollars, and the imprisonment shall not exceed thirty Days.

2. If any tax authorized by any by-law, or any part thereof, is not paid at the time prescribed by the by-law, the amount unpaid, with the addition of one-half of one per centum thereof, may be paid by the Superintendent General to the treasurer out of the share in any money of the band of the Indian in default; and, if such share is insufficient to pay the tax, or any portion thereof so remaining unpaid, the defaulter shall be deemed to have violated the by-law imposing the tax, and shall incur a penalty therefor equal to the amount of the tax or the balance thereof remaining unpaid, as the case may be.

3. The proceedings for the imposition of any punishment authorized by this section, or the by-laws, rules or regulations approved and confirmed thereunder, may be taken before one justice of the peace, under Part XV. of the Criminal Code. and the amount of any such penalty shall be paid over to the treasurer of the band to 'which the Indian incurring it belongs for the use of such hand.

4. The by-laws, rules and regulations by this section authorized to be made shall, when approved and confirmed by the Superintendent General, have the force of law within and with respect to the reserve, and the Indians residing thereon. R.S., c. 44, s. 10; 53 V., c. 30, s. 2.

Evidence.

195. A copy of any by-law, rule or regulation under this Part, approved by the Superintendent Gen-

eral, and purporting To be certified by the agent for the band to which it relates to be a true copy thereof, shall be evidence of such by-law, rule or regulation, and of such approval, without proof of the signature -of such agent; and no such by-law, rule or regulation shall be invalidated by any defect of form, if it is substantially consistent with the intent and meaning of this Part. R.S., c. 44, s. 12.

8. The said Act is further amended by adding thereto as Part Three thereof the following provisions: —

"PART THREE.

"SOLDIER SETTLEMENT.

"196. (1) The Soldier Settlement Act, 1919, (excepting sections three, four, eight, nine, ten, eleven, fourteen, twenty-nine, subsection two of fifty-one, and sixty thereof, and excepting the whole of Part Three thereof) with such amendments as may from time to time be made to said Act shall, with respect to any 'settler' as defined by said Act who is an 'Indian' as defined by this Act, be administered by the Superintendent General of Indian Affairs.

(2) For the purpose of such administration, the Deputy Superintendent General of Indian Affairs shall have the same powers as the Soldier Settlement Board have under The Soldier Settlement Act, 1919, the words 'Deputy Superintendent General of Indian Affairs' being, for such purpose, read in the said Act as substituted for the words 'The Soldier Settlement Board' and for the words 'The Board.'

(3) Said Act, with such exceptions as aforesaid, shall for such purpose, be read as one with this Part of this Act.

"197. (1) The Deputy Superintendent General may acquire for a settler who is an Indian, land as well without as within an Indian reserve, and shall have authority to panted. grant to such settler a location ticket for common lands of the band without the consent of the Council of the band, and, in the event of land being acquired or provided for such settler in an Indian reserve, the Deputy Superintendent General shall have power to take security as provided by The Soldier Settlement Act, 1919, and to exercise all other- wise lawful rights and powers with respect to such lands, notwithstanding any provisions of the Indian Act to the contrary.

(2) Every such grant shall be in accordance with the provisions of said Soldier Settlement Act, 1919, and of this Part.

2. Section one hundred and ninety-seven of the said Act, as enacted by chapter fifty-six of the statutes of 1919 (First session), is repealed, and the following is substituted therefor: —

"197. The Deputy Superintendent General may acquire for a settler who is an Indian, land as well without as within an Indian reserve, and shall have authority to set apart for such settler a portion of the common lands of the band without the consent of the council of the band. In the event of land being so acquired or set apart on an Indian reserve, the Deputy Superintendent General shall have power to take the said land as security for any advances made to such settler, and the provisions of The Soldier Settlement Act, 1919, shall, as far as applicable, apply to such transactions. It shall, however, be only the individual Indian interest in such lands that is being acquired or given as security, and the interest of the band in such lands shall not be in any way affected by such transactions."

"198. The Soldier Settlement Board and its officers and employees shall, upon request of the Deputy

Superintendent General of Indian Affairs, aid and assist him, to the extent requested, in the execution of the purposes of this Act, and the said Board may sell, convey and transfer to the said Deputy, for the execution of any such purposes, at such prices as may be. agreed, any property held for disposition by such Board.

"199. (1) In the event of any doubt or difficulty arising with respect to the administration by the Superintendent General of Indian Affairs of the provisions of The Soldier Settlement Act, 1919, or as to the powers of the Deputy Superintendent General of Indian Affairs, as by this Act authorized or granted, the Governor in Council may, by order, resolve such doubt or difficulty and may define powers and procedure.

(2) Such order shall not extend the powers which are by The Soldier Settlement Act, 1919, provided."

INDIAN ACT. R.S.C. 1927, c. 98.

(See S.C. 1951, c. 29, ss. 123-124.)
CHAPTER 98
An Act respecting Indians.
SHORT TITLE.
1. This Act may be cited as the Indian Act. R.S., Short title, c. 81, s. 1.
INTERPRETATION.
2. In this Act, unless the context otherwise requires,
(a) "agent" or "Indian agent" means and includes a commissioner, assistant commissioner, superintendent, agent or other officer acting under the instructions of the Superintendent General.
(b) "band" means any tribe, band or body of Indians who own or are interested in a reserve or in Indian? lands in common, of which the legal title is vested in the Crown, or who share alike in the distribution of any annuities or interest moneys for which the Government of Canada is responsible; and, when action is being taken by the band as such, means the band in council.
(c) "Department" means the Department of Indian Affairs.
(d) "Indian" means
(i) any male person of Indian blood reputed to be- long to a particular band,
(ii) any child of such person,
(iii) any woman who is or was lawfully married to such person.
(e) "Indian lands" means any reserve or portion of a reserve which has been surrendered to the Crown.
(f) "intoxicants" means and includes all spirits, strong spirituous liquors, wines, or fermented or com- pounded liquors, or intoxicating drink of any kind whatsoever, and any intoxicating liquor or fluid, and opium, and any preparation thereof, whether liquid or solid, and any other intoxicating drug or substance, and tobacco or tea mixed or compounded or impregnated with opium or with other intoxicating drugs, spirits or substances, and whether the same or any of them are liquid or solid.
(g) "irregular band" means any tribe, band or body of persons of Indian blood who own no interest

in any reserve or lands of which the legal title is vested in the Crown, who possess no common fund managed by the Government of Canada, and who have not had any treaty relations with the Crown.

(h) "non-treaty Indian" means any person of Indian blood who is reputed to belong to an irregular band, or who follows the Indian mode of life, even if such person is only a temporary resident in Canada.

(i) "person" means an individual other than an Indian.

(j) "reserve" means any tract or tracts of land set apart by treaty or otherwise for the use or benefit of or granted to a particular band of Indians, of which the legal title is in the Crown, and which remains so set apart and has not been surrendered to the Crown, and includes all the trees, wood, timber, soil, stone, minerals, metals and other valuables thereon or therein.

(k) "special reserve" means any tract or tracts of land, and everything belonging thereto, set apart for the use or benefit of and held in trust for any band or irregular band of Indians, the title of which is vested in a society, corporation or community legally established, and capable of suing and being sued, or in a person or persons of European descent.

(l) "Superintendent General" means the Superintendent General of Indian Affairs, and "Deputy Superintendent General" means the Deputy Superintendent General of Indian Affairs.

(m) "Territories" means the Northwest Territories and the Yukon Territory. R.S., c. 81, s. 2; 1920, c. 50, s. 3.

PART I.

INDIANS.

Application.

3. The Governor in Council may, by proclamation, from time to time, exempt from the operation of this Part, or from the operation of any one or more of the sections of this Part, Indians or non-treaty Indians, or any of them, or any band or irregular band of them, or the reserves or special reserves, or Indian lands, or any portions of them, in any province or in the territories, or in any of them. and may again, by proclamation, from time to time, re- move such exemption. R.S., c. 81, s. 3.

Department of Indian Affairs.

4. The Minister of the Interior, or the head of any other department appointed for that purpose by the Governor in Council, shall be the Superintendent General of Indian Affairs, and shall, as such, have the control and management of the lands and property of the Indians in Canada.

2. The Superintendent General of Indian Affairs shall have charge of Eskimo affairs. R.S., c. 81, s. 4; 1924, c. 47, s. 1.

1. Subsection two of section four of the Indian Act, chapter ninety-eight of the Revised Statutes of Canada, 1927, is repealed.

5. Here shall be a department of the government of Canada which shall be called the Department of Indian Affairs, over which the Superintendent General shall pre-. R.S., c. 81, a 5. S.C. 1936, c. 32, s. 11(2).

(2) Sections three, six, seven and nine of the Geology and Mines Act, chapter eighty-three of the Revised Statutes of Canada, 1927, and section five and paragraph (a) of subsection one and subsec-

tion two of section seven of the Indian Act, chapter ninety-eight of the Revised Statutes of Canada, 1927, are repealed.

6. The Department of Indian Affairs shall have the management, charge and direction of Indian affairs. R.S., c. 81, s. 6.

7. The Governor in Council may appoint

(a) an officer who shall be called the Deputy of the Superintendent General of Indian Affairs.

(b) a deputy governor.

2. Such other officers, clerks and servants as are requisite for the proper conduct of the business of the Department may be appointed in the manner authorized by law. R.S., c. 81, s. 7; 1918, c. 12.

(2) Sections three, six, seven and nine of the Geology Mines Act, chapter eighty-three of the Revised Statutes of Canada, 1927, and section five and paragraph (a) of subsection one and subsection two of section seven of the Indian Act, chapter ninety-eight of the Revised Statutes of Canada, 1927, are repealed.

8. The Deputy Governor shall have the power, in the absence of or under instructions of the Governor General, to sign letters patent for Indian lands.

2. The signature of the Deputy Governor to such patents shall have the same force and virtue as if such patents were signed by the Governor General. R.S., c. 81, s. 8.

Schools.

9. The Governor in Council may establish

(a) day schools in any Indian reserve for the children of such reserve.

(b) industrial or boarding schools for the Indian children of any reserve or reserves or any district or territory designated by the Superintendent General.

2. Any school or institution the managing authorities of which have entered into a written agreement with the Superintendent General to admit Indian children and provide them with board, lodging and instruction may be declared by the Governor in Council to be an industrial school or a boarding school for the purposes of this Act.

3. The Superintendent General may provide for the transport of Indian children to and from the boarding or industrial schools to which they are assigned, including transportation to and from such schools for the annual vacations.

4. The Superintendent General shall have power to make regulations prescribing a standard for the buildings, equipment, teaching and discipline of and in all schools, and for the inspection of such schools.

5. The chief and council of any band that has children in a school shall have the right to inspect such school at such reasonable times as may be agreed upon by the Indian agent and the principal of the school.

6. The Superintendent General may apply the whole or any part of the annuities and interest moneys of Indian children attending an industrial or boarding school to the maintenance of such school or to the maintenance of the children themselves. 1920, c. 50, s. 1.

2. Subsection six of section nine of the said Act is repealed and the following substituted therefor:

"(6) The Superintendent General may apply the whole or any part of the annuities and interest moneys of Indian children attending an industrial or boarding school to the maintenance of such children."

10. Every Indian child between the ages of seven and fifteen years who is physically able shall attend such day, industrial or boarding school as may be designated by the Superintendent General for the full periods during which such school is open each year.

3. Subsection one of section ten of the said Act is repealed and the following substituted therefor:

10. (1) Every Indian child between the full ages of seven and sixteen years who is physically able shall attend such day, industrial or boarding school as may be designated by the Superintendent General for the full periods during such school is open each year; provided that were it has been made to appear to the satisfaction of the Super- intendent General that it would be detrimental to any particular Indian child to have it discharged from school on attaining the full age of sixteen years, the Superintendent General may direct that such child be detained at school for such further period as may seem to be advisable, but not beyond the full age of eighteen years, and in such case the provisions of this section with respect to truancy shall apply to such child and its parents, guardians or persons with whom such child resides during such further period of school attendance."

2. Such school shall be the nearest available school of the kind required, and no Protestant child shall be assigned to a Roman Catholic school or a school conducted under Roman Catholic auspices, and no Roman Catholic child shall be assigned to a Protestant school or a school con- ducted under Protestant auspices.

3. The Superintendent General may appoint any officer or person to be a truant officer to enforce the attendance of Indian children at school, and for such purpose a truant officer shall be vested with the powers of a peace officer, and shall have authority to enter any place where he has reason to believe there are Indian children between the ages of seven and fifteen years, and when requested by the Indian agent, a schoolteacher or the chief of a band shall examine into any case of truancy, shall warn the truants, their parents or guardians or the person with whom any Indian child resides, of the consequences of truancy, and notify the parent, guardian or such person in writing to cause the child to attend school.

4. Any parent, guardian or person with whom an Indian child is residing who fails to cause such child, be- tween the ages aforesaid, to attend school as required by this section after having received three days' notice so to do by a truant officer shall, on the complaint of the truant officer, be liable on summary conviction before a justice of the peace or Indian agent to a fine of not more than two dollars and costs, or imprisonment for a period not exceeding ten days or both, and such child may be arrested without a warrant and conveyed to school by the truant officer.

5. No parent or other person shall be liable to such penalties if such child

(a) is unable to attend school by reason of sickness or other unavoidable cause.

(b) has passed the entrance examination for high schools; or

(c) has been excused in writing by the Indian agent or teacher for temporary absence to assist in husbandry or urgent and necessary household duties. 1920, c. 50, s. 1.

1.Section ten of the Indian Act, chapter ninety-eight of the Revised Statutes of Canada, 1927, is amended by adding thereto the following subsection: —

"(6) For the purposes of this section, every member of the Royal Canadian Mounted Police Force and any special constable appointed for police duty on an Indian reserve, shall be a truant officer."

11. The Governor in Council may take the land of an Indian held under location ticket or otherwise, for school purposes, upon payment to such Indian of the compensation agreed upon, or in case of disagreement such compensation as may be determined in such manner as the Superintendent General may direct. 1914, c. 35, s. 2.

Membership of Band.

12. Any illegitimate child may, unless he has, with the consent of the band whereof the father or mother of such child is a member, shared in the distribution moneys of such band for a period exceeding two years, be, at any time, excluded from the membership thereof by the Super- intendent General. R.S., c. 81, s. 12.

13. Any Indian who has for five years continuously re- sided in a foreign country without the consent, in writing, of the Superintendent General or his agent, shall cease to be a member of the band of which he was formerly a member and he shall not again become a member of that band, or of any other band, unless the consent of such band, with the approval of the Superintendent General or his agent, is first obtained. R.S., c. 81, s. 13.

14. Any than an Indian woman, who marries any person other than Indian or a non-treaty Indian, shall cease to be an Indian in every respect within the meaning of this Act, except that she shall be entitled to share equally with the members of the band to which she formerly belonged, in the annual or semi-annual distribution of their annuities, interest moneys and rents; but such income may be to her at any time at ten years' purchase, with the approval of the Superintendent General. 1920, c. 50, s.2

15. Any Indian woman who marries an Indian of any other band, or a non-treaty Indian, shall cease to be a member of the band to which she formerly belonged, and shall become a member of the band or irregular band of which her husband is a member.

2. If she marries a non-treaty Indian, while becoming a member of the irregular band of which her husband is a member, she shall be entitled to share equally with the members of the band of which she was formerly a member, in the distribution of their moneys; but such income may be commuted to her at any time at ten years' purchase, with the consent of the band. R.S., c. 81, s. 15.

16. No half-breed in Manitoba who has shared in the distribution of half-breed lands shall be accounted an Indian.

2. No half-breed head of a family, except the widow of an Indian or a half-breed who has already been admitted into a treaty, shall, unless under very special circumstances, which shall be determined by the Superintendent General or his agent, be accounted an Indian or entitled to be ad- mitted into any Indian treaty.

3. Any half-breed who has been admitted into a treaty shall, on obtaining the consent in writing of the Superintendent General, be allowed to withdraw therefrom on signifying his desire so to do in writing, signed by him in the presence of two witnesses, who shall attest his signature on oath before some person authorized by law to ad- minister such oath.

4. Such withdrawal shall include the wife and minor unmarried children of such half-breed. R.S., c. 81, s. 16. 1914, c. 35, ss. 3 and 4.

17. When, of a band, an Indian of one band is admitted into membership in another band, and his admission thereinto is assented to by the Superintendent General, such Indian shall cease to have

any interest in the lands or moneys of the band of which he was formerly a member, and shall be entitled to share in the lands and moneys of the band to which he is so admitted.

2. The Superintendent General may cause to be deducted from the capital of the band of which such Indian was formerly a member his per capita share of such capital and place the same to the credit of the capital of the band into membership in which he has been admitted in the manner aforesaid. R.S., c. 81, s. 17.

18. The Superintendent General, may from time to time upon the report of an officer, or other person specially appointed by him to make an inquiry, determine who is or who is not a member of any band of Indians entitled to share in the property and annuities of the band.

2. The decision of the Superintendent General in any such matter shall be final and conclusive, subject to the Governor in Council. R.S., c. 81, s. 18.

Reserves.

19. All reserves for Indians, or for any band of Indians, or held in trust for their benefit, shall be deemed to be re- served and held for the same purposes as they were held heretofore, but shall be subject to the provisions of this Part. R.S., c. 81, s. 19.

20. The Superintendent General may authorize surveys. plans and reports to be made of any reserve for Indians. showing and distinguishing the improved lands, the forests subdivision and lands fit for settlement, and such other information as reserves is required; and may authorize the whole or any portion of a reserve to be subdivided into lots. R.S., c. 81, s. 20.

21. No Indian shall be deemed to be lawfully in pos- session of any land in a reserve, unless he has been or is reserve, located for the same by the band, or council of the band, with the approval of the Superintendent General; but no Indian shall be dispossessed of any land on which he has improvements, without receiving compensation for such improvements, at a valuation approved by the Superintendent General, from the Indian who obtains the land, or from the funds of the band, as is determined by the Superintendent General.

2. Prior to the location of an Indian under this section, in the province of Manitoba, Saskatchewan or Alberta, or the Territories, the Indian commissioner may issue a certificate of occupancy to any Indian belonging to a band residing upon a reserve in the aforesaid provinces or territories, of so much land, not exceeding in any case one hundred and sixty acres, as the Indian, with the approval of the commissioner, selects.

3. Such certificate may be cancelled at any time by the Indian commissioner, but shall, while it remains in force, entitle the holder thereof, as against all others, to possession of the lands described therein. R.S., c. 81, s. 21.

22. When the Superintendent General approves of any location as aforesaid, he shall issue, in triplicate, a granting a location title to such Indian, one triplicate of which he shall retain in a book to be kept for the purpose. and the other two of which he shall forward to the local agent.

2. The local agent shall deliver to the Indian in whose favour it is issued one of such duplicates so forwarded, and shall cause the other to be copied into a register of the band, provided for the purpose, and shall file the same. R.S., c. 81, s. 22.

23. The conferring of any such location title shall not have the effect of rendering the land covered thereby subject to seizure under legal process, and such title shall be transferable only to an Indian of

the same band, and then only with the consent and approval of the Superintendent General, whose consent and approval shall be given only by the issue of a ticket, in the manner prescribed in the last preceding section. R.S., c. 81, s. 23.

24. Every Indian and every non-treaty Indian, in the province of Manitoba, British Columbia, Saskatchewan or Alberta, or the Territories, who had, previously to the selection of a reserve, possession of and who has made permanent improvements on a plot of land which upon such selection becomes included in, or surrounded by, a reserve, shall have the same privileges, in respect of such plot, as an Indian enjoys who holds under a location title. R.S., c. 81, s. 24.

Descent of Property.

25. Indian's may devise or bequeath property of any kind in the same manner as other persons.

2. No will be purporting to dispose of land in a reserve or any interest therein shall be of any force or effect unless or until the will has been approved by the Superintendent General, and if a will be disapproved by the Superintendent General the Indian making the will shall be deemed to have died intestate; and the Superintendent General may approve of a will generally and disallow any disposition thereby made of land in a reserve or of any interest in such land, in which case the will so approved shall have force and effect except so far as such disallowed disposition is concerned, and the Indian making the will shall be deemed to have died intestate as to the land or interest the disposition of which is so disallowed.

3. No one who is not entitled to reside on the reserve shall by reason of any devise or bequest or by reason of any intestacy be entitled to hold land in a reserve, but any land in a reserve devised by will or devolving on an intestacy, to someone not entitled to reside on the reserve, shall be sold by the Superintendent General to some member of the band and the proceeds thereof shall be paid to such devisee or heir. R.S., c. 81, s. 25; 1918, c. 26, s. 1.

1. Subsection three of section twenty-five of the Indian Act chapter ninety-eight of the Revised Statutes of Canada, 1927 is repealed and the following substituted therefor: — "(3) No one who is not entitled to reside on the reserve still by reason of any devise or bequest or by reason of any intestacy be entitled to hold land in a reserve, but any land in a reserve devised by will or devolving on an intestacy, to someone not entitled to reside on the reserve, Fhft11 be sold by the Superintendent General to the band or to some member of the band and the proceeds thereof shall be paid to such devisee or heir."

26. Upon the death of an Indian intestate his property of all kinds, real and personal, movable and immovable, including any recognized interest, he may have in land in a reserve, shall descend as follows:

(a) One-third of the inheritance shall devolve upon his one-third widow, if she is a woman of good moral character, and the remainder upon his children, if all are living, or, if any who are dead have died without issue.

(b) If there is no widow, or if the widow is not of good otherwise moral character, the whole inheritance shall devolve upon his children in equal shares, if all are living, or, if any who are dead have died without issue.

(c) If one or more of the children are living, and one are dead, having had lawful issue, the inheritance so far as the same does not descend to the widow, shall devolve upon the children who are living, and the descendants of such children as have died, so that each child who is living shall receive such share as would have descended to him if all the children of the intestate who have died leaving issue had been living, and? so that the descendants of each child who is dead shall inherit in equal shares the share which their parent would have received if living.

(d) If the descendants of the intestate entitled to share in the inheritance are of unequal degrees of consanguinity to the intestate, the inheritance shall devolve so that those who are in the nearest degree of consanguinity shall take the shares which would have descended to them, had all the descendants in the same degree of consanguinity who have died leaving issue, been living, and so that the issue of the descendants who have died shall respectively take the shares which their parents, if living, would have received. but the Superintendent General may, in his discretion direct that the widow, if she is of good moral character, shall have the right, during her widowhood, to occupy any land in the reserve of the band to which deceased belonged of which he was the recognized owner, and to have the use of any property of the deceased for which, under the provisions of this Part, he was not liable to taxation.

2. The Superintendent General shall be the sole and judge as to the moral character of the widow of any intestate Indian. R.S., c. 81, s. 26.

27. During the minority of the children of an Indian who dies intestate, the administration and charge of the? property to which they are entitled as aforesaid shall devolve upon the widow, if any, of the intestate, if she is of good moral character; and, in such case, as each male child attains the age of twenty-one years, and as each female child attains that age, or with the consent of the widow, marries before that age, the share of such child shall, subject to the approval of the Superintendent General, be conveyed or delivered to him or her.

2. The Superintendent General may, at any time, remove the widow from such administration and charge and confer the same upon some other person, and, in like manner, may remove such other person and appoint another, and so, from time to time, as occasion requires.

3. The Superintendent General may, whenever there are minor children, appoint a fit and proper person to take charge of such children and their property, and may remove such person and appoint another, and so, from time to time, as occasion requires. R.S., c. 81, s. 27.

28. The Superintendent General may appoint a person or persons to administer the estate of any deceased or insane Indian, and may make such general regulations and such orders in particular cases as he deems necessary to secure the satisfactory administration of such estates. 1924, c. 47, s. 2.

2. Section twenty-eight of the said Act is amended by, adding thereto the following subsection:

"(2) The Superintendent General may remove an executor of an estate who neglects or refuses to carry out the of the will in such time as may be considered reasonable by the Superintendent and appoint someone in the place of such executor."

29. In case any Indian dies intestate without issue, leaving a widow, all his property of whatever kind shall without devolve upon her, and if he leaves no widow the same shall devolve upon the nearest of kin to the deceased: Provided that any interest which he may have had in land in a reserve shall be vested in His Majesty for the benefit of the band owning such reserve if his nearest of kin is more remote than a brother or sister. 1924, c. 47, s. 3.

30. The property of a married Indian woman who dies intestate shall descend in the same manner and be distributed in the same proportions as that of a male Indian who dies intestate, her widower, if any, taking the share which the widow of such male Indian would take.

2. The other provisions of this Part respecting the descent of property shall in like manner apply to the case of an intestate married woman, the word widower being substituted for the word widow in each case.

3. The property of an unmarried Indian woman who dies intestate shall descend in the same manner as if she had been a male. R.S., c. 81, s. 29. .

31. A claimant of land in a reserve or of any interest in any therein as devisee or legatee or heir of a deceased Indian shall not be held to be lawfully in possession thereof or be the recognized owner thereof until he shall have obtained a location ticket therefor from the Superintendent General. R.S., c. 81, s. 30.

32. The Superintendent General may decide all ques- which arise under this Part, respecting the distribution among those entitled thereto of the property of a deceased Indian, and he shall be the sole and final judge as to who the persons so entitled are.

2. The Superintendent General may do whatsoever in his judgment will best give to each claimant his share according to the true intent and meaning of this Part, and to that end, if he thinks fit, may direct the sale, lease or other disposition of such property or any part thereof, and the distribution or application of the proceeds or income thereof, regard being always had in any such disposition to the restriction upon the disposition of property in a reserve. RS., c. 81, s. 31.

33. Notwithstanding anything in this Part, the courts having jurisdiction in the case of persons other than Indians, with but not without the consent of the Superintendent General, may grant probate of the wills of Indians and letters of administration of the estate and effects of intestate Indians, in which case such courts and the executors and administrators obtaining such probate, or thereby appointed, shall have the like jurisdiction and powers as in other cases, except that no disposition shall, without the consent of the Superintendent General, be made of or dealing had with regard to any right or interest in land in a reserve or any property for which, under the provisions of this Part, an Indian is not liable to taxation. R.S., c. 81, s. 32.

Trespassing on Reserves.

34. No person, or Indian other than an Indian of the band, shall without the authority of the Superintendent General, reside or hunt upon, occupy or use any land or reside on marsh, or reside upon or occupy any road, or allowance for road, running through any reserve belonging to or occupied by such band.

2. All deeds, leases, contracts, agreements or instruments of whatsoever kind made, entered into, or consented to by any Indian, purporting to permit persons or Indian's void. other than Indians of the band to reside or hunt upon such reserve, or to occupy or use any portion thereof, shall be void. R.S., c. 81, s. 33.

35. If any Indian is illegally in possession of any land on a reserve, or if any person, or Indian other than an Indian of the band, without the license of the Superintendent General,

(a) settles, resides or hunts upon, occupies, uses, or causes or permits any cattle or other animals owned by him, or in his charge, to trespass on any such land or marsh.

(b) fishes in any marsh, river, stream or creek on or running through a reserve; or

(c) settles, resides upon or occupies any road, or allowance for road, on such reserve.

the Superintendent General or such other officer or person as he thereunto deputes and authorizes, shall, on complaint made to him, and on proof of the fact to his satisfaction, Warrant. issue his warrant, signed and sealed, directed to any literate person willing to act in the premises, commanding him forthwith as the case may be,

(a) to remove from the said land, marsh or road, or allowance for road, every such person or Indian and his family, so settled, or who is residing or hunting upon, or occupying, or is illegally in possession of the same.

(b) to remove such cattle or other animals from such land or marsh.

(c) to cause such person or Indian to cease fishing in any marsh, river, stream or creek, as aforesaid; or

(d) to notify such person or Indian to cease using, as aforesaid, the said land, river, stream, creek or marsh, road or allowances for road.

2. The person to whom such warrant is directed, shall execute the same, and, for that purpose, shall have the same powers as in the execution of criminal process.

3. The expenses incurred in any such removal or notification, or causing to cease fishing, shall be borne, as the case may be, by the person removed or notified, or caused to cease fishing, or who owns the cattle or other animals removed, or who has them in charge, and may be recovered from him as the costs in any ordinary action or suit, or if the trespasser is an Indian, such expenses may be deducted from his share of annuity and interest money, if any such are due to him.

4. Any such person or Indian other than an Indian of the band may be required orally or in writing by an Indian agent, a chief of the band occupying the reserve, or a constable, as the case may be,

(a) to remove with his family, if any, from the land, marsh or road, or allowance for road, upon which he is or has so settled, or is residing or hunting, or which he so occupies.

(b) to remove his cattle from such land or marsh. S.C. 1930, c. 25, c. 4.

4. Paragraph "b" of subsection four of section thirty-five of the said Act is repealed and the following substituted therefor:

"(b) to remove any cattle or other animals owned by him or in his charge from such land or marsh."

(c) to cease fishing in any such marsh, river, stream or creek as aforesaid; or

(d) to cease using as aforesaid any such land, river stream, creek, marsh, road or allowance for road. R.S., c. 81, s. 34.

36. If any person or Indian, after he has been removed or notified as aforesaid, or after any cattle or other animals owned by him or in his charge have been removed as aforesaid,

(a) returns to, settles, resides or hunts upon or occupies or uses as aforesaid any of the said land or marsh.

(b) causes or permits any cattle or other animals owned by him or in his charge to return to any of the said land or marsh.

(c) returns to any marsh, river, stream or creek on or running through a reserve, for the purpose of fishing therein, or

(d) returns to, settles or resides upon or occupies any of the said roads or allowances for roads.
the Superintendent General, or any officer or person deputed or authorized, as aforesaid, upon view, or upon proof on oath before him, to his satisfaction, that the person or Indian has,
(a) returned to, settled, resided or hunted upon or occupied or used as aforesaid any of the said lands or marshes.
(b) caused or permitted any cattle or other animals owned by him, or in his charge, to return to any of the said land or marsh.
(c) returned to any marsh, river, stream or creek on or running through a reserve for the purpose of fishing therein, or
(d) returned to, settled or resided upon or occupied any of the said roads or allowances for roads.
shall direct and send his warrant, signed and sealed, to the sheriff of the proper county or district, or to any literate person therein, commanding him forthwith to arrest sulci person or Indian, and bring him before any stipendiary magistrate, police magistrate, justice of the peace or Indian agent, who may, on summary conviction, commit him to the common goal of the said county or district, or if there is no goal in the said county or district, or if the reserve? is not situated within any county or district, then the goal nearest to the said reserve in the province, there to remain for the time ordered in the warrant of commitment.
2. The length of imprisonment aforesaid shall not exceed thirty days for the first offence, and thirty days additional for each subsequent offense.
3. If the said reserve is not situated within any county or district, such warrant shall be directed and sent to some literate person within such reserve. R.S., c. 81, s. 35.
37. Such sheriff or other person shall accordingly arrest the said person or Indian, and deliver him to the keeper of the proper goal, who shall receive such person or Indian, and imprison him in the said goal for the term aforesaid. R.S., c. 81, s. 36.
38. The Superintendent General, or such officer or person aforesaid, shall cause the judgment or order against the offender to be drawn up and filed in his office.
2. Such judgment shall not be appealed from, or removed by certiorari or otherwise but shall be final. R.S., c. 81, s. 37.
Recovery of Possession of Reserves.
39. If the possession of any lands reserved or claimed to be reserved for the Indians, or of any lands of which the Indians or any Indian or any band or tribe of Indians claim the possession or any right of possession, is withheld, or if any such lands are adversely occupied or claimed by any person, or if any trespass is committed thereon, the possession may be recovered for the Indians or Indian or band or tribe of Indians, or the conflicting claims may be adjudged and determined or damages may be recovered in an action at the suit of His Majesty on behalf of the Indians or Indian or of the band or tribe of Indians entitled to or claiming the possession or right of possession or entitled to or claiming the declaration, relief or damages.
2. The Exchequer Court of Canada shall have jurisdiction to hear and determine any such action.
3. Any such action may be instituted by information of the Attorney General of Canada upon the instructions of the Superintendent General of Indian Affairs.
4. Nothing in this section shall impair, abridge or in anywise affect any existing remedy or mode of

procedure provided for cases, or any of them, to which this section applies. 1910, c. 28, s. 1; 1911, c. 14, s. 4.

Sale or Barter.

40. The Governor in Council may make regulations for prohibiting or regulating the sale, barter, exchange or gift by any band or irregular band of Indians, or by any Indian of any band or irregular band, in the province of Manitoba, Saskatchewan or Alberta, or the Territories, of any grain or root crops, or other produce grown upon any reserve, and may further provide that such sale, barter, exchange or gift shall be null and void, unless the same are made in accordance with such regulations. R.S., c. 81, s. 38.

5. Section forty of the said Act is repealed and the following substituted therefor: —

"40. No person shall buy or otherwise acquire from any band or irregular band of Indians or from any Indian any cattle or other animals of any kind from any reserve in the Province of Manitoba, Saskatchewan or Alberta or the Territories without the written consent of the Indian agent.

3. Section forty of the said Act, as enacted by section five of chapter twenty-five of the statutes of 1930, is repealed and the following is substituted therefor: —

"40. No person shall buy or otherwise acquire from any band or irregular band of Indians or from any Indian and no Indian shall sell or otherwise dispose of to any one other than a member of the band, any cattle or other animals of any kind from any reserve in the province of Manitoba, Saskatchewan or Alberta or the Territories without the written consent of the Indian Agent."

41. No person shall buy or otherwise acquire from any band or irregular band of Indians, or from any Indian, any grain, root crops, or other produce from upon any reserve in the province of Manitoba, Saskatchewan or Alberta, or the Territories. R.S., c. 81, s. 39.

6. Section forty-one of the said Act, as enacted by section six of chapter twenty-five of the statutes of 1930, is repealed and the following is substituted therefor: —

" 41. No person shall buy or otherwise acquire from Buying any band or irregular band of Indians, or from any Indian, and no Indian shall sell or otherwise dispose of to any one other than a member of the band, any grain, root crops, or other produce from upon any reserve in the Province of Manitoba, Saskatchewan or Alberta, or the Territories, without the written consent of the Indian Agent."

42. If any such grain or root crops, or other produce as, are unlawfully in the possession of any person within the intent and meaning of this Part, or of any regulations made by the Governor in Council under this Part, any person acting under the authority, either general or special, of the Superintendent General, may, with such assistance in that behalf as he thinks necessary, seize and take possession of the same; and he shall deal therewith as the Superintendent General, or any officer or person thereunto by him authorized, directs. R.S., c. 81, s. 40.

7. Section forty-two of the said Act is repealed and ten following substituted therefor: —

"42. If any such cattle or other animals or such grain, root crops, or other produce, as aforesaid, are unlawfully in the possession of any person within the intent and meaning of this part, any person acting under the authority, either general or special, of the Superintendent General, me with such assistance in that behalf as he thinks necessary, seize and take possession of the same and he shall deal therewith as the Superintendent General or any officer or person thereunto by him authorized, directs."

1. The Indian Act, chapter ninety-eight of the Revised Statutes of Canada, 1927, is amended by inserting immediately after section forty-two thereof, the following section: —

(1) The Governor in Council may make regulations to prohibit and control the buying or otherwise acquiring from any Indian, non-treaty Indian or band or irregular band of Indians any wild animal or the skin or other part of such animal. Without restricting the generality the foregoing the regulations may prescribe: —

(a) that the Superintendent General or Agent acting on his behalf may issue permits to buy or otherwise acquire any wild animal or parts thereof as aforesaid and may fix the terms upon which such permits may be issued.

(b) that a fine not exceeding five hundred dollars or imprisonment for a term not exceeding six months or both fine and imprisonment may be imposed for any violation of such regulations.

(2) Where the Superintendent General, or Agent acting on his behalf, has reason to believe that the regulations been contravened in respect of any wild animal or the skin or other part of such animal he may seize such animal or any part or parts thereof wherever found and bring the same before any judge, police or stipendiary magistrate, two justices of the peace or Indian Agent and on proof that such contravention has occurred such animal or part or parts shall be declared forfeited to His Majesty. Any animal or part thereof declared forfeited hereunder shall be disposed of as the Superintendent General may direct.

(3) Such regulations may from time to time by order of the Superintendent General be declared to apply to any area in the Dominion of Canada and copies of every such order shall be posted in all post offices in or adjacent to the area therein specified.

(4) The Superintendent General may at any time without prior notice revokes any permit issued in accordance with any regulation made under the provisions of this section.

(5) The regulations made by the Governor in Council and every order made by the Superintendent General under the provisions of this section shall be published in the Canada Gazette

43. The Governor in Council may make regulations for prohibiting the cutting, carrying away or removing from any reserve or special reserve, of any hard or sugar-maple tree or sapling. R.S., c. 81, s. 41.

44. No official or employee connected with the inside or outside service of the Department, and no missionary in the employ of any religious denomination, or otherwise employed in mission work among Indians, and no school teacher on an Indian reserve, shall, without the special license in writing of the Superintendent General, trade with any Indian, or sell to him directly or indirectly, any goods or supplies, cattle or other animals.

2. The Superintendent General may at any time revoke the license so given by him. R.S., c. S1, s. 42.

45. No person shall barter directly or indirectly with any Indian on a reserve in the province of Manitoba, Saskatchewan or Alberta, or the Territories, or sell to any such Indian any goods or supplies, cattle or other animals without the special license in writing of the Superintendent General.

2. The Superintendent General may, at any time, revoke the license by him given.

3. Upon prosecution of any offender against the pro- visions of this and the last preceding section, the evidence of the Indian to whom the sale was made, and the production to, or view by, the magistrate or Indian agent of the article or animal sold, shall be sufficient evidence on which to convict.

R.S., c. 81, s. 43.

Roads and Bridges.

46. Indians residing upon any reserve shall be liable, if so, directed by the Superintendent General, or any officer or person by him thereunto authorized, to perform labor upon the public roads laid out or used in or through, or abutting upon such reserve, which labor shall be performed under the sole control of the Superintendent General, or officer or person aforesaid, who may direct when, where and how and in what manner such labor shall be applied, and to what extent the same shall be imposed upon any Indian who is a resident upon the reserve.

2.The Superintendent General, or person or officer afore said shall have the like power to enforce the performance of such labor by imprisonment or otherwise, as may be done by any power or authority under any law, rule or regulation in force in the province or territory in which such reserve is situated, for the non-performance of statute labor; but the labor to be so required of any such Indian shall not exceed in amount or extent what may be required of other inhabitants of the same province, territory, county or other local division, under the laws requiring and regulating such labor and the performance thereof. R.S., c. 81, s. 44.

47. Every band of Indians shall cause the roads, bridges, ditches and fences within its reserve to be put and maintained in proper order, in accordance with the instructions received, from time to time, from the Superintendent General, or from the agent of the Superintendent General.

2. Whenever in the opinion of the Superintendent General Such roads, bridges, ditches and fences are not so put or maintained in order, he may cause the work to be performed at the cost of the band, or of the particular Indian in default, as the case may be, either out of its or his annual allowances or otherwise. R.S., c. 81, s. 45.

5. Section forty-seven of the said Act is amended by adding thereto the following subsection: —

"(3) The Superintendent General shall have the authority to determine where roads shall be established on a reserve."

Lands taken for Public Purposes.

48. No portion of any reserve shall be taken for the purpose of any railway, road, public work, or work designed for any public utility without the consent of the Governor in Council, but any company or municipal or local authority having statutory power, either Dominion or provincial, for taking or using lands or any interest in lands without the consent of the owner may, with the consent of the Governor in Council as aforesaid, and subject to the terms and conditions imposed by such consent, exercise such statutory power with respect to any reserve or portion of a reserve.

2. In any such case compensation shall be made there- for to the Indians of the band, and the exercise of such power, and the taking of the lands or interest therein and the determination and payment of the compensation shall, unless otherwise provided by the order in council evidencing the consent of the Governor in Council, be governed by the requirements applicable to the like proceedings by such company, municipal or local authority in ordinary cases.

3. The Superintendent General shall, in any case in an arbitration is had, name the arbitrator on behalf of the Indians, and shall act for them in any matter relating to the settlement of such compensation.

4. The amount awarded in any case shall be paid to the Minister of Finance for the use of the band of Indians for whose benefit the reserve is held, and for the benefit of any Indian who has improvements taken or injured. R.S., c. 81, s. 46; 1911, c. 14, s. 1.

Surrender and Forfeiture of Lands in Reserve.
49. If, by the violation of the conditions of any trust respecting any special reserve, or by the breaking up of any society, corporation or community, or, if by the death title of any person or persons without a legal succession or Zeldin trusteeship, in whom the title to a special reserve is held in trust, the said title lapses or becomes void in law, the legal title shall become vested in His Majesty in trust, and the property shall be managed for the band or irregular band previously interested therein as an ordinary reserve.

2. The trustees of any special reserve may, at any time, surrender the same to His Majesty in trust, whereupon the property shall be managed for the band or irregular His band previously interested therein as an ordinary reserve. R.S., c. 81, s. 47.

50. Except as in this Part otherwise provided, no reserve or portion of a reserve shall be sold, alienated or leased until it has been released or surrendered to the Crown for the purposes of this Part; but the Superintendent General may lease, for the benefit of any Indian, upon his application for that purpose, the land to which he is entitled without such land being released or surrendered, and may, without surrender, dispose to the best advantage, in the interests of the Indians, of wild grass and dead or fallen timber.

2. The Governor in Council may make regulations of enabling the Superintendent General without surrender to issue leases for surface rights on Indian reserve, upon such terms and conditions as may be considered proper in the interest of the Indians covering such area only as may be necessary for the mining of the precious metals by any one otherwise authorized to mine such metals, said terms to include provision of compensating any occupant of land for any damage that may be caused thereon as determined by the Superintendent General. R.S., c. 81, s. 48; 1919, c. 56, s. 1.

1. Subsection two of section fifty of the Indian Act, chapter ninety-eight of the Revised Statutes of Canada, 1927, is repealed and the following substituted therefor: —

"(2) The Governor in Council may make regulations enabling the Superintendent General in respect of any Indian reserve, to issue leases upon such terms as may be considered proper in the interest of the Indians and of any other lessee or licensee of surface rights,

(a) upon surrender in accordance with this part, of any land deemed to contain salt, petroleum, natural gas, coal, gold, silver, copper, iron or other minerals and to grant in respect of such land the right to prospect for, mine, recover and take away any or all such mineral, and

(b) without surrender, to any person authorized to mine any of the minerals in this section mentioned, of surface rights over such area of any land within a reserve containing any such minerals as may be necessary for the mining thereof."

51. Except as in this Part otherwise provided, no release or surrender of a reserve, or a portion of a reserve, held for the use of the Indians of any band, or of any individual Indian, shall be valid or binding, unless the release or surrender shall be assented to by a majority of the male members of the band of the full age of twenty-one years, at a meeting or council thereof summoned for that

purpose, according to the rules of the band, and held in the presence of the Superintendent General, or of any officer duly authorized to attend such council, by the Governor in Council or by the Superintendent General.

2. No Indian shall be entitled to vote or be present at such council, unless he habitually resides on or near, and is interested in the reserve in question.

3. The fact that such release or surrender has been assented to by the band at such council or meeting shall be certified on oath by the Superintendent General, or by the officer authorized by him to attend such council or meeting, and by some of the chiefs or principal men present thereat and entitled to vote, before any person having authority to take affidavits and having jurisdiction within the place where the oath is administered.

4. When such assent has been so certified, as aforesaid, such release or surrender shall be submitted to the Governor in Council for acceptance or refusal. R.S., c. 81, s. 49; 1918, c. 26, s. 2.

52. In the case of an Indian reserve which adjoins or is situated wholly or partly within an incorporated town or city having a population of not less than eight thousand, and which reserve has not been released or surrendered by the Indians, the Governor in Council may, upon the recommendation of the Superintendent General, refer to the judge of the Exchequer Court of Canada for inquiry and report the question as to whether it is expedient, having regard to the interest of the public and of the Indians of the band for whose use the reserve is held, that the Indians should be removed from the reserve or any part of it.

2. The order in council made in the case shall be certified by the Clerk of the Privy Council to the Registrar of the Exchequer Court of Canada, and the judge of the court shall thereupon proceed as soon as convenient to fix a time and place, of which due notice shall be given by publication in the Canada Gazette, and otherwise as may be directed by the judge, for taking the evidence and hearing and investigating the matter.

3. The judge shall have the like powers to issue subpoenas, compel the attendance and examination of witnesses, take evidence, give directions, and generally to hear and determine the matter and regulate the procedure as in proceedings upon information by the Attorney General within the ordinary jurisdiction of the court, and shall assign counsel to represent and act for the Indians who may be opposed to the proposed removal.

4. If the judge finds that it is expedient that the band of Indians should be removed from the reserve or any part of it, he shall proceed, before making his report, to ascertain the amounts of compensation, if any, which should be paid respectively to individual Indians of the band for the special loss or damages which they will sustain in respect of the buildings or improvements to which they are entitled upon the lands of the reserve for which they are located, and the judge shall, moreover, consider and report upon any of the other facts or circumstances of the case which he may deem proper or material to be considered by the Governor in Council.

5. The judge shall transmit his findings, with the a report of the proceedings, to the Governor in Council, who shall lay a full report of the proceedings, the evidence and the findings before Parliament at the then current or next ensuing session thereof, and upon such findings being approved by resolution of Parliament the Governor in Council may thereupon give effect to the said findings and cause the reserve, or any part thereof from which it is found expedient to remove the Indians, to

be sold or leased by public auction after three months advertisement in the public press, upon the best terms which, in the opinion of the Governor in Council, may be obtained therefor.

6. The proceeds of the sale or lease, after deducting the usual percentage for management fund, shall be applied in compensating individual Indians for their buildings or improvements as found by the judge, in purchasing a new reserve for the Indians removed, in transferring the said Indians with their effects thereto, in erecting buildings upon the new reserve, and in providing the Indians with such other assistance as the Superintendent General may consider advisable; and the balance of the proceeds, if any, shall be placed to the credit of the Indians; but the Governor in Council shall not cause the Indians to be removed, Exception, or disturb their possession, until a suitable reserve has been obtained and set apart for them in lieu of the reserve from which the expediency of removing the Indians is so established as aforesaid.

7. For the purpose of selecting, appropriating and acquiring the lands necessary to be taken, or which it may be deemed expedient to take, for any new reserve to be acquired for the Indians as authorized by the last preceding subsection, whether they are Crown lands or not, the Superintendent General shall have all the powers conferred upon the Minister by the Expropriation Act, and such new reserve shall, for the purposes aforesaid, be deemed to be a public work within the definition of that expression in the Expropriation Act; and all the provisions of the Expropriation Act, in so far as applicable and not inconsistent with this Act, shall apply in respect of the proceedings for the selection, survey, ascertainment and acquisition of the lands required and the determination and payment of the compensation therefor.

8. The Superintendent General shall not exercise the power of expropriation unless authorized by the Governor in Council. 1911, c. 14, s. 2.

53. Nothing in this Part shall confirm any release or surrender which, but for this Part, would have been invalid; and no release or surrender of any reserve, or portion of a reserve, to any person other than His Majesty, shall be valid. R.S., c. 81, s. 50.

54. All Indian lands which are reserves or portions of reserves surrendered, or to be surrendered, to His Majesty, shall be deemed to be held for the same purpose as heretofore. and shall be managed, leased and sold as the Governor in Council directs, subject to the conditions of surrender and the provisions of this Part. R.S., c. 81, s. 51.

Sale and Transfer of Indian Lands.

55. Every certificate of sale or receipt for money received on the sale of Indian lands granted or made by the Superintendent General or any agent of, his, so long as the sale to which such certificate or receipt relates is in force and not rescinded, shall entitle the person to whom the same is granted, or his assignee, by instrument registered under this or any former Act providing for registration in such cases, to take possession of and occupy the land therein comprised, subject to the conditions of such sale, and unless the same has been revoked or cancelled, to maintain thereunder actions and suits against any wrongdoer or trespasser, as effectually as he could do under a patent from the Crown; but the same shall have no force against a license to cut timber existing at the time of the granting or making thereof.

2. Such certificate or receipt shall be prima facie evidence of possession by such person, or the as-

signee, under an instrument registered as aforesaid in any such action or suit. R.S., c. 81, s. 52.

56. The Superintendent General shall keep a book for registering, at the option of the persons interested, the particulars of any assignment made, as well by the original purchaser or lessee of Indian lands, or his heirs or legal representatives, as by any subsequent assignee of any such lands, or the heirs or legal representatives of such assignee. R.S., c. 81, s. 53.

57. Upon any such assignment being produced too the Superintendent General, and, except in cases where such assignment is made under a corporate seal, with an affidavit of due execution thereof, and of the place of such execution, and the names, residences and occupations of the witnesses, or, as to lands in the province of Quebec, upon the production of any such assignment executed in notarial form, or of a notarial copy thereof, the Superintendent General shall cause the material parts of the assignment to be registered in the said book, and shall cause to be endorsed on the assignment a certificate of such registration signed by himself or by the Deputy Superintendent General, or any other officer of the Department by him authorised to sign such certificates. R.S., c. 81, s. 54.

58. Every such assignment so registered shall be valid against any assignment previously executed, which is subsequently registered or is unregistered.

2. No such registration shall be made until all the conditions of the sale, grant or location are complied with or dispensed with by the Superintendent General.

3. Every assignment registered as aforesaid shall be unconditional in its terms. R.S., c. S1, s. 55.

59. If any subscribing witness to any such assignment is dead, or is absent from Canada, the Superintendent General may register such assignment upon the production of an affidavit proving the death or absence of such witness, and his handwriting, or the handwriting of the person making such assignment. R.S., c. 81, s. 56.

60. No agent for the sale of Indian lands shall, within his division, directly or indirectly, except under an order of the Governor in Council, purchase any land which he is appointed to sell, or become proprietor of or interested in any such land, during the time of his agency; and every such purchase or interest shall be void. R.S., c. 81, s. 57.

Tax Sales.

61. Whenever the proper municipal officer having, by the law of the province in which the land affected is situate, authority to make or execute deeds or conveyances of lands sold for taxes, makes or executes any deed or conveyance purporting to grant or convey Indian lands which have been sold or located, but not patented, or the interest therein of the locate or purchaser from the Crown, and such deed or conveyance recites or purports to be based upon a sale of such lands or such interest in taxes, the Superintendent General may approve of such deed or conveyance, and act upon and treat it as a valid transfer of all the right and interest of the original locate or purchaser from the Crown, and of every person claiming under him in or to such land to the grantee named in such deed or conveyance.

2. When the Superintendent General has signified his approval of such deed or conveyance by endorsement thereon, the grantee shall be substituted in all respects, in relation to the land so conveyed, for the original locate or purchaser from the Crown, but no such deed or conveyance shall be deemed to confer upon the grantee any greater right or interest in the land than that possessed by the original locate or purchaser from the Crown. R.S., c. 81, 8. 58.

62. The Superintendent General may cause a patent to be issued to the grantee named in such deed or conveyance on the completion of the original conditions of the location or sale, unless such deed or conveyance is declared invalid by a court of competent jurisdiction in a suit or action instituted by some person interested in such land within two years after the date of the sale for taxes, and unless within such delay notice of such contestation has been given to the Superintendent General. R.S., c. 81, s. 59.

63. Every such deed or conveyance shall be registered in the office of the Superintendent General within two years from the date of the sale for taxes; and unless the same is so registered, it shall not be deemed to have preserved its priority, as against a purchaser in good faith from the original locate or purchaser from the Crown, in virtue of an assignment registered prior to the date of the registration of the deed or conveyance based upon a sale for taxes as aforesaid. R.S., c. 81, s. 60.

Cancellation.

64. If the Superintendent General is satisfied that any purchaser or lessee of any Indian lands, or any person claiming under or through him, has been guilty of any fraud or imposition, or has violated any of the conditions of the sale or lease, or if any such sale or lease has been made or issued in error or mistake, he may cancel such sale or lease and resume the land therein mentioned, or dispose of it as if no sale or lease thereof had ever been made.

2. In any case where the Superintendent or the Deputy Superintendent General gives or has given notice to a purchaser or lessee of Indian lands or to his assignee, agent, executor, administrator or representative, of his intention to cancel a sale or lease under the provisions of this section, and in pursuance of such notice enters or has entered in the records of the Department the formal cancellation of such sale or lease, such entry of cancellation shall be and be deemed to have been effective from the date thereof to cancel and annul the said sale or lease, and any payments made on account of such sale or lease shall be and be deemed to have been forfeited.

3. In any such case as described in the preceding subsection the notice of cancellation shall be deemed to be and to have been sufficient if signed by the Superintendent General, the Deputy Superintendent General, or by any officer of the Department by the direction and with the authority of the Superintendent General or the Deputy Superintendent General: and moreover, the notice shall be deemed to be and to have been duly given and served upon or delivered to the purchaser or lessee, or to his assignee, agent, executor, administrator or representative as aforesaid if posted prepaid or franked to his last known address.

4. No action, suit or other proceeding, either at law or in equity, shall lie or be instituted, prosecuted or maintained against His Majesty or against the Superintendent General, or the Attorney General, or any officer of the Government of Canada, claiming any relief or declaration against or in respect of the cancellation or forfeiture of any such sale or lease, or payments on account thereof by means of any such notice as aforesaid, unless the same was or shall have been instituted within one year from the date of the giving of the said notice.

5. Within the first fifteen days of each session of Parliament, the Superintendent General shall cause to be laid before both Houses of Parliament, a list of all such sales or leases, cancelled during the twelve months next preceding that session, or since the date of the beginning of the then last session. R.S., c. 81, s. 61; 1924, c. 47, s. 4.

Ejectment.

65. Whenever any purchaser, lessee or other person refuses or neglects to deliver up possession of any land after revocation or cancellation of the sale or lease thereof, as aforesaid, or whenever any person is wrongfully in possession of any Indian lands and refuses to vacate or abandon possession of the same, the Superintendent General may apply to the judge of the county court of the county or district in which the land lies, or to any judge of a superior court, or in the Northwest Territories to any stipendiary magistrate, for an order in the nature of a writ of habere facias possessionem, or writ of possession.

2. The said judge or magistrate, upon proof to his satisfaction that the right or title of the person to hold such land has been revoked or cancelled, as aforesaid, or that such person is wrongfully in possession of Indian lands, shall grant an order requiring the purchaser, lessee or person in possession to deliver up the same to the Superintendent General, or person by him authorized to receive such possession.

3. The order shall have the same force as a writ of habere facias possessionem, or writ of possession.

4. The sheriff, or any bailiff or person to whom it has been entrusted for execution by the Superintendent General, shall execute the same in like manner as he would execute such writ in an action of ejectment or a possessory action.

5. The costs of an incident to any proceedings under this section or any part thereof shall be paid by any party to such proceedings or by the Superintendent General, as the judge or magistrate orders. R.S., c. 81, s. 62.

Rent.

66. Whenever any rent payable to the Crown on any lease of Indian lands is in arrear, the same may be recovered

(a) by warrant of distress issued by the Superintendent General or any agent or officer appointed under this Part and authorized by the Superintendent General to act in such cases, and with like proceedings thereon as in ordinary cases of landlord and tenant directed to any person or persons by him named therein.

(b) by warrant of distress, and with like proceedings thereon as in case of a distress warrant by a justice of the peace for non-payment of a pecuniary penalty issued by him and directed as aforesaid; or

(c) by action of debt, as in ordinary cases of rent in arrear, brought therefor in the name of the Superintendent General.

2. Demand of rent shall not be necessary in any case. R.S.., c. 81, 63.

Powers of Superintendent General

67. When by law or by any deed, lease or agreement relating to Indian lands, any notice is required to be given, or any act to be done by or on behalf of the Crown, such notice may be given, and act done by or by the authority, of the Superintendent General. R.S., c. 81, s. 64.

68. Whenever it is found that, by reason of false survey or error in the books or plans in the Department or in the late Indian branch of the Department of the Interior, any grant, sale or appropriation of land is deficient, or whenever any parcel of land contains less than the quantity of land mentioned in the patent therefor, the Superintendent General may order the purchase money of so much land as is deficient with the interest thereon from the time of the application therefor to be paid to the

original purchaser in land or money as the Superintendent General directs.

2. If the land has passed from the original purchaser, and the claimant was ignorant of a deficiency at the time of his purchase, the Superintendent General may order payment as aforesaid of the purchase money for so much of the land as is deficient which the claimant has paid.

3. No such claim shall be entertained unless application is made within five years from the date of the patent, and unless the deficiency is equal to one-tenth of the whole quantity described as contained in the particular lot or parcel of land granted. R.S., c. 81, s. 65.

69. The Superintendent General may, from time to time, by public notice, declare that, on and after a day therein named, the laws respecting game in force in the province of Manitoba, Saskatchewan or Alberta, or the Territories, or respecting such game as is specified in such notice, shall apply to Indians within the said province or Territories, as the case may be, or to Indians in such parts thereof as to him seems expedient. R.S., c. 81, s. 66.

2. Section sixty-nine of the said Act is repealed and the following is substituted therefor: —

"69. (1) The Superintendent General, subject to the approval of the Governor in Council, may, as in this section provided, make regulations which, upon publication thereof in the Canada Gazette, shall apply with the same force as if the terms of such regulations had been herein enacted.

(2) The regulations may provide for appropriate Penalties, not exceeding, as to imprisonment, three months and not exceedingly as to fine, one hundred dollars, for violation or non-observance of any provision of any regulation.

(3) Without restricting the generality of the provisions of subsection one of this section, the regulations may provide, inter alia, for the incorporation by reference, as part, of such regulations, of any specific and indicated law or regulation of and in force within any province of Canada, and in particular, and whether or not by way of the incorporation by reference of provincial laws or regulations, such regulations may provide—

(a) with relation to Indians within the province of Manitoba, Saskatchewan or Alberta or within the Territories, as the case may be, or to Indians in such parts of such provinces and Territories as to him seems expedient, that laws either in the same terms as, or in like terms to, or in other terms than, those in force in such provinces and territories, respectively, with relation to game in general or to specific game, shall apply, upon publication thereof in the Canada Gazette, with the same force as if enacted in this Act, to such Indians as such regulations shall prescribe.

(b) for the destruction of noxious weeds and the prevention of the breeding, spreading or prevalence of any insect, pest or disease which may or might be destructive of or injurious to vegetation on Indian Reserves.

(c) governing the speed and operation of vehicles on highways within Indian Reserves."

70. The Superintendent General, his deputy, or other person specially authorized by the Governor in Council, may, by subpoena issued by him, require any person or Indian to appear before him, and to bring with him any papers or writings relating to any matter affecting Indians, and examine such person under oath in respect to any such matter.

2. If any person or Indian duly summoned by subpoena as aforesaid neglects or refuses to appear at the time and place specified in the subpoena, or refuses to give evidence or to produce the papers or writings demanded of him, the Superintendent General, his deputy or such other person may, by

warrant under his hand and seal, cause such person or Indian so refusing or neglecting to be taken into custody and to be imprisoned in the nearest common goal as for contempt of court, for a period not exceeding fourteen days. R.S., c. 81, s. 67; 1918, c. 26, s. 3.

Patents.

71. Every patent for Indian lands shall be prepared in the Department, and shall 'be signed by the Superintendent General or his deputy or by some other person thereunto specially authorized by order of the Governor in Council, and, when so signed, shall be registered by an officer specially appointed for that purpose by the Registrar General, and then transmitted to the Secretary of State of Canada, by whom, or by the Under Secretary of State, the same shall be countersigned and the Great Seal thereto caused to be affixed.

2. Every such patent for land shall be signed by the Governor or by the Deputy Governor appointed under this Part for that purpose. R.S., c. 81, s, 68.

72. On any application for a patent by the heir, assignee or devisee of the original purchaser from the Crown, the Superintendent General may receive proof, in such manner as he directs and requires, in support of any claim for a patent, when the original purchaser is dead; and upon being satisfied that the claim has been equitably and justly established, may allow the same, and cause a patent to issue accordingly.

2. Nothing in this section shall limit the right of a person claiming a patent to land in the province of Ontario to make application at any time to the Commissioner, under the Act respecting claims to lands in Upper Canada for which no patents have been issued, being chapter eighty of the Consolidated Statutes of Upper Canada. R.S., c. 81, s. 69.

73. Whenever letters patent have been issued to or in The name of the wrong person, through mistake, or contain any clerical error or misnomer, or wrong description of any material fact therein, or of the land thereby intended to be granted, the Superintendent General, if there is no adverse claim, may direct the defective letters patent to be cancelled, and a minute of such cancellation to be entered in the margin of the registry of the original letters patent, and correct letters patent to be issued in their stead.

2. Such correct letters patent shall relate back to the date of those so cancelled, and have the same effect as if issued at the date of such cancelled letters patent. R.S., c. 81, s. 70.

74. In all cases, in which grants, or letters patent have issued for the same land, inconsistent with each other, through error, and in all cases of sales or appropriations of the same land, inconsistent with each other, the Superintendent General may, in cases of sale, cause a repayment of the purchase money, with interest.

2. When the land has passed from the original purchaser, has been improved before a discovery of the error, the Superintendent General may, in substitution, assign land or grant a certificate entitling the person to purchase Indian lands of such value, and to such extent as he deems just and equitable under the circumstances; but no such claim shall be entertained unless it is preferred within five years from the discovery of the error. R.S., c. 81, s. 71.

75. Whenever patents for Indian lands have issued through fraud or in error or improvidence, the Exchequer Court of Canada or a superior court in any province may, in respect of lands situate within its jurisdiction, upon information, action, bill or plaint, respecting such lands, and upon

hearing the parties interested, or upon default of the said parties after such notice of proceeding as the said courts shall respectively order, decree such patents to be void: and, upon a registry of such decree in the Department, such patents shall be void to all intents.

2. The practice in such cases shall be regulated by orders, from time to time, made by the said courts respectively. R.S., c. 81, s. 72.

Timber Lands

76. The Superintendent General, or any officer or agent authorized by him to that- effect, may grant licenses to cut trees on ungranted Indian lands, or on reserves at such rates and subject to such conditions, regulations and restrictions, as are, from time to time, established by the Governor in Council, and such conditions, regulations and restrictions shall be adapted to the locality in which such reserves or lands are situated. R.S., c. 81, s. 73.

77. No license shall be so granted for a longer period than twelve months from the date thereof; and if, in consequence of any incorrectness of survey or other error or cause whatsoever, a license is found to comprise land included in a license of a prior date, or land not being reserve, or ungranted Indian lands, the license granted shall be void in so far as it comprises such land, and the holder or proprietor of the license so rendered void shall have no claim upon the Crown for indemnity or compensation by reason of such avoidance. R.S., c. 81, s. 74.

78. Every license shall describe the lands upon which the trees may be cut, and the kind of trees which may be cut, and shall confer, for the time being, on the licensee the right to take and keep possession of the land so described, subject to such regulations as are made.

2. Every license shall vest in the holder thereof all rights of property in all trees of the kind specified, cut within the limits of the license during the term thereof, whether such trees are cut by the authority of the holder of such license or by any other person, with or without his consent.

3. Every license shall entitle the holder thereof to seize, in revendication or otherwise, such trees and the logs, timber or other product thereof, if found in the possession of any unauthorized person, and also to institute any action or suit against any wrongful possessor or trespasser, and to prosecute all trespassers and other offenders to punishment, and to recover damages, if any.

4. All proceedings pending at the expiration of any license may be continued to final termination, as if the license had not expired. R.S., c. 81, s. 75.

79. Every person who obtains a license shall, at the expiration thereof, make to the officer or agent granting the same, or to the Superintendent General, a return of the number and kinds of trees cut, and of the quantity and description of sawlogs, or of the number and description of sticks of square or other timber, manufactured and carried away under such license, which return shall be sworn to by the holder of the license or his agent, or by his foreman.

2. Every person who refuses or neglects to make such return, or who evades, or attempts to evade, any regulation made by the Governor in Council in that behalf, shall be held to have cut without authority, and the timber or other product made shall be dealt with accordingly. R.S., c. 81, 3. 76.

80. All trees cut, and the logs, timber or other product thereof, shall be liable for the payment of the dues thereon, so long as and wheresoever the same, or any part thereof, are found, whether in the original logs or manufactured into deals, boards or other stuff.

2. All officers or agents entrusted with the collection of such dues may follow and seize and detain

the same wherever they are found until the dues are paid or secured. R.S., c. 81, s. 77.

81. No instrument or security taken for dues, either before or after the cutting of the trees, as collateral security, or to facilitate collection, shall in any way affect the lien for such dues, but the lien shall subsist until the said dues are actually discharged. R.S., c. 81, s. 78.

82. If any timber so seized and detained for non-payment of dues remains more than twelve months in the Custody of the agent or person appointed to guard the same, without the dues and expenses being paid, the Superintendent General may order a sale of the said timber to be made after sufficient notion.

2. The net proceeds of such sale, after deducting the number of dues, expenses, and costs incurred, shall be handed over to the owner or claimant of such timber, upon his applying therefor and proving his right thereto. R.S., c. 81, s. 79.

83. Any officer or agent acting under the Superintendent General may seize or cause to be seized in His Majesty's name any logs, timber, wood or other products of trees, or any trees themselves, cut without authority on Indian lands or on a reserve, wherever they are found, and place the same under proper custody until a decision can be had in the matter from competent authority. R.S., c. 81, s. 80.

84. When the logs, timber, wood, or other products of trees, or the trees themselves cut without authority on Indian lands or on a reserve, have been made up or inter- mingled with other trees, wood, timber, logs, or other pro- ducts of trees into a crib, dram or raft, or in any other manner, so that it is difficult to distinguish the timber cut on Indian lands or on a reserve without license, from the other timber with which it is made up or intermingled, the whole of the timber so made up or intermingled shall be held to have been cut without authority on Indian lands or on a reserve, and shall be seized and forfeited and sold by the Superintendent General or any officer or agent acting under him, unless evidence satisfactory to him is adduced showing the probable quantity not cut on Indian lands or on a reserve. R.S., c. 81, s. 81.

85. Every officer or person seizing trees, logs, timber or other products of trees in the discharge of his duty under this Part may, in the name of the Crown, call in any assistance necessary for securing and protecting the same. R.S., c. 81, s. 82.

86. Whenever any trees, logs, timber or other product of trees are seized for non-payment of Crown dues, or for any other cause of forfeiture, or whenever any prosecution Is brought in respect of any penalty or forfeiture under this Part, and any question arises whether said dues have been paid or whether the trees, logs, timber or other product were cut on lands other than any of the lands aforesaid, the burden of proving payment, or on what land the same were cut, as the case may be, shall lie on the owner or claimant and not on the officer who seizes the same, or the person who brings such prosecution. R.S., c. 81, s. 83.

87. All trees, logs, timber or other product of trees seized under this Part shall be deemed to be condemned unless the person from whom they are seized, or the owner thereof within one month from the day of the seizure, gives notice to the seizing officer, or nearest officer or agent of the Superintendent General that he claims, or intends to claim them, and unless within one month from the day of giving such notice he initiates, in some court of competent jurisdiction, proceedings for the purpose of establishing his claim.

2. In default of such notice and initiation of proceedings, the officer or agent seizing shall report the circumstances to the Superintendent General, who may order the sale by the said officer or agent of such trees, logs, timber or other products. R.S., c. 81, s. 84.

88. Any judge of any superior, county or district court, or any stipendiary magistrate, police magistrate or Indian agent, may, in a summary way, under the provisions of the Criminal Code relating to summary convictions, try and determine such seizures; and may, pending the trial, Delivery on order the delivery of the trees, or the logs, timber or other product to the alleged owner, on receiving security by bond, with two good and sufficient sureties, first approved by the said agent, to pay double the value of such trees, logs, timber or other product, in case of their condemnation.

2. Such bond shall be taken in the name of the Superintendent General, for His Majesty, and shall be delivered up to and kept by the Superintendent General.

3. If such seized trees, logs, timber or other product are condemned, the value thereof shall be paid forthwith to the Superintendent General or agent, and the bond cancelled, otherwise the penalty of such bond shall be enforced and recovered. R.S., c. 81, s. 85.

89. Everyone who avails himself of any false statement or false oath to evade the payment of dues under this Part, shall forfeit the timber in respect of which the dues are attempted to be evaded. R.S., c. 81, s. 86.

Management of Indian Moneys.

90. All moneys or securities of any kind applicable to the support or benefit of Indians, or any band of Indians, and all moneys accrued or hereafter to accrue from the sale of any Indian lands or the proceeds of any timber on any Indian lands or a reserve shall, subject to the provisions of this Part, be applicable to the same purposes, and be dealt with in the same manner as they might have been applied to or dealt with but for the passing of this Part.

2. No contract or agreement binding or purporting to bind, or in any way dealing with the moneys or securities referred to in this section, or with any moneys appropriated by Parliament for the benefit of Indians, made either by the chiefs or councilors of any band of Indians or by the members of the said band, other than and except as authorized by and for the purposes of this part shall be valid or of any force or effect unless and until it has been approved in writing by the Superintendent General. R.S.V c. 81, s. 87; 1910, c. 28, s. 2.

91. The Governor in Council may reduce the purchase money due or to become due on sales of Indian lands, or reduce or remit the interest on such purchase money, or reduce the rent at which Indian lands have been leased, when he considers the same excessive.

2. A return setting forth all the reductions and remissions made under this section during the fiscal year shall be submitted to both Houses of Parliament within twenty days after the expiration of such year, if Parliament is then sitting, and if Parliament is not then sitting, within twenty days after the opening of the next ensuing session of Parliament. R.S., c. 81, s. 88.

92. With the exception of such sum not exceeding fifty centum of the proceeds of any land, timber or other property, as is agreed at the time of the surrender to be paid to the members of the band interested therein, the Governor in Council may, subject to the provisions of this Part, direct how and in what manner, and by whom, the moneys arising from the disposal of Indian lands, or of property held or to be held in trust for Indians, or timber on Indian lands or reserves, or from any other

source for the benefit of Indians, shall be invested from time to time, and how the payments or assistance to which the Indians are entitled shall be made or given.

2. The Governor in Council may provide for the general management of such moneys, and direct what percentage or proportion thereof shall be set apart, from time to time, to cover the cost of and incidental to the management of reserves, lands, property and moneys under the provisions of this Part, and may authorize and direct the expenditure of such moneys for surveys, for compensation to Indians for improvements or any interest, they had in lands taken from them, for the construction or repair of roads, bridges, ditches and watercourses on such reserves or lands, for the construction and repair of school buildings and charitable institutions, and by way of contribution to schools attended by such Indians: Provided that where the capital standing to the credit of a band does not exceed the sum of two thousand dollars the Governor in Council may direct and authorize the expenditure of such capital for any purpose which may be deemed to be for the general welfare of the band. R.S., c. 81. s. 89: 1919. c. 56. s. 2: 1927 c. 32 s. 1

93. The Governor in Council may, with the consent of a band, authorize and direct the expenditure of any capital expenditure moneys standing at the credit of such band, in the purchase of land as a reserve for the band or as an addition to its reserve, or in the purchase of cattle, implements or machinery for the band, or in the construction of permanent improvements upon the reserve of the band, or such works thereon or in connection therewith as, in his opinion, will be of permanent value to the band, or will, when completed, properly represent capital or in the making of loans to members of the band to promote progress, no such loan, however, to exceed in amount one-half of the appraised value of the interest of the borrower in the lands held by him.

3. Subsection one of section ninety-three of the said Act is repealed and the following substituted therefor: —

"(1) The Governor in Council may, with the consent of a band, authorize and direct the expenditure of any capital moneys standing at the credit of such band, in the purchase of land as a reserve for the band or as an addition to its reserve, or the possessory right of a member of the band in respect of any particular parcel of land on the reserve, or in the purchase of cattle, implements or machinery for the band, or in the construction of permanent improvements upon the reserve of the band, or such works thereon or in connection therewith as, in his opinion, will be of permanent value to the band, or will, when completed, properly represent capital, or in the making of loans to members of the band to promote progress, no such loan, however, to exceed in amount one-half of the appraised value of the interest of the borrower in the lands held by him."

2. In the event of a band refusing to consent to the expenditure of such capital moneys as the Superintendent General may consider advisable for any of the purposes mentioned in subsection one of this section, and it is appearing to the Superintendent General that such refusal is detrimental to the progress or welfare of the band, the Governor in Council may, without the consent of the band, authorize and direct the expenditure of such capital for such of the said purposes as may be considered reasonable and proper.

3. Whenever any land in a reserve whether held in common or by an individual Indian is uncultivated and the band or individual is unable or neglects to cultivate the same, the Superintendent

General, notwithstanding anything in this Act to the contrary, may, without a surrender, grant a lease of such lands for agricultural or grazing purposes for the benefit of the band or individual, or may employ such persons as may be considered necessary to improve or cultivate such lands during the pleasure of the Superintendent General, and may authorize and direct the expenditure of so much of the capital funds of the band as may be considered necessary for the improvements of such land, or for the purchase of such stock, machinery, material or labor as may be considered necessary for the cultivation or grazing of the same, and in such case all the proceeds derived from such lands, except a reasonable rent to be paid for any individual holding, shall be placed to the credit of the band.

4. In the event of improvements being made on the lands of an individual the Superintendent General may deduct the value of such improvements from the rental payable for such lands. 1918, c. 26, s. 4; 1924, c. 47, s. 5.

94. The proceeds arising from the sale or lease of any Indian lands, or from the timber, hay, stone, minerals or other valuables thereon, or on a reserve, shall be paid to the Minister of Finance to the credit of the Indian fund. R.S., c. 81, s. 91.

8. The said Act is amended by inserting therein the following section: —

"94A. The Superintendent General may operate farms On Indian Reserves, employing such persons as may be considered necessary, for the purpose of instructing the Indians in farming and for the supply of pure seed for Indian farmers and may from time to time apply any Profits arising therefrom in the extension of such operations or in making loans to Indians to enable them to engage in Farming or other operations or apply such proceeds in any other way for their progress and development."

2. The said Act is further amended by inserting immediately after section ninety-four A the following:

94B.(1) For the purpose of granting loans to Indian Bands, group or groups of Indians, or individual Indians and for the expenditure of moneys for co-operative projects on their behalf, the Minister of Finance may, from time to time, authorize the advance to the Superintendent General of Indian Affairs out of the Consolidated Revenue Fund of Canada of such sums of money as the said Superintendent General may require enabling him to make loans to Indian Banda, group or groups of Indians or individual Indians, for the purchase of farm implements, machinery, livestock, fishing and other equipment, seed grain and materials to be used in native handicrafts and to expend and loan money for the carrying out of co-operative projects on behalf of the Indians. All expenditures made under such advances shall be made under regulations established from time to time by the Governor in Council and shall be accounted for in the like manner as other public moneys. Any moneys received by the Superintendent General of Indian Affairs from the Indian Bands, group or groups of Indians, individual Indians or co-operative projects, for aid furnished under the provisions of this section shall be remitted by him to the Minister of Finance in repayment of such advances. The number of outstanding advances to the said Superintendent General including all amounts owing by the Indian Bands, group or groups of Indians, individual Indians or outstanding on co-operative projects shall at no time exceed the sum of three hundred and fifty thousand Dollars.

(2) The Superintendent General shall annually prepare a report with regard to loans made under

the provisions of subsection one of this section, during the preceding calendar year, and such report shall be laid before parliament within fifteen days or, if parliament is not then sitting, within fifteen days after the beginning of the next session."

95. The Superintendent General may

(a) stop the payment of the annuity and interest money tendent' of, as well as deprive of any participation in the real General, property of the band, any Indian who is proved, to the satisfaction of the Superintendent General, guilty of deserting his family, or of conduct justifying his wife or family in separating from him, or who is separated from his family by imprisonment, and apply the same towards the support of the wife or family of such Indian.

(b) stop the payment of the annuity and interest money of any Indian parent of an illegitimate child, and apply the same to the support of such child.

(c) stop the payment of the annuity and interest money of. as well as deprive of any participation in the real property of the band, any woman who deserts her husband or family and lives immorally with another man. and apply the same to the support of the family so deserted.

(d) whenever sick or disabled, or aged or destitute Indians are not provided for by the band of which they are members, furnish sufficient aid from the funds of the band for the relief of such sick, disabled, aged or destitute Indians.

(e) make such regulations as he deems necessary for the prevention or mitigation of disease the frequent and effectual cleansing of streets, yards and premises. the removal of nuisances and unsanitary conditions. the cleansing, purifying, ventilating and disinfecting of premises by the owners and occupiers or other persons having the care or ordering thereof; the supplying of such medical aid, medicine and other articles and accommodation as the Superintendent General may deem necessary for preventing or mitigating an outbreak of any communicable disease; entering and inspecting any premises used for human habitation in any locality in which conditions exist which in the opinion of the Superintendent General is unsanitary, or such as to render the inhabitants especially liable to disease, and for directing the alteration or destruction of any such building which is, in the opinion of the Superintendent General, unfit for human habitation. preventing the overcrowding of premises used for human habitation by limiting the number of dwellers in such premises; preventing and regulating the departure of persons from, and the access of persons to, infected localities; preventing persons or conveyances from passing from one locality to another; detaining persons or conveyances who or which have been exposed to infection for inspection or disinfection until the danger of infection is past; the removal or keeping under surveillance of persons living in infected localities; and any other matter which, in the opinion of the Superintendent General, the general health of the Indians of any locality may require.

(f) make by-laws for the taxation, control and destruction of dogs and for the protection of sheep, and such by-laws may be applied to such reserves or parts thereof from time to time as the Superintendent General may direct.

(g) make regulations governing the operation of pool rooms, dance halls and other places of amusement on Indian Reserves.

2. In the event of any conflict between any regulation made by the Superintendent General and any rule or regulation made by any band; the regulations made by the Superintendent General shall pre-

vail

3. In any regulations or by-laws made under the pro- visional of this section, the Superintendent General may provide for the imposition of a fine not exceeding thirty dollars or imprisonment not exceeding thirty days, for the violation of any of the provisions thereof. R.S., c. 81, s. 92; 1914, c. 35, s. 6; 1918, c. 26, s. 5; 1927, c. 32, s. 2.

Election of Chiefs.

96. Whenever the Governor in Council deems it ad- visible for the good government of a band, to introduce the elective system of chiefs and councilors or headmen, he may provide that the chief and councilors or headmen of any band shall be elected, as hereinafter provided, at such time and place as the Superintendent General direct. and they shall in such case be elected for a term of three years.

2. The councilors or headmen may be in the proportion of two for every two hundred Indians.

3. No band shall have more than one chief and fifteen councilors or headmen.

4. Any band composed of at least thirty members may have a chief. R.S., c. 81, s. 93. 4. Section ninety-six of the said Act is amended by adding thereto the following subsection: —

"(5) In any case of an equality of votes at any such election the agent or person presiding thereat shall have the casting votes."

97. Life chiefs and councilors or headmen now living may continue to hold rank until death or resignation, or until their removal by the Governor in Council for dishonesty, intemperance, immorality or incompetency.

2. In the event of the Governor in Council providing that the chief and councilors or headmen of a band shall be elected, the life chiefs and councilors or headmen shall not exercise powers as such unless elected under the provision aforesaid. R.S., c. 81, s. 94.

98. An election may be set aside by the Governor in Council, on a report of the Superintendent General, if it is proved by two witnesses before the Indian agent for the or such other person as is deputed by the Superintendent General to take evidence in the matter, that fraud or gross irregularity was practiced at the said election.

2. Every Indian who is proved guilty of such fraud or irregularity, or connivance thereat, may be declared in- eligible for re-election for a period not exceeding six years if the Governor in Council, on the report of the Superintendent General, so directs. R.S., c. 81, s. 95.

99. Any elected or life chief and any councillor or head- man, or any chief or councillor or headman chosen according to the custom of any band, may, on the ground of dis- honesty, intemperance, immorality or incompetency, be deposed by the Governor in Council and declared ineligible to hold the office of chief or councillor or headman for a period not exceeding three years. R.S., c. 81, s. 96.

5. The said Act is amended by inserting the following section immediately after section ninety-nine thereof: —

"99A. (1) At meetings of the council the agent for the reserve, or his deputy appointed for the purpose with the consent of the Superintendent General, shall

(a) preside and record the proceedings.

(b) control and regulate all matters of procedure and form, and adjourn the meeting to a time named

or sine die.
(c) report and certify all by-laws and other acts and proceedings of the council to the Superintendent General.
(d) address the council and explain and advise the members thereof upon their powers and duties.
(2) No such agent or deputy shall vote on any question to be decided by the council."
Regulations to be made by Chiefs.
100. The chief or chiefs of any band in council may, subject to confirmation by the Governor in Council, make rules and regulations as to the religious denomination to which the teacher at the school established on the reserve shall belong.
2. If the majority of the band belongs to any one religious denomination, the teacher at the school established on the reserve shall belong to the same denomination.
3. The Protestant or Catholic minority of any band may, with the approval of and under regulations made by the Governor in Council, have a separate school established on the reserve. R.S., c. 81, a. 97.

101. The chief or chiefs of any band in council may likewise, and subject to such confirmation, make rules and regulations as to
(a) the care of the public health.
(b) the observance of order and decorum at assemblies of the Indians in general council, or on other occasions.
(c) the prevention of disorderly conduct and nuisances.
(d) the prevention of trespass by cattle, and the protection of sheep, horses, mules and cattle.
(e) the construction and maintenance of watercourses, roads, bridges, ditches and fences.
(f) the construction and repair of schoolhouses, council houses and other Indian public buildings, and the attendance at school of children between the ages of six and fifteen years.
(g) the establishment of pounds and the appointment of pound-keepers.
(h) the locating of the band in their reserves, and the establishment of a register of such locations.
(i) the repression of noxious weeds.
9. Subsection one of section one hundred and one of the said Act is amended by adding thereto the following paragraph: —
"(j) Controlling or prohibiting participation in, or attendance at, public games, sports, races, athletic contests or other such amusements on the Sabbath."
6. Section one hundred and one of the said Act is amended by adding thereto, the following paragraph: —
"(k) Regulating the operations of hawkers, peddlers or others coming on the reserve to sell, or take orders for, wares or merchandise."
2. The Governor in Council may by the rules and regulations aforesaid provide for the imposition of punishment by fine, penalty or imprisonment, or both for violation of any of such rules or regulations.
3. The fine or penalty shall in no case exceed thirty dollars, and the imprisonment shall in no case exceed thirty days.

4. The proceedings for the imposition of such punishment shall be taken under the provisions of the Criminal Code relating to summary convictions. R.S., c. 81, s. 98. 1927, c. 32, s. 3.

Taxation.

102. No Indian or non-treaty Indian shall be liable to be taxed for any real or personal property, unless he holds, in his individual right, real estate under a lease or in fee simple, or personal property outside of the reserve or special reserve, in which case he shall be liable to be taxed for such real or personal property at the same rate as other persons in the locality in which it is situate. R.S., c. 81, s. 99.

103. No taxes shall be levied on the real property of any Indian, acquired under the enfranchisement clauses of this Part, until the same has been declared liable to taxation by proclamation of the Governor in Council, published in the Canada Gazette. R.S., c. 81, s. 100.

104. All land vested in the Crown or in any person in trust or for the use of any Indian or non-treaty Indian or any band or irregular band of Indians or non-treaty Indians shall be exempt from taxation, except those lands which, having been surrendered by the bands owning them, though unpatented, have been located by or sold or agreed to be sold to any person; and, except as against the Crown and any Indian located on the land, the same shall be liable to taxation in like manner as other lands in the same locality.

2. Nothing herein contained shall interfere with the right of the Superintendent General to cancel the original sale or location of any land, or shall render such land liable to taxation until it is again sold or located. R.S., c. 81, s. 101.

Legal Rights of Indians.

105. No person shall take any security or otherwise obtain any lien or charge, whether by mortgage, judgment or otherwise, upon real or personal property of any Indian or non-treaty Indian, except on real or personal property subject to taxation under the last three preceding sections: Provided that any person selling any article to an Indian or non-treaty Indian may take security on such article for any part of the price thereof which is unpaid. R.S., c. 81, s. 102.

10. Section one hundred and five of the said Act is repealed and the following section substituted therefor: —

"105 No one other than an Indian or non-treaty Indian shall take any security or otherwise obtain any lien or charge, whether by mortgage, judgment or otherwise, upon real or personal property of any Indian or non-treaty Indian, except on real or personal property subject to taxation under the last three preceding sections: Provided that any person selling any article to an Indian or non-treaty Indian may take security on such article for any part of the price thereof which is unpaid."

106. Indians and non-treaty Indians shall have the right to sue for debts due to them, or in respect of any tort or wrong inflicted upon them, or to compel the performance of obligations contracted with them.

2. In any suit or action between Indians, or in any case of assault in which the offender is an Indian, no appeal shall lie from any judgment, order or conviction by any police magistrate, stipendiary magistrate, or two justices of the peace or an Indian agent, when the sum adjudged or the penalty imposed does not exceed ten dollars. R.S., c. 81, s. 103.

107. No pawn taken from any Indian or non-treaty Indian for any intoxicant shall be retained by the person to whom such pawn is delivered; but the thing so pawned may be sued for and shall be recoverable, with costs of suit, in any court of competent jurisdiction by the Indian or non-treaty Indian who pawned the same. R.S., c. 81, s. 104.

108. No presents given to Indians or non-treaty Indians, and no annuities or interest on funds, and no moneys appropriated by Parliament, held for any band of Indians, and no property purchased or acquired with or by means of any such annuities or income or moneys, and whether in the possession of any band of such Indians or of any Indian of any band or irregular band or not, shall be liable to be taken, seized, distrained, attached or in any way made the subject of judicial process for any debt, matter or cause whatsoever.

2. No such presents or property shall, in the province of Manitoba, British Columbia, Saskatchewan or Alberta, or in the Territories be sold, bartered, exchanged, or given by any band or irregular band of Indians, or any Indian of any such band to any person or Indian other than an Indian of such band.

3. Animals given to Indians under treaty stipulations, and the progeny thereof, and farming implements, tools and any other articles given to Indians under treaty stipulations shall be held to be presents within the meaning of this section.

4. Every such sale, barter, exchange or gift shall be null and void unless such sale, barter, exchange or gift is made with the written assent of the Superintendent General or his agent.

5. No Indian or non-treaty Indian in the province of Manitoba, British Columbia, Saskatchewan or Alberta, or in the Territories, shall without the written consent of this Indian Agent sell, barter, exchange or give to any person or Indian other than an Indian of such band, or kill or destroy any animal or the progeny thereof given to him or to the band under treaty stipulations, or loaned or conditionally given to him or to the band by the Government.

6. Any Indian who violates any of the provisions of the last preceding subsection shall be liable on summary conviction to a penalty, not exceeding twenty-five dollars with costs of prosecution or to imprisonment not exceeding two months, or to both fine and imprisonment. R.S., c. 81, s. 105; 1910, c. 28, s. 3; 1914, c. 35, s. 7.

109. If any presents given to Indians or non-treaty Indians, or any property purchased or acquired with or by means of any annuities granted to Indians, are or is unlaw- fully in the possession of any person, within the true intent and meaning of the last preceding section, any person acting under the authority of the Superintendent General may with such assistance in that behalf as he thinks necessary seize and take possession of the same, and shall deal therewith as the Superintendent General directs.

2. No title to any Indian grave-house, carved grave-pole, totem-pole, carved house-post or large rock embellished with paintings or carvings on an Indian reserve, shall be acquired by any means whatsoever by any person without the written consent of the Superintendent General, and no Indian grave-house, carved grave-pole, totem pole, carved house-post or large rock embellished with paintings or carvings, on an Indian reserve shall be removed, taken away, mutilated, disfigured, defaced or destroyed without such written consent.

3. Any person violating any of the provisions of sub- section two hereof shall be liable on summary

conviction to a penalty not exceeding two hundred dollars, with costs of prosecution, and in default of payment to imprisonment for a term not exceeding three months, and any article removed or taken away contrary to the provisions of the said subsection may be seized on the instructions of the Superintendent General and dealt with as he may direct. R.S., c. 81, & 106; 1927, c. 32, s. 4.

110. Upon the application of an Indian of any band, or upon the application of a band on a vote of a majority of the male members of such band of the full age of twenty- one years at a meeting or council thereof summoned for that purpose, according to the rules of the band and held in the presence of the Superintendent General or of an officer duly authorized to attend such council, by the Governor in Council or by the Superintendent General, a Board may be appointed by the Superintendent General to consist of two officers of the Department and a member of the band to which the Indian or Indians under investigation belongs, to make enquiry and report as to the fitness of any Indian or Indians to be enfranchised.

2. The Indian member of the Board shall be nominated by the council of the band, within thirty days after the date of notice having been given to the council, and in default of such nomination, the appointment shall be made by the Superintendent General.

3. In the course of such enquiry it shall be the duty of the Board to take into consideration and report upon the attitude of any such Indian towards his enfranchisement, attitude shall be a factor in determining the question of fitness.

4. Such report shall contain a description of the land occupied by each Indian, the amount thereof and the improvements thereon, the names, ages and sex of every Indian whose interests it is anticipated will be affected, and such other information as the Superintendent General may direct such Board to obtain.

5. On the report of the Superintendent General that any Indian, male or female, over the age of twenty-one years is fit for enfranchisement, the Governor in Council may by order direct that such Indian shall be and become enfranchised at the expiration of two years from the date of such order or earlier if requested by such Indian, and from the date of such enfranchisement the provisions of this and of any other Act or law making any distinction between the legal rights, privileges, disabilities and liabilities of Indians and those of His Majesty's other subjects, shall cease to apply to such Indian or to his or her minor unmarried children, or, in the case of a married male Indian, to the wife of such Indian, and every such Indian and child and wife shall thereafter have, possess and enjoy all the legal powers, rights and privileges of His Majesty's other subjects, and shall no longer be deemed to be Indians within the meaning of any laws relating to Indians.

6. Where a wife is living apart from her husband, the enfranchisement of the husband shall not carry with it the enfranchisement of his wife except on her own written request to be so enfranchised.

7. An Indian over the age of twenty-one years shall have the right to choose the Christian name and surname by which he or she wishes to be enfranchised and thereafter known, and from the date of the order of enfranchisement such Indian shall thereafter be known by such names, and if no such choice is made such Indian shall be enfranchised by and bear the name or names by which he or she has been theretofore commonly known.

8. Upon the issue of an order of enfranchisement the Superintendent General shall, if any Indian enfranchised holds any land on a reserve, cause letters patent to be issued to such Indian for such

land; and such Indian shall pay to the funds of the band such amount per acre for the land he holds as the Superintendent General considers to be the value of the common interest of the band in such land, and such payment shall be a charge against the share of such Indian in the funds of the band.

9. The Superintendent General shall also pay to each Indian upon enfranchisement his or her share of the funds to the credit of the band, including such amount as the Superintendent General determines to be his or her share of the value of the common interest of the band in the lands of the reserve or reserves, or share of the principal of the annuities of the band capitalized at five per centum, out of such moneys as are provided by Parliament for the purpose or which may be otherwise available for such purpose.

10. The land and money of any minor, unmarried children may be held for the benefit of such minor or may be granted or paid in whole or in part to the father, or, if the father is dead, to the mother, or in either case to such person as the Superintendent General may select for such purpose for the maintenance of such minor, and the land and money of the wife shall be granted and paid to the husband, unless in any case the Superintendent General shall direct that the whole or any part thereof be granted or paid to the wife herself, in which case the same shall be granted or paid to the wife.

11. If such Indian holds no land in a reserve, he or she shall be paid from the funds of the band such amount as the Superintendent General determines to be his or her share of the value of the common interest of the band in the lands of the reserve or reserves, and shall also be paid his or her share of the funds or annuities of the band capitalized as aforesaid.

12. Every Indian who is not a member of the band and every non-treaty Indian who, with the acquiescence of the band and approval of the Superintendent General, has been permitted to reside on the reserve or to obtain a holding or location thereon, may be enfranchised and given letters patent for such land as a member of the band, provided that such Indian or non-treaty Indian shall pay to the credit of the band the value of the common interest of the band in the land for which he receives a patent.

13. On the issue of the letters patent to any enfranchised Indian for any land he may be entitled to, or the payment from the capital funds or annuities of the band, as above provided, such Indian and his or her minor un- married children and, in the case of a male married Indian, the wife of such Indian shall cease to have any further claims whatsoever against any common property or funds of the band. 1920, c. 50, s. 3; 1922, c. 26, s. 1; 1924, c. 47, s. 6.

7. Section one hundred and ten of the said Act is amended by adding thereto, the following subsection:

(14) In respect of an Indian or Indians of any band who has not or have not made application for enfranchisement under this section or under section one hundred and fourteen of this Act, the Superintendent General may appoint a Board to consist of any judge of any superior court or any judge of any circuit, district or county court, an officer of the Department and a member of the band to be selected by the band to which the Indian or Indians under investigation belongs or belong, or, failing the selection of such member for a period of thirty days after the date of notice having been given to the Council, the member shall be appointed by the Superintendent General, to make enquiry and report as to the fitness of any Indian or Indians to be enfranchised, and such report shall

have the same force and effect and shall be dealt with in the same manner as if the same had been made upon the application of an Indian or Indians under this section: Provided that no enfranchisement of any Indian or Indians shall be made under this subsection in violation of the terms of any treaty, agreement or undertaking that may have been entered into or made between or by the Crown and the Indians of the band in question."

111. When. a majority of the members of a band is enfranchised, the common land or other public property of the band shall be equitably allotted to members of the band, and thereafter the residue, if any, of such land or public property may be sold by the Superintendent General and the proceeds of such sale placed to the credit of the funds of the band to be divided as provided in the last preceding section, but the Governor in Council may reserve and set apart from the funds of the band such sum as the Superintendent General may consider necessary for the perpetual care and protection of any Indian cemetery or burial plot belonging to such Indians, and any other common property which in the opinion of the Superintendent General should be preserved as such.

2. No part of such land or other property shall be sold to any person other than a member of the band except by public auction after three months' advertisement in the public press. 1920, c. 50, s. 3.

112. The Governor in Council may make regulations for the carrying out of the provisions. of the two sections immediately preceding this section, and subject to the provisions of this Act for determining how the land, capital moneys and other property of a band, or any part thereof, shall be divided, granted and paid, upon the enfranchisement of any Indian or Indians belonging to such band or having any interest in any of the property of such band, and decide any questions arising under the said sections, and the decision of the Governor in Council thereon shall be final and conclusive. 1920, c. 50, s. ,3.

113. The Superintendent General shall, within fifteen days after the opening of each session of Parliament, submit to both Houses of Parliament, a list of the Indians enfranchised under this Act during the previous fiscal year, and the amount of land and money granted and paid to each Indian so enfranchised. 1920, c. 50, s. 3.

114. If an Indian who holds no land in a reserve, does not reside on a reserve and does not follow the Indian mode of life, makes application to be enfranchised, and satisfies the Superintendent General that he is self-supporting and fit to be enfranchised, and surrenders all claims whatsoever to any interest in the lands of, the band to which he belongs, and accepts his share of the funds at the credit of the band including the principal of the annuities of. the band, to which share he would have been entitled had he been enfranchised under the foregoing sections of the Act, in full of all claims to the property of 'The band, or in case the band to which Jhe belongs has no funds or principal of annuities, surrenders all claims whatsoever to any property of the band, the Governor in Council may order that such Indian be enfranchised and paid his said share if any, and from the date of such order such Indian, together with his wife and unmarried minor children, shall be held to be enfranchised.

2. Any unmarried Indian woman of the age of twenty- one years, and any Indian widow and her minor unmarried children, may be enfranchised in the like manner in every respect as a male Indian and his said children. 3. This section shall apply to the Indians in any part of Canada. 1918, c. ,26, s. 6.

Offences and Penalties.

115. Every person, or Indian other than an Indian of, the band, who, without the authority of the Superintendent General, resides or hunts upon, occupies or uses any land or marsh, or who resides upon or occupies any road, or allowance for road, running through any reserve belonging to or occupied by such band shall be pliable, upon summary conviction, to imprisonment for a term not exceeding one month or to a penalty not exceeding ten dollars and not less than five dollars, with costs of prosecution, half of which penalty shall belong to the informer. R.S., c. 81, s. 124.

8. Section one hundred and fifteen of the said Act is repealed and the following is substituted therefor: —

"115. Every person, or Indian other than an Indian the band, who, without the authority of the Superintendent General, resides or hunts upon, occupies or uses any land or marsh, or who resides upon or occupies any road, or allowance for road, running through any reserve belonging to or occupied by such band, or who is found on the reserve and is unable to prove that he is there for some legitimate purpose, shall be liable, upon summary conviction, to imprisonment for a term not exceeding one month or to a penalty not exceeding ten dollars and not less than five dollars, with costs of prosecution, half of which penalty shall belong to the informer."

116. Any person or Indian who, being lawfully required by an Indian agent, a chief of the band occupying a reserve, or a constable,

(a) to remove with his family, if any, from the land, marsh, road, or allowance for road upon which he is or has settled or is residing or hunting, or which he occupies.

(b) to remove his cattle from such land or marsh.

11. Paragraph (b) of section one hundred and sixteen of the said Act is repealed and the following substituted therefor: —

"(b) to remove any cattle or other animals owned by him or in his charge from such land or marsh."

(c) to cease fishing in any marsh, river, stream or creek on or running through a reserve; or

(d) to cease using, occupying, settling or residing upon any land, river, stream, creek, marsh, road or allowance for a road in a reserve;

fails to comply with such requirement, shall, upon summary conviction, be liable to a penalty of not less than five dollars and not more than ten dollars for every day during which such failure continues, and, in default of payment, to be imprisoned for a term not exceeding three months. R.S., c. 81, s. 125.

117. Every Indian, not being an Indian of the band, who, in the case where shooting privileges over a reserve or part of a reserve, or fishing privileges in any marsh, pond, river, stream or creek upon or running through a reserve, have with the consent of the Indians of the band, been leased or granted to any person, and, in such case, every person not, under such lease or grant, entitled so to do, who hunts, shoots, kills or destroys any game animals or birds, or who fishes for takes, catches or kills any fins to which such exclusive privilege extends, upon the reserve or part of a reserve, or in any marsh, pond, river, stream or creek covered by such lease or grant, shall, in addition to any other penalty or liability thereby incurred, be liable, on summary conviction, for every such offence to a penalty not exceeding ten dollars and not less than five dollars, and, in default of payment, to imprisonment for any term not exceeding one month. R.S., c. 81, s. 126.

118. Every person, or Indian, other than an Indian of the band to which the reserve belongs, who, without the license in writing of the Superintendent General, or of some officer or person deputed by him for that purpose, cuts, carries away or removes from any of the lands, roads or allowances for roads in a reserve, any of the trees, saplings, shrubs, underwood, timber, cordwood or part of a tree, or hay, or removes any of the stone, soil, minerals, metals or other valuables from the said lands, roads or allowances for roads, shall, on summary conviction thereof before any stipendiary magistrate, police magistrate or any two justices of the peace or an Indian agent, incur in each case the costs of prosecution and

(a) for every tree he cuts, carries away or removes, a penalty of twenty dollars.

(b) for cutting, carrying away or removing any of the saplings, shrubs, underwood, timber, cordwood or part of a tree or hay, if under the value of one dollar, a penalty of four dollars; and, if over the value of one dollar. a penalty of twenty dollars.

(c) for removing any of the stone, soil, minerals, metals, or other valuables aforesaid, a penalty of twenty dollars.

2. In default of immediate payment of the said penalties and costs, such magistrate, justices of the peace, or Indian agent may issue a warrant directed to any person or persons by him or them named therein, to levy the amount of the said penalties and costs by distress and sale of the goods and chattels of the person or Indian liable to pay the same, or may, without proceeding by distress and sale, upon non-payment of such penalties and costs, order the person or Indian liable therefor to be imprisoned in the common goal of the county or district in which the said reserve or any part thereof lies for a term not exceeding thirty days, if the penalty does not exceed twenty dollars, or for a term not exceeding three months, if the penalty exceeds twenty dollars.

3. The Superintendent General, or such other officer or person as he shall authorize in that behalf may issue the warrant on any such conviction; or may, without proceeding by distress and sale, make such order upon such conviction as such magistrate, justices of the peace or Indian agent could make; and similar proceedings may be had upon the warrant so issued as if it had been issued by the magistrate, justices of the peace or Indian agent before whom the person was convicted.

4. If upon the return of any warrant for distress and sale, the amount thereof has not been made, or if any part of it remains unpaid, such magistrate, or justices of the peace, or Indian agent, or the Superintendent General, or such other officer or person as aforesaid, may commit the person in default to the common goal, as aforesaid, for a term not exceeding thirty days, if the sum claimed upon the said warrant does not exceed twenty dollars, or for a term not exceeding three months if the sum exceeds twenty dollars.

5. All such penalties shall be paid to the Minister of Finance, and shall be disposed of for the use and benefit of the band of Indians for whose benefit the reserve is held, in such manner as the Governor in Council directs. R.S., c. 81, s. 127.

119. Every Indian of the band who, without the license in writing of the Superintendent General, or of some officer or person deputed by him for that purpose,

(a) cuts, carries away or removes from land in a reserve held by another Indian under a location title or by an Indian otherwise recognized by the Department as the occupant thereof any of the trees, cordwood, or part of a tree, saplings, shrubs, underwood, timber or hay thereon, or removes from such land any of the stone, soil, minerals, metals or other valuables.

(b) cuts, carries away or removes from any portion of the reserve of his band, for sale and not for the immediate use of himself and his family any trees, timber, cordwood or part of a tree, saplings, shrubs, underwood or hay thereon, or removes any of the stone, soil, minerals, metals or other valuables therefrom, for sale, as aforesaid; or

(c) unless with the consent of the band and the approval of the Superintendent General, cute or uses any pine or large timber for any purpose other than for building on his own location or farm shall incur the penalties providing in the last preceding. section in respect to Indians of other bands and other persons.

2. The same proceedings may be had for the recovery thereof as are provided for in the said section. R S c 81 for 8. 128

120. Every person who buys or otherwise acquires from any Indian or band or irregular band of Indians in the province of Manitoba, Saskatchewan or Alberta, or the Territories, any grain, root crops or other produce contrary to regulations made by the Governor in Council in that behalf, shall, on summary conviction before a stipendiary magistrate, police magistrate or two justices of the peace or an Indian agent, be liable to a penalty not exceeding one hundred dollars, or to imprisonment for a term not exceeding three months, or to both. R.S., c. 81, s. 129.

12. Section one hundred and twenty of the said Act is repealed and the following substituted therefor:

120. Every person who buys or otherwise acquires from any Indian or band or irregular band of Indians in the province of Manitoba, Saskatchewan, or Alberta, or the Territories any cattle or other animals or any grain, root crops or other produce or sells to any such Indian any goods or supplies, cattle or other animals contrary to the provisions of this Act, shall, on summary conviction, be liable to a penalty not exceeding one hundred dollars, or to imprisonment for a term not exceeding three months, or to both."

9. Section one hundred and twenty of the said Act, as enacted by section twelve of chapter twenty-five of the statutes of 1930, is repealed and the following is substituted therefor: —

"120. Every person who buys or otherwise acquires from any Indian or band or irregular band of Indians in the Province of Manitoba, Saskatchewan, or Alberta, or the Territories, or sells to any such Indian, any cattle or other animals or any grain, root crops or other produce, and every Indian who sells any cattle or other animals or any grain, root crops or other produce, contrary to the provisions of this Act, shall on summary conviction be liable to a penalty not exceeding fifty dollars or to pronate for a term not exceeding thirty days, or to Both."

121. Every person who cuts, carries away or removes from any reserve or special reserve, any hard or sugar maple tree or sapling, or buys or otherwise acquires from any Indian or non-treaty Indian, or other person, any hard or sugar-maple tree or sapling so cut, carried away or removed from any reserve or special reserve in the province of Manitoba, Saskatchewan or Alberta, or the Territories, contrary to regulations made in that behalf by the Governor in Council, shall, on summary conviction before a stipendiary magistrate, police magistrate, or two justices of the peace or an Indian agent, be liable to a penalty not exceeding one hundred dollars or to imprisonment for a term not exceeding three months, or to both. R.S., c. 81, s. 130.

122. Every person being
(a) an official or employee connected with the Department.
(b) a missionary in the employ of any religious denomination, or otherwise employed in mission work among Indians; or
(c) a schoolteacher on an Indian reserve; and
(d) in the province of Manitoba, Saskatchewan or Alberta, or the Territories
who, on a reserve, without the special license in writing of the Superintendent General, trades with any Indian or directly or indirectly sells to him any goods or supplies, cattle or other animals, shall be liable to a fine equal in amount to double the sum received for the goods, supplies, cattle or other animals sold, and, in addition, to the costs of prosecution before a police magistrate, a stipendiary magistrate, a justice of the peace or the Indian agent for the locality where the offence occurs. R.S., c. 81, s. 131.

123. If any person without authority, cuts or employs, or induces any other person to cut, or assists in cutting any trees of any kind on Indian lands or on any reserve, or removes or carries away, or employs, or induces or assists any other person to remove or carry away any trees of any kind so cut from any Indian lands or reserve, he shall not acquire any right to the trees so cut, or any claim to any remuneration for cutting or preparing the same for market, or conveying the same to or towards market.

2. When the trees or logs or timber or any products thereof have been removed, so that the same cannot, in the opinion of the Superintendent General, conveniently be seized, he Bhall, in addition to the loss of his labor and disbursements, incur a penalty of three dollars for each tree, rafting stuff excepted, which he is proved to have cut or caused to be cut or carried away.

3. Such penalty shall be recoverable with costs at the suit and in the name of the Superintendent General or resident agent in any court having jurisdiction in civil matters to the amount of the penalty.

4. In all such cases, it shall be incumbent on the person charged to prove his authority to cut.

5. The averment of the person seizing or prosecuting that he is duly employed under the authority of this Part shall be sufficient proof thereof, unless the defendant proves the contrary. R.S., c. 81, s. 132.

124. Every person or Indian other than an Indian of the band who, without the written consent of the Superintendent General or his agent, the burden of proof concerning which shall be on the accused, buys or otherwise acquires any presents given to Indians or non-treaty Indians, or any property purchased or acquired with or by means of any annuities granted to Indians or any part thereof, is guilty of an offence, and liable on summary conviction, to a fine not exceeding two hundred dollars, or to, imprisonment for a term not exceeding six months. R.S., c. 81, s. 133.

125. Every agent for the 6ale of Indian lands who, within his division, directly or indirectly, except under an order of the Governor in Council, purchases any land which he is appointed to, sell, or becomes proprietor of or interested in any such land, during the time of his agency shall forfeit his office and incur a penalty of four hundred dol- , lars for every such offence, recoverable in an action of debt by any person who sues for the same. R.S., c. 81, s. 134.

126. Everyone who by himself, his clerk, servant or agent, and everyone who in the employment or

on the premises of another directly or indirectly on any pretense or by any device,

(a) sells, barters, supplies or gives to any Indian or non-treaty Indian, or to any person, male or female, who is reputed to belong to a particular band, or who follows the Indian mode of life, or any child of such person any intoxicant, or causes or procures the same to be done or attempts the same or connives thereat.

(b) opens or keeps or causes to be opened or kept on any reserve or special reserve a tavern, house or building in which any intoxicant is sold, supplied or given.

(c) is found in possession of any intoxicant in the house, tent, wigwam, or place of abode of any Indian or nontreaty Indian or of any person on any reserve or special reserve, or on any other part of any reserve or special reserve; or

6. Paragraph (c) of subsection one of section one hundred and twenty-six of the said Act is repealed and the following substituted therefor: —

"(c) is found in possession of any intoxicant in the Having house, room, tent, wigwam, or place of abode of any Indian or non-treaty Indian whether on or off a reserve, or of any person on any reserve or special reserve, or on any other part of any reserve or special reserve; or

(d) sells, barters, supplies or gives to any person on any reserve or special reserve any intoxicant.

shall, on summary conviction before any judge, police magistrate, stipendiary magistrate, or two justices of the peace or Indian agent, be liable to imprisonment for a term not exceeding six months and not less than one month, with or without hard labor, or to a penalty not exceeding three hundred dollars and not less than fifty dollars with costs of prosecution, or to both penalty and imprisonment in the discretion of the convicting judge, magistrate, justices of the peace or Indian agent.

2. A moiety of every such penalty shall belong to the informer or prosecutor, and the other moiety thereof to His Majesty, to form part of the fund for the benefit of that body of Indians or non-treaty Indians with respect to one or more members of which the offence was committed. R.S., c. 81, s. 135.

18. Subsection two of section one hundred and twenty-six of the said Act is repealed and the following substituted therefor:

"(2) A moiety of every such penalty shall belong to the informer or prosecutor."

7. Subsection two of section one hundred and twenty- six of the said Act is repealed.

127. The commander or person in charge of any steamer or other vessel, or boat, from or on board of which any intoxicant has been sold, bartered, exchanged, supplied or given to any Indian or non-treaty Indian, shall, on summary conviction before any judge, police magistrate, stipendiary magistrate or two justices of the peace, or Indian agent, be liable to a penalty not exceeding three hundred dollars and not less than fifty dollars for each such offence, with costs of prosecution, and in default of immediate payment of such penalty and costs, any person so convicted shall be committed to any common goal, house of correction, lock-up or other place of confinement by the judge, magistrate or two justices of the peace, or Indian agent, before whom the conviction has taken place, for a term not exceeding six months and not less than one month, with or without hard labor, or until such penalty and costs are paid.

2. The penalty shall be applied as provided in the last preceding section. R.S., c. 81, s. 136.

8. Subsection two of section one hundred and twenty-seven of the said Act is repealed.

128. Every Indian or non-treaty Indian who makes or manufactures any intoxicant, or who has in his possession, or concealed, or who sells, exchanges with, barters, supplies or gives to any other Indian or non-treaty Indian, any intoxicant, shall, on summary conviction before any judge, police magistrate, stipendiary magistrate or two justices of the peace, or Indian agent, be liable to imprisonment for a term not exceeding six months and not less than one month, with or without hard labour, or to a penalty not exceeding one hundred dollars and not less than twenty five dollars, or to both penalty and imprisonment, in the discretion of the convicting judge, magistrate, or justices of the peace or Indian agent. R.S., c. 81, s. 137.

129. No penalty shall be incurred when the intoxicant is made use of in case of sickness under the sanction of a medical man or under the directions of a minister of religion.

2. The burden of proof that the intoxicant has been so made use of shall be on the accused. R.S., c. 81, s. 138.

130. Any constable or peace officer may arrest without warrant any person or Indian found gambling, or drunk, or with intoxicants in his possession, on any part of a reserve, and may detain him until he can be brought before a justice of the peace, and such person or Indian shall be liable upon summary conviction to imprisonment for a term not exceeding three .months or to a penalty not exceeding fifty dollars and not less than ten dollars, with costs of prosecution, half of which pecuniary penalty shall belong to the informer.

9. Subsection one of section one hundred and thirty of the said Act is amended by striking out the words of which pecuniary penalty shall belong to the informer."

2. Any person or Indian who has been gambling or has been drunk on an Indian reserve, or has had liquor in his possession on an Indian reserve, shall be liable on summary conviction to imprisonment for any term not exceeding three months, or to a penalty not exceeding fifty dollars and not less than ten dollars, with costs of prosecution. half of which pecuniary penalty shall belong to the informer. R.S., c. 81, s. 139; 1920, c. 50, s. 4.

10. Subsection two of section one hundred and thirty of the said Act is amended by striking out the words "half of which pecuniary penalty shall belong to the informer."

131. The keg, barrel, case, box, package or receptacle from which any intoxicant has been sold, exchanged, bartered. supplied or given, as well that in which the original supply was contained as the vessel wherein any portion of such original supply was supplied as aforesaid, and the remainder of the contents thereof, if such barrel, keg, case, box, package, receptacle or vessel aforesaid, respectively can be identified; and any intoxicant imported, manufactured or brought into and upon any reserve or special reserve, or into the house, tent, wigwam or place of abode, or on the person of any Indian or non-treaty Indian, or suspected to be upon any reserve or special reserve, may be searched for under a search warrant in that behalf granted by any judge, police magistrate, stipendiary magistrate or justice of the peace, and, if found, seized by any Indian superintendent, agent or bailiff, or other officer connected with the Department, or by any constable, where so ever found on such land or in such place or on the person of such Indian or non-treaty Indian.

2. On complaint before any judge, police magistrate, stipendiary magistrate, justice of the peace or Indian agent, he may, on evidence that this Act has been violated in respect of any such intoxicant or of any such keg, barrel, case, box, package, receptacle or vessel, or contents thereof, declare the same

forfeited, and cause the same to be forthwith destroyed.

3. Such judge, magistrate, justice of the peace or Indian agent may condemn the Indian or person in whose possession the same is found to pay a penalty not exceeding one hundred dollars and not less than fifty dollars, and the costs of prosecution; and, in default of immediate payment, the offender may be committed to any common gaol, house of correction, lock-up or other place of confinement, with or without hard labour, for any term not exceeding six months, and not less than two months, unless such penalty and costs are sooner paid.

4. A moiety of such penalty shall belong to the prosecutor, and the other moiety to His Majesty for the purpose hereinbefore mentioned. R.S., c. 81, a. 140.

11. Subsection four of section one hundred and thirty- one of the said Act is repealed.

132. If it is proved before any judge, police magistrate, stipendiary magistrate or two justices of the peace, or Indian agent, that any vessel, boat, canoe or conveyance of any description, upon the sea or sea-coast, or upon any river, lake or stream, is employed in carrying any intoxicant, to be supplied to Indians or non-treaty Indians, such vessel, boat, canoe or conveyance so employed may be seized and declared forfeited, as in the last preceding section mentioned, and sold, and the proceeds thereof paid to His Majesty for the purpose hereinbefore mentioned. R.S., c. 81, s. 141.

14. Section one hundred and thirty-two of the said Act is repealed and the following substituted therefor:—

"132. If it is proved before any judge, police magistrate, stipendiary magistrate or two justices of the peace or Indian agent that any vehicle, motor car, automobile, can vessel, boat, canoe or conveyance of any description is employed in carrying any intoxicant to be supplied to Indians or non-treaty Indians, such vehicle, motor car, automobile, vessel, boat, canoe or conveyance so employed may be seized and declared forfeited, as in the last preceding section mentioned and sold, and the proceeds thereof paid to His Majesty for "the purpose hereinbefore mentioned."

133. Every article, chattel, commodity or thing in the purchase, acquisition, exchange, trade or barter of which, in violation of this Act, the consideration, either wholly or in part, is an intoxicant, shall be forfeited to His Majesty and may be seized, as is hereinbefore provided in respect to any receptacle of any intoxicant, and may be sold, and the proceeds thereof paid to His Majesty, for the purpose hereinbefore mentioned. R.S., c. 81, s. 142.

134. Every person who introduces any intoxicant at any council or meeting of Indians held for the purpose of discussing or assenting to a release or surrender of a re- serve or portion thereof or for the purpose of assenting to the issuing of a license, and every agent or officer employed by the Superintendent General, or by the Governor in Council, who introduces, allows or countenances by his presence the use of such intoxicant among such Indians during the week before or at or the week after such council or meeting, shall incur a penalty of two hundred dollars recoverable by action in any court of competent jurisdiction.

2. A moiety of such penalty shall belong to the in- former. RS., c. 81, s. 143.

12. Subsection two of section one hundred and thirty- four of the said Act is repealed.

135. Every Indian who is found in a state of intoxication shall be liable on summary conviction thereof to imprisonment for any term not exceeding one month, or to a penalty not exceeding thirty dollars and not less than five dollars, or to both penalty and imprisonment, in the discretion of the

convicting judge, magistrate, justice of the peace or Indian agent. R.S., c. 81, s. 144.

136. Any constable or other peace officer may, without warrant, arrest any Indian or non-treaty Indian found in a state of intoxication, and convey him to any common gaol, house of correction, lock-up, or other place of confinement, there to be kept until he is sober; and such Indian or non-treaty Indian shall, when sober, be brought for trial before any judge, police magistrate, stipendiary magistrate, or justice of the peace or Indian agent. R.S., c. 81, s. 145.

137. If any Indian or non-treaty Indian who has been so convicted, refuses, upon examination, to state or give information of the person from whom, the place where, and the time when, he procured such intoxicant, and if from any other Indian or non-treaty Indian, then, if within his knowledge, from whom, where and when such intoxicant was originally procured or received, he shall be liable to imprisonment as aforesaid for a further period not exceeding fourteen days, or to an additional penalty not exceeding fifteen dollars and not less than three dollars, or to both penalty and imprisonment, in the discretion of the convicting judge, magistrate, justice of the peace or Indian agent.

2. In any prosecution under this Act the certificate of analysis of a provincial or dominion analyst shall be accepted as prima facie evidence of the fact stated therein as to the alcoholic or narcotic content of the sample analyzed. R.S., c. 81, s. 146; 1927, c. 32, s. 5.

15. Subsection two of section one hundred and thirty- seven of the said Act is repealed and the following substituted therefor:—

"(2) In any prosecution under this Act, a certificate of analysis signed or purporting to be signed by a provincial or dominion analyst, shall be accepted as prima facie evidence of the facts stated therein, as to the analysis or the alcoholic or narcotic content of the sample or preparation therein referred to as having been analyzed, and of the authority of the person signing such certificate without any proof of appointment or signature."

138. Every agent who knowingly and falsely information, or causes to be informed, any person applying to him to purchase any land within his division and agency, that the same has already been purchased, or who refuses to permit the person so applying to purchase the same according to existing regulations, shall be liable therefor to the person so applying, in the sum of five dollars for each acre of land which the person so applying offered to purchase, recoverable by action of debt in any court of competent jurisdiction. R.S., c. 81, s. 147.

139. Every person who, after public notice by the Superintendent General prohibiting the sale, gift, or other disposal to Indians in any part of the province of Manitoba, Saskatchewan or Alberta, or the Territories, of any fixed ammunition or ball cartridge, without the permission in writing of the Superintendent General, sells or gives, or in any other manner conveys to any Indian, in the portion of the said provinces or Territories to which such notice applies, any fixed ammunition or ball cartridge, shall, on summary conviction before any stipendiary or police magistrate or by any two justices of the peace, or by an Indian agent, be liable to a penalty not exceeding two hundred dollars, or to imprisonment for a term not exceeding six months, or to both penalty and imprisonment, within the limits aforesaid, at the discretion of the court before which the conviction is had. R.S., c. 81, s. 148.

140. Every Indian or other person who engages in, or assists in celebrating or encourages either directly or indirectly another to celebrate any Indian festival, dance or other ceremony of which the giving away or paying or giving back of money, goods or articles of any sort forms a part, or is a feature, whether such gift of money, goods or articles takes place before, at, or after the celebration of the same, or who engages or assists in any celebration or dance of which the wounding or mutilation of the dead or living body of any human being or animal forms a part or is a feature, is guilty of an offence and is liable on summary conviction to imprisonment for a term not exceeding six months and not less than two months.

2. Nothing in this section shall be construed to prevent the holding of any agricultural show or exhibition or the giving of prizes for exhibits thereat.

3. Any Indian in the province of Manitoba, Saskatchewan, Alberta, or British Columbia, or in the Territories who participates in any Indian dance outside the bounds of his own reserve, or who participates in any show, exhibition, performance, stampede or pageant in aboriginal costume without the consent of the Superintendent General or his authorized agent, and any person who induces or employs any Indian to take part in such dance, show, exhibition, performance, stampede or pageant, or induces any Indian to leave his reserve or employs any Indian for such a purpose, whether the dance, show, exhibition, stampede or pageant has taken place or not, shall on summary conviction be liable to a penalty not exceeding twenty-five dollars, or to imprisonment for one month, or to both penalty and imprisonment. R.S., c. 81, s. 149; 1914, c. 35, a. 8; 1918, c. 26, s. 7.

10. Subsection three of section one hundred and forty of the said Act is amended by striking out the words "in aboriginal costume" in the fifth line thereof.

16. The said Act is amended by inserting therein section 140A as follows:—

"140A. Where it is made to appear in open court that any Indian, summoned before such court, by inordinate frequenting of a poolroom either on or off an Indian reserve, misspends or wastes his time or means to the detriment of himself, his family or household, of which he is a member, the police magistrate, stipendiary magistrate, Indian agent, or two justices of the peace holding such court, shall, by writing under his or their hand or hands forbid the owner or person in charge of a poolroom which such Indian is in the habit of frequenting to allow such Indian to enter such poolroom for the space of one year from the date of such notice.

Any owner or person in charge of a poolroom who allows an Indian to enter a poolroom in violation of such notice, and any Indian who enters a poolroom where his admission has been so forbidden, shall be liable on summary conviction to a penalty not exceeding twenty-five dollars and costs or to imprisonment for a term not exceeding thirty days."

141. Every person who, without the consent of the Superintendent General expressed in writing, receives, obtains, solicits or requests from any Indian any payment or contribution or promise of any payment or contribution the purpose of raising a fund or providing money for the prosecution of any claim which' the tribe or band of Indians to which such Indian belongs, or of which he is a member, has or is represented to have for the recovery of any claim or money for the benefit of the said tribe or band, shall be guilty of an offence and liable upon summary conviction for each such offence to a penalty not exceeding two hundred dollars and not less than fifty dollars or to imprisonment for any term not exceeding two months. 1927, c. 32, s. 6.

142. Every fine, penalty or forfeiture under this Act, except so much thereof as is payable to an informer or per- son suing therefor, shall belong to His Majesty for the benefit of the band of Indians with respect to which or to one or more members of which the offence was committed, or to which the offender, if an Indian, belongs: Provided that the Governor in Council may from time to time direct that the same be paid to any provincial, municipal or local authority which wholly or in part bears the expense of administering the law under which such fine, penalty or forfeiture is imposed, or that the same be applied in any other manner deemed best adapted to attain the objects of such law or to secure its clue administration, and may in case of doubt decide what band is entitled to the benefit of any such fine, penalty or forfeiture. R.S., c. 81, s. 150.

Evidence and Procedure.

143. Upon any inquest, or upon any inquiry into any matter involving a criminal charge, or upon the trial of any crime or offence whatsoever or by whomsoever committed, any court, judge, police or stipendiary magistrate, recorder, coroner, justice of the peace or Indian agent, may receive the evidence of any Indian or non-treaty Indian, who is destitute of the knowledge of God or of any fixed and clear belief in religion, or in a future state of rewards and punishments, without administering the usual form of oath to any such Indian or non-treaty Indian, as aforesaid, upon his solemn affirmation or declaration to tell the truth, the whole truth, and nothing but the truth, or in such form as is approved by such court, judge, magistrate, recorder, coroner, justice of the peace or Indian agent, as most binding on the conscience of such Indian or non-treaty Indian. R.S., c. 81, s. 151.

144. In the case of any inquest, or upon any inquiry into any matter involving a criminal charge, or upon the trial of any crime or offence whatsoever, the substance of the evidence or information of any such Indian or non- treaty Indian, as aforesaid, shall be reduced to writing and signed by the Indian, by mark if necessary, giving the same, and verified by the signature or mark of the person acting as interpreter, if any, and by the signature of the judge, magistrate, recorder, coroner, justice of the peace, Indian agent or person before whom such evidence or information is given. R.S., c. 81, s. 152.

145. The court, judge, magistrate, recorder, coroner, justice of the peace or Indian agent shall, before taking any such evidence, information or examination, caution every such Indian or non-treaty Indian, as aforesaid, that he will be liable to incur punishment if he does not tell the truth, the whole truth and nothing but the truth.

2. Every solemn affirmation or declaration, in what soever form made or taken, by any Indian or non-treaty Indian, as aforesaid, shall be of the same force and effect as if such Indian or non-treaty Indian had taken an oath in the usual form. R.S., c. 81, ss. 153 and 154.

146. The written declaration or examination so made, taken and verified, of any such Indian or non-treaty Indian, as aforesaid, may be lawfully read and received as evidence upon the trial of any criminal proceeding when under the like circumstances the written affidavit, examination, deposition or confession of any person might be lawfully read and received as evidence.

2. Copies of any records, documents, books or papers belonging to or deposited in the Department, attested under the signature of the Superintendent General or of the Deputy of the Superintendent General, shall be evidence in all cases in which the original records, documents, books or papers would be evidence. R.S., c. 81, s. 155.

147. In any order, writ, warrant, summons and proceeding whatsoever made, issued or taken by the Superintendent General, or any officer or person by him deputed as aforesaid, or by any stipendiary magistrate, police magistrate, justice of the peace or Indian agent, it shall not be necessary to insert or express the name of the person or Indian summoned, arrested, distained upon, imprisoned or otherwise proceeded against therein, except when the name of such person or Indian is truly given to or known by the Superintendent General, or such officer or person, or such stipendiary magistrate, police magistrate, justice of the peace or Indian agent.

2. If the name is not truly given to or known by him, he may name or describe the person or Indian by any part of the name of such person or Indian given to or known by him.

3. If no part of the name is given to or known by him, he may describe the person or Indian proceeded against in any manner by which he may be identified.

4. All such proceedings containing or purporting to give the name or description of any such person or Indian, as shall prima facie be sufficient. R.S., c. 81, s. 156.

148. All sheriffs, gaolers or peace officers, to whom any such process is directed by the Superintendent General, or by any officer or person by him deputed as aforesaid, or by any stipendiary magistrate, police magistrate, justice of the peace or Indian agent, and all other persons to whom such process is directed with their consent, shall obey the same; and all other officers shall, upon reasonable requisition so to do, assist in the execution thereof. R.S., c. 81, s. 157.

149. In all cases of encroachment upon, or of violation of trust respecting any special reserve, proceedings may be taken in the name of His Majesty, in any superior court, notwithstanding the legal title is not vested in His Majesty. R.S., c. 81, s. 158.

150. Any judge of a court, judge of sessions of the peace, recorder, police magistrate or stipendiary magistrate, shall have full power to do alone whatever is authorized by this Part to be done by a justice of the peace or by two justices of the peace. R.S., c. 81, s. 159.

151. Any recorder, police magistrate or stipendiary magistrate, appointed for or having jurisdiction to act in any city or town shall, with respect to offences and matters under this Part, have and exercise jurisdiction over the whole county or union of counties or judicial district in which the city or town for which he has been appointed or in which he has jurisdiction is situate. R.S., c. 81, a 160.

152. Every Indian agent shall for all the purposes of this Act or of any other Act respecting Indians, and with justice of respect to

(a) any offence against the provisions of this Act or any other Act respecting Indians;

(b) any offence against the provisions of the Criminal Code respecting the inciting of Indians to commit riotous acts; or

(c) any offence by any Indian or non-treaty Indian against any of the provisions of those parts of the Criminal Code relating to vagrancy and offences against morality;

be ex officio a justice of the peace and have the power and authority of two justices of the peace, anywhere within the territorial limits of his jurisdiction as a justice, as defined in his appointment or otherwise defined by the Governor in Council, whether the Indian or non-treaty Indian charged with or in any way concerned in or affected by the offence, matter or thing to be tried, investigated or dealt with, is or is not within his ordinary jurisdiction, charge or supervision as an Indian agent. R.S., c. 81, s. 161.

153. In the provinces of Manitoba, British Columbia, Saskatchewan and Alberta, and in the Territories, every Indian agent shall, for all such purposes and with respect to any such offence, be ex officio a justice of the peace and have the power and authority of two justices of the peace, whether or not the territorial limits of his jurisdiction as a justice, as defined in his appointment or otherwise defined as aforesaid, extend to the place where he may have occasion to act as such justice or to exercise such power or authority, and whether the Indians charged with or in any way concerned in or affected by the offence, matter or thing, to be tried, investigated or otherwise dealt with, are or are not within his ordinary jurisdiction, charge or supervision as Indian agent. R.S., c. 81, s. 162.

154. If any Indian is convicted of any crime punishable by imprisonment in a penitentiary or other place of confinement, the costs incurred in procuring such conviction, and in carrying out the various sentences recorded, may be, defrayed by the Superintendent General, and paid out of any annuity or interest coming to such Indian, or to the band, as the case may be. R.S., c. 81, a 163.

General.

155. No Indian or non-treaty Indian resident in the province of Manitoba, Saskatchewan or Alberta, or the Territories, shall be held capable of having acquired or of acquiring a homestead or pre-emption right under any Act respecting Dominion lands, to a quarter-section, or any parcel of land in any surveyed or unsurveyed lands in the said provinces or territories, or the right to share in the distribution of any lands allotted to half-breeds: Provided that

(a) he shall not be disturbed in the occupation of any plot on which he had permanent improvements prior to his becoming a party to any treaty with the Crown;

(b) nothing in this section shall prevent the Superintendent General, if found desirable, from compensating any Indian for his improvements on such a plot land, without obtaining a formal surrender thereof from the band; and

(c) nothing in this section shall apply to any person who withdrew from any Indian treaty prior to the first day of October, in the year one thousand eight hundred and seventy-four. R.S., c. 81, s. 164.

156. Where shooting privileges over a reserve or part of a reserve, or fishing privileges thereon have, with the consent of the Indians of the band, been leased or granted to any person, it shall not be lawful for any person, not under such lease or grant entitled so to do, or for any Indian other than an Indian of the band, to hunt, shoot, kill or destroy any game animals or birds, or to fish for, take, catch or kill any fish to which such, exclusive privilege extends, upon the reserve or part of a reserve. R.S., c. 81, s. 165.

157. At the election of a chief or chiefs, or at the granting of any ordinary consent required of a band under this Part, those entitled to vote at the council or meeting thereof shall be the male members of the band, of the full age of twenty-one years; and the vote of a majority of such members, at a council or meeting of the band summoned according to its rules, and held in the presence of the Superintendent General, or of an agent acting under his instructions, shall be sufficient to determine such election or grant such consent. R.S., c. 81, s. 166.

158. If any brand has a council of chiefs or councilors, any ordinary consent required of the band may be granted by a vote of a majority of such chiefs or councilors, at a council summoned according to its rules, and held in the presence of the Superintendent General or his agent. R.S., c. 81, s. 167.

159. No one shall introduce any intoxicant at any council or meeting of Indians held for the purpose of discussing or of assenting to a release or surrender of a reserve or portion thereof, or for the purpose of assenting to the issuing of a timber or other license. R.S., c. 81, s. 168.

160. All affidavits required under this Act or intended to be used in reference to any claim, business or transaction in connection with Indian affairs, may be taken before the judge or clerk of any county or circuit court, or any justice of the peace, or any commissioner for taking affidavits in any court, or the Superintendent General, or the Deputy of the Superintendent General, or any inspector of Indian agencies, or any Indian agent, or any surveyor duly licensed and sworn, appointed by the Superintendent General to inquire into, or to take evidence, or report in any matter submitted to or pending before the Superintendent General, or if made out of Canada, before the mayor or chief magistrate of, or the British consul in, any city, town or municipality, or before any notary public. R.S., c. 81, s. 169.

161. All regulations made by the Governor in Council under this Part shall be published in the Canada Gazette, and shall be laid before both Houses of Parliament within the first fifteen days of the session next after the date thereof. R.S., c. 81, s. 170.

162. The annuities payable to Indians in pursuance of the conditions of any treaty expressed to have been entered into on behalf of His Majesty or His predecessors, and for the payment of which the Government of Canada is responsible, shall be a charge upon the Consolidated Revenue Fund of Canada, and be payable out of any unappropriated moneys forming part thereof. 1911, c. 14, s. 3.

PART II.

INDIAN ADVANCEMENT.

Interpretation.

163. In this Part, unless the context otherwise requires

(a) "electors" means the male Indians of the full age of twenty-one years resident on any reserve to which this Part applies;

(b) "reserve" includes two or more reserves, and " band " includes two or more bands united for the purposes of this Part by the Order in Council applying it. R.S., c. 81, s. 172.

Application of this Part.

164. This Part may be made applicable, as hereinafter provided, to any band of Indians in any of the provinces, or in the Territories, except in so far as it is herein otherwise provided. R.S., c. 81, s. 173.

165. Whenever any band of Indians is declared by the. Governor in Council to be considered fit to have this Part applied to it, this Part shall so apply from the time appointed in such Order in Council. R.S., c. 81, s. 174.

Application of Part I.

166. The provisions of Part I of this Act shall continue to apply to every band to which this Part is, from time to time, declared to apply, in so far only as they are not inconsistent with this Part.

2. If it thereafter appears to the Governor in Council that this Part cannot be worked satisfactorily by any band to which it has been declared to apply, the Governor in Council may by Order in Council, declare that after a day named in the Order in Council, this Part shall no longer apply to such band, and such band shall thereafter be subject only to Part I, except that by-laws, rules and regulations theretofore made under this Part, and not ultra vires of the chiefs in council under Part I, shall

continue in force until they are repealed by the Governor in Council. R.S., c. 81, s. 175.

Division of Reserves.

167. Every reserve to which this Part is to apply may, by the Order in Council applying it, be divided into sections, the number of which shall not exceed six, and each section shall have therein, as nearly as is found convenient, an equal number of male Indians of the full age of twenty-one years, or, should the majority of the Indians of the reserve so desire, the whole reserve may form one section, the wishes of the Indians in respect thereto being first ascertained in the manner prescribed in Part I in like matters, and certified to the Superintendent General by the Indian agent.

2. Subsection one of section one hundred and sixty-seven of the Indian Act, chapter ninety-eight of the Revised Statutes of Canada, 1927, is repealed, and the following is substituted therefor:—

"167. (1) Every reserve e to which this Part is applicable, may, by Order in Council, be divided into sections, the number of which shall not exceed six, and each section shall have therein, as nearly as is found convenient, an equal number of male Indians of the full age of twenty-one years, or, should the majority of the Indians of the reserve so desire, the Governor in Council may provide that the whole reserve may form one section, the wishes of the Indians in respect thereto being first ascertained in the manner prescribed in Part I in like matters, and certified to the Superintendent General by the Indian agent. The power to divide any such reserve into sections, or to provide that the whole reserve may form one section may, subject to the provisions of this section, be exercised at any time and from time to time, as the Governor in Council may see fit."

2. The sections shall be distinguished by numbers from one upwards, and the reserve shall be designated in the Order in Council as The Indian Reserve, inserting such name as is thought proper, and the sections shall be designated by the numbers assigned to them respectively. R.S., c. 81, s. 176.

Nominations for Election of Councilors.

168. A meeting of the electors for the purpose of nominating candidates for election as councillors shall be held between the hours of ten o'clock in the forenoon and twelve o'clock at noon, at a place to be appointed by the Indian agent, on a day being one week previous to the day on which the election of councillors is to be held on any reserve as hereinafter provided.

2. Due notice of such meeting shall be given in the manner customary in the band for calling meetings for public purposes. R.S., c. 81, s. 177.

169. The Indian agent, or in his absence such person as is appointed by the Superintendent General, or failing such appointment, a chairman to be chosen by the meeting, shall preside over such meeting and shall take and keep the minutes thereof. R.S., c. S1, s. 178.

170. Only Indians nominated at such meeting shall be recognized as, or permitted to become candidates for election as aforesaid; and each nomination to be valid must be made on the motion of an elector of the section of the reserve for the representation whereof the nominee is proposed as a candidate, and the motion must be seconded by another elector of that section. R.S., c. 81, s. 179.

171. The nominations of the candidates shall, so far as practicable, be made consecutively and previously to any speeches being made by the movers and seconders or by any other persons, but nominations may be made up to the hour of twelve o'clock noon. R.S., c. 81, s. 180.

172. If only one candidate for any councillorship is proposed, the Indian agent or chairman shall, at twelve o'clock noon, declare such candidate duly elected; and if two or more candidates are pro-

posed for any councillorship, an election shall be held under the provisions of this Part. R.S., c. 81, s. 181.

Elections.

173. On a day and at a place, and between the hours prescribed in the Order in Council, the electors shall meet for the purpose of electing the members of the council of the reserve. R.S., c. 81, s. 182.

174. One or more members to represent each section of the reserve, as provided in such Order in Council, shall be elected by the electors resident in each section, and the Indian or Indians, as the case may be, having the votes of the greatest number of electors for each section, shall be the councillor or councillors, as the case may be therefor, provided he or they are respectively possessed of, and living in, a house in the reserve. R.S., c. 81, s. 183.

13. Section one hundred and seventy-four of the said Act is repealed and the following substituted therefor:—

"174. One or more members to represent each section of the reserve, as provided in such Order in Council, shall be elected by the electors resident in each section, and the Indian or Indians, as the case may be, having the votes of the greatest number of electors for each section, shall be the councillor or councillors, as the case may be, therefor, provided he or they are respectively possessed of a house on, and living on, the reserve."

175. The agent for the reserve shall preside at the election, or in his absence some person appointed by him as his deputy, with the consent of the Superintendent General, or some person appointed by the Superintendent General may preside at the said election, and shall take and record the votes of the electors, and may, subject to appeal to the Superintendent General by or on behalf of any Indian or Indians who deems himself or themselves aggrieved by the action of such agent or deputy, or of such agent or person appointed as aforesaid, admit or reject the claim of any Indian to be an elector, and may determine who are the councillors for the several sections, and shall report the same to the Superintendent General.

2. In any case of an equality of votes at any such election the agent or person residing thereat shall have the casting vote. R.S., c. 8

Meetings of Council.

176. On a day and at a place, and between the hours prescribed by the Superintendent General, if the day fixed for the same is within eight days from the date at which the councillors were elected, the said councillors shall meet and elect one of their number to act as chief councillor, and the councillor so elected shall be the chief councillor. R.S., 81, s. 185.

177. The council shall meet for the dispatch of business, at such place on the reserve and at such times as the agent for the reserve appoints, but which shall not exceed twelve times or be less than four times in the year for which it is elected, and due notice of the time and place of each meeting shall be given to each councillor by the agent. R.S., 81, s. 86.

178. At such meeting of the council the agent for the reserve, or his deputy appointed for the purpose with the consent of the Superintendent General, shall

(a) preside, and record the proceedings;

(b) control and regulate all matters of procedure and form and adjourn the meeting to a time named or sine die;

(c) report and certify all by-laws and other acts and proceedings of the council to the Superintendent General;

(d) address the council and explain and advise the members thereof upon their powers and duties.

2. No such agent or deputy shall vote on any question to be decided by the council. R.S., c. S1, s. 187.

179. Full faith and credence shall be given in all courts and places whatsoever to any certificate given by such agent or deputy under the provisions of paragraph (c) of the last preceding section. R.S., c. 81, s. 188.

180. Each councillor present shall have a vote on every question to be decided by the council, and such question shall be decided by the majority of votes, the chief councillor voting as a councillor and having also a casting vote, in case the votes would otherwise be equal.

2. Four councillors shall be a quorum for the despatch of any business. R.S., c. 81, s. 189.

Term of Office, Vacancies, Etc.

181. The councillors shall remain in office until others are elected in their stead, and an election for that purpose shall be held in like manner, at the same place and between the like hours on the like day, in each succeeding year, if it is not a Sunday or holiday, in which case it shall be held on the next day thereafter which is not a Sunday or a holiday.

2. If there is a failure to elect on the day appointed for the election, the Superintendent General shall appoint another day on which it shall be held. R.S., c. 81, s. 190.

182. In the event of a vacancy in the council, by the death or inability to act of any councillor, more than three months before the time for the next election, an election to fill such vacancy shall be held by the agent or his deputy, after such notice to the electors concerned as the Superintendent General directs, at which only the electors of the section represented by the councillor to be replaced shall vote, and to such election the provisions respecting other elections shall apply, so far as they are applicable.

2. If the councillor to be replaced is the chief councillor, then an election of a chief councillor shall be held in the manner already provided, but the day fixed for such election shall be at least one week after the date when the new councillor is elected. R.S., c. 81, s. 191.

183. During the time of any vacancy in the council the remaining councillors shall constitute the council, and they may, in the event of a vacancy in the office, appoint a chief from among themselves for the time being. R.S., c. 81, s. 192.

184. Every member of a council elected under the provisions of this Part, who is proved to be a habitual drunkard or to be living in immorality, or to have accepted a bribe, or to have been guilty of dishonesty or of malfeasance of office of any kind, shall, on proof of the fact to the satisfaction of the Superintendent General, be disqualified from acting as a member of the council, and shall, on being notified, cease forthwith so to act; and the vacancy occasioned thereby shall be filled in the manner hereinbefore provided. R.S., c. 81, s. 193.

Powers of Council.

185. The council may, by by-law, rule or regulation. approved and confirmed by the Superintendent General. provide that the religious denomination to which the teacher or teachers of the school or schools established on the reserve shall belong, shall be that of the majority of the Indians resident

on the reserve ; but the Protestant or Roman Catholic minority on the reserve may also have a separate school or schools, with the approval of and under regulations made by the Governor in Council.

2. The council may also make by-laws, rules and regulations, approved and confirmed by the Superintendent General, regulating all or any of the following subjects and purposes, that is to say:—

(a) The care of the public health;

(b) The observance of order and decorum at elections of councillors, meetings of the council, and assemblies of Indians on other occasions, or generally, on the reserve, by the appointment of constables and erection of lock-up houses, or by the adoption of other legitimate means;

(c) The prevention of disorderly conduct and nuisances:

(d) The subdivision of the land in the reserve, and the distribution of the same amongst the members of the band; also, the setting apart, for common use, of woodland and land for other purposes;

(e) The protection of and the prevention of trespass by cattle, sheep, horses, mules and other domesticated animals; and the establishment of pounds, the appointment of pound keepers and the regulation of their duties, fees and charges;

(f) The construction and repairs of school houses, council houses and other buildings for the use of the In- on the reserve, and the attendance at school of children between the ages of six and fifteen years;

(g) The construction, maintenance and improvement of roads and bridges, and the contributions, in money or labour, and other duties of residents on the reserve, in respect thereof; the size and kind of sleighs to be used on the roads in the winter season, and the manner in which the horse or horses or other beasts of burden shall be harnessed to such sleighs; and the appointment of roadmasters and fence-viewers, and their powers and duties;

(h) The construction, maintenance and improvement of water, sewerage and lighting works and systems;

(i) The construction and maintenance of watercourses, ditches and fences, and the obligations of vicinage, the destruction and repression of noxious weeds and the preservation of the wood on the various holdings, or elsewhere, in the reserve;

(j) The removal and punishment of persons trespassing upon the reserve, or frequenting it for improper purposes;

17. Subsection two of section one hundred and eighty five of the said Act is amended by adding thereto after paragraph (j) thereof the following paragraph:—

"(jj) Controlling or prohibiting participation in, or attendance at, public games, sports, races, athletic contests or other such amusements on the Sabbath."

(k) The raising of money for any or all of the purposes for which the council may make by-laws as aforesaid, by assessment and taxation of the lands of Indians enfranchised, or in possession of lands by location ticket in the reserve: Provided that the valuation for assessment shall be made yearly, in such manner and at such times as are appointed by the by-law in that behalf, and be subject to revision and correction by the agent for the reserve, and shall come into force only after it has been submitted to him and corrected, if and as he thinks justice requires, and approved by him. and that the tax shall be imposed for the year in which the by-law is made, and shall not exceed one-half of one per centum on the assessed value of the land on which it is to be paid; and provided also that any Indian deeming himself aggrieved by the decision of the agent, made as hereinbefore provided, may appeal to the Superintendent General, whose decision in the matter shall be final;

(l) The appropriation and payment to the local agent, as treasurer, by the Superintendent General, of so much of the moneys of the band as are required for defraying expenses necessary for carrying out the bylaws made by the council, including those incurred for assistance absolutely necessary for enabling the council or the agent to perform the duties assigned to them;

(m) The imposition of punishment by penalty or by imprisonment, or by both, for any violation of or disobedience to any law, rule or regulation made under this Part, committed by any Indian of the reserve; but such penalty shall, in no case, except for non-payment of taxes, exceed thirty dollars, and the imprisonment shall not exceed thirty days.

11. Subsection two of section one hundred and eighty-five of the said Act is amended by adding thereto the following paragraph:—

"(n) Regulating the operations of hawkers, peddlers or others coming on the Reserve to sell, or take orders for. wares or merchandise."

3. If any tax authorized by any by-law, or any part thereof, is not paid at the time prescribed by the by-law, the amount unpaid, with the addition of one-half of one per centum thereof, may be paid by the Superintendent General to the treasurer out of the share in any money of the band of the Indian in default; and, if such share is insufficient to pay the tax, or any portion thereof so remaining unpaid, the defaulter shall be deemed to have violated the by-law imposing the tax, and shall incur a penalty therefor equal to the amount of the tax or the balance thereof remaining unpaid, as the case may be.

4. The proceedings for the imposition of any punishment authorized by this section, or the by-laws, rules or regulations approved and confirmed thereunder, may be taken before one justice of the peace, under the provisions of the Criminal Code relating to summary convictions; and the amount of any such penalty shall be paid over to the treasurer of the band to which the Indian incurring it belongs for the use of such band.

5. The by-laws, rules and regulations by this section authorized to be made shall, when approved and confirmed by the Superintendent General, have the force of law within and with respect to the reserve, and the Indians residing thereon. R.S., c. 81, s. 194; 1920, c. 50, s. 5; 1927, c. 32, s. 7.

Evidence.

186. A copy of any by-law, rule or regulation under this Part, approved by the Superintendent General, and purporting to be certified by the agent for the band to which it relates to be a true copy thereof, shall be evidence of such by-law, rule or regulation, and of such approval, without proof of the signature of such agent; and no such by-law, rule or regulation shall be invalidated by any defect of form, if it is substantially consistent with the intent and meaning of this Part. R.S., c. 81, a 195.

PART III.

SOLDIER SETTLEMENT.

187. The Soldier Settlement Act, excepting sections three, four, eight, nine, ten, eleven, fourteen, twenty-nine, subsection two of fifty-one, and sixty-one thereof, and excepting the whole of Part III thereof, with such amendments as may from time to time be made to said Act shall, with respect to

any " settler " as defined by said Act who is an " Indian " as defined by this Act, be administered by the Superintendent General.

2. For the purpose of such administration, the Deputy Superintendent General of Indian Affairs shall have the same powers as the Soldier Settlement Board has under the Soldier Settlement Act, the words "Deputy Superintendent General of Indian Affairs " being, for such purpose, read in the said Act as substituted for the words " The Soldier Settlement Board" and for the words "The Board".

3. Said Act, with such exceptions as aforesaid, shall for such purpose, be read as one with this Part of this Act. 1919, c. 56, s. 3.

188. The Deputy Superintendent General may acquire for a settler who is an Indian, land as well without as with- in an Indian reserve, and shall have authority to set apart for such settler a portion of the common lands of the band without the consent of the council of the band.

2. In the event of land being so acquired or set apart on an Indian reserve, the Deputy Superintendent General shall have power to take the said land as security for any advances made to such settler, and the provisions of the Soldier Settlement Act, shall, as far as applicable, apply to such transactions.

3. It shall, however, be only the individual Indian interest in such lands that is being acquired or given as security, and the interest of the band in such lands shall not be in any way affected by such transactions. 1922, c. 26, s. 2.

189. The Soldier Settlement Board and its officers and employees shall, upon request of the Deputy Superintendent General, aid and assist him, to the extent requested, in the execution of the purposes of this Act, and the said Board may sell, convey and transfer to the said Deputy, for the execution of any such purposes, at such prices as may be agreed, any property held for disposition by such Board. 1919, c. 56, s. 3.

190. In the event of any doubt or difficulty arising with respect to the administration by the Superintendent General of the provisions of the Soldier Settlement Act, or as to the powers of the Deputy Superintendent General as by this Act authorized or granted, the Governor in Council may, by order, resolve such doubt or difficulty and may define powers and procedure.

2. Such order shall not extend the powers which are by the Soldier Settlement Act, provided. 1919, c. 56, a. 3.

N.B.: R.S.C. 1927, c. 98 is affected by the following provisions of S.C. 1951, c. 29, proclaimed on 4 September 1951:
REPEAL.
123. (1) Section one of the Indian Act, chapter ninety-eight of the Revised Statutes of Canada, 1927, is repealed and the following substituted therefor:
"1. This Act may be cited as the Indian (Soldier Settlement) Act."
(2) Sections two to one hundred and eighty-six of the said Act are repealed.
(3) Where in sections one hundred and eighty-seven to one hundred and ninety of the said Act
(a) reference is made to the Indian Act, it shall be deemed to be a reference to this Act, and
(b) reference is made to the Superintendent General or Deputy Superintendent General of Indian

Affairs, it shall be deemed to be a reference to the Minister.

Paragraph (6) of subjection (3) of section 123 is amended by substituting the Minister of Indian Affair and Northern Development for the Minister therein mentioned

PRIOR GRANTS.

124. Where, prior to the coming into force of this Act,

(a) a reserve or portion of a reserve was released or surrendered to the Crown pursuant to Part I of the Indian Act, chapter ninety-eight of the Revised Statutes of Canada, 1927, or pursuant to the provisions of the statutes relating to the release or surrender of reserves in force at the time of the release or surrender,

(b) Letters Patent under the Great Seal of Canada were issued purporting to grant a reserve or portion of a reserve so released or surrendered, or any interest therein, to any person, and

(c) the Letters Patent have not been declared void or inoperative by any Court of competent jurisdiction, the Letters Patent shall, for all purposes, be deemed to have been issued at the date thereof under the direction of the Governor in Council.

COMING INTO FORCE.

125. This Act shall come into force on a day to be fixed by proclamation of the Governor in Council.

The Indian Act. S.C. 1951, c. 29

15 GEORGE VI.

CHAP. 29.

An Act respecting Indians.

[Assented to 20th June, 1951.]

HIS Majesty, by and with the advice and consent of the Senate and House of Commons of Canada, enacts as follows:

SHORT TITLE.

1. This Act may be cited as The Indian Act.

INTERPRETATION.

2. (1) In this Act,

(a) "band" means a body of Indians

(i) for whose use and benefit in common, lands, the legal title to which is vested in His Majesty, have been set apart before or after the coming into force of this Act,

(ii) for whose use and benefit in common, moneys are held by His Majesty, or

(iii) declared by the Governor in Council to be a band for the purposes of this Act;

(b) "child" includes a legally adopted Indian child:

(c) "council of the band" means

(i) in the case of a band to which section seventy-three applies, the council established pursuant to that section,

(ii) in the case of a band to which section seventy-three does not apply, the council chosen according to the custom of- the band, or, where there is no council, the chief of the band chosen according to the custom of the band;

(d) "Department" means the Department of Citizenship and Immigration;

(e) "elector" means a person who
(i) is registered on a Band List,
(ii) is of the full age of twenty-one years, and
(iii) is not disqualified from voting at band elections;
(f) "estate" includes real and personal property and any interest in land;
(g) "Indian" means a person who persuant to this Act is registered as an Indian or is entitled to be registered as an Indian;
(h) "Indian moneys" means all moneys collected, received or held by His Majesty for the use and benefit of Indians or bands;
(i) "intoxicant" includes alcohol, alcoholic, spirituous, vinous, fermented malt or other intoxicating liquor or combination of liquors and mixed liquor a part of which is spirituous, vinous, fermented or otherwise intoxicating and all drinks or drinkable liquids and all preparations or mixtures capable of human consumption that are intoxicating;
(j) "member of a band" means a person whose name appears on a Band List or who is entitled to have his name appear on a Band List;
(k) "mentally incompetent Indian" means an Indian who, pursuant to the laws of the province in which he resides, has been found to be mentally defective or incompetent for the purposes of any laws of that province providing for the administration of estates of mentally defective or incompetent persons;
(l) "Minister" means the Minister of Citizenship and Immigration;
(m) "registered" means registered as an Indian in the Indian Register ;
(n) "Registrar" means the officer of the Department who is in charge of the Indian Register;
(o) "reserve" means a tract of land, the legal title to which is vested in His Majesty, that has been set apart by His Majesty for the use and benefit of a band;
(p) "superintendent" includes a commissioner, regional supervisor, Indian superintendent, assistant Indian superintendent and any other person declared by the Minister to be a superintendent for the purposes of this Act, and with reference to a band or a reserve, means the superintendent for that band or reserve;
(q) "surrendered lands" means a reserve or part of a reserve or any interest therein, the legal title to which remains vested in His Majesty, that has been released or surrendered by the band for whose use and benefit it was set apart.
(2) The expression "band" with reference to a reserve or surrendered lands means the band for whose use and benefit the reserve or the surrendered lands were set apart.
(3) Unless the context otherwise requires or this Act otherwise provides
(a) a power conferred upon a band shall be deemed not to be exercised unless it is exercised pursuant to the consent of a majority of the electors of the band, and
(b) a power conferred upon the council of a band shall be deemed not to be exercised unless it is exercised pursuant to the consent of a majority of the councillors of the band present at a meeting of the council duly convened.
ADMINISTRATION.
3. (1) This Act shall be administered by the Minister of Citizenship and Immigration, who shall be

the superintendent general of Indian affairs.

(2) The Minister may authorize the Deputy Minister of Citizenship and Immigration or the chief officer in charge of the branch of the Department relating to Indian affairs to perform and exercise any of the duties, powers and functions that may be or are required to be performed or exercised by the Minister under this Act or any other Act of the Parliament of Canada relating to Indian affairs.

APPLICATION OF ACT.

4. (1) This Act does not apply to the race of aborigines commonly referred to as Eskimos.

(2) The Governor in Council may by proclamation declare that this Act or any portion thereof, except sections thirty- seven to forty-one, shall not apply to

(a) any Indians or any group or band of Indians, or

(b) any reserve or any surrendered lands or any part thereof, and may by proclamation revoke any such declaration.

DEFINITION AND REGISTRATION OF INDIANS.

5. An Indian Register shall be maintained in the Department, which shall consist of Band Lists and General Lists and in which shall be recorded the name of every person who is entitled to be registered as an Indian.

6. The name of every person who is a member of a band and is entitled to be registered shall be entered in the Band List for that band, and the name of every person who is not a member of a band and is entitled to be registered shall be entered in a General List.

7. (1) The Registrar may at any time add to or delete from a Band List or a General List the name of any person who, in accordance with the provisions of this Act, is entitled or not entitled, as the case may be, to have his name included in that List.

(2) The Indian Register shall indicate the date on which each name was added thereto or deleted therefrom.

8. Upon the coming into force of this Act, the band lists then in existence in the Department shall constitute the Indian Register, and the applicable lists shall be posted in a conspicuous place in the superintendent's office that serves the band or persons to whom the list relates and in all other places where band notices are ordinarily displayed.

9. (1) Within six months after a list has been posted in accordance with section eight or within three months after the name of a person has been added to or deleted from a Band List or a General List pursuant to section seven

(a) in the case of a Band List, the council of the band, any ten electors of the band, or any three electors if there are less than ten electors in the band,

(b) in the case of a posted portion of a General List, any adult person whose name appears on that posted portion, and

(c) the person whose name was included in or omitted from the list referred to in section eight, or whose name was added to or deleted from a Band List or a General List, may, by notice in writing to the Registrar, containing a brief statement of the grounds therefor, protest the inclusion, omission, addition, or deletion, as the case may be, of the name of that person.

(2) Where a protest is made to the Registrar under this section he shall cause an investigation to be made into the matter and shall render a decision, and subject to a reference under subsection three,

the decision of the Registrar is final and conclusive.

(3) Within three months from the date of a decision of the Registrar under this section

(a) the council of the band affected by the Registrar's decision, or

(b) the person by or in respect of whom the protest was made,

may, by notice in writing, request the Registrar to refer the decision to a judge for review, and thereupon the Registrar shall refer the decision, together with all material considered by the Registrar in making his decision, to the judge of the county or district court of the county or district in which the band is situated or in which the person in respect of whom the protest was made resides, or such other county or district as the Minister may designate, or in the Province of Quebec, to the judge of the Superior Court for the district in which the band is situated or in which the person in respect of whom the protest was made resides, or such other district as the Minister may designate.

(4) The judge of the country, district or Superior Court, as the case may be, shall inquire into the correctness of the Registrar's decision, and for such purposes may exercise all the powers of a commissioner under Part I of the Inquiries Act; the judge shall decide whether the person in respect of whom the protest was made is, in accordance with the provisions of this Act, entitled or not entitled, as the case may be, to have his name included in the Indian Register, and the decision of the judge is final and conclusive.

10. Where the name of a male person is included in, omitted from, added to or deleted from a Band List or a General List, the names of his wife and his minor children shall also be included, omitted, added or deleted, as the case may be.

11. Subject to section twelve, a person is entitled to be registered if that person

(a) on the twenty-sixth day of May, eighteen hundred and seventy-four, was, for the purposes of An Act providing fur the organization of the Department of the Secretary of State of Canada, and for the management of Indian and Ordnance Lands, chapter forty-two of the statutes of 1868, as amended by section six of chapter six of the statutes of 1869, and section eight of chapter twenty-one of the statutes of 1874, considered to be entitled to hold, use or enjoy the lands and other immovable property belonging to or appropriated to the use of the various tribes, bands or bodies of Indians in Canada,

(b) is a member of a band

(i) for whose use and benefit, in common, lands have been set apart or since the twenty-sixth day of May, eighteen hundred and seventy-four have been agreed by treaty to be set apart, or

(ii) that has been declared by the Governor in Council to be a band for the purposes of this Act,

(c) is a male person who is a direct descendant in the male line of a male person described in paragraph (a) or (b),

(d) is the legitimate child of

(i) a male person described in paragraph (a) or (b), or

(ii) a person described in paragraph (c),

(e) is the illegitimate child of a female person described in paragraph (a), (b) or (d), unless the Registrar is satisfied that the father of the child was not an Indian and the Registrar has declared that the child is not entitled to be registered, or

(j) is the wife or widow of a person who is entitled to be registered by virtue of paragraph (a), (b), (c), (d) or (e).

12. (1) The following persons are not entitled to be registered, namely,

(a) a person who

(i) has received or has been allotted half-breed lands or money scrip,

(ii) is a descendant of a person described in sub-paragraph (i),

(iii) is enfranchised, or

(iv) is a person born of a marriage entered into after the coming into force of this Act and has attained the age of twenty-one years, whose mother and whose father's mother are not persons described in paragraph (a), (b), (d), or entitled to be registered by virtue of paragraph (e) of section eleven, unless, being a woman, that person is the wife or widow of a person described in section eleven, and

(b) a woman who is married to a person who is not an Indian.

(2) The Minister may issue to any Indian to whom this Act ceases to apply, a certificate to that effect.

13. (1) Subject to the approval of the Minister, a person whose name appears on a General List may be admitted into membership of a band with the consent of the band or the council of the band.

(2) Subject to the approval of the Minister, a member of a band may be admitted into membership of another band with the consent of the latter band or the council of that band.

14. A woman who is a member of a band ceases to be a member of that band if she marries a person who is not a member of that band, but if she marries a member of another band, she thereupon becomes a member of the band of which her husband is a member.

15. (1) Subject to subsection two, an Indian who becomes enfranchised or who otherwise ceases to be a member of a band is entitled to receive from His Majesty

(a) one per capita share of the capital and revenue moneys held by His Majesty on behalf of the band, and

(b) an amount equal to the amount that in the opinion of the Minister he would have received during the next succeeding twenty years under any treaty then in existence between the band and His Majesty if he had continued to be a member of the band.

(2) A person is not entitled to receive any amount under subsection one

(a) if his name was removed from the Indian register pursuant to a protest made under section nine, or

(b) if he is not entitled to be a member of a band by reason of the application of paragraph (e) of section eleven or subparagraph (iv) of paragraph (a) of section twelve.

(3) Where by virtue of this section moneys are payable to a person who is under the age of twenty-one, the Minister may

(a) pay the money's to the parent, guardian or other person having the custody of that person, or

(b) cause payment of the moneys to be withheld until that person reaches the age of twenty-one.

(4) Where the name of a person is removed from the Indian Register and he is not entitled to any payment under t subsection one, the Minister shall, if he considers it equitable to do so, authorize payment, out of moneys appropriated by Parliament, of such compensation as the Minister may determine for any permanent improvements made by that person on lands in a reserve.

16. (1) Section fifteen does not apply to a person who ceases to be a member of one band by reason of his becoming a member of another band, but, subject to subsection three, there shall be transferred to the credit of the latter band the amount to which that person would, but for this section, have been entitled under section fifteen.

(2) A person who ceases to be a member of one band by reason of his becoming a member of another band is not entitled to any interest in the lands or moneys held by His Majesty on behalf of the former band, but he is entitled to the same interest in common in lands and moneys held by His Majesty' on behalf of the latter band as other members of that band.

(3) Where a woman who is a member of one band becomes a member of another band by reason of marriage, and the per capita share of the capital and revenue moneys held by His Majesty on behalf of the first-mentioned band is greater than the per capita share of such moneys so held for the second-mentioned band, there shall be transferred to the credit of the second-mentioned band an amount equal to the per capita share held for that band, and the remainder of the money to which the woman would, but for this section, have been entitled under section fifteen shall be paid to her in such manner and at such times as the Minister may determine.

17. (1) The Minister may, whenever he considers it desirable,

(a) constitute new bands and establish Band Lists with respect thereto from existing Band Lists or General Lists, or both, and

(b) amalgamate bands that, by a vote of a majority of their electors, request to be amalgamated.

(2) Where pursuant to subsection one a new band has been established from an existing band or any part thereof, such portion of the reserve lands and funds of the existing band as the Governor in Council determines shall be held for the use and benefit of the new band.

RESERVES

18. (1) Subject to the provisions of this Act, reserves shall be held by His Majesty for the use and benefit of the respective bands for which they were set apart; and subject to this Act and to the terms of any treaty or surrender, the Governor in Council may determine whether any purpose for which lands in a reserve are used or are to be used is for the use and benefit of the band.

(2) The Governor in Council may authorize the use of lands in a reserve for the purpose of Indian schools, the administration of Indian affairs, Indian health projects or for any other purpose for the general welfare of the band, and may take any lands in a reserve required for such purposes, but where an individual Indian, immediately prior to such taking, was entitled to the possession of such lands, compensation for such use shall be paid to the Indian, in such amount as may be agreed between the Indian and the Minister, or, failing agreement, as may be determined in such manner as the Minister may direct.

19. The Minister may

(a) authorize surveys of reserves and the preparation of plans and reports with respect thereto,

(b) divide the whole or any portion of a reserve into lots or other subdivisions, and

(c) determine the location and direct the construction of roads in a reserve.

POSSESSION OF LANDS IN RESERVES.

20. (1) No Indian is lawfully in possession of land in a reserve unless, with the approval of the Minister, possession of the land has been allotted to him by the council of the band.

(2) The Minister may issue to an Indian who is lawfully in possession of land in a reserve a certificate, to be called a Certificate of Possession, as evidence of his right to possession of the land described therein.

(3) For the purposes of this Act, any person who, at the commencement of this Act, holds a valid and subsisting location ticket issued under The Indian Act, 1880, or any statute relating to the same subject matter, shall be deemed to be lawfully in possession of the land to which the location ticket relates and to hold a Certificate of Possession with respect thereto.

(4) Where possession of land in a reserve has been allotted to an Indian by the council of the band, the Minister may, in his discretion, withhold his approval and may authorize the Indian to occupy the land temporarily and may prescribe the conditions as to use and settlement that are to be fulfilled by the Indian before the Minister approves of the allotment.

(5) Where the Minister withholds approval pursuant to subsection four, he shall issue a Certificate of Occupation to the Indian, and the Certificate entitles the Indian, or those claiming possession by devise or descent, to occupy the land in respect of which it is issued for a period of two years from the date thereof.

(6) The Minister may extend the term of a Certificate of Occupation for a further period not exceeding two years, and may, at the expiration of any period during which a Certificate of Occupation is in force

(a) approve the allotment by the council of the band and issue a Certificate of Possession if in his opinion the conditions as to use and settlement have been fulfilled, or

(b) refuse approval of the allotment by the council of the band and declare the land in respect of which the Certificate of Occupation was issued to be available for re-allotment by the council of the band.

21. There shall be kept in the Department a register, to be known as the Reserve Land Register, in which shall be entered particulars relating to Certificates of Possession and Certificates of Occupation and other transactions respecting lands in a reserve.

22. Where an Indian who is in possession of lands at the time they are included in a reserve made permanent improvements thereon before that time, he shall be deemed to be in lawful possession of such lands at the time they are so included.

23. An Indian who is lawfully removed from lands in a reserve upon which he has made permanent improvements may, if the Minister so directs, be paid compensation in respect thereof in an amount to be determined by the Minister, either from the person who goes into possession or from the funds of the band, at the discretion of the Minister.

24. An Indian who is lawfully in possession of lands in a reserve may transfer to the band or to another member of the band the right to possession of the land, but no transfer or agreement for the transfer of the right to possession of lands in a reserve is effective until it is approved by the Minister.

25. (1) An Indian who ceases to be entitled to reside on a reserve may, within six months or such further period as the Minister may direct, transfer to the band or another member of the band the right to possession of any lands in tire reserve of which he was lawfully in possession.

(2) Where an Indian does not dispose of his right of possession in accordance with subsection one,

the right to possession of the land reverts to the band, subject to the payment to the Indian who was lawfully in possession of the land, from the funds of the band, of such compensation for permanent improvements as the Minister may determine.

26. Whenever a Certificate of Possession or Occupation was, in the opinion of the Minister, issued to or in the name of the wrong person, through mistake, or contains any clerical error or misnomer, or wrong description of any material fact therein, the Minister may cancel the Certificate and issue a corrected Certificate in lieu thereof.

27. The Minister may, with the consent of the holder thereof, cancel any Certificate of Possession or Occupation, and may cancel any Certificate of Possession or Occupation that in his opinion was issued through fraud or in error.

28. (1) Subject to subsection two, a deed, lease, contract, instrument, document or agreement of any kind whether written or oral, by which a band or a member of a band purports to permit a person other than a member of that band to occupy or use a reserve or to reside or otherwise exercise any rights on a reserve is void.

(2) The Minister may by permit in writing authorize any person for a period not exceeding one year to occupy or use a reserve or to reside or otherwise exercise rights on a reserve.

29. Reserve lands are not subject to seizure under legal process.

TRESPASS ON RESERVES.

30. A person who trespasses on a reserve is guilty of an offence and is liable on summary conviction to a fine not exceeding fifty dollars or to imprisonment for a term not exceeding one month or to both fine and imprisonment.

31. (1) Without prejudice to section thirty, where an Indian or a band alleges that persons other than Indians are or have been

(a) unlawfully in occupation or possession of,

(b) claiming adversely the right to occupation or possession of, or

(c) trespassing upon a reserve or part of a reserve, the Attorney General of Canada may exhibit an Information in the Exchequer Court of Canada claiming, on behalf of the Indian or the band, the relief or remedy sought.

(2) An Information exhibited under subsection one shall, for all purposes of the Exchequer Court Act, be deemed to be an action or suit by the Crown within the meaning of, paragraph (d) of section thirty of that Act.

(3) Nothing in this section shall be construed to impair, abridge or otherwise affect any right or remedy that, but for this section, would be available to His Majesty or to an Indian or a band.

SALE OR BARTER OF PRODUCE.

32. (1) A transaction of any kind whereby a band or a member thereof purports to sell, barter, exchange, give or otherwise dispose of cattle or other animals, grain or hay, whether wild or cultivated, or root crops or plants or their products from a reserve in Manitoba, Saskatchewan or Alberta, to a person other than a member of that band, is void unless the superintendent approves the transaction in writing.

(2) The Minister may at any time by order exempt a band and the members thereof or any member thereof from the operation of this section, and may revoke any such order.

33. Every person who enters into a transaction that is void under subsection one of section thirty-two is guilty of an offence.

ROADS AND BRIDGES.

31. (1) A band shall ensure that the roads, bridges, ditches and fences within the reserve occupied by that band are maintained in accordance with instructions issued from time to time by the superintendent.

(2) Where, in the opinion of the Minister, a band has not carried out the instructions of the superintendent given under subsection one, the Minister may cause the instructions to be carried out at the expense of the band or any member thereof and may recover the cost thereof from any amounts that are held by His Majesty and are payable to the band or such member.

LANDS TAKEN FOK PUBLIC PURPOSES.

35. (1) Where by an Act of the Parliament of Canada or a provincial legislature His Majesty in right of a province, a municipal or local authority or a corporation is empowered to take or to use lands or any interest therein without the consent of the owner, the power may, with the consent of the Governor in Council and subject to any terms that may be prescribed by the Governor in Council, be exercised in relation to lands in a reserve or any interest therein.

(2) Unless the Governor in Council otherwise directs, all matters relating to compulsory taking or using of lands in a reserve under subsection one shall be governed by the statute by which the powers are conferred.

(3) Whenever the Governor in Council has consented to the exercise by a province, authority or corporation of the powers' referred to in subsection one, the Governor in Council may, in lieu of the province, authority or corporation taking or using the hands without the consent of the owner, authorize a transfer or grant of such lands to the province, authority or corporation, subject to any terms that may be prescribed by the Governor in Council.

(4) Any amount that is agreed upon or awarded in respect of the compulsory taking or using of land under this section or that is paid for a transfer or grant of land pursuant to this section shall be paid to the Receiver General of Canada for the use and benefit of the band or for the use and benefit of any Indian who is entitled to compensation or payment as a result of the exercise of the powers referred to in subsection one.

SPECIAL RESERVES.

36. Where lands have been set apart for the use and benefit of a band and legal title thereto is not vested in His Majesty, this Act applies as though the lands were a reserve within the meaning of this Act.

SURRENDERS.

37. Except where this Act otherwise provides, lands in a reserve shall not be sold, alienated, leased or otherwise disposed of until they have been surrendered to His Majesty by the band for whose use and benefit in common the reserve was set apart.

38. (1) A band may surrender to His Majesty any right or interest of the band and its members in a reserve.

(2) A surrender may be absolute or qualified, conditional or unconditional.

39. (1) A surrender is void unless

(a) it is made to His Majesty,

(b) it is assented to by a majority of the electors of the band at

(i) a general meeting of the band called by the council of the band, or

(ii) a special meeting of the band called by the Minister for the purpose of considering a proposed surrender, and

(c) it is accepted by the Governor in Council.

(2) Where a majority of the electors of a band did not vote at a meeting called pursuant to subsection one of this section or pursuant to section fifty-one of the Indian Act, chapter ninety-eight of the Revised Statutes of Canada, 1927, the Minister may, if the proposed surrender was assented to by a majority of the electors who did vote, call another meeting by giving thirty days' notice thereof.

(3) Where a meeting is called pursuant to subsection two and the proposed surrender is assented to at the meeting by a majority of the members voting, the surrender shall be deemed, for the purpose of this section, to have been assented to by a majority of the electors of the band.

(4) The Minister may, at the request of the council of the band or whenever he considers it advisable, order that a vote at any meeting under this section shall be by secret ballot.

(5) Every meeting under this section shall be held in the presence of the superintendent or some other officer of the Department designated by the Minister.

40. When a proposed surrender has been assented to by the band in accordance with section thirty-nine, it shall be certified on oath by the superintendent or other officer who attended the meeting and by the chief or a member of the council of the band, and shall then be submitted to the Governor in Council for acceptance or refusal.

41. A surrender shall be deemed to confer all rights that are necessary to enable His Majesty to carry out the terms of the surrender.

DESCENT OF PROPERTY.

42. Unless otherwise provided in this Act, all jurisdiction and authority in relation to matters and causes testamentary, with respect to deceased Indians, is vested exclusively in the Minister, and shall be exercised subject to and in accordance with regulations of the Governor in Council.

43. Without restricting the generality of section forty two, the Minister may

(a) appoint executors of wills and administrators of estates of deceased Indians, remove them and appoint others in their stead,

(b) authorize executors to carry out the terms of the wills of deceased Indians,

(c) authorize administrators to administer the property of Indians who die intestate,

(d) carry out the terms of wills of deceased Indians and administer the property of Indians who die intestate, and

(e) make or give any order, direction or finding that in his opinion it is necessary or desirable to make or give with respect to any matter referred to in section forty two.

44. (i) The court that would have jurisdiction if the jurisdiction deceased were not an Indian may, with the consent of the Minister, exercise, in accordance with this Act, the jurisdiction and authority conferred in relation to matters and causes testamentary upon the Minister by this Act and any

other powers, jurisdiction and authority ordinarily vested in that court.

(2) The Minister may direct in any particular case that an application for the grant of probate of the will or letters of administration shall be made to the court that would have jurisdiction if the deceased were not an Indian, and the Minister may refer to such court any question arising out of any will or the administration of any estate.

(3) A court that is exercising any jurisdiction or authority under this section shall not without the consent in writing of the Minister enforce any order relating to real property on a reserve.

WILLS.

45. (1) Nothing in this Act shall be construed to prevent or prohibit an Indian from devising or bequeathing his property by will.

(2) The Minister may accept as a will any written instrument signed by an Indian in which he indicates his wishes or intention with respect to the disposition of his property upon his death.

(3) No will executed by an Indian shall be of any legal force or effect as a disposition of property until the Minister has approved the will or a court has granted probate thereof pursuant to this Act.

46. (1) The Minister may declare the will of an Indian to be void in whole or in part if he is satisfied that

(a) the will was executed under duress or undue influence,

(b) the testator at the time of execution of the will lacked testamentary capacity,

(c) the terms of the will would impose hardship on persons for whom the testator had a responsibility to provide,

(d) the will purports to dispose of land in a reserve in a manner contrary to the interest of the band or contrary to this Act,

(e) the terms of the will are so vague, uncertain or capricious that proper administration and equitable distribution of the estate of the deceased would be difficult or impossible to carry out in accordance with this Act, or

(f) the terms of the will are against the public interest.

(2) Where a will of an Indian is declared by the Minister or by a court to be wholly void, the person executing the will shall be deemed to have died intestate, and where the will is so declared to be void in part only, any bequest or devise affected thereby, unless a contrary intention appears in the will, shall be deemed to have lapsed.

APPEALS.

47. (1) A decision of the Minister made in the exercise of the jurisdiction or authority conferred upon him by section forty-two, forty-three or forty-six may, within two months from the date thereof, be appealed by any person affected thereby to the Exchequer Court of Canada, if the amount in controversy in the appeal exceeds five hundred dollars or if the Minister consents to an appeal.

(2) The judges of the Exchequer Court may make rules respecting the practice and procedure governing appeals under this section.

DISTRIBUTION OF PROPERTY ON INTESTACY.

48. (1) Where the net value of the estate of an intestate does not, in the opinion of the Minister, exceed in value two thousand dollars, the estate shall go to the widow,

(2) Where the net value of the estate of an intestate, in the opinion of the Minister, is two thousand dollars or more, two thousand dollars shall go to the widow, and the remainder shall go as follows, namely,

(a) if the intestate left no issue, the remainder shall go to the widow.

(b) if the intestate left one child, one-half of the remainder shall go to the widow,

(c) if the intestate left more than one child, one-third of the remainder shall go to the widow, and where a child has died leaving issue and such issue is alive at the date of the intestate's death, the widow shall take the same share of the estate as if the child had been living at that date.

(3) Notwithstanding subsections one and two,

(a) where in any particular case the Minister is satisfied that any children of the deceased will not be adequately provided for, he may direct that all or any part of the estate that would otherwise go to the widow shall go to the children, and

(b) the Minister may direct that the widow shall have the right, during her widowhood, to occupy any lands on a reserve that were occupied by her deceased husband at the time of his death.

(4) Where an intestate dies leaving issue his estate shall be distributed, subject to the rights of the widow, if any, per stirpes among such issue.

(5) Where an intestate dies leaving no widow or issue his estate shall go to his father and mother in equal shares if both are living, but if either of them is dead the estate shall go to the survivor.

(6) Where an intestate dies leaving no widow or issue or father or mother his estate shall go to his brothers and sisters in equal shares, and if any brother or sister is dead the children of the deceased brother or sister shall take the share their parent would have taken if living, but where the only persons entitled are children of deceased brothers and sisters, they shall take per capita.

(7) Where an intestate dies leaving no widow, issue, father, mother, brother or sister, and no children of any deceased brother or sister, his estate shall go to his next-of-kin.

(8) Where the estate goes to the next-of-kin it shall be distributed equally among the next-of-kin of equal degree of consanguinity to the intestate and those who legally represent them, but in no case shall representation be admitted after brothers' and sisters' children, and any interest in land in a reserve shall vest in His Majesty for the benefit of the band if the nearest of kin of the intestate is more remote than a brother or sister.

(9) For the purposes of this section, degrees of kindred shall be computed by counting upward from the intestate to the nearest common ancestor and then downward to the relative, and the kindred of the half-blood shall inherit equally with those of the whole-blood in the same degree.

(10) Descendants and relatives of the intestate begotten before his death but born thereafter shall inherit as if they had been born in the lifetime of the intestate and had survived him.

(11) All such estate as is not disposed of by will shall be distributed as if the testator had died intestate and had left no other estate.

(12) No widow is entitled to dower in the land of her deceased husband dying intestate, and no husband is entitled to an estate by curtesy in the land of his deceased wife so dying, and there is no community of real or personal property situated on a reserve.

(13) Illegitimate children and their issue shall inherit from the mother as if the children were legitimate, and shall inherit as if the children were legitimate, through the mother, if dead, any real or

personal property that she would have taken, if living, by gift, devise or descent fro many other person.

(14) Where an intestate, being an illegitimate child, dies leaving no widow or issue, his estate shall go to his mother, if living, but if the mother is dead his estate shall go to the other children of the same mother in equal shares, and where any child is dead the children of the deceased child shall take the share their parent would have taken if living; but where the only persons entitled are children of deceased children of the mother, they shall take per capita.

(15) This section applies in respect of an intestate woman as it applies in respect of an intestate male, and for the purposes of this section the word "widow" includes "widower".

(16) In this section "child" includes a legally adopted child.

49. A person who claims to be entitled to possession or occupation of lands in a reserve by devise or descent shall be deemed not to be in lawful possession or occupation of that land until the possession is approved by the Minister.

50. (1) A person who is not entitled to reside on a reserve does not by devise or descent acquire a right to possession or occupation of land in that reserve.

(2) Where a right to possession or occupation of land in a reserve passes by devise or descent to a person who is not entitled to reside on a reserve, that right shall be offered for sale by the superintendent to the highest bidder among persons who are entitled to reside on the reserve and the proceeds of the sale shall be paid to the devisee or descendant, as the case may be.

(3) Where no tender is received within six months or such further period as the Minister may direct after the date when the right to possession or occupation is offered for sale under subsection two, the right shall revert to the band free from any claim on the part of the devisee or descendant, subject to the payment, at the discretion of the Minister, to the devisee or descendant, from the funds of the band, of such compensation for permanent improvements as the Minister may determine.

(4) The purchaser of a right to possession or occupation of land under subsection two shall be deemed not to be in lawful possession or occupation of the land until the possession is approved by the Minister.

MENTALLY INCOMPETENT INDIANS.

51. (1) Subject to the section, all jurisdiction and authority in relation to the property of mentally incompetent Indians is vested exclusively in the Minister.

(2) Without restricting the generality of subsection one. the Minister may

(a) appoint persons to administer the estates of mentally incompetent Indians,

(b) order that any property of a mentally incompetent Indian shall be sold, leased, alienated, mortgaged, disposed of or otherwise dealt with for the purpose of

(i) paying his debts or engagements,

(ii) discharging encumbrances on his property,

(iii) paying debts or expenses incurred for his maintenance or otherwise for his benefit, or

(iv) paying or providing for the expenses of future maintenance, and

(c) make necessary to secure the satisfactory management of the estates of mentally incompetent Indians.

(3) The Minister may order that any property situated off a reserve and belonging to a mentally incompetent Indian shall be dealt with under the laws of the province in which the property is situated.

GUARDIANSHIP.

52. The Minister may administer or provide for the administration of any property to which infant children of Indians are entitled, and may appoint guardians for such purpose.

MANAGEMENT OP RESERVES AND SURRENDERED LANDS.

53. (1) The Minister or a person appointed by him for the purpose may manage, sell, lease or otherwise dispose of surrendered lands in accordance with this Act and the terms of the surrender.

(2) Where the original purchaser of surrendered lands is dead and the heir, assignee or devisee of the original purchaser applies for a grant of the lands, the Minister may, upon receipt of proof in such manner as he directs and requires in support of any claim for the grant and upon being satisfied that the claim has been equitably and justly established, allow the claim and authorize a grant to issue accordingly.

(3) No person who is appointed to manage, sell, lease or otherwise dispose of surrendered lands or who is an officer or servant of His Majesty employed in the Department may, except with the approval of the Governor in Council, acquire directly or indirectly any interest in surrendered lands.

54. Where surrendered lands have been agreed to be sold or otherwise disposed of and Letters Patent relating thereto have not issued, or where surrendered lands have been leased, the purchaser, lessee or other person having an interest in the surrendered lands may, with the approval of the Minister, assign his interest in the surrendered lands or a part thereof to any other person.

55. (1) There shall be kept in the Department a register, to be known as the Surrendered Lands Register, in which shall be entered particulars in connection with any lease or other disposition of surrendered lands by the Minister or any assignment thereof.

(2) A conditional assignment shall not be registered.

(3) Registration of an assignment may be refused until proof of its execution has been furnished.

(4) An assignment against an unregistered assignment or an assignment subsequently registered.

56. Where an assignment is registered there shall be endorsed on the original copy thereof a certificate of registration signed by the Minister or by an officer of the Department authorized by him to sign such certificates.

57. The Governor in Council may make regulations

(a) authorizing the Minister to grant licenses to cut timber on surrendered lands, or, with the consent of the council of the band, on reserve lands,

(b) imposing terms, conditions and restrictions with respect to the exercise of rights conferred by licenses granted under paragraph (a),

(c) providing for the disposition of surrendered mines and minerals underlying lands in a reserve,

(d) prescribing the penalty not exceeding one hundred dollars or imprisonment for a term of three months or both fine and imprisonment that may be imposed on summary conviction for violation of any regulation made under this section, and

(e) providing for the seizure and forfeiture of any timber or minerals taken in violation of any regulation made under this section.

58. (1) Where land in a reserve is uncultivated or unused or remains uncultivated or unused for a period of two years, the Minister may, with the consent of the council of the band,

(a) improve or cultivate such land and employ persons therefor, authorize and direct the expenditure of so much of the capital funds of the band as he considers necessary for such improvement or cultivation including the purchase of such stock, machinery or material or for the employment of such labour as the Minister considers necessary,

(b) where the land is in the lawful possession of any individual, grant a lease of such land for agricultural or grazing purposes or for any purpose that is for the benefit of the person in possession, and

(c) where the land is not in the lawful possession of any individual, grant for the benefit of the band a lease of such land for agricultural or grazing purposes.

(2) Out of the proceeds derived from the improvement or cultivation of lands pursuant to paragraph (b) of subsection one, a reasonable rent shall be paid to the individual in lawful possession of the lands or any part thereof, and the remainder of the proceeds shall be placed to the credit of the band, but if improvements are made on the lands occupied by an individual, the Minister may deduct the value of such improvements from the rent payable to such individual under this subsection.

(3) The Minister may lease for the benefit of any Indian at upon his application for that purpose, the land of which he is lawfully in possession without the land being surrendered.

(4) Notwithstanding anything in this Act, the Minister may, without a surrender

(a) dispose of wild grass or dead or fallen timber,

(b) with the consent of the council of the band, dispose of sand, gravel, clay and other non-metallic substances upon or under lands in a reserve, or, where such consent cannot be obtained without undue difficulty or delay, may issue temporary permits for the taking of sand, gravel, clay and other non-metallic substances upon or under lands in a reserve, renewable only with the consent of the council of the band, and the proceeds of such transactions shall be credited to band funds or shall be divided between the band and the individual Indians in lawful possession of the lands in such shares as the Minister may determine.

59. The Minister may, with the consent of the council of a band

(a) reduce or adjust the amount payable to His Majesty in respect of a sale, lease or other disposition of surrendered lands or a lease or other disposition of lands in a reserve or the rate of interest payable thereon, and

(b) reduce or adjust the amount payable to the band by an Indian in respect of a loan made to the Indian from band funds.

60. (1) The Governor in Council may at the request of a band grant to the band the right to exercise such control and management over lands in the reserve occupied by that band as the Governor in Council considers desirable.

(2) The Governor in Council may at any time withdraw from a band a right conferred upon the band under subsection one.

MANAGEMENT OF INDIAN MONEYS.

61. (1) Indian moneys shall be expended only for the benefit of the Indians or bands for whose use

and benefit in common the moneys are received or held, and subject to this Act and to the terms of any treaty or surrender, the Governor in Council may determine whether any purpose for which Indian moneys are used or are to be used is for the use and benefit of the band.

(2) Interest upon Indian moneys held in the Consolidated Revenue Fund shall be allowed at a rate to be fixed from time to time by the Governor in Council.

62. All Indian moneys derived from the sale of sur- rendered lands or the sale of capital assets of a band shall be deemed to be capital moneys of the band and all Indian moneys other than capital moneys shall be deemed to be revenue moneys of the band.

63. Notwithstanding The Consolidated Revenue and Audit Act, 1931, where moneys to which an Indian is entitled are paid to a superintendent under any lease or agreement made under this Act, the superintendent may pay the moneys to the Indian.

64. With the consent of the council of a band, the Minister may authorize and direct the expenditure of capital moneys of the band

(a) to distribute per capita to the members of the band an amount not exceeding fifty per cent of the capital moneys of the band derived from the sale of surrendered lands,

(b) to construct and maintain roads, bridges, ditches and water courses on the reserves or on surrendered lands,

(c) to construct and maintain outer boundary fences on reserves,

(d) to purchase land for use by the band as a reserve or as an addition to a reserve,

(e) to purchase for the band the interest of a member of the band in lands on a reserve,

(f) to purchase livestock and farm implements, farm equipment, or machinery for the band,

(g) to construct and maintain on or in connection with a reserve such permanent improvements or works as in the opinion of the Minister will be of permanent value to the band or will constitute a capital investment,

(h) to make to members of the band, for the purpose of promoting the welfare of the band, loans not exceeding one-half of the total value of

(i) the chattels owned by the borrower, and

(ii) the land with respect to which he holds or is eligible to receive a Certificate of Possession, and may charge interest and take security therefor.

(i) to meet expenses necessarily incidental to the management of lands on a reserve, surrendered lands and any band property, and

(j) for any other purpose that in the opinion of the Minister is for the benefit of the band.

65. The Minister may pay from capital moneys

(a) compensation to an Indian in an amount that is determined in accordance with this Act to be payable to him in respect of land compulsorily taken from him for band purposes, and

(b) expenses incurred to prevent or suppress grass or forest fires or to protect the property of Indians in cases of emergency.

66. (1) With the consent of the council of a band, the Minister may authorize and direct the expenditure of revenue moneys for any purpose that in his opinion will promote the general progress and welfare of the band or any member of the band.

(2) The Minister may make expenditures out of the revenue moneys of the band to assist sick, dis-

abled, aged or destitute Indians of the band and to provide for the burial of deceased indigent members of the band.

(3) The Governor in Council may authorize the expenditure of revenue moneys of the band for all or any of the following purposes, namely,

(a) for the destruction of noxious weeds and the prevention of the spreading or prevalence of insects, pests or diseases that may destroy or injure vegetation on Indian reserves.

(b) to prevent, mitigate and control the spread of diseases on reserves, whether or not the diseases are infectious or communicable,

(c) to provide for the inspection of premises on reserves and the destruction, alteration or renovation thereof,

(d) to prevent overcrowding of premises on reserves used as dwellings,

(e) to provide for sanitary conditions in private premises on reserves as well as in public places on reserves, and

(f) for the construction and maintenance of boundary fences.

67. (1) Where the Minister is satisfied that a male Indian

(a) has deserted his wife or family without sufficient cause,

(b) has conducted himself in such a manner as to justify the refusal of his wife or family to live with him, or

(c) has been separated by imprisonment from his wife and family, he may order that payments of any annuity or interest money to which that Indian is entitled shall be applied to the support of the wife or family or both the wife and family of that Indian.

(2) Where the Minister is satisfied that a female Indian has deserted her husband or family, he may order that payments of any annuity or interest money to which that Indian is entitled shall be applied to the support of her family.

(3) Where the Minister is satisfied that one or both of the parents of an illegitimate child is an Indian, he may stop payments out of any annuity or interest moneys to which either or both of the parents would otherwise be entitled and apply the moneys to the support of the child, but not so as to prejudice the welfare of any legitimate child of either Indian.

68. (1) The Governor in Council may by order permit a band to control, manage and expend in whole or in part its revenue moneys and may amend or revoke any such order.

(2) The Governor in Council may make regulations to give effect to subsection one and may declare therein the extent to which this Act and The Consolidated Revenue and Audit Act, 1981, shall not apply to a band to which an order made under subsection one applies.

LOANS TO INDIANS.

69. (1) The Minister of Finance may from time to time advance to the Minister out of the Consolidated Revenue Fund such sums of money as the Minister may require to enable him

(a) to make loans to bands, groups of Indians or individual Indians for the purchase of farm implements, machinery, livestock, motor vehicles, fishing equipment, seed grain, fencing materials, materials to be used in native handicrafts, any other equipment, and gasoline and other petroleum products, or for the making of repairs or the payment of wages, or

PART I

1. Paragraph (a) of subsection (1) of section 69 of The Indian Act, chapter 29 of the statutes of 1951, is repealed and the following substituted therefor:

"(a) to make loans to bands, groups of Indians or individual Indians for the purchase of farm implements, machinery, livestock, motor vehicles, fishing equipment, seed grain, fencing materials, materials to be used in native handicrafts, any other equipment, and gasoline and other petroleum products, or for the making of repairs or the payment of wages, or for the clearing and breaking of land within reserves, or"

(b) to expend or to lend money for the carrying out of co-operative projects on behalf of Indians.

(2) The Governor in Council may make regulations to give effect to subsection one.

(3) Expenditures that are made under subsection one shall be accounted for in the same manner as public moneys.

(4) The Minister shall pay to the Minister of Finance all moneys that he receives from bands, groups of Indians or individual Indians by way of repayments of loans made under subsection one.

(5) The total amount of Outstanding advances to the Minister under this section shall not at any one time exceed three hundred and fifty thousand dollars.

(6) The Minister shall within fifteen days after the termination of each fiscal year or, if Parliament is not then in session, within fifteen days after the commencement of the next ensuing session thereof, lay before Parliament a report setting out the total number and amount of loans made under subsection one during that year.

FARMS.

70. (1) The Minister may operate farms on reserves and may employ such persons as he considers necessary to instruct Indians in farming and may purchase and distribute without charge, pure seed to Indian farmers.

(2) The Minister may apply any profits that result from the operation of farms pursuant to subsection one on reserves to extend farming operations on the reserves or to make loans to Indians to enable them to engage in farming or other agricultural operations or he may apply such profits in any way that he considers to be desirable to promote the progress and development of the Indians.

TREATY MONEY.

71. Moneys that are payable to Indians or to Indian bands under a treaty between His Majesty and the band and for the payment of which the Government of Canada is responsible, may be paid out of the Consolidated Revenue Fund.

REGULATIONS.

72. (1) The Governor in Council may make regulations

(a) for the protection and preservation of fur-bearing animals, fish and other game on reserves,

(b) for the destruction of noxious weeds and the prevention of the spreading or prevalence of insects, pests or diseases that may destroy or injure vegetation on Indian reserves,

(c) for the control of the speed, operation and parking of vehicles on roads within reserves,

(d) for the taxation, control and destruction of dogs and for the protection of sheep on reserves,

(e) for the operation, supervision and control of pool rooms, dance halls and other places of amusement on reserves,

(f) to prevent, mitigate and control the spread of diseases on reserves, whether or not the diseases are infectious or communicable,

(g) to provide medical treatment and health services for Indians,

(h) to provide compulsory hospitalization and treatment for infectious diseases among Indians,

(i) to provide for the inspection of premises on reserves and the destruction, alteration or renovation thereof,

(j) to prevent overcrowding of premises on reserves used as dwellings,

(k) to provide for sanitary conditions in private premises on reserves as well as in public places on reserves, and

(l) for the construction and maintenance of boundary fences.

(2) The Governor in Council may prescribe the penalty, not exceeding a fine of one hundred dollars or imprisonment for a term not exceeding three months or both fine and imprisonment, that may be imposed on summary conviction for violation of a regulation made under subsection one.

(3) The Governor in Council may make orders and regulations to carry out the purposes and provisions of this Act.

ELECTIONS OF CHIEFS AND BAND COUNCILS.

73. (1) Whenever he deems it advisable for the good government of a band, the Governor in Council may declare by order that after a day to be named therein the council of the band, consisting of a chief and councillors, shall be selected by elections to be held in accordance with this Act.

(2) The council of a band in respect of which an order has been made under subsection one shall consist of one chief, and one councillor for every one hundred members of the band, but the number of councillors shall not be less than two nor more than twelve and no band shall have more than one chief.

(3) The Governor in Council may, for the purposes of giving effect to subsection one, make orders or regulations to provide

(a) that the chief of a band shall be elected by

(i) a majority of the votes of the electors of the band, or

(ii) a majority of the votes of the elected councillors of the band from among themselves, but the chief so elected shall remain a councillor,

(b) that the councillors of a band shall be elected by

(i) a majority of the votes of the electors of the band, or

(ii) a majority of the votes of the electors of the band in the electoral section in which the candidate resides and that he proposes to represent on the council of the band,

(c) that a reserve shall for voting purposes be divided into not more than six electoral sections containing as nearly as may be an equal number of Indians eligible to vote, and

(d) for the manner in which electoral sections established under paragraph (c) shall be distinguished or identified.

(4) Where the Minister is satisfied that a majority of the electors of a band do not desire to have the reserve divided into electoral sections and reports to the Governor in Council accordingly, the Governor in Council may order that the reserve shall for voting purposes consist of one electoral section.

74. (1) No person other than an elector who resides in a section may be nominated for the office of councillor to represent that section on the council of the band.

(2) No person may be candidate for election as chief or councillor unless his nomination is moved and seconded by persons who are themselves eligible to be nominated.

75. (1) The Governor in Council may make orders and regulations with respect to band elections and, without restricting the generality of the foregoing, may make regulations with respect to

(a) meetings to nominate candidates,

(b) the appointment and duties of electoral officers,

(c) the manner in which voting shall be carried out,

(d) election appeals, and

(e) the definition of residence for the purpose of determining the eligibility of voters.

(2) The regulations made under paragraph (c) of sub- section one shall make provision for secrecy of voting.

76. (1) A member of a band who is of the full age of twenty-one years and is ordinarily resident on the reserve is qualified to vote for a person nominated to be chief of the band, and where the reserve for voting purposes consists of one section, to vote for persons nominated as councillors.

(2) A member of a band who is of the full age of twenty- one years and is ordinarily resident in a section that has been established for voting purposes is qualified to vote for a person nominated to be councillor to represent that section.

77. (1) Subject to this section, chiefs and councillors shall hold office for two years.

(2) The office of chief or councillor becomes vacant when

(a) the person who holds that office

(i) is convicted of an indictable offence,

(ii) dies or resigns his office, or

(iii) is or becomes ineligible to hold office by virtue of this Act, or

(b) the Minister declares that in his opinion the person who holds that office

(i) is unfit to continue in office by reason of his having been convicted of an offence,

(ii) has been absent from meetings of the council for three consecutive meetings without being authorized to do so, or

(iii) was guilty, in connection with an election, of corrupt practice, accepting a bribe, dishonesty or malfeasance.

(3) The Minister may declare a person who ceases to hold office by virtue of subparagraph (iii) of paragraph (b) of subsection two to be ineligible to be a candidate for chief or councillor for a period not exceeding six years.

(4) Where the office of chief or councillor becomes vacant more than three months before the date when another election would ordinarily be held, a special election may be held in accordance with this Act to fill the vacancy.

78. The Governor in Council may set aside the election of a chief or a councillor on the report of the Minister that he is satisfied that

(a) there was corrupt practice in connection with the election,

(b) there was a violation of this Act that might have affected the result of the election, or

(c) a person nominated to be a candidate in the election was ineligible to be a candidate.

79. The Governor in Council may make regulations with respect to band meetings and council

meetings and, without restricting the generality of the foregoing, may meetings. make regulations with respect to

(a) presiding officers at such meetings,

(b) notice of such meetings,

(c) the duties of any representative of the Minister at such meetings, and

(d) the number of persons required at the meeting to constitute a quorum.

POWERS OF THE COUNCIL.

80. The council of a band may make by-laws not inconsistent with this Act or with any regulation made by the Governor in Council or the Minister, for any or all of the following purposes, namely,

(a) to provide for the health of residents on the reserve and to prevent the spreading of contagious and infectious diseases,

(b) the regulation of traffic,

(c) the observance of law and order,

(d) the prevention of disorderly conduct and nuisances,

(e) the protection against and prevention of trespass by cattle and other domestic animals, the establishment of pounds, the appointment of pound-keepers, the regulation of their duties and the provision for fees and charges for their services,

(f) the construction and maintenance of water courses, roads, bridges, ditches, fences and other local works,

(g) the dividing the reserve or a portion thereof into zones and the prohibition of the construction or maintenance of any class of buildings or the carrying on of any class of business, trade or calling in any such zone,

(h) the regulation of the construction, repair and use of buildings, whether owned by the band or by individual members of the band,

(i) the survey and allotment of reserve lands among the members of the band and the establishment of a register of Certificates of Possession and Certificates of Occupation relating to allotments and the setting apart of reserve lands for common use, if authority therefor has been granted under section sixty,

(j) the destruction and control of noxious weeds,

(k) the regulation of beekeeping and poultry raising,

(l) the construction and regulation of the use of public wells, cisterns, reservoirs and other water supplies,

(m) the control and prohibition of public games, sports, races, athletic contests and other amusements,

(n) the regulation of the conduct and activities of hawkers, peddlers or others who enter the reserve to buy, sell or otherwise deal in wares or merchandise,

(o) the preservation, protection and management of furbearing animals, fish and other game on the reserve,

(p) the removal and punishment of persons trespassing upon the reserve or frequenting the reserve for prescribed purposes,

(q) with respect to any matter arising out of or ancillary to the exercise of powers under this section, and

(r) the imposition on summary conviction of a fine not exceeding one hundred dollars or imprisonment for a term not exceeding thirty days or both fine and imprisonment for violation of a by-law made under this section.

81. (1) A copy of every by-law made under the authority of section eighty shall be forwarded by mail by the chief or a member of the council of the band to the Minister within four days after it is made.

(2) A by-law made under section eighty shall come into force forty days after a copy thereof is forwarded to the Minister pursuant to subsection one, unless it is disallowed by the Minister within that period, but the Minister may declare the by-law to be in force at any time before the expiration of that period.

82. (1) Without prejudice to the powers conferred by section eighty, where the Governor in Council declares that a band has reached an advanced stage of development, the council of the band may, subject to the approval of the Minister, make by-laws for any or all of the following purposes, namely,

(a) the raising of money by

(i) the assessment and taxation of interests in land in the reserve of persons lawfully in possession thereof, and

(ii) the licensing of businesses, callings, trades and occupations,

(b) the appropriation and expenditure of moneys of the band to defray band expenses,

(c) the appointment of officials to conduct the business of the council, prescribing their duties and providing for their remuneration out of any moneys raised pursuant to paragraph (a),

(d) the payment of remuneration, in such amount as may be approved by the Minister, to chiefs and councillors, out of any moneys raised pursuant to paragraph (a),

(e) the imposition of a penalty for non-payment of taxes imposed pursuant to this section, recoverable on summary conviction, not exceeding the amount of the tax or the amount remaining unpaid, and

(f) with respect to any matter arising out of or ancillary to the exercise of powers under this section.

(2) No expenditures shall be made out of moneys raised pursuant to paragraph (a) of subsection one except under the authority of a by-law of the council of the band.

83. Where a tax that is imposed upon an Indian by or under the authority of a by-law made under section eighty-two is not paid in accordance with the by-law, the Minister may pay the amount owing together with an amount equal to one-half of one per cent thereof out of moneys payable out of the funds of the band to the Indian.

84. The Governor in Council may revoke a declaration made under section eighty-two whereupon that section shall no longer apply to the band to which it formerly applied, but any by-law made under the authority of that section and in force at the time the declaration is revoked shall be deemed to continue in force until it is revoked by the Governor in Council.

85. A copy of a by-law made by the council of a band under this Act, if it is certified to be a true copy by the superintendent, is prima facie evidence that the by-law was duly made by the council and approved by the Minister, without proof of the signature or official character of the superintendent, and no such by-law is invalid by reason of any defect in form.

TAXATION.

86. (1) Notwithstanding any other Act of the Parliament of Canada or any Act of the legislature of a province, but subject to subsection two of this section and to section eighty-two, the following property is exempt from taxation, namely,

(a) the interest of an Indian or a band in reserve or surrendered lands, and

(b) the personal property of an Indian or band situated on a reserve,

and no Indian or band is subject to taxation in respect of the ownership, occupation, possession or use of any property mentioned in paragraph (a) or (b) or is otherwise subject to taxation in respect of any such property; and no succession duty, inheritance tax or estate duty is payable on the death of any Indian in respect of any such property or the succession thereto if the property passes to an Indian, nor shall any such property be taken into account in determining the duty payable under The Dominion Succession Duly Act on or in respect of other property passing to an Indian.

(2) Subsection one does not apply to or in respect of the personal property of an Indian who has executed a waiver. under the provisions of paragraph (f) of subsection two of section fourteen of The Dominion Elections Act, 1938.

LEGAL RIGHTS.

87. Subject to the terms of any treaty and any other Act of the Parliament of Canada, all laws of general application from time to time in force in any province are applicable to and in respect of Indians in the province, except to the extent that such laws are inconsistent with this Act or any order, rule, regulation or by-law made thereunder, and except to the extent that such laws make provision for any matter for which provision is made by or under this Act.

88. (1) Subject to this Act, the real and personal property of an Indian or a band situated on a reserve is not subject to charge, pledge, mortgage, attachment, levy,. seizure, distress or execution in favour or at the instance of any person other than an Indian.

(2) A person who sells to a band or a member of a band a chattel under an agreement whereby the right of property or right of possession thereto remains wholly or in part in the seller, may exercise his rights under the agreement not with standing that the chattel is situated on a reserve.

89. (1) For the purposes of sections eighty-six and eighty-eight, personal property that was

(a) purchased by His Majesty with Indian moneys or moneys appropriated by Parliament for the use and benefit of Indians or bands, or

(b) given to Indians or to a band under a treaty or agreement between a band and His Majesty, shall be deemed always to be situated on a reserve.

(2) Every transaction purporting to pass title to any property that is by this section deemed to be situated on a reserve, or any interest in such property, is void unless the transaction is entered into with the consent of the Minister or is entered into between members of a band or between the band and a member thereof.

(3) Every person who enters into any transaction that is void by virtue of subsection two is guilty of an offence, and every person who, without the written consent of the Minister, destroys personal property that is by this section deemed to be situated on a reserve, is guilty of an offence.

TRADING WITH INDIANS.

90. (1) No person may, without the written consent of the Minister, acquire title to any of the following property situated on a reserve, namely,
(a) an Indian grave house,
(b) a carved grave pole,
(c) a totem pole,
(d) a carved house post, or
(e) a rock embellished with paintings or carvings.
(2) Subsection one does not apply to chattels referred to There in that are manufactured for sale by Indians.
(3) No person shall remove, take away, mutilate, disfigure, deface or destroy any chattel referred to in subsection one without the written consent of the Minister.
(4) A person who violates this section is guilty of an offence and is liable on summary conviction to a fine not exceeding two hundred dollars or to imprisonment for a term not exceeding three months.
91. (1) No person who is
(a) an officer or employee in the Department,
(b) a missionary engaged in mission work among Indians, or
(c) a school teacher on a reserve,
shall, without a licence from the Minister or his duly authorized representative, trade for profit with an Indian or sell to him directly or indirectly goods or chattels, but no such licence shall be issued to a full-time officer or employee in the Department.
(2) The Minister or his duly authorized representative may at any time cancel a licence given under this section.
(3) A person who violates subsection one is guilty of an offence and is liable on summary conviction to a fine not exceeding five hundred dollars.
(4) Without prejudice to subsection three, an officer or employee in the Department who contravenes subsection one may be dismissed ' from office.
PENALTIES.
92. A person who, without the written permission of the Minister or his duly authorized representative,
(a) removes from a reserve
(i) minerals, stone, sand, gravel, clay or soil, or
(ii) trees, saplings, shrubs, underbrush, timber, cordwood or hay, or
(b) has in his possession anything removed from a reserve contrary to this section, is guilty of an offence and is liable on summary conviction to a fine not exceeding five hundred dollars or to imprisonment for a term not exceeding three months or to both fine and imprisonment.
93. A person who directly or indirectly by himself or by any other person on his behalf knowingly
(a) sells, barters, supplies or gives an intoxicant to
(i) any person on a reserve, or
(ii) an Indian outside a reserve,
(b) opens or keeps or causes to be opened or kept on a reserve a dwelling house, building, tent, or place in which intoxicants are sold, supplied or given to any person, or

(c) makes or manufactures intoxicants on a reserve, is guilty of an offence and is liable on summary conviction to a fine of not less than fifty dollars and not more than three hundred dollars or to imprisonment for a term of not less than one month and not more than six months, with or without hard labour, or to both fine and imprisonment.

94. An Indian who
(a) has intoxicants in his possession,
(b) is intoxicated, or
(c) makes or manufactures intoxicants
off a reserve, is guilty of an offence and is liable on summary conviction to a fine of not less than ten dollars and not more than fifty dollars or to imprisonment for a term not exceeding three months or to both fine and imprisonment.

95. (1) No offence is committed against subparagraph (ii) of paragraph (a) of section ninety-three or paragraph (a) of section ninety-four if intoxicants are sold to an Indian for consumption in a public place in accordance with a law of the province where the sale takes place authorizing the sale of intoxicants to a person for consumption in a public place.

(2) This section shall not come into force in any province until a proclamation bringing it into force in the province is issued by the Governor in Council at the request of the Lieutenant-Governor in Council of the province.

96. A person who is found
(a) with intoxicants in his possession, or
(b) intoxicated
on a reserve, ,is guilty of an offence and is liable on summary conviction to a fine of not less than ten dollars and not more than fifty dollars or to imprisonment for a term not exceeding three months or to both fine and imprisonment.

97. The provisions of this Act relating to intoxicants do not apply where the intoxicant is used or is intended to be used in cases of sickness or accident.

98. In any prosecution under this Act the burden of proof that an intoxicant was used or was intended to be used in a case of sickness or accident is upon the accused.

99. In every prosecution under this Act a certificate of analysis furnished by an analyst employed by the Government of Canada or by a province shall be accepted as prima facie evidence of the facts stated therein and of the authority of the person giving or issuing the certificate, without proof of the signature of the person appearing to have signed the certificate or his official character, and without further proof thereof.

100. Every person who is guilty of an offence against any provision of this Act or any regulation made by the Governor in Council or the Minister for which a penalty is not provided elsewhere in this Act or the regulations, is liable on summary conviction to a fine not exceeding two hundred dollars or to imprisonment for a term not exceeding three months or to both fine and imprisonment.

101. (1) Whenever a peace officer or a superintendent or a person authorized by the Minister believes on reasonable grounds that an offence against section thirty-three, eighty-nine, ninety-three, ninety-four or ninety-six has been committed, he may seize all goods and chattels by means of or in relation to which he reasonably believes the offence was committed.

2. Subsection (1) of section 101 of the said Act is repealed and the following substituted therefor:
"101. (1) Whenever a peace officer or a superintendent or a person authorized by the Minister believes on reasonable grounds that an offence against section thirty-three, eighty-nine, ninety-two, ninety-three, ninety-four or ninety-six has been committed, he may seize all goods and chattels by means of or in relation to which he reasonably believes the offence was committed, and he may enter, open and search any place or thing in or upon which he reasonably believes any such goods or chattels may be found."

(2) All goods and chattels seized pursuant to subsection Detention, one may be detained for a period of three months following the day of seizure unless during that period proceedings under this Act in respect of such offence are undertaken, in which case the goods and chattels may be further detained until such proceedings are finally concluded.

(3) Where a person is convicted of an offence against the sections mentioned in subsection one, the convicting court or judge may order that the goods and chattels by means of or in relation to which the offence was committed, in addition to any penalty imposed, are forfeited to His Majesty.

102. Every fine, penalty or forfeiture imposed under this Act belongs to His Majesty for the benefit of the band with respect to which or to one or more members of which the offence was committed or to which the offender, if an Indian, belongs, but the Governor in Council may from time to time direct that the fine, penalty or forfeiture shall be paid to a provincial, municipal or local authority that bears in whole or in part the expense of administering the law under which the fine, penalty or forfeiture is imposed, or that the fine, penalty or forfeiture shall be applied in the manner that he considers will best promote the purposes of the law under which the fine, penalty or forfeiture is imposed, or the administration of that law.

103. In any order, writ, warrant, summons or proceeding issued under this Act it shall be sufficient if the name of the person or Indian referred to therein is the name given to, or the name by which the person or Indian is known by, the person who issues the order, writ, warrant, summons or proceedings, and if no part of the name of the person is given to or known by the person issuing the order, writ, warrant, summons or proceedings, it is sufficient if the person or Indian is described in any manner by which he may be identified.

104. A police magistrate or a stipendiary magistrate shall have and may exercise, with respect to matters arising under this Act, jurisdiction over the whole county, union of counties or judicial district in which the city, town or other place for which he is appointed or in which he has jurisdiction under provincial laws is situated.

105. The Governor in Council may appoint persons to be, for the purposes of this Act, justices of the peace and those persons shall have and may exercise the powers and authority of two justices of the peace with regard to

(a) offences under this Act,

(b) offences under the Criminal Code with respect to inciting Indians on reserves to commit riotous acts, and robbing of Indian graves, and

(c) any offence against the provisions of the Criminal Code relating to cruelty to animals, common assault, breaking and entering and vagrancy, where the offence is committed by an Indian or relates to the person or property of an Indian.

106. Where, immediately prior to the coming into force of this Act, an Indian agent was ex officio a justice of the peace under the Indian Act, chapter ninety-eight of the Revised Statutes of Canada, 1927, he shall be deemed, for the purposes of this Act. to have been appointed under section one hundred and five, and he may exercise the powers and authority conferred by that section until his appointment is revoked by the Minister.

107. For the purposes of this Act or any matter relating to Indian affairs

(a) persons appointed by the Minister for the purpose,

(b) superintendents, and

(c) the Minister, Deputy Minister and the chief officer in charge of the branch of the Department relating to Indian affairs are ex officio commissioners for the taking of oaths.

108. (1) On the report of the Minister that an Indian has applied for enfranchisement and that in his opinion the Indian

(a) is of the full age of twenty-one years,

(b) is capable of assuming the duties and responsibilities of citizenship, and

(c) when enfranchised, will be capable of supporting himself and his dependants,

the Governor in Council may by order declare that the Indian and his wife and minor unmarried children are enfranchised.

(2) On the report of the Minister that an Indian woman married a person who is not an Indian, the Governor in Council may by order declare that the woman is enfranchised as of the date of her marriage.

(3) Where, in the opinion of the Minister, the wife of an Indian is living apart from her husband, the names of his wife and his minor children who are living with the wife shall not be included in an order under subsection one that enfranchises the Indian unless the wife has applied for enfranchisement, but where the Governor in Council is satisfied that such wife is no longer living apart from her husband, the Governor in Council may by order declare that the wife and the minor children are enfranchised.

(4) A person is not enfranchised unless his name appears in an order of enfranchisement made by the Governor in Council.

109. A person with respect to whom an order for enfranchisement is made under section one hundred and eight shall, from the date thereof, be deemed not to be an Indian within the meaning of this Act or any other statute or law.

110. (1) Upon the issue of an order of enfranchisement, any interest in land and improvements on an Indian reserve of which the enfranchised Indian was in lawful possession or over which he exercised rights of ownership, at the time of his enfranchisement, may be disposed of by him by gift or private sale to the band or another member of the band, but if not so disposed of within thirty days after the date of the order of enfranchisement such land and improvements shall be offered for sale by tender by the superintendent and sold to the highest bidder and the proceeds of such sale paid to him; and if no bid is received and the property remains unsold after six months from the date of such offering, the land, together with improvements, shall revert to the band free from any interest of the enfranchised person therein, subject to the payment, at the discretion of the Minister, to the

enfranchised Indian, from the funds of the band, of such compensation for permanent improvements as the Minister may determine.

(2) When an order of enfranchisement issues or has issued, the Governor in Council may, with the consent of the council of the band, by order declare that any lands within a reserve of which the enfranchised Indian had formerly been in lawful possession shall cease to be Indian reserve lands.

(3) When an order has been made under subsection two, the enfranchised Indian is entitled to occupy such lands for a period of ten years from the date of his enfranchisement, and the enfranchised Indian shall pay to the funds of the band, or there shall, out of any money payable to the enfranchised Indian under this Act, be transferred to the funds of the band, such amount per acre for the lands as the Minister considers to be the value of the common interest of the band in the lands.

(4) At the end of the ten-year period referred to in subsection three the Minister shall cause a grant of the lands to be made to the enfranchised Indian or to his legal representatives.

111. (1) Where the Minister reports that a band has applied for enfranchisement, and has submitted a plan for the disposal or division of the funds of the band and the lands in the reserve, and in his opinion the band is capable of managing its own affairs as a municipality or part of a municipality, the Governor in Council may by order approve the plan, declare that all the members of the band are enfranchised, either as of the date of the order or such later date as may be fixed in the order, and may make regulations for carrying the plan and the provisions of this section into effect.

(2) An order for enfranchisement may not be made under subsection one unless more than fifty per cent of the electors of the band signify, at a meeting of the band called for the purpose, their willingness to become enfranchised under this section, and their approval of the plan.

(3) The Governor in Council may, for the purpose of giving effect to this section, authorize the Minister to enter into an agreement with a province or a municipality, or both, upon such terms as may be agreed upon by the Minister and the province or municipality, or both.

(4) Without restricting the generality of subsection three, an agreement made thereunder may provide for financial assistance to be given to the province or the municipality or both to assist in the support of indigent, infirm or aged persons to whom the agreement applies, and such financial assistance, or any part thereof, shall, if the Minister so directs, be paid out of moneys of the band, and any such financial assistance not paid out of moneys of the band shall be paid out of moneys appropriated by Parliament.

112. (1) The Minister may appoint a committee to inquire into and report upon the desirability of enfranchising within the meaning of this Act an Indian or a band, whether or not the Indian or the band has applied for enfranchisement.

(2) A committee appointed under subsection one shall consist of

(a) a judge or retired judge of a superior, surrogate, district or county court,

(b) an officer of the Department, and

(c) a member of the band to be appointed by the council of the band, but if no appointment is made by the council of the band within thirty days after a request therefor is sent by the Minister to the band, a member of the band appointed by the Minister.

(3) Where the committee or a majority thereof reports

(a) in the case of an Indian, that in its opinion the Indian is qualified under paragraphs (a), (b) and

(c) of subsection one of section one hundred and eight to be enfranchised,
(b) in the case of a band, that in the opinion of the committee the band is capable of managing its own affairs as a municipality or part of a municipality, and the committee has submitted a plan for the disposal or division of the funds of the band and the lands in the reserve, and
(c) that it is desirable that the Indian or the band, as the case may be, should be enfranchised, the report, if approved by the Minister, shall be deemed to be an application for enfranchisement by the Indian or by the band and shall be dealt with as such in accordance with this Act, except that, in the case of a band, the provisions of subsection two of section one hundred and eleven, are not applicable.
(4) An Indian or the members of a band shall not be enfranchised under this section contrary to the terms of any treaty, agreement or undertaking between a band and His Majesty that is applicable.

SCHOOLS.

113. The Governor in Council may authorize the Minister, in accordance with this Act,
(a) to establish, operate and maintain schools for Indian children,
(b) to enter into agreements on behalf of His Majesty for the education in accordance with this Act of Indian children, with
(i) the government of a province,
(ii) the council of the Northwest Territories,
(iii) the council of the Yukon Territory,
(iv) a public or separate school board, and
(v) a religious or charitable organization.

114. The Minister may
(a) provide for and make regulations with respect to standards for buildings, equipment, teaching, education, inspection and discipline in connection with schools,
(b) provide for the transportation of children to and from school,
(c) enter into agreements with religious organizations for the support and maintenance of children who are being educated in schools operated by those organizations, and
(d) apply the whole or any part of moneys that would otherwise be payable to or on behalf of a child who is attending a residential school to the maintenance of that child at that school.

115. (1) Subject to section one hundred and sixteen, every Indian child who has attained the age of seven years shall attend school,
(2) The Minister may
(a) permit an Indian who has attained the age of six years to attend school,
(b) require an Indian who becomes sixteen years of age during the school term to continue to attend school until the end of that term, and
(c) require an Indian who becomes sixteen years of age to attend school for such further period as the Minister considers advisable, but no Indian shall be required to attend school after he becomes eighteen years of age.

116. An Indian child is not required to attend school if the child
(a) is, by reason of sickness or other unavoidable cause that is reported promptly to the principal, unable to attend school,

(b) has passed entrance examinations for high school,

(c) is, with the permission in writing of the superintendent, absent from school for a period not; exceeding six weeks in each term for the purpose of assisting in husbandry or urgent and necessary household duties,

(d) is under efficient instruction at home or elsewhere, within one year after the written approval by the Minister of such instruction, or

(e) is unable to attend school because there is insufficient accommodation in the school that the child is entitled or directed to attend.

117. Every Indian child who is required to attend school shall attend such school as the Minister may designate, but no child whose parent is a Protestant shall be assigned to a school conducted under Roman Catholic auspices and no child whose parent is a Roman Catholic shall be assigned to a school conducted under Protestant auspices, except by written direction of the parent.

118. (1) The Minister may appoint persons, to be called truant officers, to enforce the attendance of Indian children at school, and for that purpose a truant officer shall have the powers of a peace officer.

(2) Without restricting the generality of subsection one, a truant officer may

(a) enter any place where he believes, on reasonable grounds, that there are Indian children who are between the ages of seven and sixteen years of age, or who are required by the Minister to attend school,

(b) investigate any case of truancy, and

(c) serve written notice upon the parent, guardian or other person having the care or legal custody of a child to cause the child to attend school regularly thereafter.

(3) Where a notice has been served in accordance with paragraph (c) of subsection two with respect to a child who is required by this Act to attend school, and the child does not within three days after the service of notice attend school and continue to attend school regularly thereafter, the person upon whom the notice was served is guilty of an offence and is liable on summary conviction to a fine of not more than five dollars or to imprisonment for a term not exceeding ten days or to both fine and imprisonment.

(4) Where a person has been served with a notice in accordance with paragraph (c) of subsection two, it is not necessary within a period of twelve months thereafter to serve that person with any other notice in respect of further non-compliance with the provisions of this Act, and whenever such person within the period of twelve months fails to cause the child with respect to whom the notice was served or any other child of whom he has charge or control to attend school and continue in regular attendance as required by this Act, such person is guilty of an offence and liable to the penalties imposed by subsection three as if he had been served with the notice.

(5) A child who is habitually late for school shall be deemed to be absent from school.

(6) A truant officer may take into custody a child whom he believes on reasonable grounds to be absent from school contrary to this Act and may convey the child to school, using as much force as the circumstances require.

119. An Indian child who

(a) is expelled or suspended from school, or

(b) refuses or fails to attend school regularly, shall be deemed to be a juvenile delinquent within the meaning of The Juvenile Delinquents Act, 1929.

120. (1) Where the majority of the members of a band belongs to one religious denomination the school established on the reserve that has been set apart for the use and benefit of that band shall be taught by a teacher of that denomination.

(2) Where the majority of the members of a band are not members of the same religious denomination and the band by a majority vote of those electors of the band who were present at a meeting called for the purpose requests that day schools on the reserve should be taught by a teacher belonging to a particular religious denomination, the school on that reserve shall be taught by a teacher of that denomination.

121. A Protestant or Roman Catholic minority of any band may, with the approval of and under regulations to be made by the Minister, have a separate day school or day school classroom established on the reserve unless, in the opinion of the Governor in Council, the number of children of school age does not so warrant.

122. In sections one hundred and thirteen to one hundred and twenty-one

(a) "child" means an Indian who has attained the age of six years but has not attained the age of sixteen years, and a person who is required by the Minister to attend school,

(b) "school" includes a day school, technical school, high school and residential school, and

(c) "truant officer" includes

(i) a member of the Royal Canadian Mounted Police,

(ii) a special constable appointed for police duty on a reserve, and

(iii) a school teacher and a chief of the band, when authorized by the superintendent.

REPEAL.

123. (1) Section one of the Indian Act, chapter ninety-eight of the Revised Statutes of Canada, 1927, is repealed and the following substituted therefor:

"1. This Act may be cited as the Indian (Soldier Settlement) Act."

(2) Sections two to one hundred and eighty-six of the said Act are repealed.

(3) Where in sections one hundred and eighty-seven to one hundred and ninety of the said Act

(a) reference is made to the Indian Act, it shall be deemed to be a reference to this Act, and

(b) reference is made to the Superintendent General or Deputy Superintendent General of Indian Affairs, it shall be deemed to be a reference to the Minister.

PRIOR GRANTS.

Paragraph (b) of subsection (3) of section 123 is amended by substituting the Minister of Indian Affairs and Northern Development for the Minister therein mentioned.

PRIOR GRANTS

124. Where, prior to the coming into force of this Act,

(a) a reserve or portion of a reserve was released or surrendered to the Crown pursuant to Part I of the Indian Act, chapter ninety-eight of the Revised Statutes of Canada, 1927, or pursuant to the provisions of the statutes relating to the release or surrender of reserves in force at the time of the release or surrender,

(b) Letters Patent under the Great Seal of Canada were issued purporting to grant a reserve or portion of a reserve so released or surrendered, or any interest therein, to any person, and

(c) the letters Patent have not been declared void or inoperative by any Court of competent jurisdiction, the Letters Patent shall, for all purposes, be deemed to have been issued at the date thereof under the direction of the Governor in Council.

3. Section 124 of the said Act is repealed and the following substituted therefor:

"124. Where, prior to the fourth day of September, nineteen hundred and fifty-one, a reserve or portion of a reserve was released or surrendered to the Crown pursuant to Part I of the Indian Ad, chapter ninety-eight of the Revised Statutes of Canada, 1927, or pursuant to the provisions of the statutes relating to the release or surrender of reserves in force at the time of the release or surrender, and

(a) prior to that date Letters Patent under the Great Seal of Canada were issued purporting to grant a reserve or portion of a reserve so released or surrendered, or any interest therein, to any person, and the Letters Patent have not been declared void or inoperative by any Court of competent jurisdiction, or

(b) prior to that date a reserve or portion of a reserve so released or surrendered, or any interest therein, was sold or agreed to be sold by the Crown to any person, and the sale or agreement for sale has not been cancelled or by any Court of competent jurisdiction declared void or inoperative,

the Letters Patent or the sale or agreement for sale, as the case may be, shall, for all purposes, be deemed to have been issued or made at the date thereof under the direction of the Governor in Council."

COMING INTO FORCE.

125. This Act shall come into force on a day to be fixed by proclamation of the Governor in Council.

INDIAN ACT. R.S.C. 1952, c. 149.

    see also   Government Organization Act

    S.C. 1966-67, c. 25

    S.C. 1968-69, c. 28

    CHAPTER 149.

An Act respecting Indians.

SHORT TITLE.

1. This Act may be cited as the Indian Act. 1951, c. 29, Short title, s. 1.

INTERPRETATION.

2. (1) In this Act,

(a) "band" means a body of Indians

(i) for whose use and benefit in common, lands, the legal title to which is vested in Her Majesty, have been set apart before or after the coming into force of this Act,

(ii) for whose use and benefit in common, moneys are held by Her Majesty, or

(iii) declared by the Governor in Council to be a band for the purposes of this, Act;

(b) "child" includes a legally adopted Indian child;

(c) "council of the band" means "Council of

(i) in the case of a band to which section 73 applies, he council established pursuant to that section,

(ii) in the case of a band to which section 73 does not apply, the council chosen according to the custom of the band, or, where there is no council, the chief of the band chosen according to the custom of the band;

(d) "Department" means the Department of Citizenship Immigration;

(e) "elector" means a person who

(i) is registered on a Band List,

(ii) is of the full age of twenty-one years, and

(iii) is not disqualified from voting at band elections;

(f) "estate" includes real and personal property and any interest in land;

(g) "Indian" means a person who pursuant to this Act is registered as an Indian or is entitled to be registered as an Indian;

(h) "Indian moneys" means all moneys collected, received or held by Her Majesty for the use and benefit of Indians or bands;

(i) "intoxicant" includes alcohol, alcoholic, spirituous, vinous, fermented malt or other intoxicating liquor or combination of liquors and mixed liquor a part of which is spirituous, vinous, fermented or otherwise intoxicating and all drinks or drinkable liquids and all preparations or mixtures capable of human consumption that are intoxicating;

(j) "member of a band" means a person whose name appears on a Band List or who is entitled to have his name appear on a Band List;

(k) "mentally incompetent Indian" means an Indian who. pursuant to the laws of the province in which he resides, has been found to be mentally defective or incompetent for the purposes of any laws of that province providing for the administration of estates of mentally defective or incompetent persons;

(l) "Minister" means the Minister of Citizenship and Immigration;

(m) "registered" means registered as an Indian in the Indian Register:

(n) "Registrar" means the officer of the Department who is in charge of the Indian Register;

(o) "reserve" means a tract of land, the legal title to which is vested in Her Majesty, that has been set apart by Her Majesty for the use and benefit of a band;

(p) "superintendent" includes a commissioner, regional supervisor, Indian superintendent, assistant Indian superintendent and any other person declared by the Minister to be a superintendent for the purposes of this Act. and with reference to a band or a reserve, means the superintendent for that band or reserve;

(q) "surrendered lands" means a reserve or part of a reserve or any interest therein, the legal title to which remains vested in Her Majesty, that has been released or surrendered by the band for whose use and benefit it was set apart

(2) The expression "band" with reference to a reserve or surrendered lands means the band for whose use and benefit the reserve or the surrendered lands were set apart.

(3) Unless the context otherwise requires or this Act Otherwise provides

(a) a power conferred upon a band shall be deemed not council, to be exercised unless it is exercised pursuant to the consent of a majority of the electors of the band, and

(b) a power conferred upon the council of a band shall be deemed not to be exercised unless it is exercised t pursuant to the consent of a majority of the councillors of the band present at a meeting of the council duly convened. 1951, c. 29, 8. 2.

ADMINISTRATION.

3. (1) This Act shall be administered by the Minister of Citizenship and Immigration, who shall be the superintendent general of Indian affairs.

(2) The Minister may authorize the Deputy Minister of Authority Citizenship and Immigration or the chief officer in charge Minister and of the branch of the Department relating to Indian affairs to perform and exercise any of the duties, powers and functions that may be or are required to be performed or exercised by the Minister under this Act or any other Act of the Parliament of Canada relating to Indian affairs. 1951. c. 29, s. 3.

APPLICATION OF ACT.

4. (1) This Act does not apply to the race of aborigines commonly referred to as Eskimos.

1. (1) Subsection (1) of section 4 of the Indian Ad is repealed and the following substituted therefor:

"4. (1) A reference in this Act to an Indian does not Application include any person of the race of aborigines commonly referred to as Eskimos.

(2) The Governor in Council may by proclamation declare that this Act or any portion thereof, except sections 37 to 41, shall not apply to

(a) any Indians or any group or band of Indians, or

(b) any reserve or any surrendered lands or any part thereof, and may by proclamation revoke any such declaration. 1951. c. 29, 8. 4.

(2) Section 4 of the said Act is further amended by adding thereto the following subsection:

"(3) Sections 113 to 122 and, unless the Minister other wise orders, sections 42 to 52 do not apply to or in respect of any Indian who does not ordinarily reside on a reserve or on lands belonging to Her Majesty in right of Canada or a province."

DEFINITION AND REGISTRATION OF INDIANS.

5. An Indian Register shall be maintained in the Department, which shall consist of Band Lists and General Lists and in which shall be recorded the name of every person who is entitled to be registered as an Indian. 1951, c. 29. s. 5.

6. The name of every person who is a member of a band is entitled to be registered shall be entered in the Band List for that band, and the name of every person who is not a member of a band and is entitled to be registered shall be entered in a General List. 1951, c. 29, a. 6.

7. (i) The Registrar may at any time add to or delete , from a Band List or a General List the name of any person who, in accordance with the provisions of this Act, is entitled or not entitled, as the case may be, to have his name included in that List.

(2) The Indian Register shall indicate the date on which each name was added thereto or deleted therefrom. 1951,c.29,s.7

8, Upon the coming into force of this Act, the band lists then in existence in the Department shall constitute the Indian Register, and the applicable lists shall be posted in a conspicuous place in the superintendent's office that serves the band or persons to whom the list relates and in all other places where band notices are ordinarily displayed. 1951, c. 29, s. 8.

9. (1) Within six months after a list has been posted in accordance with section 8 or within three

months after the name of a person has been added to or deleted from a Band List or a General List pursuant to section 7

(a) in the case of a Band List, the council of the band, any ten electors of the band, or any three electors if there are less than ten electors in the band,

(b) in the case of a posted portion of a General List, any adult person whose name appears on that posted portion, and

(c) the person whose name was included in or omitted from the list referred to in section 8, or whose name was added to or deleted from a Band List or a General List,

may, by notice in writing to the Registrar, containing a brief statement of the grounds therefor, protest the inclusion, omission, addition, or deletion, as the case may be, of the name of that person.

2. (1) Subsection (1) of section 9 of the said Act is amended by deleting all the words after the end of paragraph

(c) thereof and substituting therefor the following: "may, by notice in writing to the Registrar, containing a brief statement of the grounds therefor, protest the inclusion, omission, addition, or deletion, as the case may be, of the name of that person, and the onus of establishing those grounds lies on the person making the protest."

(2) Where a protest is made to the Registrar under this section he shall cause an investigation to be made into the matter and shall render a decision, and subject to a reference under subsection (3), the decision of the Registrar is final and conclusive.

(3) Within three months from the date of a decision Reference of the Registrar under this section

(a) the council of the band affected by the Registrar's decision, or

(b) the person by or in respect of whom the protest was made,

may, by notice in writing, request the Registrar to refer the decision to a judge for review, and thereupon the Registrar shall refer the decision, together with all material considered by the Registrar in making his decision, to the judge of the county or district court of the county or district in which the band is situated or in which the person in respect of whom the protest was made resides, or such other county or district as the Minister may designate, or in the Province of Quebec, to the judge of the Superior Court for the district in which the band is situated or in which the person in respect of whom the protest was made resides, or such other district as the Minister may designate.

(4) The judge of the county, district or Superior Court, inquiry and as the case may be, shall inquire into the correctness of the Registrar's decision, and for such purposes may exercise all the powers of a commissioner under Part I of the Inquiries Act; the judge shall decide whether the person in respect of whom the protest was made is, in accordance with the provisions of this Act, entitled or not entitled, as the case may be, to have his name included in the Indian Register, and the decision of the judge is final and conclusive. 1951, c. 29, s. 9.

(2) Section 9 of the said Act is further amended by adding thereto the following subsections:

"(5) Not more than one reference of a Registrar's decision in respect of a protest may be made to a judge under this section.

"(6) Where a decision of the Registrar has been inferred to a judge for review under this section, the burden of establishing that the decision of the Registrar is erroneous is on the person who requested that the decision be so referred."

10. Where the name of a male person is included in, omitted from, added to or deleted from a Band List or a General List, the names of his wife and his minor children shall also be included, omitted, added or deleted, as the

11. Subject to section 12, a person is entitled to be registered if that person

(a) on the 26th day of May, 1874, was, for the purposes of An Act providing for the organization of the Department of the Secretary of State of Canada, and for the management of Indian and Ordnance Lands, chapter 42 of the statutes of 1868, as amended by section 6 of chapter 6 of the statutes of 1869. and section 8 of chapter 21 of the statutes of 1874, considered to be entitled to hold, use or enjoy the lands and other immovable property belonging to or appropriated to the use of the various tribes, bands or bodies of Indians in Canada;

(b) is a member of a band

(i) for whose use and benefit, in common, lands have been set apart or since the 26th day of May, 1874, have been agreed by treaty to be set apart, or

(ii) that has been declared by the Governor in Council to be a band for the purposes of this Act;

(c) is a male person who is a direct descendant in the male line of a male person described in paragraph (a) or (b);

(d) is the legitimate child of

(i) a male person described in paragraph (a) or (b), or

(ii) a person described in paragraph (c);

(e) is the illegitimate child of a female person described in paragraph (a), (b) or (d), unless the Registrar is satisfied that the father of the child was not an Indian and the Registrar has declared that the child is not entitled to be registered ; or

3. (1) Paragraph (e) of section 11 of the said Act is repealed and the following substituted therefor:

"(e) is the illegitimate child of a female person described in paragraph (a), (b) or (d) or

(f) is the wife or widow of a person who is entitled to be registered by virtue of paragraph (a), (b), (c), (d) or (e). 1951, c. 29, s. 11.

12 (1) The following persons are not entitled to be registered, namely,

(2) Section 12 of the said Act is amended by adding thereto, immediately after subsection (1) thereof, the following subsection :

(1a) The addition to a Band List of the name of an illegitimate child described in paragraph (e) of section 11 may be protested at any time within twelve months after the addition, and if upon the protest it is decided that the father of the child was not an Indian, the child is not entitled to be registered under paragraph (e) of section 11."

(3) This section applies only to persons born after the coming into force of this Act.

(a) a person who

(i) has received or has been allotted half-breed lands or money scrip,

(ii) is a descendant of a person described in subparagraph (i),

(iii) is enfranchised, or

(iv) is a person born of a marriage entered into after the 4th day of September, 1951, and has attained the age of twenty-one years, whose mother and whose father's mother are not persons described in paragraph (a), (b), (d), or entitled to be registered by virtue of paragraph (e) of section 11, unless, being a woman, that person is the wife or widow of a person described in section 11, and

(b) a woman who is married to a person who is not an Indian.

4. Paragraph (b) of subsection (1) of section 12 of the said Act is repealed and the following substituted therefor:

"(b) a woman who married a person who is not an Indian, unless that woman is subsequently the wife or widow of a person described in section 11."

(2) The Minister may issue to any Indian to whom this Act ceases to apply, a certificate to that effect. 1951, c. 29, s. 12.

1. Section 12 of the Indian Act is amended by adding thereto the following subsection:

"(3) Subparagraphs (i) and (ii) of paragraph (a) of subsection (1) do not apply to a person who

(a) pursuant to this Act is registered as an Indian on the day this subsection comes into force, or

(b) is a descendant of a person described in paragraph (o) of this subsection."

13. (1) Subject to the approval of the Minister, a person whose name appears on a General List may be admitted into membership of a band with the consent of general the band or the council of the band.

(2) Subject to the approval of the Minister, a member Transfer of of a band may be admitted into membership of another band with the consent of the latter band or the council of that band. 1951, c. 29, s. 13.

5. Section 13 of the said Act is repealed and the following substituted therefor:

"13. Subject to the approval of the Minister and, if the Minister so directs, to the consent of the admitting band,

(a) a person whose name appears on a General List may be admitted into membership of a band with the consent of the council of the band ; and

(b) a member of a band may be admitted into membership of another band with the consent of the council of the latter band."

14. A woman who is a member of a band ceases to be a member of that band if she marries a person who is not a member of that band, but if she marries a member of bomber, another band, she thereupon becomes a member of the band of which her husband is a member. 1951, c. 29, s. 14.

15. (1) Subject to subsection (2), an Indian who becomes enfranchised or who otherwise ceases to be a ceasing to be member of a band is entitled to receive from Her Majesty

(a) one per capita share of the capital and revenue moneys held by Her Majesty on behalf of the band, and

(b) an amount equal to the amount that in the opinion of the Minister he would have received during the next succeeding twenty years under any treaty then in existence between the band and Her Majesty if he had continued to be a member of the band.

(2) A person is not entitled to receive any amount under subsection (1) made in

(a) if his name was removed from the Indian register pursuant to a protest made under section 9, or

(b) if he is not entitled to be a member of a band by reason of the application of paragraph (e) of section 11 or subparagraph (iv) of paragraph (a) of section 12.

(3) Where by virtue of this section moneys are payable to a person who is under the age of twenty-one. the Minister may

(a) pay the moneys to the parent, guardian or other person having the custody of that person, or

6. (1) Paragraph (a) of subsection (3) of section 15 of the said Act is repealed and the following substituted therefor:

"(a) pay the moneys to the parent, guardian or other person having the custody of that person or to the public trustee, public administrator or other like official for the province in which that person resides, or"

(b) cause payment of the moneys to be withheld until that person reaches the age of twenty-one.

(4) Where the name of a person is removed Indian Register and he is not entitled to any payment under subsection (1), the Minister shall, if he considers it equitable to do so, authorize payment, out of moneys appropriated by Parliament, of such compensation as the Minister may determine for any permanent improvements made by that person on lands in a reserve. 1951, c. 29, s. 15.

(2) Section 15 of the said Act is further amended by adding thereto the following subsection:

"(5) Where, prior to the coming into force of this Act, Commutation any woman became entitled, under section 14 of the Indian Ad, chapter 98 of the Revised Statutes of Canada, 1927, or any prior provisions to the like effect, to share in the distribution of annuities, interest moneys or rents, the Minister may, in lieu thereof, pay to such woman out of the moneys of the band an amount equal to ten times the average annual amounts of such payments made to her during the ten years last preceding or, if they were paid for less than ten years, during the years they were paid."

16. (1) Section 15 does not apply to a person who ceases to be a member of one band by reason of his becoming a member of another band, but, subject to subsection

(3), there shall be transferred to the credit of the latter band the amount to which that person would, but for this section, have been entitled under section 15.

(2) A person who ceases to be a member of one band by reason of his becoming a member of another band is not entitled to any interest in the lands or moneys held by Her Majesty on behalf of the former band, but he is entitled to the same interest in common in lands and moneys held by Her Majesty on behalf of the latter band as other members of that band.

(3) Where a woman who is a member of one band becomes a member of another band by reason of marriage, and the per capita share of the capital and revenue moneys held by Her Majesty on behalf of the first-mentioned band is greater than the per capita share of such moneys so held for the second-mentioned band, there shall be transferred to the credit of the second-mentioned band an amount equal to the per capita share held for that band, and the remainder of the money to which the woman would, but for this section, have been entitled under section 15 shall be paid to her in such manner and at such times as the Minister may determine. 1951, c. 29, s. 16.

17. (1) The Minister may, whenever he considers it, desirable,

(a) constitute new bands and establish Band Lists with respect thereto from existing Band Lists or General Lists, or both, and

(b) amalgamate bands that, by a vote of a majority of their electors, request to be amalgamated.

7. (1) Subsection (1) of section 17 of the said Act is amended by striking out the word "and" at the end of paragraph (a) thereof, by inserting the word "and" at the end of paragraph (b) thereof and by adding thereto the following paragraph:

"(c) where a band has applied for enfranchisement, remove any name from the Band List and add it to the General List."

(2) Where pursuant to subsection (1) a new band has been established from an existing band or any part thereof, such portion of the reserve lands and funds of the existing band as the Governor in Council determines shall be held for the use and benefit of the new band. 1951, c. 29, s. 17.

(2) Subsection (2) of section 17 of the said Act is repealed and the following substituted therefor:

"(2) Where pursuant to subsection (1) a new band has been established from an existing band or any part thereof, such portion of the reserve lands and funds of the existing band as the Minister determines shall be held for the use and benefit of the new band.

(3) No protest may be made under section 9 in respect of the deletion from or addition to a list consequent upon the exercise by the Minister of any of his powers under subsection (1)."

RESERVES.

18. (1) Subject to the provisions of this Act, reserves shall be held by Her Majesty for the use and benefit of the respective bands for which they were set apart; and subject to this Act and to the terms of any treaty or surrender, the Governor in Council may determine whether any purpose for which lands in a reserve are used or are to be used is for the use and benefit of the band.

(2) The Governor in Council may authorize the use of Use of lands in a reserve for the purpose of Indian schools, the administration of Indian affairs, Indian health projects or for any other purpose for the general welfare of the band, and may take any lands in a reserve required for such purposes, but where an individual Indian, immediately prior to such taking, was entitled to the possession of such lands, compensation for such use shall be paid to the Indian, in such amount as may be agreed between the Indian and the Minister, or, failing agreement, as may be determined in such manner as the Minister may direct. 1951, c. 29, s. 18.

8. Subsection (2) of section 18 of the said Act is repealed and the following substituted therefor:

"(2) The Minister may authorize the use of lands in a reserve for the purpose of Indian schools, the administration of Indian affairs, Indian burial grounds, Indian health projects or, with the consent of the council of the band, for any other purpose for the general welfare of the band, and may take any lands in a reserve required for such purposes, but where an individual Indian, immediately prior to such taking, was entitled to the possession of such lands, compensation for such use shall be paid to the Indian, in such amount as may be agreed between the Indian and the Minister, or, failing agreement, as may be determined in such manner as the Minister may direct."

19. The Minister may

(a) authorize surveys of reserves and the preparation of plans and reports with respect thereto,

(b) divide the whole or any portion of a reserve into lots or other subdivisions, and

(c) determine the location and direct the construction of roads in a reserve. 1951, c. 29, s. 19.

POSSESSION OF LANDS IN RESERVES.

20. (1) No Indian is lawfully in possession of land in a reserve unless, with the approval of the Minister, possession session of the land has been allotted to him by the council of the band.

(2) The Minister may issue to an Indian who is lawfully Certificate in possession of land in a reserve a certificate, to be called a Certificate of Possession, as evidence of his right to possession of the land described therein.

(3) For the purposes of this Act, any person who, on Location the 4th day of September, 1951, held

a valid and subsisting location ticket issued under The Indian Act, 1880, or any statute relating to the same subject matter, shall be deemed to be lawfully in possession of the land to which the location ticket relates and to hold a Certificate of Possession with respect thereto.

(4) Where possession of land in a reserve has been allotted to an Indian by the council of the band, the Minister may, in his discretion, withhold his approval and may authorize the Indian to occupy the land temporarily and may prescribe the conditions as to use and settlement that are to be fulfilled by the Indian before the Minister approves of the allotment.

(5) Where the Minister withholds approval pursuant to subsection (4), he shall issue a Certificate of Occupation to the Indian, and the Certificate entitles the Indian, or those claiming possession by devise or descent, to occupy the land in respect of which it is issued for a period of two years from the date thereof.

(6) The Minister may extend the term of a Certificate of Occupation for a further period not exceeding two years, and approval may, at the expiration of any period during which a certificate of Occupation is in force

(a) approve the allotment by the council of the band and issue a Certificate of Possession if in his opinion the conditions as to use and settlement have been fulfilled, or

(b) refuse approval of the allotment by the council of the band and declare the land in respect of which the Certificate of Occupation was issued to be available for re-allotment by the council of the band. 1951, c. 29, s. 20.

21. There shall be kept in the Department a register, to be known as the Reserve Land Register, in which «hall be entered particulars relating to Certificates of Possession and Certificates of Occupation and other transactions respecting lands in a reserve. 1951, c. 29, s. 21.

22. Where an Indian who is in possession of lands at the time they are included in a reserve, made permanent improvements thereon before that time, he shall be deemed to be in lawful possession of such lands at the time they are so included. 1951, c. 29, s. 22.

23. An Indian who is lawfully removed from lands in a reserve upon which he has made permanent improvements may, if the Minister so directs, be paid compensation in respect thereof in an amount to be determined by the Minister, either from the person who goes into possession or from the funds of the band, at the discretion of the Minister. 1951, c. 29, s. 23.

24. An Indian who is lawfully in possession of lands In a reserve may transfer to the band or to another member of the band the right to possession of the land, but no transfer or agreement for the transfer of the right to possession of lands in a reserve is effective until it is approved by the Minister. 1951, c. 29, s. 24.

25. (1) An Indian who ceases to be entitled to reside on a reserve may, within six months or such further period as the Minister may direct, transfer to the band or another member of the band the right to possession of any lands in the reserve of which he was lawfully in possession.

(2) Where an Indian does not dispose of his right of possession in accordance with subsection (1), the right to possession of the land reverts to the band, subject to the payment to the Indian who was lawfully in possession of band, the land, from the funds of the band, of such compensation for permanent improvements as the Minister may determine. 1951, c. 29, s. 25.

26. Whenever a Certificate of Possession or Occupation was, in the opinion of the Minister, issued

to or in the name of the wrong person, through mistake, or contains any clerical error or misnomer, or wrong description of any material fact therein, the Minister may cancel the Certificate and issue a corrected Certificate in lieu thereof. 1951, c. 29, s. 26.

9. Sections 26 and 27 of the said Act are repealed and the c. 40, s. 9. following substituted therefor:

26. Whenever a Certificate of Possession or Occupation or a Location Ticket issued under The Indian Act, 1880, or Tickets. any statute relating to the same subject matter was, in the opinion of the Minister, issued to or in the name of the wrong person, through mistake, or contains any clerical error or misnomer, or wrong description of any material fact therein, the Minister may cancel the Certificate or Location Ticket and issue a corrected Certificate in lieu thereof.

27. The Minister may, with the consent of the holder Cancellation thereof, cancel any Certificate of Possession or Occupation, and may cancel any Certificate of Possession or Occupation that in his opinion was issued through fraud or in error. 1951, c. 29, s. 27.

27. The Minister may, with the consent of the holder thereof, cancel any Certificate of Possession or Occupation or Location Ticket referred to in section 26, and may cancel any Certificate of Possession or Occupation or Location Ticket that in his opinion was issued through fraud or in error."

28. (1) Subject to subsection (2), a deed, lease, con- Grant», etc. tract, instrument, document or agreement of any kind "android, whether written or oral, by which a band or a member of a band purports to permit a person other than a member of that band to occupy or use a reserve or to reside or otherwise exercise any rights on a reserve is void.

(2) The Minister may by permit in writing authorize any person for a period not exceeding one year to occupy or use a reserve or to reside or otherwise exercise rights on a reserve. 1951, c. 29, s. 28.

10. Subsection (2) of section 28 of the said Act is repealed and the following substituted therefor:

"(2) The Minister may by permit in writing authorize any person for a period not exceeding one year, or with the consent of the council of the band for any longer period, to occupy or use a reserve or to reside or otherwise exercise rights on a reserve."

29. Reserve lands are not subject to seizure under legal process. 1951, c. 29, s. 29.

TRESPASS ON RESERVES.

30. A person who trespasses on a reserve is guilty of an offence and is liable on summary conviction to a fine not exceeding fifty dollars or to imprisonment for a term not exceeding one month or to both fine and imprisonment. 1951, c. 29, s. 30.

31. (1) Without prejudice to section 30, where an Indian or a band alleges that persons other than Indians are or have been

(a) unlawfully in occupation or possession of,

(b) claiming adversely the right to occupation or possession of, or

(c) trespassing upon

a reserve or part of a reserve, the Attorney General of Canada may exhibit an Information in the Exchequer Court of Canada claiming, on behalf of the Indian or the band, the relief or remedy sought.

(2) An Information exhibited under subsection (1) shall, For all purposes of the Exchequer Court Act, be deemed to be an action or suit by the Crown within the meaning of paragraph (d) of section 29 of that Act.

(3) Nothing in this section shall be construed to impair, preserved abridge or otherwise affect any

right or remedy that, but for this section, would be available to Her Majesty or to an Indian or a band. 1951, c. 29, s. 31.

SALE OR BARTER OF PRODUCE.

32. (1) A transaction of any kind whereby a band or a member thereof purports to sell, barter, exchange, give or otherwise dispose of cattle or other animals, grain or hay, whether wild or cultivated, or root crops or plants or their products from a reserve in Manitoba, Saskatchewan or Alberta, to a person other than a member of that band, is void unless the superintendent approves the transaction in writing.

(2) The Minister may at any time by order exempt a band and the members thereof or any member thereof from the operation of this section, and may revoke any such order. 1951, c. 29, s. 32.

33. Every person who enters into a transaction that is void under subsection (1) of section 32 is guilty of an offence. 1951, c. 29, s. 33.

ROADS AND BRIDGES.

34. (1) A band shall ensure that the roads, bridges, ditches and fences within the reserve occupied by that band are maintained in accordance with instructions issued from time to time by the superintendent.

(2) Where, in the opinion of the Minister, a band has maintain not carried out the instructions of the superintendent , given under subsection (1), the Minister may cause the instructions to be carried out at the expense of the band or any member thereof and may recover the cost thereof from any amounts that are held by Her Majesty and are payable to the band or such member. 1951, c. 29, s. 34.

LANDS TAKEN FOR PUBLIC PURPOSES.

35. (1) Where by an Act of the Parliament of Canada or a provincial legislature Her Majesty in right of a province, a municipal or local authority or a corporation is lands with empowered to take or to use lands or any interest therein without the consent of the owner, the power may, with the consent of the Governor in Council and subject to any terms that may be prescribed by the Governor in Council, be exercised in relation to lands in a reserve or any interest therein.

(2) Unless the Governor in Council otherwise directs, all matters relating to compulsory taking or using of lands in a reserve under subsection (1) shall be governed by the statute by which the powers are conferred.

(3) Whenever the Governor in Council has consented to the exercise by a province, authority or corporation of the powers referred to in subsection (1), the Governor in Council may, in lieu of the province, authority or corporation taking or using the lands without the consent of the owner, authorize a transfer or grant of such lands to the province, authority or corporation, subject to any terms that may be prescribed by the Governor in Council.

(4) Any amount that is agreed upon or awarded in respect of the compulsory taking or using of land under this section or that is paid for a transfer or grant of land pursuant to this section shall be paid to the Receiver General of Canada for the use and benefit of the band or for the use and benefit of any Indian who is entitled to compensation or payment as a result of the exercise of the powers re-

ferred to in subsection (1). 1951, c. 29, s. 35.

SPECIAL RESERVES.

36. Where lands have been set apart for the use and benefit of a band and legal title thereto is not vested in Her Majesty, this Act applies as though the lands were a reserve within the meaning of this Act. 1951, c. 29, s. 36.

SURRENDERS.

37. Except where this Act otherwise provides, lands in No sale etc., a reserve shall not be sold, alienated, leased or otherwise disposed of until they have been surrendered to Her Majesty by the band for whose use and benefit in common the reserve was set apart. 1951, c. 29. s. 37.

38. (1) A band may surrender to Her Majesty any right Or interest of the band and its members in a reserve.

(2) A surrender may be absolute or qualified, conditional or unconditional. 1951, c. 29, s. 38.

39. (1) A surrender is void unless

(a) it is made to Her Majesty,

(b) it is assented to by a majority of the electors of the band at

(i) a general meeting of the band called by the council of the band, or

(ii) a special meeting of the band called by the Minister for the purpose of considering a proposed surrender, and

(c) it is accepted by the Governor in Council.

11. Subsections (1), (2) and (3) of section 39 of the said Act are repealed and the following substituted therefor:

"39. (1) A surrender is void unless

(a) it is made to Her Majesty,

(b) it is assented to by a majority of the electors of the band

(i) at a general meeting of the band called by the council of the band,

(ii) at a special meeting of the band called by the Minister for the purpose of considering a proposed surrender, or

(iii) by a referendum as provided in the regulations, and

(c) it is accepted by the Governor in Council.

(2) Where a majority of the electors of a band did not meeting called pursuant to subsection (1) of this section or pursuant to section 51 of the Indian Act, chapter 98 of the Revised Statutes of Canada, 1927, the Minister may, if the proposed surrender was assented to by a majority of the electors who did vote, call another meeting by giving thirty days' notice thereof.

(2) Where a majority of the electors of a band did not vote at a meeting or referendum called pursuant to subsection (1) of this section or pursuant to section 51 of the Indian Act, chapter 98 of the Revised Statutes of Canada, 1927, the Minister may, if the proposed surrender was assented to by a majority of the electors who did vote, call another meeting by giving thirty days' notice thereof or another referendum as provided in the regulations.

(3) Where a meeting is called pursuant to subsection (2) and the proposed surrender is assented to at the meeting by a majority of the members voting, the surrender shall be deemed, for the purpose of this section, to have been assented to by a majority of the electors of the band.

(3) Where a meeting is called pursuant to subsection (2) and the proposed surrender is assented to at the meeting or referendum by a majority of the electors voting, the surrender shall be deemed, for the purpose of this section, to have been assented to by a majority of the electors of the band."

(4) The Minister may, at the request of the council of the band or whenever he considers it advisable, order that a vote at any meeting under this section shall be by secret ballot.

(5) Every meeting under this section shall be held in the presence 0f the superintendent or some other officer of the Department designated by the Minister. 1951, c. 29, s. 39.

40. When a proposed surrender has been assented to by band in accordance with section 39, it shall be certified on oath by the superintendent or other officer who attended the meeting and by the chief or a member of the council of the band, and shall then be submitted to the Governor in Council for acceptance or refusal. 1951, c. 29, s. 40.

41. A surrender shall be deemed to confer all rights that are necessary to enable Her Majesty to carry out the terms of the surrender. 1951, c. 29, s. 41.

DESCENT OF PROPERTY.

42. Unless otherwise provided in this Act, all jurisdiction and authority in relation to matters and testamentary, with respect to deceased Indians, is vested exclusively in the Minister, and shall be exercised subject to and in accordance with regulations of the Governor in Council. 1951, c. 29, s. 42.

12. Section 42 of the said Act is amended by adding thereto the following subsections:

"(2) The Governor in Council may make regulations for providing that a deceased Indian who at the time of his death was in possession of land in a reserve shall, in such deemed to circumstances and for such purposes as the regulations prescribe, be deemed to have been at the time of his death possession lawfully in possession of that land.

"(3) Regulations made under this section may be made Application or applicable to estates of Indians who died before or after the coming into force of this Act."

43. Without restricting the generality of section 42, the Minister may

(a) appoint executors of wills and administrators of estates of deceased Indians, remove them and appoint others in their stead,

(b) authorize executors to carry out the terms of the wills of deceased Indians,

(c) authorize administrators to administer the property of Indians who die intestate,

(d) carry out the terms of wills of deceased Indians and administer the property of Indians who die intestate, and

(e) make or give any order, direction or finding that in his opinion it is necessary or desirable to make or give with respect to any matter referred to in section 42. 1951, c. 29, s. 43.

44. (1) The court that would have jurisdiction if the deceased were not an Indian may, with the consent of the Minister, exercise, in accordance with this Act, the jurisdiction and authority conferred in relation to matters and causes testamentary upon the Minister by this Act and any other powers, jurisdiction and authority ordinarily vested in that court.

(2) The Minister may direct in any particular case that an application for the grant of probate of the will or letters of administration shall be made to the court that would have jurisdiction if the deceased were not an Indian, and the Minister may refer to such court- any question arising out of any will or the administration of any estate.

(3) A court that is exercising any jurisdiction or authority under this section shall not without the consent in writing of the Minister enforce any order relating to real property on a reserve. 1951, c. 29, s. 44.

WILLS.

45. (1) Nothing in this Act shall be construed to prevent or prohibit an Indian from devising or bequeathing his property by will.

(2) The Minister may accept as a will any written instrument signed by an Indian in which he indicates his wishes or intention with respect to the disposition of his property upon his death.

(3) No will executed by an Indian is of any legal force or effect as a disposition of property until the Minister has approved the will or a court has granted probate thereof pursuant to this Act. 1951, c. 29, s. 45.

46. (1) The Minister may declare the will of an Indian to be void in whole or in part if he is satisfied that

(a) the will was executed under duress or undue influence,

(b) the testator at the time of execution of the will lacked testamentary capacity,

(c) the terms of the will would impose hardship on persons for whom the testator had a responsibility to provide,

(d) the will purports to dispose of land in a reserve in a manner contrary to the interest of the band or contrary to this Act,

(e) the terms of the will are so vague, uncertain or capricious that proper administration and equitable distribution of the estate of the deceased would be difficult or impossible to carry out in accordance with this Act, or

(f) the terms of the will are against the public interest.

(2) Where a will of an Indian is declared by the Minister or by a court to be wholly void, the person executing the will shall be deemed to have died intestate, and where the will is so declared to be void in part only, any bequest or devise affected thereby, unless a contrary intention appears in the will, shall be deemed to have lapsed. 1951, c. 29, s. 46.

APPEALS

47 (1) A decision of the Minister made in the exercise of the jurisdiction or authority conferred upon him by section 42, 43 or 46 may, within two months from the date thereof, be appealed by any person affected thereby to the Exchequer Court of Canada, if the amount in controversy in the appeal exceeds five hundred dollars or if the Minister consents to an appeal.

(2) The judges of the Exchequer Court may make rules respecting the practice and procedure governing appeals under this section. 1951, c. 29, s. 47.

DISTRIBUTION OF PROPERTY ON INTESTACY.

48. (1) Where the net value of the estate of an intestate does not, in the opinion of the Minister, exceed in value two thousand dollars, the estate shall go to the widow.

(2) Where the net value of the estate of an intestate, in the opinion of the Minister, is two thousand dollars or more, two thousand dollars shall go to the widow, and the remainder shall go as follows, namely,

(a) if the intestate left no issue, the remainder shall go to the widow,

(b) if the intestate left one child, one-half of the remainder shall go to the widow, and
(c) if the intestate left more than one child, one-third of the remainder shall go to the widow, and where a child has died leaving issue and such issue is alive at the date of the intestate's death, the widow shall take the same share of the estate as if the child had been living at that date.
(3) Notwithstanding subsections (1) and (2),
(a) where in any particular case the Minister is satisfied that any children of the deceased will not be adequately provided for, he may direct that all or any part of the estate that would otherwise go to the widow shall go to the children, and
(b) the Minister may direct that the widow shall have the right, during her widowhood, to occupy any lands on a reserve that were occupied by her deceased husband at the time of his death.
(4) Where an intestate dies leaving issue his estate shall be distributed, subject to the rights of the widow, if any, per stirpes among such issue.
(5) Where an intestate dies leaving no widow or issue his estate shall go to his father and mother in equal shares if both are living, but if either of them is dead the estate shall go to the survivor.
(6) Where an intestate dies leaving no widow or issue or father or mother his estate shall go to his brothers and sisters in equal shares, and if any brother or sister is dead the children of the deceased brother or sister shall take the share their parent would have taken if living, but where the only persons entitled are children of deceased brothers and sisters, they shall take per capita.
(7) Where an intestate dies leaving no widow, issue, father, mother, brother or sister, and no children of any deceased brother or sister, his estate shall go to his next of- kin.
(8) Where the estate goes to the next-of-kin it shall be distributed equally among the next-of-kin of equal degree of consanguinity to the intestate and those who legally represent them, but in no case shall representation be admitted after brothers' and sisters' children, and any interest in land in a reserve shall vest in Her Majesty for the benefit of the band if the nearest of kin of the intestate is more remote than a brother or sister.
(9) For the purposes of this section, degrees of kindred shall be computed by counting upward from the intestate to the nearest common ancestor and then downward to the relative, and the kindred of the half-blood shall inherit equally with those of the whole-blood in the same degree.
(10) Descendants and relatives of the intestate begotten before his death but born thereafter shall inherit as if they had been born in the lifetime of the intestate and had survived him.
(11) All such estate as is not disposed of by will shall be distributed as if the testator had died intestate and had left no other estate.
(12) No widow is entitled to dower in the land of her deceased husband dying intestate, and no husband is entitled to an estate by curtesy in the land of his deceased wife so dying, and there is no community of real or personal property situated on a reserve.
(14) Where an intestate, being an illegitimate child, dies leaving no widow or issue, his estate shall go to his mother, child. if living, but if the mother is dead his estate shall go to the other children of the same mother in equal shares, and where any child is dead the children of the deceased child shall take the share their parent would have taken if living; but where the only persons entitled are children of deceased children of the mother, they shall take per capita.
(15) This section applies in respect of an intestate woman as it applies in respect of an intestate male,

and for the purposes of this section the word "widow" includes "widower".

(16) In this section "child" includes a legally adopted child. 1951, c. 29, s. 48.

18. Subsection (16) of section 48 of the said Act is repealed and the following substituted therefor: "(16) In this section "child" includes a legally adopted "Child and a child adopted in accordance with Indian custom."

49. A person who claims to be entitled to possession or occupation of lands in a reserve by devise or descent shall be deemed not to be in lawful possession or occupation of that land until the possession is approved by the Minister. 1951, c. 29, s. 49.

50. (1) A person who is not entitled to reside on a reserve does not by devise or descent acquire a right to possession or occupation of land in that reserve.

(2) Where a right to possession or occupation of land in a reserve passes by devise or descent to a person who is not entitled to reside on a reserve, that right shall be offered for sale by the superintendent to the highest bidder among persons who are entitled to reside on the reserve and the proceeds of the sale shall be paid to the devisee or descendant, as the case may be.

(3) Where no tender is received within six months or such further period as the Minister may direct after the date when the right to possession or occupation is offered for sale under subsection (2), the right shall revert to the band free from any claim on the part of the devisee or descendant, subject to the payment, at the discretion of the Minister, to the devisee or descendant, from the funds of the band, of such compensation for permanent improvements as the Minister may determine.

(4) The purchaser of a right to possession or occupation of land under subsection(2) shall be deemed not to be in lawful possession or occupation of the land until the possession is approved by the Minister. 1951, c. 29, s. 50.

MENTALLY INCOMPETENT INDIANS.

51. (1) Subject to this section, all jurisdiction and authority in relation to the property of mentally incompetent Indians is vested exclusively in the Minister.

(2) Without restricting the generality of subsection (1) the Minister may

(a) appoint persons to administer the estates of mentally incompetent Indians,

(b) order that any property of a mentally incompetent Indian shall be sold, leased, alienated, mortgaged, disposed of or otherwise dealt with for the purpose of

(i) paying his debts or engagements.

(ii) discharging encumbrances on his property.

(iii) paying debts or expenses incurred for his maintenance or otherwise for his benefit, or

(iv) paying or providing for the expenses of future maintenance, and

(c) make such orders and give such directions as he considers necessary to secure the satisfactory management of the estates of mentally incompetent Indians.

(3) The Minister may order that any property situated on a reserve and belonging to a mentally incompetent Indian shall be dealt with under the laws of the province in which the property is situated. 1951, c. 29, s. 51.

GUARDIANSHIP.

52. The Minister may administer or provide for the administration of any property to which infant children of Indians are entitled, and may appoint guardians for such purpose. 1951, c. 29, s. 52.

MANAGEMENT OF RESERVES AND SURRENDERED LANDS.

53. (1) The Minister or a person appointed by him for the purpose may manage, sell, lease or otherwise dispose of surrendered lands in accordance with this Act and the terms of the surrender.

(2) Where the original purchaser of surrendered lands is dead and the heir, assignee or devisee of the original purchaser applies for a grant of the lands, the Minister may. upon receipt of proof in such manner as he directs and requires in support of any claim for the grant and upon being satisfied that the claim has been equitably and justly established, allow the claim and authorize a grant to issue accordingly.

(3) No person who is appointed to manage, sell, lease or otherwise dispose of surrendered lands or who is an officer or servant of Her Majesty employed in the Department may. except with the approval of the Governor in Council, acquire directly or indirectly any interest in surrendered lands. 1951, c. 29, s. 53.

54. Where surrendered lands have been agreed to be sold or otherwise disposed of and Letters Patent relating thereto have not issued, or where surrendered lands have been leased, the purchaser, lessee or other person having an interest in the surrendered lands may, with the approval of the Minister, assign his interest in the surrendered lands or a part thereof to any other person. 1951, c. 29, s. 54.

55. (1) There shall be kept in the Department a register, to be known as the Surrendered Lands Register, in which shall be entered particulars in connection with any lease or other disposition of surrendered lands by the Minister or any assignment thereof.

(2) A conditional assignment shall not be registered.

(3) Registration of an assignment may be refused until proof of its execution has been furnished.

(4) An assignment registered under this section is valid against an unregistered assignment or an assignment subsequently registered. 1951, c. 29, s. 55.

56. Where an assignment is registered there shall be endorsed on the original copy there of a certificate of registration signed by the Minister or by an officer of the Department authorized by him to sign such certificates. 1951, c. 29, s. 56.

57. The Governor in Council may make regulations

(a) authorizing the Minister to grant licenses to cut timber on surrendered lands, or, with the consent of the council of the band, on reserve lands,

(b) imposing terms, conditions and restrictions with respect to the exercise of rights conferred by licenses granted under paragraph (a),

(c) providing for the disposition of surrendered mines and minerals underlying lands in a reserve,

(d) prescribing the penalty not exceeding one hundred dollars or imprisonment for a term of three months or both fine and imprisonment that may be imposed on summary conviction for violation of any regulation made under this section, and

(e) providing for the seizure and forfeiture of any timber or minerals taken in violation of any regulation made under this section. 1951, c. 29, s. 57.

58. (1) Where land in a reserve is uncultivated or unused or remains uncultivated or unused for a period of two years, the Minister may, with the consent of the council of the band,

14. The portion of subsection (1) of section 58 of the said Act that precedes paragraph (a) thereof is repealed and the following substituted therefor:

"58. (1) Where land in a reserve is uncultivated or unused, the Minister may, with the consent of the council of the band,"
(a) improve or cultivate such land and employ persons therefor, authorize and direct the expenditure of so much of the capital funds of the band as he considers necessary for such improvement or cultivation including the purchase of such stock, machinery or material or for the employment of such labour as the Minister considers necessary,
(b) where the land is in the lawful possession of any individual, grant a lease of such land for agricultural or grazing purposes or for any purpose that is for the benefit of the person in possession, and
(c) where the land is not in the lawful possession of any individual, grant for the benefit of the band a lease of such land for agricultural or grazing purposes.
(2) Out of the proceeds derived from the improvement or cultivation of lands pursuant to paragraph (b) of subsection (1), a reasonable rent shall be paid to the individual in lawful possession of the lands or any part thereof, and the remainder of the proceeds shall be placed to the credit of the band, but if improvements are made on the lands occupied by an individual, the Minister may deduct the value of such improvements from the rent payable to such individual under this subsection.
(3) The Minister may lease for the benefit of any Indian upon his application for that purpose, the land of which he is lawfully in possession without the land being surrendered.
(4) Notwithstanding anything in this Act, the Minister may, without a surrender
(a) dispose of wild grass or dead or fallen timber, and
(b) with the consent of the council of the band, dispose of sand, gravel, clay and other non-metallic substances upon or under lands in a reserve, or, where such consent cannot be obtained without undue difficulty or delay, may issue temporary permits for the taking of sand, gravel, clay and other non-metallic substances upon or under lands in a reserve, renewable only with the consent of the council of the band, and the proceeds of such transactions shall be credited to band funds or shall be divided between the band and the individual Indians in lawful possession of the lands in such shares as the Minister may determine. 1951, c. 29, s. 58.
59. The Minister may, with the consent of the council of a band.
(a) reduce or adjust the amount payable to Her Majesty in respect of a sale, lease or other disposition of surrendered lands or a lease or other disposition of lands in a reserve or the rate of interest payable thereon, and
(b) reduce or adjust the amount payable to the band by an Indian in respect of a loan made to the Indian from band funds. 1951, c. 29, s. 59.
60(1) The Governor in Council may at the request of a band grant to the band the right to exercise such control and management over lands in the reserve occupied by that band as the Governor in Council considers desirable.
(2) The Governor in Council may at any time withdraw from a band a right conferred upon the band under subsection (1). 1951, c. 29, s. 60.
MANAGEMENT OF INDIAN MONEYS.
61. (1) Indian moneys shall be expended only for the benefit of the Indians or bands for whose use and benefit in common the moneys are received or held, and subject to this Act and to the terms

of any treaty or surrender, the Governor in Council may determine whether any purpose for which Indian moneys are used or are to be used is for the use and benefit of the band.

(2) Interest upon Indian moneys held in the Consolidated Revenue Fund shall be allowed at a rate to be fixed from time to time by the Governor in Council. 1951, c. 29, s. 61.

62. All Indian moneys derived from the sale of surrendered lands or the sale of capital assets of a band shall be deemed to be capital moneys of the band and all Indian moneys other than capital moneys shall be deemed to be revenue moneys of the band. 1951, c. 29, s. 62.

63. Notwithstanding the Financial Administration Act, where moneys to which an Indian is entitled are paid to a superintendent under any lease or agreement made under this Act, the superintendent may pay the moneys to the Indian. 1951, c. 29, s. 63.

64. With the consent of the council of a band, the Minister may authorize and direct the expenditure of capital moneys of the band

(a) to distribute per capita to the members of the band an amount not exceeding fifty per cent of the capital moneys of the band derived from the sale of surrendered lands,

(b) to construct and maintain roads, bridges, ditches and water courses on the reserves or on surrendered lands,

(c) to construct and maintain outer boundary fences on reserves,

(d) to purchase land for use by the band as a reserve or as an addition to a reserve,

(e) to purchase for the band the interest of a member of the band in lands on a reserve,

(f) to purchase livestock and farm implements, farm equipment, or machinery for the band,

(g) to construct and maintain on or in connection with a reserve such permanent improvements or works as in the opinion of the Minister will be of permanent value to the band or will constitute a capital investment,

(h) to make to members of the band, for the purpose of promoting the welfare of the band, loans not exceeding one-half of the total value of

(i) the chattels owned by the borrower, and

(ii) the land with respect to which he holds or is eligible to receive a Certificate of Possession, and may charge interest and take security therefor,

(i) to meet expenses necessarily incidental to the management of lands on a reserve, surrendered lands and any band property, and

(j) for any other purpose that in the opinion of the Minister is for the benefit of the band. 1951, c. 29, s. 64.

15. Section 64 of the said Act is amended by deleting the word "and" at the end of paragraph (i) thereof, by re-lettering paragraph (j) thereof as paragraph (k) and by adding thereto, immediately after paragraph (i) thereof, the following paragraph:

"(j) to construct houses for members of the band, to make loans to members of the band for building purposes with or without security and to provide for the guarantee of loans made to members of the band for building purposes, and".

65. The Minister may pay from capital moneys

(a) compensation to an Indian in an amount that is determined in accordance with this Act to be payable to him in respect of land compulsorily taken from him for band purposes, and

(b) expenses incurred to prevent or support grass or forest fires or to protect the property of Indians in cases of emergency. 1951, c. 29, s. 65.

66. (1) With the consent of the council of a band, the Minister may authorize and direct the expenditure of revenue moneys for any purpose that in his opinion will promote the general progress and welfare of the band or any member of the band.

(2) The Minister may make expenditures out of the revenue moneys of the band to assist sick, disabled, aged or destitute Indians of the band and to provide for the burial of deceased indigent members of the band.

16. (1) Subsection (2) of section 66 of the said Act is repealed and the following substituted therefor:

(2) The Minister may make expenditures out of the revenue moneys of the band to assist sick, disabled, aged or destitute Indians of the band and to provide for the burial of deceased indigent members of the band and to provide for the payment of contributions under the Unemployment Insurance Act on behalf of employed persons who are paid in respect of their employment out of moneys of the band."

(3) The Governor in Council may authorize the expenditure of revenue moneys of the band for all or any of the following purposes, namely:

(2) The portion of subsection (3) of section 66 of the said Act that precedes paragraph (a) thereof is repealed and the following substituted therefor:

(3) The Minister may authorize the expenditure of revenue moneys of the band for all or any of the following purposes namely,".

(a) for the destruction of noxious weeds and the prevention of the spreading or prevalence of insects, pests or diseases that may destroy or injure vegetation on Indian reserves;

(b) to prevent, mitigate and control the spread of diseases on reserves, whether or not the diseases are infectious or communicable;

(c) to provide for the inspection of premises on reserves and the destruction, alteration or renovation thereof;

(d) to prevent overcrowding of premises on reserves used as dwellings;

(e) to provide for sanitary conditions in private premises on reserves as well as in public places on reserves ; and

(f) for the construction and maintenance of boundary fences. 1951, c. 29, s. 66.

17. The said Act is further amended by adding thereto, immediately after section 66 thereof, the following section:

"66A. Where money is expended by Her Majesty for ' the purpose of raising or collecting Indian moneys, the Minister may authorize the recovery of the amount so expended from the moneys of the band."

67. (1) Where the Minister is satisfied that a male Indian .

(a) has deserted his wife or family without sufficient cause,

(b) has conducted himself in such a manner as to justify the refusal of his wife or family to live with him, or

(c) has been separated by imprisonment from his wife and family,

he may order that payments of any annuity or interest money to which that Indian is entitled shall be applied to the support of the wife or family or both the wife and family of that Indian.

(2) Where the Minister is satisfied that a female Indian has deserted her husband or family, he may order that payments of any annuity or interest money to which that Indian is entitled shall be applied to the support of her family.

(3) Where the Minister is satisfied that one or both of the parents of an illegitimate child is an Indian, he may stop payments out of any annuity or interest moneys to which either or both of the parents would otherwise be entitled and apply the moneys to the support of the child, but not so as to prejudice the welfare of any legitimate child of either Indian. 1951. c. 29, s. 67.

68. (1) The Governor in Council may by order permit a band to control, manage and expend in whole or in part its revenue moneys and may amend or revoke any such, order.

(2) The Governor in Council may make regulations to , give effect to subsection (1) and may declare therein the extent to which this Act and the Financial Administration Act shall not apply to a band to which an order made under subsection (1) applies. 1951. c. 29, s. 68.

LOANS TO INDIANS.

69. (1) The Minister of Finance may from time to time advance to the Minister out of the .Consolidated Revenue Fund such sums of money as the Minister may require to enable him

(a) to make loans to bands, groups of Indians or individual Indians for the purchase of farm implements, machinery, livestock, motor vehicles, fishing equipment, seed grain, fencing materials, materials to be used in native handicrafts, any other equipment, and gasoline and other petroleum products, or for the making of repairs or the payment of wages, or

4. Paragraph (a) of subsection (1) of section 69 of the Indian Act, chapter 149 of the Revised Statutes of Canada, 1952, is repealed and the following substituted therefor:

"(a) to make loans to bands, groups of Indians or individual Indians for the purchase of farm implements, machinery, livestock, motor vehicles, fishing equipment, seed grain, fencing materials, materials to be used in native handicrafts, any other equipment, and gasoline and other petroleum products, or for the making of repairs or the payment of wages, or for the clearing and breaking of land within reserves, or"

(b) to expend or to lend money for the carrying out of co-operative projects on behalf of Indians.

18. (1) Subsection (1) of section 69 of the said Act is amended by striking out the word "or" at the end of paragraph (a) thereof, by inserting the word "or" at the end of paragraph (b) thereof, and by adding thereto the following paragraph :

"(c) to provide for any other matter prescribed by the Governor in Council."

(2) The Governor in Council may make regulations to give effect to subsection (1).

(3) Expenditures that are made under subsection (1) shall be accounted for in the same manner as public moneys.

(4) The Minister shall pay to the Minister of Finance all moneys that he receives from bands, groups of Indians or individual Indians by way of repayments of loans made under subsection (1).

105. The Acts and portions of Acts set out in Schedule B are repealed or amended in the manner and to the extent indicated in that Schedule.

Subsection 69(4) is amended by substituting the Receiver General for the Minister of Finance.

(5) The total amount of outstanding advances to the Minister under this section shall not at any one time exceed three hundred and fifty thousand dollars.

(2) Subsection (5) of section 69 of the said Act is repealed and the following substituted therefor:

(5) The total amount of outstanding advances to the Minister under this section shall not at any one time exceed one million dollars."

(6) The Minister shall within fifteen days after the termination of each fiscal year or, if Parliament is not then in session, within fifteen days after the commencement of the next ensuing session, lay before Parliament a report setting out the total number and amount of loans made under subsection (1) during that year. 1951, c. 29, s. 69.

FARMS

70. (1) The Minister may operate farms on reserves and may employ such persons as he considers necessary to instruct Indians in farming and may purchase and distribute without charge, pure seed to Indian farmers.

(2) The Minister may apply any profits that result from the operation of farms pursuant to subsection (1) on reserves to extend farming operations on the reserves or to make loans to Indians to enable them to engage in farming or other agricultural operations or he may apply such profits in any way that he considers to be desirable to promote the progress and development of the Indians. 1951, c. 29, s. 70.

TREATY MONEY.

71. Moneys that are payable to Indians or to Indian bands under a treaty between Her Majesty and the band and for the payment of which the Government of Canada is responsible, may be paid out of the Consolidated Revenue Fund. 1951, c. 29, s. 71.

REGULATIONS.

72. (1) The Governor in Council may make regulations

(a) for the protection and preservation of fur-bearing animals, fish and other game on reserve,

(b) for the destruction of noxious weeds and the prevention of the spreading or prevalence of insects, pests or diseases that may destroy or injure vegetation on Indian reserves,

(c) for the control of the speed, operation and parking of vehicles on roads within reserves,

(d) for the taxation, control and destruction of dogs and for the protection of sheep on reserves,

(e) for the operation, supervision and control of pool rooms, dance halls and other places of amusement on reserves,

(f) to prevent, mitigate and control the spread of diseases on reserves, whether or not the diseases are infectious or communicable,

(g) to provide medical treatment and health services for Indians,

(h) to provide compulsory hospitalization and treatment for infectious diseases among Indians,

(i) to provide for the inspection of premises on reserves and the destruction, alteration or renovation thereof,

(j) to prevent overcrowding of premises on reserves used as dwellings,

(k) to provide for sanitary conditions in private premises on reserves as well as in public places on reserves, and

(l) for the construction and maintenance of boundary fences.

19. Subsection (1) of section 72 of the said Act is amended by striking out the word "and" at the end of paragraph (k) thereof, by adding the word "and" at the end of paragraph (l) thereof and by adding thereto the following paragraph:

"(m) for empowering and authorizing the council of a band to borrow money for band projects or housing purposes and providing for the making of loans out of moneys so borrowed to members of the band for housing purposes."

(2) The Governor in Council may prescribe the penalty, not exceeding a fine of one hundred dollars or imprisonment for a term not exceeding three months or both fine and imprisonment, that may be imposed on summary conviction for violation of a regulation made under subsection(1).

(3) The Governor in Council may make orders and regulations to carry out the purposes and provisions of this Act. 1951, c. 29, s. 72.

ELECTIONS OF CHIEFS AND BAND COUNCILS.

(73) 1 Whenever he deems it advisable for the good government of a band, the Governor in Council may declare by order that after a day to be named therein the council of the band, consisting of a chief and councillors, shall be selected by elections to be held in accordance with this Act.

20. (1) Subsections (1) and (2) of section 73 of the said Act are repealed and the following substituted therefor:

73. (1) Whenever he deems it advisable for the good government of a band, the Minister may declare by order that after a day to be named therein the council of the band, consisting of a chief and councillors, shall be selected by elections to be held in accordance with this Act.

(2) The council of a band in respect of which an order has been made under subsection (1) shall consist of one chief, and one councillor for every one hundred members of the band, but the number of councillors shall not be less than two nor more than twelve and no band shall have more than one chief.

"(2) Unless otherwise ordered by the Minister, the council of a band in respect of which an order has been made under subsection (1) shall consist of one chief, and one councillor for every one hundred members of the band, but the number of councillors shall not be less than two nor more than twelve and no band shall have more than one chief."

(3) The Governor in Council may, for the purposes of giving effect to subsection (1), make orders or regulations to provide

(a) that the chief of a band shall be elected by

(i) a majority of the votes of the electors of the band, or

(ii) a majority of the votes of the elected councillors of the band from among themselves, but the chief so elected shall remain a councillor,

(b) that the councillors of a band shall be elected by

(i) a majority of the votes of the electors of the band, or

(ii) a majority of the votes of the electors of the band in the electoral section in which the candidate resides and that he proposes to represent on the council of the band,

(c) that a reserve shall for voting purposes be divided into not more than six electoral sections containing as nearly as may be an equal number of Indians eligible to vote, and

(d) for the manner in which electoral sections established under paragraph (c) shall be distinguished or identified.

(2) Paragraphs (c) and (d) of subsection (3) of section 73 of the said Act are repealed.

(4) Where the Minister is satisfied that a majority of the electors of a band do not desire to have the reserve divided into electoral sections and reports to the Governor in Council accordingly, the Governor in Council may order that the reserve shall for voting purposes consist of one electoral section, 1951, c. 29, s. 73.

(3) Subsection (4) of section 73 and the said act is repealed and following substituted therefor:

(4) A reserve shall for voting purposes consist of one electoral section, except that where the majority of the electors of a band who were present and voted at a referendum or a special meeting held and called for the purpose in accordance with the regulations have decided that the reserve should for voting purposes be divided into electoral sections and the Minister so recommends, the Governor in Council may make orders or regulations to provide that the reserve shall for voting purposes be divided into not more than six electoral sections containing as nearly as may be an equal number of Indians eligible to vote and to provide for the manner in which electoral sections so established shall be distinguished or identified."

74. (1) No person other than an elector who resides in a section may be nominated for the office of councillor to represent that section on the council of the band.

(2) No person may be a candidate for election as chief or councillor unless his nomination is moved and seconded by persons who are themselves eligible to be nominated. 1951, c. 29, s. 74.

75. (1) The Governor in Council may make orders and regulations with respect to band elections and, without restricting the generality of the foregoing, may make regulations with respect to

(a) meetings to nominate candidates,

(b) the appointment and duties of electoral officers,

(c) the manner in which voting shall be carried out,

(d) election appeals, and

(e) the definition of residence for the purpose of determining the eligibility of voters.

(2) The regulations made under paragraph (c) of subsection (1) shall make provision for secrecy of voting 1951, c. 29, s. 75.

76. (1) A member of a band who is of the full age of twenty-one years and is ordinarily resident on the reserve is qualified to vote for a person nominated to be chief of the band, and where the reserve for voting purposes consists of one section, to vote for persons nominated as councillors.

(2) A member of a band who is of the full age of twenty-one years and is ordinarily resident in a section that has been established for voting purposes is qualified to vote for a person nominated to be councillor to represent that section. 1951, c. 29, s. 76.

77. (1) Subject to this section, chiefs and councillors hold office for two years.

(2) The office of chief or councillor becomes vacant when

(a) the person who holds that office

(i) is convicted of an indictable offence,

(ii) dies or resigns his office, or

(iii) is or becomes ineligible to hold office by virtue of this Act; or

(b) the Minister declares that in his opinion the person who holds that office

(i) is unfit to continue in office by reason of his having been convicted of an offence,
(ii) has been absent from meetings of the council for three consecutive meetings without being authorized to do so, or
(iii) was guilty, in connection with an election, of corrupt practice, accepting a bribe, dishonesty or malfeasance.
(3) The Minister may declare a person who ceases to hold office by virtue of subparagraph (iii) of paragraph (b)of subsection (2) to be ineligible to be a candidate for chief or councillor for a period not exceeding six years.
(4) Where the office of chief or councillor becomes vacant more than three months before the date when another election would ordinarily be held, a special election may be held in accordance with this Act to fill the vacancy. 1951, c. 29, s. 77.
78. The Governor in Council may set aside the election of a chief or a councillor on the report of the Minister that he is satisfied that
(a) there was corrupt practice in connection with the election,
(b) there was a violation of this Act that might have affected the result of the election, or
(c) a person nominated to be a candidate in the election was ineligible to be a candidate. 1951, c. 29, s. 78.
79. The Governor in Council may make regulations with respect to band meetings and council meetings and, without restricting the generality of the foregoing, may make regulations with respect to
(a) presiding officers at such meetings,
(b) notice of such meetings,
(c) the duties of any representative of the Minister at such meetings, and
(d) the number of persons required at the meeting to constitute a quorum. 1951, c. 29, s. 79.
POWERS OF THE COUNCIL.
80. The council of a band may make by-laws not inconsistent with this Act or with any regulation made by the Governor in Council or the Minister, for any or all of the following purposes, namely:
(a) to provide for the health of residents on the reserve and to prevent the spreading of contagious and infectious diseases;
(b) the regulation of traffic;
(c) the observance of law and order;
(d) the prevention of disorderly conduct and nuisances;
(e) the protection against and prevention of trespass by cattle and other domestic animals, the establishment of pounds, the appointment of pound-keepers, the regulation of their duties and the provision for fees and charges for their services;
(f) the construction and maintenance of water courses, roads, bridges, ditches, fences and other local works;
(g) the dividing the reserve or a portion thereof into zones and the prohibition of the construction or maintenance of any class of buildings or the carrying on of any class of business, trade or calling in any such zone ;
(h) the regulation of the construction, repair and use of buildings, whether owned by the band or

by individual members of the band;

(i) the survey and allotment of reserve lands among the members of the band and the establishment of a register of Certificates of Possession and Certificates of Occupation relating to allotments and the setting apart of reserve lands for common use. if authority therefor has been granted under section 60;

(j) the destruction and control of noxious weeds;

(k) the regulation of beekeeping and poultry raising;

(l) the construction and regulation of the use of public wells, cisterns, reservoirs and other water supplies;

(m) the control and prohibition of public games, sports, races, athletic contests and other amusements;

(n) the regulation of the conduct and activities of hawkers, peddlers or others who enter the reserve to buy, sell or otherwise deal in wares or merchandise;

(o) the preservation, protection and management of furbearing animals, fish and other game on the reserve;

(p) the removal and punishment of persons trespassing upon the reserve or frequenting the reserve for prescribed purposes;

(q) with respect to any matter arising out of or ancillary to the exercise of powers under this section; and

(r) the imposition on summary conviction of a fine not exceeding one hundred dollars or imprisonment for a term not exceeding thirty days or both fine and imprisonment for violation of a by-law made under this section. 1951, c. 29, s. 80.

81. (1) A copy of every by-law made under the authority of section 80 shall be forwarded by mail by the chief or a member of the council of the band to the Minister within four days after it is made.

(2) A by-law made under section 80 shall come into force forty days after a copy thereof is forwarded to the Minister pursuant to subsection (1), unless it is disallowed by the Minister within that period, but the Minister may declare the by-law to be in force at any time before the expiration of that period. 1951, c. 29, s. 81.

82. (1) Without prejudice to the powers conferred by section 80, where the Governor in Council declares that a band has reached an advanced stage of development, the council of the band may, subject to the approval of the Minister, make by-laws for any or all of the following purposes, namely:

(a) the raising of money by

(i) the assessment and taxation of interests in land in the reserve of persons lawfully in possession thereof, and

(ii) the licensing of businesses, callings, trades and occupations;

(b) the appropriation and expenditure of moneys of the band to defray band expenses;

(c) the appointment of officials to conduct the business of the council, prescribing their duties and providing for their remuneration out of any moneys raised pursuant to paragraph (a) ;

(d) the payment of remuneration, in such amount as may be approved by the Minister, to chiefs and councillors, out of any moneys raised pursuant to paragraph (a);

(e) the imposition of a penalty for non-payment of taxes imposed pursuant to this section, recoverable on summary conviction, not exceeding the amount of the tax or the amount remaining unpaid; and

21. Subsection (1) of section 82 of the said Act is amended by striking out the word "and" at the end of paragraph (e) thereof, by re-lettering paragraph (f) thereof as paragraph (g) and by adding thereto, immediately after paragraph (e) thereof, the following paragraph: (f) the raising of money from band members to support band projects; and".

(f) with respect to any matter arising out of or ancillary to the exercise of powers under this section.

(2) No expenditure shall be made out of moneys raised pursuant to paragraph (a) of subsection (1) except under the authority of a by-law of the council of the band 1951 c. 29, s. 82.

(83) where a tax that is imposed upon an Indian by or under the authority of a by-law, the minister may pay the amount owing together with an amount equal to one-half of one per cent thereof out of moneys payable out of the funds of the band to the Indian. 1951, c. 29, s. 83.

84. The Governor in Council may revoke a declaration made under section 82 whereupon that section shall no authority longer apply to the band to which it formerly applied, but to make any by-law made under the authority of that section and in force at the time the declaration is revoked shall be deemed to continue in force until it is revoked by the Governor in Council. 1951, c. 29, s. 84.

85. A copy of a by-law made by the council of a band under this Act, if it is certified to be a true copy by the superintendent, is prima facie evidence that the by-law was duly made by the council and approved by the Minister, without proof of the signature or official character of the superintendent, and no such by-law is invalid by reason of any defect in form. 1951, c. 29, s. 85.

TAXATION.

86. (1) Notwithstanding any other Act of the Parliament of Canada or any Act of the legislature of a province, but subject to subsection (2) and to section 82, the following property is exempt from taxation, namely,

(a) the interest of an Indian or a band in reserve or surrendered lands, and

(b) the personal property of an Indian or band situated on a reserve,

and no Indian or band is subject to taxation in respect of the ownership, occupation, possession or use of any property mentioned in paragraph (a) or (b) or is otherwise subject to taxation in respect of any such property; and no succession duty, inheritance tax or estate duty is payable on the death of any Indian in respect of any such property or the succession thereto if the property passes to an Indian, nor shall any such property be taken into account in determining the duty payable under the Dominion Succession Duty Act on or in respect of other property passing to an Indian.

(2) Subsection (1) does not apply to or in respect of the personal property of an Indian who has executed a waiver under the provisions of paragraph (e) of subsection (2) of section 14 of the Canada Elections Act. 1951, c. 29, s. 86.

1. Subsection (2) of section 86 of the Indian Act is repealed.

87. Subject to the terms of any treaty and any other Act of the Parliament of Canada, all laws of general application from time to time in force in any province are applicable to and in respect of Indians in the province, except to the extent that such laws are inconsistent with this Act or any order, rule,

regulation or by-law made thereunder, and except to the extent that such laws make provision for any matter for which provision is made by or under this Act. 1951, c. 29, s. 87.

88. (1) Subject to this Act, the real and personal property of an Indian or a band situated on a reserve is not subject to charge, pledge, mortgage, attachment, levy, seizure, distress or execution in favour or at the instance of any person other than an Indian.

(2) A person who sells to a band or a member of a band a chattel under an agreement whereby the right of property or right of possession thereto remains wholly or in part in the seller, may exercise his rights under the agreement notwithstanding that the chattel is situated on a reserve. 1951, c. 29, s. 88.

89. (1) For the purposes of section 86 and 88, personal property that was

(a) purchased by Her Majesty with Indian moneys or moneys appropriated by Parliament for the use and benefit of Indians or bands, or

(b) given to Indians or to a band under a treaty or agreement between a band and Her Majesty, shall be deemed always to be situated on a reserve.

(2) Every transaction purporting to pass title to any property that is by this section deemed to be situated on a reserve, or any interest in such property, is void unless the transaction is entered into with the consent of the Minister or is entered into between members of a band or between the band and a member thereof.

(3) Every person who enters into any transaction that is void by virtue of subsection (2) is guilty of an offence, and every person who, without the written consent of the Minister, destroys personal property that is by this section deemed to be situated on a reserve, is guilty of an offence. 1951, c. 29, s. 89.

TRADING WITH INDIANS.

90. (1) No person may, without the written consent of the Minister, acquire title to any of the following property situated on a reserve, namely,

(a) an Indian grave house,

(b) a carved grave pole,

(c) a totem pole,

(d) a carved house post, or

(e) a rock embellished with paintings or carvings.

(2) Subsection (1) does not apply to chattels referred to therein that are manufactured for sale by Indians.

(3) No person shall remove, take away, mutilate, dis- Removal, figure, deface or destroy any chattel referred to in subsection (1) without the written consent of the Minister.

(4) A person who violates this section is guilty of an, offence and is liable on summary conviction to a fine not exceeding two hundred dollars or to imprisonment for a term not exceeding three months. 1951, c. 29, s. 90.

91. (1) No person who is

(a) an officer or employee in the Department,

(b) a missionary engaged in mission work among Indians, or

(c) a school teacher on a reserve, shall, without a licence from the Minister or his duly authorized representative, trade for profit with an Indian or sell to him directly or indirectly goods or chattels, but no such licence shall be issued to a full-time officer or employee in the Department.

(2) The Minister or his duly authorized representative may at any time cancel a licence given under this section.

(3) A person who violates subsection (1) is guilty of an offence and is liable on summary conviction to a fine not exceeding five hundred dollars.

(4) Without prejudice to subsection (3), an officer or employee in the Department who contravenes subsection (1) may be dismissed from office. 1951, c. 29, s. 91.

PENALTIES.

92. A person who, without the written permission of the Minister or his duly authorized representative,

(a) removes

 (i) minerals, stone, sand, gravel, clay or soil, or

(ii) trees, saplings, shrubs, underbrush, timber, cordwood or hay, or

(b) has in reserve contrary to this section, Offence and is guilty of an offence and is liable on summary conviction to a fine not exceeding five hundred dollars or to imprisonment for a term not exceeding three months or to both fine and imprisonment. 1951, c. 29, s. 92.S.C. 1956,

22. Section 92 of the said Act and the heading immediately preceding that section are repealed and the following substituted therefor:

"REMOVAL OF MATERIALS FROM RESERVES.

92. A person who, without the written permission of the Minister or his duly authorized representative, from"

(a) removes or permits anyone to remove from a reserve

 (i) minerals, stone, sand, gravel, clay or soil, or

(ii) trees, saplings, shrubs, underbrush, timber, cordwood or hay, or

(b) has in his possession anything removed from a reserve contrary to this section,

is guilty of an offence and is liable on summary conviction to a fine not exceeding five hundred dollars or to imprisonment for a term not exceeding three months or to both fine and imprisonment."

93. A person who directly or indirectly by himself or any 0ther person on his behalf knowingly

(a) sells, barters, supplies or gives an intoxicant to

(i) any person on a reserve, or

(ii) an Indian outside a reserve,

(b) opens or keeps or causes to be opened or kept on a reserve a dwelling house, building, tent, or place in which intoxicants are sold, supplied or given to any person, or

(c) makes or manufactures intoxicants on a reserve,

is guilty of an offence and is liable on summary conviction to a fine of not less than fifty dollars and not more than three hundred dollars or to imprisonment for a term of not less than one month and not more than six months, with or without hard labour, or to both fine and imprisonment. 1951, c. 29, s. 93.

94. An Indian who

(a) has intoxicants m his possession,

(b) is intoxicated, or

(c) makes or manufactures intoxicants

off a reserve, is guilty of an offence and is liable on summary conviction to a fine of not less than ten dollars and not more than fifty dollars or to imprisonment for a term not exceeding three months or to both fine and imprisonment. 1951, c. 29, s. 94.

95. (1) No offence is committed against subparagraph (i) of paragraph (a) of section 93 or paragraph (a) of section 94 if intoxicants are sold to an Indian for consumption in a public place in accordance with a law of t province where the sale takes place authorizing the sale of intoxicants to a person for consumption in a public place.

(2) This section shall not come into force in any province until a proclamation bringing it into force in the province is issued by the Governor in Council at the request of the Lieutenant-Governor in Council of the province. 1951, c. 29, s. 95.

23. (1) Section 95 of the said Act is repealed and the following substituted therefor:

"95. (1) Subsection (2) or subsection (3) shall come into force, or cease to be in force, in a province or in a part thereof only if a proclamation declaring it to be in force, or to cease to be in force, as the case may be, in the province or part thereof is issued by the Governor in Council at the request of the Lieutenant-Governor in Council of the province.

(2) No offence is committed against subparagraph (ii) of paragraph (a) of section 93 or paragraph (a) of section 94 if intoxicants are sold to an Indian for consumption in a public place in accordance with the law of the province where the sale takes place.

(3) No offence is committed against subparagraph (ii) of paragraph (a) of section 93 or paragraph (a) of section 94 if intoxicants are sold to or had in possession by an Indian in accordance with the law of the province where the sale takes place or the possession is had."

96. A person who is found

(a) with intoxicants in his possession, or

(b) intoxicated

on a reserve, is guilty of an offence and is liable on summary conviction to a fine of not less than ten dollars and not more than fifty dollars or to imprisonment for a term not exceeding three months or to both fine and imprisonment. 1951, c. 29, s. 96.

(2) The said Act is further amended by adding thereto, immediately after section 96 thereof, the following section: 96A. (1) Subsection (2) shall come into force, or cease to be in force, in a reserve only if a proclamation declaring it to be in force, or to cease to be in force, as the case may be, in the reserve, is issued by the Governor in Council.

(2) No offence is committed against paragraph (a) of section 96 if intoxicants are had in possession by any person in accordance with the law of the province where the possession is had.

(3) A proclamation in respect of a reserve shall not be issued under subsection (1) except in accordance with the wishes of the band, as expressed at a referendum of the electors of the band by a majority of the electors who voted thereat.

(4) The Governor in Council may make regulations

(a) respecting the taking of votes and the holding of a referendum for the purposes of this section; and

(b) defining a reserve for the purposes of subsection (1) to consist of one or more reserves or any part thereof.

(5) No proclamation bringing subsection (2) into force in a reserve shall be issued unless the council of the band has transmitted to the Minister a resolution of the council requesting that subsection (2) be brought into force in the reserve, and either

(a) the reserve is situated in a province or part thereof in which subsection (3) of section 95 is in force, or

(b) the Minister has communicated the contents of the resolution to the Attorney General of the province in which the reserve is situated, the Lieutenant-Governor in Council of the province has not, within sixty days after such communication, objected to the granting of the request, and the Governor in Council has directed that the wishes of the band with respect thereto be ascertained by a referendum of the electors of the band.

(6) Where subsection (2) is in force in a reserve no offence is committed against subparagraph (ii) of paragraph (a) of section 93 or paragraph (a) of section 94 if intoxicants are sold to or had in possession by a member of the band in accordance with the law of the province in which the reserve is situated."

97. The provisions of this Act relating to intoxicants do not apply where the intoxicant is used or is intended to be used in cases of sickness or accident. 1951, c. 29, s. 97

98. In any prosecution under this Act the burden of proof that an intoxicant was used or was intended to be used in a case of sickness or accident is upon the accused. 1951, c. 29, s. 98.

99. In every prosecution under this Act a certificate of analysis furnished by an analyst employed by the Government of Canada or by a province shall be accepted as prima facie evidence of the facts stated therein and of the authority of the person giving or issuing the certificate, without proof of the signature of the person appearing to have signed the certificate or his official character, and without further proof thereof. 1951, c. 29, s. 99.

100. Every person who is guilty of an offence against any provision of this Act or any regulation made by the Governor in Council or the Minister for which a penalty is not provided elsewhere in this Act or the regulations, is liable on summary conviction to a fine not exceeding two hundred dollars or to imprisonment for a term not exceeding three months or to both fine and imprisonment. 1951, c. 29, s. 100.

101. (1) Whenever a peace officer or a superintendent or a person authorized by the Minister believes on reasonable grounds that an offence against section 33, 89, 93, 94 or 96 has been committed, he may seize all goods and chattels by means of or in relation to which he reasonably believes the offence was committed.

5. Subsection (1) of section 101 of the said Act k repealed and the following substituted therefor:

"101. (1) Whenever a peace officer or a superintendent or a person authorized by the Minister believes on reasonable grounds that an offence against section 33, 89, 92, 93, 94 or 96 has been committed, he may seize all goods and chattels by means of or in relation to which he reasonably believes the offence was committed, and he may enter, open and search any place or thing in or upon which he reasonably believes any such goods or chattels may be found."

24. (1) Subsection (1) of section 101 of the said Act k repealed and the following substituted there-

for:

"FORFEITURES AND PENALTIES.

101. (1) Whenever a peace officer or a superintendent or a person authorized by the Minister believes on reasonable grounds that an offence against section 33, 89, 92, 93, 94 or 96 has been committed, he may seize all goods and chattels by means of or in relation to which he reasonably believes the offence was committed."

(2) All goods and chattels seized pursuant to subsection (1) may be detained for a period of three months following the day of seizure unless during that period proceedings under this Act in respect of such offence are undertaken, in which case the goods and chattels may be further detained until such proceedings are finally concluded.

(3) Where a person is convicted of an offence against the sections mentioned in subsection (1), the convicting court or judge may order that the goods and chattels by means of or in relation to which the offence was committed, in addition to any penalty imposed, are forfeited to Her Majesty. 1951, c. 29, s. 101.

(2) Subsection (3) of section 101 of the said Act is repealed and the following substituted therefor:

(3) Where a person is convicted of an offence against the sections mentioned in subsection (1), the convicting court or judge may order that the goods and chattels by means of or in relation to which the offence was committed, in addition to any penalty imposed, are forfeited to Her Majesty and may be disposed of as the Minister directs.

(4) A justice who is satisfied by information upon oath that there is reasonable ground to believe that there are upon a reserve or in any building, receptacle or place any goods or chattels by means of or in relation to which an offence against any of the sections mentioned in subsection (1) has been, is being or is about to be committed, may at any time issue a warrant under his hand authorizing a person named therein or a peace officer at any time to search the reserve, building, receptacle or place for any such goods or chattels."

102. Every fine, penalty or forfeiture imposed under this Act belongs to Her Majesty for the benefit of the band with respect to which or to one or more members of which the offence was committed or to which the offender, if an Indian, belongs, but the Governor in Council may from time to time direct that the fine, penalty or forfeiture shall be paid to a provincial, municipal or local authority that bears in whole or in part the expense of administering the law under which the fine, penalty or forfeiture is imposed, or that the fine, penalty or forfeiture shall be applied in the manner that he considers will best promote the purposes of the law under which the fine, penalty or forfeiture is imposed, or the administration of that law. 1951, c. 29, s. 102.

103. In any order, writ, warrant, summons or proceeding issued under this Act it is sufficient if the name of the person or Indian referred to therein is the name given to, or the name by which the person or Indian is known by, the person who issues the order, writ, warrant, summons or proceedings, and if no part of the name of the person is given to or known by the person issuing the order, writ, warrant, summons or proceedings, it is sufficient if the person or Indian is described in any manner by which he may be identified. 1951, c. 29, s. 103.

104. A police magistrate or a, stipendiary magistrate has and may exercises with respect to matters arising under this Act, jurisdiction over the whole county, union of counties or judicial district in

which the city, town or other place for which he is appointed or in which he has jurisdiction under provincial laws is situated. 1951, c. 29, s. 104.

105. The Governor in Council may appoint persons to be, for the purposes of this act justices of the peace and those persons have and may exercise the powers and authority of two justices of the peace with regard to

(a) offences under this Act,

(b) offences under the Criminal Code with respect to inciting Indians on reserves to commit riotous acts, and robbing of Indian graves, and

25. paragraph (b) of section 105 of the said act is repealed

(c) any offence against the provision of the criminal code relating to cruelty to animals, common assault, breaking and entering and vagrancy, where the offence is committed by an Indian or relates to the person or property of an Indian. 1951, c. 29, s. 105.

106. Where, immediately prior to the 4th day of Indian agent September, 1951, an Indian agent was ex officio a justice of the peace under the Indian Act, chapter 98 of the Revised Statutes of Canada, 1927, he shall be deemed, for the purposes of this Act, to have been appointed under section 105, and he may exercise the powers and authority conferred by that section until his appointment is revoked by the Minister. 1951, c. 29, s. 106.

107. For the purposes of this Act or any matter relating to Indian affairs

(a) persons appointed by the Minister for the purpose,

(b) superintendents, and

(c) the Minister, Deputy Minister and the chief officer in charge of the branch of the Department relating to Indian affairs are ex officio commissioners for the taking of oaths. 1951, c. 29, s. 107.

ENFRANCHISEMENT.

108. (1) On the report of the Minister that an Indian has applied for enfranchisement and that in his opinion the Indian

(a) is of the full age of twenty-one years,

(b) is capable of assuming the duties and responsibilities of citizenship, and

(c) when enfranchised, will be capable of supporting himself and his dependants, the Governor in Council may by order declare that the Indian and his wife and minor unmarried children are enfranchised.

(2) On the report of the Minister that an Indian woman married a person who is not an Indian, the Governor in Council may by order declare that the woman is enfranchised as of the date of her marriage.

26. Subsection (2) of section 108 of the said Act is repealed and the following substituted therefor:

(2) On the report of the Minister that an Indian woman married a person who is not an Indian, the Governor in Council may by order declare that the woman is enfranchised as of the date of her marriage and, on the recommendation of the Minister may by order declare that all or any of her children are enfranchised as of the date of the marriage or such other date as the order may specify."

(3) Where, in the opinion of the Minister, the wife of an Indian is living apart from her husband, the names of his wife and his minor children who are living with the wife shall not be included in an order under subsection (1) that enfranchises the Indian unless the wife has applied for enfranchise-

ment, but where the Governor in Council is satisfied that such wife is no longer living apart from her husband, the Governor in Council may by order declare that the wife and the minor children are enfranchised.

(4) A person is not enfranchised unless his name appears in an order of enfranchisement made by the Governor in Council. 1951, c. 29, s. 108.

109. A person with respect to whom an order for enfranchisement is made under section 108 shall, from the date thereof, be deemed not to be an Indian within the meaning of this Act or any other statute or law. 1951, c. 29, s. 109.

27. Section 100 of the said Act is repealed and the following substituted therefor:

109. A person with respect to whom an order for enfranchisement is made under this Act shall, from the date thereof, or from the date of enfranchisement provided for therein, be deemed not to be an Indian within the meaning of this Act or any other statute or law."

110. (1) Upon the issue of an order of enfranchisement, any interest in land and improvements on an Indian reserve of which the enfranchised Indian was in lawful possession or over which he exercised rights of ownership, at the time of his enfranchisement, may be disposed of by him by gift or private sale to the band or another member of the band, but if not so disposed of within thirty days after the date of the order of enfranchisement such land and improvements shall be offered for sale by tender by the superintendent and sold to the highest bidder and the proceeds of such sale paid to him ; and if no bid is received and the property remains unsold after six months from the date of such offering, the land, together with improvements, shall revert to the band free from any interest of the enfranchised person therein, subject to the payment, at the discretion of the Minister, to the enfranchised Indian, from the funds of the band, of such compensation for permanent improvements as the Minister may determine.

(2) When an order of enfranchisement issues or has issued, the Governor in Council may, with the consent of the council of the band, by order declare that any lands within a reserve of which the enfranchised Indian had formerly been in lawful possession shall cease to be Indian reserve lands.

(3) When an order has been made under subsection (2), the enfranchised Indian is entitled to occupy such lands for a period of ten years from the date of his enfranchisement, and the enfranchised Indian shall pay to the funds of the band, or there shall, out of any money payable to the enfranchised Indian under this Act, be transferred to the funds of the band, such amount per acre for the lands as the Minister considers to be the value of the common interest of the band in the lands.

(4) At the end of the ten-year period referred to in subsection (3) the Minister shall cause a grant of the lands to be made to the enfranchised Indian or to his legal representatives. 1951, c. 29, s. 110.

111. (1) Where the Minister reports that a band has applied for enfranchisement, and has submitted a plan for the disposal or division of the funds of the band and the lands in the reserve, and in his opinion the band is capable of managing its own affairs as a municipality or part of a municipality, the Governor in Council may by order approve the plan, declare that all the members of the band are enfranchised, either as of the date of the order or such later date as may be fixed in the order, and may make regulations for carrying the plan and the provisions of this section into effect.

(2) An order for enfranchisement may not be made under subsection (1) unless more than fifty per cent of the electors . of the band signify, at a meeting of the band called for the purpose, their will-

ingness to become enfranchised under this section, and their approval of the plan.

(3) The Governor in Council may, for the purpose of giving effect to this section, authorize the Minister to enter into an agreement with a province or a municipality, or both, upon such terms as may be agreed upon by the Minister and the province or municipality, or both.

(4) Without restricting the generality of subsection (3), an agreement made thereunder may provide for financial assistance to be given to the province or the municipality or both to assist in the support of indigent, infirm or aged persons to whom the agreement applies, and such financial assistance, or any part thereof, shall, if the Minister so directs, be paid out of moneys of the band, and any such financial assistance not paid out of money of the band shall be paid out of moneys appropriated by Parliament. 1951, c. 29, s. 111.

112. (1) The Minister may appoint a committee to Commute inquire into and report upon the desirability of enfranchising within the meaning of this Act an Indian or a band, whether or not the Indian or the band has applied for enfranchisement.

(2) A committee appointed under subsection (1) shall consist of

(a) a judge or retired judge of a superior, surrogate, district or county court,

(b) an officer of the Department, and

(c) a member of the band to be appointed by the council of the band, but if no appointment is made by the council of the band within thirty days after a request therefor is sent by the Minister to the band, a member of the band appointed by the Minister.

(3) Where the committee or a majority thereof reports

(a) in the case of an Indian, that in its opinion the Indian is qualified under paragraphs (a), (b) and (c) of subsection (1) of section 10S to be enfranchised,

(b) in the case of a band, that in the opinion of the committee the band is capable of managing its own affairs as a municipality or part of a municipality, and the committee has submitted a plan for the disposal or division of the funds of the band and the lands in the reserve, and

(c) that it is desirable that the Indian or the band, as the case may be, should be enfranchised, the report, if approved by the Minister, shall be deemed to be an application for enfranchisement by the Indian or by the band and shall be dealt with as such in accordance with this Act, except that, in the case of a band, the provisions of subsection (2) of section 111 are not applicable.

(4) An Indian or the members of a band shall not be enfranchised under this section contrary to the terms of any treaty, agreement or undertaking between a band and Her Majesty that is applicable. 1951, c. 29, s. 112.

1. Section 112 of the Indian Act is repealed and the following substituted therefor:

112. (1) Where a band has applied for enfranchisement within the meaning of this Act and has submitted a plan for the disposal or division of the funds of the band and the lands in the reserve, the Minister may appoint a committee to inquire into and report upon any or all of the following matters, namely:

(a) the desirability of enfranchising the band;

(b) the adequacy of the plan submitted by it; and

(c) any other matter relating to the application for enfranchisement or to the disposition thereof.

(2) A committee appointed under subsection (1) shall consist of

(a) a judge or retired judge of a superior, surrogate, district or county court,

(b) an officer of the Department, and

(c) a member of the band to be designated by the council of the band."

SCHOOLS.

113. The Governor in Council may authorize the Minister, in accordance with this Act,

(a) to establish, operate and maintain schools for Indian children,

(b) to enter into agreements on behalf of Her Majesty for the education in accordance with this Act of Indian children, with

(i) the government of a province,

(ii) the council of the Northwest Territories,

(iii) the council of the Yukon Territory,

(iv) a public or separate school board, and

(v) a religious or charitable organization. 1951, c. 29, s. 113.

28. Section 113 of the said Act is repealed and the following substituted therefor:

113. (1) The Governor in Council may authorize the Minister, in accordance with this Act, to enter into agreements on behalf of Her Majesty for the education in accordance with this Act of Indian children, with

(a) the government of a province,

(b) the Commissioner of the Northwest Territories,

(c) the Commissioner of the Yukon Territory,

(d) a public or separate school board,, and

(e) a religious or charitable organization.

(2) The Minister may, in accordance with this Act, establish, operate and maintain schools for Indian children."

114. The Minister may

(a) provide for and make regulations with respect to standards for buildings, equipment, teaching, education, inspection and discipline in connection with schools,

(b) provide for the transportation of children to and from school,

(c) enter into agreements with religious organizations for the support and maintenance of children who are being educated in schools operated by those organizations, and

(d) apply the whole or any part of moneys that would otherwise be payable to or on behalf of a child who is attending a residential school to the maintenance of that child at that school. 1951, c. 29, s. 114.

115. (1) Subject to section 116, every Indian child who has attained the age of seven years shall attend school.

(2) The Minister may

(a) permit an Indian who has attained the age of six years to attend school,

20. Paragraph (a) of subsection (2) of section 115 of the said Act is repealed and the following substituted therefor:

(a) require an Indian who has attained the age of six years to attend school,"

(b) require an Indian who becomes sixteen years of age during the school term to continue to attend school until the end of that term, and

(c) require an Indian who becomes sixteen years of age to attend school for such further period as the Minister considers advisable, but no Indian shall be required to attend school after he becomes eighteen years of age. 1951, c. 29, s. 115.

116. An Indian child is not required to attend school When if the child

(a) is, by reason of sickness or other unavoidable cause that is reported promptly to the principal, unable to attend school,

(b) has passed entrance examinations for high school,

30. Paragraph (b) of section 116 of the said Act is repealed

(c) is, with the permission in writing of the superintendent, absent from school for a period not exceeding six weeks in each term for the purpose of assisting in husbandry or urgent and necessary household duties,

(d) is under efficient instruction at home or elsewhere, within one year after the written approval by the Minister of such instruction, or

(e) is unable to attend school because there is insufficient accommodation in the school that the child is entitled or directed to attend. 1951, c. 29, s. 116.

117. Every Indian child who is required to attend school shall attend such school as the Minister may designate but no child whose parent is a Protestant shall be assigned to a school conducted under Homan Catholic auspices and no child whose parent is a Roman Catholic shall be assigned to a school conducted under Protestant auspices, except by written direction of the parent. 1951, c. 29,s. 117.

118. (1) The Minister may appoint persons, to be called truant officers, to enforce the attendance of Indian children at school, and for that purpose a truant officer has the powers of a peace officer.

(2) Without restricting the generality of subsection (1), a truant officer may

(a) enter any place where he believes, on reasonable grounds, that there are Indian children who are between the ages of seven and sixteen years of age, or who are required by the Minister to attend school,

(b) investigate any case of truancy, and

(c) serve written notice upon the parent, guardian or other person having the care or legal custody of a child to cause the child to attend school regularly thereafter.

(3) Where a notice has been served in accordance with paragraph (c) of subsection (2) with respect to a child who is required by this Act to attend school, and the child does not within three days after the service of notice attend school and continue to attend school regularly thereafter, the person upon whom the notice was served is guilty of an offence and is liable on summary conviction to a fine of not more than five dollars or to imprisonment for a term not exceeding ten days or to both fine and imprisonment.

(4) Where a person has been served with a notice in accordance with paragraph (c) of subsection (2), it is not necessary within a period of twelve months thereafter to serve that person with any other notice in respect of further non-compliance with the provisions of this Act, and whenever such person within the period of twelve months fails to cause the child with respect to whom the notice was served or any other child of whom he has charge or control to attend school and continue in regular

attendance as required by this Act, such person is guilty of an offence and liable to the penalties imposed by subsection (3) as if he had been served with the notice.

(5) A child who is habitually late for school shall be deemed to be absent from school.

(6) A truant officer may take into custody a child whom he believes on reasonable grounds to be absent from school contrary to this Act and may convey the child to school, using as much force as the circumstances require. 1951, c. 29, s. 118.

119. An Indian child who

(a) is expelled or suspended from school, or

(b) refuses or fails to attend school regularly, shall be deemed to be a juvenile delinquent within meaning of the Juvenile Delinquents Act. 1951, c. s. 119.

120. (1) Where the majority of the members of a band belongs to one religious denomination the school established on the reserve that has been set apart for the use and benefit of that band shall be taught by a teacher of that denomination.

(2) Where the majority of the members of a band are, not members of the same religious denomination and the band by a majority vote of those electors of the band who were present at a meeting called for the purpose requests that day schools on the reserve should be taught by a teacher belonging to a particular religious denomination, the school on that reserve shall be taught by a teacher of that denomination. 1951, c. 29, s. 120.

121. A Protestant or Roman Catholic minority of any band may, with the approval of and under regulations to made by the Minister, have a separate day school or day school classroom established on the reserve unless, in the opinion of the Governor in Council, the number of children of school age does not so warrant. 1951, c. 29, s. 121.

122. In sections 113 to 121

(a) "child" means an Indian who has attained the age of six years but has not attained the age of sixteen years, and a person who is required by the Minister to attend school,

(b) "school" includes a day school, technical school, high school and residential school, and

(c) "truant officer" includes

(i) a member of the Royal Canadian Mounted Police

(ii) a special constable appointed for police duty on a reserve, and

(iii) a school teacher and a chief of the band, when authorized by the superintendent. 1951, c. 29, s. 122.

PRIOR GRANTS.

123. Where, prior to the 4th day of September, 1951,

(a) a reserve or portion of a reserve was released or surrendered to the Crown pursuant to Part I of the Indian Act, chapter 98 of the Revised Statutes of Canada, 1927, or pursuant to the provisions of the statutes relating to the release or surrender of reserves in force at the time of the release or surrender,

(b) Letters Patent under the Great Seal of Canada were issued purporting to grant a reserve or portion of a reserve so released or surrendered, or any interest therein, to any person, and

(c) the Letters Patent have not been declared void or inoperative by any Court of competent jurisdiction, the Letters Patent shall, for all purposes, be deemed to have been issued at the date thereof under the direction of the Governor in Council. 1951, c. 29, s. 124.

6. Section 123 of the said Act is repealed and the following substituted therefor:

"123. Where, prior to the 4th day of September, 1951, Prior grants a reserve or portion of a reserve was released or surrendered to the Crown pursuant to Part I of the Indian Act, chapter. 98 of the Revised Statutes of Canada, 1927, or pursuant to the provisions of the statutes relating to the release or surrender of reserves in force at the time of the release or surrender, and

(a) prior to that date Letters Patent under the Great Seal of Canada were issued purporting to grant a reserve or portion of a reserve so released or surrendered, or any interest therein, to any person, and the Letters Patent have not been declared void or inoperative by any Court of competent jurisdiction, or

(b) prior to that date a reserve or portion of a reserve so released or surrendered, or any interest therein, was sold or agreed to be sold by the Crown to any person, and the sale or agreement for sale has not been cancelled or by any Court of competent jurisdiction declared void or inoperative, the Letters Patent or the sale or agreement for sale, as the case may be, shall, for all purposes, be deemed to have been issued or made at the date thereof under the direction of the Governor in Council."

7. This Part shall come into force, and Part I is repealed, on the day the Revised Statutes of Canada, 1952, come into force.

INDIAN ACT. R.S.C. 1970, c. 1-6.
    CHAPTER 1-6
An Act respecting Indians
SHORT TITLE
Short title 1. This Act may be cited as the Indian Act. R.S., c. 149, s. 1.
Interpretation
2. (1) In this Act "band" means a body of Indians
(a) for whose use and benefit in common, lands, the legal title to which is vested in Her Majesty, have been set apart before, on or after the 4th day of September 1951,
(b) for whose use and benefit in common, moneys are held by Her Majesty, or
(c) declared by the Governor in Council to be a band for the purposes of this Act ; "child" includes a legally adopted Indian child; "council of the band" means
(a) in the case of a band to which section 74 applies, the council established pursuant to that section,
(b) in the case of a band to which section 74 does not apply, the council chosen according to the custom of the band, or, where there is no council, the chief of the band chosen according to the custom of the band;
"Department" means the Department of Indian Affairs and Northern Development ; "elector" means a person who
(a) is registered on a Band List,
(b) is of the full age of twenty-one years, and
(c) is not disqualified from voting at band elections;
"estate" includes real and personal property and any interest in land ;

"Indian" means a person who pursuant to this Act is registered as an Indian or is entitled to be registered as an Indian;

"Indian moneys" means all moneys collected, received or held by Her Majesty for the use and benefit of Indians or bands;

"intoxicant" includes alcohol, alcoholic, spirituous, vinous, fermented malt or other intoxicating liquor or combination of liquors and mixed liquor a part of which is spirituous, vinous, fermented or otherwise intoxicating and all drinks or drinkable liquids and all preparations or mixtures capable of human consumption that are intoxicating;

"member of a band" means a person whose name appears on a Band List or who is entitled to have his name appear on a Band List;

"mentally incompetent Indian" means an Indian who, pursuant to the laws of the province in which he resides, has been found to be mentally defective or incompetent for the purposes of any laws of that province providing for the administration of estates of mentally defective or incompetent persons;

"Minister" means the Minister of Indian Affairs and Northern Development; "registered" means registered as an Indian in the Indian Register;

"Registrar" means the officer of the Department who is in charge of the Indian

"reserve" means a tract of land, the legal title to which is vested in Her Majesty, that has been set apart by Her Majesty for the use and benefit of a band;

"superintendent" includes a commissioner, regional supervisor, Indian superintendent, assistant Indian superintendent and any other person declared by the Minister to be a superintendent for the purposes of this Act, and with reference to a band or a reserve, means the superintendent for that band or reserve;

"surrendered lands" means a reserve or part of a reserve or any interest therein, the legal title to which remains vested in Her Majesty, that has been released or surrendered by the band for whose use and benefit it was set apart.

(2) The expression "band" with reference to a reserve or surrendered lands means the band for whose use and benefit the reserve or the surrendered lands were set apart.

(3) Unless the context otherwise requires or this Act otherwise provides

(a) a power conferred upon a band shall be deemed not to be exercised unless it is exercised pursuant to the consent of a majority of the electors of the band, and

(b) a power conferred upon the council of a band shall be deemed not to be exercised unless it is exercised pursuant to the consent of a majority of the councillors of the band present at a meeting of the council duly convened. R.S., c. 149, s. 2; 1966-67, c. 25, s. 40.

ADMINISTRATION

3 (1) This Act shall be administered by the Minister of Indian Affairs and Northern Development, who shall be the superintendent general of Indian affairs.

(2) The Minister may authorize the Deputy Minister of Indian Affairs and Northern Development or the chief officer in charge of the branch of the Department relating to Indian affairs to perform and exercise any of the duties, powers and functions that may be or are required to be performed or exercised by the Minister under this Act or any other Act of the Parliament of Canada relating to

Indian affairs. R.S., c. 149, s. 3; 1966-67, c. 25, s. 40.

APPLICATION OF ACT

4 (1) A reference in this Act to an Indian does not include any person of the race of aborigines commonly referred to as Eskimos.

(2) The Governor in Council may by proclamation declare that this Act or any portion thereof, except sections 37 to 41, shall not apply to

(a) any Indians or any group or band of Indians, or

(b) any reserve or any surrendered lands or any part thereof, and may by proclamation revoke any such declaration.

(3) Sections 114 to 123 and, unless the Minister otherwise orders, sections 42 to 52 do not apply to or in respect of any Indian who does not ordinarily reside on a reserve or on lands belonging to Her Majesty in right of Canada or a province. R.S., c. 149, s. 4; 1956, c. 40, s. 1.

DEFINITION AND REGISTRATION OF INDIANS

5. An Indian Register shall be maintained in the Department, which shall consist of Band Lists and General Lists and in which shall be recorded the name of every person who is entitled to be registered as an Indian. R.S., c. 149, s. 5.

6. The name of every person who is a member of a band and is entitled to be registered shall be entered in the Band List for that band, and the name of every person who is not a member of a band and is entitled to be registered shall be entered in a General List. R.S., c. 149, s. 6.

7. (i) The Registrar may at any time add to or delete from a Band List or a General List the name of any person who, in accordance with this Act, is entitled or not entitled, as the case may be, to have his name included in that List.

(2) The Indian Register shall indicate the date on which each name was added thereto or deleted therefrom. R.S., c. 149, s. 7.

8. The band lists in existence in the Department on the 4th day of September 1951 shall constitute the Indian Register, and the applicable lists shall be posted in a conspicuous place in the superintendent's office that serves the band or persons to whom the List relates and in all other places where band notices are ordinarily displayed. R.S., c. 149, s. 8.

9. (i) Within six months after a list has y been posted in accordance with section 8 or within three months after the name of a person has been added to or deleted from a Band List or a General List pursuant to section 7

(a) in the case of a Band List, the council of the band, any ten electors of the band, or any three electors if there are less than ten electors in the band,

(b) in the case of a posted portion of a General List, any adult person whose name appears on that posted portion, and

(c) the person whose name was included in or omitted from the List referred to in section 8, or whose name was added to or deleted from a Band List or a General List, may, by notice in writing to the Registrar, containing a brief statement of the grounds therefore, protest the inclusion, omission, addition, or deletion, as the case may be, of the name of that person, and the onus of establishing those grounds lies on the person making the protest.

(2) Where a protest is made to the Registrar under this section he shall cause an investigation to be

made into the matter and shall render a decision, and subject to a reference under subsection (3), the decision of the Registrar is final and conclusive.

(3) Within three months from the date of a decision of the Registrar under this section

(a) the council of the band affected by the Registrar's decision, or

(b) the person by or in respect of whom the protest was made,

may, by notice in writing, request the Registrar to refer the decision to a judge for review, and thereupon the Registrar shall refer the decision, together with all material considered by the Registrar in making his decision, to the judge of the county or district court of the county or district in which the band is situated or in which the person in respect of whom the protest was made resides, or such other county or district as the Minister may designate, or in the Province of Quebec, to the judge of the Superior Court for the district in which the band is situated or in which the person in respect of whom the protest was made resides, or such other district as the Minister may designate.

25. (1) The Acts mentioned in Schedule II to this Act are amended in the manner and to the extent indicated in that Schedule.

(2) Proceedings to which any of the provisions amended by Schedule II apply that were commenced before the coming into force of this section shall be continued in accordance with those amended provisions without any further formality.

(3) A reference in any Act, other than this Act, or in any document, instrument, regulation, proclamation or order in council, to a County Court of Judicature of Prince Edward Island shall be held, as regards any transaction, matter or thing subsequent to the coming into force of this section, to be a reference to the Supreme Court of Prince Edward Island.

Subsections 9(3) and (4) are repealed and the following substituted therefor:

"(3) Within three months from the date of a decision of the Registrar under this section,

(a) the council of the band affected by the Registrar's decision, or

(b) the person by or in respect of whom the protest was made,

may, by notice in writing, request the Registrar to refer the decision to a judge for review, and thereupon the Registrar shall refer the decision, together with all material considered by the Registrar in making his decision,

(c) in the Province of Prince Edward Island, to a judge of the Supreme Court,

(d) in the Province of Quebec, to a judge of the Superior Court for the district in which the band is situated or in which the person in respect of whom the protest was made resides, or for such other district as the Minister may designate, or

(e) in any other province, to a judge of the county or district court of the county or district in which the band is situated or in which the person in respect of whom the protest was made resides, or of such other county or district as the Minister may designate.

(4) The judge of the county, district or Superior Court, as the case may be, shall inquire into the correctness of the Registrar's decision, and for such purposes may exercise all the powers of a commissioner under Part I of the Inquiries Act; the judge shall decide whether the person in respect of whom the protest was made is, in accordance with this Act, entitled or not entitled, as the case may be, to have his name included in the Indian Register, and the decision of the judge is final and conclusive.

(4) The judge of the Supreme Court, Superior Court, county or district court, as the case may be, shall inquire into the correctness of the Registrar's decision, and for such purposes may exercise all the powers of a commissioner under Part I of the Inquiries Act; the judge shall decide whether the person in respect of whom the protest was made is, in accordance with this Act, entitled or not entitled, as the case may be, to have his name included in the Indian Register, and the decision of the judge is final and conclusive."

(5) Not more than one reference of a Registrar's decision in respect of a protest may be made to a judge under this section.

(6) Where a decision of the Registrar has been referred to a judge for review under this section, the burden of establishing that the decision of the Registrar is erroneous is on the person who requested that the decision be so referred. R.S., c. 149, s. 9; 1956, c. 40, s. 2.

10. Where the name of a male person is included in, omitted from, added to or deleted from a Band List or a General List, the names of his wife and minor children shall also be included, omitted, added or deleted, as the case may be. R.S., c. 149, s. 10.

11 (1) Subject to section 12, a person is entitled to be registered to registered if that person

(a) on the 26th day of May 1874 was, for the purposes of An Act providing for the organization of the Department of the Secretary of State of Canada, and for the management of Indian and Ordnance Lands, being chapter 42 of the Statutes of Canada, 1868, as amended by section 6 of chapter 6 of the Statutes of Canada, 1869, and section 8 of chapter 21 of the Statutes of Canada, 1874, considered to be entitled to hold, use or enjoy the lands and other immovable property belonging to or appropriated to the use of the various tribes, bands or bodies of Indians in Canada ;

(b) is a member of a band

(i) for whose use and benefit, in common, lands have been set apart or since the 26th day of May 1874, have been agreed by treaty to be set apart, or

(ii) that has been declared by the Governor in Council to be a band for the purposes of this Act ;

(c) is a male person who is a direct descendant in the male line of a male person described in paragraph (a) or (b)

(d) is the legitimate child of

(i) a male person described in paragraph (a) or (b), or

(ii) a person described in paragraph (c);

(e) is the illegitimate child of a female person described in paragraph (a), (b) or (d); or

(f) is the wife or widow of a person who is entitled to be registered by virtue of paragraph (a), (6), (c), (d) or (e).

(2) Paragraph (1) (e) applies only to persons born after the 13th day of August 1956. R.S., c. 149, s. 11; 1956, c. 40, s. 3.

12. (1) The following persons are not entitled to be registered, namely,

(a) a person who

(i) has received or has been allotted half breed lands or money scrip,

(ii) is a descendant of a person described in subparagraph (i),

(iii) is enfranchised, or

(iv) is a person born of a marriage entered into after the 4th day of September 1951 and has attained the age of twenty-one years, whose mother and whose father's mother are not persons described in paragraph 11 (1)(a),(b) or (d) or entitled to be registered by virtue of paragraph 11(1)(e), unless, being a woman, that person is the wife or widow of a person described in section 11, and

(b) a woman who married a person who is not an Indian, unless that woman is subsequently the wife or widow of a person described in section 11.

(2) The addition to a Band List of the name of an illegitimate child described in paragraph 11 (1)(e) may be protested at any time within twelve months after the addition, and if upon the protest it is decided that the father of the child was not an Indian, the child is not entitled to be registered under that paragraph.

(3) The Minister may issue to any Indian to whom this Act ceases to apply, a certificate to that effect.

(4) Subparagraphs (1)(a)(i) and (ii) do not apply to a person who

(a) pursuant to this Act is registered as an Indian on the 13th day of August 1958, or

(b) is a descendant of a person described in paragraph (a) of this subsection.

(5) Subsection (2) applies only to persons born after the 13th day of August 1956. R.S., c. 149, s. 12; 1956, c. 40, ss. 3, 4; 1958, c. 19, s. 1.

13, Subject to the approval of the Minister and, if the Minister so directs, to the consent of the admitting band,

(a) a person whose name appears on a General List may be admitted into membership of a band with the consent of the council of the band, and

(b) a member of a band may be admitted into membership of another band with the consent of the council of the latter band. 1956, c. 40, s. 5.

14. A woman who is a member of a band ceases to be a member of that band if she marries a person who is not a member of that band, but if she marries a member of another band, she thereupon becomes a member of the band of which her husband is a member. R.S., c. 149, s. 14.

15. (1) Subject to subsection (2), an Indian who becomes enfranchised or who otherwise ceases to be a member of a band is entitled to receive from Her Majesty

(a) one per capita share of the capital and revenue moneys held by Her Majesty on behalf of the band, and

(b) an amount equal to the amount that in the opinion of the Minister he would have received during the next succeeding twenty years under any treaty then in existence between the band and Her Majesty if he had continued to be a member of the band.

(2) A person is not entitled to receive any amount under subsection (1)

(a) if his name was removed from the Indian register pursuant to a protest made under section 9, or

(b) if he is not entitled to be a member of a band by reason of the application of paragraph 11 (1)(e) or subparagraph 12(1) (a)(iv).

(3) Where by virtue of this section moneys are payable to a person who is under the age of twenty-one, the Minister may

(a) pay the moneys to the parent, guardian or other person having the custody of that person or to the public trustee, public administrator or other like official for the province in which that person resides, or (b) cause payment of the moneys to be withheld until that person reaches the age of twenty-one.

(4) Where the name of a person is removed from the Indian Register and he is not entitled to any payment under subsection (1), the Minister shall, if he considers it equitable to do so, authorize payment, out of moneys appropriated by Parliament, of such compensation as the Minister may determine for any permanent improvements made by that person on lands in a reserve.

(5) Where, prior to the 4th day of September 1951, any woman became entitled, under section 14 of the Indian Act, chapter 98 of the Revised Statutes of Canada, 1927, or any prior provisions to the like effect, to share in the distribution of annuities, interest moneys or rents, the Minister may, in lieu thereof, pay to such woman out of the moneys of the band an amount equal to ten times the average annual amounts of such payments made to her during the ten years last preceding or, if they were paid for less than ten years, during the years they were paid. R.S., c. 149, s. 15; 1956, c. 40, s. 6.

16. (1) Section 15 does not apply to a person who ceases to be a member of one band by reason of his becoming a member of another band, but, subject to subsection (3), there shall be transferred to the credit of the latter band the amount to which that person would, but for this section, have been entitled under section 15.

(2) A person who ceases to be a member of one band by reason of his becoming a member of another band is not entitled to any interest in the lands or moneys held by Her Majesty on behalf of the former band, but he is entitled to the same interest in common in lands and moneys held by Her Majesty on behalf of the latter band as other members of that band.

(3) Where a woman who is a member of one band becomes a member of another band by reason of marriage, and the per capita share of the capital and revenue moneys held by Her Majesty on behalf of the first-mentioned band is greater than the per capita share of such moneys so held for the second-mentioned band, there shall be transferred to the credit of the second-mentioned band an amount equal to the per capita share held for that band, and the remainder of the money to which the woman would, but for this section, have been entitled under section 15 shall be paid to her in such manner and at such times as the Minister may determine. R.S., c. 149, s. 16.

17. (1) The Minister may, whenever he considers it desirable,

(a) constitute new bands and establish Band Lists with respect thereto from existing Band Lists or General Lists, or both,

(b) amalgamate bands that, by a vote of a majority of their electors, request to be amalgamated, and

(c) where a band has applied for enfranchisement, remove any name from the Band List and add it to the General List.

(2) Where pursuant to subsection (1) a new band has been established from an existing band or any part thereof, such portion of the reserve lands and funds of the existing band as the Minister determines shall be held for the use and benefit of the new band.

(3) No protest may be made under section 9 in respect of the deletion from or addition to a list consequent upon the exercise by the Minister of any of his powers under subsection (1). R.S., c. 149, s. 17; 1956, c. 40, s. 7.

REVERSE

18. (1) Subject to this Act, reserves are held by Her Majesty for the use and benefit of the respective bands for which they were set apart; and subject to this Act and to the terms of any treaty or surrender, the Governor in Council may determine whether any purpose for which lands in a reserve are

used or are to be used is for the use and benefit of the band.

(2) The Minister may authorize the use of lands in a reserve for the purpose of Indian schools, the administration of Indian affairs, Indian burial grounds, Indian health projects or, with the consent of the council of the band, for any other purpose for the general welfare of the band, and may take any lands in a reserve required for such purposes, but where an individual Indian, immediately prior to such taking, was entitled to the possession of such lands, compensation for such use shall be paid to the Indian, in such amount as may be agreed between the Indian and the Minister, or, failing agreement, as may be determined in such manner as the Minister may direct. R.S., c. 149, s. 18; 1956, c. 40, s. 8.

19. The Minister may

(a) authorize surveys of reserves and the preparation of plans and reports with respect thereto,

(b) divide the whole or any portion of a reserve into lots or other subdivisions, and

(c) determine the location and direct the construction of roads in a reserve. R.S., c. 149, s. 19.

POSSESSION OF LANDS IN RESERVES

20. (1) No Indian is lawfully in possession of land in a reserve unless, with the approval of the Minister, possession of the land has been allotted to him by the council of the band.

(2) The Minister may issue to an Indian who is lawfully in possession of land in a reserve a certificate, to be called a Certificate of Possession, as evidence of his right to possession of the land described therein.

(3) For the purposes of this Act, any person who, on the 4th day of September 1951, held a valid and subsisting Location Ticket issued under The Indian Act, 1980, or any statute relating to the same subject-matter, shall be deemed to be lawfully in possession of the land to which the location ticket relates and to hold a Certificate of Possession with respect thereto.

(4) Where possession of land in a reserve has been allotted to an Indian by the council of the band, the Minister may, in his discretion, withhold his approval and may authorize the Indian to occupy the land temporarily and may prescribe the conditions as to use and settlement that are to be fulfilled by the Indian before the Minister approves of the allotment.

(5) Where the Minister withholds approval pursuant to subsection (4), he shall issue a Certificate of Occupation to the Indian, and the Certificate entitles the Indian, or those claiming possession by devise or descent, to occupy the land in respect of which it is issued for a period of two years from the date thereof.

(6) The Minister may extend the term of a approval Certificate of Occupation for a further period not exceeding two years, and may, at the expiration of any period during which a Certificate of Occupation is in force

(a) approve the allotment by the council of the band and issue a Certificate of Possession if in his opinion the conditions as to use and settlement have been fulfilled, or

(b) refuse approval of the allotment by the council of the band and declare the land in respect of which the Certificate of Occupation was issued to be available for reallotment by the council of the band. R.S., c. 149, s. 20.

21. There shall be kept in the Department a register, to be known as the Reserve Land Register, in which shall be entered particulars relating to Certificates of Possession and Certificates of Occupa-

tion and other transactions respecting lands in a reserve. R.S., c.149, s. 21.

22. Where an Indian who is in possession of lands at the time are included in a reserve, made permanent improvements thereon before that time, he shall be deemed to be in lawful possession of such lands at the time they are so included. R.S., c. 149, s. 22.

23. An Indian who is lawfully removed from lands in a reserve upon which he has made permanent improvements may, if the Minister so directs, be paid compensation in respect thereof in an amount to be determined by the Minister, either from the person who goes into possession or from the funds of the band, at the discretion of the Minister. R.S., c. 149, s. 23.

24. An Indian who is lawfully in possession of lands in a reserve may transfer to the band or to another member of the band the right to possession of the land, but no transfer or agreement for the transfer of the right to possession of lands in a reserve is effective until it is approved by the Minister. R.S., c. 149, s. 24.

25. (1) An Indian who ceases to be entitled to reside on a reserve may, within six months or such further period as the Minister may direct, transfer to the band or another member of the band the right to possession of any lands in the reserve of which he was lawfully in possession.

(2) Where an Indian does not dispose of his right of possession in accordance with subsection (1), the right to possession of the land reverts to the band, subject to the payment to the Indian who was lawfully in possession of the land, from the funds of the band, of such compensation for permanent improvements as the Minister may determine. R.S., c. 149,s. 25.

26. Whenever a Certificate of Possession or Occupation or a Location Ticket issued under The Indian Act, 1880, or any statute relating to the same subject-matter was, in the opinion of the Minister, issued to or in the name of the wrong person, through mistake, or contains any clerical error or misnomer, or wrong description of any material fact therein, the Minister may cancel the Certificate or Location Ticket and issue a corrected Certificate in lieu thereof. 1956, c.40, s. 9.

27. The Minister may, with the consent of the holder thereof, cancel any Certificate of Possession or Occupation or Location Ticket referred to in section 26, and may cancel any Certificate of Possession or Occupation or Location Ticket that in his opinion was issued through fraud or in error. 1956, c. 40, s. 9.

28. (1) Subject to subsection (2), a deed, lease, contract, instrument, document or agreement of any kind whether written or oral, by which a band or a member of a band purports to permit a person other than a member of that band to occupy or use a reserve or to reside or otherwise exercise any rights on a reserve is void.

(2) The Minister may by permit in writing authorize any person for a period not exceeding one year, or with the consent of the council of the band for any longer period, to occupy or use a reserve or to reside or otherwise exercise rights on a reserve. R.S., c. 149, s. 28; 1956, c. 40, s. 10.

29. Reserve lands are not subject to seizure under legal process. R.S., c. 149, s. 29.

TRESPASS ON RESERVES

30. A person who trespasses on a reserve is guilty of an offence and is liable on summary conviction to a fine not exceeding fifty dollars or to imprisonment for a term not exceeding one month, or to both. R.S., c. 149, s. 30.

31. (1) Without prejudice to section 30, where an Indian or a band alleges that persons other than Indians are or have been

(a) unlawfully in occupation or possession of,

(b) claiming adversely the right to occupation or possession of, or

(c) trespassing upon

a reserve or part of a reserve, the Attorney General of Canada may exhibit an Information in the Exchequer Court of Canada claiming, on behalf of the Indian or the band, the relief or remedy sought.

(2) An Information exhibited under subsection (1) shall, for all purposes of the Exchequer Court Act, be deemed to be an action or suit by the Crown within the meaning of paragraph 29(d) of that Act.

65. The Acts mentioned in Schedule II to this Act are amended in the manner and to the extent indicated in that Schedule.

1. Subsection 31(2) is repealed and the following substituted therefor:

"(2) An Information exhibited under subsection (1) shall, for all purposes of the Federal Court Act, be deemed to be a proceeding by the Crown within the meaning of that Act."

(3) Nothing in this section shall be construed to impair, abridge or otherwise affect any right or remedy that, but for this section, would be available to Her Majesty or to an Indian or a band. R.S., c. 149, s. 31.

SALE OR BARTER OF PRODUCE

32. (1) A transaction of any kind whereby produce a band or a member thereof purports to sell, barter, exchange, give or otherwise dispose of cattle or other animals, grain or hay, whether wild or cultivated, or root crops or plants or their products from a reserve in Manitoba, Saskatchewan or Alberta, to a person other than a member of that band, is void unless the superintendent approves the transaction in writing.

(2) The Minister may at any time by order exempt a band and the members thereof or any member thereof from the operation of this section, and may revoke any such order. R.S., c. 149, s. 32.

33. Every person who enters into a transaction that is void under subsection 32(1) is guilty of an offence. R.S., c. 149, s. 33.

ROADS AND BRIDGES

34. (1) A band shall ensure that the roads, bridges, ditches and fences within the reserve occupied by that band are maintained in accordance with instructions issued from time to time by the superintendent.

(2) Where, in the opinion of the Minister, a band has not carried out the instructions of the superintendent given under subsection (1), the Minister may cause the instructions to be carried out at the expense of the band or any member thereof and may recover the cost thereof from any amounts that are held by Her Majesty and are payable to the band or such member. R.S., c. 149, s. 34.

LANDS TAKEN FOR PUBLIC PURPOSES

35. (1) Where by an Act of the Parliament authorities Canada or a provincial legislature, Her Majesty in right of a province, a municipal or local authority or a corporation is empowered to take or to use lands or any interest therein without the consent of the owner, the power may, with the consent of the Governor in Council and subject to any terms that may be prescribed by the Gover-

nor in Council, be exercised in relation to lands in a reserve or any interest therein.

(2) Unless the Governor in Council otherwise directs, all matters relating to compulsory taking or using of lands in a reserve under subsection (1) are governed by the statute by which the powers are conferred.

(3) Whenever the Governor in Council has compulsory consented to the exercise by a province, authority or corporation of the powers referred to in subsection (1), the Governor in Council may, in lieu of the province, authority or corporation taking or using the lands without the consent of the owner, authorize a transfer or grant of such lands to the province, authority or corporation, subject to any terms that may be prescribed by the Governor in Council.

(4) Any amount that is agreed upon or awarded in respect of the compulsory taking or using of land under this section or that is paid for a transfer or grant of land pursuant to this section shall be paid to the Receiver General for the use and benefit of the band or for the use and benefit of any Indian who is entitled to compensation or payment as a result of the exercise of the powers referred to in subsection (1). R.S., c. 149, s. 35.

SPECIAL RESERVES

36, Where lands have been set apart for benefit of a band and legal title thereto is not vested in Her Majesty, this Act applies as though the lands were a reserve within the meaning of this Act. R.S., c. 149,s. 36.

SURRENDERS

37. Except where this Act otherwise provides, lands in a reserve shall not be sold, alienated, leased or otherwise disposed of until they have been surrendered to Her Majesty by the band for whose use and benefit in common the reserve was set apart. R.S., c.149, s. 37.

38. (1) A band may surrender to Her Majesty any right or interest of the band and its members in a reserve.

(2) A surrender may be absolute or qualified, conditional or unconditional. R.S., c. 149, s. 38.

39. (1) A surrender is void unless

(a) it is made to Her Majesty,

(b) it is assented to by a majority of the electors of the band

(i) at a general meeting of the band called by the council of the band,

(ii) at a special meeting of the band called by the Minister for the purpose of considering a proposed surrender, or

(iii) by a referendum as provided in the regulations, and

(c) it is accepted by the Governor in Council.

(2) Where a majority of the electors of a band did not vote at a meeting or referendum called pursuant to subsection (1) of this section or pursuant to section 51 of the Indian Act, chapter 98 of the Revised Statutes of Canada, 1927, the Minister may, if the proposed surrender was assented to by a majority of the electors who did vote, call another meeting by giving thirty days notice thereof or another referendum as provided in the regulations.

(3) Where a meeting is called pursuant to subsection (2) and the proposed surrender is assented to

at the meeting or referendum by a majority of the electors voting, the surrender shall be deemed, for the purpose of this section, to have been assented to by a majority of the electors of the band.

(4) The Minister may, at the request of the council of the band or whenever he considers it advisable, order that a vote at any meeting under this section shall be by secret ballot.

(5) Every meeting under this section shall be held in the presence of the superintendent or some other officer of the Department designated by the Minister. R.S., c. 149, s. 39; 1956, c. 40,s. 11.

40. When a proposed surrender has been assented to by the band in accordance with section 39, it shall be certified on oath by the superintendent or other officer who attended the meeting and by the chief or a member of the council of the band, and shall then be submitted to the Governor in Council for acceptance or refusal. R.S., c. 149, s. 40.

41. A surrender shall be deemed to confer all rights that are necessary to enable Her Majesty to carry out the terms of the surrender. R.S., c. 149, s. 41.

DESCENT OF PROPERTY

42. (1) Unless otherwise provided in this Act, all jurisdiction and authority in relation to matters and causes testamentary, with respect to deceased Indians, is vested exclusively in the Minister, and shall be exercised subject to and in accordance with regulations of the Governor in Council.

(2) The Governor in Council may make regulations for providing that a deceased Indian who at the time of his death was in possession of land in a reserve shall, in such circumstances and for such purposes as the regulations prescribe, be deemed to have been at the time of his death lawfully in possession of that land.

(3) Regulations made under this section may be made applicable to estates of Indians who died before, on or after the 4th day of September 1951. R.S., c. 149, s. 42; 1956, c. 40, s. 12.

43. Without restricting the generality of section 42, the Minister may

(a) appoint executors of wills and administrators of estates of deceased Indians, remove them and appoint others in their stead ;

(b) authorize executors to carry out the terms of the wills of deceased Indians;

(c) authorize administrators to administer the property of Indians who die intestate ;

(d) carry out the terms of wills of deceased Indians and administer the property of Indians who die intestate; and

(e) make or give any order, direction or finding that in his opinion it is necessary or desirable to make or give with respect to any matter referred to in section 42. R.S., c. 149, s. 43.

44. (1) The court that would have jurisdiction if the deceased were not an Indian may, with the consent of the Minister, exercise, in accordance with this Act, the jurisdiction and authority conferred upon the Minister by this Act in relation to testamentary matters and causes and any other powers, jurisdiction and authority ordinarily vested in that court.

(2) The Minister may direct in any particular case that an application for the grant of probate of the will or letters of administration shall be made to the court that would have jurisdiction if the deceased were not an Indian, and the Minister may refer to such court any question arising out of any will or the administration of any estate.

(3) A court that is exercising any jurisdiction or authority under this section shall not without the consent in writing of the Minister enforce any order relating to real property on a reserve. R.S., c.

149, s. 44.

WILLS

45. (1) Nothing in this Act shall be construed to prevent or prohibit an Indian from devising or bequeathing his property by will.

(2) The Minister may accept as a will any written instrument signed by an Indian in which he indicates his wishes or intention with respect to the disposition of his property upon his death.

(3) No will executed by an Indian is of any legal force or effect as a disposition of property until the Minister has approved the will or a court has granted probate thereof pursuant to this Act. R.S., c. 149, s. 45.

46. (1) The Minister may declare the will of an Indian to be void in whole or in part if he is satisfied that

(a) the will was executed under duress or undue influence ;

(b) the testator at the time of execution of the will lacked testamentary capacity;

(c) the terms of the will would impose hardship on persons for whom the testator had a responsibility to provide;

(d) the will purports to dispose of land in a reserve in a manner contrary to the interest of the band or contrary to this Act ;

(e) the terms of the will are so vague, uncertain or capricious that proper administration and equitable distribution of the estate of the deceased would be difficult or impossible to carry out in accordance with this Act ; or

(f) the terms of the will are against the public interest.

(2) Where a will of an Indian is declared by the Minister or by a court to be wholly void, the person executing the will shall be deemed to have died intestate, and where the will is so declared to be void in part only, any bequest or devise affected thereby, unless a contrary intention appears in the will, shall be deemed to have lapsed. R.S., c. 149, s. 46.

APPEALS

47. (1) A decision of the Minister made in the exercise of the jurisdiction or authority conferred upon him by section 42, 43 or 46 may, within two months from the date thereof, be appealed by any person affected thereby to the Exchequer Court of Canada, if the amount in controversy in the appeal exceeds five hundred dollars or if the Minister consents to an appeal.

(2) The judges of the Exchequer Court may make rules respecting the practice and procedure governing appeals under this section. R.S., c. 149, s. 47.

65. The Acts mentioned in Schedule II to this Act are amended in the manner and to the extent indicated in that Schedule.

2. Subsection 47(2) is repealed.

DISTRIBUTION OF PROPERTY ON INTESTACY

48. (1) Where the net value of the estate of an intestate does not, in the opinion of the Minister, exceed in value two thousand dollars, the estate shall go to the widow.

(2) Where the net value of the estate of an intestate, in the opinion of the Minister, is two thousand dollars or more, two thousand dollars shall go to the widow, and the remainder shall go as follows, namely:

(a) if the intestate left no issue, the remainder shall go to the widow ;
(b) if the intestate left one child, one-half of the remainder shall go to the widow; and
(c) if the intestate left more than one child, one-third of the remainder shall go to the widow ; and where a child has died leaving issue and such issue is alive at the date of the intestate's death, the widow shall take the same share of the estate as if the child had been living at that date.

(3) Notwithstanding subsections (1) and (2), (a) where in any particular case the Minister is satisfied that any children of the deceased will not be adequately provided for, he may direct that all or any part of the estate that would otherwise go to the widow shall go to the children, and
(b) the Minister may direct that the widow shall have the right, during her widowhood, to occupy any lands on a reserve that were occupied by her deceased husband at the time of his death.

(4) Where an intestate dies leaving issue his estate shall be distributed, subject to the rights of the widow, if any, per stirpes among such issue.

(5) Where an intestate dies leaving no widow or issue his estate shall go to his father and mother in equal shares if both are living, but if either of them is dead the estate shall go to the survivor.

(6) Where an intestate dies leaving no widow or issue or father or mother his estate shall go to his brothers and sisters in equal shares, and if any brother or sister is dead the children of the deceased brother or sister shall take the share their parent would have taken if living, but where the only persons entitled are children of deceased brothers and sisters, they shall take per capita.

(7) Where an intestate dies leaving no widow, issue, father, mother, brother or sister, and no children of any deceased brother or sister, his estate shall go to his next-of-kin.

(8) Where the estate goes to the next-of-kin It shall be distributed equally among the next-of-kin of equal degree of consanguinity to the intestate and those who legally represent them, but in no case shall representation be admitted after brothers' and sisters' children, and any interest in land in a reserve shall vest in Her Majesty for the benefit of the band if the nearest of kin of the intestate is more remote than a brother or sister.

(9) For the purposes of this section, degrees of kindred shall be computed by counting upward from the intestate to the nearest common ancestor and then downward to the relative, and the kindred of the half-blood shall inherit equally with those of the whole blood in the same degree.

(10) Descendants and relatives of intestate begotten before his death but born thereafter shall inherit as if they had been born in the lifetime of the intestate and had survived him.

(11) All such estate as is not disposed of by Will shall be distributed as if the testator had died intestate and had left no other estate.

(12) No widow is entitled to dower in the Land of her deceased husband dying intestate, and no husband is entitled to an estate by curtesy in the land of his deceased wife so dying, and there is no community of real or personal property situated on a reserve.

(13) Illegitimate children and their issue shall inherit from the mother as if the children were legitimate, and shall inherit as if the children were legitimate, through the mother, if dead, any real or personal property that she would have taken, if living, by gift, devise or descent from any other person.

(14) Where an intestate, being an illegitimate Child, dies leaving no widow or issue, his estate shall go to his mother, if living, but if the mother is dead his estate shall go to the other children of the

same mother in equal shares, and where any child is dead the children of the deceased child shall take the share their parent would have taken if living; but where the only persons entitled are children of deceased children of the mother, they shall take per capita.

(15) This section applies in respect of an intestate woman as it applies in respect of an intestate male, and for the purposes of this section the word "widow" includes "widower".

(16) In this section "child" includes a legally adopted child and a child adopted in accordance with Indian custom. R.S., c. 149, s. 48; 1956, c. 40, s. 13.

49. A person who claims to be entitled to possession or occupation of lands in a reserve by devise or descent shall be deemed not to be in lawful possession or occupation of that land until the possession is approved by the Minister. R.S., c. 149, s. 49.

50. (1) A person who is not entitled to reside on a reserve does not by devise or descent acquire a right to possession or occupation of land in that reserve.

(2) Where a right to possession or occupation of land in a reserve passes by devise or descent to a person who is not entitled to reside on a reserve, that right shall be offered for sale by the superintendent to the highest bidder among persons who are entitled to reside on the reserve and the proceeds of the sale shall be paid to the devisee or descendant, as the case may be.

(3) Where no tender is received within six months or such further period as the Minister may direct after the date when the right to possession or occupation is offered for sale under subsection (2), the right shall revert to the band free from any claim on the part of the devisee or descendant, subject to the payment, at the discretion of the Minister, to the devisee or descendant, from the funds of the band, of such compensation for permanent improvements as the Minister may determine.

(4) The purchaser of a right to possession or occupation of land under subsection (2) shall be deemed not to be in lawful possession or occupation of the land until the possession is approved by the Minister. R.S., c. 149, s. 50.

MENTALLY INCOMPETENT INDIANS

51. (1) Subject to this section, all jurisdiction and authority in relation to the property of mentally incompetent Indians is vested exclusively in the Minister.

(2) Without restricting the generality of subsection (1), the Minister may

(a) appoint persons to administer the estates of mentally incompetent Indians;

(b) order that any property of a mentally incompetent Indian shall be sold, leased, alienated, mortgaged, disposed of or otherwise dealt with for the purpose of

(i) paying his debts or engagements,

(ii) discharging encumbrances on his property,

(iii) paying debts or expenses incurred for his maintenance or otherwise for his benefit, or

(iv) paying or providing for the expenses of future maintenance ; and

(c) make such orders and give such directions as he considers necessary to secure the satisfactory management of the estates of mentally incompetent Indians.

(3) The Minister may order that any property situated off a reserve and belonging to a mentally incompetent Indian shall be dealt with under the laws of the province in which the property is situ-

ated. R.S., c. 149, s. 51.

GUARDIANSHIP

52. The Minister may administer or provide for administration of any property to which infant children of Indians are entitled, and may appoint guardians for such purpose. R.S., c. 149, s. 52.

MANAGEMENT OF RESERVES AND SURRENDERED LANDS

53. (1) The Minister or a person appointed by him for the purpose may manage, sell, lease or otherwise dispose of surrendered lands in accordance with this Act and the terms of the surrender.

(2) Where the original purchaser of surrendered lands is dead and the heir, assignee or devisee of the original purchaser applies for a grant of the lands, the Minister may, upon receipt of proof in such manner as he directs and requires in support of any claim for the grant and upon being satisfied that the claim has been equitably and justly established, allow the claim and authorize a grant to issue accordingly.

(3) No person who is appointed to manage, sell, lease or otherwise dispose of surrendered lands or who is an officer or servant of Her Majesty employed in the Department may, except with the approval of the Governor in Council, acquire directly or indirectly any interest in surrendered lands. R.S., c. 149, s. 53.

54. Where surrendered lands have been agreed to be sold or otherwise disposed of and letters patent relating thereto have not issued, or where surrendered lands have been leased, the purchaser, lessee or other person having an interest in the surrendered lands may, with the approval of the Minister, assign his interest in the surrendered lands or a part thereof to any other person. R.S., c. 149, s. 54.

55. (1) There shall be kept in the Department a register, to be known as the Surrendered Lands Register, in which shall be entered particulars in connection with any lease or other disposition of surrendered lands by the Minister or any assignment thereof.

(2) A conditional assignment shall not be registered.

(3) Registration of an assignment may be refused until proof of its execution has been furnished.

(4) An assignment registered under this section is valid against an unregistered assignment or an assignment subsequently registered. R.S., c. 149, s. 55.

56. Where an assignment is registered there shall be endorsed on the original copy thereof a certificate of registration signed by the Minister or by an officer of the Department authorized by him to sign such certificates. R.S., c. 149, s. 56.

57. The Governor in Council may make Regulations

(a) authorizing the Minister to grant licences to cut timber on surrendered lands, or, with the consent of the council of the band, on reserve lands;

(b) imposing terms, conditions and restrictions with respect to the exercise of rights conferred by licence granted under paragraph (a);

(c) providing for the disposition of surrendered mines and minerals underlying lands in a reserve;

(d) prescribing the penalty not exceeding one hundred dollars or imprisonment for a term of three months, or both, that may be imposed on summary conviction for violation of any regulation made under this section; and

(e) providing for the seizure and forfeiture of any timber or minerals taken in violation of any regulation made under this section. R.S., c. 149, s. 57.

58. (1) Where land in a reserve is uncultivated or unused, the Minister may, with the consent of the council of the band,

(a) improve or cultivate such land and employ persons therefor, and authorize and direct the expenditure of so much of the capital funds of the band as he considers necessary for such improvement or cultivation including the purchase of such stock, machinery or material or for the employment of such labour as the Minister considers necessary ;

(b) where the land is in the lawful possession of any individual, grant a lease of such land for agricultural or grazing purposes or for any purpose that is for the benefit of the person in possession ; and

(c) where the land is not in the lawful possession of any individual, grant for the benefit of the band a lease of such land for agricultural or grazing purposes.

(2) Out of the proceeds derived from the improvement or cultivation of lands pursuant to paragraph (1)(b), a reasonable rent shall be paid to the individual in lawful possession of the lands or any part thereof, and the remainder of the proceeds shall be placed to the credit of the band, but if improvements are made on the lands occupied by an individual, the Minister may deduct the value of such improvements from the rent payable to such individual under this subsection.

(3) The Minister may lease for the benefit of any Indian upon his application for that purpose, the land of which he is lawfully in possession without the land being surrendered.

(4) Notwithstanding anything in this Act, the Minister may, without a surrender

(a) dispose of wild grass or dead or fallen timber, and

(b) with the consent of the council of the band, dispose of sand, gravel, clay and other non-metallic substances upon or under lands in a reserve, or, where such consent cannot be obtained without undue difficulty or delay, may issue temporary permits for the taking of sand, gravel, clay and other non-metallic substances upon or under lands in a reserve, renewable only with the consent of the council of the band, and the proceeds of such transactions shall be credited to band funds or shall be divided between the band and the individual Indians in lawful possession of the lands in such shares as the Minister may determine. R.S., c. 149, s. 58; 1956, c. 40, s. 14.

59. The Minister may, with the consent of the council of a band,

(a) reduce or adjust the amount payable to Her Majesty in respect of a sale, lease or other disposition of surrendered lands or a lease or other disposition of lands in a reserve or the rate of interest payable thereon, and

(b) reduce or adjust the amount payable to the band by an Indian in respect of a loan made to the Indian from band funds. R.S., c. 149, s. 59.

60. (1) The Governor in Council may at the request of a band grant to the band the right to exercise such control and management over lands in the reserve occupied by that band as the Governor in Council considers desirable.

(2) The Governor in Council may at any time withdraw from a band a right conferred upon the band under subsection (1). R.S., c.149, s. 60.

MANAGEMENT OF INDIAN MONEYS

61. (1) Indian moneys shall be expended only for the benefit of the Indians or bands for whose use and benefit in common the moneys are received or held, and subject to this Act and to the terms

of any treaty or surrender, the Governor in Council may determine whether any purpose for which Indian moneys are used or are to be used is for the use and benefit of the band.

(2) Interest upon Indian moneys held in the Consolidated Revenue Fund shall be allowed at a rate to be fixed from time to time by the Governor in Council. R.S., c. 149, s. 61.

62. All Indian moneys derived from the sale of surrendered lands or the sale of capital assets of a band shall be deemed to be capital moneys of the band and all Indian moneys other than capital moneys shall be deemed to be revenue moneys of the band. R.S., c. 149, s. 62.

63. Notwithstanding the Financial Administration Act, where moneys to which an Indian is entitled are paid to a superintendent under any lease or agreement made under this Act, the superintendent may pay the moneys to the Indian. R.S., c. 149, s. 63.

64. With the consent of the council of a band, the Minister may authorize and direct the expenditure of capital moneys of the band

(a) to distribute per capita to the members of the band an amount not exceeding fifty per cent of the capital moneys of the band derived from the sale of surrendered lands;

(b) to construct and maintain roads, bridges, ditches and water courses on the reserves or on surrendered lands ;

(c) to construct and maintain outer boundary fences on reserves ;

(d) to purchase land for use by the band as a reserve or as an addition to a reserve ;

(e) to purchase for the band the interest of a member of the band in lands on a reserve;

(f) to purchase livestock and farm implements, farm equipment, or machinery for the band ;

(g) to construct and maintain on or in connection with a reserve such permanent improvements or works as in the opinion of the Minister will be of permanent value to the band or will constitute a capital investment ;

(h) to make to members of the band, for the purpose of promoting the welfare of the band, loans not exceeding one-half of the total value of

(i) the chattels owned by the borrower, and

(ii) the land with respect to which he holds or is eligible to receive a Certificate of Possession, and may charge interest and take security therefor;

(i) to meet expenses necessarily incidental to the management of lands on a reserve, surrendered lands and any band property ;

(j) to construct houses for members of the band, to make loans to members of the band for building purposes with or without security and to provide for the guarantee of loans made to members of the band for building purposes ; and

(k) for any other purpose that in the opinion of the Minister is for the benefit of the band. R.S., c. 149, s. 64 ; 1956, c. 40, 8. 15.

65. The Minister may pay from capital moneys

(a) compensation to an Indian in an amount that is determined in accordance with this Act to be payable to him in respect of land compulsorily taken from him for band purposes, and

(b) expenses incurred to prevent or suppress grass or forest fires or to protect the property of Indians in cases of emergency. R.S., c. 149, s. 65.

66. (1) With the consent of the council of a band, the Minister may authorize and direct bond

the expenditure of revenue moneys for any purpose that in his opinion will promote the general progress and welfare of the band or any member of the band.

(2) The Minister may make expenditures out of the revenue moneys of the band to assist sick, disabled, aged or destitute Indians of the band and to provide for the burial of deceased indigent members of the band and to provide for the payment of contributions under the Unemployment Insurance Act on behalf of employed persons who are paid in respect of their employment out of moneys of the band.

(3) The Minister may authorize the expenditure of revenue moneys of the band for ail of Minister or any of the following purposes, namely:

(a) for the destruction of noxious weeds and the prevention of the spreading or prevalence of insects, pests or diseases that may destroy or injure vegetation on Indian reserves ;

(b) to prevent, mitigate and control the spread of diseases on reserves, whether or not the diseases are infectious or communicable;

(c) to provide for the inspection of premises on reserves and the destruction, alteration or renovation thereof ;

(d) to prevent overcrowding of premises on reserves used as dwellings ;

(e) to provide for sanitary conditions in private premises on reserves as well as in public places on reserves; and

(f) for the construction and maintenance of boundary fences. R.S., c. 149, s. 66; 1956, c. 40, s. 16.

67. Where money is expended by Her Majesty for the purpose of raising or collecting Indian moneys, the Minister may authorize the recovery of the amount so expended from the moneys of the band. 1956, c. 40, s. 17.

68. (1) Where the Minister is satisfied that A male Indian

(a) has deserted his wife or family without sufficient cause,

(b) has conducted himself in such a manner as to justify the refusal of his wife or family to live with him, or

(c) has been separated by imprisonment from his wife and family, he may order that payments of any annuity or interest money to which that Indian is entitled shall be applied to the support of the wife or family or both the wife and family of that Indian.

(2) Where the Minister is satisfied that a female Indian has deserted her husband or family, he may order that payments of any annuity or interest money to which that Indian is entitled shall be applied to the support of her family.

(3) Where the Minister is satisfied that one children or 0f the parents of an illegitimate child is an Indian, he may stop payments out of any annuity or interest moneys to which either or both of the parents would otherwise be entitled and apply the moneys to the support of the child, but not so as to prejudice the welfare of any legitimate child of either Indian. R.S., c. 149, s. 67.

69. (1) The Governor in Council may by order permit a band to control, manage and expend in whole or in part its revenue moneys and may amend or revoke any such order.

(2) The Governor in Council may make regulations to give effect to subsection (1) and may declare therein the extent to which this Act and the Financial Administration Act shall not apply to a band to which an order made under subsection (1) applies. R.S., c. 149, s. 68.

LOANS TO INDIANS

70. (1) The Minister of Finance may from time to time authorize advances to the Minister out of the Consolidated Revenue Fund of such sums of money as the Minister may require to enable him

(a) to make loans to bands, groups of Indians or individual Indians for the purchase of farm implements, machinery, livestock, motor vehicles, fishing equipment, seed grain, fencing materials, materials to be used in native handicrafts, any other equipment, and gasoline and other petroleum products, or for the making of repairs or the payment of wages, or for the clearing and breaking of land within reserves,

(b) to expend or to lend money for the carrying out of cooperative projects on behalf of Indians, or

(c) to provide for any other matter prescribed by the Governor in Council.

(2) The Governor in Council may make regulations to give effect to subsection (1).

(3) Expenditures that are made under subsection (1) shall be accounted for in the same manner as public moneys.

(4) The Minister shall pay to the Receiver General all moneys that he receives from bands, groups of Indians or individual Indians by way of repayments of loans made under subsection (1).

(5) The total amount of outstanding advances to the Minister under this section shall not at any one time exceed six million and fifty thousand dollars.

(6) The Minister shall within fifteen days after the termination of each fiscal year or, if Parliament is not then in session, within fifteen days after the commencement of the next ensuing session, lay before Parliament a report setting out the total number and amount of loans made under subsection (1) during that year. R.S., c. 149, s. 69; 1952-53, c. 41, s. 4; 1956, c. 40, s. 18; 1968-69, c. 28, s. 105; 1969-70, c. 2, Sch. vote L50a. [See 1969- 70, c. 24, Sch. vote L53b.]

FARMS

71. (i) The Minister may operate farms on reserves and may employ such persons as he considers necessary to instruct Indians in farming and may purchase and distribute without charge, pure seed to Indian farmers.

(2) The Minister may apply any profits that result from the operation of farms pursuant to subsection (1) on reserves to extend farming operations on the reserves or to make loans to Indians to enable them to engage in farming or other agricultural operations or he may apply such profits in any way that he considers to be desirable to promote the progress and development of the Indians. R.S., c. 149, s. 70.

TREATY MONEY

72. Moneys that are payable to Indians or to Indian bands under a treaty between Her Majesty and the band and for the payment of which the Government of Canada is responsible, may be paid out of the Consolidated Revenue Fund. R.S., c. 149, s. 71.

REGULATIONS

Regulations 73. (i) The Governor in Council may make regulations

(a) for the protection and preservation of fur-bearing animals, fish and other game on reserves;

(b) for the destruction of noxious weeds and the prevention of the spreading or prevalence of insects, pests or diseases that may destroy or injure vegetation on Indian reserves;

(c) for the control of the speed, operation and parking of vehicles on roads within reserves;

(d) for the taxation, control and destruction of dogs and for the protection of sheep on reserves;

(e) for the operation, supervision and control of pool rooms, dance halls and other places of amusement on reserves;

(f) to prevent, mitigate and control the spread of diseases on reserves, whether or not the diseases are infectious or communicable

(g) to provide medical treatment and health services for Indians;

(h) to provide compulsory hospitalization and treatment for infectious diseases among Indians;

(i) to provide for the inspection of premises on reserves and the destruction, alteration or renovation thereof;

(j) to prevent overcrowding of premises on reserves used as dwellings;

(k) to provide for sanitary conditions in private premises on reserves as well as in public places on reserves;

(l) for the construction and maintenance of boundary fences; and

(m) for empowering and authorizing the council of a band to borrow money for band projects or housing purposes and providing for the making of loans out of moneys so borrowed to members of the band for housing purposes.

(2) The Governor in Council may prescribe the penalty, not exceeding a fine of one hundred dollars or imprisonment for a term not exceeding three months, or both, that may be imposed on summary conviction for violation of a regulation made under subsection (1)

(3) The Governor in Council may make orders and regulations to carry out the purposes and provisions of this Act. R.S., c. 149, s.72; 1956, c. 40, s. 19.

ELECTIONS OF CHIEFS AND BAND COUNCILS

74. (1) Whenever he deems it advisable for the good government of a band, the Minister may declare by order that after a day to be named therein the council of the band, consisting of a chief and councillors, shall be selected by elections to be held in accordance with this Act.

(2) Unless otherwise ordered by the Minister, the council of a band in respect of which an order has been made under subsection (1) shall consist of one chief, and one councillor for every one hundred members of the band, but the number of councillors shall not be less than two nor more than twelve and no band shall have more than one chief.

(3) The Governor in Council may, for the purposes of giving effect to subsection (1), make orders or regulations to provide

(a) that the chief of a band shall be elected by

(i) a majority of the votes of the electors of the band, or

(ii) a majority of the votes of the elected councillors of the band from among themselves, but the chief so elected shall remain a councillor; and

(b) that the councillors of a band shall be elected by

(i) a majority of the votes of the electors of the band, or

(ii) a majority of the votes of the electors of the band in the electoral section in which the candidate resides and that he proposes to represent on the council of the band.

(4) A reserve shall for voting purposes consist of one electoral section, except that where the majority of the electors of a band who were present and voted at a referendum or a special meeting held and

called for the purpose in accordance with the regulations have decided that the reserve should for voting purposes be divided into electoral sections and the Minister so recommends, the Governor in Council may make orders or regulations to provide that the reserve shall for voting purposes be divided into not more than six electoral sections containing as nearly as may be an equal number of Indians eligible to vote and to provide for the manner in which electoral sections so established shall be distinguished or identified. R.S., c. 149, s. 73; 1956, c. 40, s. 20.

75. (1) No person other than an elector who resides in a section may be nominated for the office of councillor to represent that section on the council of the band.

(2) No person may be a candidate for election as chief or councillor unless his nomination is moved and seconded by persons who are themselves eligible to be nominated. R.S., c. 149, s. 74.

76. (1) The Governor in Council may make orders and regulations with respect to band elections and, without restricting the generality of the foregoing, may make regulations with respect to

(a) meetings to nominate candidates;

(b) the appointment and duties of electoral officers;

(c) the manner in which voting shall be carried out;

(d) election appeals; and

(e) the definition of residence for the purpose of determining the eligibility of voters.

(2) The regulations made under paragraph (1)(c) shall make provision for secrecy of voting. R.S., c. 149, s. 75.

77, (i) A member of a band who is of the full age 0f twenty-one years and is ordinarily resident on the reserve is qualified to vote for a person nominated to be chief of the band, and where the reserve for voting purposes consists of one section, to vote for persons nominated as councillors.

(2) A member of a band who is of the full age of twenty-one years and is ordinarily resident in a section that has been established for voting purposes is qualified to vote for a person nominated to be councillor to represent that section. R.S., c. 149, s. 76.

78. (j) Subject to this section, chiefs and councillors hold office for two years.

(2) The office of chief or councillor becomes vacant when

(a) the person who holds that office

(i) is convicted of an indictable offence,

(ii) dies or resigns his office, or

(iii) is or becomes ineligible to hold office by virtue of this Act; or

(b) the Minister declares that in his opinion the person who holds that office

(i) is unfit to continue in office by reason of his having been convicted of an offence,

(ii) has been absent from meetings of the council for three consecutive meetings without being authorized to do so, or

(iii) was guilty, in connection with an election, of corrupt practice, accepting a bribe, dishonesty or malfeasance.

(3) The Minister may declare a person who ceases to hold office by virtue of subparagraph (2)(b)(iii) be ineligible to be a candidate for chief or councillor for a period not exceeding six years.

(4) Where the office of chief or councillor becomes vacant more than three months before the date when another election would ordinarily be held, a special election may be held in accordance with

this Act to fill the vacancy. R.S., c. 149, s. 77.

79. The Governor in Council may set aside election of a chief or a councillor on the report of the Minister that he is satisfied that

(a) there was corrupt practice in connection with the election ;

(b) there was a violation of this Act that might have affected the result of the election ; or

(c) a person nominated to be a candidate in the election was ineligible to be a candidate. R.S., c. 149, s. 78.

80. The Governor in Council may make regulations with respect to band meetings and council meetings and, without restricting the generality of the foregoing, may make regulations with respect to

(a) presiding officers at such meetings;

(b) notice of such meetings ;

(c) the duties of any representative of the Minister at such meetings; and (d) the number of persons required at the meeting to constitute a quorum. R.S., c. 149, s. 79.

POWERS OF THE COUNCIL

81. The council of a band may make bylaws not inconsistent with this Act or with any regulation made by the Governor in Council or the Minister, for any or all of the following purposes, namely:

(a) to provide for the health of residents on the reserve and to prevent the spreading of contagious and infectious diseases;

(b) the regulation of traffic;

(c) the observance of law and order;

(d) the prevention of disorderly conduct and nuisances;

(e) the protection against and prevention of trespass by cattle and other domestic animals, the establishment of pounds, the appointment of pound-keepers, the regulation of their duties and the provision for fees and charges for their services;

(f) the construction and maintenance of water courses, roads, bridges, ditches, fences and other local works;

(g) the dividing of the reserve or a portion thereof into zones and the prohibition of the construction or maintenance of any class of buildings or the carrying on of any class of business, trade or calling in any such zone ;

(h) the regulation of the construction, repair and use of buildings, whether owned by the band or by individual members of the band ;

(i) the survey and allotment of reserve lands among the members of the band and the establishment of a register of Certificates of Possession and Certificates of Occupation relating to allotments and the setting apart of reserve lands for common use, if authority therefor has been granted under section 60;

(j) the destruction and control of noxious weeds ;

(k) the regulation of bee-keeping and poultry raising ;

(l) the construction and regulation of the use of public wells, cisterns, reservoirs and other water supplies;

(m) the control and prohibition of public games, sports, races, athletic contests and other amusements;

(n) the regulation of the conduct and activities of hawkers, peddlers or others who enter the reserve to buy, sell or otherwise deal in wares or merchandise ;

(o) the preservation, protection and management of fur-bearing animals, fish and other game on the reserve ;

(p) the removal and punishment of persons trespassing upon the reserve or frequenting the reserve for prescribed purposes ;

(q) with respect to any matter arising out of or ancillary to the exercise of powers under this section ; and

(r) the imposition on summary conviction of a fine not exceeding one hundred dollars or imprisonment for a term not exceeding thirty days, or both, for violation of a bylaw made under this section. R.S., c. 149, s. 80.

82. (1) A copy of every by-law made under the authority of section 81 shall be forwarded by mail by the chief or a member of the council of the band to the Minister within four days after it is made.

(2) A by-law made under section 81 comes into force forty days after a copy thereof is forwarded to the Minister pursuant to subsection (1), unless it is disallowed by the Minister within that period, but the Minister may declare the by-law to be in force at any time before the expiration of that period. R.S., c. 149, s. 81.

83. (1) Without prejudice to the powers conferred by section 81, where the Governor in Council declares that a band has reached an advanced stage of development, the council of the band may, subject to the approval of the Minister, make by-laws for any or all of the following purposes, namely

(a) the raising of money by

(i) the assessment and taxation of interests in land in the reserve of persons lawfully in possession thereof, and

(ii) the licensing of businesses, callings, trades and occupations;

(b) the appropriation and expenditure of moneys of the band to defray band expenses ;

(c) the appointment of officials to conduct the business of the council, prescribing their duties and providing for their remuneration out of any moneys raised pursuant to paragraph (a);

(d) the payment of remuneration, in such amount as maybe approved by the Minister, to chiefs and councillors, out of any moneys raised pursuant to paragraph (a);

(e) the imposition of a penalty for nonpayment of taxes imposed pursuant to this section, recoverable on summary conviction, not exceeding the amount of the tax or the amount remaining unpaid;

(f) the raising of money from band members to support band projects; and

(g) with respect to any matter arising out of or ancillary to the exercise of powers under this section.

(2) No expenditure shall be made out of moneys raised pursuant to paragraph (1)(a) except under the authority of a by-law of the council of the band. R.S., c. 149, s. 82; 1956, c. 40, s. 21.

84. Where a tax that is imposed upon an Indian by or under the authority of a by-law made under section 83 is not paid in accordance with the by-law, the Minister may pay the amount owing together with an amount equal to one-half of one per cent thereof out of moneys payable out of the funds of the band to the Indian. R.S., c. 149, s. 83.

85. The Governor in Council may revoke a declaration made under section 83 whereupon that sec-

tion no longer applies to the band to which it formerly applied, but any by-law made under the authority of that section and in force at the time the declaration is revoked shall be deemed to continue in force until it is revoked by the Governor in Council. R.S., c. 149, s. 84.

86. A copy of a by-law made by the council of a band under this Act, if it is certified to be a true copy by the superintendent, is evidence that the by-law was duly made by the council and approved by the Minister, without proof of the signature or official character of the superintendent, and no such by-law is invalid by reason of any defect in form. R.S., c. 149, s. 85.

TAXATION

87. Notwithstanding any other Act of the Parliament of Canada or any Act of the legislature of a province, but subject to subsection (2) and to section 83, the following property is exempt from taxation, namely :

(a) the interest of an Indian or a band in reserve or surrendered lands ; and

(b) the personal property of an Indian or band situated on a reserve ;

and no Indian or band is subject to taxation in respect of the ownership, occupation, possession or use of any property mentioned in paragraph (a) or (6) or is otherwise subject to taxation in respect of any such property; and no succession duty, inheritance tax or estate duty is payable on the death of any Indian in respect of any such property or the succession thereto if the property passes to an Indian, nor shall any such property be taken into account in determining the duty payable under the Dominion Succession Duty Act, being chapter 89 of the Revised Statutes of Canada, 1952, or the tax payable under the Estate Tax Act, on or in respect of other property passing to an Indian. R.S., c. 149, s. 86; 1958, c. 29, s. 59; 1960, c. 8, s. 1.

LEGAL RIGHTS

88. Subject to the terms of any treaty and any other Act of the Parliament of Canada, all laws of general application from time to time in force in any province are applicable to and in respect of Indians in the province, except to the extent that such laws are inconsistent with this Act or any order, rule, regulation or by-law made thereunder, and except to the extent that such laws make provision for any matter for which provision is made by or under this Act. R.S., c. 149, s. 87.

89. (1) Subject to this Act, the real and personal property of an Indian or a band situated on a reserve is not subject to charge, pledge, mortgage, attachment, levy, seizure, distress or execution in favour or at the instance of any person other than an Indian.

(2) A person who sells to a band or a member of a band a chattel under an agreement whereby the right of property or right of possession thereto remains wholly or in part in the seller, may exercise his rights under the agreement notwithstanding that the chattel is situated on a reserve. R.S., c. 149, s. 88.

90. (1) For the purposes of sections 87 and 89, personal property that was

(a) purchased by Her Majesty with Indian moneys or moneys appropriated by Parliament for the use and benefit of Indians or bands, or

(b) given to Indians or to a band under a treaty or agreement between a band and Her Majesty, shall be deemed always to be situated on a reserve.

(2) Every transaction purporting to pass title to any property that is by this section deemed to be

situated on a reserve, or any interest in such property, is void unless the transaction is entered into with the consent of the Minister or is entered into between members of a band or between the band and a member thereof.

(3) Every person who enters into any transaction that is void by virtue of subsection (2) is guilty of an offence, and every person who, without the written consent of the Minister, destroys personal property that is by this section deemed to be situated on a reserve, is guilty of an offence. R.S., c. 149, s. 89.

TRADING WITH INDIANS

91. (1) No person may, without the written consent of the Minister, acquire title to any of the following property situated on a reserve, namely:

(a) an Indian grave house;

(b) a carved grave pole;

(c) a totem pole;

(d) a carved house post; or

(e) a rock embellished with paintings or carvings.

(2) Subsection (1) does not apply to chattels referred to therein that are manufactured for sale by Indians.

(3) No person shall remove, take away, mutilate, disfigure, deface or destroy any chattel referred to in subsection (1) without the written consent of the Minister.

(4) A person who violates this section is guilty of an offence and is liable on summary conviction to a fine not exceeding two hundred dollars or to imprisonment for a term not exceeding three months. R.S., c. 149, s. 90.

92. (1) No person who is

(a) an officer or employee in the Department,

(b) a missionary engaged in mission work among Indians, or

(c) a school teacher on a reserve, shall, without a licence from the Minister or his duly authorized representative, trade for profit with an Indian or sell to him directly or indirectly goods or chattels, but no such licence shall be issued to a full-time officer or employee in the Department.

(2) The Minister or his duly authorized representative may at any time cancel a licence given under this section.

(3) A person who violates subsection (1) is guilty of an offence and is liable on summary conviction to a fine not exceeding five hundred dollars.

(4) Without prejudice to subsection (3), an officer or employee in the Department who contravenes subsection (1) may be dismissed from office. R.S., c. 149, s. 91.

REMOVAL OF MATERIALS FROM RESERVES

93. A person who, without the written permission of the Minister or his duly authorized representative,

(a) removes or permits anyone to remove from a reserve

(i) minerals, stone, sand, gravel, clay or soil, or

(ii) trees, saplings, shrubs, underbrush, timber, cordwood or hay, or

(b) has in his possession anything removed from a reserve contrary to this section, is guilty of an offence and is liable on summary conviction to a fine not exceeding five hundred dollars or to imprisonment for a term not exceeding three months, or to both. 1956, c. 40, s. 22.

94. A person who directly or indirectly by himself or by any other person on his behalf knowingly

(a) sells, barters, supplies or gives an intoxicant to

(i) any person on a reserve, or

(ii) an Indian outside a reserve,

(b) opens or keeps or causes to be opened or kept on a reserve a dwelling-house, building, tent, or place in which intoxicants are sold, supplied or given to any person, or

(c) makes or manufactures intoxicants on a reserve, is guilty of an offence and is liable on summary conviction to a fine of not less than fifty dollars and not more than three hundred dollars or to imprisonment for a term of not less than one month and not more than six months, with or without hard labour, or to both fine and imprisonment. R.S., c. 149, s. 93.

95. An Indian who

(a) has intoxicants in his possession,

(b) is intoxicated, or

(c) makes or manufactures intoxicants, off a reserve, is guilty of an offence and is liable on summary conviction to a fine of not less than ten dollars and not more than fifty dollars or to imprisonment for a term not exceeding three months or to both fine and imprisonment. R.S., c. 149, s. 94.

96. (1) Subsection (2) or subsection (3) comes into force, or ceases to be in force, in a province or in a part thereof only if a proclamation declaring it to be in force, or to cease to be in force, as the case may be, in the province or part thereof is issued by the Governor in Council at the request of the lieutenant governor in council of the province.

(2) No offence is committed against sub paragraph 94(a)(ii) or paragraph 95(a) if intoxicants are sold to an Indian for consumption in a public place in accordance with the law of the province where the sale takes place.

(3) No offence is committed against subparagraph 94(a)(ii) or paragraph 95(a) if intoxicants are sold to or had in possession by an Indian in accordance with the law of the province where the sale takes place or the possession is had. 1956, c. 40, s. 23.

97. A person who is found

(a) with intoxicants in his possession, or

(b) intoxicated, on a reserve, is guilty of an offence and is liable on summary conviction to a fine of not less than ten dollars and not more than fifty dollars or to imprisonment for a term not exceeding three months or to both fine and imprisonment. R.S., c. 149, s. 96.

98. (1) Subsection (2) comes into force, or ceases to be in force, in a reserve only if a proclamation declaring it to be in force, or to cease to be in force, as the case may be, in the reserve, is issued by the Governor in Council.

(2) No offence is committed against paragraph 97(a) if intoxicants are had in possession by any person in accordance with the law of the province where the possession is had.

(3) A proclamation in respect of a reserve shall not be issued under subsection (1) except in accordance with the wishes of the band, as expressed at a referendum of the electors of the band by a majority of the electors who voted thereat.

(4) The Governor in Council may make regulations

(a) respecting the taking of votes and the holding of a referendum for the purposes of this section, and

(b) defining a reserve for the purposes of subsection (1) to consist of one or more reserves or any part thereof.

(5) No proclamation bringing subsection (2) into force in a reserve shall be issued unless the council of the band has transmitted to the Minister a resolution of the council requesting that subsection (2) be brought into force in the reserve, and either

(a) the reserve is situated in a province or part thereof in which subsection 96(3) is in force, or

(b) the Minister has communicated the contents of the resolution to the attorney general of the province in which the reserve is situated, the lieutenant governor in council of the province has not, within sixty days after such communication, objected to the granting of the request, and the Governor in Council has directed that the wishes of the band with respect thereto be ascertained by a referendum of the electors of the band.

(6) Where subsection (2) is in force in a reserve no offence is committed against subparagraph 94(a)(ii) or paragraph 95(a) if intoxicants are sold to or had in possession by a member of the band in accordance with the law of the province in which the reserve is situated. 1956, c. 40, s. 23.

99. The provisions of this Act relating to intoxicants do not apply where the intoxicant is used or is intended to be used in cases of sickness or accident. R.S., c. 149, s. 97.

100. In any prosecution under this Act the burden of proof that an intoxicant was used or was intended to be used in a case of sickness or accident is upon the accused. R.S., c. 149, s. 98.

101. In every prosecution under this Act a certificate of analysis furnished by an analyst employed by the Government of Canada or by a province shall be accepted as evidence of the facts stated therein and of the authority of the person giving or issuing the certificate, without proof of the signature of the person appearing to have signed the certificate or his official character, and without further proof thereof. R.S., c. 149, s. 99.

102. Every person who is guilty of an offence against any provision of this Act or any regulation made by the Governor in Council or the Minister for which a penalty is not provided elsewhere in this Act or the regulations, is liable on summary conviction to a fine not exceeding two hundred dollar or to imprisonment for a term not exceeding three months, or to both. R.8., c. 149, *. 100.

FORFEITURES AND PENALTIES

103. (1) Whenever a peace officer or a superintendent or a person authorized by the Minister believes on reasonable grounds that an offence against section 33, 90, 93, 94, 95 or 97 has been committed, he may seize all goods and chattels by means of or in relation to which he reasonably believes the offence was committed.

(2) All goods and chattels seized pursuant to subsection (1) may be detained for a period of three months following the day of seizure unless during that period proceedings under this Act in respect of such offence are undertaken, in which case the goods and chattels may be further detained until such proceedings are finally concluded.

(3) Where a person is convicted of an offence against the sections mentioned in subsection (1), the convicting court or judge may order that the goods and chattels by means of or in relation to which

the offence was committed, in addition to any penalty imposed, are forfeited to Her Majesty and may be disposed of as the Minister directs.

(4) A justice who is satisfied by information upon oath that there is reasonable ground to believe that there are upon a reserve or in any building, receptacle or place any goods or chattels by means of or in relation to which an offence against any of the sections mentioned in subsection (1) has been, is being or is about to be committed, may at any time issue a warrant under his hand authorizing a person named therein or a peace officer at any time to search the reserve, building, receptacle or place for any such goods or chattels. R.S., c. 149, s. 101; 1952-53, c. 41, s. 5; 1956, c. 40, s. 24.

104. Every fine, penalty or forfeiture imposed under this Act belongs to Her Majesty for the benefit of the band with respect to which or to one or more members of which the offence was committed or to which the offender, if an Indian, belongs, but the Governor in Council may from time to time direct that the fine, penalty or forfeiture shall be paid to a provincial, municipal or local authority that bears in whole or in part the expense of administering the law under which the fine, penalty or forfeiture is imposed, or that the fine, penalty or forfeiture shall be applied in the manner that he considers will best promote the purposes of the law under which the fine, penalty or forfeiture is imposed, or the administration of that law. R.S., c. 149, s. 102.

105. In any order, writ, warrant, summons or proceeding issued under this Act it is sufficient if the name of the person or Indian referred therein is the name given to, or the name [b] which the person or Indian is known by, the person who issues the order, writ, warrant, summons or proceedings, and if no part of the name of the person is given to or known by the person issuing the order, writ, warrant, summons or proceedings, it is sufficient if the person or Indian is described in any manner by which he may be identified. R.S., c. 149, s. 103.

106. A police magistrate or a stipendiary magistrate has and may exercise, with respect to matters arising under this Act, jurisdiction over the whole county, union of counties or judicial district in which the city, town or other place for which he is appointed or in which he has jurisdiction under provincial laws is situated. R.S., c. 149, s. 104.

107. The Governor in Council may appoint persons to be, for the purposes of this Act, justices of the peace and those persons have and may exercise the powers and authority of two justices of the peace with regard to

(a) offences under this Act, and

(b) any offence against the provisions of the Criminal Code relating to cruelty to animals, common assault, breaking and entering and vagrancy, where the offence is committed by an Indian or relates to the person or property of an Indian. R.S., c. 149,s. 105; 1956, c. 40, s. 25.

108. For the purposes of this Act or any matter relating to Indian affairs

(a) persons appointed by the Minister for the purpose,

(b) superintendents, and

(c) the Minister, Deputy Minister and the chief officer in charge of the branch of the Department relating to Indian affairs, are ex officio commissioners for the taking of oaths. R.S., c. 149, s. 107.

ENFRANCHISEMENT

109. (1) On the report of the Minister that an Indian has applied for enfranchisement and that in his opinion the Indian

(a) is of the full age of twenty-one years,
(b) is capable of assuming the duties and responsibilities of citizenship, and
(c) when enfranchised, will be capable of supporting himself and his dependants, the Governor in Council may by order declare that the Indian and his wife and minor unmarried children are enfranchised.
(2) On the report of the Minister that an Indian woman married a person who is not an Indian, the Governor in Council may by order declare that the woman is enfranchised as of the date of her marriage and, on the recommendation of the Minister may by order declare that all or any of her children are enfranchised as of the date of the marriage or such other date as the order may specify.
(3) Where, in the opinion of the Minister, the wjfe 0f an indian is living apart from her husband, the names of his wife and his minor children who are living with the wife shall not be included in an order under subsection (1) that enfranchises the Indian unless the wife has applied for enfranchisement, but where the Governor in Council is satisfied that such wife is no longer living apart from her husband, the Governor in Council may by order declare that the wife and the minor children are enfranchised.
(4) A person is not enfranchised unless his name appears in an order of enfranchisement made by the Governor in Council. R.S., c. 149, s. 108; 1956, c. 40, s. 26.
110. A person with respect to whom an order for enfranchisement is made under this Act shall, from the date thereof, or from the date of enfranchisement provided for therein, be deemed not to be an Indian within the meaning of this Act or any other statute or law. 1956, c. 40, s. 27.
111. (1) Upon the issue of an order of enfranchisement, any interest in land and improvements on an Indian reserve of which the enfranchised Indian was in lawful possession or over which he exercised rights of ownership, at the time of his enfranchisement, may be disposed of by him by gift or private sale to the band or another member of the band, but if not so disposed of within thirty days after the date of the order of enfranchisement such land and improvements shall be offered for sale by tender by the superintendent and sold to the highest bidder and the proceeds of such sale paid to him; and if no bid is received and the property remains unsold after six months from the date of such offering, the land, together with improvements, shall revert to the band free from any interest of the enfranchised person therein, subject to the payment, at the discretion of the Minister, to the enfranchised Indian, from the funds of the band, of such compensation for permanent improvements as the Minister may determine.
(2) When an order of enfranchisement issues or has issued, the Governor in Council may, with the consent of the council of the band, by order declare that any lands within a reserve of which the enfranchised Indian had formerly been in lawful possession shall cease to be Indian reserve lands.
(3) When an order has been made under subsection (2), the enfranchised Indian is entitled to occupy such lands for a period of ten years from the date of his enfranchisement, and the enfranchised Indian shall pay to the funds of the band, or there shall, out of any money payable to the enfranchised Indian under this Act, be transferred to the funds of the band, such amount per acre for the lands as the Minister considers to be the value of the common interest of the band in the lands.
(4) At the end of the ten-year period referred to in subsection (3) the Minister shall cause a grant of the lands to be made to the enfranchised Indian or to his legal representatives. R.S., c. 149, s. 110.

112. (1) Where the Minister reports that a band has applied for enfranchisement, and has submitted a plan for the disposal or division of the funds of the band and the lands in the reserve, and in his opinion the band is capable of managing its own affairs as a municipality or part of a municipality, the Governor in Council may by order approve the plan, declare that all the members of the band are enfranchised, either as of the date of the order or such later date as may be fixed in the order, and may make regulations for carrying the plan and the provisions of this section into effect.

(2) An order for enfranchisement may not be made under subsection (1) unless more than fifty per cent of the electors of the band signify, at a meeting of the band called for the purpose, their willingness to become enfranchised under this section, and their approval of the plan.

(3) The Governor in Council may, for the purpose of giving effect to this section, authorize the Minister to enter into an agreement with a province or a municipality, or both, upon such terms as may be agreed upon by the Minister and the province or municipality, or both.

(4) Without restricting the generality of subsection (3), an agreement made thereunder may provide for financial assistance to be given to the province or the municipality or both to assist in the support of indigent, infirm or aged persons to whom the agreement applies, and such financial assistance, or any part thereof, shall, if the Minister so directs, be paid out of moneys of the band, and any such financial assistance not paid out of moneys of the band shall be paid out of moneys appropriated by Parliament. R.S., c. 149, s. 111.

113. (1) Where a band has applied for enfranchisement within the meaning of this Act and has submitted a plan for the disposal or division of the funds of the band and the lands in the reserve, the Minister may appoint a committee to inquire into and report upon any or all of the following matters, namely:

(a) the desirability of enfranchising the band;

(b) the adequacy of the plan submitted by it; and

(c) any other matter relating to the application for enfranchisement or to the disposition thereof.

(2) A committee appointed under subsection (1) shall consist of

(a) a judge surrogate, district or county court,

(b) an officer of the Department, and

(c) a member by the council of the band. 1960-61, c. 9, s. 1.

SCHOOLS

114. (i) The Governor in Council may authorize the Minister, in accordance with this Act, to enter into agreements on behalf of Her Majesty for the education in accordance with this Act of Indian children, with

(a) the government of a province,

(b) the Commissioner of the Northwest Territories,

(c) the Commissioner of the Yukon Territory,

(d) a public or separate school board, and

(e) a religious or charitable organization.

(2) The Minister may, in accordance with this Act, establish, operate and maintain schools for Indian children. 1956, c. 40, s. 28.

115. The Minister may

(a) provide for and make regulations with respect to standards for buildings, equipment, teaching, education, inspection and discipline in connection with schools;
(b) provide for the transportation of children to and from school;
(c) enter into agreements with religious organizations for the support and maintenance of children who are being educated in schools operated by those organizations; and
(d) apply the whole or any part of moneys that would otherwise be payable to or on behalf of a child who is attending a residential school to the maintenance of that child at that school. R.S., c. 149, s. 114.
116. (1) Subject to section 117, every Indian child who has attained the age of seven years shall attend school.
(2) The Minister may
(a) require an Indian who has attained the age of six years to attend school;
(b) require an Indian who becomes sixteen years of age during the school term to continue to attend school until the end of that term; and
(c) require an Indian who becomes sixteen years of age to attend school for such further period as the Minister considers advisable, but no Indian shall be required to attend school after he becomes eighteen years of age. R.S., c. 149, s. 115; 1956, c. 40, s. 29.
117. An Indian child is not required to attend school if the child
(a) is, by reason of sickness or other unavoidable cause that is reported promptly to the principal, unable to attend school;
(b) is, with the permission in writing of the superintendent, absent from school for a period not exceeding six weeks in each term for the purpose of assisting in husbandry or urgent and necessary household duties;
(c) is under efficient instruction at home or elsewhere, within one year after the written approval by the Minister of such instruction; or
(d) is unable to attend school because there is insufficient accommodation in the school that the child is entitled or directed to attend. R.S., c. 149, 6. 116; 1956, c. 40, s. 30.
118. Every Indian child who is required to attend school shall attend such school as the Minister may designate, but no child whose parent is a Protestant shall be assigned to a school conducted under Roman Catholic auspices and no child whose parent is a Roman Catholic shall be assigned to a school conducted under Protestant auspices, except by written direction of the parent. R.S., c. 149, s. 117.
119. (1) The Minister may appoint persons, to be called truant officers, to enforce the attendance of Indian children at school, and for that purpose a truant officer has the powers of a peace officer.
(2) Without restricting the generality of subsection (1), a truant officer may
(a) enter any place where he believes, on reasonable grounds, that there are Indian children who are between the ages of seven and sixteen years of age, or who are required by the Minister to attend school;
(b) investigate any case of truancy; and
(c) serve written notice upon the parent, guardian or other person having the care or legal custody of a child to cause the child to attend school regularly thereafter.

(3) Where a notice has been served in accordance with paragraph (2)(c) with respect to a child who is required by this Act to attend school, and the child does not within three days after the service of notice attend school and continue to attend school regularly thereafter, the person upon whom the notice was served is guilty of an offence and is liable on summary conviction to a fine of not more than five dollars or to imprisonment for a term not exceeding ten days, or to both.

(4) Where a person has been served with a notice in accordance with paragraph (2)(c), it is not necessary within a period of twelve months thereafter to serve that person with any other notice in respect of further noncompliance with the provisions of this Act, and whenever such person within the period of twelve months fails to cause the child with respect to whom the notice was served or any other child of whom he has charge or control to attend school and continue in regular attendance as required by this Act, such person is guilty of an offence and liable to the penalties imposed by subsection (3) as if he had been served with the notice.

(5) A child who is habitually late for school shall be deemed to be absent from school.

(6) A truant officer may take into custody a child whom he believes on reasonable grounds to be absent from school contrary to this Act and may convey the child to school, using as much force as the circumstances require. R.S., c. 149, s. 118.

120. An Indian child who

(a) is expelled or suspended from school, or

(b) refuses or fails to attend school regularly, shall be deemed to be a juvenile delinquent within the meaning of the Juvenile Delinquent Act. R.S., c. 149, s. 119.

121. (1) Where the majority of the members of a band belongs to one religious denomination, the school established on the reserve that has been set apart for the use and benefit of that band shall be taught by a teacher of that denomination.

(2) Where the majority of the members of a band are not members of the same religious denomination and the band by a majority vote of those electors of the band who were present at a meeting called for the purpose requests that day schools on the reserve should be taught by a teacher belonging to a particular religious denomination, the school on that reserve shall be taught by a teacher of that denomination. R.S., c. 149, 8. 120.

122, A Protestant or Roman Catholic minority of any band may, with the approval of and under regulations to be made by the Minister, have a separate day school or day school classroom established on the reserve unless, in the opinion of the Governor in Council, the number of children of school age does not so warrant. R.S., c. 149, s. 121.

123. In sections 114 to 122 "child" means an Indian who has attained the age of six years but has not attained the age of sixteen years, and a person who is required by the Minister to attend school; "school" includes a day school, technical school, high school and residential school; "truant officer" includes

(a) a member of the Royal Canadian Mounted Police,

(b) a special constable appointed for police duty on a reserve ; and

(c) a school teacher and a chief of the band, when authorized by the superintendent. R.S., c. 149, s. 122.

PRIOR GRANTS

124. Where, prior to the 4th day of September 1951, a reserve or portion of a reserve was released or surrendered to the Crown pursuant to Part I of the Indian Act, chapter 98 of the Revised Statutes of Canada, 1927, or pursuant to the provisions of the statutes relating to the release or surrender of reserves in force at the time of the release or surrender, and

(a) prior to that date Letters Patent under the Great Seal were issued purporting to grant a reserve or portion of a reserve so released or surrendered, or any interest therein, to any person, and the Letters Patent have not been declared void or inoperative by any Court of competent jurisdiction, or

(b) prior to that date a reserve or portion of a reserve so released or surrendered, or any interest therein, was sold or agreed to be sold by the Crown to any person, and the sale or agreement for sale has not been cancelled or by any Court of competent jurisdiction declared void or inoperative, the Letters Patent or the sale or agreement for sale, as the case may be, shall, for all purposes, be deemed to have been issued or made at the date thereof under the direction of the Governor in Council. 1952-53, c. 41, s. 6.

www.ingramcontent.com/pod-product-compliance
Lightning Source LLC
Chambersburg PA
CBHW060418010526
44118CB00017B/2261